CONTENTS

SECTION I

UNITED KINGDOM HYDROGRAPHIC OFFICE (UKHO), CHARTING, NAUTICAL PUBLICATIONS, PROMULGATION AND RECEIPT OF INFORMATION

CHAPTER 1

The United Kingdom Hydrographic Office, Surveying and Charting

CHAPTER 2

Admiralty Charts

CHAPTER 3

Admiralty Publications

CHAPTER 4

Promulgation of information by, and rendering of information to the UKHO

SECTION II

THE MARITIME ENVIRONMENT

CHAPTER 5

The sea

CHAPTER 6

Ice

CHAPTER 7

Meteorology

SECTION III

REGULATION OF THE MARITIME ENVIRONMENT

CHAPTER 8

International organisations

CHAPTER 9

Constraints on navigation

CHAPTER 10

Maritime pollution and conservation (MARPOL)

NP 100

THE MARINER'S HANDBOOK

NINTH EDITION
2009

PUBLISHED BY THE UNITED KINGDOM HYDROGRAPHIC OFFICE

DIRECTIONS FOR UPDATING THIS VOLUME

This volume is kept up to date in a "Continuous Revision" cycle. This means that it will be continuously revised by its Editor for a period of approximately five years using information received in the Hydrographic Office, and then republished. Publication is announced in Part 1 of *Admiralty Notices to Mariners,* and a listing of all current editions is updated and published quarterly in Part 1B of *Admiralty Notices to Mariners* and 6-monthly in NP 234 *Cumulative List of Admiralty Notices to Mariners*. Additionally, this list is continuously updated and available on the UKHO website at www.ukho.gov.uk.

During the life of the book, it is amended as necessary by notices published weekly in Section IV of *Admiralty Notices to Mariners*.

A check-list of all extant Notices, but not the text, is published quarterly at Section IB of *Admiralty Notices to Mariners*. The full text of all extant Section IV Notices are published annually in January in NP247(2) *Annual Summary of Admiralty Notices to Mariners - Amendments to Sailing Directions.*

These amendments will normally be restricted to those critical to the safety of navigation, and information required to be published as a result of changes to national legislation affecting shipping, and to port regulations.

It is recommended that amendments issued in this way are cut out and pasted into the book. Mariners may, however, prefer to keep amendments in a separate file, and annotate the text of the book in the margin to indicate the existence of an amendment. This latter method may be more appropriate in some volumes where significant numbers of amendments, sometimes overlapping, may make the cut-and-paste method unwieldy and confusing.

RECORD OF AMENDMENTS

The table below is to record Section IV Notices to Mariners amendments affecting this volume.
Sub-paragraph numbers in the margin of the body of the book are to assist the user when making amendments to this volume.

Weekly Notices to Mariners (Section IV)

2010	2011	2012	2013	2014

SECTION IV

OPERATIONS AT SEA

CHAPTER 11

Navigation and Aids to Navigation

CHAPTER 12

Military Operations

CHAPTER 13

Commercial Operations

ANNEXES, GLOSSARIES, INDEX AND SUPPLEMENTARY TABLES

PREFACE

The Ninth Edition of *The Mariner's Handbook* has been compiled by Lieutenant Commander S B Lewis, Royal Navy. The United Kingdom Hydrographic Office has used all reasonable endeavours to ensure that this publication contains all the information obtained by and assessed by it at the date shown below. Information received or assessed after that date will be included in *Admiralty Notices to Mariners* where appropriate.

This edition supersedes the Eigth Edition (2004), which is cancelled.

Information on climate and currents has been based on data provided by the Met Office, Exeter.

Copyright for some of the material in this publication is owned by the authority named under the item and permission for its reproduction must be obtained from the owner.

The following sources of information, other than UKHO Publications and Ministry of Defence papers, have been consulted:
  Ice Navigation in Canadian Waters, Canadian Coast Guard (1999)
  Ice Seamanship, Captain G Q Parnell (Nautical Institute) (1986)
  Svensk Lots del A, Swedish Hydrographic Office (1992)

Photography:
  Views of cloud formations and aural forms reprinted courtesy of the Met Office, Exeter.
  Views of sea states reprinted courtesy of the Met Office, Exeter and Environment Canada.
  Views of ice formations reprinted courtesy of British Antarctic Survey.

Mr M. S. Robinson
Chief Executive United Kingdom Hydrographic Office

The United Kingdom Hydrographic Office
Admiralty Way
Taunton
Somerset TA1 2DN
England
18th September 2009

HOW TO REPORT NEW OR SUSPECTED DANGERS TO NAVIGATION OR CHANGES OBSERVED IN AIDS TO NAVIGATION

A Hydrographic Note, Form H.102, with instructions, is contained in the back of the Weekly Edition of Admiralty Notices to Mariners. This form can also be downloaded from the UKHO Website. The form should be used to report all observations, including new or suspected dangers to navigation or changes to aids to navigation.

FEEDBACK

In order to maintain and improve the accuracy of information contained within this volume, The United Kingdom Hydrographic Office welcomes general comments, new, additional or corroborative information and digital images from mariners and other users. Such information should be forwarded by post, fax or e-mail to the address below giving, where possible, the source for the information if this is not based on personal observation.

UKHO CONTACT DETAILS

Helpdesk
United Kingdom Hydrographic Office
Admiralty Way
TAUNTON
Somerset
TA1 2DN
United Kingdom

e-mail: helpdesk@ukho.gov.uk
Tel: +44 (0)1823 723366
Fax: +44 (0)1823 350561
Website: www.ukho.gov.uk

Admiralty Sailing Directions
e-mail: sailingdirections@ukho.gov.uk
Tel: +44 (0)1823 33790   extension 3518
Fax: +44 (0)1823 351865
(Book Support Unit)

Head of Sailing Directions
Tel: +44 (0)1823 33790   extension 3382

HOW TO OBTAIN ADMIRALTY CHARTS AND PUBLICATIONS

A complete list of Admiralty Charts and Publications (both paper and digital), together with a list of authorised Admiralty Distributors for their purchase, is contained in the "Catalogue of Admiralty Charts and Publications" (NP131), which is published annually. The Admiralty Digital Catalogue is available to download free of charge from the UKHO Website.

Details of authorised Admiralty Distributors can also be obtained from the UKHO Helpdesk.

RELATED ADMIRALTY PUBLICATIONS AND THEIR CONTENTS

Admiralty Notices to Mariners (NMs):

Weekly Notices to Mariners
Navigationally significant changes to nautical charts, lights, fog signals, radio signals and Sailing Directions

Reprint of all Radio Navigational Warnings in force and a summary of charts and publications being published

Cumulative List of Notices to Mariners
Published in January and July of each year

A list of all nautical charts available and a complete list of all NMs affecting them during the previous two years

Annual Summary of Notices to Mariners
Published at the beginning of the year in two parts

Annual Notices to Mariners, Temporary and Preliminary notices

Cumulative summary of amendments to Sailing Directions

Admiralty Sailing Directions (Pilots):

Waterway directions

Port facilities

Directions for port entry

Navigational hazards

Buoyage

Climatological data

Admiralty List of Radio Signals:

Maritime Radio Stations

Radio Aids to Navigation

Standard time

Maritime Safety Information

Radio weather services

Global Maritime Distress and Safety System (GMDSS)

Pilot services

Vessel Traffic Services

Port operations

Admiralty List of Lights:

Lighthouses, lightships, lit floating marks

Characteristics and intensity

Elevation

Range of light

Description of structure

Fog signals

For more information, please visit www.ukho.gov.uk

ABBREVIATIONS

The following abbreviations are used in the text:

AIS	Automatic Identification System
ALC	Articulated loading column
ALP	Articulated loading platform
AMVER	Automated Mutual Assistance Vessel Rescue System
ARCS	Admiralty Raster Chart Service
ASL	Archipelagic Sea Lane
ATBA	Area To Be Avoided
ATLAS	autonomous temperature line acquisition system
AVCS	Admiralty Vector Chart Service
°C	degrees Celsius
CALM	Catenary anchor leg mooring
CBM	Conventional buoy mooring
CDC	Certain Dangerous Cargo
CHA	Competent Harbour Authority
cm	centimetre(s)
COTP	Captain of the Port
CVTS	Co-operative Vessel Traffic System
DART	Deep-ocean Assessment and Reporting Tsunamis
DF	direction finding
DG	degaussing
DGPS	Differential Global Positioning System
DMA	Dynamic Management Area
DPG	Dangerous and Polluting Goods
DSC	Digital Selective Calling
DW	Deep Water
dwt	deadweight tonnage
DZ	danger zone
E	east (easterly, eastward, eastern, easternmost)
ECDIS	Electronic Chart Display and Information System
EEZ	exclusive economic zone
ELSBM	Exposed location single buoy mooring
ENC	Electronic Navigational Chart
ENE	east-north-east
EPIRB	Emergency Position Indicating Radio Beacon
ESE	east–south–east
ETA	estimated time of arrival
ETD	estimated time of departure
EU	European Union
FAD	fish aggregating device
feu	forty foot equivalent unit
fm	fathom(s)
FPSO	Floating production storage and offloading vessel
FPU	Floating production unit
FSO	Floating storage and offloading vessel
ft	foot (feet)
g/cm³	gram per cubic centimetre
GMDSS	Global Maritime Distress and Safety System
GNNS	Global Navigation Satellite Systems
GPS	Global Positioning System

GRP	glass reinforced plastic
grt	gross register tonnage (obsolete)
gt	gross tonnage
HAT	Highest Astronomical Tide
HF	high frequency
hm	hectometre
HMS	Her (His) Majesty's Ship
hp	horse power
hPa	hectopascal
HSC	High Speed Craft
HW	High Water
IALA	International Association of Lighthouse Authorities
IHO	International Hydrographic Organization
IMDG	International Maritime Dangerous Goods
IMO	International Maritime Organization
ISPS	International Ship and Port Facility Security Code
ITCZ	Intertropical Convergence Zone
ITZ	Inshore traffic zone
JRCC	Joint Rescue Co-ordination Centre
kHz	kilohertz
km	kilometre(s)
kn	knot(s)
kW	kilowatt(s)
LANBY	Large Automatic Navigation Buoy
LASH	Lighter Aboard Ship
LAT	Lowest Astronomical Tide
LF	low frequency
LHG	Liquefied Hazardous Gas
LMT	Local Mean Time
LNG	Liquefied Natural Gas
LOA	Length overall
LPG	Liquefied Petroleum Gas
LW	Low Water
m	metre(s)
m³	cubic metre(s)
mb	millibar(s)
MCTS	Marine Communications and Traffic Services Centres
MF	medium frequency
MHz	megahertz
MHHW	Mean Higher High Water
MHLW	Mean Higher Low Water
MHW	Mean High Water
MHWN	Mean High Water Neaps
MHWS	Mean High Water Springs
MLHW	Mean Lower High Water
MLLW	Mean Lower Low Water
MLW	Mean Low Water
MLWN	Mean Low Water Neaps
MLWS	Mean Low Water Springs
mm	millimetre(s)
MMSI	Maritime Mobile Service Identity
MRCC	Maritime Rescue Co-ordination Centre
MRSC	Maritime Rescue Sub-Centre

m/s	metres per second		SBM	Single buoy mooring
MSI	Marine Safety Information		SE	south-east
MSL	Mean Sea Level		SHA	Statutory Harbour Authority
MSR	Mandatory Ship Reporting		SMA	Seasonal Management Area
MV	Motor Vessel		SPM	Single point mooring
MW	megawatt(s)		sq	square
MY	Motor Yacht		SRR	Search and Rescue Region
			SS	Steamship
N	north (northerly, northward, northern, northernmost)		SSCC	Ship Sanitation Control Certificate
			SSCEC	Ship Sanitation Control Exemption Certificate
NATO	North Atlantic Treaty Organization			
Navtex	Navigational Telex System		SSE	south-south-east
NE	north-east		SSW	south-south-west
NGA	National Geospatial-Intelligence Agency		STL	Submerged turret loading
NNE	north-north-east		STS	ship to ship
NNW	north-north-west		SW	south-west
No(s)	number(s)		SWATH	small waterplane area twin hull ship
NOAA	National Oceanic and Atmospheric Administration		teu	twenty foot equivalent unit
nrt	net register tonnage (obsolete)		TRITON	Triangle Trans-Ocean Buoy Network
nt	net tonnage		TSS	Traffic Separation Scheme
NW	north-west			
			UHF	ultra high frequency
ODAS	Ocean Data Acquisition System		UKC	under-keel clearance
OPL	off port limits		UKHO	United Kingdom Hydrographic Office
			ULCC	Ultra Large Crude Carrier
PEC	Pilotage Exemption Certificate		UN	United Nations
PEL	Port Entry Light		UT	Universal Time
PLEM	Pipe line end manifold		UTC	Co-ordinated Universal Time
PMSC	Port Marine Safety Code			
POL	Petrol, Oil & Lubricants		VDR	Voyage Data Recorder
PSSA	Particularly Sensitive Sea Areas		VHF	very high frequency
PWC	Personal watercraft		VLCC	Very Large Crude Carrier
			VMRS	Vessel Movement Reporting System
RCC	Rescue Co-ordination Centre		VTC	Vessel Traffic Centre
RMS	Royal Mail Ship		VTMS	Vessel Traffic Management System
RN	Royal Navy		VTS	Vessel Traffic Services
RoRo	Roll-on, Roll-off			
RT	radio telephony		W	west (westerly, westward, western, westernmost)
S	south (southerly, southward, southern, southernmost)		WGS	World Geodetic System
			WMO	World Meteorological Organization
SALM	Single anchor leg mooring system		WNW	west-north-west
SALS	Single anchored leg storage system		WSW	west-south-west
SAR	Search and Rescue		WT	radio (wireless) telegraphy
Satnav	Satellite navigation			

SECTION I

UNITED KINGDOM HYDROGRAPHIC OFFICE (UKHO), CHARTING, NAUTICAL PUBLICATIONS, PROMULGATION AND RECEIPT OF INFORMATION

NOTES

2

Chapter 1

The United Kingdom Hydrographic Office (UKHO), surveying and charting

General information

History
1.1

1   Before the establishment of a dedicated hydrographic service within the Admiralty, there had been hydrographers by appointment to reigning monarchs (from King Charles II onwards), though these were grants of titular privileges rather than salaried appointments. In 1751, the post of Admiralty Surveyor was created for the charting of home waters. The first occupant of this post was Murdoch Mackenzie, who was succeeded in 1771 by his nephew, also called Murdoch Mackenzie, a serving Lieutenant in the Royal Navy.

2   The United Kingdom Hydrographic Office (UKHO) can trace its origins to the appointment by order in council of Alexander Dalrymple FRS as the first Hydrographer to the Admiralty, by King George III, in 1795. Dalrymple set to work reviewing "...the difficulties and dangers to His Majesty's fleet in the navigation of ships". The first Admiralty Chart (of Quiberon Bay in Brittany) was published in 1800.

3   Dalrymple served (apart from a brief period in 1804, when as a result of ill-health, the work of the Office was overseen by William Bligh of *HMS Bounty* fame) until 1808. Dalrymple was replaced by Captain Thomas Hurd Royal Navy, under whose leadership charts were first sold to the general public (a major change from the days when national security or the interests of the individual surveyor were considered by the Admiralty to be paramount!), the first chart catalogue was produced, and the first editions of Sailing Directions and Light Lists were published between 1823 and 1829.

4   Perhaps the best known of all UK Hydrographers was Rear Admiral Sir Francis Beaufort KCB, FRS, who served from 1829 until 1855. Among his many achievements, apart from the establishment of the Beaufort Scale of wind strength (7.3) which is still in use today and for which he is most famous, were his instigation of the conduct of surveys world-wide, and the promotion of international co-operation. Under his leadership, Tide Tables were introduced in 1833, and Notices to Mariners were first published in 1834.

5   Also under his tenure, the Admiralty set up a scientific branch consisting of the Hydrographic Department, the Royal Greenwich Observatory, the Nautical Almanac Office and the Chronometer Office. He also established a Compass branch in 1842, with its own observatory at Woolwich, and a Harbour branch which became responsible for the tidal waters of the UK. By the time of his retirement in 1855, the Admiralty had nearly 2000 charts in print.

6   For over a century, the printing of Admiralty charts and related publications was undertaken by agents, until 1922, when His Majesty's Stationery Office (HMSO) took over responsibility, and the Admiralty Chart Establishment was formed at Cricklewood, north London. This operation was brought under the direct control of the Hydrographer in 1929.

The onset of war in 1939 prompted the relocation of the printing facility to purpose-built premises in a safer location in Taunton, Somerset in 1941, and the Hydrographic Office subsequently consolidated its entire operation on the Taunton site in 1968.

7   The UKHO was established as a Defence Support Agency of the Ministry of Defence in 1990, and became a Trading Fund in 1996.

Recent developments
1.2

1   Advances in technology over the years have facilitated incremental improvements in the accuracy and quality of the navigational information provided by the UKHO. In particular, the development of echo sounders in the 1930s, sidescan sonar in the 1960s and the use of satellites for precise navigation from the 1970s onwards have given surveyors and hydrographers the capability to provide charting of unprecedented accuracy.

2   The establishment of international bodies such as the International Maritime Organisation and the International Hydrographic Organisation, and the globalisation of maritime trade since the Second World War has encouraged and facilitated international co-operation, and the sharing of hydrographic information to an unprecedented extent, enabling compilation of charts and nautical publications to a level of accuracy and detail not possible in previous eras.

Function and purpose
1.3

1   The UKHO exists primarily to provide hydrographic services which enable the Royal Navy and other UK Ministry of Defence customers to meet current and potential future operational tasks in times of peace, crisis or war.

2   It also provides wider value to the UK Government in support of the UK Maritime and Coastguard Agency (MCA), which is the responsible authority for the UK's Treaty obligations under the United Nations SOLAS Convention.

Scope of UKHO activity
1.4

1   The core business of the UKHO lies in supporting national defence and the international merchant marine, producing a portfolio of over 3200 paper charts and about 160 publications as well as an increasing number of digital products including ENCs (2.87), AVCS (2.98), ARCS (2.106), TotalTide (3.33)

and the Admiralty Digital Lights List (3.18).

2   In addition, the business continues to operate in a number of related market segments such as Admiralty Leisure and training. It also offers consultancy services in Hydrographic Expertise and Law of the Sea.

As part of the UK's SOLAS obligations, the UKHO operates a round-the-clock Navigation Warning service for NAVAREA 1 (4.7) from its Taunton base.

Surveying

Data quality

Charted depths
1.5

1   Before using a chart to plan or navigate a passage, mariners should make themselves aware of the quality of the survey data that has been used to place the soundings and contours on the chart, since not all sea areas have been surveyed to modern standards or even systematically surveyed at all. Indeed large areas of sea, especially in offshore areas, have never been systematically surveyed to any standard. The chart will have been compiled from the best data available but this does not mean that shoal areas dangerous to navigation will not exist.

2   To help with this assessment, each chart carries a statement, below the title, referring to the origin of the data used to compile it. Where known, sources of hydrographic information are shown by means of a source diagram (see 1.6). ENCs do not carry a source diagram but instead include data fields with information about the reliability of "objects". The object "Category of Zone of Confidence" (CATZOC) in an ENC gives an estimate of the reliability of the source data (see 1.7–1.8).

Use of source diagrams
1.6

1   The source diagrams on Admiralty charts and ARCS are scaled replicas of the chart, showing the coverage, dates, scales and authority for the various types of source material since these can give an indication of the quality of the survey(s) used to compile the chart, and hence the reliability of the depicted sea floor. The source diagram may also show areas of shallow banks or routeing measures to assist

in relating the sources to the chart. Where insufficient information is available to include a source diagram, details of the source material used for the chart are given in a written summary.

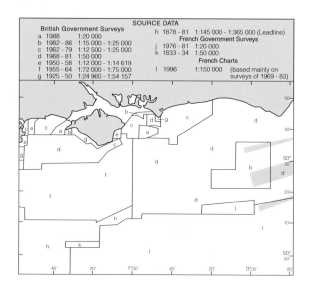

Source Diagram (1.6)

CATZOC
1.7

1   CATZOC allows a hydrographic authority to encode data against five categories (ZOC A1, A2, B, C, D), with a sixth category (U) for data which has not been assessed.

The categorisation of hydrographic data is based on three factors (position accuracy, depth accuracy, and sea floor coverage), as shown in the table below:

CATEGORY OF ZONES OF CONFIDENCE
(ZOC TABLE)

1	2	3		4	5
ZOC[1]	Position Accuracy[2]	Depth Accuracy[3]		Seafloor Coverage	Typical Survey Characteristics[5]
A1	± 5m + 5% depth	**0·5m + 1% depth**		Full area search undertaken. Significant seafloor features detected[4] and depths measured.	Controlled, systematic survey[6]. High position and depth accuracy achieved using DGPS or a minimum of three high quality lines of position (LOP) and a multibeam, channel or mechanical sweep system.
		Depth (m)	Accuracy (m)		
		10	± 0·6		
		30	± 0·8		
		100	± 1·5		
		1000	± 10·5		
A2	± 20m	**1·0m + 2% depth**		Full area search undertaken. Significant seafloor features detected[4] and depths measured.	Controlled, systematic survey[6] achieving position and depth accuracy less than ZOC A1 and using a modern survey echo sounder[7] and a sonar or mechanical sweep system.
		Depth (m)	Accuracy (m)		
		10	± 1·2		
		30	± 1·6		
		100	± 3·0		
		1000	± 21·0		
B	± 50m	**1·0m + 2% depth**		Full area search not achieved; uncharted features, hazardous to surface navigation are not expected, but may exist.	Controlled, systematic survey achieving similar depth but lesser position accuracies than ZOC A2 using a modern survey echo sounder but no sonar or mechanical sweep system.
		Depth (m)	Accuracy (m)		
		10	± 1·2		
		30	± 1·6		
		100	± 3·0		
		1000	± 21·0		
C	± 500m	**= 2·0m + 5% depth**		Full area search not achieved; depth anomalies may be expected.	Low accuracy survey or data collected on an opportunity basis such as soundings on passage.
		Depth (m)	Accuracy (m)		
		10	± 2·5		
		30	± 3·5		
		100	± 7·0		
		1000	± 52·0		
D	Worse than ZOC C	Worse than ZOC C		Full area search not achieved, large depth anomalies may be expected.	Poor quality data or data that cannot be quality assessed due to lack of information.
U	Unassessed - the quality of the bathymetric data has yet to be assessed.				

To decide on a ZOC category, all conditions outlined in columns 2-4 of the table must be met.

Footnotes

1. The allocation of a ZOC indicates that particular data meets minimum criteria for position and depth accuracy and seafloor coverage defined in this table. ZOC categories reflect a charting standard and not just a hydrographic survey standard. Depth and position accuracies specified for each ZOC category refer to the errors of the final depicted soundings and include not only survey errors but also other errors introduced in the chart production process. Data may be further qualified by Object Class 'Quality of Data' (M_QUAL) sub-attributes as follows:

    a. Positional Accuracy (POSACC) and Sounding Accuracy (SOUACC) may be used to indicate that a higher position or depth accuracy has been achieved than defined in this table (eg a survey where full sea floor coverage was not achieved could not be classified higher than ZOC B; however if the position accuracy was, for instance, ±15 m, the sub-attribute POSACC could be used to indicate this.

    b. Swept areas where the clearance depth is accurately known but the actual seabed depth is not accurately known may be accorded a higher ZOC (ie A1 or A2) providing positional and depth accuracies of the swept depth meets the criteria in this table. In this instance, Depth Range Value 1 (DRVAL1) may be used to specify the swept depth. The position accuracy criteria apply to the boundaries of swept areas.

    c. SURSTA, SUREND and TECSOU may be used to indicate the start and end dates of the survey and the technique of sounding measurement.

2. Position Accuracy of depicted soundings at 95% CI (2·45 Sigma) with respect to the given datum. It is the cumulative error and includes survey, transformation and digitising errors etc. Position accuracy need not be rigorously computed for ZOCs B, C and D but may be estimated based on type of equipment, calibration regime, historical accuracy etc.

3. Depth accuracy of depicted soundings = a + (b·d)/100 at 95% CI (2·00 sigma), where d = depth in metres, at the critical depth. Depth accuracy need not be rigorously computed for ZOCs B, C and D but may be estimated based on type of equipment, calibration regime, historical accuracy etc.

4. Significant sea floor features are defined as those rising above depicted depths by more than:

Depth	Significant feature
< 40 m	2 m
> 40 m	10% depth

A full sea floor search indicates that a systematic survey was conducted using detection systems, depth measurement systems, procedures, and trained personnel designed to detect and measure depths on significant sea floor features. Significant features are included on the chart as scale allows. It is impossible to guarantee that no significant feature could remain undetected, and significant features may have become present in the area since the time of the survey.

5. Typical survey characteristics. These descriptions should be seen as indicative examples only.

6. Controlled systematic surveys (ZOCs A1, A2 and B) are surveys comprising planned survey lines, on a geodetic datum which can be transformed to WGS84.

7. Modern survey echo sounder. A high precision, single beam depth measuring equipment, generally including all survey echo sounders designed post-1970.

1.8

1   ZOC A1 and A2 require very high accuracy standards which were rarely, if ever, achieved before the advent of satellite positioning in the 1980s. Therefore, many sea lanes which have been regarded as adequately surveyed for many years may carry a ZOC B classification.

Note. The ZOC classification attained by a survey is for the survey at the date it was conducted. In areas of mobile seabed the actual seabed may differ markedly from what has been charted, even if the survey is only a few months old (see 1.23).

2   **ZOC U.** In the early days of ENC production, hydrographic authorities created ENCs by digitising the existing paper charts. Although this allowed for a rapid expansion in the numbers of ENC cells that were available, it meant that the compilers creating the ENC did not have to hand all the information required to assess which ZOC classification the different parts of the ENC should have. Rather than expend time researching this information, hydrographic authorities categorized the entire ENC as ZOC U, meaning that the category of the data had not been assessed. Although this situation is improving, it will be some time before early ENC cells are revisited and have all soundings categorised with an appropriate CATZOC.

Scale of survey

1.9

1   The scale is the scale of the survey fair sheet provided by the surveyor to the UKHO. This only had any real relevance where the survey covered the fair sheet with no gaps.

For almost all surveys conducted before 1865, and inshore surveys conducted before 1905, the quoted scale has no particular relevance since the surveyor would not have covered his plotting sheet fully. Between 1905 and 2000, the scale provides an indication of the line spacing between soundings.

2   Surveys were generally plotted so that the survey lines were 5 mm apart on the plotting sheet. Thus a survey with a scale of 1:12 500 would have lines run at 62·5 m intervals. The scale for a survey was generally selected so that it would detect changes in the sea floor topography that were expected in the area: for example, in areas where rock pinnacles were expected, a larger scale survey (and hence narrower line spacings) would be chosen in comparison to flat sandy areas.

3   It should be noted that for surveys conducted before side–scan sonar (1.17) became available, dangers to shipping could still exist between the lines. For a single beam echo sounder survey conducted at a line spacing of 62·5 m, a wreck the size of a large tanker could remain undetected if it lay parallel to and between two adjacent lines. Recently, there have been several instances of uncharted shoals being found in areas where comprehensive surveys, up to scales of 1:5000, had been carried out, but before side scan technology was available.

4   In one case, a shoal of 0·2 m was discovered lying between two survey lines, each of which showed depths of greater than 10 m. The scale of this survey was 1:5000, with line spacings of only 25 m. See diagram 1.9.

5   With the advent of swathe survey systems (1.14), the surveyor became able to cover the sea floor fully. At this time, the concept of scale of survey becomes meaningless and the term *'full sea floor coverage'* is used on source diagrams to indicate that this is the case.

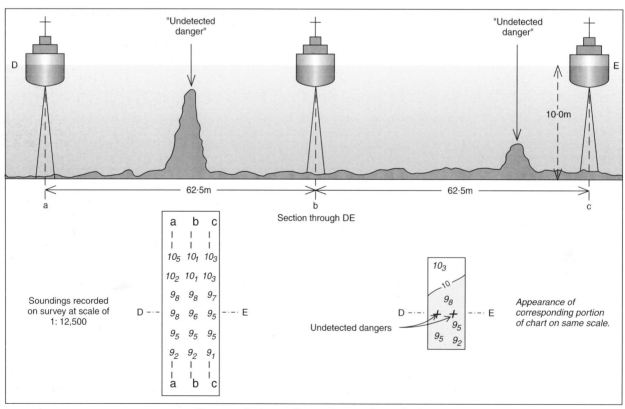

Dangers between lines of soundings (1.9)

6   Where a swathe system has been used, but there are concerns that it may not have detected all objects (ie there are small gaps in the coverage), or a bathymetric LIDAR system (1.15) has been used, the source diagram will be annotated *'partial sea floor coverage'*.

Date of survey
1.10

1   Over time, the technology available to conduct hydrographic surveys has improved and this has allowed the surveyor to survey areas with greater accuracy and certainty. New technology tends to remain in use for relatively long periods of time before a further advance is introduced which may enable a step change in capability. Following such a step change, this further improvement in capability is also likely to remain relatively stable for a significant period. This means that there have been several "technology horizons", the dates of which are a useful indication of the surveying accuracy likely to have been achieved, although these dates can only be approximate due to the time taken to phase in new technology.

2   The following table shows significant dates on the technology horizon:

Date	Sounding Method	Fixing Method	Remarks
Pre-1865	lead line	Angles to local landmarks	Surveys were mainly concerned with recording previously undiscovered land. More attention was given to fixing the coast than to provide soundings. Soundings, where present at all, tend to be sparse, with irregular gaps between them. The quoted scale is largely irrelevant when used to judge sounding density.
1865	lead line	Angles to local landmarks	Steam replaced sail in British survey ships and regular lines of soundings begin to appear. Offshore, the scale of the survey will give an indication of the expected density of soundings. Inshore, where boats were used instead of ships, oars remained the method of propulsion, and sounding lines continued to be irregular.
1905	lead line	Angles to local landmarks	Steam replaced oars as the propulsion method for survey boats, allowing regular lines of soundings to be extended to all areas of the survey. The scale of the survey gives an indication for the first time of the expected density of soundings.
1935	single beam echo sounder	Angles to local landmarks	Greater ease of collecting soundings allowed far denser surveys to be gathered. The scale of the survey gives an indication of the expected density of soundings.
1950	single beam echo sounder	Electronic position-fixing	Greater accuracy and consistency of position fixing extending farther offshore than was possible with angles to shore marks.
1973	single beam echo sounder and side-scan sonar	Electronic position-fixing	Side-scan sonar allows surveyor to locate hazards that exist between lines of soundings. For the first time, surveys will have covered the entire sea floor.
1985	single beam echo sounder and side-scan sonar	Satellite position-fixing	Introduction of satellite positioning allows surveyor to accurately position his ship anywhere in the world to a common datum.
2000	Swathe echo sounder	Satellite position-fixing	Swathe systems replace single beam echo sounders and side-scan sonar. Swathe systems permit the surveyor to detect obstructions between survey lines and to gather depths over them.

It should be noted that the date when a survey was conducted is of particular relevance in area where the seabed is composed of unstable materials and is therefore liable to move.

3   The maximum draught of vessels in service at the time of a survey affected the depths to which soundings were taken, and the depths of shoals examined. Until 1858, the year in which the SS *Great Eastern,* with an intended draught of 9·1 m, was launched, the draught of a vessel rarely exceeded 6 m. Draughts of 15 m were considered a maximum until about 1958. Now, the largest vessels in service may have draughts of up to around 30 m.

4   In spite of the advances in modern surveying methods, and the many reports received from vessels at sea, undiscovered dangers, particularly to deep-draught vessels, must still be expected, even on well-frequented routes. For example, Walter Shoals, on the route from Cape of Good Hope to Selat Sunda, with a least depth of 18 m, were not discovered until 1962.

Sounding methods

General information
1.11

1   There are four sounding methods used to obtain depth data for use on Admiralty charts: lead line, single beam echo sounder, swathe echo sounder, and LIDAR (LIght Detection And Ranging) (see 1.15). Additionally, Wire Sweep and Sidescan sonar are included here, for although they are not sounding methods in themselves, they aid the surveyor in providing a better understanding of the seabed and associated depths.

An illustration of the data quality obtainable by some of these sounding methods can be seen in the examples of sandwaves at 5.53.

Lead line
1.12

1   This is the oldest method of obtaining depth information. The surveyor lowers a lead weight, into the sea, attached to a graduated line. When the weight touches the bottom, the depth is recorded

Unsurveyed

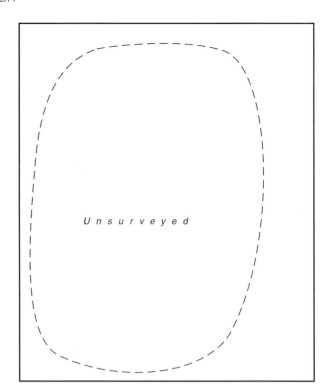

Unsurveyed

Lead Line

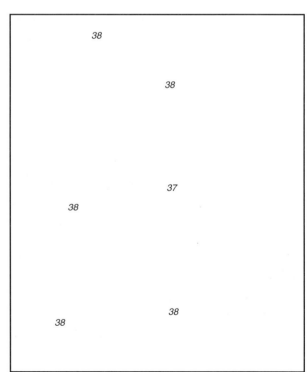

Lead Line sounding selection

Sounding Methods (1.11)

Single Beam

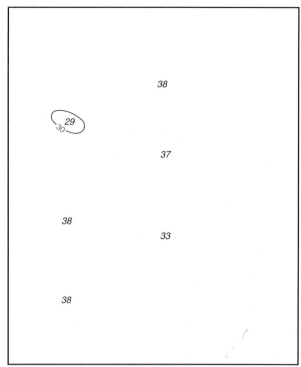

Single Beam sounding selection

Multibeam

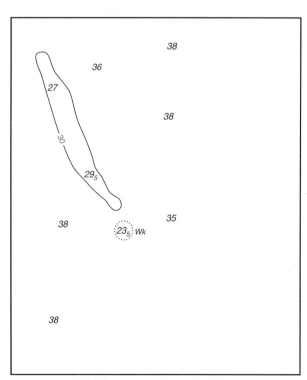

Multibeam sounding selection

Sounding Methods (1.11)

using the graduations on the line. The method is simple, and can be highly accurate. The problem with using a lead line is that it only measures the depth in the position where the line is lowered and gives no information about depths in other areas.

Single beam echo sounder
1.13

1   The single beam echo sounder transmits a pulse of acoustic energy vertically below the vessel and times the interval between transmission and reception of the returning echo. Provided that the speed of sound in the water column is known, the time interval can be used to calculate the depth of water.

2   Vessels equipped with a single beam echo sounder are able to gather a complete profile off the sea floor directly beneath them. The depths along this profile are generally of high accuracy, although, like the lead line, single beam echo sounders provide no information about depths either side of the vessel's track.

Swathe echo sounder
1.14

1   There are two types of swathe echo sounders, interferometric and beam-forming. Although the technologies are different, the result of their use in surveying is similar, so they are considered together here. Swathe echo sounders transmit a swathe of acoustic energy along a narrow fan ahead and astern, and in a wider fan on either beam. The reflected energy from the sea floor is processed and the position for each depth, relative to the transducer, is computed from the angle of reception and the time.

2   The major benefit of swathe echo sounding is that close to 100% coverage of the sea floor can be achieved, so that uncertainties between adjacent sounding lines can be greatly minimised. In addition, the acoustic processing technology used in swathe echo sounding equipment results in a much higher resolution of sea floor features, resulting in a much better understanding of the seabed topography. See also 11.102.

LIDAR
1.15

1   LIDAR is a laser pulsing device, normally mounted in fixed or rotary-wing aircraft, which uses timed pulses of energy to measure the distance between the transmitter and the ground or sea floor. There are two types in use: topographic and bathymetric. Information from both may exist on Admiralty charts.

    Topographic LIDAR. As the name implies, topographic equipment can only be used to measure heights of land, but if used at low water, can provide useful information on drying sandbanks.

2   The equipment uses a low power infra-red laser that can be pulsed very quickly (10 kHz) and has a very narrow beamwidth, allowing highly detailed data to be collected. The density of the data results in surveys that are normally as good or better than the highest quality swathe echo sounder surveys. The infra-red laser used in these systems will not penetrate any water, so any survey carried out can only take place when the sea floor is dry.

3   **Bathymetric LIDAR.** This equipment works in a similar way to topographic LIDAR except that in order for the laser pulse to penetrate the water, it uses a blue-green laser. Also, because of the greater difficulty in penetrating water, more power is required. This creates two problems: firstly, because the greater power output generates more heat, the laser cannot be pulsed as quickly (1 kHz is the more common speed, but there are some which operate around 3 kHz). Secondly, The wavelength and power of the pulse must be diffused in order to make it eye safe.

4   For these reasons, the laser has a spot diameter of about 2 m when it hits the sea surface, much broader than the narrow beam of the infra-red laser. Refraction within the water column also affects the spot diameter, so that it expands to around half the water depth; for example in 20 m of water, the spot diameter of the pulse will be in the order of 10 m. This limits the ability of system to detect small features, and it is therefore not possible to say with any certainty that small features (up to around ⅓ of the area of the spot) have been detected.

5   Furthermore, because LIDAR works by effectively shining light through water, the opacity of the water limits the depth to which the laser can penetrate. In exceptionally clear water, the maximum depth is about 70 m, whereas typically in UK waters 20-30 m is the maximum achievable penetration. Black rocks and kelp will also further limit the maximum effective depth of the system.

6   The foregoing constraints can combine to make the system less able to produce high-resolution sea floor mapping than than a swathe system, although it is still substantially better than a single beam echo sounder survey. Nevertheless, being aircraft mounted, LIDAR is useful for surveying shallow areas which it is difficult for boats to reach. Also, aircraft speeds allow large areas to be covered (up to 65 km^2 per hour) much more quickly.

Wire sweep or wire drag
1.16

1   Depths obtained from wire sweeps appear on Admiralty charts, notably over wrecks. When a wreck is discovered, it may not be possible to obtain an accurate depth using a single beam echo sounder, because some narrow or thin features such as masts or derricks may represent a danger but do not necessarily register on the sounder. In order to establish the presence of such dangers, the survey vessel will lower a thin wire to a predetermined depth and slowly traverse the position of the wreck. If the wire does not snag, it is lowered in stages and the process is repeated until it does. The deepest depth at which the wire did not snag is then recorded as the "swept" depth.

Side-scan sonar
1.17

1   Side-scan sonar is not used for obtaining depths. It is, however, a tool which can look sideways and allows the surveyor to detect the presence of features either side of the vessel's track. Once detected, the surveyor must run extra sounding lines over the detected feature in order to obtain its depth.

Fixing methods

Angles to local landmarks
1.18

1 Before satellite or electronic position fixing systems were available, surveyors would position their boats by measuring angles to prominent local landmarks. If done carefully, this can be a very accurate method, although it only positions the boat relative to the local landmark.

Electronic position fixing
1.19

1 In the 1950s, electronic position fixing became available. The first such systems used three or more land–based transmitting stations which allowed the surveyor to position himself using special charts drawn up with lattices overlaid on the charted detail. This method of fixing was not necessarily more accurate than the angles used earlier, but it did have the advantage that it worked farther offshore, and in all weather conditions.

Satellite position fixing
1.20

1 With the advent of satellite positioning, the surveyor became independent of shore stations for the first time, because satellite derived positions were related to a global horizontal datum eg WGS84. Initially, the accuracy of these systems were no greater than those derived from electronic position fixing, but they had the advantage of being able to be used worldwide. The disadvantage was that for the first time the relationship between the global horizontal datum in use and local land datums, to which all previous surveys had been related, had to be defined. Sometimes the difference could be in the order of several hundred metres. This problem was resolved by converting positions from one datum to the other before plotting. Recently, advances in processing methods have led to a significant increase in the accuracy obtainable from satellite positioning systems, and surveys can now be positioned with an accuracy of better than 5 m.

2 On charts based on older surveys, it may therefore be expected that some dangers within the 20 m depth contour may have been missed, and that even when the survey is modern every danger may not have been located.

Depths

Accuracy and quality of information
1.21

1 Outside the 20 m depth contour there may be known shoal depths which were not significant when they were found, but which, if fully examined. could prove to be dangers with less water than charted over them.

2 Offshore surveys seldom attain the precision of those in sheltered inshore waters due to difficulties in fixing, in sounding in a seaway, and the almost invariable requirement to reduce soundings to chart datum using interpolation between distant tide gauges.

3 Due caution should therefore be exercised when in parts of the world which have not been recently surveyed or where isolated pinnacles or shoals are common.

Deep draught vessels in particular should exercise due caution when within the 200 m depth contour in parts of the world which are imperfectly surveyed, or where many reported shoals are shown on the charts.

4 Within the 20 m depth contour, for the same reason, it must be assumed that some dangers may not have been detected. Vessels of normal draught should not therefore approach the shore within the 20 m depth contour without taking due precaution to avoid a possible danger. Outside the 20 m depth contour there may be not only similar dangers, but others discovered by older surveys, but not then being significant to shipping on account of their depths, not examined to modern standards.

5 Even with plans of harbours and channels which have been surveyed in detail on scale of 1:12 500 or larger, vessels should avoid if possible passing over isolated soundings appreciably shoaler than surrounding ones, as some rocks are so sharp that the shoalest part may not have been found by the lead, or the echo sounder may not have passed directly over the peak. Depths over wrecks (1.38) should be treated with caution for the same reason, unless they have been obtained by wire sweep.

6 Soundings which do not originate from a regular survey are shown as "Reported" on Admiralty charts, or "Doubtful" on International charts. They may prove to be incorrect in depth or position, or totally false. In the case of a newly-discovered feature it is unlikely that the least depth will have been found. Such soundings should therefore be taken to indicate that similar, or less depths, may be encountered in the vicinity.

Seabed

Nature of the seabed
1.22

1 Too much trust should not be placed on the quality of the seabed shown on charts, since the majority of samples will have been obtained by means of a lead armed with tallow, and are therefore only representative of the surface layer. More reliable are seabed symbols shown in the vicinity of anchorages, or qualities of the seabed described with the holding ground in *Admiralty Sailing Directions*, as the samples will probably have been obtained from the anchor flukes of the vessel that did the original survey. More reliance can also be placed on symbols showing one type of seabed over another, as the sample must have been larger than that usually obtained from an armed lead.

Areas of mobile seabed
1.23

1 In certain areas where the nature of the seabed is unstable, depths may change by several metres in a matter of weeks. In these cases, even when surveys are conducted to a modern standard (i.e. 1973 onwards), if the seabed is mobile, significant differences may still exist between depths as charted and depths as they presently exist. In areas where the seabed is very changeable, the chart will carry a legend such as "Changeable Depths". In such areas, the mariner should exercise due caution and obtain the latest known depths from local authorities, even when the charted depths along the intended track indicate sufficient depth of water, proceeding only when safe to do so.

2   Coral reefs (5.46) can grow by as much as 0·05 m in a year, or 5 m in a century. Shifting banks or sandwaves (5.53) may themselves appreciably alter depths, or may move or uncover wrecks near them.

Charting

Navigational information

Use of information received
1.24

1   Increased offshore operations and interest in the sea floor, the continuous development and construction of ports and terminals, the deeper draught of vessels using coastal waters, increased traffic management, and more efficient and rapid methods of surveying, are among the reasons for the growing amount of information reaching the UKHO.

2   This information is closely examined on receipt before being promulgated in the wide range of paper and electronic charts, diagrams, books, pamphlets and digital products published by the UKHO. In this way it is sought to keep hydrographic products up-to-date.

Disclaimer
1.25

1   While the UKHO makes all reasonable efforts to ensure that data supplied is accurate, it should be appreciated that the data may not always be complete, up-to-date or positioned to modern surveying standards and therefore no warranty can be given as to its accuracy.

2   The mariner must be the final judge of the reliance he places on the information given, bearing in mind his particular circumstances, the need for safe and prudent navigation, local pilotage guidance and the judicious use of available navigational aids. The appearance and content of the data depicted on paper and digital charts may vary with the scale of the chart and may be different when depicted in a digital chart system (see 2.87).

Digital products
1.26

1   Increasing use is being made of new digital techniques for displaying, transmitting, and updating navigational information used at sea. Digital data products include electronic charts (see 2.77 to 2.110), *Admiralty TotalTide* (3.33), the *Admiralty Digital List of Lights* (3.18), and services such as *Admiralty Notices to Mariners* (4.25) to be found on the UKHO website www.ukho.gov.uk

2   Within the UKHO, strenuous efforts are made to ensure that the data provided through these services are as accurate as they can be. Data received on CD-ROM will have been checked before issue. Data on the web is checked before posting to the website and regular checks of the data on the website are maintained. There remains a small risk that such data may be corrupted by hitherto unforeseen means or even by the user's own digital equipment.

Software
1.27

1   In addition to the increasing supply of digital navigational information, the UKHO is finding the need to develop products which embody software which generates data and information for use in navigation. The most obvious case is the supply of software for tidal prediction, such as Admiralty TotalTide (3.33). In other cases, search facilities are incorporated in products to enable the user to locate particular items of information.

2   The UKHO normally commissions the development of such software and all possible means are used to ensure that the information generated within such a product is correct and reliable. However, with increasingly complex software, it is important that the user should only operate it on suitable equipment, as stated in the individual guidance notes for the product. It is also important that other applications should not be running on the user's machine at the same time.

3   Guidance notes and advice relating to software and data are included with the product information for each individual product.

Methods and standards

Scale
1.28

1   The nature and importance of the area concerned govern the thoroughness with which the area must be examined and therefore the selection of the scale of the survey.
     Ports and harbours are usually surveyed on a scale of between 1:12 500 and 1:5000, and anchorages on a scale of only 1:25 000.

2   A general survey of a coast which vessels only pass in proceeding from one place to another is seldom made on a scale larger than 1:50 000. In such general surveys of coasts or little frequented anchorages, the surveyor does not contemplate that ships will approach the shore without taking special precautions.

3   Survey systems which collect data in a digital form, and multibeam echo sounders which can achieve total ensonification of the sea floor, do not themselves guarantee complete and rigorous coverage of an area. The method by which the data obtained is processed is particularly important in assessing the completeness of coverage and is therefore carefully considered by the chart compiler before eliminating any pre-existing shoal depths.

4   Charts may be published on a smaller scale than the surveys on which they are based, though modern large scale charts are often published on the same scale as the original surveys. With an older chart it would be unwise to assume the original survey was on a larger scale than that of the chart itself.

5   Very rarely is it necessary for the scale of any part of a chart to be larger than the scale of the survey: if such extrapolation has been necessary the fact is stated in the title block of the chart to warn against the false sense of accuracy such extrapolation gives.

Scale accuracy
1.29

1   The accuracy of the scale of a chart depends on the accuracy of the original base measurement and early surveys in difficult terrain often used methods that were less accurate than modern electronic means. This resulted in small unknown errors in scale and therefore distances throughout the survey, which should be borne in mind when fixing by radar in remote areas. For example, whilst an error of 5% in the length of the base would have no practical effect on fixes based on bearings or angles, distances obtained by radar would need to be adjusted by 5% to agree with charted distances.

2   Positions plotted on, or extracted from, a chart will contain an element of imprecision related to the scale of the chart.

Examples:

At a scale of 1:600 000, a chart user who is capable of plotting to a precision of 0·3 mm must appreciate that this represents approximately 120 m on the ground.

3   At a scale of 1:25 000, the same plotting error will be only about 5 m on the ground.

Thus, if the difference between a WGS84 Datum position and the horizontal datum of the chart is, say 50 m, this would not be plottable at the smaller scale, (the chart could effectively be said to be on WGS84 Datum) but would be plottable (2·0 mm), and therefore significant, at the larger scale.

4   This explains why it is not uncommon for small and medium scale approach charts to be referenced to WGS84 Datum while the larger scale port plans have no quoted horizontal datum. Similarly, some charts at scales of 1:50 000 and smaller just quote a reference to WGS Datum (without a year date) since the positional difference between WGS72 and WGS84 Datums is not plottable at these scales.

Chart Datums and the accuracy of charted positions
1.30

1   The International Maritime Organization offers the following advice:

"Many different definitions of a horizontal datum (also known as geodetic datum) exist. However, a practical working definition in use is:
A horizontal datum is a reference system for specifying positions on the Earth's surface. Each datum is associated with a particular reference spheroid that can be different in size, orientation and relative position from the spheroids associated with other horizontal datums. Positions referred to different datums can differ by several hundred metres."

2   The practical result is that a given geographical position, not associated with a specific datum, could refer to different physical objects. In other words, a physical object can have as many geographical positions as there are datums.

3   For example, South Foreland Lighthouse, United Kingdom, has the following positions:

Geographical Position	Horizontal Datum
51°08'·39N 1°22'·37E	Referred to OSGB(36) Datum (the former local datum for the United Kingdom)
51°08'·47N 1°22'·35E	Referred to European (1950) Datum (the Continental datum)
51°08'·42N 1°22'·27E	Referred to World Geodetic System 1984 (WGS84) Datum (the world-wide datum used by Global Positioning System (GPS))

4   Most paper charts world–wide are not yet referred to WGS84 Datum. This means that, in those cases, positions obtained from satellite navigation receivers will not be directly compatible with the chart and must not be used without adjustment. Hydrographic offices are attempting to refer as many new charts as possible to WGS84, but there remain many areas of the world where information does not exist to enable the transformation to be performed.

5   When known, the horizontal datum of the chart is usually named in the chart title block although, on its own, this information is of limited benefit to the mariner. Since 1982 many hydrographic offices have been adding "Satellite-Derived Positions" notes (usually situated close to the title) when charts have been revised. This note provides a latitude and longitude adjustment to be applied to positions obtained directly from satellite navigation systems (such as GPS) to make them compatible with the horizontal datum of the chart.

6   The following provides a worked example:

Satellite-derived position	4°22'·00N	21°30'·00W
Lat/Long adjustments	0'·07S	0'·24E
Adjusted position (compatible with Chart Datum)	4°21'·93N	21°29'·76W

In this example, the shift equates to approximately 230 m which can be plotted at scales larger than 1:1 000 000.

7   Where known, these adjustments are an average value for the whole area covered by the chart and are quoted to 2 decimal places of a minute in both latitude and longitude, so that the maximum uncertainty is about 10 m in both latitude and longitude (0·005' and 0·014' will both be rounded to 0·01'). This uncertainty can be plotted at scales larger than 1:30 000 (where it is represented by 0·3 mm on the chart).

8   Inevitably, cases exist where overlapping charts show different latitude or longitude shift values. For example, one chart might show 0·06' and its neighbour 0·07'; for each individual chart the value will be an average, but in the area common to both charts the value will range from 0·064' to 0·066'.

9   In cases where an adjustment cannot be determined because of the lack of knowledge about the relationship between WGS84 Datum and the datum of the chart, the hydrographic office may add a note to that effect, warning that adjustments "may be significant to navigation". The largest difference between satellite navigation derived and charted position reported so far is 7 miles in the Pacific Ocean, but even larger undiscovered differences may exist. Where charts do not contain any note about position adjustment it must not be assumed that no adjustment is required.

10   Most manufacturers of GPS receivers are now incorporating datum transformations into their software which enable users to (apparently) receive positions referred to datums other than WGS84 Datum. Unfortunately, many cases exist where a single transformation will not be accurate for a large regional datum. For example, the relationship between WGS84 Datum and European Datum (1950) is very different between the north and south of the region, despite the datum name being the same.

11   Therefore, the position transformed to WGS84 Datum in the receiver by means of a Europe-wide average may differ from the WGS84 Datum position output by the receiver, amended to European Datum (1950) by the shift note on an individual chart. This is a source of error and may be of major significance for navigation.

12   It must not be assumed that all charts in a region are referred to the regional datum. For example, although most metric charts of mainland European waters are referred to European Datum (1950), many charts are also referred to local datums, such as Norwegian Datum 1948. Additionally, as there are no international standards defining the conversion parameters between different horizontal datums, the parameters used by the GPS devices may be different. Hydrographic offices use the best available parameters, so mariners are advised to keep their GPS receiver referred to WGS84 Datum, or, in the case of GLONASS to PZ90 Datum, and apply the datum adjustment note from the chart.

13   Apart from the differences in positions between different horizontal datums, two other aspects affect charted positional accuracy. These aspects are:

The accuracy to which features are surveyed (see 1.31).

The accuracy to which they are compiled on to a chart (see 1.32).

Surveying
1.31

1   Hydrographic surveys are generally conducted using the best position-fixing technology available at the time. Until the Second World War, this was limited to accurate visual fixing. Subsequently, terrestrial based electronic position fixing (such as Decca, Hifix, Hyperfix, and Trisponder) were used until the 1980s. DGPS is the current standard for most hydrographic surveys.

2   Generally, position fixing for surveying was more accurate than that for navigation in the first two categories, but DGPS (1.34 and 11.41) is widely available for use by all mariners with the appropriate equipment. The result is that current navigation with DGPS is, commonly, more accurate than position-fixing used for surveys conducted before 1980.

3   The consequence is that, although a modern vessel may know its position to an accuracy of better than 10 metres, the position of objects on the sea floor may only be known to an accuracy of 200 metres or much

worse, depending on the age of the latest survey and/or its distance from the coast.

4   Furthermore, it is only since the 1980s that surveying systems have had the computer processing capacity to enable the observations to be analysed to enable an estimate of the accuracy of position fixing to be generated. The result is that, although the current accuracy standard of position fixing surveys can be stated, it is impossible to provide anything other than general estimates for older surveys.

5   The current accuracy standard for positioning is ±13 metres for most surveys with the standard of plus or minus 5 metres (both 95% of the time) for certain special purpose surveys. It can be confidently stated that the former value is often significantly improved upon. Further improvements will undoubtedly be made as a result of technological developments, but at present there has to be a balance between the cost of a survey and the quality and quantity of the results achieved.

6   In summary, although the position of maritime objects derived from modern surveys will be accurate to better than 10 metres, this cannot be used as a general statement about all such objects.

Chart compilation
1.32

1   Most paper charts and their derived digital versions are assembled from a variety of sources such as maps, surveys, and photogrammetric plots. The intention is to provide the mariner with the best available information for all parts of that chart and the usual procedure is to start with the most accurate sources, but it is often impossible to complete the whole chart without recourse to older, less accurate, sources.

2   When sources are referred to different datums, transformations have to be calculated and applied to make the sources compatible. The intention is for such transformations to have an accuracy of 0·3 mm at chart scale, this being the effective limit of manual cartography. But, depending on the information available, this may not always be possible.

3   When the positions of navigationally significant objects are accurately known, the intention is that they are located on a chart to an accuracy of 0·3 mm. The obvious consequence is that accuracy varies with chart scale. Thus:

0·3 mm at a scale of 1:10 000 is 3 m;
0·3 mm at a scale of 1:50 000 is 15 m;
0·3 mm at a scale of 1:150 000 is 45 m.

4   The situation will change as chart data becomes available digitally, but much of the early digital data will derive from these paper charts and the limitations will remain. Furthermore, a pixel on a computer display screen is approximately 0·2 mm square, roughly equivalent to the accuracy available on the paper chart.

5   The situation for mariners is improving with recent surveys referred directly to WGS84 Datum, increasing numbers of charts referred to WGS84 Datum (or to ETRS89 or other WGS84 compatible datums) which for all practical purposes is the same) and increased international co-operation in the exchange of information. It will be many years before all areas are re-surveyed and all charts revised.

6   Until such time, mariners should remain alert to danger. A satellite navigation receiver may output a position to a precision of three decimal places of a minute, but that does not mean that all its positions are accurate to 2 m or that the resulting position is compatible with the positions of objects shown on modern charts (paper or digital) which may have been established 100 years ago and not surveyed since. The chart title notes and cautions and the source diagram, which shows the ages of surveys, must always be consulted for indications of limitations.

Positions from satellite navigation systems
1.33

1   Positions obtained from GPS (11.36) are normally referred to WGS84, whilst positions obtained from GLONASS (11.44) are referred to SGS90 or PZ90, whose agreement with WGS84 Datum is less than 15 m with a mean average of about 5 metres. As a result, at present, neither can be plotted on those Admiralty paper charts (currently almost half the total) which are referred to local horizontal datums. The intention is to refer all charts to WGS84 Datum, but this will be a lengthy process, and one that can proceed only when the relationships between existing surveys and WGS84 Datum have been established. In advance of achieving this aim, all New Charts and New Editions of charts on scales of 1:2 000 000 and larger, published since 1981, carry a note indicating the magnitude and direction of the shift between satellite-derived positions (referred to WGS84 Datum) and chart positions.

2   The latest wording of the shift note includes an example, unique for each chart, which depicts how the shift should be applied.

3   There remain many charts, some carrying a note stating that a satellite-derived position shift cannot be determined, where sufficient details of horizontal datum are not known. It is important to note that in the worst cases, such as isolated islands or charts of great antiquity, there may be a discrepancy of several miles in charted positions from those derived from GNSS. This means that approximately 1000 charts carry a note which, in its latest wording, states that:

4   *"Mariners are warned that these differences MAY BE SIGNIFICANT TO NAVIGATION and are therefore advised to use alternative sources of positional information, particularly when closing the shore or navigating in the vicinity of dangers".*

5   However, the absence of such notes must not be taken to imply that WGS84 Datum positions can be plotted directly on a chart, simply that the chart has not been examined and updated since 1981.

6   Mariners who visit areas where the charts carry no note, or have the note stating that differences cannot be determined, are requested to report observed differences between positions referenced to chart graticule and those from GPS, referenced to WGS84 Datum using Form H102b (see 4.52). The results of these observations are examined and may provide evidence for notes detailing approximate differences between WGS84 Datum and the datum of the chart.

Differential Global Positioning System (DGPS)
1.34

1   Whereas GPS produces a quoted accuracy in the order of metres, DGPS has the potential to produce positions accurate to less than a metre when referred to WGS84 Datum. Admiralty charts are compiled from the best source data available, but these sources are of varying age and scale. Also, in different parts of the world, charts are referred to a variety of different datums. These factors may each introduce apparent inaccuracies between the chart and the GPS if the mariner relies solely on GPS for navigation and attempts to navigate to the quoted GPS accuracy.

2   Mariners are warned against over reliance on the quoted accuracy of GNSS systems when using some large and medium scale Admiralty charts, both paper and ARCS (2.106) versions, particularly when closing the coast or approaching off lying dangers such as wrecks.

3   In many parts of the world, including some parts of the British Isles, the most recent data available may have been gathered when survey methods were less sophisticated than they are now and the sort of accuracy currently available with GPS was not possible. In these cases, the absolute accuracy of the positioning of this data to modern standards is doubtful. However, where recent survey data exists (in most significant ports and their approaches and in other areas where modern surveys are indicated in the Source Diagram on the appropriate chart) this should be less of a problem.

Graduations on plans
1.35

1   Graduations are now inserted on all plans, and on all previously published ungraduated ones as opportunity offers. On old plans, these graduations are often based on imperfect information. Consequently, whenever an accurate geographical position is quoted, it is necessary to quote the number of the chart from which the position has been derived.

Distortion of charts
1.36

1   The paper on which charts are printed is subject to distortion, but the effect of this is seldom sufficient to affect navigation. It must not however be expected that accurate series of angles taken to different points will always exactly agree when carefully plotted on the chart, especially if the lines are to be objects at some distance.

Ocean charting
1.37

1   While most charts of the continental shelf are based on surveys of varying age and quality, very little survey work of a systematic nature has been carried out beyond the edge of the continental shelf (200 m depth contour). With the completion of the two series of International Charts on scales of 1:3 500 000 and 1:10 000 000, augmented by the series of Admiralty 1:3 500 000 mid-ocean charts and 1:10 000 000 Southern Ocean charts, the oceans have been systematically charted for the first time to common specifications.

2   These charts, however, still represent only a "best guess" in their portrayal of the depths and shape of the ocean floor. They are for the most part still based on sparse and inadequate sounding data, and many significant bathymetric features, including shoals, have doubtless still to be found and charted.

3   The International Hydrographic Organization estimated in 1976 that for only 16% of the oceans was there sufficient sounding data to determine the sea floor topography with reasonable accuracy; for a further 22% the data were only sufficient for showing major sea floor features; while for the remaining 62% the sounding data were considered too sparse to describe the sea floor with any degree of completeness. Despite more lines of ocean soundings from ships on passage since then, the situation is much the same today.

4   Nearly all ocean soundings available are from random lines of soundings from a wide variety of sources of varying reliability and accuracy. Sounding coverage is best along well-frequented routes, but even in these waters undiscovered dangers may still exist, especially for deep-draught vessels.

5   For example, the existence of Muirfield Seamount which lies on the route from Cape of Good Hope to Selat Sunda, 75 miles SW of Cocos Islands, was not suspected until 1973 when MV *Muirfield* reported having struck an "obstruction" and sustained considerable damage to her keel. At the time, she was travelling at 13½ kn, with a draught of 16 m in a 2 to 3 m swell, and in charted depths of over 5000 m. A subsequent survey by HMAS *Moresby* in 1983 found a least depth of 18 m over the seamount, the summit being level and about 5 cables in extent rising sharply on all sides from deep water.

6   Particular care is needed when navigating in the vicinity of oceanic dangers or seamounts as very few of these features have been fully surveyed to modern standards to determine their correct position, full extent, or the least depth over them.

Many charted ocean dangers and shoals are from old sketch surveys and reports, often dating from the nineteenth century. Positions from such reports may be grossly in error; their probable positional error, if prior to the general introduction of radio time signals for shipping in the 1920s, is considered to be of the order of ±10–20 miles, but may be greater.

7   Furthermore, many ocean dangers are pinnacle-shaped pillars of rock or coral rising steeply from deep water, crowning the summits of seamounts and ocean ridges: little or no warning is given from soundings in their approach. Consequently the detection of dangerous pinnacles in time to take avoiding action will be extremely difficult, especially for modern deep-draught ocean-going vessels travelling under normal conditions. A dangerous pinnacle in ocean depths could possibly exist 2 cables from depths of 1000 m, 5 cables from depths of 2000 m, and 2 miles from depths of 3000 m.

Depth criteria for wrecks
1.38

1   Modern charting standards specify that new wrecks will be charted showing the least depth over them, if known. Depicting wrecks in this manner, in preference to the use of the symbols for dangerous (⊞) and non-dangerous (⧾) wrecks, provides the mariner with the maximum useful information, and allows him to assess what degree of danger the particular wreck represents for his particular vessel.

2   Mariners should be aware, however, that the symbols for dangerous and non-dangerous wrecks remain in common usage on charts published by the UKHO and other hydrographic offices and, furthermore, that the different hydrographic organisations may use different criteria to differentiate between these two classifications of wreck.

3   The depth criteria used by the UKHO to differentiate between the two classifications of wreck have changed over the years. If the depth of water over a wreck was thought to be equal to, or less than, the depth criteria in the table below, then the wreck would have been charted as dangerous (⊞).

Date	Depth criteria
Before 1960	14·6 m (8 fathoms)
1960 – 1963	18·3 m (10 fathoms)
1963 – 1968	20·1 m (11 fathoms)
1968 onwards	28·0 m (15 fathoms)

4   The progressive changes above were a reflection of the ever increasing sizes of vessel which were entering service during the period.

Mariners should be aware, however, that circumstances exist which result in wrecks with a depth of less than 28 m over them being charted as non-dangerous wrecks (less-dangerous wrecks might be a more appropriate term) on present day editions of Admiralty charts. Such circumstances include:

5   Admiralty charts which have been compiled either partially or entirely using data from a foreign chart where different criteria have been used for wreck assessment. In such cases the foreign criteria, and the associated chart symbols, will be carried forward on to the Admiralty chart.

6   Similarly, a foreign government Notice to Mariners may promulgate information concerning a wreck in an area covered by an Admiralty chart. If the UKHO decides that it is appropriate to re-issue the information in an Admiralty Notice to Mariners for the Admiralty chart(s) concerned, the original foreign government criteria, assessment and resulting chart symbol will be retained.

7   Earlier wrecks, originally assessed and charted with reference to the criteria of the day, may be charted on subsequent New Editions and New Charts without the benefit of present day re-assessment and, in consequence, will retain the symbol appropriate to the criteria of the time. An extreme example might be a 1959 wreck with a depth of 15·5 m (8½ fathoms) over it, which was assessed and charted as non-dangerous at the time, continuing to be charted as non-dangerous today.

8   Wrecks with less than 28 m over them may, in certain circumstances, be assessed by the UKHO using more subjective criteria in addition to depth, and, as a result, be classified and charted as non-dangerous.

In light of the foregoing, mariners are advised that wrecks charted as non-dangerous nevertheless remain worthy of caution, and that a value for the minimum depth over them cannot be derived simply by inspection of the chart.

System of names

System
1.39

1   Geographical names are rendered in UKHO publications in accordance with the general rules

followed by the Permanent Committee on Geographical Names for British Official Use (PCGN) and on the Technical Resolutions and Chart Specifications of the IHO.

2   The principal function of the PCGN is to advise the British government on policies and procedures for the proper writing of geographical names for places outside the UK, excluding the Antarctic. It also provides a unique toponymic perspective on current global political affairs.

    Internet. http://www.pcgn.org.uk

Definitions
1.40

1   **Toponym:** A word or group of words constituting a proper name designating a natural or artificial topographic feature, e.g. London, Deutsche Bucht, Southsea Castle.

2   **Exonym:** A toponym used by one country to designate a geographical feature that lies wholly or partly outside the bounds of its national sovereignty, and which may be situated in territory under the jurisdiction of another state which uses a different form, e.g. Londres, Copenhagen, Finland, Atlantic Ocean.

    Generic term: The term in a legend or toponym which describes the type of geographic feature, e.g. Channel, Bank, Castle.

3   **State:** The term includes an independent country or colonial territory, or protectorate, protected state or trust territory.

General principles
1.41

1   The approved name of any administrative division of a state, or federation of states, or any natural or artificial geographical feature or any place lying wholly within one state, or federation of states, is that adopted by the supreme administrative authority concerned with that state or federation of states; e.g. Kaliningrad not Königsberg.

2   Where states officially use varieties of the Roman alphabet, toponyms are accepted in their official spelling. If accents or diacritical marks are used in these alphabets, they are shown on both upper and lower case letters.

3   Where states use partly-Roman alphabets, the non-Roman letters in toponyms may be transliterated into Roman letters in accordance with the conventions of the respective partly Roman alphabets, e.g. Icelandic ð=dh, þ=th, Maltese ħ=h.

    In Norwegian, ø (not ö) and å (not aa) are to be used; in Danish, ø (not ö) is to be used, but the use of å or aa in Danish is now a matter of choice for the relevant local authority and spellings should be in accordance with the latest Danish chart or map.

    Note that the earlier forms may still be found on some older charts of Denmark and Norway.

4   Where the official alphabet of the administering authority is not Roman, the spelling of names is to be in accordance with the current official Romanisation acceptable to PCGN. If no official Romanisation exists, but a system of Roman transliteration has been accepted by PCGN, the official forms of names are to be transliterated in accordance with it.

5   Where the official script of a state is not alphabetical, e.g. Chinese, the official forms of names

are rendered in Roman letters in accordance with the system of transcription approved by PCGN.

6   For generic terms the official spelling used by the state having sovereignty is used, e.g. Isola d'Iscia (not Island of Iscia).

Exonyms
1.42

1   English conventional names are used for:
Water areas extending beyond the territorial limits of recognised governments, e.g. Gulf of Mexico, North Sea, Bay of Biscay.
Geographical regions or features extending over more than one state, or which are in dispute between nations, e.g. Europe, Sahara Desert.

2   Boundary features which have different national names, e.g. The Alps, River Danube, Pyrenees. Sailing Directions give the various national or alternative names as well.
Names of places where more than one official language is in use, and names of places differ, e.g. Antwerp (not Anvers or Antwerpen). National forms are also given in *Admiralty Sailing Directions*.

3   Names of states on charts: If the name of a foreign state is shown in the title of a chart, the English exonym is used. In the body of the chart the exonym is also used and the national form in a subordinate style below it, e.g. FINLAND with Suomi subordinate. However, on charts of the small scale International series the form, SUOMI with Finland subordinate, is retained. In either case the national form may be transliterated.

4   Underwater features and drying features on the continental shelf lying wholly or partly outside the limits of recognised governments, though where features do not extend far beyond the limits of territorial seas this rule is not applied rigorously.

5   Exonyms of a third nation are used when that nation has held sovereignty in the past over the area in question and official names in the national language cannot be obtained. In general, the change to the national language is made only when an official gazetteer or mapping in that language is available.

Obsolete or alternative names
1.43

1   **On charts.** For certain important and well known places, and where confusion could occur, former names are retained in a subordinate style, in brackets, adjacent to the national name until the new name is accepted internationally.

    In the case of certain international features, the conventional name may be retained e.g. Malacca Strait.

2   **In Sailing Directions and other publications.** When a new name is accepted, the old name is shown in brackets until the new name has been adopted on all charts of the area concerned. Both names are indexed in *Admiralty Sailing Directions*.

    When a new or revised edition of a volume is being prepared, however, names are normally revised throughout.

3   When an old name is well known but has been superseded by a new name or form, consideration is given to retaining both names in Sailing Directions for a considerable time, e.g. Çanakkale Boğazi, formerly known as The Dardanelles.

Symbology on charts

Conventions
1.44

1   The symbology used on Admiralty paper charts is fully decribed and illustrated with examples in *Chart 5011 Symbols and Abbreviations Used on Admiralty Paper Charts.* It is based on "Chart Specifications of the International Hydrographic Organisation (IHO)", adopted in 1982, and it is laid out and the symbols numbered in accordance with the official IHO version of Chart INT 1 (English version produced by Germany).

2   Names and other legends referring to fixed (i.e. above water and land) features are normally in upright text, and those relating to floating and water features are normally in forward-sloping (italic) text. Tor features which are difficult to define as either "land" or "water", such as locks or docks, the text will be according to the principal characteristic of the feature. The same principle applies to many symbols e.g. buoys slope and beacons are upright.

Chapter 2

ADMIRALTY CHARTS

General information

Use of the most appropriate chart

General information
2.1

1　The mariner should always use the largest scale chart appropriate for his purpose.

In closing the land or dangerous banks, regard must always be had to the scale of the chart used. A small error in laying down a position may mean only a few metres on a large scale chart, whereas on a small scale the same amount of displacement on the paper may mean several cables.

2　For the same reason bearings to near objects should be used in preference to objects farther off, although the latter may be more prominent, as a small error in bearing or in laying it down on the chart has a greater effect in misplacing the position the longer the line to be drawn.

Scale
2.2

1　The larger the scale of the chart, the greater the detail that can be shown on it.

Each Admiralty chart, or series of charts, is designed for a particular purpose. Large scale charts are intended to be used for entering harbours or anchorages or for passing close to navigational hazards. Medium scale charts are usually published as series of charts intended for navigation along coasts, while small scale charts are intended for offshore navigation and passage planning.

2　The mariner using the medium scale charts for passage along a coast need not transfer on to a large scale for short distances, except where this depicts more clearly intricate navigational hazards close to his intended route. Although the larger scale chart depicts information in more detail, those on the next smaller scale show adequately all the dangers, traffic separation schemes, aids to navigation, etc, that are necessary for the purpose for which the chart is designed.

3　The principle followed in planning Admiralty charts of foreign coasts is that they should be on a scale adequate for coastal navigation or to give access to the major trading ports: this principle is generally adopted by other Hydrographic Offices which chart areas outside their own waters.

4　In some parts of the world, charts on a larger scale than those of the Admiralty series are published by national Hydrographic Offices covering their coasts and ports. The mariner intending to navigate in an area where the largest scale Admiralty chart is not adequate for his particular purpose should take steps to acquire the appropriate foreign charts (see 2.42–2.46).

5　A type approved ECDIS (2.81) will display a warning if the mariner attempts to use ENCs at scales larger than that of the source chart.

Accuracy and reliability

Reliance on charts
2.3

1　Whilst every effort is made to ensure the accuracy of the information on Admiralty charts and in other publications, it should be appreciated that the information may not always be complete, up-to-date or positioned to modern surveying standards and that information announced by Navigational Warnings or *Admiralty Notices to Mariners* because of its immediate importance cannot always be verified before promulgation. Furthermore, it is sometimes necessary to defer the promulgation of certain less important information, see 4.1 and 3.4. **Attention is drawn to paragraph 1.25.**

2　No chart is infallible. Every chart is liable to be incomplete, either through imperfections in the survey on which it is based, or through subsequent alterations to the topography or sea floor. However, in the vicinity of recognised shipping lanes charts may be used with confidence for normal navigational needs. The mariner must be the final judge of the reliance he can place on the information given, bearing in mind his particular circumstances, safe and prudent navigation, local pilotage guidance and the judicious use of available navigational aids.

3　Ships take the ground when the draught exceeds the depth of water. The practice of running and observing the echo sounder when anywhere near shoal water considerably reduces the possibility of grounding due to navigational error.

Assessing the reliability of a chart
2.4

1　Apart from any suspicious inconsistencies disclosed in the course of using a chart, the only means available to the mariner of assessing its reliability is by examining it.

Charts should be used with prudence: there are areas where the source data are old, incomplete or of poor quality.

2　The mariner should use the largest scale appropriate for his particular purpose; apart from being the most detailed, the larger scales are usually updated first. When extensive new information (such as a new hydrographic survey) is received, some months may elapse before it can be fully incorporated in published charts.

3   On small scale charts of ocean areas where hydrographic information is, in many cases, still sparse, charted shoals may be in error as regards position, least depth and extent. Undiscovered dangers may exist, particularly away from well-established routes.

4   Data used on Admiralty charts comes from a variety of sources; surveys conducted by the Royal Navy specifically for charts, those conducted by port authorities, and those conducted by oil companies, for example. Recent surveys have used DGPS as the position-fixing aid, but earlier surveys used systems such as Trisponder and Hifix with lesser accuracies, particularly at greater distances from land. Furthermore, it is only comparatively recently that surveying systems have had the computer processing capacity to enable more than the minimum number of observations to be analysed to enable an estimate of the accuracy of position fixing to be generated. This means that it is impossible to provide anything other than general accuracy estimates for older surveys, particularly those conducted out of sight of land or relative to a coastline which is itself poorly surveyed. Older surveys are often more accurate in relative terms than in absolute terms i.e. the soundings are positioned accurately in relation to each other, but as a whole may have absolute differences from modern datums such as WGS84. In these cases, conventional navigation using charted features gives better results than modern techniques such as GPS. Although a navigator may know his position relative to satellites to an accuracy of 10 m, the shoals in which he may be navigating may only be known to an accuracy of 200 m or worse.

5   Data from many other sources, positioned by various methods, is routinely included, when appropriate, so that there is no single standard accuracy to which every position on an individual chart can be quoted. However, the intention is that navigationally significant features should be plotted as accurately as possible, within ±0·3 mm of their quoted positions.

Even these considerations can only suggest the degree of reliance to be placed on it. These observations apply equally to ENCs and RNCs such as those in ARCS which may include the same data as shown on a nineteenth century fathoms chart.

6   Furthermore, it should be noted that where a chart carries the magenta legend "WGS84" or "WGS84 positions can be plotted directly on this chart", it means only that the graduation has been adjusted to be consistent with the WGS84 datum. It does not mean necessarily that any part of the area covered by the chart has been resurveyed to the same accuracy as used by GPS and equivalent systems, nor does it mean that the source data has been re-computed to remove the errors derived from earlier survey methods (which would not be possible in any case without conducting a resurvey). Therefore while GPS positions may be plotted directly onto charts that are referred to WGS84, their likely relationship to charted objects must be assessed with reference to the source statement or source diagram carried by the chart where this is available (see 1.5 and 1.6).

Horizontal datums on charts and satellite derived positions

General information

Definition of a horizontal datum
2.5

1   A horizontal, or geodetic, datum is a reference system for specifying positions on the Earth's surface. A datum is always associated with a particular reference spheroid. Different spheroids vary in size, orientation and relative position.

Note. Positions referred to different datums can differ by several hundred metres.

Background
2.6

1   In recent years the accuracy of navigation has been improved by the introduction of global navigation satellite navigation systems (GNSS) such as the Global Positioning System (GPS) (11.36). The Standard Positioning Service (SPS) is capable of horizontal positioning accurate to 20m for 95% of the time and Differential GPS (DGPS) (11.41), a refinement of GPS, allows a typical accuracy better than 5 m; some systems are capable of sub metre accuracy.

2   Because of these improvements, mariners need to be aware of the relevance of geodetic datums and the practical limitations of the depiction of charted detail.

History of datums

General information
2.7

1   For safety of navigation, it is important that all positions are accurately related to each other. It has only been since the launching of artificial earth satellites that truly world-wide horizontal datums, such as World Geodetic System 1984 (WGS84 Datum), have become a practical reality. In historical terms, datums were constructed from terrestrially observed triangulations carried out on the Earth's surface, but transferred to a theoretical surface known as the spheroid (or the ellipsoid). This is the simplest mathematical shape that most closely matches the Earth's surface and can be thought of either as a sphere compressed at the poles or as a rotated ellipse.

2   The construction of horizontal datums has passed through three distinct phases: local datums covering single countries, regional datums covering groups of countries and world-wide datums.

Local datums
2.8

1   In the era before artificial earth satellites, it was only possible to observe all points within a given datum from at least two other points within that datum using angles and distances. Thus datums could only be

developed over areas limited by geography or by territorial concerns.

The geographical limitation was any large area of water; for example, it was possible to observe between points on either side of the English Channel, but not possible to observe across the North Sea. Terrain such as forest, mountains or desert caused difficulties, but these could be overcome.

Territorial concerns limited the willingness of adjoining countries to divulge details of their surveys to their neighbours.

2   Because of irregularities in the Earth's shape and the limited area over which that shape could be observed, different countries calculated or adopted differently sized spheroids for their own triangulation. Thus the Airy spheroid matches the shape of the Earth well in the British Isles, the Everest spheroid in the Indian subcontinent and the Clarke spheroid in North America. Since they were differently sized and positioned, the theoretical centres of these spheroids are offset relative to each other in three dimensions. None of these was "wrong" for the areas in which they were used, but could not all be "right" for the whole Earth; see diagram below.

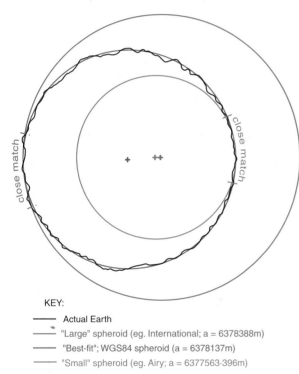

KEY:

————— Actual Earth

————— "Large" spheroid (eg. International; a = 6378388m)

————— "Best-fit"; WGS84 spheroid (a = 6378137m)

————— "Small" spheroid (eg. Airy; a = 6377563·396m)

Relative sizes and offsets of spheroids (greatly exaggerated) (2.8)

3   Irregularities in the Earth's shape and gravity field also cause anomalies in the direction of the vertical (particularly on isolated islands or near mountain ranges). Any uncertainty in the direction of the vertical will result in an error in any astronomical observations, traditionally used as the origin of a datum.

4   The final difficulty faced in the production of a coherent system of latitudes and longitudes was the calculation of the positions from a large number of angle and distance observations. Ideally such calculations would all be carried out simultaneously but, when they had to be carried out by hand with the use of tables, this was clearly impractical. The solution

was to split the area into a series of manageable blocks, calculate one and then move on to an adjacent block, holding points on the border fixed. Unfortunately, this caused errors to build up throughout the calculations leading to local distortions in the datum, shown in the diagram in paragraph 2.14.

5   Datums thus suffered from problems of origin (from the differing astronomical observations), calculation (from the large number of terrestrial observations) and surface (from the differing spheroids)

When the different geographical positions of an object on different datums are known, it is possible to calculate a transformation between the datums and then convert all positions from one datum to another. However, if the only common points fall in a small region, the resulting transformation is likely to become inaccurate away from that region.

Regional datums
2.9

1   Following World War Two, all the basic observations of most of the countries of W Europe were re-examined and extended, with the use of early electronic computers, to form European Datum 1950 (ED50), one example of a regional datum.

The next force for change was the launch of the first artificial Earth satellites which required an observation and control network on a unified datum and, eventually, provided the means of obtaining such a unified datum.

World-wide datums
2.10

1   In the early 1960s the USA launched a series of Transit satellites to improve the navigation of submarines. Methods were soon developed to exploit a series of observations of the signals to establish an accurate position for a fixed object, referred to the same datum as that used by the satellites. This datum was initially known as World Geodetic System (1960) (WGS60) which was subsequently refined to WGS66, WGS72 and, following many additional observations and calculations, WGS84.

2   There remain several older Admiralty charts which still carry a note giving positional shifts from WGS72 derived positions. These notes will be altered to refer to WGS84 as New Charts and New Editions are published. Until these are published, as an interim measure, in order to establish the shift from WGS84 to the datum of any of these charts, the longitude shift in the note should be altered by 0·01 minutes W. For example:

A shift of 0·14 minutes E from WGS72 becomes a shift of 0·13 minutes E from WGS84.

A shift of 0·24 minutes W from WGS72 becomes a shift of 0·25 minutes W from WGS84.

3   The difference between WGS72 and WGS84 is a maximum of 4·5 m in latitude and 17·1 m in longitude at the Equator reducing to zero at the poles. For all practical purposes WGS84 is likely to be the definitive datum for many years to come. WGS84 refers to both datum and spheroid; on average, the spheroid provides the closest match to the Earth's surface, although in specific areas it may not match as well as a previously calculated spheroid.

4   WGS84 is that used by the GPS (Global Positioning System) satellites and thus the datum to which positions from those satellites are normally referred.

Although navigation positions from the Standard Positioning Service (SPS) of GPS are only accurate to ± 20 m (for 95% of the time), it is possible to establish positions to geodetic (better than 1 m) accuracy. This makes it possible to compare positions on different datums and compute a transformation.

5 Some countries are adopting their own regional or continental equivalent of WGS84 to take account of tectonic plate movement. Two such equivalents are North American Datum 1983 (NAD83) and European Terrestrial Reference System 1989 (ETRS89). For practical purposes, other than precise operations such as surveying or automated docking, the differences between these datums and WGS84 will remain insignificant for the foreseeable future. Charts referred to these datums carry the magenta marginal note "WGS84", indicating that WGS84 positions may be plotted directly onto the chart.

Datums in worldwide use

Adoption of WGS84
2.11

1 Many hydrographic authorities have decided to transfer their charts to WGS84 or a WGS84 compatible datum. It is impractical to convert single, isolated charts from one datum to another as it would result in incompatibilities when moving between charts in an area. The UKHO solution has therefore been to convert groups of charts (ie all of those in an area such as the approaches to a port) at the same time. Thus, all the charts of the United Kingdom are in the process of being transformed from local datums (e.g. Ordnance Survey of Great Britain 1936 Datum (OSGB36)) to ETRS89 which is compatible with WGS84 (2.10).

2 There remain, however, many areas of the world where insufficient information exists to enable new charts to be referred to WGS84. Thus, for example, the datum used for 25% (2009) of the 6500 panels on paper charts published by the UKHO is not WGS84 (or WGS84 compatible datums), but one of over 60 regional or local datums.

3 Mariners should therefore:
Always confirm periodically that a GNSS-derived position is correctly plotted by use of relative navigation techniques such as visual fixing, radar range and bearing or a transferred ARPA target. Keep the GNSS receiver set to display WGS84 positions, applying datum shifts from the chart in use as necessary, and particularly when navigating close to coastlines and or other dangers.

4 Be aware of the limitations of the chart in use at all times, particularly in relation to the age and accuracy of the data used in its compilation. Assumptions should not be made if the datum of the chart is not stated.

Undetermined datums
2.12

1 A significant proportion (approximately 20%) of Admiralty charts are of parts of the world which cannot be related to any known datum. Effort continues to be made by hydrographic authorities to establish these relationships, but the quality and quantity of data varies from region to region, and in some cases is simply unavailable.

2 Despite recent improvements, warnings continue to be required on paper charts of those regions, and are displayed in ECDIS if ENCs are being used. On Admiralty charts, the warning states that "...the differences between satellite-derived positions and positions on this chart cannot be determined..." and that "...differences may be significant to navigation...". The largest difference found to date (2009) is 7 miles in the Pacific Ocean, but larger shifts may exist.

3 **Caution.** Despite ongoing improvements, it will be many years before all areas covered by charts of undetermined datum can be resurveyed and recharted. Chart title notes, cautions and Source Data Diagrams should therefore always be consulted in order to establish the limitations of the chart in use.

Effect of using different datums
2.13

1 The reasons for the differences between datums are described at 2.5, but the practical result is that a physical object can have as many geographical positions as there are datums and these positions can differ by hundreds, and sometimes thousands, of metres. For example, South Foreland Light, in the Dover Strait, has the following positions:

Geographical Position	Horizontal Datum
51°08'·39N 1°22'·37E	OSGB36 (The regional datum for UK)
51°08'·48N 1°22'·35E	ED50 (The regional datum for continental Europe)
51°08'·42N 1°22'·26E	WGS72 (the obsolete global datum)
51°08'·42N 1°22'·27E	WGS84 (the global datum used by GNSS)

A diagrammatic representation of this example is given below:

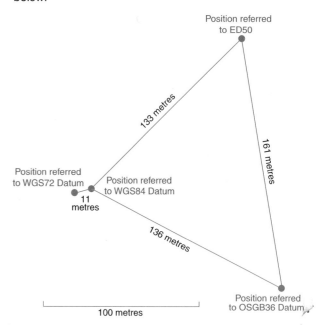

Horizontal Datum Discrepancies, South Foreland Lt, UK (2.13)

Datum differences
2.14

1 The differences between datums shown above are not constant, but vary around the coastline. For example, the UKHO uses 11 different sets of

transformation values for charts and surveys of the UK to obtain the best accuracies. Diagram 2.14.1 shows the differences in metres between a WGS84 position and the equivalent charted position referred to OSGB36 at 13 points along the coast of Great Britain.

2   Not only does the difference between OSGB36 and WGS84 vary around the coasts of Great Britain, but it varies in an irregular manner. This can be seen in diagram 2.14.2, which shows lines joining points of

equal difference; the values shown are in seconds of latitude and longitude.

3   An example of the effect such differences can make to charting is demonstrated in diagram 2.14.3, a portion of Chart 1273 (St. Lucia in the West Indies) which shows the positions of the coastline determined in 1888 by astronomical observations and recalculated with respect to WGS84.

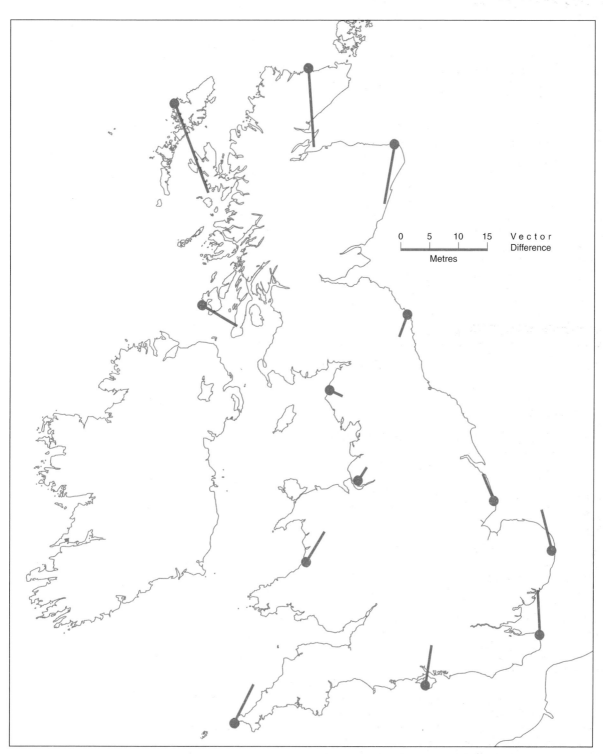

Differences between a General and Several Specific Datum Transformations (2.14.1)

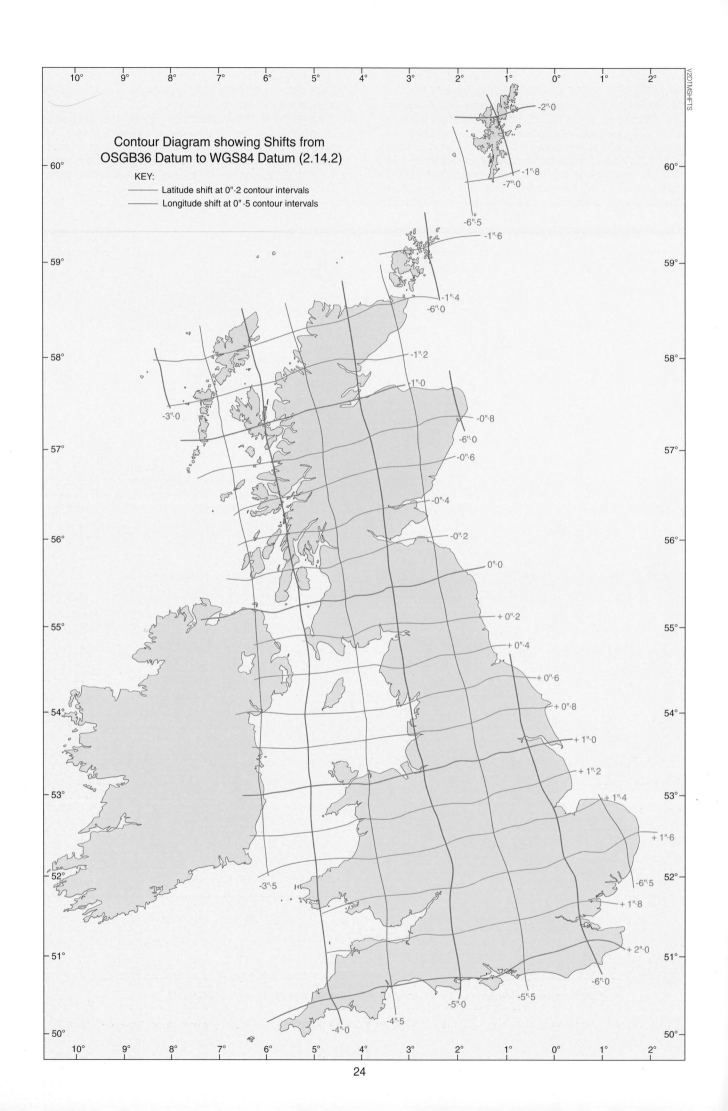

Contour Diagram showing Shifts from
OSGB36 Datum to WGS84 Datum (2.14.2)

KEY:

——— Latitude shift at 0".2 contour intervals
——— Longitude shift at 0".5 contour intervals

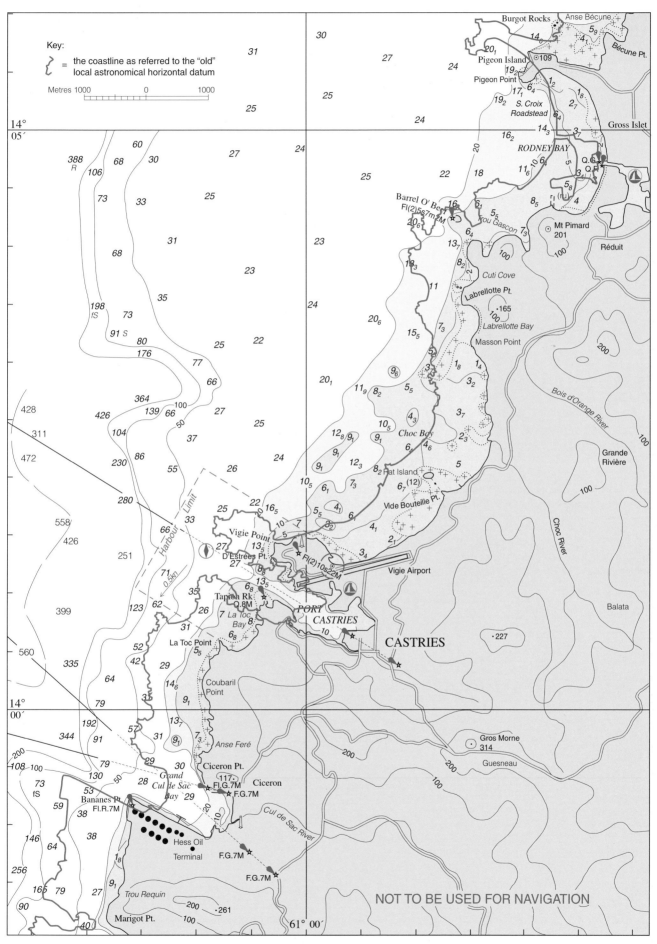

Old and New Versions of BA Chart 1273 referred to local astronomical and WGS84 Datums respectively (2.14.3)

Transferring positions between charts
2.15

1   When transferring positions from one chart to another, mariners should bear in mind that the datums of the two charts may be different, or that the datum on one or the other may be unknown. Where this is the case, Admiralty charts carry a Position Note stating the shift required to be applied in transferring positions between the charts concerned. For example:

CHART(S) [NUMBER(S)]: POSITIONS

To agree with the larger scale / smaller scale/ adjoining* chart(s) [number(s)] which is/are* referred to [name] Datum, positions read from chart[number] must be adjusted by [value] minutes NORTHWARD / SOUTHWARD* and [value] minutes EASTWARD / WESTWARD*.

2   Transferring positions by latitude and longitude may be appropriate when small scale charts are in use, but when using larger scale charts, a more accurate transfer of position is likely to be achieved if the range and bearing from a known position is used.

Additionally, if the scale difference between the two charts is large, any position taken from the small scale chart may have a significant error when plotted on the larger scale chart.

Guidance on the use of satellite-derived positional data provided in notes on charts should always be followed.

Charts of the British Isles
2.16

1   Some older charts of waters around the British Isles are still referred to OSGB36. There has been a programme in place since 2000 to update all these charts to a WGS84 compatible datum, and much of this work is now complete. The charts which have yet to be updated cover some of the waters of the Western Isles of Scotland and the Irish coast. Inevitably, this means that some adjoining charts in these areas will be referred to different datums until the programme is complete. Positions between the two can differ by as much as 130 m.

2   For the duration of the conversion programme, when transferring positions between adjoining charts on different datums, mariners should take care to ensure that any corrections applied to a position prior to transfer are applied in the correct direction.

Reporting differences between observed and charted positions
2.17

1   In order to improve the quality of charting in areas where little positional data is held, and particularly in areas where the chart has an undetermined datum, the UKHO welcomes reports of observed differences between the chart and satellite-derived observed positions, which may enable approximate shift values to be calculated. Such reports can be made on Form H102b which is reproduced at the end of Chapter 4 and can also be found on the UKHO website at www.ukho.gov.uk. Submission instructions are included on the form.

Datums used by GNSS
2.18

1   GNSS are fully described at 11.23. The most widely used is GPS NavStar, the positions from which are referenced to WGS84. GLONASS positions are referenced to PZ-90. However, most receivers in use worldwide, including GLONASS, have the ability to output positions referenced to WGS84.

However, because not all charts are referred to WGS84 as discussed at 2.9-2.12, positions obtained from GNSS will not always be compatible with the chart, and must not be used without correction, as the differences may be significant to navigation.

Relating the position of a point to WGS 84
2.19

1   There are only two ways to relate the position of a point to WGS84. These are:

To observe it directly (by GPS observation or surveyed from GPS observations) or remotely sensed (fixed to WGS84 points); or

To transform it by established mathematical techniques from some other datum using published parameters. These parameters must have a known or estimated accuracy associated with them.

Applying corrections
2.20

1   When known, the horizontal datum of the chart is usually named in the chart title although, on its own, this information is of limited benefit to the mariner. Since 1982 many hydrographic offices have been adding "Satellite-Derived Positions" notes (usually situated close to the title) when charts have been revised. This note provides a latitude and longitude adjustment to be applied to positions obtained directly from satellite navigation systems (such as GPS) to make them compatible with the horizontal datum of the chart.

2   The following provides a worked example:

WGS84 position	4°22'·00N	21°30'·00W
Lat/Long adjustments	0'·07S	0'·24E
Adjusted position	4°21'·93N	21°29'·76W

In this example, the shift equates to approximately 230 m which can be plotted at scales larger than 1:1 000 000.

Scale of chart and plotting accuracy
2.21

1   Adjustments such as those above are an average value for the whole area covered by the chart and are quoted to 2 decimal places of a minute in both latitude and longitude (three decimal places for some charts at scales larger than 1:15 000). The result is that the maximum uncertainty is about 10 metres in both latitude and longitude (0'·005 and 0'·014 will both be rounded to 0'·01).

2   This uncertainty can be plotted at scales larger than 1:30 000 (where it is represented by 0·3 mm on the chart), which is considered to be the normal achievable plotting accuracy. Inevitably, cases exist where overlapping charts show different latitude or longitude shift values. For example, one chart might show 0'·06 and its neighbour 0'·07; for each individual

chart the value will be an average, but in the area common to both charts the value will range from 0'·064 to 0'·066.

GPS receivers with built-in datum correction
2.22
1   Most manufacturers of GPS receivers are now incorporating datum transformations into their software which enable users to (apparently) receive positions referred to datums other than WGS84. Unfortunately, many cases exist where a single transformation will not be accurate for a large regional datum. For example, the relationship between WGS84 and ED50 is very different between the north and south of the region, despite the datum name being the same.

2   Therefore, the position transformed to WGS84 in the receiver by means of a Europe-wide average may differ from the WGS84 position output by the receiver, amended to ED50 by the shift note on an individual chart. This is a source of error and may be of major significance for navigation.

Regional datums, and datums used on charts
2.23
1   It must not be assumed that all charts in a region are referred to the regional datum. For example, although most metric charts of mainland European waters are referred to ED50, many charts are also referred to local datums. Additionally, as there are no international standards defining the conversion parameters between different horizontal datums, the parameters used by the GNSS receivers may be different. Hydrographic authorities use the best adopted parameters, so mariners are advised to keep their GNSS receiver referenced to WGS84 and apply the datum adjustment note from the chart.

Survey accuracy in relation to positional accuracy of GNSS
2.24
1   It should be remembered that while GNSS systems enable a vessel's position to be known to an accuracy of 20 m or better, this may not be reflected in the accuracy of the chart they are using. Apart from the differences in positions between different horizontal datums, two other aspects affect charted positional accuracy:
     The accuracy to which features are surveyed.
     The accuracy with which they are compiled onto a chart.
For further information see 1.20–1.21.

Differences in position caused by different methods of transformation
2.25
1   Diagram 2.25 shows the differences in metres between positions transformed from WGS84 to OSGB36 by means of the UKHO's method of multiple transformations (see 2.13) compared with those transformed by means of the uniform countrywide shift promulgated in the S-60 publication by the IHO.

Datums in electronic charting systems (ECS)

General information
2.26
1   As there are many different makes and types of ECS/ECDIS equipment, mariners should consult their system manuals in conjunction with the information which follows, which is only intended as general guidance.

     Most ECS process and display positions using WGS84 for horizontal reference, largely because they have been designed to work with GPS receivers as the primary positioning source. In systems which can be switched to other datums, WGS84 is normally the default. However a significant proportion of paper charts and thus their digital equivalents are not yet accurately related to WGS84. This obliges the ECS/ECDIS to be able to identify when position source and chart are working on different datums and take action either to make appropriate adjustments or provide a warning to the user.

2   ECS/ECDIS systems designed to use WGS84 will normally expect position inputs to be related to that datum. These inputs could be vessel position data direct from a navigation aid such as GPS or user entered data such as routeing or waypoint information. **Caution.** If data referred to other datums is used, it is likely to result in the vessel position or any overlay information being offset relative to the displayed chart data.

Admiralty Raster Chart Service (ARCS)
2.27
1   ARCS charts (facsimile copies of the Admiralty paper chart) contain the same position shift information as that shown on the paper chart. Where a shift to WGS84 is available, the ARCS chart carries this information. This enables the ECS/ECDIS to automatically make the appropriate adjustment to allow the vessel's position from GPS to be correctly displayed on the ARCS chart. Where the shift to WGS84 is unknown, this is explicitly recorded in the ARCS chart data and the ECS/ECDIS should display a warning that the plotted position is liable to be inaccurate. Further details are included in the ARCS User Guide. See also 2.106.

Electronic Navigational Charts (ENCs)
2.28
1   The IMO specification for ECDIS requires that all ENCs be referred to WGS84. The lack of geodetic information for some parts of the world may further delay the availability of ENCs for these areas. See also 2.87.

Other electronic chart data
2.29
1   Electronic chart data is available from a wide variety of sources. Users are advised to check the user documentation with regard to the horizontal datum used by these products. It is advisable to bear in mind the statements elsewhere in this chapter with regard to the accuracy of shifts to WGS84 for certain areas of the world.

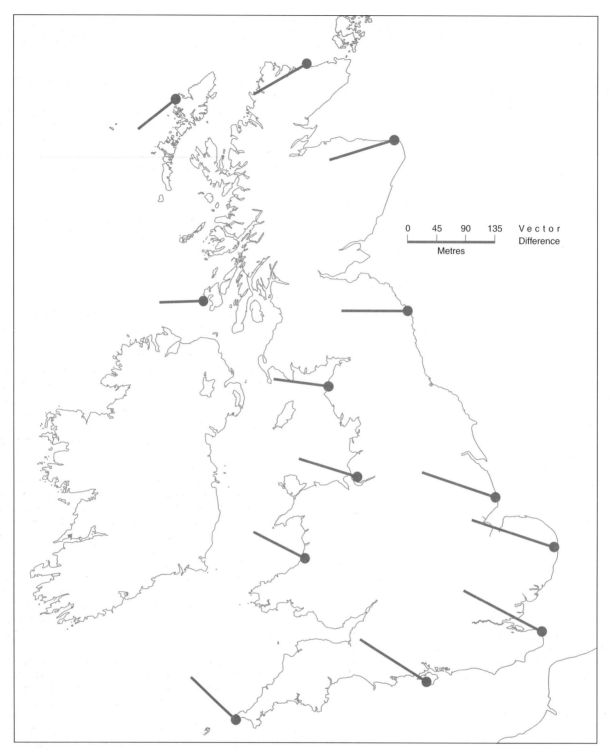

Differences between WGS84 Datum and OSGB36 Datum positions (2.25)

GPS input to ECS/ECDIS

2.30

1   Many GPS receivers have the capability to provide positions referred to any datum selected by the operator. It is advisable to only use WGS84 settings when the GNSS receiver is interfaced to ECS/ECDIS. This is because, as outlined in paragraph 2.22, receiver manufacturers often use average shifts and more importantly, in most cases, the GNSS does not tell the ECS/ECDIS which datum is being input.

2   **Caution.** The use of settings other than WGS84 is likely to result in the vessel's position being incorrectly displayed in ECS/ECDIS.

Paper Charts and Diagrams

Charts of the Admiralty Series

General information

Metric charts
2.31

1 From 1800 to 1968 Admiralty charts were published with fathoms and feet as the units for depths, and feet as the units for heights. However, since 1968 Admiralty charts have gradually been converted to metres, thus conforming with charts of almost all other countries. It will be many years before all charts are converted, but 86% of Admiralty charts were in metres by 2009.

2 The policy is to metricate blocks of charts in specific areas, but at the same time almost all new charts outside these areas will also be published in metres (or metric style in US waters).

Symbols and abbreviations
2.32

1 *Chart 5011 — Symbols and Abbreviations used on Admiralty Paper Charts* is published as an A4-sized book, and can be conveniently kept with this book. The numbering convention follows that of International Chart 1 (INT1).

It is treated as a chart, and is updated by *Admiralty Notices to Mariners*.

Primary and derived sources
2.33

1 The Admiralty world-wide chart series comprises a mixture of charts compiled using both primary and derived sources and methods. In waters where the United Kingdom has the responsibility or where there are, as yet, no other chart producers, charts are compiled from 'raw' or primary data (e.g. surveys, maps). Outside these areas, derived charts are either re-compiled using the data shown on the chart produced by another Hydrographic Office (HO), or are published as a modified reproduction in the familiar Admiralty style.

International charts
2.34

1 These modified reproductions may form part of the International (INT) Chart Series in which members of the International Hydrographic Organization (IHO) publish charts with internationally agreed limits and scales. Each chart carries a unique INT number in addition to the UKHO or foreign national number allocated to it. Modified reproductions of INT charts also carry three seals:

The originating HO.
The IHO.
The UKHO.

2 International charts originally produced by the UKHO will carry two seals:

The IHO.
The UKHO.

International boundaries and national limits
2.35

1 The international boundaries and national limits shown on reproductions are the responsibility of the producer Hydrographic Office, ie the country of origin. The portrayal of these limits does not imply United Kingdom recognition. See 9.15 and 9.16.

Chart coverage

Admiralty charts
2.36

1 The policy followed by the United Kingdom, UK Overseas Territories and certain Commonwealth countries and other areas, is to chart all waters, ports and harbours on a scale sufficient for the safe navigation of all vessels. Elsewhere overseas, Admiralty charts are schemed to enable ships to cross the oceans and proceed along the coasts of the world to reach the approaches to ports, using the most appropriate scales.

2 On large scale charts, all navigationally significant features, including depths, dangers and aids to navigation are shown.

On coastal charts, full details of only the principal lights and fog signals, and those lights, fog signals, light vessels, light floats, LANBYs and buoys that are likely to be used for navigation on the chart are usually shown. Significant depths are also shown, but aids to navigation in harbours and other inner waters are not usually inserted.

3 If the use of a larger scale chart is essential (e.g. for navigation close inshore, or for anchoring), details are given of those aids which must be identified before changing to it, even though short range aids to navigation and minor sea floor obstructions are usually omitted.

It also sometimes happens that a small scale chart is the largest scale on which a new harbour can be shown, in which case it may be appropriate to insert on it full details of certain aids, such as a landfall buoy.

4 Limits of larger scale charts in the Admiralty series are shown in magenta on most fathoms charts, and on all metric charts. Where the limits are too small to show, a textual reference to the larger scale chart may be given. Occasionally, limits of larger scale charts of other nations may be shown on Admiralty charts, the chart number being prefixed by the national 2 or 3 letter ISO code.

5 Foreign ports, in general, are charted on a scale adequate for ships under pilotage, but major ports are charted on larger scales commensurate with their importance or intricacy.

Under a series of bi-lateral agreements, many charts produced by foreign government hydrographic offices have been adopted into the Admiralty series (see 2.44).

Categories of Chart

New Chart (NC)
2.37

1 A New Chart (NC) is issued if it embraces an area not previously charted to the scale shown, or it embraces an area different from the existing chart, or it introduces different depth units, or it is the adoption of a national or international (INT) chart.

When a new chart is published, the Date of Publication is shown outside its bottom margin, in the middle.

e.g. Published at Taunton, United Kingdom 5th September 2009

New Edition (NE)
2.38

1 A New Edition is published when there is a large amount of navigationally-significant new data. In these circumstances, a (P)NM would normally be issued immediately to cover the period when the chart is being re-compiled, and would be cancelled when the chart is published. A NE would also be published once a significant amount of other received data had accumulated.

2 Once a NE has been published, all notations of previous updates are erased, and the previous edition is cancelled. Once cancelled, a previous edition must not be used.

When a NE of an Admiralty Chart is published, the Edition number and the date of publication are shown in the Customer Information box in the bottom left corner of the chart, outside the margin:

Edition Number:	3
Edition Date:	4th November 2009

Current editions
2.39

1 The date of publication of a chart and the date, where applicable, of its current edition are given in the *Catalogue of Admiralty Charts and Publications* and *Cumulative List of Admiralty Notices to Mariners* (4.39). Details of New Charts and New Editions published after the date to which the catalogue and the list are updated will be found in the announcements in Section I of the *Weekly Editions of Admiralty Notices to Mariners*.

Admiralty Notices to Mariners
2.40

1 From the time a chart is published, it is kept up–to–date for all information essential to navigation by *Admiralty Notices to Mariners* until it is either withdrawn or replaced by a New Edition or New Chart. See 2.69.

Describing a chart
2.41

1 To describe a particular copy of a chart, the following details should be stated:
Number of the chart.
Title.
Date of Printing (on the reverse of the chart).
Date of Publication.
Date of last New Edition (if any).
Number of last Notice to Mariners.

Foreign Government Charts

Foreign charts
2.42

1 In areas not covered in detail by Admiralty charts, other Hydrographic Offices may publish charts of the country concerned, giving larger scale coverage than Admiralty charts. Certain foreign government charts may, however, be adopted into the Admiralty series.

The international use of standard chart symbols and abbreviations enables the charts of foreign countries to be used with little difficulty by the mariner of any nation. Most foreign charts express depths and heights in metres, but the unit is invariably stated below the title of the chart.

2 The vertical chart datum of a foreign chart should, however, be carefully noted as some use a datum below which the tide sometimes falls, e.g. in their own waters, USA uses Mean Lower Low Water (see 5.15).

Foreign charts may not always be referred to the same horizontal datum as Admiralty charts, and if this is the case positions should be transferred by bearing and distance from common charted objects and not by latitude and longitude. See also 1.30.

Each hydrographic office has a system similar to *Admiralty Notices to Mariners* (4.25) for keeping their charts and publications updated.

Availability
2.43

1 Foreign government charts and plans are usually available only from national agencies at the larger ports and from the appropriate hydrographic office.

Hydrographic offices have their addressees listed in *Catalogue of Admiralty Charts and Publications* (see 2.56).

2 Although larger scale foreign government charts may be available for their own waters, they are often not readily available before arrival in the area and corrections may also be hard to obtain on a regular basis. The mariner using Admiralty charts has the advantages of using one homogeneous series, readily available from agents throughout the world, updated by a single series of Notices to Mariners and supported by a corresponding world-wide series of nautical publications.

Modified reproductions of foreign government charts
2.44

1 In accordance with International Chart Regulations and bilateral arrangements between the UK and many other Hydrographic Offices, facsimile or modified reproductions of selected foreign government charts are published by the UKHO and form part of the Admiralty series of charts. The selected charts are those considered to be required by international shipping. These charts are usually given numbers in the Admiralty series, but in some cases, eg Australia, New Zealand and Japan, they retain their national chart numbers with an identifying prefix. For Australia, New Zealand and some other countries, all chart correcting Notices to Mariners issued by that country which affect these charts are re-issued in *Admiralty Notices to Mariners*. For most reproduced charts, however, only selected NMs are re-issued, as appropriate, for international shipping.

2　Increasingly as the standardisation of charts improves, the UKHO is accepting into its series more modified reproductions of national charts produced by other HOs. This move also reflects the closer relationship which the UKHO seeks to establish with these HOs. The benefits to the user of this policy include better coverage in certain areas and quicker turn round times for new editions. As with INT charts, these charts are modified to reflect the standard UKHO practice for style and symbology. Modified reproductions of National charts carry two seals:

　　The originating HO.
　　The UKHO.

3　All modified reproductions of charts which have been adopted into the Admiralty series are listed in the *Catalogue of Admiralty Charts and Publications* under their BA, AUS, NZ and JP chart numbers, and are updated by Notices to Mariners in the usual way.

Australian and New Zealand charts
2.45

1　The full range of Australian and New Zealand charts is given in their respective chart catalogues which are available on the following websites:

　　www.hydro.gov.au
　　www.linz.govt.nz

Australia and New Zealand have agreed with the United Kingdom to adopt responsibility for chart coverage in the areas shown in Diagram 2.45; these areas extend to Antarctica. All medium and large scale Admiralty charts of these areas are reproductions of Australian and New Zealand charts.

Canadian and United States charts
2.46

1　Canadian Charts and Publications Regulations and US Navigation Safety Regulations require ships in Canadian and US waters to use and maintain appropriate charts and navigational publications. In certain areas, only Canadian or US charts and publications will suffice.

Summaries of these Regulations are given in *Annual Summary of Admiralty Notices to Mariners Part I* (see 4.38).

Charts for Specific Purposes

Routeing charts
2.47

1　Routeing charts are published for the N and S Atlantic, Indian, and N and S Pacific Oceans. Each chart has twelve versions, one for each month, and assists the navigator to plan an ocean passage for any time of year by providing:

　　An outline of the surrounding land areas and the positions of the major ports.

2　The recognised shipping routes between major ports, with distances.
Data on wind speed, direction and force, incidence of low visibility and frequency of storms.
Data on sea and air temperature, air pressure and ice limits.
Data on ocean currents.
The limits of loadline zones and the locations of ocean weather ships.

Oceanic charts and plotting sheets
2.48

1　**Ocean Plotting Sheets,** published by the United Kingdom Hydrographic Office, form a series of eight blank graduated sheets on a scale of 1:1 000 000 covering the world. Six of the sheets are graduated on the Mercator projection and two, of the polar regions, on a stereographic projection. The six Mercator graduated sheets can be supplied with compass roses printed on them.

A further series, linked to the Mercator sheets, are also published on a scale of 1:250 000.

These sheets are well suited to field use and the collection and compilation of soundings when making reports.

2　**Ocean Sounding Charts.** Consisting of approximately 600 plotting sheets covering the world's oceans, Ocean Sounding Charts (OSCs) are records of the oceanic soundings held by the UKHO. The series has not been maintained since 1991, however, and no additional soundings have been added since then. Copies of the 1:1 000 000 charts continue to be available in their present form and can be ordered by specifying the area number given on *Chart 5330 - Index of Plotting Areas and Ocean Sounding sheets,* prefixed by the letter C (eg C594). For the Mediterranean area, 1:250 000 sheets are similarly available from the national hydrographic authorities shown in diagram 2.48.

3　**General Bathymetric Charts of the Oceans (GEBCO)** were initiated at the beginning of the 20th century by Prince Albert I of Monaco. Now, by agreement reached through the IHO, various maritime countries are responsible for co-ordinating the collection of oceanic soundings for the compilation of this world-wide bathymetric series. It consists of 16 sheets on Mercator projection at a scale of 1:10 000 000 at the equator, covering the world's oceans between latitudes 72°N and 72°S, as well as 2 sheets on Polar Stereographic projection at a scale of 1:6 000 000 at latitude 75°, covering the N and S polar regions. These sheets form the basis for a World Chart (sheet 5.00) at a scale of 1:35 000 000, which includes the polar regions at a scale of 1:25 000 000.

4　These 19 sheets are also produced on CD-ROM as the GEBOC Digital Atlas (GDA), a seamless bathymetric contour chart of the world's oceans. The GDA is avaialble from:

　　British Oceanographic Data Centre (BODC),
　　Joseph Proudman Building, 6 Brownlow Street,
　　Liverpool, L3 5DA, United Kingdom.
　　Internet: www.bodc.ac.uk

The areas for which co-ordinating countries are responsible are detailed in the *Catalogue of Admiralty Charts and Publications*.

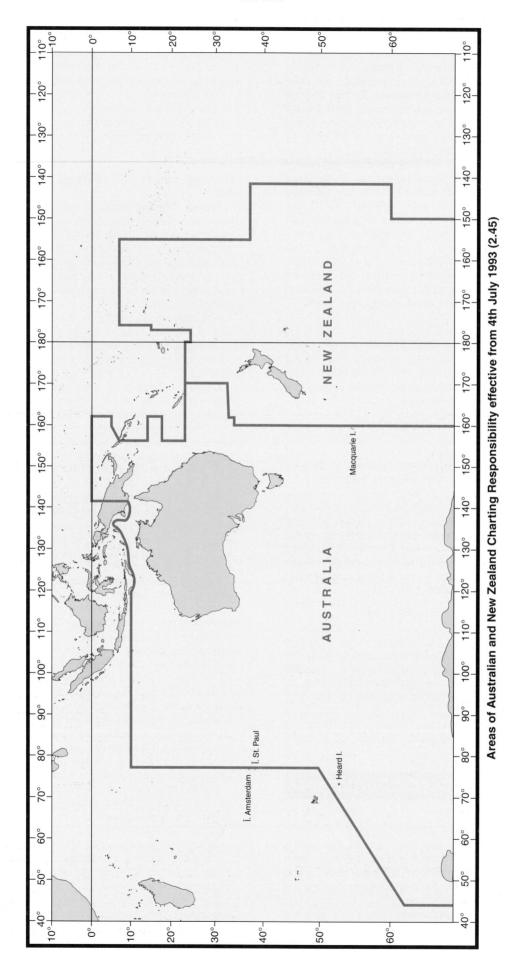

Areas of Australian and New Zealand Charting Responsibility effective from 4th July 1993 (2.45)

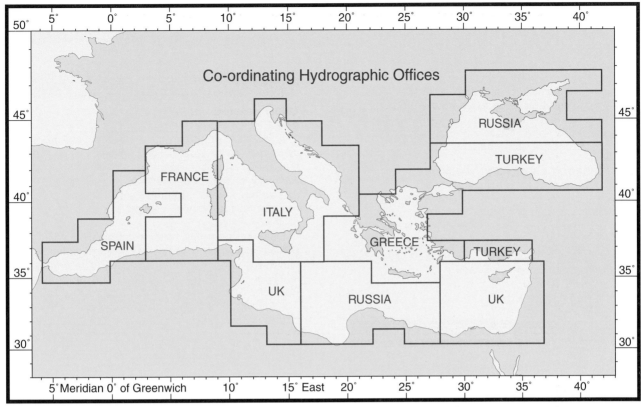

Mediterranean: Ocean Sounding Charts at 1:250,000 (2.48)

5   **International Bathymetric Charts of the Mediterranean (IBCM).** This series compiled in 1981 and printed by the former USSR under the auspices of the Intergovernmental Oceanographic Commission (IOC) of UNESCO, consists of 10 sheets on the Mercator projection at a scale of 1:1 million at 38°N and a single sheet covering the whole area at a scale of 1:5 million. Co-ordinating maritime countries collect oceanic sounding data and maintain the master sounding sheets in their area of responsibility on 1:250 000 plotting sheets. Copies of these master sounding sheets form a comprehensive collection of ocean soundings of the Mediterranean Sea.

6   **Availability.** Ocean Plotting Sheets are available through Admiralty Distributors.

    Ocean Sounding Charts and IBCM Sounding Charts which are the responsibility of the UKHO are also available through Admiralty Distributors. They will be reproduced to order on either paper or plastic from master copies and prices quoted on application. It should be noted that in areas where data is readily available and master copies are full, continuation copies have been started.

7   Ocean and IBCM Sounding Charts maintained by co-ordinating offices other than the United Kingdom can be obtained from those offices, their addresses being given in *Catalogue of Admiralty Charts and Publications*.

    GEBCO sheets can be obtained either as unfolded sheets or as a folded boxed set from the following:

8   Geopubs Ltd
    4, Glebe Crescent
    Minehead
    Somerset TA24 5SN
    United Kingdom;

The International Hydrographic Bureau,
4 Quai Antoine Ier,
B.P. 445,
MC 98011 MONACO CEDEX,
Principality of Monaco;

9   CHS Client Services,
    615 Booth,
    Ottawa,
    Ontario K1A OE6
    Canada.

Gnomonic charts
2.49

1   For great circle sailing, 15 gnomonic charts are published covering the Atlantic, Pacific and Indian Oceans, except for an equatorial belt in each ocean.

    A great circle course can alternatively be laid off on a Mercator chart by using *Chart 5029 — Great Circle Diagram* which enables the latitudes and longitudes of a series of positions along the course to be determined graphically.

Ships' Boats' charts
2.50

1   The oceans of the world are covered by a set of six *Ships' Boats' charts* printed on waterproof paper. Each chart shows the coastline, the approximate strengths and directions of prevailing winds and currents, limits of ice, and isogonic lines. On the reverse of each are elementary directions for the use of the chart, remarks on the management of boats, and on wind, weather and currents.

2   They are available as a set in a polythene wallet, together with paper, pencil, eraser, protractor and tables of sunset and sunrise.

Azimuth diagrams
2.51
1   Azimuth diagrams are published to enable the true bearing of a heavenly body to be obtained graphically from its local hour angle and declination.

Charts 5000 and *5001* are azimuth diagrams covering latitudes 0°–65°, and 65°–90° respectively.

Miscellaneous charts and diagrams
2.52
1   Among the other series of charts published are:
   Star Charts and Diagrams.
   Magnetic Variation Charts.
   Practice and Exercise Area (PEXA) Charts (United Kingdom area only).
   Co-Tidal and Co-range Charts.
   Instructional Charts.
   Time Zone Chart.

Supply and distribution

Admiralty Distributors
2.53
1   All Admiralty Distributors supply any of the Admiralty, Australian, New Zealand or Japanese charts listed in *Catalogue of Admiralty Charts and Publications*.

The range and quantity of charts and publications stocked by Distributors varies considerably. Distributors in major ports in the United Kingdom and on the principal trade route overseas keep fully updated stocks to meet all reasonable day-to-day requirements. These Distributors are identified as International Admiralty Chart Agents in *Catalogue of Admiralty Charts and Publications*. Agents at smaller ports and small craft sailing centres in the United Kingdom keep only restricted stocks.

2   Distributors are spread throughout the world: their addresses are given in *Annual Summary of Admiralty Notices to Mariners* and are listed in *Catalogue of Admiralty Charts and Publications*.

Orders
2.54
1   An order for charts or publications should be placed at least seven days before the items are required. This enables the Distributor to obtain copies of any item not in stock or not fully updated. The prompt supply service between the United Kingdom Hydrographic Office, Chart Distributors and others, such as ship owners and their agents, usually ensures timely delivery to most ports of the world by air mail, air freight or similar means.

2   The prudent mariner will however, make sure that a comprehensive outfit of charts and publications is carried on board to cover the expected area of operations.

Chart Update Services
2.55
1   Certain Distributors also have the facilities to check and bring up-to-date complete folios or outfits of charts, replacing obsolete charts as necessary, and supplying, unprompted, New Editions of charts required for a ship's outfit.

Overlay tracings (2.70) to make chart updates easier are also obtainable from Admiralty Distributors.

Selection of charts

Chart catalogues
2.56
1   *Catalogue of Admiralty Charts and Publications* gives the limits and details, including the dates of publication and the dates of current editions, of all Admiralty charts, plotting sheets and diagrams, and of Australian, New Zealand and Japanese charts reprinted in the Admiralty series. It also lists the prices of the products.

2   Lists of countries with established Hydrographic Offices publishing charts of their national waters, places where *Admiralty Notices to Mariners* are available for consultation, and the addresses of Admiralty Distributors are also contained in it.

Admiralty Charts and Hydrographic Publications — Home Edition, gives detail of charts and publications covering the coasts of the British Isles and part of the coast of NW Europe. This leaflet is obtainable gratis from Admiralty Distributors.

Carriage requirements
2.57
1   *The International Convention for the Safety of Life at Sea, (SOLAS) 1974* states: "All ships shall carry adequate and up-to-date charts, sailing directions, lists of lights, notices to mariners, tide tables and all other nautical publications necessary for the intended voyage."

The publications required to be carried by ships registered in the United Kingdom under the *Merchant Shipping (Safety of Navigation) Regulations 2002* are given in Annex A.

Chart folios
2.58
1   Charts can be supplied individually or made up into folios.

Standard Admiralty Chart Folios have their limits shown in *Catalogue of Admiralty Charts and Publications*. These folios are arranged geographically and together provide cover for the world. Each folio contains all relevant navigational charts for the area concerned.

2   The charts comprising a folio are contained in a buckram cover. They are either half-size sheets, or full-size sheets folded, with normal overall dimensions in each case of 710 x 520 mm.

State of charts on supply

General information
2.59
1   Once a chart is published and leaves the UKHO, it is kept updated by *Admiralty Notices to Mariners* and New Editions by an International Admiralty Distributor until it is supplied to the mariner. The chart supplied will invariably be the latest edition and up-to-date for all Permanent Notices to Mariners, but not for Temporary or Preliminary Notices.

To confirm that the chart is the latest edition and has been updated, the latest *Cumulative List of*

Admiralty Notices to Mariners (4.39) and subsequent Weekly Editions can be consulted.

2   To enable a complete new outfit of charts to be updated for the Temporary and Preliminary Notices affecting it, and to bring all its associated publications up-to-date, the current edition of *Annual Summary of* *Admiralty Notices to Mariners* and appropriate sections of Weekly Editions of Notices for the current calendar year and as necessary prior to that for updates to particular volumes of *Admiralty List of Lights and Fog Signals*, (see 4.27), will be required. These should be supplied with the outfit.

Upkeep of the paper chart outfit

Chart Outfit Management

Chart outfits
2.60

1   An outfit of charts, in addition to the necessary Standard Admiralty Folios, or selected charts made up into folios as required, should include the following publications:

Paper Chart Maintenance Record (2.62).
Weekly Editions of Admiralty Notices to Mariners subsequent to the most recent *Annual Summary of Admiralty Notices to Mariners, Parts 1 and 2*. Earlier editions may be required to amend a volume of *Admiralty List of Lights* approaching its re-publication date. See 3.17.

2   Chart 5011 — *Symbols and Abbreviations used on Admiralty Paper Charts*.
Appropriate volumes of:
Admiralty Sailing Directions.
Admiralty List of Lights and Fog Signals.
Admiralty List of Radio Signals.
Admiralty Tide Tables.
Tidal Stream Atlases.
The Mariner's Handbook.

3   The supplier of the outfit will state the number of the last Notice to Mariners to which it has been amended.

Chart management system
2.61

1   A system is required to keep an outfit of charts up-to-date. It should include arrangements for the supply of New Charts, New Editions of charts and extra charts, as well as new editions and Supplements to *Admiralty Sailing Directions* and other nautical publications, if necessary at short notice.

2   On notification by *Admiralty Notice to Mariners* that a new edition of a book has been published, it should be obtained as soon as possible. Amendments to a book subsequent to such a Notice will refer to the new edition or to the book as amended by the Supplement.

Arrangements should be made for the continuous receipt of Navigational Warnings, *Admiralty Notices to Mariners*, and notices affecting any foreign charts carried.

3   A system of documentation is required which shows quickly and clearly that all relevant updates have been received and applied, and that New Charts, New Editions and the latest editions of publications and their supplements have been obtained or ordered.

Paper Chart Maintenance Record
2.62

1   For users of Standard Admiralty Folios of charts, *Paper Chart Maintenance Record* offers a convenient method to manage a chart outfit. It contains sheets providing a numerical index of charts, indicates in which folio they are held, and has space against chart for logging Notices to Mariners affecting it. Where only a selection of the charts in standard Admiralty Folios are held, the method can be readily adapted. It is divided into two parts:

Part I is divided into two sections: Section 1 is used to record receipt of the chart outfit/folios and *Weekly Editions of Admiralty Notices to Mariners*. Section 2 is used to record New Charts and New Editions published.

2   Part 2 is divided into three sections: Section 1 is used to record *Admiralty Notices to Mariners* affecting Admiralty Charts numbered 1–4999. Section 2 is used to record *Admiralty Notices to Mariners* affecting Australian, New Zealand and Japanese charts reproduced by the UKHO. Section 3 is used to record *Admiralty Notices to Mariners* affecting miscellaneous Admiralty Charts numbered from 5000 onwards.

Action on receiving a chart outfit
2.63

1   **Charts.** Enter the number of the Notice to which the outfit has been updated in the *Paper Chart Maintenance Record*, and insert the Folio Number on the thumb-label of each chart.

If not using Standard Admiralty Folios, enter the Folio Number against each chart of the Maintenance Record.

2   Consult the Index of Charts Affected in the Weekly Edition of Notices to Mariners containing the last Notice to which the outfit has been updated, and all subsequent Weekly Editions. If any charts held are mentioned, enter the numbers of the Notices affecting them against the charts concerned in the Maintenance Record, and then update the charts.

3   Consult the latest monthly Notice listing Temporary and Preliminary Notices in force, and the Temporary and Preliminary Notices in each Weekly Edition subsequent to it. If any charts are affected by those Notices, enter in pencil the numbers of the Notices against the charts in the Maintenance Record, and then update the charts for them (also in pencil).

Extract all Temporary and Preliminary Notices from *Weekly Editions of Admiralty Notices to Mariners* subsequent to the current *Annual Summary of Admiralty Notices to Mariners* and make them into a 'Temporary and Preliminary Notices' file.

4   **Navigational Warnings.** From all Weekly Editions of the current year, detach Section III and file, or list the messages by their areas. Determine which messages are still in force from the Weekly Edition issued monthly, which lists them and insert the information from these messages on any relevant charts.

Admiralty Sailing Directions. From Weekly Editions subsequent to the current *Annual Summary of*

Admiralty Notices to Mariners, detach Section IV and file (see 3.10).

5   **Admiralty List of Lights.** From Weekly Editions subsequent to those supplied with the volumes, detach Section V and insert all amendments in the volumes.

Admiralty List of Radio Signals. From Weekly Editions subsequent to those announcing publication of the volumes, detach Section VI and insert all amendments in the volumes.

Admiralty Tide Tables. From *Annual Summary of Admiralty Notices to Mariners* for the year in progress, insert any corrigenda to the volume. If the Summary for the year has not yet been received, see 3.31.

Chart 5011 — Symbols and Abbreviations used on Admiralty Paper Charts. Use any Notices supplied with the book to update it.

Action on notification of the publication of a New Chart or New Edition
2.64

1   When a New Chart or New Edition is published, this is announced by a Notice giving the Date of Publication and the numbers of any Temporary and Preliminary Notices affecting it. From such Notices, enter on the appropriate page of Part I of the Maintenance Record:

Number of the Chart.
Date of Publication.
Number of the Notice announcing publication.
Numbers of any Temporary and Preliminary Notices affecting the chart (in pencil).

2   Until the chart is received, the numbers of any subsequent Permanent, Temporary or Preliminary Notices affecting it should be recorded with the above entry.

Action on receipt of a New Chart or New Edition
2.65

1   Enter the following details in the *Paper Chart Maintenance Record*:

If a New Chart, enter the Folio Number against the Chart Number in the Index.
On the sheet at the beginning of Part I, enter the date of receipt of the chart.
Against the Chart Number in the Notices to Mariners column of the Index Sheet, enter "NC" or "NE" with the date of publication, followed by a double vertical line to close the space.

2   In the Notices to Mariners column of the chart in the Index, enter the numbers of any Notices recorded against the chart on the sheet at the beginning of Part I.
Enter the Folio Number on the thumb-label of the chart.
Update the chart for any Notices transferred from Part I as described above, and for any Radio Navigational Warnings affecting it.
Destroy all copies of the previous edition. **Once a New Edition of a chart is received, the superseded edition must NOT be used for navigation.**

Action on receipt of a chart additional to the outfit
2.66

1   Enter the Folio Number on the thumb-label of the chart. If not using Standard Admiralty Folios, enter the Folio Number against the chart in the Index of the Log.

Enter the number of the last Notice to which the chart has been updated against the chart in the Index of the Log.

2   Consult the Index of Charts Affected in each *Weekly Edition of Admiralty Notices to Mariners* from the one including the last Notices to Mariners entered on the chart (see also 4.39). If any Notices affecting the chart have been issued since the last Notice for which it has been updated, enter them against the chart in the Log and update the chart for them.

3   Consult the file of Temporary and Preliminary Notices (2.63). If any affect the chart, enter their numbers against the chart in the Log, and update the chart for them.

From the file or list of Navigational Warnings (4.8), see if any affect the chart. If so, annotate the chart accordingly.

Action on receipt of a replacement chart
2.67

1   Insert the Folio Number on the thumb-label of the chart.

From the record kept in the Log, update the replacement chart for any Notices affecting it published after the last Notice entered on it under Notices to Mariners.

Consult the file of Temporary and Preliminary Notices, enter any affecting the chart in the Log, and update the chart if relevant.

Consult the file or list of Navigational Warnings. If any Warnings affect the chart, annotate it accordingly.

Action on receipt of a Weekly Edition of Admiralty Notices to Mariners
2.68

1   Check that the serial number of the Weekly Edition is in sequence with Editions already received, then:

From the Index of Charts Affected, enter in the Log the numbers of the Notices affecting the charts held.

Turn to the end of Section II to see if any Temporary or Preliminary Notices have been published or cancelled. If they have been, add to or amend the entries in the Log against the charts accordingly.

2   Examine the "Admiralty Publications" Notice to see if any relevant New Charts or New Editions have been published, or charts withdrawn. If they have, take action as at 2.65.

Detach and use Sections III to VI as follows:
Section III. Check printed text of messages against any signalled versions. File Section, or note down messages by their areas, and bring up-to-date previous information on the file and any notations made on charts;

3   Section IV: Add to file or list (3.10);
Section V: Cut up and use to amend *Admiralty List of Lights*;
Section VI: Cut up and use to amend *Admiralty List of Radio Signals*;
Re-secure chart updating blocks to Section II.
From folios affected, extract and update charts for the appropriate Notices in Section II.

Correcting Charts

General information
2.69

1 Only updates given in Section II of *Weekly Editions of Admiralty Notices to Mariners* should be used to correct any chart in ink.

Updates to charts from information received from authorities other than the UKHO may be noted in pencil, but no charted danger should be expunged without the authority of the UKHO.

2 All updates given in *Weekly Editions of Admiralty Notices to Mariners* should be inserted on the charts affected. When they have been completed the numbers of the Notices should be entered (2.76) clearly and neatly; permanent Notices in waterproof violet ink, Temporary and Preliminary Notices in pencil.

Temporary and Preliminary Notices should be rubbed out as soon as a Notice is received cancelling them.

3 *Chart 5011 — Symbols and Abbreviations used on Admiralty Paper Charts* should be followed to ensure uniformity of updates. These symbols are invariably indicated on overlay update tracings (2.70).

If several charts are affected by one Notice, the largest scale chart should be updated first to appreciate the detail of the update.

Overlay update tracings
2.70

1 Overlay update tracings are produced by the UKHO and used by Admiralty Distributors to update their stocks of nautical charts.

The tracing show graphically the precise update required to be made to a chart by an NM, and enable positions to be "pricked through" onto the chart. Copies of the tracings are reprinted under licence from the UKHO and can be purchased from Admiralty Distributors.

2 When using these tracings, the text of the printed NM must invariably be consulted. See also *How to Keep Your Admiralty Charts Up-to-date.*

Terms used in updates
2.71

1 The main text of the update starts with one of the following commands, usually in the order shown:

INSERT is used for the insertion of all new data or, together with the **DELETE** command (see below), when a feature has moved position sufficiently that the **MOVE** command (see below) is not appropriate. For example: Delete feature and Insert in a different position. Note: The exact text to be written on a chart by insertion will appear in Italics in the printed notice.

2 **AMEND** is used when a feature remains in its existing charted position but has a change of characteristic, for example:
Amend light to Fl.3s25m10M 32 ̊36 ́9S 60 ̊54 ́2E.
When only the range of a light changes:
Amend range of light to 10M 32 ̊36 ́9S 60 ̊54 ́2E.

SUBSTITUTE is used when one feature replaces an existing feature and the position remains as charted. The new feature is always shown first, for example: Substitute e for s (where e is the **new** feature).

3 **MOVE** is used for features whose characteristics or descriptions remain unchanged, but they are to be moved small distances, for example:
Move starboard-hand conical buoy from 56 ̊00 ́62N 4 ̊46 ́47W to 56 ̊00 ́93N 4 ̊46 ́85W.

DELETE is used when features are to be removed from the chart or, together with the **INSERT** command (see above), when features are moved a significant distance such that the **MOVE** command is inappropriate.

Full details of chart updating methods can be found in *How to Keep Your Admiralty Charts Up-to-Date.*

Previous updates
2.72

1 When updating a chart, first check that the previous published update has been made to the chart. This information is given at the end of the new Notice.

Detail required
2.73

1 The amount of detail shown on a chart varies with its scale. On a large scale chart, for example, full details of all lights and fog signals are shown, but on smaller scales the order of reduction of information is Elevation, Period, Range, until on an ocean chart of the area only lights with a range of 15 miles or more will normally be inserted, and then only their light-star and magenta flare. On the other hand, radio beacons are omitted from large scale charts where their use would be inappropriate, and, unless they are long range beacons, from ocean charts.

2 Notices adding detail to charts indicate how much detail should be added to each chart, but Notices deleting detail do not always make this distinction.

If a shortened description would result in ambiguity between adjacent aids, detail should be retained.

The insertion of excessive detail not only clutters the chart, but can lead to errors, since the charts quoted as affected in each Notice assume the mariner has reduced with the scale of the charts the details inserted by previous Notices.

Alterations
2.74

1 Erasures should never be made. Where necessary, detail should be crossed through, or in the case of lines, such as depth contours or limits, crossed with a series of short double strokes, slanting across the line. Typing correction fluids should not be used.

Alterations to depth contours, deletion of depths to make way for detail, etc, are not mentioned in Notices unless they have some navigational significance.

2 Where tinted depths contours require amendment, the line should be amended, but the tint, which is only intended to draw attention to the line, can usually remain untouched.

Where information is displaced for clarity, its proper position should be indicated by a small circle and arrow.

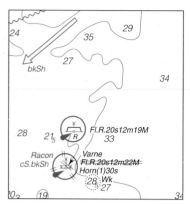

Displaced Correction (2.74)

3   Further information on updating charts is available in *How to Keep Your Admiralty Charts Up-to-Date*.

Blocks
2.75

1   Some Notices are accompanied by reproductions of portions of charts (known as "Blocks"). When updating charts from blocks, the following points should be borne in mind.

A block may not only indicate the insertion of new information, but also the omission of matter previously shown. The text of the accompanying Notice should invariably be read carefully.

2   The limiting lines of a block are determined for convenience of reproduction. They need not be strictly adhered to when cutting out for pasting on the chart, provided that the preceding paragraph is taken into consideration.

Owing to distortion the blocks do not always fit the chart exactly. When pasting a block on a chart, therefore, care should be taken that the more important navigational features fit as closely as possible. This is best done by fitting the block while it is dry and making two or three pencil ticks round the edges for use as fitting marks after the paste is applied to the chart.

Completion of updates
2.76

1   Whenever an update has been made to a chart the number of the Notice and the year (if not already shown) should be entered in the bottom left-hand corner of the chart. The entries for Temporary and Preliminary Notices should be entered in pencil, below the line of Notices.

Electronic charts and display systems

General information

Introduction
2.77

1   Unlike paper-based navigation, digital navigation involves the use of electronic chart display systems which are capable of displaying the position of a vessel superimposed on a chart image displayed on a computer screen.

Mariners should note that, as is explained in the following paragraphs, whilst there are many varieties of both electronic display systems and electronic charts, only ECDIS systems (2.81) using ENCs (2.88) meet the strict IMO SOLAS requirements for the carriage of charts and that any other systems can only be used as aids to navigation.

Chart display systems
2.78

1   There are many systems which are capable of displaying charts electronically. These fall into two classes. The first is ECDIS (Electronic Chart Display and Information System) which can meet IMO definition of a carriage-compliant system. For a full definition, see 2.81.

The second is an Electronic Chart System (ECS), a generic term for a system which does not conform to the IMO definition of an ECDIS, does not meet SOLAS chart carriage requirements, and which may not therefore be used for primary paperless navigation.

Electronic charts
2.79

1   **General information.** Electronic charts are manufactured and distributed by both government Hydrographic Offices and by private companies.

Only officially produced electronic charts (i.e. those manufactured by, or on the authority of, government Hydrographic Offices), may be used for primary, paperless navigation, provided that they are installed on ECDIS equipment which meets IMO performance standards.

2   Electronic charts are of two distinct types, vector and raster.

Vector charts. Each point on a vector chart has been digitally mapped, allowing the information to be used in a sophisticated way such as clicking on a feature to obtain all the information relating to the displayed feature. ENCs are vector charts.

Raster charts are electronic facsimiles of paper charts and therefore present navigational information in the same familiar style. In order to meet IMO performance standards when used in ECDIS, they must be originated by, or distributed on the authority of a government authorised Hydrographic Office. They are then termed Raster Navigational Charts (RNCs). The Admiralty Raster Chart Service (ARCS) (see 2.106) is made up of RNCs which fully conform to IHO standards.

Official and unofficial data
2.80

1   When the terms "official" and "unofficial" are applied to electronic charts, "official" is the term used to mean that the chart is compliant with SOLAS carriage

requirements (see Annex A) which requires that such a chart is "...issued officially by or on the authority of a Government, authorised Hydrographic Office or other relevant Government institution and is designed to meet the requirements of marine navigation."

2 While private sector producers of electronic charts may make their charts under licence from hydrographic offices, this does not mean that they are "authorised" by those offices. This means that they cannot satisfy the carriage requirements of SOLAS and are therefore "unofficial".

"Unofficial" electronic charts cannot be used in ECDIS for primary navigation. They may be used as a supplementary aid to navigation, but if used in this way, primary navigation must be undertaken using paper charts in order to comply with the regulations.

ECDIS

Definition
2.81

1 An Electronic Chart Display and Information System (ECDIS) is a navigation information system which, with adequate back-up arrangements, can be accepted as complying with the up-to-date chart required by regulations V/19 and V/27 of the 1974 SOLAS Convention. It displays selected information from a SENC (2.89) with positional information from navigation sensors to assist the mariner in route planning and route monitoring, and if required, can display additional navigation-related information. To comply with IMO requirements, an ECDIS must be type approved to IEC 61174 as laid down in the IMO performance standard.

Performance standards
2.82

1 The ECDIS Performance Standard, developed jointly by the IMO and the IHO, was approved by the IMO in 1995 and updated in 1998 and 2006. It requires the displayed ENC data to be compliant with S-57 (2.88), and also requires that the ECDIS equipment displays the data in accordance with S-52 – *Specifications for Chart Content and Display Aspects of ECDIS.* This standard has been produced by the IHO for the chart content and display aspects of ECDIS in order to ensure that hydrographic data supplied by member state Hydrographic Offices is used in a manner that will enhance the safety and efficiency of navigation by satisfying the requirements set out in the *IMO Performance Standards for ECDIS.* It should be read in conjunction with S-57.

2 Many ECDIS systems installed on vessels will have been type approved against early versions of the type approval standard (IEC 61174) and also may not be compliant with current versions of IHO standards. Mariners using ECDIS should be aware that as a result of this some features within the ENC may not display in ECDIS as intended. See 2.94 for implications of different versions on Temporary and Preliminary NMs and 2.95 for routeing measures implications. IMO Safety of Navigation Circular 266 (SN Circ266) underlines the importance of maintaining software to current versions of IHO standards.

Carriage requirements
2.83

1 ENCs conform to International Hydrographic Organisation (IHO) specifications and if used with a type-approved ECDIS, together with adequate back-up arrangements, satisfy the chart carriage requirements under SOLAS Chapter V. As such, signatory nations may accept such ENCs as fully acceptable for navigation in their waters.

2 Vessels which are obliged to comply with SOLAS regulations should note that the IMO has approved the use of ECDIS in Raster Chart Display System (RCDS) mode of operation when RNCs, such as those provided by ARCS, are displayed. Approval is subject to two conditions:

RNCs can only be used when ENCs are not available.

When operating in the RCDS mode, ECDIS must be used together with an appropriate folio of up to date paper charts.

3 All other forms of digital charts and display systems are designated as Electronic Chart Systems (ECS) which do not satisfy the SOLAS chart carriage requirements. ECS may only be used as a navigation aid; a full complement of paper charts must still be kept up to date and be used for navigation.

Guidance regarding the use of ECDIS and ENC can be found in the document *Facts about Charts and Carriage Requirements* published jointly by IC-ENC and Primar Stavanger and is available at www.ukho.gov.uk/2012compliance.

Mandatory carriage of ECDIS
2.84

1 In 2009, the 86th meeting of the Maritime Safety Committee (MSC) of the IMO agreed to the formal adoption of a mandatory carriage requirement for ECDIS. The change to SOLAS Regulation V19, which will come into force in July 2011, will require the fitting of ECDIS in a range of vessel types and sizes, starting in 2012 and phased over a 6-year period.

Settings and alarms
2.85

1 It is vitally important that safety values, particularly relating to depth contours and depths are correctly set in the ECDIS equipment. Failure to do so could lead the mariner to believe that, due to the absence of an alarm, he is in safe water when the opposite is true. Similarly, if erroneously set in the opposite sense, the mariner may restrict himself unnecessarily when more safe water is available than is indicated by the display.

2 The mariner should always set safety contours and/or safety depths. In both cases the system will display these contour depths in emphasised symbology when selected. If safety contours are not selected, the system will display a safety contour of 30 m by default.

A look ahead range, expressed either as a distance or a time should also be set by the mariner to control how far in advance an alert is given before a distance limit is violated. The same look ahead range should be set for approaching boundaries of prohibited areas, areas where special conditions apply, and crossing a safety contour or proximity to danger. This range should never be set to zero.

Experience with ECDIS and ENCs
2.86

1   Although ECDIS has been in use at sea for some years, its employment is not yet widespread and many mariners remain unpractised in its use. This situation is expected to change significantly over the next few years, particularly with a mandatory carriage requirement for ECDIS by IMO from 2012 (2.84), and as newly qualified Deck Officers graduate from colleges and universities.

2   In the meantime, there remains some lack of confidence in the new technology which makes it vitally important that mariners work to ensure that they are fully conversant with the capabilities and limitations of their equipment and its functionality, and taking extra care until full confidence is attained. All available sources of advice should be utilised, including, for UK mariners, the publication *Safety of Navigation - Implementation of SOLAS Chapter V*" published by the UK Maritime and Coastguard Agency (MCA).

ENCs

General information
2.87

1   ENCs are vector electronic charts that conform to IMO and IHO specifications. They are compiled from a database of individual items ("objects") of digitized chart data which can be displayed as a seamless chart. When used in ECDIS, the data is re-assembled to display either the chart image or a user-selected combination of data. ENCs are "intelligent" in that systems using them can be set up to give warning of impending danger in relation to the vessel's position and movement.

Definitions
2.88

1   The following definitions are established by the IMO in regard to electronic charting:

Electronic Navigational Chart (ENC) is a database, standardised in content, structure and format, issued for use with ECDIS on the authority of government authorised Hydrographic Offices. The ENC contains all the chart information necessary for safe navigation and may contain supplementary information in addition to that contained in the paper chart (e.g. Sailing Directions) which may be considered necessary for safe navigation.

2   **S-57.** *S-57 - IHO Transfer Standard for Digital Hydrographic Data* is the IHO publication which describes the standard to be used for the exchange of digital hydrographic data between national Hydrographic Offices and for its distribution to manufacturers, mariners and other data users. It is intended to be used for the supply of data for ECDIS.

3   **S-63.** *S-63 - IHO Data Protection Scheme* is the IHO standard for the encryption and authentication of ENC information. It defines security constructs and operating procedures which must be followed to ensure that the data protection scheme is operated correctly and to provide specifications which allow participants to build S-63 compliant

systems and distribute data in a secure and commercially viable manner. The purpose of data protection is threefold:

4   To prevent unauthorised use of data by encrypting the ENC information.
To restrict access to ENC information to only those cells for which a customer holds a licence.
To provide assurance that the ENC data has come from approved sources.

System Electronic Navigational Chart (SENC)
2.89

1   SENC is the navigation database which is derived from the conversion of the ENC from its S-57 format (or from the S-63 encrypted form of this) to the ECDIS manufacturer's equipment specific format. It is normally generated by the ECDIS as the ENCs are loaded onto the system; however in some cases the conversion may be carried out ashore and the data delivered to a vessel in the required SENC format. The SENC must contain all of the ENC data and any updates to it; it may be supplemented with information from other sources.

Cell usage bands and identifiers
2.90

1   Each ENC has a unique 8-character identifier. The first two characters indicate the producer nation (eg GB for a UK-produced cell, NL for a Netherlands cell etc), the 3rd character indicates the navigational purpose of the ENC, commonly referred to as the "Usage Band" into which the cell is categorised, and the last 5 characters are used as the unique identifier for that ENC.

The usage band designator indicates the intended navigational purpose of the ENC and will take one of the following values:

Usage Band	Purpose
1	Overview
2	General
3	Coastal
4	Approach
5	Harbour
6	Berthing

2   Thus an ENC with an identifier GB500005 is UK-produced in the harbour usage band.

Category of Zone of Confidence (CATZOC)
2.91

1   The CATZOC attribute is the mechanism by which the ENC gives an estimate of the reliability of source data. This is designed to give the mariner the same degree of understanding as the Source Data Diagram on an equivalent paper chart (1.7). The information is displayed in ECDIS as a series of asterisks in an enclosing shape; the number of asterisks relates directly to the CATZOC diagram at 1.7 as described in the following table:

ENC Symbol	CATZOC Equivalent

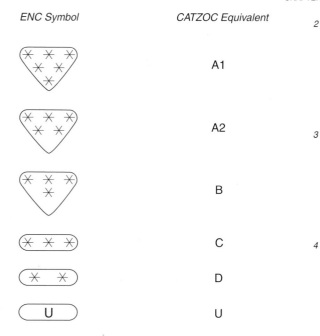

A1

A2

B

C

D

U

Category of Zone of Confidence (CATZOC) (2.91)

Appearance of ENC displayed data in ECDIS
2.92

1   It should be noted that the appearance and content of the ENC data displayed on ECDIS may differ substantially from the same or similar data in the paper chart form.

Examples include:

Scale Minimum (SCAMIN). The SCAMIN attribute defines the minimum (smallest) scale at which particular objects in an ENC are displayed in an ECDIS. It must be set to a smaller scale than the compilation scale, which is the scale at which the ENC is intended to be used for safe navigation. It is a very powerful ENC attribute that can be set against particular objects with the aim of reducing ECDIS screen clutter when zooming out. It does not apply to objects designated as minimum requirements for the base display. Generally speaking, clutter is not a problem when navigating at or near compilation scale.

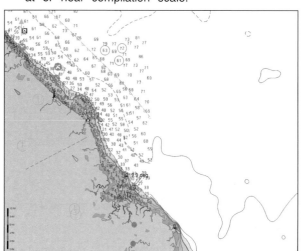

Screenshot of ECDIS display showing SCAMIN set in the E ENC cell but not in the W ENC cell (2.92.1)

2   The IHO has recommended best practice for setting SCAMIN, which has been accepted by the majority of HOs. This may take some time to implement, and until implementation is complete there may be instances of display such as can be seen in Diagram 2.92.1. In this case SCAMIN has been set in the eastern ENC cell, but not the western cell.

3   Whilst this view can be somewhat disconcerting, one solution is to switch the ECDIS display to standard mode. This will suppress the soundings which will result in a perfectly safe and usable display at such small viewing scales. Remember, what cannot be seen is still continuously monitored by the ECDIS either on passage or whilst passage planning.

4   **Contour intervals.** Adjoining paper charts can often use depth contours of different values and these have been used by mariners for many years without particular problems. However, when different contour intervals are used in adjoining ENC cells, an odd stepping effect can result when the ECDIS-generated safety contour crosses from one cell to the next. Diagram 2.92.2 clearly demonstrate the problems where safety contours are defaulted to a deeper value where depth contours are discontinuous between adjacent ENC cells.

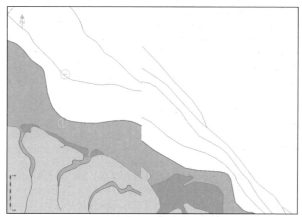

Screenshot of ECDIS display showing mis-match of contour intervals between ENC cells (2.92.2)

5   These problems exist on paper charts, but are more obvious in ENCs because of the seamless nature of the electronic chart. The main advantage of the ENC is that the safety contour can be fine tuned by applying appropriate values to the safety depth. This enables ECDIS to monitor both depth area and sounding values.

A best practice for encoding contour intervals has been issued by the IHO, but it may be some time before this is implemented universally owing to the varied sources from which ENCs are created.

6   **Overlapping ENCs.** There are instances where ENC data from different suppliers overlaps within the same Usage Band. Mariners should be aware that where such overlapping data conflicts, different ECDIS systems handle and display the data in different ways, and that an ECDIS might display data which has not been updated in preference to data which has. In some cases, two overlapping chart cells may be displayed at the same time. The UKHO makes every effort to minimise the impact of overlapping data in its

AVCS service, but under constraints imposed by the IHO, is not permitted to modify ENC data from the hydrographic authorities of other nations.

7 Details of all known instances of overlapping data are listed under Safety Information in the README.TXT file issued with each weekly update CD.

ENC updating
2.93

1 Theoretically, an ENC should be updated in line with the paper chart series of the producing nation. Most of the inconsistencies in the updating of ENCs and paper charts result from differences in the production methods of the producing HO.

2 The UKHO weekly updating service for ENCs within the AVCS and ECDIS services include all updates issued by other GHOs for ENCs they have produced. Mariners should note that updates for some GHO ENCs lag significantly behind updates for their paper charts of the same area. In such cases, ENCs within AVCS and the Admiralty ECDIS service may be less up to date than the corresponding paper chart.

3 Normally, the UKHO publishes New Editions to the ENCs it produces at the same time as a New Edition to the equivalent paper chart. Mariners should note that in some circumstances, such as where a NM block or some particularly complex NM is issued for the paper chart, an additional New Edition of the ENC may be required. The UKHO cannot guarantee that other GHOs will synchronise publication of New Editions for their paper charts and their ENCs.

4 Not all HOs update weekly; some have, for example, a monthly updating system. This can simplify ENC and paper chart synchronisation since there is more time available to perform the necessary tasks.

Mariners must take care when updating ENCs to ensure that they familiarise themselves with the nature of the change made to the charted detail. Some ECDIS systems will highlight changes in orange though it must be noted that the detail of the change made may not always be clear.

5 Information giving the update status for all GB cells can be obtained from the UKHO website by downloading the ENC Cell Update List from www.ukho.gov.uk/AVCS. The information provided for each cell includes:

Edition number and issue date.

Latest update number and issue date.

Latest NM included in the cell.

Other value added resellers (VAR) of GB ENCs may provide this information in other forms.

Specific information on the updating of ENCs is given in the README.txt file (2.104) included in ENC service media such as AVCS CD-ROMs.

6 Mariners should be aware of the significant changes in navigational practice required by the introduction of ECDIS and of the need to manage these updates in a careful and prudent manner.

Temporary and Preliminary Notices to Mariners
2.94

1 ENC producers use a variety of different methods to promulgate Temporary and Preliminary Notices to Mariners (T&P NMs). Some known examples of this are:

2 Producing T&P NMs in exactly the same way as normal NMs, using standard chart features.

The use of standard chart features in combination with the time varying attributes Date Start (DATSTA), Date End (DATEND), Period Start (PERSTA) and Period End (PEREND). In ECDIS systems not implementing the time varying attributes, these features will be permanently displayed.

3 The use of a combination of a Caution Area (CTNARE) feature and text description feature attribute (TXTDSC) which provides the full text of the NM. Temporary or Preliminary feature objects are provided and enclosed by a CTNARE to which a TXTDSC is attributed with a value pointing to an external text file. This file contains the text of the T&P NM.

4 ENCs published by the UKHO (GB country code prefix) will, wherever possible, provide T&P NMs in the same way as normal chart correcting notices. Only in certain circumstances where this is not possible will caution areas be used. All features changed by a T&P NM will carry the following Source Indication (SORIND)attribute:

GB.GB.NMrpt.nnnn(T) or (P)/yy

5 Not all government Hydrographic Offices (GHO) issue T & P NMs for their ENCs. Where this is the case, relevant GHO paper Notices to Mariner bulletins or websites (if available) should be consulted. Detailed information on specific issues relating to the use of ENCs from all HOs is given in the README.txt file contained in the \INFO folder on every AVCS and ECDIS Service data disk.

Routeing measures
2.95

1 The varying attributes Date Start (DATSTA) and Date End (DATEND) are used by UKHO and some other Hydrographic Offices to notify mariners in advance of new or amended routeing measures. ECDIS approved to IEC 61174 Edition 2 (2002) or later should be able to display the time–related features correctly. ECDIS type approved prior to IEC 61174 Edition 2 may display both old and new routeing measures simultaneously or fail to give any indication of the changes.

Information from nautical publications
2.96

1 IHO specifications permit ENCs to include information from nautical publications. The UKHO is presently (2009) developing the technology to enable this feature. However, until it is fully developed and available, in order to meet SOLAS requirements mariners using ENCs must continue to use related official publications.

Use of navigational information provided by UKHO
2.97

1 Attention is drawn to paragraph 1.25 concerning the use of navigational information provided by the UKHO.

Admiralty Vector Chart Service (AVCS)

General information
2.98

1   AVCS brings together ENCs from national Hydrographic Offices around the world and ENC coverage produced by UKHO in co-operation with foreign governments to provide extensive worldwide coverage. It comprises only ENCs which conform to the definition of a nautical chart set out in SOLAS Chapter V Regulation 2.2, which means that they can be used with a type-approved ECDIS for primary navigation.

2   Data is supplied on CD-ROM or DVD and maintained by a weekly update CD or on-line through the Admiralty Updating Service (an installable application contained on the Admiralty Utilities CD). Data can be supplied in S-57 format, protected by S-63 encryption (2.82), or a SENC format (2.89) depending on the requirement of the mariner. In either case, the scope of this service can also be viewed on the *Admiralty Digital Catalogue* (also available on the Utilities CD). The Catalogue can be used to order new ENCs and maintain an inventory of holdings.

3   The service is normally licensed for periods of 12 months, but licenses are available for shorter periods.

ENC availability
2.99

1   All ENCs in AVCS are available on a chart-by-chart basis as ENC Units. These Units are the smallest unit of sale allowed by the ENC producer, and usually contain ENC data approximately equivalent to a paper chart. Each unit will contain one or more individual ENCs, called cells.

AVCS is also available in a series of managed folios, each of which contains all the ENCs required for a specific purpose.

Folios
2.100

1   AVCS is provided in geographically based folios giving worldwide coverage. There are 3 types of folio available, designed to maximise utility and minimise the carriage of redundant data. A mix of all 3 folio types is required for most voyages.

Transit Folios. For the purposes of AVCS, the world is divided into "Transit Areas" representing convenient and well-understood ocean regions (see diagram 2.100.1). These contain predominantly Overview (Usage Band 1) and General (Usage Band 2) cell coverage, with Coastal (Usage Band 3) coverage where appropriate (at selected choke points, capes, straits and complex coasts).

2   Transit Folios are intended to save mariners the expense of purchasing detailed coverage for regions that they are just passing through, whilst including more coverage to negotiate choke points. Approach and Harbour band cells are available either in the appropriate Regional or Port Folio (see below), or individually.

Regional Folios. These folios are of much smaller geographical footprint than Transit Folios, of which they are usually a sub-area (see diagram 2.100.2). They generally include all Coastal (Usage Band 3) coverage within the folio's footprint and, where Coastal band coverage is not available (eg Scandinavia), include Approach band coverage.

3   ENC coverage at Regional scales is expanding rapidly. Where Regional Folios can be schemed so that they provide sufficient coverage to populate a useful folio, they will be released in AVCS. Until

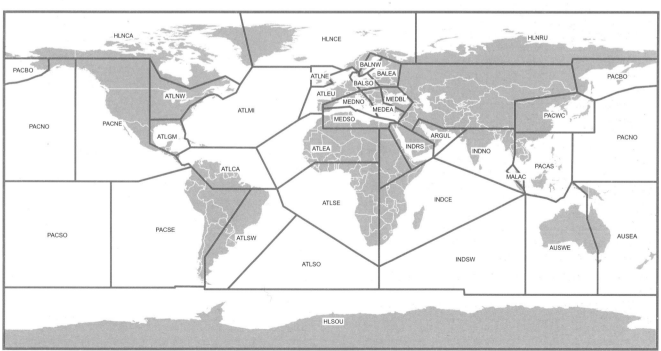

AVCS Transit Folios (2.100.1)

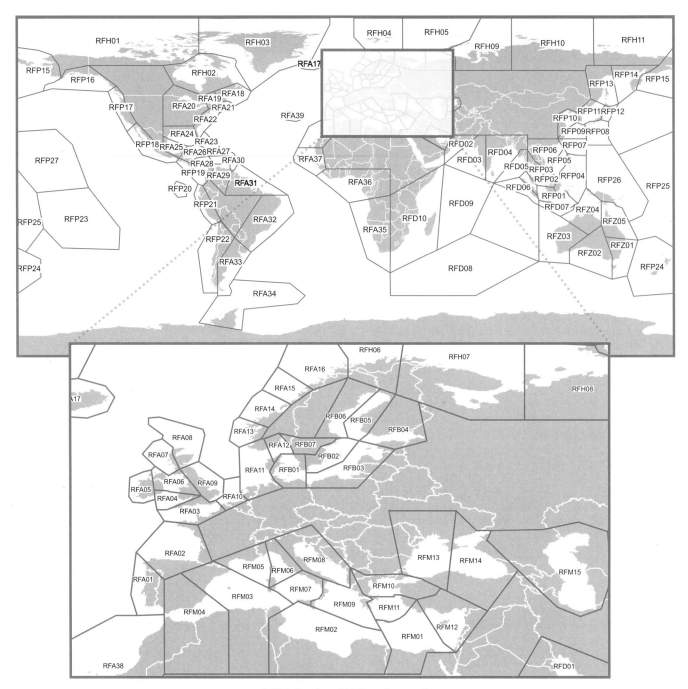

AVCS Regional Folios (2.100.2)

then, limited coverage will be provided by means of individual Units.

Port Folios. Coverage of the world's ports is schemed into a set of Port Folios. Each contains the coverage necessary to enter the port, with Approach (Usage Band 4), Harbour (Usage Band 5) and Berthing (Usage Band 6) ENCs grouped together into a single folio.

4   In very complex areas where a number of ports share approaches, a single Port Folio has been schemed to provide the coverage for all the ports in the area. See Diagram 2.100.3

Typically, the mariner will be able to choose only the Transit Folios necessary to get him from his present location to a particular destination port, plus one or more Regional Folios to provide more detail where necessary. He may then choose specific detailed coverage appropriate to the port(s) being visited.

Admiralty Information Overlay
2.101

1   The Admiralty Information Overlay (AIO) is a new concept under development by the UKHO which will provide access to additional safety and NM information which is navigationally significant and can be used in conjunction with ENCs to improve safety of navigation when using ECDIS. It should be used for voyage planning, and can be referred to whilst on passage.

Example of an AVCS port folio

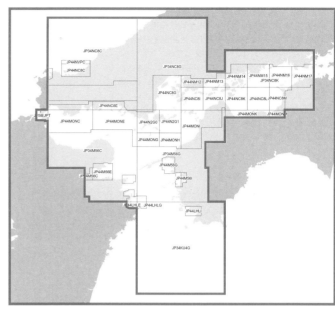

Example of an AVCS 'superport' folio

AVCS Port Folios (2.100.3)

2   The Overlay, which is expected to become available in early 2010, will contain information about changes or hazards of a temporary nature, such as changes to aids to navigation, advance notice of permanent changes, new survey information which will later be issued as an ENC update, and additional information of relevance to mariners which has not been included in national ENCs.

3   The AIO will not, initially, be able to be displayed in all ECDIS equipment. www.ukho.gov.uk/AVCS will list ECDIS equipment able to display the AIS as ECDIS manufacturers develop the facility. Alternatively, the ECDIS manufacturer should be consulted.

Licensing
2.102
1   AVCS licences are valid for 12 months. Within this period, folios and units may be added at any time for shorter periods, or until the expiry of the licence. There is no requirement for all data to expire at the same time, so mariners can tailor their holdings to that which is appropriate for their operations at any given time.

Thus, when folios and units are added to a licence for a shorter period than the overall licence period, they can be renewed or allowed to expire at the end of their term. For example, a vessel whose operational area is changed may allow data in one area to expire while simultaneously adding data for another area, all within the original AVCS licence period.

AVCS Start-Up Pack
2.103
1   On first commencement of a licence period, the mariner will receive an AVCS Start-up Pack, chart permit files which unlock the folios, and units ordered and an End User Licence Agreement.

Included in the AVCS Start-up Pack are a Quick-Start Guide, a User Guide and multiple AVCS Base disks, containing all available official ENC data. These are supplied either as CD-ROMs or DVDs, depending on the mariner's requirement.

2   The pack also includes an Admiralty Utilities installation CD containing the Admiralty Updating Service and the *Admiralty Digital Catalogue*, and the first weekly Update CD (see 2.105).

README file
2.104
1   All AVCS Base and Update CD-ROMs contain a README file which includes important safety information which should be read before using the service. For example, it includes a caution concerning ENCs derived from charts which are not on WGS 84 or a compatible datum.

The file is located in the \ENC ROOT folder on each CD-ROM and contains the following information:
Specific charting practices of some ENC producers which may be significant to navigation.
Specific updating practices of some ENC producers such as delays between the issue of paper NMs and ENC updates.

2   Identified overlaps between ENCs which may cause problems in display systems.
ENCs which have been withdrawn from service for any reason and which should not be used (permits will not normally be issued for these ENCs).
Specific licence and disclaimer text required by some ENC producers.

The README file is updated every week and changes are highlighted in a "Latest Corrections" section at the beginning. The file should be read as part of the weekly ENC update process to ensure that all relevant changes are understood.

Updating
2.105
1   Update CDs are supplied weekly, enabling data to be maintained for Notices to Mariners. Additionally, New Editions and replacement charts within the licensed folios and units will be supplied automatically.

Any new ENC which becomes available, whose coverage falls within a licensed folio will be supplied automatically at no additional cost to the mariner.

2   The issue of New Editions and new ENCs may require a new Chart Permit File to be issued. Where this is the case, it will be sent to the mariner by email. It is important that the correct permit file, corresponding to the week of issue of the updates being installed, is loaded into ECDIS before the updates are installed.

These updates are also available by email and over the internet by using the Admiralty Updating Service, supplied as part of the AVCS.

Admiralty Raster Chart Service (ARCS)

General information
2.106

1   ARCS is the digital reproduction of Admiralty charts for use in a wide range of digital navigational systems both at sea and in shore-based applications. ARCS charts are direct digital reproductions of paper Admiralty charts and they retain the same standards of accuracy, reliability and clarity.

Updating service
2.107

1   ARCS is supported by a comprehensive updating service which mirrors the Notices to Mariners used to update Admiralty charts. Updating is achieved with the minimum of effort. Weekly Notices to Mariners updates are supplied on an update CD-ROM. The updates are applied automatically and the updating information is cumulative so only the latest update CD-ROM needs to be used.

2   These updates are also available by email and over the internet by using the Admiralty Updating Service.

Format
2.108

1   ARCS charts are provided on CD-ROM allowing their use in a wide range of equipment, from full integrated bridge systems to stand alone personal computers. World-wide coverage is held on 10 regional CDs and one CD for small-scale charts.

Service levels
2.109

1   Owners of ARCS compatible equipment can subscribe to one of two service levels:

ARCS-Navigator is designed for users requiring access to the latest updating information. This is a complete chart supply and updating service which is provided under licence to the user. On joining the service the user will be supplied with the regional CDs that are required and, for the period of the licence, the weekly Update CDs. These contain all the necessary Notices to Mariners information, chart New Editions, and Preliminary and Temporary Notices to Mariners information needed to maintain the full ARCS chart outfit up to date. Periodically the user will be supplied with re-issues of the regional chart CDs.

2   Additional charts can be added to the outfit at any time. Selective access to individual charts on the regional CDs will be provided by a series of "keys", allowing the user to pay for only those charts required.

3   **ARCS-Skipper** is designed for users having less need for frequent updates. This service provides users with access to ARCS charts without the automatic update service. Charts will be licensed without time limit; it is for the user to decide when updated ARCS images are required. Many system suppliers may incorporate manual update facilities into their equipment allowing users to overlay new information onto the ARCS chart. Additionally, regional chart CDs will be re-issued on a regular basis and users wishing to obtain new editions or updated images will be able to licence the revised CDs.

Coverage
2.110

1   The coverage provided by each CD-ROM is shown in the following diagram:

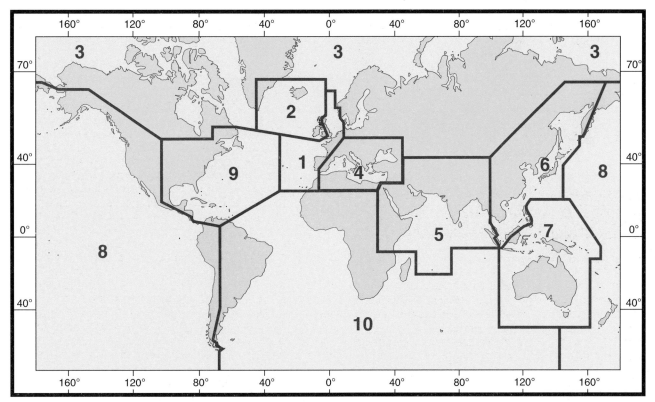

Regional Coverage of ARCS CD-ROMs (2.110)

RC 1. North Sea and English Channel to Gibraltar
RC 2. British Isles (west coast) and Iceland
RC 3. Northern waters and Baltic Sea
RC 4. Mediterranean and Black Seas
RC 5. Indian Ocean (northern part) and Red Sea
RC 6. Singapore to Japan

RC 7. Australia, Borneo and Philippines
RC 8. Pacific Ocean
RC 9. North America (east coast) and Caribbean
RC 10. South Atlantic and Indian Ocean (southern part)
RC 11. Ocean Charts (1:3,500,000 and smaller)

NOTES

Chapter 3

ADMIRALTY PUBLICATIONS

General information

Availability
3.1

1   All the books described below, listed in *Catalogue of Admiralty Charts and Publications,* are published by The UKHO except where indicated, and are obtainable from Admiralty Distributors.

Time used in Admiralty publications
3.2

1   The term "UT" is being introduced into Admiralty Publications to replace "GMT", initially as "UT (GMT)".

Universal Time (UT or UT1) is the mean solar time of the prime meridian obtained from direct astronomical observation and corrected for the effects of small movements of the Earth relative to the axis of rotation (polar variation).

Greenwich Mean Time (GMT) may be regarded as the general equivalent of UT or UT1.

2   Since these timescales correspond directly with the angular position of the Earth around its axis of diurnal rotation, they are used for astronomical navigation and forms the basis of the time argument in the *Nautical Almanac* and *Admiralty Tide Tables.*

Details of other time scales, including Local Times, are given in *Admiralty List of Radio Signals Volume 2.*

Admiralty Sailing Directions

General information

Scope
3.3

1   *Admiralty Sailing Directions* are are published in 74 volumes, providing world-wide coverage. The limits of each volume are shown in Diagram 3.3.

2   They are complementary to the chart and to the other navigational publications of the UKHO and are written with the assumption that the reader has the appropriate chart before him and other relevant publications to hand.

3   The information in Sailing Directions is intended primarily for use by mariners in vessels of 150 gt or more. It may, however, like the information on charts, be useful to those in any vessel, but does not take into account the special needs of hovercraft, submarines under water, deep draught tows and other special vessels.

Currency
3.4

1   Of the vast amount of information needed to keep charts up-to-date in every detail, only the most important items can be used to update the charts by Notices to Mariners. Some less important information may not reach the chart until its next edition, but may nevertheless be included in New Editions. It is therefore possible that in some less important detail, Sailing Directions may be more up-to-date than the chart.

Units of measurement
3.5

1   **Depths, heights, elevations and short distances** are given in metric units. Where the reference chart quoted is in fathoms and feet, the depths and dimensions from the chart are given in brackets after the metric depth to simplify comparison between the chart and the book.

2   **Distances** at sea are given in sea miles and cables (see Glossary), and on land in kilometres.

Maintenance of Sailing Directions

Use of Sailing Directions
3.6

1   Before using *Admiralty Sailing Directions,* the mariner must always:

Check that the most recent edition of the volume, and its Supplement where relevant, are held.

Check that all the amendments in *Annual Notices to Mariners Part 2 - Amendments to Sailing Directions* have been applied.

Check that all amendments published at Section IV of *Weekly Editions of Admiralty Notices to Mariners* subsequent to the publication of the most recent edition of *Annual Notices to Mariners Part 2 - Amendments to Sailing Directions* have been applied, using the most recent quarterly check-list at Section IB of the weekly edition, and the most recent edition of *Cumulative List of Admiralty Notices to Mariners.*

2   Where it is found that the most up to date information is not held, the most recent editions of all Admiralty publications can be obtained from Admiralty Distributors, and back copies of *Weekly Editions of Admiralty Notices to Mariners* can also be downloaded from the UKHO website www.ukho.gov.uk.

New Editions
3.7

1   Sailing Directions are updated by a process of Continuous Revision, with titles republished as new editions at approximately three yearly intervals. Some volumes, indicated in the *Catalogue of Admiralty Charts and Publications* are on an extended cycle of approximately 5 years.

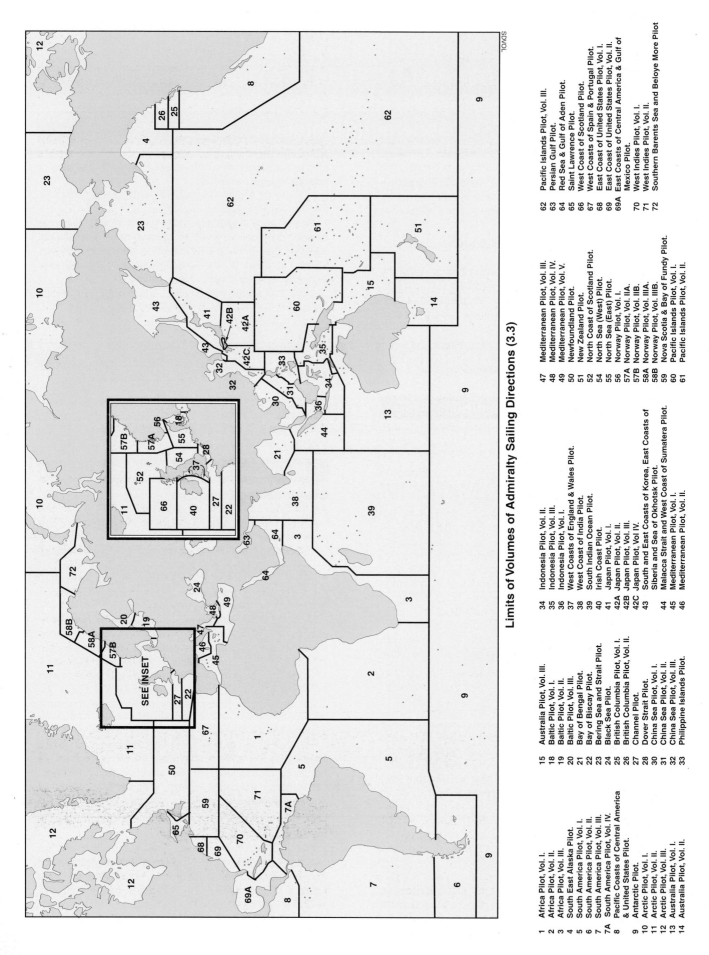

Limits of Volumes of Admiralty Sailing Directions (3.3)

1 Africa Pilot, Vol. I.
2 Africa Pilot, Vol. II.
3 Africa Pilot, Vol. III.
4 South East Alaska Pilot.
5 South America Pilot, Vol. I.
6 South America Pilot, Vol. II.
7 South America Pilot, Vol. III.
7A South America Pilot, Vol. IV.
8 Pacific Coasts of Central America & United States Pilot.
9 Antarctic Pilot.
10 Arctic Pilot, Vol. I.
11 Arctic Pilot, Vol. II.
12 Arctic Pilot, Vol. III.
13 Australia Pilot, Vol. I.
14 Australia Pilot, Vol. II.

15 Australia Pilot, Vol. III.
18 Baltic Pilot, Vol. I.
19 Baltic Pilot, Vol. II.
20 Baltic Pilot, Vol. III.
21 Bay of Bengal Pilot.
22 Bay of Biscay Pilot.
23 Bering Sea and Strait Pilot.
24 Black Sea Pilot.
25 British Columbia Pilot, Vol. I.
26 British Columbia Pilot, Vol. II.
27 Channel Pilot.
28 Dover Strait Pilot.
30 China Sea Pilot, Vol. I.
31 China Sea Pilot, Vol. II.
32 China Sea Pilot, Vol. III.
33 Philippine Islands Pilot.

34 Indonesia Pilot, Vol. II.
35 Indonesia Pilot, Vol. III.
36 Indonesia Pilot, Vol. I.
37 West Coasts of England & Wales Pilot.
38 West Coast of India Pilot.
39 South Indian Ocean Pilot.
40 Irish Coast Pilot.
41 Japan Pilot, Vol. I.
42A Japan Pilot, Vol. II.
42B Japan Pilot, Vol. III.
42C Japan Pilot, Vol IV.
43 South and East Coasts of Korea, East Coasts of Siberia and Sea of Okhotsk Pilot.
44 Malacca Strait and West Coast of Sumatera Pilot.
45 Mediterranean Pilot, Vol. I.
46 Mediterranean Pilot, Vol. II.

47 Mediterranean Pilot, Vol. III.
48 Mediterranean Pilot, Vol. IV.
49 Mediterranean Pilot, Vol. V.
50 Newfoundland Pilot.
51 New Zealand Pilot.
52 North Coast of Scotland Pilot.
54 North Sea (West) Pilot.
55 North Sea (East) Pilot.
56 Norway Pilot, Vol. I.
57A Norway Pilot, Vol. IIA.
57B Norway Pilot, Vol. IIB.
58A Norway Pilot, Vol. IIIA.
58B Norway Pilot, Vol. IIIB.
59 Nova Scotia & Bay of Fundy Pilot.
60 Pacific Islands Pilot, Vol. I.
61 Pacific Islands Pilot, Vol. II.

62 Pacific Islands Pilot, Vol. III.
63 Persian Gulf Pilot.
64 Red Sea & Gulf of Aden Pilot.
65 Saint Lawrence Pilot.
66 West Coast of Scotland Pilot.
67 West Coasts of Spain & Portugal Pilot.
68 East Coast of United States Pilot, Vol. I.
69 East Coast of United States Pilot, Vol. II.
69A East Coasts of Central America & Gulf of Mexico Pilot.
70 West Indies Pilot, Vol. I.
71 West Indies Pilot, Vol. II.
72 Southern Barents Sea and Beloye More Pilot

Supplements
3.8

1   Some older volumes have, in the past, been updated by publication of a Supplement. Each Supplement was cumulative so that each successive supplement superseded the previous one. These volumes have all now been taken into Continuous Revision, and no further Supplements will be published.

Until these older volumes have been published as New Editions, any volume demanded for which a Supplement has been published, will automatically be supplied with the most recent Supplement.

Current editions
3.9

1   To determine the current editions of Sailing Directions, and their latest supplements, if applicable, and for information regarding the publication dates of new editions, see *Annual Notices to Mariners Part 2 - Amendments to Sailing Directions*. This information can also be found in *Catalogue of Admiralty Charts and Publications, Cumulative List of Admiralty Notices to Mariners,* and quarterly at Section 1B of *Weekly Editions of Admiralty Notices to Mariners.*

Amendment by Notices to Mariners
3.10

1   Section IV of *Weekly Editions of Admiralty Notices to Mariners* contains amendments to Sailing Directions that cannot wait until the next new edition. These amendments will normally be restricted to those deemed navigationally significant, and information required to be published as a result of changes to national legislation affecting shipping, and to port regulations. Information that is made clear by a chart updating Notice will not always be repeated in a Section IV Notice unless it requires elaboration in Sailing Directions.

2   **Extant amendments published in Section IV** of *Weekly Editions of Admiralty Notices to Mariners* are listed in a Notice published quarterly in that Section. Those in force at the end of the year are reprinted in full in *Annual Notices to Mariners Part 2 - Amendments to Sailing Directions*.

Amendment procedure
3.11

1   It is recommended that amendments are cut out and pasted into the parent book. Mariners may, however, prefer to keep amendments in a separate file, and annotate the text of the book in the margin to indicate the existence of an amendment. This latter method is preferred in volumes which still have Supplements, and may be more appropriate in some other volumes where significant numbers of amendments, sometimes overlapping, may make the cut-and-paste method unwieldy and confusing.

Ocean Passages for the World

Contents
3.12

1   For the mariner planning an ocean passage, *Ocean Passages for the World* provides a selection of commonly used routes with their distances between principal ports and important positions. It contains details of weather, currents and ice hazards appropriate to the routes, and so links the volumes of Sailing Directions. It also gives other useful information on Load Line Rules, Weather Routeing, etc.

2   The volume is laid out to provide recommended routes for both full-powered vessels, and low-powered and sailing vessels, in separate chapters.

The book is updated by Section IV of *Weekly Editions of Admiralty Notices to Mariners*.

Admiralty Distance Tables

Contents
3.13

1   *Admiralty Distance Tables* (NP 350) are published in three volumes:

Volume 1: Atlantic Ocean, NW Europe, Mediterranean Sea, Caribbean Sea and Gulf of Mexico.

Volume 2: Indian Ocean and part of the Southern Ocean from South Africa to New Zealand, Red Sea, Persian Gulf and Eastern Archipelago.

2   **Volume 3:** Pacific Ocean and seas bordering it.

The tables give the shortest navigable distances in International Nautical Miles (1852 m) between important positions and chief ports of the world. These distances may differ from those used in *Ocean Passages for the World* (3.12) which, though longer, take advantage of favourable climatic conditions and currents.

Admiralty List of Lights and Fog Signals

Contents
3.14

1   *Admiralty List of Lights and Fog Signals (ALL),* usually termed 'Admiralty List of Lights' is published in 12 regional volumes (A-M), providing world-wide coverage. Between them, they contain the latest known details of lights, light structures, light vessels, light floats, LANBYs and fog signals. Light buoys of a height of 8 m or greater may also be listed and some with a height of less than 8 m are occasionally included in the list, as are light buoys considered to be of primary navigational significance. Certain minor lights, in little frequented parts of the world covered only by small scale charts, are included in the list though they are not charted.

A Geographical Range Table for determining Dipping Distances, and a Luminous Range Diagram for obtaining the range at which a light can be seen allowing for its power and the prevailing visibility, are contained in each volume.

2   The limits of each volume are shown on Diagram 3.14.

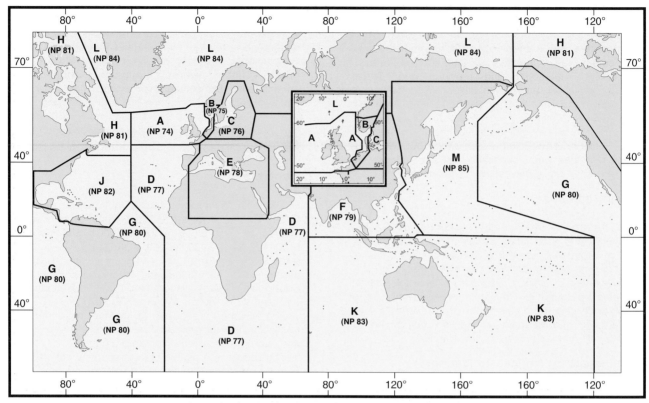

Limits of Admiralty List of Lights and Fog Signals (3.14)

Positions
3.15

1 Positions given in *Admiralty List of Lights* use either WGS84 or undetermined datums. Positions are obtained from the best sources available, usually Lists of Lights published by national authorities. Where datum shifts are known, they are applied to obtain the WGS84 position. Consequently, *Admiralty List of Lights* positions may not always exactly agree with those given in *Admiralty Sailing Directions* which are taken from the largest scale reference chart. In all cases, the largest scale reference chart should be used for positional information on lights.

Amendment
3.16

1 Changes of any SOLAS significance to lights or fog signals in *Admiralty List of Lights* are incorporated in the various volumes by Section V of the first *Weekly Editions of Admiralty Notices to Mariners* published after the information is received.

2 SOLAS/navigationally significant updates to lights shown on charts will also be issued as Section II NMs and in digital chart update CDs. This information is usually issued in a later Weekly Edition than that of the corresponding Section V NM or ADLL (3.18).

New Editions
3.17

1 A new edition of each volume is published annually. The new edition will include all of the minor light changes accumulated over the previous year, as well as all of the SOLAS light changes published by Section V Notice. The amendments which have accumulated after the volume has gone to print will be found in Section V of the Weekly Edition of *Notices to Mariners* which announces the publication of the volume.

Admiralty Digital List of Lights
3.18

1 Admiralty Digital List of Lights (ADLL), part of the Admiralty Digital Products (ADP) range, is a PC-based programme using exactly the same official data as that provided in paper form. The programme has been approved by the MCA as meeting SOLAS carriage requirements (see Annex A).

2 Global coverage is provided across nine Area Data Sets contained on a single CD-ROM. Users initially specify the areas for which coverage is required; additional area coverage is available at short notice by electronic transmission direct to the vessel.

3 The ADLL weekly update includes all SOLAS and minor light changes. Updates are promulgated weekly by CD-ROM, email or via the UKHO website at www.ukho.gov.uk.

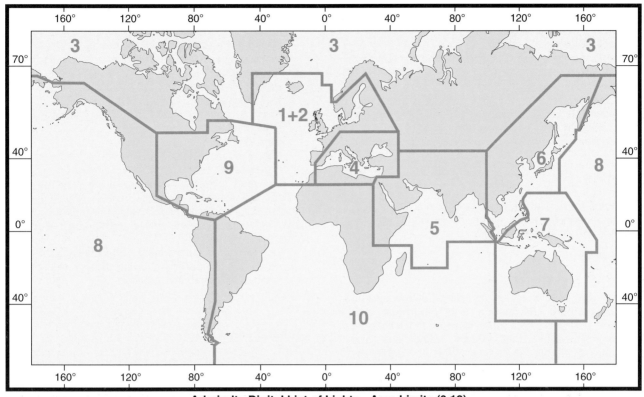

Admiralty Digital List of Lights - Area Limits (3.18)

AREAS 1+2.	Northern Europe and the Baltic	AREA 6.	Singapore to Japan
AREA 3.	Northern waters	AREA 7.	Australia, Borneo and Philippines
AREA 4.	Mediterranean and Black Seas	AREA 8.	Pacific Ocean
AREA 5.	Indian Ocean (northern part) and Red Sea	AREA 9.	North America (east coast) and Caribbean
		AREA 10.	South Atlantic and Indian Ocean (southern part)

Admiralty List of Radio Signals

General information
3.19

1   *Admiralty List of Radio Signals* (ALRS) are published in six volumes. A new edition of each volume is published annually, except for Volume 4 which is published at approximately 18 month intervals. Together they provide a comprehensive source of information on all aspects of maritime radio communications.

Volume 1
3.20

1   Volume 1, Maritime Radio Stations, is published in two parts:
   Part 1 covers Europe, Africa and Asia (excluding the Far East).
   Part 2 covers Americas, Far East and Oceania.
   Each part contains particulars of:
   Global Marine Communications Services.
   Maritime Radio Stations.

2   Coast Guard Radio Stations.
   Medical Advice by Radio.
   Arrangements for Quarantine Reports.
   Locust Reports and Pollution Reports.
   Maritime Satellite Services.
   Piracy and Armed Robbery Reports.

Regulations for the use of Radio in Territorial Waters.
Extract from the International Radio Regulations.

Volume 2
3.21

1   Volume 2, Radio Aids to Navigation, Satellite Navigation Systems, Legal Time, Radio Time Signals and Electronic Position Fixing Systems, contains particulars of:
   VHF Radio Direction-finding Stations (RG).
   Radar Beacons (Racons and Ramarks).
   Automatic Identification System (AIS).
   Satellite Navigation Systems (including a listing of radio beacons world-wide that transmit DGPS corrections).
2   Legal Time.
   Radio Time Signals.
   Electronic Position Fixing System: LORAN-C.
   Associated Diagrams are shown with the text.

Volume 3
3.22

1   Volume 3, Maritime Safety Information Services, is published in two parts:
   Part 1 covers Europe, Africa and Asia (excluding the Far East).

Part **2** covers Americas, Far East and Oceania.
Each part contains particulars of:
Radio Facsimile Broadcasts.
2   Radio Weather Services.
Radio Navigational Warnings (including NAVTEX and WWNWS).
GUNFACTS and SUBFACTS broadcasts.
Global Marine Meteorological Services.
Certain Meteorological Codes provided for the use of shipping.
Associated diagrams and tables are shown with the text.

Volume 4
3.23
1   Volume 4, Lists of Meteorological Observation Stations, contains a full listing of all meteorological observation stations world-wide.

Volume 5
3.24
1   Volume 5, Global Maritime Distress and Safety System (GMDSS), contains particulars of the system with associated information and diagrams, and includes extracts from the relevant International Telecommunications Union Radio Regulations and services available to assist vessels using or participating in the GMDSS.

Volume 6
3.25
1   Volume 6, Pilot Services, Vessel Traffic Services and Port Operations, is published in six parts:

Part **1** covers United Kingdom and Ireland (including European Channel Ports).
Part **2** covers Europe (excluding UK, Ireland, Channel Ports and Mediterranean).
2   Part **3** covers Mediterranean and Africa (including Persian Gulf).
Part **4** covers the Indian sub-continent, SE Asia and Australasia.
Part **5** covers North America, Canada and Greenland.
Part **6** covers North East Asia.
Part **7** covers Central and South America and the Caribbean.
3   Each part contains particulars of the maritime radio procedures essential to assist vessels requiring pilots and/or entering port. Also included is information on ship reporting systems, vessel traffic services (VTS) and port operations.
The text is supplemented with many associated diagrams and illustrations showing the key elements of the many individual procedures.

Amendment
3.26
1   When a newly-published volume is received, it should be amended from Section VI of *Weekly Editions of Admiralty Notices to Mariners*.
Cumulative List of Amendments. A summary, issued quarterly in Section VI, lists stations which have been amended.

Admiralty Tide Tables

Arrangement
3.27
1   *Admiralty Tide Tables* are published in four volumes annually as follows:
Volume 1: United Kingdom and Ireland (including European Channel Ports).
Volume 2: Europe (excluding United Kingdom and Ireland), Mediterranean Sea and Atlantic Ocean.
Volume 3: Indian Ocean and South China Sea (including Tidal Stream Tables).
Volume 4: Pacific Ocean (including Tidal Stream Tables).
2   Each volume is divided into three parts. Part I gives daily predictions of the times and heights of high and low water for a selection of Standard Ports.
In addition, Part Ia of Volume 1 contains hourly height predictions at a selection of Standard Ports, and in Volumes 3 and 4, Part Ia contains daily predictions of the times and rates of a number of tidal stream stations.
Part II contains the time and height differences which are to be applied to the Standard Port predictions, in order to derive predictions at a much larger number of Secondary Ports.
3   Part III lists the principal harmonic constants for all those ports where they are known, intended for use with the Simplified Harmonic Method (SHM). In addition, in Volumes 2, 3 and 4, Part IIIa contains

similar information for a number of tidal stream stations.
Also included are templates to assist in the prediction of tides by the time and height difference method and Simplified Harmonic Method (SHM).

Simplified Harmonic Method (SHM) for Windows
3.28
1   SHM for Windows is a Windows-based tidal prediction program using the Simplified Harmonic Method of Prediction.
Following input of the harmonic constants for the port in question, obtainable by the user from either *Admiralty Tide Tables*, or *Tidal Harmonic Constants for European Waters*, the program displays graphical predictions of height against time for a period of up to seven consecutive days, as well as a range of other features useful as aids to navigation.

Accuracy
3.29
1   Data for the Secondary Ports vary considerably in completeness and accuracy. In general, where full data is given, it can be assumed that predictions will satisfy the normal demands of navigation. Where incomplete data is given, it is prudent to regard the information obtained as approximate. Relevant symbols, footnotes and other notes are provided to alert the user where incomplete data is given.

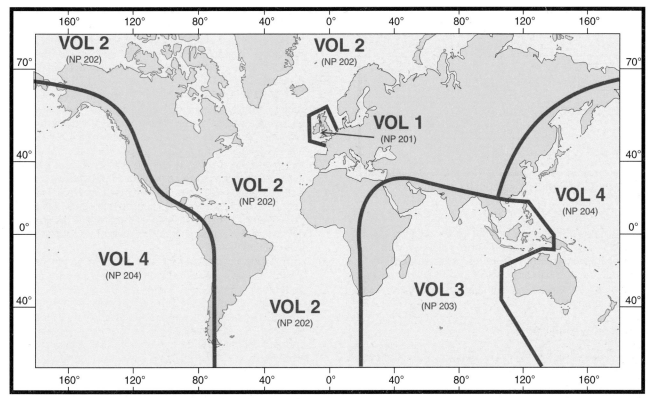

Limits of volumes of Admiralty Tide Tables (3.27)

Coverage
3.30
1   *Admiralty Tide Tables Vol 1* provides comprehensive coverage of predictions for the British Isles. Some individual harbour authorities publish daily predictions for places which are not Standard Ports in *Admiralty Tide Tables*.

Outside the British Isles, the general principle is to publish only a selection of the Standard Port predictions published in foreign tide tables, and those foreign tables should be consulted where appropriate.

2   Foreign tide tables are obtainable from the appropriate national Hydrographic Office (2.43), and usually from national agencies at the larger ports. A note of those places for which daily predictions are given in foreign tables is included in Part II of all four volumes.

Amendment
3.31
1   Latest additions and any amendments to *Admiralty Tide Tables* are published in *Annual Summary of Admiralty Notices to Mariners*. If any amendments affect the early part of the year before the Summary has been issued, they are published in a Notice issued during the previous November.

2   Information in *Admiralty Tide Tables* on subjects such as tidal levels, harmonic constants, chart datum etc, is subject to continual revision and information from obsolete editions should never be used.

Tidal Stream Atlases
3.32
1   A series of 22 Tidal Stream Atlases show the direction and strength of tidal streams in parts of NW Europe at hourly intervals in diagrammatic form. Each diagram is referenced to the time of HW at a specified Standard Port, and a method is included for assessing the rate of the stream depending upon the range of the specific tide in question.

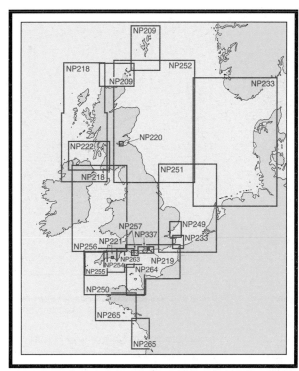

Tidal Stream Atlases of NW Europe (3.32.1)

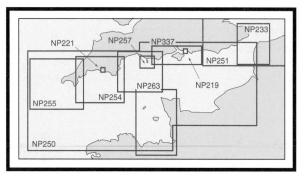

Tidal Stream Atlases – English Channel (3.32.2)

2   The data is the same as that given on large scale charts, but the diagrammatic presentation is advantageous when planning and executing a passage through an area, as it provides interpolated estimates of stream movements in between the observed points.

Admiralty TotalTide
3.33

1   Admiralty TotalTide is a PC-based tidal prediction program which uses the same prediction algorithms and Harmonic Constants as the *Admiralty Tide Tables*, and has been designed to meet SOLAS carriage requirements.

Tidal heights for both Standard and Secondary Ports are displayed in graphical and tabular form.

Tidal stream rates are presented on a chart-based diagram.

2   TotalTide permits the mariner to select and simultaneously calculate tidal heights for multiple ports for up to seven days. Output from the system also includes periods of daylight and nautical twilight, moon phases and a springs and neaps indicator. Underkeel and overhead clearance can be displayed in a graphic form to aid passage planning. Tidal levels output includes both HAT and LAT (where available) at all ports, as opposed to only being available at Standard Ports in ATT. Also available are statistical displays of data such as extreme predicted events over a specific time period.

3   TotalTide is supplied in the form of a single CD which contains the calculation program and the seven geographic Area Data Sets (ADS) providing global coverage (see diagram). A permit system then provides access to the areas required. Annual updates for TotalTide are available from Admiralty Distributors, and are necessary due to the annual nature of the product.

4   Further details are given at the end of each volume of *Admiralty Tide Tables.*

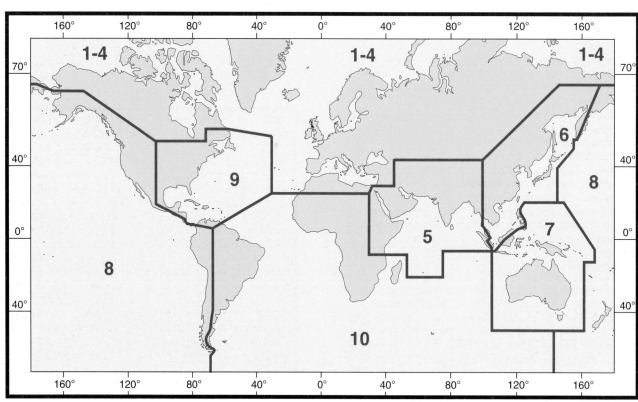

Limits of Admiralty TotalTide Area Data Sets (3.33)

Areas 1-4 **Europe, Northern Waters and Mediterranean**	**Area 8** **Pacific Ocean including New Zealand**
Area 5 **Indian Ocean (Northern Part) and Red Sea**	**Area 9** **North America (East Coast) and Caribbean**
Area 6 **Singapore to Japan**	**Area 10** **South Atlantic and Indian Ocean**
Area 7 **Australia, Borneo and Philippines**	

Admiralty EasyTide
3.34

1   Admiralty EasyTide is an on-line tidal prediction service intended primarily for the leisure mariner. Free predictions are available for 7 days (current +6), and predictions over longer periods are available for an appropriate charge.

Further details are available at www.ukho.gov.uk.

Other tidal publications
3.35

1   A list of Admiralty Tidal Publications is given at the end of each volume of *Admiralty Tide Tables*. These include Co-tidal charts and atlases, instructional handbooks on tidal subjects and other miscellaneous tidal publications.

Publications supporting celestial navigation

HM Nautical Almanac Office (HMNAO)
3.36

1   Since 2006, HM Nautical Almanac Office (www.hmnao.com) has been repositioned within the UKHO, and its publications are now produced as part of the Admiralty series of Nautical Publications, available from Admiralty Distributors.

HMNAO produces astronomical data in a number of formats suitable for a wide range of users.

2   It is jointly responsible, with the US Nautical Almanac Office within the Astronomical Applications Department of the US Naval Observatory, for producing the annual volumes of *The Astronomical Almanac* (3.37), *The Nautical Almanac* (3.38) and *Astronomical Phenomena* (3.39).

HMNAO also produces *NavPac and Compact Data* (3.40) and *Rapid Sight Reduction Tables for Navigation* (3.41).

The Astronomical Almanac
3.37

1   *The Astronomical Almanac* contains a wide variety of both technical and general astronomical information. The book is a world-wide resource for fundamental astronomical data and is jointly the flagship publication of the Nautical Almanac Offices of both the UK and the USA. It contains positions of the Sun, Moon and planets to milli-arcsecond precision, and the positions of minor planets and planetary satellites for each year, together with data relating to Earth orientation, timescales and coordinate systems.

2   Phenomena including eclipses of the Sun and Moon, sunrise/set, moonrise/set and twilight times are provided as well as fundamental astronomical reference data for stars and stellar systems, observatories and related astronomical constants and techniques.

It is available through Admiralty Distributors.

The Nautical Almanac
3.38

1   *The Nautical Almanac* contains tabulations of the Sun, Moon, navigational planets (3.40) and stars for use in the determination of position at sea from sextant observations. In addition it gives times of sunrise, sunset, twilights, moonrise and moonset, phases of the Moon and eclipses of the Sun and Moon for use in the planning of observations. All the necessary interpolation and altitude correction tables are provided as well as pole star tables and diagrams and notes for the identification of stars and planets. A concise set of sight reduction tables and a sight reduction form are also included.

Astronomical Phenomena
3.39

1   *Astronomical Phenomena* provides a summary of astronomical events several years ahead of the publication of the corresponding edition of the *Astronomical Almanac* (3.37). It contains Section A of the *Astronomical Almanac* ie the phases of the Moon, eclipses of the Sun and Moon, principal occulations, planetary phenomena, elongations and magnitudes of the planets, times of sunrise/set, moonrise/set, and the times of civil, nautical and astronomical twilights in addition to the equation of time, the declination of the Sun and the Greenwich hour angle (GHA) of the pole stars, Polaris and Sigma Octantis.

2   It is published annually by the US Government Printing Office, and is available through Admiralty Distributors..

NavPac and Compact Data
3.40

1   *NavPac and Compact Data* was first produced in 1981, in book form, by HMNAO whilst part of the Royal Greenwich Observatory. It provides mariners with simple and efficient methods for calculating the positions of the Sun, Moon, navigational planets Venus, Mars, Jupiter and Saturn, the 57 bright stars and the pole stars Polaris and Sigma Octantis over several years to a consistent level of precision. It includes a variety of astronomical algorithms including determination of position from sextant observations.

2   *NavPac*, the accompanying software package, which enables mariners to compute their position at sea from observations made with a marine sextant, was added in 1995. In addition, *NavPac* has functions which will enable mariners to calculate the times of twilight, rising and setting times for the Sun and Moon, times for checking compass bearings, as well as displaying the altitudes and azimuths of celestial bodies. The latter function is particularly useful for the planning of sextant observations and includes the selection of the best seven stars to use for a fix (see 3.41). Spherical great circle and spheroidal rhumb line tracks, which are not described in the book, may also be calculated. *Navpac* operates on Windows PCs and laptops.

3   An operating manual for *NavPac* is provided on the CD-ROM together with the relevant extract from *The Admiralty Manual of Navigation Volume 2*. The astronomical data files are in a format which can be loaded on any computer.

The data in *NavPac* is updated by the production of a new edition at approximately 5 year intervals. A new edition will always retain historical data back to 1986, and add new data for the forthcoming 5 years.

Further information can be found at www.hmnao.com/navpac.

Rapid Sight Reduction Tables for Navigation
3.41

1 *Rapid Sight Reduction Tables for Navigation* are designed for the rapid reduction of astronomical sights. They use the intercept (Marcq Saint Hilaire) method of sight reduction, such that interpolation for position and time (latitude and local hour angle (LHA)) are not required. Explanatory material, examples and auxiliary tables are included in each volume.

2 **Volume 1** Selected Stars for a Given Epoch, may be used without *The Nautical Almanac*. It tabulates the calculated altitude to 1' of arc and true bearing to 1° of arc for the seven stars most suitable for obtaining a position by sextant observation, for the complete range of latitudes and LHA Aries.
It is intended for use for 2½ years either side of the epoch for which it is published.

3 **Volumes 2 and 3** contain values of the altitude to 1' of arc, and true bearing to 1° of arc, for integral degrees of declination from 29°N to 29°S, for the complete range of latitudes and for all hour angles at which the zenith distance is less than 95° (97° between latitudes 70° and the poles), providing for sights of the Sun, Moon, planets and stars not included in Volume 1. *The Nautical Almanac* (3.38) is required to provide the position of the observed body. Volume 2 covers latitudes from 0° to 40°, and Volume 3 covers latitudes between 39° and 89°.

Sight Reduction Tables for Marine Navigation
3.42

1 *Sight Reduction Tables for Marine Navigation* are designed to support celestial navigation at sea by the intercept (Marcq Saint Hilaire) method of sight reduction. The tables tabulate the calculated altitude to 0'·1 and true bearing to 0°·1, and are arranged to facilitate rapid position finding. They are intended for use with *the Nautical Almanac* (3.38).

2 Explanatory material and auxiliary tables are included in all volumes, each of which covers a latitude (N or S) band of 15°, as follows:

Volume	NP	Latitude band
1	401(1)	0°–15°
2	401(2)	15°–30°
3	401(3)	30°–45°
4	401(4)	45°–60°
5	401(5)	60°–75°
6	401(6)	75°–90°

Star Finder and Identifier
3.43

1 *Star Finder and Identifier* consists of diagrams on which are plotted the 57 stars listed on the daily pages of *The Nautical Almanac*, and on which the positions of the planets and other stars can be added. For a given LHA Aries and latitude, the elevation and true bearing of a star can be obtained by inspection.

Chapter 4

PROMULGATION OF INFORMATION BY AND RENDERING OF INFORMATION TO THE UKHO

Promulgation of information

Navigationally significant information

General information
4.1

1   Hydrographic information, both temporary and permanent, is an important aid to navigation, but the volume of such information world-wide is considerable. If all the data available were promulgated immediately to update UKHO products, the quantity would overload most users and limit the usefulness of those products.

2   Strict control is therefore exercised in selecting that which is necessary for immediate or relatively rapid promulgation. That which is considered desirable but not essential for safe navigation is usually included in the next full new edition of the product when it is published.

3   Each item of new data received in the UKHO is assessed on a scale of potential danger or significance to the mariner (ie how *navigationally significant*) taking into consideration the wide variety of users of UKHO products in the area affected and the different emphasis which those users place on the information contained in the products. For example, the master of a large merchant vessel may be far more concerned with data regarding traffic routes and deep water channels than the recreational user, who may in turn have a greater interest in shoaler areas where the merchantman would never intentionally venture. The fisherman may have a greater interest in sea floor hazards.

4   During 1997, the criteria used to assess whether hydrographic information required immediate or relatively rapid promulgation to update Admiralty products were revised and made more stringent in response to increases in the size of vessels and changes in navigational practice by chart users. However, chart users should note that information assessed prior to 1997 and not yet included in a full new edition of the chart does not benefit from these changes in criteria. For details of the revised criteria see 4.2.

5   Mariners are warned that in all cases prudent positional and vertical clearance should be given to any charted features which might present a danger to their vessel.

Selection of navigationally significant information
4.2

1   In all areas of UKHO national charting responsibility (the United Kingdom, UK Overseas Territories and many Commonwealth countries) and in other areas of significance to international shipping, decisions are made within the UKHO to proceed with one or more of the methods of promulgation outlined in 4.3. The following types of information are deemed to be navigationally significant and will normally be promulgated by Notice to Mariners with or without an accompanying block, or prompt the issue of a New Edition of a chart if the information is sufficiently extensive or detailed to be impractical to issue as a block:

2   Reports of new dangers significant to surface navigation e.g. shoal depths and obstructions with less than 31 m of water over them and wrecks with a depth of 28 m or less.
Note. On some Admiralty charts, based on older information or on information from hydrographic offices currently using different criteria, certain wrecks which have significantly less water over them than 28 m may be portrayed by the symbol K29 in *Symbols and Abbreviations used on Admiralty Charts*. For further information regarding depths over wrecks, see 1.38.

3   Changes in general charted depths significant to submarines, fishing vessels and other commercial operations (depths to about 800 m) including reports of new dangers, sub-sea structures and changes to least depths of wellheads, manifolds and templates, pipelines and permanent platform anchors in oil exploration areas such as the North Sea and the Gulf of Mexico.

4   Changes to the significant characteristics (character, period, colour of a light or range if change is generally over 5 miles) of important aids to navigation, e.g. major lights, buoys in critical positions.
New or amended routeing measures.
Works in progress outside harbour areas.
Changes in regulated areas, e.g. restricted areas, anchorages.

5   Changes in radio aids to navigation.
Additions or deletions of conspicuous landmarks.
In harbour areas, changes to wharves, reclaimed areas, updated date of dredging if previous date more than 3-4 years old, works in progress. Also new ports/port developments.
In UK home waters, all cables and pipelines, both overhead (with clearances) and seabed to a depth of 200 m. Outside UK home waters, all overhead cables and pipelines (with clearances); seabed telecommunication cables to a depth of 40 m; seabed power cables and pipelines to a depth of 200 m.

6   Offshore structures, e.g. production platforms, wind turbines, marine farms.

Pilotage services.

Vertical clearances of bridges. Also horizontal clearances in US waters.

7   Areas where there is another national charting authority are termed derived charting areas; in some of these areas there is an obligation to follow the national charting authority in promulgating navigationally significant information. This is particularly relevant for countries where there are statutory regulations in force which govern the carriage of authorised charts and publications.

Promulgation
4.3

1   The following methods are used to promulgate new information for the updating of paper charts which meets the criteria at 4.2; the method of promulgation used will depend upon the urgency, scope and complexity of the data. For the updating of electronic charts see 2.93 and 2.94. For details of AVCS see 2.98 and for ARCS see 2.106.

Navigational Warning (See 4.8).

2   Preliminary Notice to Mariners ((P)NM) (See 4.29). Temporary Notice to Mariners ((T)NM) (See 4.30). Permanent chart updating Notice to Mariners (NM) (See 4.32). An NM is issued for the prompt dissemination of textual, permanent, navigationally significant information which is not of a complex nature. An explanation of terms used in Notices to Mariners is at 2.71. A Notice may be accompanied by an NM Block where there is a significant amount of new, complex, navigationally significant data in a relatively small area or where the volume of change would clutter the chart unacceptably if amended by hand (see 2.75).

3   New Edition (NE). (See 2.38). New Chart (NC). (See 2.37).

Information which is not navigationally significant
4.4

1   Information which is assessed as being not navigationally significant or is judged inappropriate for promulgation by Navigational Warning, NM (permanent, block, preliminary or temporary), or New Edition because of its nature, is recorded to await the next routine update by NE or NC.

Sources of information
4.5

1   Information is received by the UKHO from a variety of sources. These include:

The Royal Navy and other surveying organisations. Overseas hydrographic offices and/or national charting authorities.

Other functional authorities e.g. lighthouse authorities and port authorities.

Commercial organisations e.g. communications companies, oil and gas operators.

Vessels and/or shipping companies.

Private individuals e.g. leisure sailors.

2   Of the above sources of information, the first four provide the broad base of hydrographic information, but reports from vessels and individuals are no less important for keeping the published information up-to-date.

3   Mariners are encouraged to notify the UKHO when new or suspected dangers to navigation are discovered, changes are observed in aids to navigation, or updates to charts or publications are seen to be necessary. Information on how information should be reported is given at 4.41 and subsequent paragraphs.

Navigational Warnings and weather information

World-wide Navigation Warning Service (WWNWS)

Introduction
4.6

1   The World-Wide Navigational Warning Service (WWNWS), established through the joint efforts of the International Hydrographic Organization (IHO) and the International Maritime Organization (IMO), is a co-ordinated global service for the promulgation of Navigational Warnings. Documents giving advice and information on this service are available from the International Hydrographic Organization at www.iho-ohi.net/english/home.

2   Navigational Warnings are designed to give the mariner early information of important incidents which may constitute a danger to navigation.

3   Masters are recommended to arrange, whenever possible, for the Navigational Warning broadcast to be monitored prior to sailing in case any dangers affecting their routes are notified.

4   The attention of masters is called to the necessity for making arrangements to ensure that all Navigational Warnings or other matters relating to safety of life at sea are brought to their notice, or that of the navigating officer on watch at the time, immediately on receipt. The provisions relating to the official log provide for a certificate to the effect that the master's attention has been called to all signals of importance or interest and observance of the requirement should ensure that this important matter is not overlooked.

5   The language used in both NAVAREA and coastal warnings is invariably English, although warnings may additionally be transmitted in one or more of the official languages of the United Nations. Navigational Warnings are of three types – NAVAREA warnings, coastal warnings and local warnings.

NAVAREAs
4.7

1   For the purposes of the WWNWS, the world is divided into 16 geographical sea areas, termed NAVAREAs, each identified by the roman numerals I - XVI, and one sub-area (the Baltic Sea). The authority charged with collating and issuing long range navigational warnings within a NAVAREA is is called the NAVAREA (or Sub-Area) Coordinator are given in *Admiralty List of Radio Signals Volumes 3 and 5.*

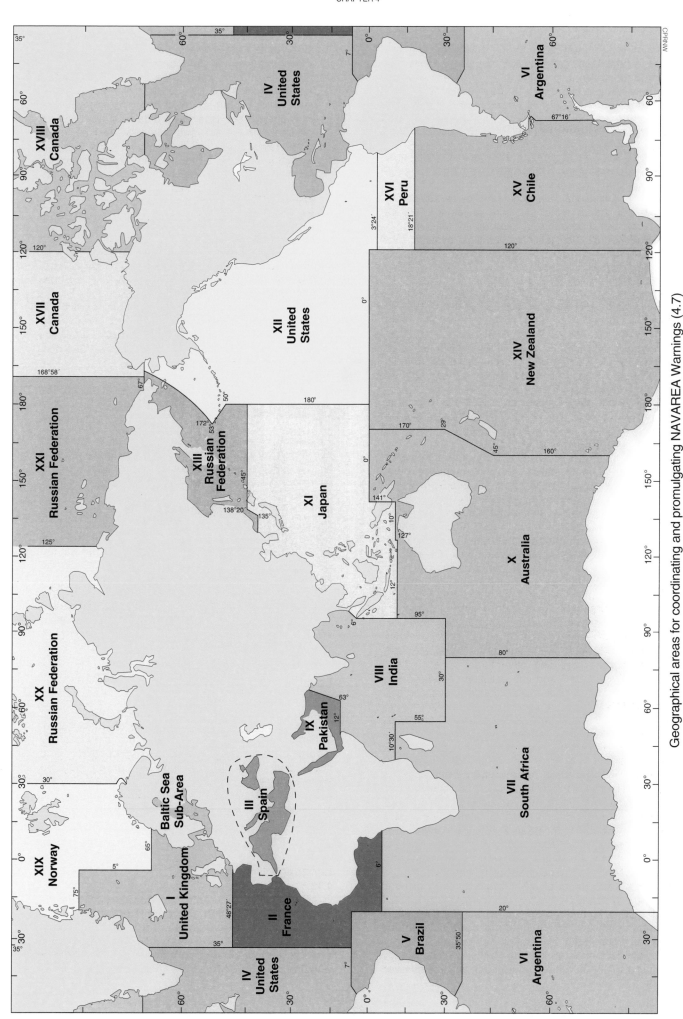

Geographical areas for coordinating and promulgating NAVAREA Warnings (4.7)

The delimitation of these NAVAREAS is not related to and shall not prejudice the delimitations of any boundaries between States
Arctic NAVAREAS Nos XVII, XVIII, XIX and XX have been agreed and are expected to become operational in 2012

2   A further 5 NAVAREAs (XVII - XXI), covering the Arctic region, have been agreed and are expected to become operational in 2012.

    The areas are shown, along with nation responsible for providing the Coordinator, at diagram 4.7.

Types of Navigational Warnings (NW)
4.8

1   There are four types of Navigational Warnings: NAVAREA warnings, Sub-Area Warnings, coastal warnings and local warnings.

    Many navigational warnings are of a temporary nature, but others remain in force for several weeks and may be succeeded by Notices to Mariners.

2   Details of all Navigational Warnings systems are given in *Admiralty List of Radio Signals Volume 3*.

NAVAREA Warnings
4.9

1   NAVAREA Warnings are concerned with information detailed below which mariners require for safe navigation.

    They are prepared in a numbered series for each calendar year. A list of those Warnings which remain in force is promulgated each week and should be recorded in a log.

2   In particular, they include new navigational hazards and failures of important aids to navigation as well as information which may require changes to planned navigational routes.

    This list is not exhaustive, and should be regarded only as a guide. Furthermore, it pre-supposes that sufficient precise information has not been previously disseminated by Notices to Mariners:

3   Casualties to lights, fog signals, buoys and other aids to navigation affecting main shipping lanes.

    The presence of dangerous wrecks in or near main shipping lanes, and, if relevant, their marking.

    The establishment of major new aids to navigation or significant changes to existing ones, when such establishment or change might be misleading to mariners.

    The presence of large or unwieldy tows in congested waters.

4   Drifting hazards (including derelict vessels, ice, mines, containers and other large items).

    Areas where SAR and anti-pollution operations are being carried out (for the avoidance of such areas).

    The presence of newly discovered rocks, shoals, reefs and wrecks likely to constitute a danger to shipping, and, if relevant, their marking.

    Unexpected alteration, or suspension, of established routes.

5   Cable or pipe-laying activity, the towing of large items of submerged equipment for research or exploration purposes, the employment of manned or unmanned submersibles or other underwater operations which constitute a potential danger in or near shipping lanes.

    The establishment of research or scientific instruments in or near shipping lanes.

    The establishment of offshore structures in or near shipping lanes.

6   Significant malfunctioning of radio-navigation services or shore-based maritime safety information radio or satellite services.

    Information concerning special operations which might affect the safety of shipping, sometimes over wide areas, e.g. naval exercises, missile firings, space missions, nuclear tests, ordnance dumping zones etc. Where the degree of hazard is known, this information will be included in the warning. Wherever possible, this information will be promulgated not less than 5 days in advance of the scheduled event, and reference may be made to the relevant national publications in the warning.

7   Acts of piracy and armed robbery against shipping.

    Tsumamis and other natural phenomena, such as abnormal changes in sea level.

    World Health Organisation (WHO) health advisory information.

    Security-related information.

Sub-Area Warnings
4.10

1   Sub-Area Warnings broadcast information which is necessary for safe navigation within a Sub-Area. They will normally include all the subject matter listed for NAVAREA Warnings above, but will usually affect only the Sub-Area.

Coastal Warnings
4.11

1   Coastal Warnings broadcast information which is necessary for safe navigation within areas to seaward of the fairway buoy or pilot station, and are not restricted to shipping lanes. Where the area is served by NAVTEX, they provide navigational warnings for the entire NAVTEX service area. Where the area is not served by NAVTEX, all warnings relevant to coastal waters out to 250 miles from shore may be included in the International SafetyNET service broadcast for the NAVAREA. Some areas of the world have established National SafetyNET Coastal Warning areas in lieu of NAVTEX Service areas.

2   Within NAVAREA I, Coastal Warnings are numbered in a continuous sequence, and prefixed by the letters WZ.

Local Warnings
4.12

1   Local Warnings broadcast information which cover inshore waters, often within the limits of jurisdiction of a harbour or port authority. They are broadcast by means other than NAVTEX or SafetyNET and supplement Coastal Warnings by giving detailed information within inshore waters. They are usually issued by port, pilotage or coastguard authorities. The messages may be in English or only in the local language.

Language
4.13

1   All NAVAREA, Sub-Area and Coastal Warnings are broadcast **in English only** on the International NAVTEX and International SafetyNET services. National NAVTEX and SafetyNET services are available in certain areas to transmit warnings in local languages.

Warnings may also be broadcast by other means not covered by the requirements of the GMDSS, such as VHF R/T.

International SafetyNET Service
4.14

1   The International SafetyNET Service is an automatic direct-printing satellite-based service for the promulgation of maritime safety information (MSI). It forms part of the Inmarsat-C Enhanced Group Call (EGC) system to provide a simple and automated means of receiving MSI on board ships at sea. For promulgation of MSI, see *Admiralty List of Radio Signals Volume 5*.

NAVTEX
4.15

1   NAVTEX is the system for the broadcast and automatic reception of MSI by means of narrow-band direct-printing telegraphy. The International NAVTEX Service uses a single frequency 518 kHz transmission in English. National NAVTEX Services may be established by maritime authorities to meet particular national requirements. These broadcasts may be on 490 kHz, 4209·5 kHz or a nationally allocated frequency and may be in either English or the appropriate national language. For details, see *Admiralty List of Radio Signals Volume 5*.

Updating charts for Navigational Warnings
4.16

1   On charts affected, information received by Navigational Warnings should be noted in pencil and expunged when the relevant messages are cancelled or superseded by Notices to Mariners.

Charts quoted in messages are only the most convenient charts; other charts may be affected.

Weather information

World Meteorological Organisation (WMO)
4.17

1   The WMO has established a global service for the transmission of high seas weather warnings and routine weather bulletins, through the Enhanced Group Calling International SafetyNET Service. METeorological service AREAS (METAREAS) are identical to the 16 NAVAREAS within the World-Wide Navigational Warning Service (WWNWS) (4.7). Each METAREA has a designated National Meteorological Service responsible for issuing high seas weather warnings and bulletins. The designated authorities are not necessarily in the same country as the NAVAREA Co-ordinators.

2   For full details of SafetyNET METAREA services see *Admiralty List of Radio Signals Volumes 3 and 5*.

The information at paragraphs 4.18 to 4.22 is valid within METAREA I only.

Offshore Shipping Forecast
4.18

1   A bulletin for offshore shipping comprising a summary of gale warnings, a plain language synopsis of general weather conditions and forecasts for 24 hours. In addition, an Enhanced Outlook is provided to cover the period from days 3-5 for the Offshore Shipping Forecast areas.

Offshore Shipping Forecasts are broadcast through:

2   RT (MF) and VHF by HM Coastguard MRCCs in the United Kingdom and also on the International NAVTEX Service (518 kHz) (4.15). Broadcast times vary with different groups of stations. For full broadcast details see *Admiralty List of Radio Signals Volume 3*.

SafetyNET - Enhanced Group Calling International SafetyNET. METAREA I only (i.e. area outside NAVTEX coverage). For full broadcast details see *Admiralty List of Radio Signals Volumes 3 and 5*.

3   BBC Radio 4. For full broadcast details see *Admiralty List of Radio Signals Volume 3*.

The enhanced Extended (3 to 5 day) Outlook is provided on the International NAVTEX Service (518 kHz) covering the shipping forecast areas of the NAVTEX transmitters; Portpatrick, Cullercoats and Niton i.e. North Sea, English Channel and SW Approaches, West Coast and Atlantic.

Gale warnings
4.19

1   Gale warnings are issued when mean winds of at least Force 8 or gusts reaching 43 to 51 kn are expected. Gale warnings remain in force until amended or cancelled. However, if the gale persists for more than 24 hours after the time of origin, the warning will be re-issued. The term Severe Gale implies a mean wind of at least Force 9 or gusts reaching 52 to 60 kn. The term Storm implies a mean wind of at least Force 10 or gusts reaching 61 to 68 kn. The term Violent Storm implies a mean wind of at least Force 11 or gusts reaching 69 knots or more. The term Hurricane implies a mean wind speed of 64 knots or greater.

2   The term Imminent implies within 6 hours of the time of issue of the gale warning; Soon implies between 6 and 12 hours; Later implies more than 12 hours.

Promulgation. Gale warnings are broadcast through:

RT (MF) and VHF by HM Coastguard MRCCs in the United Kingdom and also on the International NAVTEX Service (518 kHz). Broadcast times vary with different groups of stations. For full broadcast details see *Admiralty List of Radio Signals Volume 3*.

3   SafetyNET - Enhanced Group Calling International SafetyNET. METAREA I only (i.e. area outside NAVTEX coverage). For full broadcast details see *Admiralty List of Radio Signals Volumes 3 and 5*. BBC Radio 4. For full broadcast details see *Admiralty List of Radio Signals Volume 3*.

High seas - Atlantic Weather Bulletins and Storm Warnings
4.20

1   High seas - Atlantic Weather Bulletins and Storm Warnings are broadcast in plain language, commencing with storm warnings, if any, followed by a plain language synopsis of weather conditions, also forecasts valid for 24 hours. Storm warnings are issued whenever winds of Storm Force 10 or more are expected during the next 24 hours in any of the areas of responsibility.

2 **Promulgation.** High seas – Atlantic Weather Bulletins and Storm Warnings are broadcast on SafetyNET – Enhanced Group Calling International SafetyNET. METAREA I only (i.e. area outside NAVTEX coverage). For full broadcast details see *Admiralty List of Radio Signals Volumes 3 and 5*.

Coastal Inshore Waters Forecast
4.21

1 Coastal Inshore Waters Forecasts are broadcast for the benefit of coastal shipping, fishing vessels and leisure craft, covering the coastal waters of the UK out to 12 miles. They provide a brief synopsis, 24 hour forecast and a 24 hour outlook for 17 coastal areas.

Note. The Shetland Isles inshore forecast covers a 60 mile range of Lerwick and consists of a 12 hour forecast and a 12 hour outlook.

2 **Promulgation.** Coastal Inshore Waters Forecasts are broadcast through:

VHF by HM Coastguard MRCCs in the United Kingdom;
National NAVTEX Service (490 kHz);
BBC Radio 4.

For full broadcast details see *Admiralty List of Radio Signals Volume 3*.

Coastal Strong Wind Warnings
4.22

1 Coastal Strong Wind Warnings will only be issued if the wind speed in an inshore waters forecast area is forecast at Force 6 or more and was not identified in the previous inshore waters forecast. These will be broadcast on receipt and may be included in the repetition broadcast and are valid until the next new inshore waters forecast. The legend 'SWW' will be included in the Inshore Forecast if winds are forecasted at Force 6 or more to indicate that a strong wind warning is in operation for the time covered by the forecast.

2 **Promulgation.** Coastal Strong Wind Warnings are broadcast on receipt through VHF by HM Coastguard MRCCs in the United Kingdom and also on the National NAVTEX Service (490 kHz). For full broadcast details see *Admiralty List of Radio Signals Volume 3*.

Ships' Weather Reports
4.23

1 Ships' Weather Reports are made from vessels which have been recruited by National Meteorological Services to participate in the WMO Voluntary Observing Ship Scheme. Full details are given in *Admiralty List of Radio Signals Volume 3*.

They can be sent through a specified Inmarsat Land Earth Station using Special Access Code 41 of Inmarsat-B or Inmarsat-C. For full Inmarsat details see *Admiralty List of Radio Signals Volumes 1 and 5*.

Met Office website
4.24

1 Latest marine observations; shipping forecasts and gale warnings; and inshore waters forecasts and strong wind warnings can also be found on the Met Office website at www.metoffice.gov.uk.

Admiralty Notices to Mariners

Promulgation

How Notices to Mariners are promulgated
4.25

1 *Weekly Editions of Admiralty Notices to Mariners* contain information which enables the mariner to keep charts and books published by the UKHO up-to-date for the latest reports received.

2 The Notices are published in Weekly Editions, and are also issued by the UKHO on a daily basis to certain Admiralty Distributors.

Weekly Editions can either be obtained from Admiralty Distributors, or by regularly despatched surface or air mail.
4.26

1 **Internet Services.** *Admiralty Notices to Mariners* are also available on the Internet, using the *Admiralty Notices to Mariners* On-Line (ANMO) service. The ANMO service provides the digital versions of the weekly Notices to Mariners Bulletin, Full-Colour Blocks, Cumulative List of *Admiralty Notices to Mariners* and *Annual Summary of Notices to Mariners*. This service is available by following the Maritime Safety Information link at www.ukho.gov.uk. The web service is in Adobe Acrobat/PDF format, and the latest version of the software, and guidance notes, are available from the NM section of the website. There is also a searchable service which allows mariners to search for Notices by Admiralty Chart number. This service is available at www.nmwebsearch.com.

2 **Electronic Courier Services.** Further to the *Admiralty Notices to Mariners* (ANMO) service on the UKHO website, the UKHO has licensed several commercial companies to electronically distribute *Admiralty Notices to Mariners* via 'L' Band broadcast, or email communication, direct to vessels at sea. These 'electronic courier' or 'value added service providers' supply customised NM Text and Tracing update datasets related to a vessel's portfolio of charts and publications. The NM datasets are derived directly from the Admiralty digital NM files.

Numbering conventions
4.27

1 Weekly Editions are consecutively numbered from the beginning of each calendar year. *Notices to Mariners* are also numbered consecutively starting at the beginning of the year, noting that *Annual Notices to Mariners* will always have the first numbers in each yearly series.

Types of Notice to Mariners

General information
4.28

1 The majority of information designed for use in correcting paper charts is promulgated by the UKHO in the form of permanent, chart-correcting notices. Under certain circumstances, however, alternative forms of Notice to Mariners are utilised.

Preliminary Notice to Mariners ((P)NM).

4.29

1 A (P)NM is used when early promulgation to the mariner is needed, and:

Action/work will shortly be taking place (e.g. harbour developments), or:

Information has been received, but it is too complex or extensive to be promulgated by permanent chart updating NM. A précis of the overall changes together with navigationally significant detailed information is given in the (P)NM. Full details are included in the next New Chart or New Edition, or:

2 Further confirmation of details is needed. A permanent chart updating NM will be promulgated or NE issued when the details have been confirmed, or:

For ongoing and changeable situations such as bridge construction across major waterways. A permanent chart updating NM will be promulgated or NE issued when the work is complete.

Temporary Notice to Mariners ((T)NM).

4.30

1 A (T)NM is used where the information will remain valid only for a limited period, but will not normally be initiated when the information will be valid for less than 3-6 months. In such circumstances, the information may be available as an Navigational Warning (4.8) or may be promulgated by means of a Local Notice to Mariners.

Structure of the Weekly Edition of Notices to Mariners

Section I - Explanatory Notes and Publications List

4.31

1 Section I, published weekly, contains:

Notes and advice on the use, update and amendment of charts and publications.

Lists of New Charts, New Editions and Navigational Publications published, and any charts withdrawn, during the week.

Publication of New Charts or New Editions, or withdrawals, scheduled to take place in the near future.

2 Section IA. This section is published monthly and contains a list of (T) and (P) NMs cancelled during the previous month and a list of T&P Notices previously published and still in force.

3 Section IB. This section is published quarterly at the end of March, June, September and December each year. It lists the current editions of:

Admiralty Sailing Directions and their latest Supplements.

Admiralty List of Lights and Fog Signals.

Admiralty List of Radio Signals.

Admiralty Tidal Publications.

Admiralty Digital Publications.

Section II - Updates to Standard Navigational Charts

4.32

1 Section II contains the permanent Admiralty chart updating Notices, the first of which is always a Notice containing Miscellaneous Updates to Charts. Notices based on original information, as opposed to those that republish information from another country, have their consecutive numbers suffixed by an asterisk. Any Temporary and Preliminary Notices are included at the end of the Section. They have their consecutive numbers suffixed (T) and (P) respectively. These Notices are preceded by a Geographical Index, an Index of Notices and Chart Folios and an Index of Charts Affected.

2 Blocks. Cautionary notes, depth tables and diagrams to accompany any of these Notices will be found at the end of the section (See also 4.3 and 2.75).

Section III - Reprints of Navigational Warnings

4.33

1 This section lists the serial numbers of all NAVAREA I messages in force with reprints of those issued during the week. Edited reprints of selected important messages in force for other NAVAREAs, together with HYDROLANT and HYDROPAC messages received, are also listed in this Section.

Section IV - Amendments to Admiralty Sailing Directions

4.34

1 This section contains amendments to *Admiralty Sailing Directions* (3.10) published during the week.

Note. The full text of all extant Section IV Notices is published annually in January in *Annual Summary of Admiralty Notices to Mariners Part 2 - Amendments to Sailing Directions.*

Section V - Amendments to Admiralty Lists of Lights and Fog Signals

4.35

1 This section contains amendments to *Admiralty List of Lights and Fog Signals.* These amendments may not be published in the same weekly Edition as those giving chart updating information in Section II.

Section VI - Amendments to Admiralty Lists of Radio Signals

4.36

1 This section contains amendments to the *Admiralty List of Radio Signals.* These amendments may not be in the same Weekly Edition as those giving chart updating information in Section II.

Note. A Cumulative List of Amendments to the current editions of the *Admiralty List of Radio Signals* is published in Section VI quarterly in March, June, September and December.

Maintenance of NM Data

Retention of back copies
4.37

1   To maintain an effective set of NM data, Weekly Editions should be retained dating back to the earliest publication date of the current volumes of *Admiralty List of Lights and Fog Signals* and *Admiralty List of Radio Signals.*

In the case of *Admiralty Sailing Directions*, corrections are reprinted in full in January each year in *Annual Summary of Notices to Mariners Part 2 (see below).*

Annual Summary of Admiralty Notices to Mariners
4.38

1   *Annual Summary of Admiralty Notices to Mariners* is published annually in January, in two parts. The first part is in two sections:

Section I contains Annual Notices to Mariners. These Notices cover important topics which are likely to remain valid for some time and may be the same or very similar to those published in previous years. If and when it becomes apparent that the information has become more enduring than was originally envisaged, it will be transferred into the most appropriate parent publication.

2   Section II contains reprints of all Admiralty Temporary and Preliminary Notices which are in force on 1st January.

The second part is also in two sections:

Section I lists the current editions of all volumes of *Admiralty Sailing Directions,* and, where appropriate, their latest supplements.

Section II contains reprints of all extant amendments to *Admiralty Sailing Directions* which have been published in Section IV of Weekly Editions of *Admiralty Notices to Mariners* and are in force on 1st January.

3   These volumes are obtainable in the same way as other *Admiralty Notices to Mariners*.

Cumulative List of Admiralty Notices to Mariners
4.39

1   *Cumulative List of Admiralty Notices to Mariners* is published 6-monthly in January and July. It lists the publication dates of the current edition of each Admiralty chart and those Australian (AUS), New Zealand (NZ) and Japanese (JP) charts republished in the Admiralty series, and the serial numbers of permanent Notices affecting them issued in the previous two years.

The quoted publication date may be that of a New Chart, New Edition or a large correction. The relevant date is given in the bottom outside margin of the chart.

Summary of periodical information
4.40

1   *Annual Summary of Admiralty Notices to Mariners* and Notices issued at regular intervals provide details of messages, updates and amendments in force.

The table shows where this information can be found.

Subject	Serial Numbers in force published Monthly in Weekly Edition Section:	Full text published Annually in:
NAVAREA, HYDROPAC and HYDROLANT messages	III	Weekly Edition No. I
Temporary and Preliminary Notices	IA	Annual Summary Part 1
Amendments to *Admiralty Sailing Directions*	IV	Annual Summary Part II
Amendments to *Admiralty List of Radio Signals*	VI	List published Quarterly

Reporting of information

Observing and reporting hydrographic information

General remarks
4.41

1   Ever since man ventured on the sea, mariners have depended upon the experience and reports of those who sailed before; in this way, through the years, an increasing amount of information was accumulated from seafarers and explorers until it became possible to set down the details in convenient form, which was on charts and in Sailing Directions.

2   It may be true to say that there are now no undiscovered lands or seas and that most coasts have, to a greater or lesser degree, been surveyed and mapped; yet it is equally true that the accuracy of charts and their associated publications depend just as much as ever on reports from sea, and from others who are responsible for inshore surveys, lights, and other aids to navigation. Without a supply of information from these sources, it would not be possible to keep the charts and publications corrected for new and changed conditions.

3   Whenever a ship is making good a track over a portion of the chart where no soundings are shown, or over an area of suspected shoal depths, it is advisable to take soundings. If the ship is fitted with a suitable echo sounder, such soundings if properly recorded and reported, will be of much value for the subsequent improvement of the chart.

4   The planning of surveys can be considerably assisted by reports from ships on the adequacy or otherwise of existing charts, particularly in the light of new or intended developments at a port. In this connection the views of Harbour Authorities and pilots can be of value.

Opportunities for reporting
4.42

1   Subject to compliance with the provisions of international law concerning innocent passage, or to national laws where appropriate, every mariner should endeavour to note where charts and publications disagree with fact and should report any differences to the UKHO. Statements confirming charted and published information which may be old, but nevertheless correct, are of considerable value and can be used to reassure other mariners visiting the area.

2   It is hoped that the mariner, by following the points mentioned below, will be able to make best use of the opportunities with which he is often presented to report information, though it is realised that all ships do not carry the same facilities and equipment.

3   Reports which cannot be confirmed, or are lacking in certain details, should not be withheld. Shortcomings should be stressed, and any firm expectation of being able to check the information on a succeeding voyage should be mentioned.

Obligatory reports

Requirements
4.43

1   *The International Convention for the Safety of Life at Sea (SOLAS), 1974*, requires the Master of every vessel which meets with any of the following to make a report:

Dangerous ice, or air temperatures below freezing associated with gale force winds causing severe icing. See 6.49 for details of the required content of the report.

A dangerous derelict. The report should include the nature of derelict or danger, its position when last observed, and the date and time when it was last observed, using UT (GMT).

Any other danger to navigation. These may include shoal soundings, uncharted dangers and navigational aids out of order. Such dangers should also be reported to the UKHO, Navigational Warnings, by telephone (+44(0)1823 353448), Fax: (+44(0)1823 322352), Telex 46464 or email at navwarnings@btconnect.com. The draught of modern tankers is such that any uncharted depth of less than 30 m may be of sufficient importance to justify such action.

A tropical storm, or winds of Force 10 and above of which there has been no warning. See 7.28 for details of the required content of the report.

2   The report is to be made by all means available to vessels in the vicinity, and to the nearest coast radio station or signal station. It should be sent, preferably in English, or by *The International Code of Signals*. If sent by VHF or MF all safety communications should consist of an announcement, known as a Safety Call Format, transmitted using DSC or RT, followed by the safety message transmitted using RT. The message should be preceded by the safety signal SECURITE (for safety) or PAN PAN (for urgency) and repeated in each case three times. Full details can be found in *Admiralty List of Radio Signals Volume 5.*

3   In cases where it is considered that urgent charting action may be required, it is recommended that such reports be copied to the UKHO by the most appropriate means.

4   These reports are obligatory for the Masters of ships registered in the United Kingdom, under Statutory Instrument No 534 of 1980 and No 406 of 1981.

Standard reporting format and procedures
4.44

1   IMO Resolution A.648(16) introduces a standard reporting format and procedures, which are designed to assist Masters making reports in accordance with the national or local requirements of different Ship Reporting Systems.

2   Vessel movements are reported through a Sailing Plan, sent prior to departure, Deviation Reports where the vessel's position varies significantly from that predicted and a Final Report on arrival at destination or when leaving a Reporting Area. Three other standard reports give the detailed requirements for reporting incidents involving dangerous goods, harmful substances and marine pollution.

3   The existing procedure for making the obligatory reports described in 4.43 remains unaltered.

Other forms of report

Hydrographic Note
4.45

1   The Hydrographic Note (Form H102) is the preferred vehicle for submission of information, to the UKHO relating to charts and publications. This form is reproduced at the end of this chapter, and includes detailed guidance on its completion. Additionally, blank copies of the form are printed at the back of each weekly edition of *Admiralty Notices to Mariners.* They can also be obtained free of charge from any Admiralty Distributor, and can be downloaded from the UKHO website www.ukho.gov.uk.

2   In addition, the following UKHO forms are used for specific purposes:

Form H102a, Hydrographic Note for Port Information, should be used to render reports on port and harbour information. It is reproduced at the end of this chapter, and may be otherwise obtained in exactly the same way as the H102 above.

Form H102b, Hydrographic Note for GPS Observations against Corresponding Chart Positions, should be used for rendering reports in accordance with para 4.52. It is also reproduced at the end of this chapter, and may be downloaded from the UKHO website.

Form H636, Marine Bioluminescence Observations Reporting Form. See 4.68.

5   Mariners should not be deterred from reporting if any of the above forms are not to hand. Manuscript or email is just as acceptable.

6   Irrespective of format, reports should be forwarded to the UKHO, Admiralty Way, Taunton, Somerset, TA1 2DN, United Kingdom (email: hdcfiles@ukho.gov.uk).

7   In addition to the foregoing, mariners can assist the UKHO to provide the latest details of maritime radio services by supplying new, additional or corroborative information for *Admiralty List of Radio Signals,* using the report form in the front of each volume of

Admiralty List of Radio Signals, or Form H.102. Such information can be forwarded, either in manuscript, or by email.

Information requiring corroboration
4.46

1   Some information, dependent on its source and completeness, will require corroboration from an authoritative source (e.g. primary charting authority or a port authority) before being acted upon. However, if corroboration is being sought, but the nature of the information is such that it needs to be promulgated urgently, an NM may be issued.

Such reports should always be followed by a completed Form H.102 giving all available information.

Positions

Charts
4.47

1   The largest scale chart available, a plotting sheet prepared to a suitable scale, or, for oceanic soundings, an ocean plotting sheet (2.48), should be used to plot the ship's position during observations.

2   A cutting from a chart, with the alterations or additions shown in red, is often the best way of forwarding detail. If required, a replacement for a chart used for forwarding information will be supplied *gratis*. If it is preferred to show the amendments on a tracing of the chart, rather than on the chart itself, they should be shown in red, but adequate detail from the chart must be traced in black to enable the tracing to be fitted correctly.

The chart used should be stated and described as at 2.41.

Geographical positions
4.48

1   Latitude and longitude should only be used specifically to position details when they have been fixed by astronomical observations or by a position-fixing system which reads out in latitude and longitude.

Astronomical positions
4.49

1   Observations should be accompanied by the names and altitudes of the heavenly bodies, and the times of the observations. A note of any corrections not already applied, and an estimate of any probable error due to conditions prevailing at the time, should also be included.

Visual fixes
4.50

1   To ensure the greatest accuracy, a fix defined by horizontal sextant angles, compass bearings (true or magnetic being specified), or ranges, should consist if possible of more than two observations. The observations should be taken as nearly as possible simultaneously, should be carefully recorded at the time and listed in the report with any corrections that have been applied to them.

Fixes from electronic positioning systems
4.51

1   Loran-C positions should be accompanied by the time and full details of the fixes obtained. It should

also be stated whether any corrections have been applied, and if so their values.

Fixes from GPS
4.52

1   The report should include information on whether the receiver was set to WGS84 Datum or was outputting positions referred to another datum, or whether any position shifts quoted on the chart have been applied. Extra information such as the receiver model, and Dilution of Position values (Indications of theoretical quality of position fixing depending upon the distribution of satellites – PDOP, HDOP and GDOP) should be supplied if available.

2   Mariners are requested to report observed differences between positions referenced to chart graticule and those from GPS, referenced to WGS84 Datum, using Form H.102b (Form for Recording GPS Observations and Corresponding Chart Positions) reproduced on pages 83 and 84. The results of these observations are examined and may provide evidence for notes detailing approximate differences between WGS84 Datum and the datum of the chart.

Channels and passages
4.53

1   When information is reported about one shore of a channel or passage, or of an island in one, every endeavour should be made to obtain a connection between the two shores by angles, bearings or ranges.

Soundings

Echo sounder
4.54

1   The following information about the echo sounder should be included in the report.
    Make, name and type of set.
    The number of revolutions per minute of the stylus (checked by stop-watch).
    Speed of sound in sea water in metres or fathoms per second equivalent to the stylus speed.

2   Whether soundings have been corrected from *Echo-sounding Correction Tables*.
    Setting of the scale zero. That is whether depths recorded are from the sea surface or from the underside of the keel. If from the keel, the ship's draught abreast the transducers at the time and the height of the transducers above the keel should be given.

3   Where the displacement of the transducers from the fixing position is appreciable, the amount of this displacement and whether allowance has been made for it.

For methods of checking the accuracy of a sounder, see 11.102—11.103.

Trace
4.55

1   The trace should be forwarded with the report. To be used to full advantage, it should be marked as follows:
    A line drawn across it each time a fix is taken, and at regular time intervals.
    The times of each fix and alteration of course inserted, and times of interval marks at not more than 15 minute intervals.

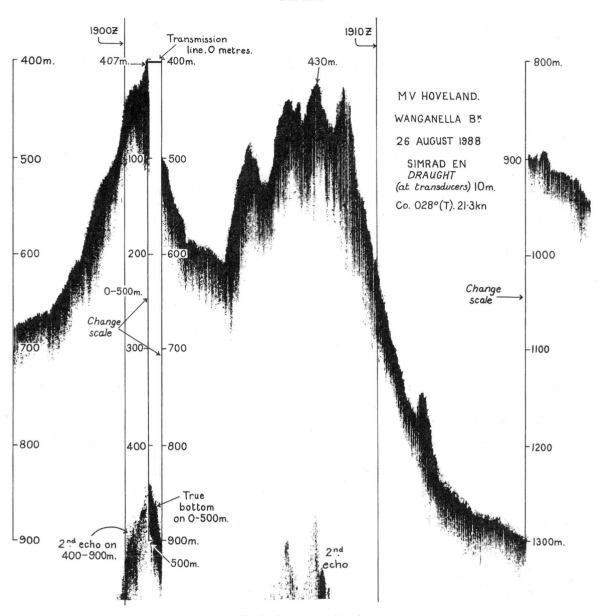

Marked up trace (4.55)

2   The position of each fix and other recorded events inserted where possible, unless a GPS printout or separate list of times and corresponding positions is enclosed with the report.

The recorded depths of all peak soundings inserted.

The limits of the phase or scale range in which the set is running marked, noting particularly when a change is made.

3   Name of the ship, date, zone time used and scale reading of the shoalest edge of the transmission line should be marked on the trace.

Diagram 4.55 shows a specimen trace with all the information required.

Investigations
4.56

1   In oceanic areas, when nearing a feature over which the depth is within the range of the ship's echo sounder, but which is approached in depths greater than that range, it is best after starting the sounder in the shoalest range scale, to increase the range and leave it set to the maximum range scale until the sea floor echo appears, and then to change scale as the depth decreases.

2   Whenever depths are found that are at variance with charted depths, the value of the report will be much enhanced by continuing to run the sounder until reasonable, or even approximate, agreement with the chart is reached. This will disclose shoal depths which are "round the clock" (11.104) or similar false echoes. However, such false echoes can still be useful if they show significant differences from charted depths, and should be submitted.

3   If an unexpected shoal or seamount is encountered, every endeavour should be made to run back over the same ground on a reciprocal course to get a further sounding with, if possible, an accurate fix of its position. If more time can be spared, several lines of soundings across the shoal area would make an even more useful report. Particularly so if the least depth over the shoal is obtained and the limits of the shoal area defined.

4   Care should be taken however not to hazard the ship when attempting to delineate a newly-discovered shoal. In oceanic areas, soundings may give little warning of the presence of a dangerous pinnacle. See 1.37.

Sandwaves
4.57

1   For remarks on sounding over areas of sandwaves, see 5.53—5.54.

Charting of reported shoals
4.58

1   When reports of shoals are received in the UKHO, they are carefully considered in the light of accompanying or other evidence before any action is taken to amend the charts. In the past much time and effort has been wasted searching for non-existent shoals. When unexpected shoal soundings are obtained in waters where the chart gives no indication of them, even though discoloured water may be seen, the only certain method of confirming their existence is by taking a cast of the lead.

2   Where, however, the charted depth is nowhere more than the scale reading of the set and the shoal is seen to rise from the sea floor on the trace, provided the speed and setting of the set is correct, the shoal sounding is usually accepted unconditionally.

Navigational marks

Lights
4.59

1   The simplest way to ensure a full report on lights is to follow the columns in the *Admiralty List of Lights* giving the information required under each heading. Some details may have to be omitted for lack of data whilst it may be possible to amplify others. Characteristics should be checked with a stop-watch.

Buoys
4.60

1   Details of buoys shown on the largest scale chart and given in *Admiralty Sailing Directions* should be verified. The position of a buoy should be checked, where possible, by fixing the ship and taking a range and bearing to the buoy, or by another suitable method.

Beacons and daymarks
4.61

1   New marks should be fixed from seaward, and the position verified where possible by responsible authorities in the area, who should be quoted in the report.

Conspicuous objects
4.62

1   Reports on conspicuous objects are required frequently since objects which were once conspicuous may later become obscured or made less conspicuous by new buildings, vegetation or other developments. The positions of conspicuous objects can sometimes be obtained from local authorities, but more often will need to be be fixed, like the new marks above, from seaward.

Wrecks
4.63

1   Stranded wrecks (which are wrecks any part of whose hull dries) or wrecks which dry should be fixed by the best available method and details recorded. The measured or estimated height of a wreck above water, or the amount which it dries, should be noted. The direction of heading and the extremities of large wrecks should be fixed if the scale of the chart is sufficiently large.

Tidal streams

Reporting
4.64

1   Reports of unexpected tidal streams should be obtained wherever possible. If only a general description of the direction can be given, it is preferable to use terms such as "east-going" and "west-going", rather than "flood" and "ebb" streams which can be ambiguous.

2   The time of the change of stream should always be referred to the time of local high water, or if this in not known, to the time of high water at the nearest port for which predictions are given in *Admiralty Tide Tables*.

Port facilities

General information
4.65

1   Form H.102a is designed as an aide-memoire for checking and collecting port information, and for rendering with Form H.102.

2   When opportunity occurs, Sailing Directions should be checked for inaccuracies, out-of-date information and omissions. Port regulations, pilotage, berthing provisions and water and other facilities are frequently subject to change. It is often only by reports from visitors that charts and publications can be kept up-to-date for such information. The value of such reports is enhanced if they can be accompanied by the local Port Handbook or a point of contact for further information.

3   When dredging operations or building work, such as that on breakwaters, wharves, docks and reclamations are described, a clear distinction should be made between work completed, work in progress, and work projected. An approximate date for the completion of unfinished or projected work is valuable.

4   Though all dimensions of piers or wharves are useful, the depths at the outer end and alongside are the most important items.

   Where dredged channels exist, the date of the last dredging and the depth obtained should be reported if found to be different from those charted.

Offshore reports

Ocean currents
4.66

1   Much useful knowledge of ocean currents (5.1—5.11) can be obtained by ships on passage. Mariners should consider reporting unusual or exceptional currents encountered using a standard Hydrographic Note (4.45).

Discoloured water

4.67

1   The legend "discoloured water" (see 5.37) appears on many charts, particularly those of the Pacific Ocean where shoals rise with alarming abruptness from great depths. Most of these legends remain on the charts from the last century when very few deep sea soundings were available, and less was known of the causes of discoloured water. Only a few of the reports of discoloured water have proved on examination to be caused by shoals.

2   Today, such reports can be compared with the accumulated information for the area concerned, a more thorough assessment made, and as a result this legend is now seldom inserted on charts.

3   Mariners are therefore encouraged, whilst having due regard to the safety of their vessels, to approach sightings of discoloured water to find whether or not the discoloration is due to shoaling.

4   If there is good reason to suppose the discoloration is due to shoal water, a Hydrographic Note (4.45), accompanied by an echo sounder trace and any other supporting evidence, should be rendered. If there is no indication of a shoal, the report should be forwarded to the Met Office, Exeter, Devon EX1 3PB, and a copy sent to the UKHO.

Bioluminescence

4.68

1   Forms of bioluminescence are discussed at 5.38—5.39. Details required in reports are as follows:
Name of vessel and observer.
Date, time and period of day (for example; early evening, night, or dawn).
Position of sighting.
Colour of phenomenon.
Description of phenomenon.
Approximate extent of phenomenon.
Means of stimulation (if any).

2   Reports should be rendered to the UKHO whenever possible. They can be submitted on a Form H636 Marine Bioluminescence Observations Reporting Form (H.636), reproduced at the end of this chapter or available from the Maritime Environment Information Centre at the UKHO, or made using a standard Hydrographic Note (4.45).

Underwater volcanoes and earthquakes

4.69

1   When tremors or shocks attributable to underwater volcanoes and earthquakes or (5.40—5.41) are experienced, reports made to the UKHO, using a standard Hydrographic Note (4.45) or by radio, are of considerable value.

Reports should give a brief description of the occurrence, its time and date, the ship's position, and the depth of water at that position.

Whales

4.70

1   Given the importance of cetacean conservation, reports of whales, porpoises and dolphins are of considerable interest.

For identifying species, useful publications are *Guide to the Identification of Whales, Dolphins and Porpoises in European Seas* (by P G H Evans) and *Whales, Dolphins and Porpoises — The visual guide to all the world's cetaceans* (by M Carwardine).

2   Details required in reports are as follows:
Name of vessel and observer
Date, time and period of day (for example; early evening, night, or dawn.)
Position of sighting
Identification and supportive description
Number sighted

3   Reports should be rendered to the UKHO whenever possible. They should be submitted on a Form H.637 Marine Life Reporting Form, reproduced at the end of this chapter or available from the Maritime Environment Information Centre at the UKHO, or made using a standard Hydrographic Note (4.45).

Turtles in British waters

4.71

1   Reports detailing sightings of turtles are of considerable interest. For identifying species, a useful publication is *The Turtle Code* (by Scottish Natural Heritage).

Reports should be made and forwarded in the same way as those described above for whales.

Ornithology

4.72

1   Those interested in ornithology can often make useful additions to the existing knowledge of bird behaviour and migration; details required can be obtained from the Hon Secretary, RN Birdwatching Society, 19 Downland Way, South Wonston, Winchester, Hants SO21 3HS.

Magnetic variation

Reporting

4.73

1   In many parts of the world there is a continuous need for more data for the plotting of isogonic curves on Admiralty Magnetic Variation charts.

All observations are valuable, but there is a particular requirement for data S of latitude 40°S, or in areas where the isogonic curves are close together, or where there are local magnetic anomalies (11.3).

2   Form H.488 — *Record of Observations for Variation* is reproduced on page 85 and can be obtained from the UKHO, is designed for rendering these observations. The methodology is described on the back of the form.

3   **Local magnetic anomalies.** Whenever a ship passes over a local magnetic anomaly (11.3), the position, extent of the anomaly, and the amount and direction of the deflection of the compass needle, should be reported, or confirmed if it is already charted, on Form H.102 to the UKHO.

Views

Introduction

4.74

1   The general availability of modern aids to navigation has reduced the need for long-range coastal views for landfalls and coastal passages, although this remains just as important for vessels not fitted with an

electronic-position-fixing system or GNSS. However, the need to change from instrument to visual navigation still occurs at some stage for all mariners, and good views are still invaluable for the speedy recognition of features when making this change.

2   New photographs are always welcome, particularly where views published in *Admiralty Sailing Directions* or on Admiralty charts are out-of-date or inadequate, or where a new view would assist the mariner. Photographs should only be taken if circumstances permit and are not forbidden by national regulations.

3   The following information is provided to rationalise the requirement for views and to assist the mariner in providing pictures which will be of most use both to other mariners and to the compilers and editors of charts and Sailing Directions, and in a usable format.

4   Even if it is not possible to comply precisely with the following guidelines, it should be borne in mind that even an imperfect photograph, correctly annotated, may well be useful in producing a view which could be of considerable value to the mariner. All material received is evaluated accordingly.

Types of view
4.75

1   The various types of view are given the following names.

Panoramic. A composite view made up from a series of overlapping photographs. This type of view is normally used to illustrate an aspect from offshore, including hinterland.

1   **Aerial oblique.** A single view taken from the air, which shows a combination of plan and elevation.

Pilotage. A single or composite view from the approach course to a harbour or narrows, showing any leading marks or transits. It may be combined with a close-up of the mark if necessary for positive identification.

Portrait. A single view of a specific object, set against its salient background.

Close-up. A single view of one object or feature with emphasis on clarity of the subject for its identification.

Panoramic views
4.76

1   Panoramic views should include, whenever possible, an identifiable feature at either end so that its geographical limits are clearly defined (see view 4.76).

2   The following measures should be adopted where possible to maximise clarity of detail:

Using additional height to increase the vertical presentation;

Closing as near as prudent to the coast whilst retaining the offshore aspect;

Using a telescopic lens;

Taking a series of photographs, overlapping by 30%, that can be built-up into a panorama.

Aerial views
4.77

1   An aerial oblique photograph gives a good general impression of a port and its berths as well as covering the pilotage aspect of identification and entry.

The most useful view will be one which is easily related to the chart and allows an assessment of the harbour size, its berths and any entrance problems. It

will also assist with the identification of navigational marks.

2   It is sometimes advantageous to show both an aerial oblique view of the harbour and a pilotage type view of the entrance.

Views of parts of harbours which are usually filled by vessels berthed at buoys or alongside, or where ferries ply regularly, should include these features wherever possible. For example:

View 4.77.1 of Grangemouth Docks shows clearly The entrances and locking arrangements and the arrangements of berths and the general layout of the harbour.

View 4.77.2, of Devonport, Tasmania, shows the entrance to a river port, and illustrates well the entrance breakwaters and marks, the berths in the middle ground and a yacht marina beyond them. View 4.77.3, of Sydney inner harbour and the bridge, is a good example of how an aerial oblique photograph can show the layout of a section of a major port from within the entrance, including the berth layout and waterway sections and ferry terminals, and areas of crossing traffic.

Pilotage views
4.78

1   These views are intended to enable the mariner to identify the features he will require as he approaches a harbour or waterway. They should be taken to show the principal navigational marks, including leading marks, and other distinguishing features.

View 4.78.1 shows the navigable channel under the Skye Bridge, with the channel markers expanded for clarity.

2   View 4.78.2 is taken on, or close to starboard of a leading line used as part of the approach to Portsmouth harbour, show the marks used (Southsea Castle Light and St Judes church spire).

3   View 4.78.3 shows the leading line used to pass through Sillette Passage in the Channel Islands, consisting of the front mark (Platte Rock Beacon) and the rear mark (the martello tower). In this case, the transit is open to starboard.

Portrait views
4.79

1   Portrait views should be taken with sufficient background to set the object in context while still showing sufficient detail to allow positive identification. Skyline and waterline both help in locating the object. View 4.79, of the lighthouse at the NE end of Kerrera island, is a good example of a portrait view.

Close-up views
4.80

1   View 4.80 shows shows the same lighthouse from View 4.79, but in close-up. It shows its features clearly and in detail, but the surroundings are cropped.

When taking such views it is beneficial to take both a portrait view and a close-up view so that the UKHO can decide which might be more suitable for publication.

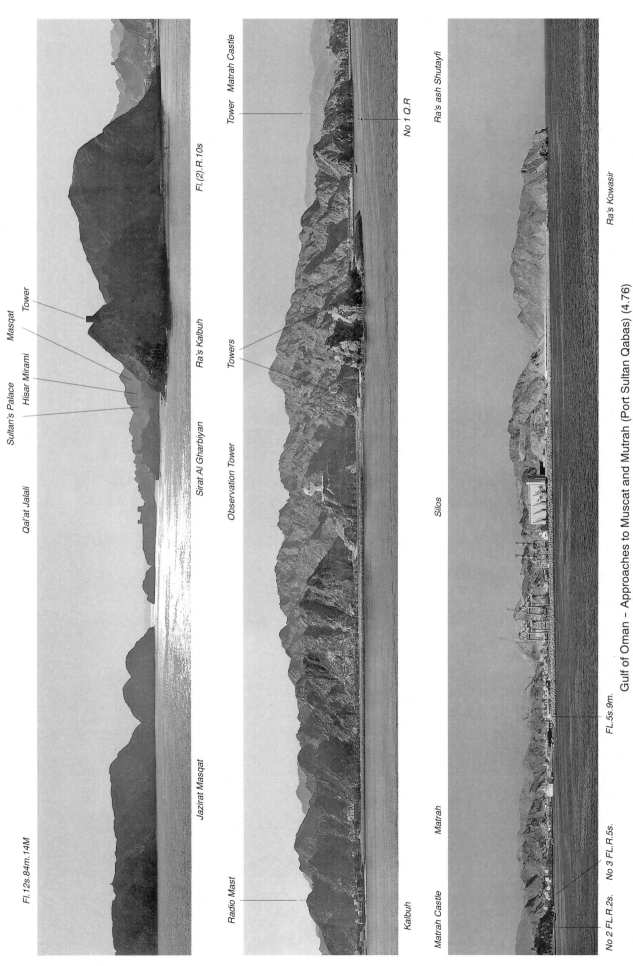

Qal'at Jalali

Sultan's Palace **Masqat** **Tower**

Hisar Mirami

Fl.12s.84m.14M

Jazirat Masqat

Sirat Al Gharbiyan

Ra's Kalbuh

Fl.(2).R.10s

Tower **Matrah Castle**

No 1 Q.R

Ra's ash Shutayfi

Observation Tower

Towers

Radio Mast

Kalbuh

Matrah Castle **Silos** **Matrah**

Ra's Kowasir

No 2 FL.R.2s. No 3 FL.R.5s. FL.5s.9m.

Gulf of Oman – Approaches to Muscat and Mutrah (Port Sultan Qabas) (4.76)

Grangemouth Docks from NE (4.77.1)

(Original dated 1997)

(Photograph - Aerial Reconnaissance) Co.)

Devonport, Tasmania from NNE (4.77.2)

(Original dated 1998)

(Photograph - McKenzie & Associates)

Sydney Harbour Bridge and inner part of Sydney Harbour from E (4.77.3)

(Original dated 1998)

(Photograph - McKenzie & Associates)

Channel Marker Port	Channel Centre Marker	Channel Marker Starboard

Skye Bridge from E (4.78.1)

(Original dated 1996)

(Photograph - HMSML Gleaner)

Leading marks for outer approach to Portsmouth bearing 0035 (4.78.2)

(Original dated 1998)

(Photograph - HMS Birmingham)

Sillette Passage Leading Marks in line 0005 (4.78.3)

(Original dated 1998)

(Photograph - Capt.F A Lawrence MRIN, Navitrom Limited)

North Spit of Kerrera Light

Kerrera – NE end (4.79)

(Original dated 1996)

(Photograph - HMSML Gleaner)

North Spit of Kerrera Light (4.80)

(Original dated 1996)

(Photograph - HMSML Gleaner)

Presentation

Quality and composition of views
4.81

1   All views in Sailing Directions are now published in colour, although there remain some legacy black and white photographs which continue to be published in the absence of suitable colour images.

Any photograph submitted, irrespective of format, should be sharp and of good contrast so that it can be reproduced to a sufficiently high quality. If it is "flat" or out of focus it will be even flatter and fuzzier when reproduced; background features may be lost and essential detail obscured.

2   Digital photography is preferred, although any kind of picture, including transparencies, negatives and polaroids can be converted to the required format if of sufficient quality. In order that digital photographs have sufficient detail, the image should be at least 300 dpi, and taken with a camera capable of 4 megapixels.

3   The object should occupy as much of the photograph as possible, with the horizon level. Some sea and sky should be included.

Attention should be given to the lighting conditions. Poor lighting can result in excessively dark photographs which may need to be repeated when the lighting improves, although it is understood that this will not always be possible.

Annotation
4.82

1   **Traditional photography.** Photographic images should be clearly annotated with as much detail as possible (see 4.83 below). If prints are being submitted, they should not be marked on the image itself. An overlay can be used, or the print mounted on plain A4 paper with the details entered in the margins.

2   **Digital photography.** Digital images should not be edited in any way. A spreadsheet should be attached to the file containing all relevant metadata.

Records
4.83

1   Accurate captioning of views published in Sailing Directions is essential. Detailed records should therefore be taken at the same time as the photograph is taken.

2   The following is the minimum information required:

Information	Remarks
Date and time	Stating zone used
Position	Bearing and distance of the camera from the object, and/or latitude and longitude.
Bearing	Approximate true bearing of axis of the camera lens.
Identification	Indications of principal landmarks and navigational aids in the photograph, with descriptions if necessary.
Miscellaneous	Any additional information available, such as wind and weather conditions, height of tide, and any imminent local developments which may alter the view.

Submission to UKHO
4.84

1   Views should be forwarded to the UKHO, accompanied by all records and charts used. They should be addressed to: Sailing Directions (BSU), United Kingdom Hydrographic Office, Admiralty Way, Taunton, Somerset, TA1 2DN. Alternatively, material can be emailed to sailingdirections@ukho.gov.uk.

2   The name of the observer, photographer and the ship should be included. The person whose name should be printed in the acknowledgement on the view when published should also be nominated.

HYDROGRAPHIC NOTE

H.102
(Oct 2008)

Forwarding information for Admiralty Charts, ENCs and Hydrographic Publications

Date		Ref. Number		
Name of ship or sender				
Address				
Tel/Fax/Telex/E-mail address of sender				
General Locality				
Subject				

Position (see Instruction 3 below)	Latitude		Longitude	
	GPS	Datum		Accuracy
Admiralty Charts affected			Edition	
Latest Weekly Edition of Notice to Mariners held				
Replacement copy of Chart No		**IS/IS NOT** required; (see Instruction 4 below.)		
ENCs affected				
Latest Update disk held	Week			
Publications affected (Edition No.)				
Date of latest supplement, page & Light List No. etc				

Details:

Signature of observer/reporter	
Tick box if not willing to be named as source of this information	☐

INSTRUCTIONS:

1. Mariners are requested to notify the United Kingdom Hydrographic Office (UKHO) *(by mail: SDRA, UKHO, Admiralty Way, Taunton, Somerset, TAI 2DN, United Kingdom or by email: hdcfiles@ukho.gov.uk)* when new or suspected dangers to navigation are discovered, changes observed in aids to navigation, or corrections to publications are seen to be necessary. The Mariner's Handbook (NP 100) Chapter 8 gives general instructions. If practicable the Mariner should also contact the originating Hydrographic Office when navigating on IMO Approved non-UKHO ENCs. The provisions of international and national laws should be complied with when forwarding such reports.

2. This form and its instructions have been designed to help both the sender and the recipient. It should be used, or followed closely, whenever appropriate. Copies of this Form may be obtained gratis from the UKHO at the above address, or principal Chart Agents (see Annual Notice to Mariners No. 2). This form is also available on the web: www.ukho.gov.uk/amd/marHNotes.asp

3. Accurate position or knowledge of positional error is of great importance. **Latitude and longitude should only be used to specifically position the details when they have been fixed by GPS or Astronomical Observations.** A full description of the method, equipment, time, estimated error and datum (where applicable) used should be given. When position is defined by sextant angles or bearings (true or magnetic to be specified), more than two should be used in order to provide a redundancy check. Where position is derived from Electronic Position Fixing (eg LORAN C) or distances observed by radar, the raw readings of the system in use should be quoted wherever possible. Where position is derived after the event, from other observations and/or Dead Reckoning, the methodology of deriving the position should be included.

4. *Paper Charts*: A cutting from the largest scale chart is the best medium for forwarding details, the alterations and additions being shown thereon in red. When requested, a new copy will be sent in replacement of a chart that has been used to forward information, or when extensive observations have involved defacement of the observer's chart. If it is preferred to show the amendments on a tracing of the largest scale chart (rather than on the chart itself) these should be in red as above, but adequate details from the chart must be traced in black ink to enable the amendments to be fitted correctly.
ENCs: A screen dump of the largest scale usage band ENC with the alterations and additions being shown thereon in red.

5. When **soundings** are obtained The Mariner's Handbook (NP 100) should be consulted. The echo sounding trace should be marked with times, depths, etc., and forwarded with the report. It is important to state whether the echo sounder is set to register depths below the surface or below the keel; in the latter case the vessel's draught should be given. Time and date should be given in order that corrections for the height of the tide may be made where necessary. The make, name and type of set should also be given.

6. **For modern sets that use electronic 'range gating', care should be taken that the correct range scale and appropriate gate width are in use.** Older electro-mechanical echo sounders frequently record signals from echoes received back after one or more rotations of the stylus have been completed. Thus with a set whose maximum range is 500m, an echo recorded at 50m may be from depths of 50m, 550m or even 1050m. Soundings recorded beyond the set's nominal range can usually be recognised by the following:

   (a) the trace being weaker than normal for the depth recorded;
   (b) the trace passing through the transmission line;
   (c) the feathery nature of the trace.

   As a check that apparently shoal soundings are not due to echoes received beyond the set's nominal range, soundings should be continued until reasonable agreement with charted soundings is reached. However, soundings received after one or more rotations of the stylus can still be useful and should be submitted if they show significant differences from charted depths.

7. **Reports which cannot be confirmed or are lacking in certain details should not be withheld**. Shortcomings should be stressed and any firm expectation of being able to check the information on a succeeding voyage should be mentioned.

8. Reports of **shoal soundings,** uncharted dangers and aids to navigation out of order should, at the mariner's discretion, also be made by radio to the nearest coast radio station. The draught of modern tankers is such that any uncharted depth under 30 metres or 15 fathoms may be of sufficient importance to justify a radio message.

9. Changes to Port Information should be forwarded on Form H.102A and any GPS/Chart Datum observations should be forwarded on Form H.102B together with Form H.102. Where there is insufficient space on the forms an additional sheet should be used.

10. Reports on ocean currents should be made in accordance with The Mariner's Handbook (NP 100) Chapter 8.

Note. - An acknowledgement or receipt will be sent and the information then used to the best advantage which may mean immediate action or inclusion in a revision in due course; for these purposes, the UKHO may make reproductions of any material supplied. When a Notice to Mariners is issued, the sender's ship or name is quoted as authority unless (as sometimes happens) the information is also received from other authorities or the sender states that they do not want to be named by using the appropriate tick box on the form. An explanation of the use made of contributions from all parts of the world would be too great a task and a further communication should only be expected when the information is of outstanding value or has unusual features.

HYDROGRAPHIC NOTE FOR PORT INFORMATION (To accompany Form H.102)	H.102A (Oct 2008)

Forwarding information for Admiralty Charts, ENCs and Hydrographic Publications

Date	Ref. Number
Name of ship or sender	
Address	
Tel/Fax/Telex/E-mail address of sender	
General Locality	

1. **NAME OF PORT**	
2. **GENERAL REMARKS** Principal activities and trade. Latest population figures and date. Number of ships or tonnage handled per year. Maximum size of vessel handled. Copy of Port Handbook *(if available)*.	
3. **ANCHORAGES** Designation, depths, holding ground, shelter afforded.	
4. **PILOTAGE** Authority for requests. Embark position. Regulations.	

5. **DIRECTIONS** Entry and berthing information. Tidal streams. Navigational aids.	
6. **TUGS** Number available.	
7. **WHARVES** Names, numbers or positions & lengths. Depths alongside.	

8. CARGO HANDLING Containers, lighters, Ro-Ro etc.	
9. REPAIRS Hull, machinery and underwater. Shipyards. Docking or slipping facilities. *(Give size of vessels handled or dimensions)* Divers.	
10. RESCUE AND DISTRESS Salvage, Lifeboat, Coastguard, etc.	

11. SUPPLIES Fuel. (with type, quantities and methods of delivery) Fresh water. (with method of delivery and rate of supply) Provisions.	
12. SERVICES Medical. Ship Sanitation. Garbage and slops. Ship chandlery, tank cleaning, compass adjustment, hull painting.	
13. COMMUNICATIONS Nearest airport or airfield. Port radio and information service. (with frequencies and hours of operating)	
14. PORT AUTHORITY Designation, address, telephone, e-mail address and website.	

HYDROGRAPHIC NOTE FOR PORT INFORMATION (To accompany Form H.102)	H.102A (Oct 2008)

15. **VIEWS** Photographs (where permitted) of the approaches, leading marks, the entrance to the harbour etc.	
16. **ADDITIONAL DETAILS**	
Signature of observer/reporter	
Tick box if not willing to be named as source of this information	

NOTES:

1. This form is designed to assist in the reporting of any observed changes to Port Information details and should be submitted as an accompaniment to Form H.102 (full instructions for the rendering of data are on Form H.102 - *email: hdcfiles@ukho.gov.uk*). In addition, the Mariner's Handbook (NP 100) Chapter 8 gives general instructions. If practicable the Mariner should also contact the originating Hydrographic Office when navigating on IMO Approved non-UKHO ENCs. The provisions of international and national laws should be complied with when forwarding such reports.

2. Form H.I02A lists the information required for Admiralty Sailing Directions and has been designed to help both sender and recipient, the sections should be used as an aide-mémoire, being used or followed closely, whenever appropriate. Where there is insufficient space on the form an additional sheet should be used.

3. **Reports which cannot be confirmed or are lacking in certain details should not be withheld**. Shortcomings should be stressed and any firm expectation of being able to check the information on a succeeding voyage should be mentioned.

HYDROGRAPHIC NOTE FOR
GPS OBSERVATIONS AGAINST CORRESPONDING CHART POSITIONS
(To accompany Form H.102)

H.102B
(Sept 2007)

Reference Number

Date

Name of ship or sender

Address

Tel/Fax/Telex/E-mail address of sender

General Locality

Time/Date of Observation (s)	BA Chart in use (SEE NOTE 3a)		Latitude/Longitude of position read from Chart (SEE NOTE 3b)	Latitude/Longitude of position read from GPS (on WGS 84) (SEE NOTE 3c)	Additional Information/Remarks (SEE NOTE 3d)
	Number	Edition Date			

Signature of observer/reporter

83

HYDROGRAPHIC NOTE FOR
GPS OBSERVATIONS AGAINST CORRESPONDING CHART POSITIONS
(To accompany Form H.102)

Forwarding information for British Admiralty Charts, ENCs and Hydrographic Publications

NOTES:

1.   This form is designed to assist in the reporting of observed differences between WGS 84 (GPS) Datum and British Admiralty Chart Datum by mariners, including yachtsmen, and should be submitted as an accompaniment to Form H.102 (full instructions for the rendering of data are on Form H.102). Where there is insufficient space on the form an additional sheet should be used. If practicable the Mariner should contact the originating Hydrographic Office when navigating on non-UKHO ENCs. The provisions of international and national laws should be complied with when forwarding such reports.

2.   **Objective of GPS Data Collection**

The UK Hydrographic Office would appreciate the reporting of GPS positions, referenced to WGS 84 Datum, at identifiable locations on charts. Such observations could be used to calculate positional shifts between WGS 84 and chart datums for those charts which it has not yet been possible to compute the appropriate shifts. These would be incorporated in future new editions or new charts and promulgated by Preliminary Notices to Mariners in the interim.

It is unrealistic to expect that a series of reported WGS 84 positions relating to a given chart will enable it to be referenced to that datum with the accuracy required for geodetic purposes. Nevertheless, this provides adequate accuracy for general navigation, considering the practical limits to the precision of 0.2mm (probably the best possible under ideal conditions – vessel alongside, good light, sharp dividers etc), this represents 10 metres on the ground at a chart scale of 1:50,000.

It is clear that users prefer to have **some** indication of the magnitude and direction of the positional shift, together with an assessment of its likely accuracy, rather than be informed that a definitive answer cannot be formulated. Consequently, where a WGS 84 version has not yet been produced, many charts now carry approximate shifts relating WGS 84 Datum to chart datum. Further observations may enable these values to be refined with greater confidence.

3.   **Details required**

a.   It is essential that the chart number, edition date and its correctional state (latest NM) are stated.

b.   Position (to 2 decimal places of a minute) of observation point, using chart graticule or, if ungraduated, relative position by bearing/distance from prominent charted features (navigation lights, trig. points, church spires etc.).

c.   Position (to 2 decimal places of a minute) of observation point, using GPS Receiver. Confirm that GPS positions are referenced to WGS 84 Datum.

d.   Include GPS receiver model and aerial type (if known). Also of interest: values of PDOP, HDOP or GDOP displayed (indications of theoretical quality of position fixing depending upon the distribution of satellites overhead) and any other comments.

RECORD OF OBSERVATIONS FOR VARIATION

Position:—

Latitude .... }

Longitude ....

Based on ....

Date ....

Compass Pattern No. ....

SHIP ....

Wind .... Sea .... Swell ....

Swinging Officer ....

SWING TO STARBOARD

Ship's Head by Standard Compass	Time G.M.T.	Bearing of		Total Compass Error
		by Standard Compass	True (Calculated)	
N 000°				
NNE 022¼°				
NE 045°				
ENE 067½°				
E 090°				
ESE 112½°				
SE 135°				
SSE 157½°				
S 180°				
SSW 202½°				
SW 225°				
WSW 247½°				
W 270°				
WNW 292½°				
NW 315°				
NNW 337½°				

Time for Swing ....

Variation = 16 | .... (Swing to Stbd.)

SWING TO PORT

Ship's Head	Time G.M.T.	Bearing of		Total Compass Error
		by Standard Compass	True (Calculated)	

Time for Swing ....

Variation = 16 | .... (Swing to Port)

Variation from swing to starboard ....

Variation from swing to port ....

2) ....

Mean Variation ....

Coefficient "A" NOT applied to observations

= ....

Approved .... Commanding Officer.

Completed forms should be forwarded to:—
The Hydrographer of the Navy, Hydrographic Department, Ministry of Defence, Taunton, Somerset, TA1 2DN

85

MARINE BIOLUMINESCENCE OBSERVATIONS REPORTING FORM

Unit:

HMOI No./Cruise Reference:

| DATE dd.mm.yy | TIME (Z) | PERIOD OF DAY | POSITION | | BIOLUMINESENCE | | | | WIND | | SEA STATE |
			LAT dd mm. mt	LONG ddd mm.m	COLOUR	DESCRIPTION	EXTENT	MEANS OF STIMULATION	Dirn	Speed	

Colour of Bioluminescence: White, blue, green, yellow, cream, orange, red, etc.

Description of Bioluminescence: Glowing sheet, Sparks (steady light), Sparkle (glittering), Small Globes, Expanding/Upwelling Blobs, Bands, Wheels, 'Milky sea' etc.

Extent: Approximate area covered by bioluminescence.

Means of Stimulation: Mechanical - either Ship's passage, or Sea Swell. Light (e.g. Aldis lamp), Active Sonar or E/S, Shaft rpm. If no stimulus apparent, insert ' ? '

Wind Direction and Speed: Use Compass point e.g. W, SW, WSW with speed in knots.

Sea State: Enter sea state from 0 – 9.

Certified free of transcription errors: Name: Rank/Rate: Signature:

Please complete this section of the form on every watch where marine mammal observing is active (either visual or acoustic), regardless of whether any contacts are observed. If an observation is made, complete Page 2 of the form below with as much detail as possible. If it is possible to take photographs of the contact, record a reference to the image in the remarks column on page 2 and return a copy of the image with the form. Completed forms should be returned (if possible by email) to UKHO at the address below.

PLATFORM: _____   SOUND SOURCE: _____

This form is to be completed by all MMOs when they have been closed up, whether marine mammals have been sighted or not.

Date dd.mm.yy	Name and Service Number	Monitoring Period Zulu Time and Lat/Long position				Monitoring Type V - visual A - acoustic O - other (? as required)	Period of Time Sonar was Transmitting (% approx)	Met Conditions Visibility in NM Beaufort sea state Beaufort wind	Marine Mammals detected? Y/N Sighting Serial Number (DTG) e.g: 251015ZDEC09 Other Remarks
		Start		Finish					
		Time	Position	Time	Position				
						V		Vis	
						A		SS	
						O		Wind	
						V		Vis	
						A		SS	
						O		Wind	
						V		Vis	
						A		SS	
						O		Wind	
						V		Vis	
						A		SS	
						O		Wind	
						V		Vis	
						A		SS	
						O		Wind	

MARINE LIFE / FISHING ACTIVITY REPORTING FORM

Version 2 January 2009

For the recording of sightings of marine mammals, sharks and other large fish, fish schools, turtles, jellyfish, sea-snakes and fishing activities.

PLATFORM

HMOI/CRUISE REF/OPERATION

Sighting Serial Number (DTG)	Watch Period	Latitude dd.mm. t	Longitude ddd. mm. t	Number Observed	Identification	Range (m) 0 – 100 100-200 200-500 500-1000 >1000	Bearing	Length (m)	Behaviour/Remarks Acoustic/Visual

Identification: Include descriptive details of the animal

Range: Approximate distance of sighted object from ship. Select one range from the list.

Bearing: Bearing of observed object from ship (in degrees):

Behaviour/Remarks: For cetaceans - general description of activities, including any bow riding, play, porpoising, acoustic activity, tail/fluke slapping, breeching, resting
For fishing boats, describe type of fishing activity observed (if any) e.g. passage, trawling etc
Indicate Acoustic or Visual observations

Completed forms and enquiries should be addressed to: Maritime Environment Information Centre, United Kingdom Hydrographic Office, Admiralty Way, TAUNTON, TA1 2DN
Tel: (01823) 337900 extension 3524
Fax: (CCITT group 3) (01823) 284077
E-mail: marine.life@ukho.gov.uk

SECTION II

THE MARITIME ENVIRONMENT

NOTES

Chapter 5

THE SEA

Ocean currents

General remarks
5.1

1   Currents flow at all depths in the oceans, but in general the stronger currents occur in an upper layer which is shallow in comparison with the general depths of the oceans.

2   Ocean current circulation takes place in three dimensions. A current at any depth in the ocean may have a vertical component as well as horizontal ones. The navigator is primarily interested in the surface currents.

Main circulations
5.2

1   The general surface current circulation of the world is shown on the World Climatic Charts in *Ocean Passages for the World* and described where appropriate in *Admiralty Sailing Directions*.

2   The main cause of surface currents in the open ocean is the direct action of the wind on the sea surface. A close correlation accordingly exists between their directions and those of the prevailing winds. Winds of high constancy blowing over extensive areas of ocean will naturally have a greater effect in producing a current than will variable or local winds. Thus the NE and SE Trade Winds of the two hemispheres are the main spring of the mid-latitude surface current circulation.

3   In the Atlantic and Pacific Oceans the two Trade Winds drive an immense body of water W over a width of some 50° of latitude, broken only by the narrow belt of the E-going Equatorial Counter-current, which is found a few degrees N of the equator in both these oceans. A similar transport of water to the W occurs in the S Indian Ocean driven by the action of the SE Trade Wind.

4   The Trade Winds in both hemispheres are balanced in higher latitudes by wide belts of variable W winds. These produce corresponding belts of predominantly E-going sets in the temperate latitudes of each hemisphere. With these E-going and W-going sets constituting the N and S limbs, there thus arise great continuous circulations of water, known as gyres, in each of the major oceans. These cells are centred in about 30°N and S, and extend from about the 10th to at least the 50th parallel in both hemispheres. The direction of the current circulation is clockwise in the N hemisphere and counter-clockwise in the S hemisphere.

Subsidiary circulations
5.3

1   Current circulations occur outside the main gyres for a number of reasons but are either associated with them or dependent upon them. For example:

Part of the North Atlantic Current branches from the main system and flows N of Scotland and N along the coast of Norway. Branching again, part

flows past Svalbard into the Arctic Ocean and part enters the Barents Sea.

2   In the main monsoon regions, the N part of the Indian Ocean, the China Seas and Eastern Archipelago, the current reverses seasonally, flowing in accordance with the monsoon blowing at the time.

The South Atlantic, South Indian and South Pacific Oceans are all open to the Southern Ocean and the Southern Ocean Current, encircling the globe in an E direction, supplements the S part of the main circulation of each of these three oceans.

Variability
5.4

1   Ocean currents undergo a continuous process of change throughout the year. In some areas such as the central parts of oceanic gyres, where latitudinal shifts amount to only a few degrees, the change is more gradual than in the monsoon regions of the Indian Ocean and SE Asia. Here, change is more abrupt and involves reversals of predominant current direction over a period of as little as a few days.

2   Over by far the greater part of all oceans, the individual currents experienced in a given region are variable, in many cases so variable that on different occasions currents may be observed to set in most, or all, directions. Even in the regions of more variable currents there is often, however, a greater frequency of current setting towards one part of the compass, so that in the long run there is a resultant flow of water through a given area in a direction which forms part of the general circulation. Some degree of variability, including occasional currents in the opposite direction to the usual flow, is to be found within the limits of the more constant currents, such as the great Equatorial Currents or the Gulf Stream.

3   The constancy of the principal currents varies to some extent in different seasons and in different parts of the current. It is usually about 50% to 75% and rarely exceeds 85%, and then only in limited areas. Current variability is mainly due to the variation of wind strength and direction. For the degree of variation to which currents are liable, reference should be made to *Ocean Passages for the World*.

Warm and cold currents
5.5

1   In general, currents which set continuously E or W acquire temperatures appropriate to the latitude concerned. Currents which set N or S over long distances, however, transport water from higher to lower latitudes, or vice versa, and so advect lower or higher temperatures from the region of origin. The Gulf Stream, for example, transports water from the Gulf of Mexico to the central part of the North Atlantic Ocean where it causes temperatures to rise to well above the latitudinal average. Between the Gulf Stream and the

American coast the water is much colder since it derives from Arctic regions by way of the Labrador Current. The transition from this cold water to the much warmer water of the Gulf Stream is marked by a very strong gradient of sea surface temperatures. Both here and elsewhere, strong temperature gradients indicated by sea temperature isotherms can be used to detect the boundaries between currents.

2   Among the principal warm currents may be listed:
Gulf Stream.
Mozambique Current.
Japan Current.
Agulhas Current.
Brazil Current.
East Australian Coast Current.

3   The principal cold currents are:
Labrador Current.
Kamchatka Current.
East Greenland Current.
Falkland Current.
Peru Current.
California Current.
Benguela Current.

4   The low temperature of the surface water of some of the cold currents is not always due to advection from lower latitudes. It is sometimes due to the upwelling of sub-surface water (5.10), as is the case in the Benguela Current.

Strengths
5.6

1   The information given below is generalised from current atlases, and refers to the currents of the open ocean, mainly between 60°N and 50°S. It does not refer to tidal streams, nor to the resultants of currents and tidal streams in coastal waters. Information about current strengths in higher latitudes is scanty.

2   The proportion of nil and very weak currents, less than ½ kn, varies considerably in different parts of the oceans. In the central areas of the main closed oceanic circulations, where current is apt to be most variable, the weakness of the resultant is, in general, not caused by an unduly high proportion of very weak currents, but by the variability of direction of the stronger currents. There is probably no region in any part of the open oceans where the currents experienced do not at times attain a rate of at least 1 kn during periods of strong winds.

3   Within the major currents of the world, maximum rates derived from ship drift records are generally found to be in the range of 2 to 4 kn although rates of 5 kn are not uncommon. The duration and extent of these higher values cannot generally be given. Higher rates occur most frequently in the following areas:
Atlantic Ocean:
In the Guinea, Guiana and Florida Currents, the Gulf Stream W of 60°W and the SE part of the Gulf of Mexico.

4   Indian Ocean:
In the Somali and East African Coast Currents, especially during the SW Monsoon. In the area of Suquṭrá are the strongest known currents in the world and rates of 7 to 8 kn have been recorded. In the Mozambique and Agulhas Currents and in the equatorial currents, particularly S of India and Sri Lanka towards the Malacca Strait.

Pacific Ocean:
In the Japan Current and locally SE of Mindanao.

Direct effect of wind
5.7

1   **Coriolis force.** When wind blows over the sea surface the frictional drag tends to cause the surface water to move with the wind. As soon as any movement is imparted, the effect of the Earth's rotation, known as the Coriolis force, is to deflect the movement towards the right in the N hemisphere and towards the left in the S hemisphere. Although theory suggests that this effect should produce a surface flow, or "wind drift current" in a direction inclined at 45° to the right or left of the wind direction in the N or S hemisphere, observations show this angle to be less in practice. Various values between 20° and 45° have been reported.

2   **Effect with increasing depth.** An effect of the movement of the surface water layer is to impart a lesser movement to the layer immediately below, in a direction to the right, left in the S hemisphere, of that of the surface layer. Thus, with increasing depth, the speed of the wind-induced current becomes progressively less but the angle between the directions of wind and current progressively increases.

3   **Relationship between wind speed and current strength.** The speed of a surface current relative to the speed of the wind responsible has been the subject of many investigations. This is a complex problem and many different answers have been put forward. An average empirical value for this ratio is about 1:40 (or 0·025). Some investigators claim a variation of the factor with latitude but the degree of any such variation is in dispute. In the main the variation with latitude is comparatively small and, in view of the other uncertainties in determining the ratio, can probably be disregarded in most cases.

4   The implication that a 40 kn wind should produce a current of about 1 kn needs qualification. The strength of the current depends on the period and the fetch over which the wind has been blowing. With the onset of wind there is initially little response in terms of water movement, which gradually builds up with time. With light winds the slight current that results takes only about 6 hours to become fully developed, but with strong winds about 48 hours is needed for the current to reach its full speed. A limited fetch, however, restricts the full development of the current.

5   It seems reasonable to expect that hurricane force winds might give rise to currents in excess of 2 kn, provided that the fetch and duration of the wind suffice. Reliable observations, however, are rare in these circumstances.

Tropical storms
5.8

1   The effect of the very high wind in tropical storms is usually reduced by the limited fetch due to the curvature of the wind path, and by the limited period within which the wind blows from a particular direction. Thus, with these storms, it is the slow-moving ones which are liable to cause the strongest currents.

2   In the vicinity of a tropical storm the set of the current may be markedly different from that normally to be expected. Comparatively little is known about such currents, particularly near the centre of the storm, since navigators avoid the centre whenever possible

3 The primary cause of the currents is the strong wind associated with the storm. The strength of the current produced by a given force of wind varies with the latitude and is greatest in low latitudes. For the latitudes of tropical storms, say 15° to 25°, a wind of force 10 would probably produce a current of about 1 kn. It is believed that the strength of the currents of tropical storms is, on the average, the same as that which a wind of similar force, unconnected with a tropical storm, would produce. These currents, at the surface, set at an angle of 45° to the right of the direction of the wind, in the N hemisphere, and therefore flow obliquely outward from the storm field, though not radially from the centre.

4 Unless due allowance is made for these sets, large errors in reckoning may arise. There have been examples of currents of abnormal strength being met in the vicinity of tropical storms which cannot be accounted for by the wind strength alone. This possibility should be borne in mind, particularly when within 100 miles of the centre.

5 Other currents, not caused directly by the wind, may flow in connection with these storms, but are likely to be negligible in comparison with the wind current.

When a tropical storm approaches or crosses an extended coastline, such as that of Florida, a strong gradient current (5.9), parallel to the coast, will be produced by the piling up of water against the coast. Under these circumstances, the sea level can rise by up to 4 m.

6 Whether the storm is in the open ocean or not there is a rise of sea level inwards to its centre as a result of the reduction of atmospheric pressure. The extent of this rise is never great, about 0·5 m, varying with the intensity of the storm. It produces no current so long as the storm is not changing in intensity. If the storm meets the coast, however, the accumulation of water at its centre will enhance the rise in sea level at the coast mentioned above and so produce a stronger gradient current along the coast.

Gradient currents
5.9

1 Pressure gradients in the water cause gradient currents. Gradient currents occur whenever the water surface develops a slope, whether under the action of wind, change of barometric pressure, or through the juxtaposition of waters of differing temperature or salinity, or both. The initial water movement is down the slope but the effect of the Earth's rotation is to deflect the movement through 90° (to the right in the N hemisphere and to the left in the S hemisphere) from the initial direction.

2 A gradient current may flow in the surface layers at the same time as a drift current is being produced by the wind. In this case the observed current will be the resultant of the two.

3 A good example of a gradient current occurs in the Bay of Bengal in February. In this month the current circulation is clockwise around the shores of the Bay, the flow being NE-going along the W shore. With the NE Monsoon still blowing, the current is setting against the wind. The explanation of this phenomenon is that the cold wind off the land cools the adjacent water. A temperature gradient thus arises between cold water in the N and warm water in the S. Because of the density difference thus created, a slope, downwards towards the N, develops. The resulting N-going flow is directed towards the right, in an E direction, and so sets up the general clockwise circulation.

Effect of wind blowing over a coastline
5.10

1 Slopes of the sea surface may be produced by wind. When a wind blows parallel with the coastline or obliquely over it, a slope of the sea surface near the coast occurs. Whether the water runs towards or away from the coast depends on which way the wind is blowing along the coast, and which hemisphere is being considered. For example, in the region of the Benguela Current, S hemisphere, the SE Trade Wind blows obliquely to seaward over the coast of SW Africa, that is to say in a NW direction. The total transport of water is 90° to the left of this, ie, in a SW direction, and therefore water is driven away from the coast.

2 The coastal currents on the E side of the main circulations are produced in this way, by removal of water from the coastal regions under the influence of the Trade Winds. Since the gradient current runs at right angles to the slope which in its turn is at right angles to the trend of the coastline, the gradient current must always be parallel with the coastline. Taking the Benguela Current as an example, the water tending to run down the slope towards the coast of SW Africa is deviated 90° to the left and therefore the gradient current is somewhat W of N, since this is the general trend of the coast. The SE Trade Wind is tending also to produce at the actual sea surface a drift current directed rather less than 45° to the left of NW or roughly W, and the actual current experienced by a ship will be the resultant of this and the gradient, approximately NW.

3 These coastal currents on the E sides of the oceans are associated with the chief regions of upwelling. In these regions colder water rises from moderate depths to replace the water drawn away from the coastal region by the wind. In consequence the sea surface temperature in these regions is lower than elsewhere in similar latitudes. The balance between the replacement of water by upwelling and its removal by the gradient current is such that the slope of the surface remains the same, so long as the wind direction and strength remain constant. The actual slope is extremely slight; it is generally less than 2·5 cm in a distance of 10 miles.

Summary
5.11

1 The factors which produce currents are very complex, and usually more than one factor will influence the surface current circulation. Observations of current by research expeditions and mariners are still insufficient to define their distribution accurately: this is especially true of sub-surface currents.

2 In middle latitudes the upper layer of water extends from the surface to depths varying from 500 to 1000 m. The greatest current generating forces act on this layer, and therefore the strongest currents, are confined to it. Wind acts upon the upper layer where it is known that the greatest changes in temperature and

and conditions within the storm field generally are unfavourable for the accurate observation of the current.

salinity exist. Hence the greatest pressure gradients are present in the upper layer.

3   Below the upper layer, the circulation at all depths, in the open ocean, is caused by density differences, and is relatively weak.

The great coastal surface currents on the W sides of the oceans also flow in the deeper layers and may reach almost to the seabed.

4   The main surface circulation of an ocean, though it forms a closed gyre, is not self-compensating. Examination of current charts makes it obvious that the same volume of water is not being transported in all parts of the gyre. There are strong and weak parts in all such circulations. Also there is some interchange between different oceans at the surface.

5   Thus a large part of the South Equatorial Current of the Atlantic passes into the North Atlantic Ocean to join the North Equatorial Current, and so contributes to the flow of the Gulf Stream. There is no adequate

compensation for this if surface currents only are considered. There must, therefore, be interchange between surface and sub-surface water. The process of upwelling has been described; in other regions, notably in high latitude, water sinks from the surface to the seabed.

6   Deep currents, including those along the ocean floors, also play their part in this process of compensation. Thus water sinking in certain places in high latitudes in the North Atlantic flows S along the ocean floor, and subsequently enters the South Atlantic.

7   Much, though not necessarily all, of the day to day variability of surface currents is due to wind variation. Seasonal variation of current is also largely due to seasonal wind changes. Abnormal weather patterns will produce abnormal currents, and it is probable that the average current will vary somewhat from year to year.

Tidal streams

Information on charts
5.12

1   Tidal stream information is treated in different ways according to the type of tidal stream and the amount of detailed information available.

On the more modern charts of the British Isles and on earlier charts which have been modernised, tidal stream information is normally given in the form of tables, which show the mean spring and mean neap rates and directions of the tidal streams at hourly intervals relative to the time of high water at a convenient Standard Port.

2   However, when the spring tidal range is greater than the mean spring range published in *Admiralty Tide Tables* (3.27), the tidal stream rates can be expected to be proportionately greater, and conversely, when the spring tidal range on the day is less than the mean spring range, the rates will be proportionately less. The same argument also applies to the neap rates. The Computation of Rates diagram at the front of any *Admiralty Tidal Stream Atlas* (3.32) will assist. In *Admiralty TotalTide* (3.33), these computations are carried out automatically. Rates and directions at intermediate times can be found by interpolation.

3   These tables are, generally speaking, based on a series of observations extending over 25 hours, preferably obtained at Spring Tides. In the case of coastal observations, any residual current found in the observations is considered fortuitous and is removed before the tables are compiled. In the case of observations in rivers and, in some cases in estuaries, the residual current is considered as the normal riverflow and is retained in the tables.

4   The observations used in the preparation of these tables and daily predictions in the relevant *Admiralty Tide Tables*, are normally taken in such a way that they give the rates and directions which may be expected by a medium-sized vessel. To this end the observations are designed to measure the average movement of a column water which extends from the surface to a depth of about 10 m. In some cases,

details of the exact methods used are not known but it can generally be assumed that similar principles have been applied. As a result of these methods, differences from the predictions may be found in the surface and near seabed movements.

5   Earlier charts show tidal stream information in the form of arrows and roses but these are being gradually removed as the information obtained from them is frequently ambiguous.

On charts of foreign waters where the tidal stream is predominantly semi-diurnal and sufficient information is available, tables similar to those in British waters are shown on the charts.

6   In a few important areas, the tidal streams are not related to the times of high water at any Standard Port and it is necessary to compute predictions of the maximum rates, slack water and directions. These predictions are included in the relevant *Admiralty Tide Tables*.

In areas where the diurnal inequality of the streams is large, they are predicted by the use of harmonic constants. These are tabulated, for places where they are known, in Part IIIa of the relevant *Admiralty Tide Tables*.

7   It should be noted that, along open coasts, the time of high water is not necessarily the same as the time of slack water, the turn more often occurring near half-tide.

Other publications
5.13

1   Tidal stream information of a descriptive nature is included in *Admiralty Sailing Directions*. It is therefore no longer included on modern charts.

For waters around the British Isles, the general circulation of the tidal stream is given in pictorial form in a series of Tidal Stream Atlases (3.32). As with charts, the largest available scale should always be used.

Tides

Chart Datum

Definition
5.14

1   Chart Datum (CD) is defined simply in the Glossary as the level below which soundings are given on Admiralty charts. CDs used for earlier surveys were based on arbitrary low water levels of various kinds.

2   Modern Admiralty surveys use as CD a level as close as possible to Lowest Astronomical Tide (LAT), which is the lowest predictable tide under average meteorological conditions. This is to conform to an IHO Technical Resolution which states that CD should be set at a level so low that the tide will not frequently fall below it.

3   The actual levels of LAT for Standard Ports are listed in *Admiralty Tide Tables*. On larger scale charts, abbreviated details showing the connection between chart datum and local land levelling datum are given in the tidal panel for the use of surveyors and engineers, where those connections are known.

Datums in use on charts
5.15

1   Large scale modern charts contain a panel giving the heights of MHWS, MHWN, MLWS and MLWN above CD, or MHHW, MLHW, MHLW and MLLW, whichever is appropriate, depending on the tidal regime in the area concerned. The definitions of all these terms are given in the Glossary. If the value of MLWS from this panel is shown as 0·0 m, CD is the same as MLWS and is not therefore based on LAT. In this case tidal levels could fall appreciably below CD on several days in a year, which happens when a CD is not based on LAT.

2   Other charts for which the UKHO is the charting authority are being converted to new CDs based on LAT as they are redrawn. The new datum is usually adopted in *Admiralty Tide Tables* about one year in advance to ensure agreement when the new charts are published. When the datum of *Admiralty Tide Tables* thus differs from that of a chart, a caution is inserted by Notice to Mariners on the chart affected drawing attention to the new datum.

3   Where foreign surveys are used for Admiralty charts, the chart datums adopted by the hydrographic authority of the country concerned are always used for Admiralty charts. This enables foreign tide tables to be used readily with Admiralty charts. In tidal waters these CDs may vary from Mean Low Water (MLW) to lowest possible low water. In non-tidal waters, such as the Baltic, CD is usually Mean Sea Level (MSL).

4   **Caution.** Many CDs are above the lowest levels to which the tide can fall, even under average weather conditions. Charts therefore do not always show minimum depths.

For further details, see the relevant *Admiralty Tidal Handbook*.

Tidal Charts

General information
5.16

1   Co-tidal and Co-range charts show lines of equal times of tides and equal range respectively, or the amplitude and phase of harmonic constants, for certain areas around the United Kingdom, North Sea, Malacca Strait and Persian Gulf. Near amphidromic points in these areas, the times of a tide may alter considerably within a short distance, so that accurate tidal predictions require considerable care, particularly for ships under way.

2   The reliability of these charts depends on the accuracy and number of tidal observations taken in the area concerned. Since offshore sites for tide-gauges, such as islands, rocks or oil rigs, are seldom suitably placed, offshore data will often depend more on interpolation than that for inshore stations.

3   Deep-draught vessels require particular attention to be paid to the limitations of these charts when predicting tides and planning passages through critical offshore areas.

Tides in Rivers and Estuaries

Abnormalities
5.17

1   Most estuaries are funnel-shaped and this causes the tidal wave to be constricted. In turn, this causes a gradual increase in the range, with high waters rising higher and low waters falling lower as the tidal wave proceeds up the estuary. This process continues up to the point where the topography of the river-bed no longer permits the low waters to continue falling.

2   Beyond this point, the behaviour of the tide will depend greatly on the topography and slope of the river-bed and the width of the river. In general, the levels of high water will continue rising but the levels of low water will rise more rapidly, thus causing a steady decrease in range until it approaches zero and the river is no longer tidal. This raising of the level of low waters is often accompanied by a low water stand, with the duration of the rising tide decreasing as the river is ascended. In extreme cases, the onset of this rising tide may be accompanied by a bore.

3   In some rivers, of which the Severn in England and the Seine in France are examples, a point is reached where the levels of low waters at springs and at neaps are the same, and above which neaps fall lower than springs.

A further complication in the upper reaches of a river is the effect of varying quantities of river water coming down-stream. This effect can be expected to be greater at low water than at high water and can also be expected to increase as the tidal range decreases.

Non-tidal Changes in Sea Level

Effect of meteorological conditions
5.18

1   Strong winds blowing steadily over the sea set up a surface current (5.7) which raises sea level in the direction in which the wind is blowing, and lowers sea level in the opposite direction.

2   Tidal predictions are computed for average conditions, including average barometric pressure. Sea level is lowered by high, and raised by low barometric pressure. A change of 34 hPa in barometric pressure can cause a change in sea level of 0·3 m but the effect of a change in pressure may not be felt immediately and may, in fact, not be experienced until after the cause of the change has ceased.

3   Since depressions are frequently accompanied by strong winds, a resulting change in sea level is often due to a combination of the effects of both wind and pressure. Such changes in sea level are superimposed on the normal tidal cycles obtained by predictions, and can be regarded as a temporary change in MSL. A rise in sea level is sometimes known as a positive surge and a fall as a negative surge.

4   Reduced tidal levels may also be experienced in settled weather, a persisting area of high pressure may reduce tidal levels by 0·3 m or more for several days. Both positive and negative surges may alter appreciably the time of high and low water from that predicted. This effect is greater where the tidal range is small. Variations from the predicted time of as much as an hour are not uncommon. For example, in 1989 a high water at Lowestoft was delayed by over 3 hours.

5   Marked seasonal changes in weather, such as occur during the monsoons, result in changes in sea level. Where sufficient data is available, the changes are given in *Admiralty Tide Tables* and are taken into account in predictions. In the estuaries of major rivers seasonal changes may also result from changes in level due to melting snow or monsoon rains, which will be more marked than seasonal changes due to winds and barometric pressure.

6   Some common effects of weather on sea level are discussed below; fuller details for particular areas are given in the appropriate volumes of *Admiralty Sailing Directions*, but the information is often scanty. Information is also given in the Introduction to *Admiralty Tide Tables*.

Positive surges
5.19

1   The greatest effects of positive surges occur in shallow water and where the resulting current from the effects of weather is confined, such as in a gulf or bight where the water can pile up. In temperate zones they are generally less than 1·5 m above astronomical predictions, but on occasions they have exceeded 3 m. Appreciable changes in sea level can be achieved by strong winds blowing over the sea from the appropriate direction for about 6 hours or so.

2   In a bight such as the North Sea, it is evident that N winds will raise the sea level in its S part, and that S winds will lower them. In confined waters such as the entrance to the Baltic, the currents resulting from the winds or barometric pressure are deflected by the numerous islands, and local knowledge may be necessary to know whether a particular wind will raise or lower sea level at a given place.

Negative surges
5.20

1   To all vessels navigating with small under-keel clearance (UKC), negative surges are of considerable importance.

Negative surges are most frequent in estuaries and areas of shallow water, and in certain places they may cause sea level to fall by as much as 1 m several times a year, and sometimes considerably more. Little, however, is known about them.

2   The effect of negative surges in tidal rivers is thought to be amplified the farther one proceeds from the sea.

It seems likely that the greatest fall in sea level will occur, however, when strong winds blow water out of a bight or similar area of enclosed water.

Negative Surge Warning Service in the southern North Sea, Thames Estuary and Dover Strait
5.21

1   Since 1973, the Negative Surge Warning Service has operated to forecast appreciable falls in tidal levels due to meteorological effects in the southern North Sea and the Thames Estuary. In 1979, the service was extended to include the Dover Strait. Warnings are issued when it is estimated that tidal levels may be 1 m or more below the astronomically predicted levels.

2   Warnings are normally issued 6 to 12 hours ahead of the event and are given in broad terms; for example "Tides expected to be appreciably below predictions in the southern North Sea and the Thames Estuary during the afternoon", or "Tides expected to be appreciably below predictions in the Dover Strait around midnight". Since 1994, an indication of the expected maximum reduction in levels has been included in the warnings; for example "Maximum reduction in levels expected to be around 1 m", or "Maximum reduction in levels expected to be between 1½ and 2 metres".

3   Where a risk of levels falling below CD is foreseen, suitable comment will be made in the warning.

Current techniques often allow the occurrence of a negative surge to be forecast up to about 30 hours ahead. In these cases, an advanced information message may be issued in the form: "Advanced information on possible Negative Surge. Forecast conditions are such that a Negative Surge is considered likely to occur...... (Location/time-frame)...... Formal warnings can be expected to follow later."

4   Negative Surge warnings are transmitted from the Coastguard stations appropriate to the Sea Regions concerned, that is to say, S North Sea, the Thames Estuary and Dover Strait, W to the Isle of Wight. Warnings are broadcast on receipt and then at each hour including the routine broadcasts. Routine schedules are described in *Admiralty List of Radio Signals Volume 3, Part 1*, where full details of broadcast times, frequencies and other relevant information will be found.

5   Negative Surge information is also included in the half hourly broadcasts of the Channel Navigation Information Service; for further details see *Admiralty List of Radio Signals Volume 6, Part 1*.

Storm surges
5.22

1   In deep water, a storm generates long waves which travel faster than the storm so that the energy put into them is soon dissipated. In shallow water, however, the speed of these long waves falls, and in depths of about 100 m their speed is reduced to about 60 kn, which may be near the speed of the storm. If the storm keeps pace with the long waves, it will continuously feed energy into them. The causes of a storm surge include not only the speed of advance, and the size and intensity of the depression, but its position in relation to the coast and the depth of water in the vicinity.

2   A severe storm surge can be expected when an intense depression moves at a critical speed across the head of a bight with storm force winds blowing into the bight. The speed of a storm surge along a coastline depends chiefly on the depth of water. In the North Sea this speed is about equal to the speed of advance of the tide. A storm surge can attain a considerable height and if its peak coincides with High Water Springs serious flooding may be caused.

3   Such a positive storm surge occurred in January 1953 when a N storm of exceptional strength and duration raised sea level by nearly 3 m along the E coast of England, and even more on the Netherlands coast, causing considerable flooding and loss of life.

4   A negative storm surge, on the other hand, can considerably reduce tidal levels. In December 1982 tidal levels in the Thames Estuary were reduced by more than 1 m for a period of just over 12 hours. The maximum "cut" in the tide during this event was 2·25 m. The winds producing this surge were associated with a depression centred to the NW of Scotland.

5   In the North Sea most storm surges occur between September and April. The average number of positive surges per year (height at least 0·6 m greater than predicted) in the twenty years to 1988 was 19. The figure for negative surges of a similar order in the S North Sea for the same period was 15.

6   In the Bay of Bengal, a far more violent positive storm surge which accompanied a cyclone in November 1970 raised sea level by about 8 m and swept over many islands with immense loss of life.

Prediction of surges
5.23

1   Mathematical models for the calculation of sea level have been developed and are now used in some countries for the prediction of both positive and negative surges. In other countries, indications of the possible onset of surges may be obtained from satellite weather pictures. Further indications may also be obtained from tide gauges. Warnings of storm surges are usually passed to the appropriate authorities for broadcast by local radio stations.

Seiches
5.24

1   Intense but minor depressions may have effects of a more localized character. The passage of a line squall, for instance, may set up an oscillation known as a seiche, having a period of anything from a few minutes to an hour or two. The height of the wave may be anything from less than a decimetre to more than a metre in extreme cases. Seiches are usually only apparent as irregularities within the tidal records of an automatic tide gauge, but large seiches can set up strong, though temporary, currents which may be a danger to small craft.

Waves

Sea

General information
5.25

1   Almost all waves at sea are caused by wind, although some may be caused by other forces of nature such as volcanic explosions, earthquakes or even icebergs calving.

   The areas where waves are formed by wind are known as generating areas, and Sea is the name given to the waves formed in it.

2   The height of sea waves depends on how long the wind has been blowing, the fetch, the currents and the wind strength. The Beaufort Wind Scale (Table 7.3) gives a guide to probable wave heights in the open sea, remote from land, when the wind has been blowing for some time.

   The effect of sea and swell on ships, and the planning of passages to put sea and swell conditions to best advantage are discussed in *Ocean Passages for the World*.

Sea state
5.26

1   Sea states are described in the table below. Photographs (5.26.1 to 5.26.14) illustrate typical appearance of the sea for a given wind strength and sea state.

Code	Description	Height in metres*	Associated wind speed (Beaufort Scale) (7.3)
0	Calm-glassy	0	0
1	Calm-rippled	0–0·1	1
2	Smooth wavelets	0·1–0·5	2
3	Slight	0·5–1·25	3–4
4	Moderate	1·25–2·5	4–5
5	Rough	2·5–4	5–7
6	Very rough	4–6	7–8
7	High	6–9	8–10
8	Very high	9–14	10–12
9	Phenomenal	Over 14	12

2   *The average wave height as obtained from the large well-formed waves of the wave system being observed.

Force 0 – Wind speed less than 1 kn (Sea like a mirror) (5.26.1)

(Photograph – M C Horner, Courtesy of the Met Office)

Force 1 – Wind speed 1 – 3 kn; mean, 2 kn
(Ripples with the appearance of scales are formed, but without foam crests) (5.26.2)

(Photograph – G J Simpson, Courtesy of the Met Office)

Force 2 – Wind speed 4 – 6 kn; mean, 5 kn
(Small wavelets, still short but more pronounced – crests have a glassy appearance and do not break) (5.26.3)

(Photograph - G J Simpson, Courtesy of the Met Office)

Force 3 – Wind speed 7 – 10 kn; mean, 9kn
(Large wavelets. Crests begin to break. Foam glassy appearance. Perhaps scattered horses) (5.26.4)

(Photograph - I G MacNeil, Courtesy of the Met Office)

Force 4 – Wind speed 11 – 16 kn; mean, 13kn
(Small waves, becoming longer; fairly frequent white horses) (5.26.5)

(Photograph - I G MacNeil, Courtesy of the Met Office)

Force 5 – Wind speed 17 – 21 kn; mean, 19 kn
(Moderate waves, taking a more pronounced long form; many white horses are formed (Chance of some spray)) (5.26.6)

(Photograph - I G MacNeil, Courtesy of the Met Office)

Force 6 - Wind speed 22-27 kn; mean 24 kn
(Large waves begin to form; the white foam crests are more extensive everywhere (Probably some spray)) (5.26.7)

(Photograph - I G MacNeil, Courtesy of the Met Office)

Force 7 - Wind speed 28 - 33 kn; mean 30 kn
(Sea heaps up and white foam from breaking waves begins to be blown in streaks along the direction of the wind) (5.26.8)

(Photograph - G J Simpson,, Courtesy of the Met Office)

Force 8 – Windspeed 34 – 40 kn; mean 37kn

(Moderate high waves of greater length; edges of crests begin to break into the spindrift.
The foam is blown in well–marked streaks along the direction of the wind) (5.26.9)

(Photograph - Environment Canada)

Force 9 – Windspeed 41 – 47 kn; mean 44kn

(High waves. Dense streaks of foam along direction of the wind.
Crests of waves begin to topple, tumble and roll over. Spray might affect visibility) (5.26.10)

(Photograph - Environment Canada)

Force 10 – Windspeed 48 – 55 kn; mean 52kn

(Very high waves with long overhanging crests. The resulting foam, in great patches, is blown in dense white streaks along the direction of the wind. On the whole, the surface of the sea takes a white appearence. The tumbling of the sea becomes heavy and shock-like. Visibility affected) (5.26.11)

(Photograph – Environment Canada)

Force 11 – Windspeed 56 – 63 kn; mean 60kn

(Exceptionally high waves. (Small and medium sized ships might be for a time lost to view behind the waves.) The sea is completely covered with long white patches of foam lying along the direction of the wind. Everywhere the edges of the wave crests are blown into froth. Visiblity affected.) (5.26.12)

(Photograph – Environment Canada)

Force 12 – Windspeed greater than 63kn
(The air is filled with foam and spray. Sea completely white with driving spray; visibility very seriously affected) (5.26.13)

(Photograph – Captain J. F. Thomson, Courtesy of the Met Office)

Force 12 – Windspeed greater than 63kn
(The air is filled with foam and spray. Sea completely white with driving spray; visibility very seriously affected) (5.26.14)

(Photograph – Captain J. F. Thomson, Courtesy of the Met Office)

Swell

General information
5.27

1 Swell is the wave motion caused by a meteorological disturbance which persists after the disturbance has died down or moved away.

Swell can travel for considerable distances from its generating area, and in deep water will maintain constant direction. As it travels away from its generating area, the height will decrease although its length and speed remain constant, thus giving rise to the long, low, regular undulations so characteristic of swell.

2 The measurement of swell is complex. Multiple swells from different generating areas are often present and these may be partially obscured by sea waves. Some climatic atlases give world-wide monthly distribution of swell, but for the reasons given above and the small number of observations in some oceans they should be used with caution.

Terminology
5.28

1 Swell is described in terms of its length and height as follows:

Length.

Short	0–100 m
Average	100–200 m
Long	over 200 m

Height.

Low	0–2 m
Moderate	2–4 m
Heavy	over 4 m

Tsunamis and abnormal waves

Tsunamis
5.29

1 Tsunamis, from the Japanese, meaning "harbour wave", are also known as seismic sea waves and are often erroneously referred to as "tidal waves". They are usually caused by submarine earthquakes, but may be caused by submarine volcanic eruptions or coastal landslips.

2 In the oceans these waves cannot be detected as they are often over 100 miles in length and less than a metre in height, travelling at tremendous speed, reaching 300 to 500 kn. On entering shallow water the waves become shorter and higher. On coasts where there is a long fetch of shallow water with oceanic depths immediately to seaward, and in V-shaped harbour mouths, the waves can reach disastrous proportions. Waves having a height of 20 m from crest to trough have been reported.

3 The first wave is seldom the highest and there is normally a succession of waves reaching a peak and then gradually disappearing. The time between crests is usually from 10 to 40 minutes. Sometimes the first noticeable part of the wave is the trough, causing an abnormal lowering of the water level. Mariners should regard such a sign as a warning that a tsunami may arrive within minutes and should take all possible precautions, proceeding to sea if at all feasible.

4 Tsunamis can travel for enormous distances, up to one-third of the circumference of the earth in the open waters of the Pacific Ocean. In 1960 a seismic disturbance of exceptional severity off the coast of Chile generated a tsunami which caused much damage and loss of life as far afield as Japan.

5 More recently, on 26 December 2004, the Great Sumatera–Andaman Earthquake, measuring up to 9·3 on the Richter Scale, with an epicentre W of Sumatera, triggered a series of devastating tsunamis along the coasts of most landmasses bordering the Indian Ocean. Waves up to 30 m in height inundated coastal communities, and nearly 250 000 people lost their lives. Whilst the majority of the devastation occurred close to the epicentre in Indonesia, Thailand, India and Sri Lanka, its direct effects were also felt in E Africa, and abnormal wave heights were registered as far afield as Mexico and Antarctica.

6 Although large tsunamis cause grave havoc, small waves in shallow water can also cause considerable damage by bumping a ship violently on a hard seabed.

7 A ship in harbour, either becoming aware of a large earthquake in the vicinity, or observing sudden marked variations in sea level, or receiving warning of an approaching tsunami, should seek safety at sea in deep water, and set watch on the local port radio frequency.

In the aftermath of a tsunami, abnormal ground swells and currents may be experienced for several days.

Tsunami warning systems
5.30

1 **History.** The first tsunami warning system was established by the USA in 1949 at Ewa Beach, Honolulu, following a tsunami originating in the Aleutian Islands in 1946. After the 1960 Chilean tsunami which caused loss of life as far afield as Hawaii and Japan, the United Nations, through the Intergovernmental Oceanographic Commission, established the Pacific Tsunami Warning System (PTWS) in 1968, based on the US facility in Honolulu, providing warnings for the Pacific rim. The system was enlarged with the establishment of the West Coast and Alaska Tsunami Warning System (WC/ATWS) in 1967.

2 **Areas of Responsibility.** WC/ATWS area of responsibility, originally only for Alaska, the British Columbia coast of Canada and the US states of Washington, Oregon and California, has now (2007) expanded to include the Caribbean Sea. In the aftermath if the Indian Ocean tsumamis of 2004, PTWC has taken on the additional responsibilities for the Indian Ocean and the South China Sea.

3 **System description.** The Tsunami Warning Centres (TWC) receive most of their data from a network of 39 (2008) DART (Deep–ocean Asessment and Reporting of Tsunamis) stations situated around the Pacific rim,

in the Caribbean Sea and in the NE Indian Ocean. The stations are all US owned apart from one by Chile, one by Australia and those in the Indian Ocean which are owned by Indonesia and Thailand.

4 **Station description.** A station consists of an anchored seabed Bottom Pressure Recorder (BPR) connected to a companion moored surface buoy for real-time communications. An acoustic link transmits data from the BPR to the buoy. The first generation stations, DART I, which became operational in 2003, had one-way satellite links to the TWCs, and transmitted data hourly. DART II, which became operational in 2005, has two-way satellite links which enhances DART I capability and enables the TWCs to interrogate buoys for data, change the operating mode in anticipation of tsunamis, and allows for real-time troubleshooting and diagnostics.

5 **Operation.** DART constitutes a vital part of the US National Oceanic and Atmospheric Administration (NOAA)'s Tsunami Program. The Tsunami Program is part of a cooperative effort to save lives and protect property through hazard assessment, warning guidance, mitigation, research capabilities and international coordination. NOAA's National Weather Service (NWS) is responsible for the overall execution of the Tsunami Program, including operation of the TWCs.

6 **Warnings.** Details of the various methods of broadcast and dissemination of warnings are given in *Admiralty List of Radio Signals Volume 3 (2).*

Abnormal waves
5.31

1 **General information.** A well-found ship properly handled is designed to withstand the longest and highest waves she is likely to encounter as long as they retain their original shapes. But when waves become distorted by meeting shoal water, a strong opposing tidal stream or current, or another wave system, abnormal steep-fronted waves must be expected. Abnormal waves may occur anywhere in the world where appropriate conditions arise. In places where waves are normally large, abnormal waves may be massive and capable of wreaking severe structural damage on the largest of ships, or even causing them to founder.

Where conditions are considered to exist which may combine to produce abnormal waves liable to endanger ocean-going craft, a warning is given in *Admiralty Sailing Directions* and in *Ocean Passages for the World.*

2 **Description.** Reports of such occurrences are very few. However, off the coast of SE Africa some research has been made into abnormal waves. To show how these waves are believed to occur in this particular case, the relevant part of *Africa Pilot Volume III* is quoted below in full.

3 "Under certain weather conditions abnormal waves of exceptional height occasionally occur off the SE coast of South Africa, causing severe damage to ships unfortunate enough to encounter them. In 1968 SS *World Glory* (28 300 gt) encountered such a wave and was broken in two, subsequently sinking with loss of life.

4 These abnormal waves, which may attain a height of 20 m or more, instead of having the normal sinusoidal wave-form have a very steep-fronted leading edge preceded by a very deep trough; the wave moving NE at an appreciable speed. These waves are known to occur between latitudes 29° and 33°30′S, mainly just to seaward of the continental shelf where the Agulhas Current runs most strongly; a ship has, however, reported sustaining damage from such a wave 30 miles to seaward of the continental shelf. Such abnormal waves can occur anywhere in the main stream of the Agulhas Current, and indeed, recent satellite imagery has shown the occurrence of very high waves in the Agulhas Current retroflection region S of the Agulhas Bank (36°00′S 21°00′E). No encounters with abnormal waves have been reported inside the 200 m depth contour. When heavy seas have been experienced outside the 200 m depth contour, much calmer seas have been found closer inshore in depths of 100 m.

5 Abnormal waves are apparently caused by a combination of sea and swell waves moving NE against the Agulhas Current, combined with the passage of a cold front. Swell waves generated from storms in high latitudes are almost always present off the SE coast of South Africa, generally moving in a NE direction. These are sometimes augmented by other swell waves from a depression in the vicinity of Prince Edward Islands (47°S 38°E) and by sea waves generated from local depressions also moving in a general NE direction.

6 Thus there may be three and sometimes more wave trains, each with widely differing wave-lengths, all moving in the same general direction. Very occasionally the crests of these different wave trains will coincide causing a wave of exceptional height to build up and last for a short time. The extent of this exceptional height will be only a few cables both along the direction the waves are travelling and along the crest of the wave. In the open sea this wave will be sinusoidal in form and a well found ship, properly handled, should ride safely over it.

7 However, when the cold front of a depression moves along the SE coast of South Africa it is preceded by a strong NE wind. If this blows for a sufficient length of time it will increase the velocity of the Agulhas Current to as much as 5 kn. On the passage of the front the wind changes direction abruptly and within 4 hours may be blowing strongly from SW. Under these conditions sea waves will rapidly build up, moving NE against the much stronger than usual Agulhas Current. If this occurs when there is already a heavy NE-going swell running, the occasional wave of exceptional height, which will build up just to seaward of the edge of the continental shelf, will no longer be sinusoidal but extremely steep-fronted and preceded by a very deep trough. A ship steering SW and meeting such a trough will find her bows still dropping into the trough with increasing momentum when she encounters the steep-fronted face of the oncoming wave, which she heads straight into, the wave eventually breaking over the

fore part of the ship with devastating force. Because of the shape of the wave, a ship heading NE is much less likely to sustain serious damage".

Long period swell waves (rissaga; infra-gravity waves)

5.32

1   Long period swell waves are a special class of waves that are longer than a typical swell wave, but shorter than a tide. Hitherto they have been difficult to measure and study, but modern computing techniques have made it possible for them to be isolated and analysed. Such waves are generated by meteorological phenomena in oceanic areas remote from coastlines, where suitable conditions may generate long swell waves with an amplitude of about 0·5 m and a period of up to 20 minutes. Interaction between swell waves may set up infra-gravity waves, with an amplitude of up to 1·5 m and a period of several minutes. Their amplitude may increase sharply as the waves approach the coast.

2   Long period swell waves may be experienced anywhere within the influence of severe weather systems in almost any oceanic area, with possible serious effects upon shipping in ports and harbours within such influence.

3   Long period swell waves cannot be felt on board a vessel, but have the effect of bodily raising or lowering the vessel relative to the sea floor in the same manner as a tide, or a storm surge. Due account should be taken of the possible effects of long period swell waves when assessing under keel clearance (11.129) required for passage through areas affected by them. Dynamic under keel clearance assessment equipment has been installed in certain New Zealand and Australian ports, from which information may be made available to mariners via the local pilot services.

Rollers

General information

5.33

1   Rollers are swell waves emanating from distant storms, which continue their progress across the oceans until they reach shallow water, where they abruptly steepen, increase in height and sweep to the shore as rollers. The shallow water may deflect or refract the swell waves so that one bay on a stretch of coast may be experiencing the full violence of rollers whilst a neighbouring one is calm and unrippled. For the same reason, rollers may come into a bay not open to the direction of an approaching swell, but facing as much as 90° from it.

2   Along the SW coast of Africa, for example, it is possible to detect the arrival of rollers by a considerable surf on the beach, by the sea breaking on the headlands of a bay before any swell is perceptible; and by large waves, like ridges on the surface of the water, visible in the offing from aloft.

3   In most other places, however, much of the danger of rollers lies in their completely unheralded and sudden onset. Mr WHB Webster, Surgeon in *Narrative of a Voyage to the Southern Atlantic Ocean in HM Sloop Chanticleer*, London, 1834, describes the rollers at Ascension Island thus:

4   *"All is tranquil in the distance, the sea breeze scarcely ripples the surface of the water, when a high swelling wave is suddenly observed rolling towards the island. At first it appears to move slowly forward, till at length it breaks on the outer reefs. The swell then increases, wave urges on wave, until it reaches the beach, where it bursts with tremendous fury."*

5   Among the places where significant rollers may be encountered are the Windward Islands, the islands of Fernando de Noronha, Saint Helena, Ascension Island and the Hawaiian Islands, and along the whole of the SW coast of Africa.

Characteristics of the sea

Density and salinity

Density

5.34

1   Grams per cubic centimetre (gm/cm^3) are normally used to express the density of the sea. Values at the surface in the open ocean range from 1·02100 to 1·02750, increasing from the equatorial regions towards the poles (see Diagrams 5.34.1—5.34.2). Lower values occur in coastal areas. At the greatest depths of the ocean, the density reaches 1·0700.

2   The density of sea water is a function of temperature, salinity and pressure; it increases with increasing salinity, increasing pressure and decreasing temperature.

Effect of density on draught

5.35

1   Change of draught due to a change of density of water may be obtained from either of the following formulae:

Increase in draught on going from salt to fresh water (sinkage).

$$\text{Sinkage} = \frac{\Delta s\text{-}\Delta f}{\Delta f} \times \frac{W}{T} \text{ linear units}$$

or,

$$\text{Draught in fresh water (Df)} = \frac{\Delta s}{\Delta f} \times Ds$$

Where:

2   Δs=Density of salt water (specific gravity or weight/unit of volume).

Δf=Density of fresh water (specific gravity or weight/unit of volume).

Ds=Draught in salt water.

Df=Draught in fresh water.

W=Displacement in tons at initial draught.

T=Tons per Linear unit Immersion at initial draught.

Salinity

5.36

1   Sea water consists of about 96·5% water and 3·5% dissolved salts. The major constituent of the salts are

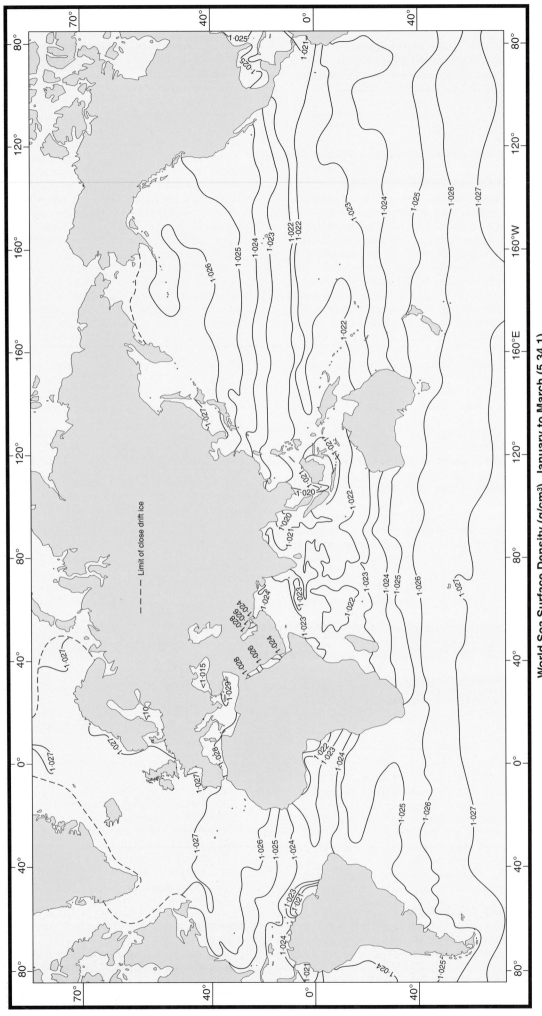

World Sea Surface Density (g/cm³) January to March (5.34.1)

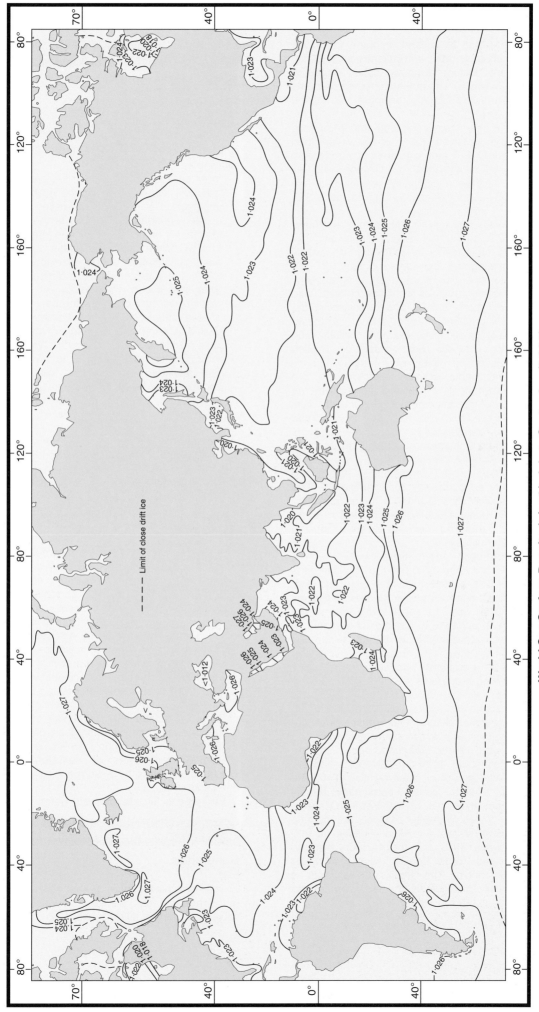

World Sea Surface Density (g/cm³) July to September (5.34.2)

ions of chloride (55·04%) and sodium (30·61%), followed by sulphate (7·68%) and magnesium (3·69%). Other constituents include dissolved gases (including oxygen, nitrogen, argon) and numerous other elements (including strontium, boron, bromine) in trace quantities.

2   The salinity of sea water is the total amount of solid material in grams contained in 1 kg of sea water when all the carbonate has been converted to oxide, the bromine and iodine replaced by chlorine and all organic matter has been completely oxidised; in the past it was usual to express salinity in parts per thousand (‰).

3   It has been known since the time of the Challenger Expedition (1873–7) that the relative composition of major dissolved constituents in sea water is virtually constant. Consequently, the determination of any single major element can be used as a measure of other elements and of the salinity. Since chloride ions make up approximately 55% of the dissolved solids, the measurement of salinity was for a long time based on the empirical relationship between salinity and chlorinity; salinity methods were based on titration techniques to determine chlorinity.

4   Now, however, most salinity determinations are made from measurements of electrical conductivity. As as result of this, the International System of Units (SI unit) for Practical Salinity (s) has been adopted and the use of parts per thousand (‰) is now declining.

5   Chlorinity is now regarded as a separate, variable property of sea water. As Practical Salinity is a ratio of two conductivities, it is dimensionless and thus expressed purely as a number; for example 35. The electrical conductivity of sea water is dependent upon both salinity and temperature, so temperature must be controlled or measured very accurately. during conductivity determinations.

6   Salinity in the open ocean averages 35·0 with a range generally between 33·0 and 37·5 (diagrams 5.36.1—5.36.2). The surface salinity in high latitudes, in regions of high rainfall, or where there is dilution by rivers or melting ice, may be considerably less; in the Gulf of Bothnia it is only 5·0. On the other hand, in isolated seas where evaporation is excessive, such as the Red Sea, salinities may reach 40·0 or more. Evaporation and precipitation, together with ocean currents and mixing processes, are the most important factors affecting salinity.

7   The large scale distribution of oceanic surface salinity follows a zonal pattern. The lowest values are in the polar regions, with a secondary minimum in a narrow equatorial zone. Maxima occur in the subtropical zones about 30°N and 20°–30°S and are highest in the Atlantic Ocean, reaching over 37·0. The salinity of the Atlantic Ocean, particularly the N Atlantic, is higher than that of the Pacific Ocean.

8   Salinity also varies vertically between the surface and the seabed. It shows a marked minimum at 600 to 1000 m between 45°S and the equator over the Atlantic, Indian and Pacific Oceans, caused by water of sub-Antarctic origin. The Pacific Ocean has a comparable salinity minimum in the N region due to the influence of sub-arctic water. Below 2000 m, the salinity is almost invariably between 34·5 and 35·0.

Colour of the Sea

Variations in colour
5.37

1   The normal colour of the sea in the open ocean in middle and low latitudes is an intense blue or ultramarine.

The following modifications in its appearance occur elsewhere:

2   In all coastal regions and in the open sea in higher latitudes, where the minute floating animal and vegetable life of the sea, called plankton, is in greater abundance, the blue of the sea is modified to shades of bluish-green and green. This results from a soluble yellow pigment, given off by the plant constituents of the plankton.

3   When the plankton is very dense such as when "blooms" occur, the colour of the organisms themselves may discolour the sea, giving it a more or less intense brown or red colour. The Red Sea, Gulf of California, the region of the Peru Current, South African waters and the Malabar coast of India are particularly liable to this, seasonally.

4   The plankton is sometimes killed more or less suddenly, by effects such as changes of sea temperature, producing dirty-brown or grey-brown discoloration and "stinking water". This occurs on an unusually extensive scale at times off the Peruvian coast, where the phenomenon is called "Aguaje". For details see *South America Pilot Volume III*. Larger masses of animate matter such as fish spawn or floating kelp may produce other kinds of temporary discolouration.

5   Mud brought down by rivers produces discolouration, which in the case of the great rivers may affect a large sea area. Soil or sand particles may be carried out to sea by wind or dust storms, and volcanic dust may fall over a sea area. In all such cases the water is more or less muddy in appearance. Submarine earthquakes may also produce mud or sand discolouration in relatively shallow water, and oil has sometimes been seen to gush up. The sea may be extensively covered with floating pumice after a volcanic eruption.

6   Isolated shoals in deep water may make the water appear discoloured, the colour varying with the depth of water over the shoal and the nature of the shoal itself. For the appearance of the water over coral reefs, see 5.47. The play of sun and cloud on the sea may often produce patches appearing at a distance convincingly like shoals.

7   Unexamined areas of discoloured water are indicated on charts by a surrounding danger line with a legend.

For reports on discoloured water, see 4.67.

Bioluminescence

Generation
5.38

1   The bioluminescence of the sea, formerly termed "phosphorescence" because phosphorus was the subject of earliest investigations, is one of the most

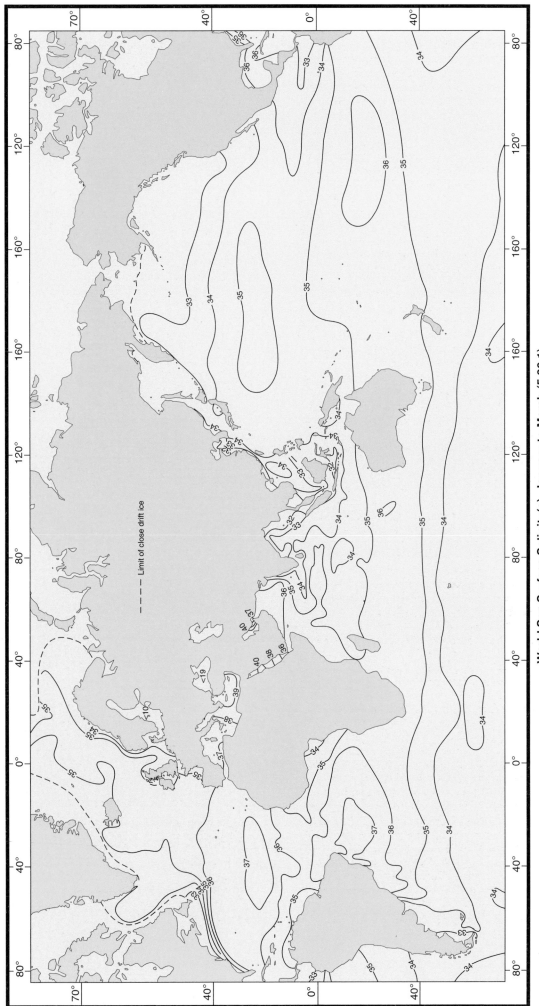

World Sea Surface Salinity(s) January to March (5.36.1)

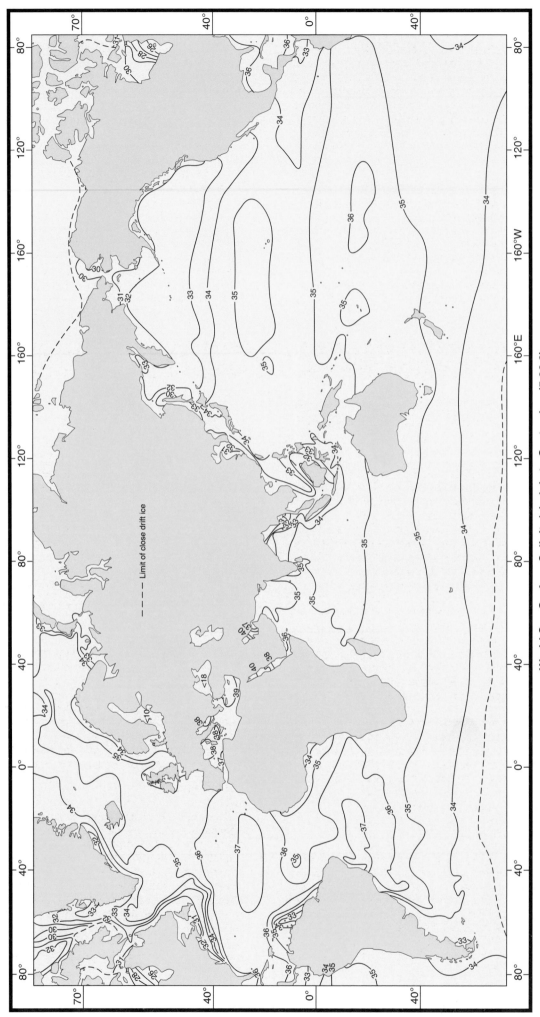

World Sea Surface Salinity(s) July to September (5.36.2)

Limit of close drift ice

remarkable of natural phenomena. The light is due to a variety of organisms, from microscopic marine life to many forms of deep-sea fish. The peculiarity of the light is that it is generated very efficiently with negligible waste of energy as heat. Its production is attributed to biochemical reactions which, though apparently automatic in the lower forms of life, are under nervous hormonal control in the higher forms.

Types and extent
5.39

1   A number of different types of the phenomena are at present recognised:
"Milky Sea". A constant, even white glow. Especially prevalent in the Arabian Sea.
Uneven sparkling patches of regular bands.
Flashing patches.
Patches apparently expanding and contracting.
"Disturbed water luminescence". Seen in breaking waves only.

2   Glowing ball type luminous masses apparently coming to the surface and exploding to light up a large area.
"Phosphorescent wheels". Beams of light moving quickly over the sea, often apparently revolving about a centre. One or more "wheels" may occur simultaneously, rotating in the same or opposite directions. Apparently confined to the Indian Ocean N of the equator and the China Seas.

3   Patches of luminescence "travelling" more or less quickly over the sea surface.
Light-stimulated luminescence.
Discrete blobs or "shapes" as from large creatures.
Research has shown that marine bioluminescence may occur anywhere, but it is most frequent in the warmer tropical seas. In the Arabian Sea it exhibits a maximum in August. In the North Atlantic maxima are associated with the seasonal increases in plankton population density during the spring and summer.
For reports on bioluminescence, see 4.68.

The seabed

Volcanoes and earthquakes

Volcanoes
5.40

1   Certain parts of the oceans are subject to volcanic activity and where these are known they are shown on charts and mentioned in *Admiralty Sailing Directions* so that ships may avoid them.

2   An example of an underwater volcano in intermittent eruption was that observed by the Japanese weather ship *Chikubu Maru* in September 1952 in the vicinity of 31°55'N 140°00'E in Izu Shoto.

3   A strong smell of sulphur was noticed, and a column of white smoke was seen to be rising out of the sea. The column of smoke became mixed with steam, but was then suddenly darkened by black smoke accompanied by flames from a violent explosion which sprang to a height of 5000 m. Almost simultaneously the sea below the column rose bodily in the form of a dome about 800 m in diameter. Volcanic ash soon began to fall from the great column of smoke.

4   Three days later a small Japanese survey vessel, sent to investigate, was lost with all hands when an even more violent eruption occurred. It is estimated that another dome of water was thrown up, rising about 10 m above the surrounding sea and nearly 2½ miles in diameter. After another two days, the volcano again erupted but less violently.

Earthquakes
5.41

1   Earthquakes can occur in the seabed just as they do on land. The effect on vessels in the vicinity will depend on the intensity of the earthquake, the distance of the vessel from the epicentre and the depth of water. These differing effects are well illustrated by the experiences of three vessels which were in in vicinity of an earthquake which occurred about 115 miles WSW of Cabo de São Vicente, Portugal, in 1969:

2   One vessel, about 100 miles NE of the epicentre and in a depth of 450 m experienced violent vibrations for about one minute.
Another, about the same distance NW of the epicentre and in a depth of 3650 m felt a severe vertical shock, as if the vessel was lifting out of the water: neither of these vessels suffered damage. Motor Tanker *Ida Knudsen* (32 000 gt), however, which was within 15 miles of the epicentre, was lifted bodily upwards, slammed violently back, and experienced very heavy vibrations; the damage was such that she was condemned as a total loss.

Submarine springs

General information
5.42

1   Submarine springs occur more frequently at sea than is generally realised. They may occur in any part of the oceans and at any depth, and may be of fresh or salt water. Fresh water springs have long been known to exist in the Persian Gulf where in the past pearl divers have used them to obtain drinking water, even when out of sight of land.
Known submarine springs are indicated on charts by a special symbol (Chart 5011 Symbol J15).

Fresh water
5.43

1   Originating from the land, fresh water submarine springs are most common off coasts where beds of permeable sedimentary rock, such as chalk or limestone, extend under the sea floor below impermeable rock strata. Such a formation allows fresh water from the land to percolate through the permeable layer until it reaches a fault or fissure in the strata above it. At this point the fresh water rises to the sea floor where it emerges as a fresh water spring, discharging water of a lower density than the surrounding sea water through which it consequently rises.

Salt water
5.44

1   If fresh water from the land absorbs dissolved materials from the rocks in its passage through the permeable layer to a submarine spring, a salt water submarine spring will occur. It will discharge water which may be just as dense as the surrounding sea water.

2   Salt water submarine springs more usually occur where geological conditions allow sea water to gain access to a permeable layer through cracks and fissures in the sea floor. As the water spreads through the permeable layer, it may become heated by magma, the molten rock below the Earth's crust, and trace elements may be leached from the surrounding layers. When the water reaches a fault in the strata over the permeable layer, it emerges as a spring, its water enriched by the dissolved salts forming a brine pool below the less dense water of the sea. Resulting chemical reactions, however, cause some of the salts of the pool, such as metal sulphides, iron silicates and magnesium oxides, to fall to the sea floor.

3   In certain parts of the oceans, however, such as near the Mid-Atlantic Ridge, in the Galapagos Rift Valley or in the Red Sea, where there is geological faulting or volcanic activity, magma lies close below the sea floor and very high temperatures may be found in salt water springs occurring there. These temperatures may be as high as 350°C, in surrounding sea water at a temperature of about 2°C, causing the hot water to rise under pressure like a geyser through the sea water in a plume, known as a "hydrothermal plume". Because of the force with which the spring water is discharged and its abrupt cooling, its salts are often deposited in the form of a chimney round the spring, as well as forming a surrounding shoal which will grow with time. In the warm water near the shoal, crabs, clams and other marine life foreign to the depth and darkness, may flourish abundantly.

4   Hydrothermal plumes are often only discharged periodically from the submarine spring, after sufficient pressure has built up below the seabed. The pattern of the plumes, whether discharged continuously or periodically, will also vary, being affected by changes in the ocean floor currents. The force with which the water is expelled from the sea floor, and the subsequent chemical reactions and changes in the concentrations of elements in solution, lead to large fluctuations in the sea water density, salinity and temperature over the whole area of the activity.

Echo sounder traces
5.45

1   Submarine springs are one of the features which can give rise to misinterpretation of echo sounder traces. Not only do the springs or hydrothermal plumes themselves give echoes which may be mistaken for shoals, but the differing water densities surrounding them will cause fluctuations in the speed of sound through salt water, giving rise to unknown errors in the depths recorded by the sounder.

Coral

Growth and erosion
5.46

1   Although depths over many coral reefs have remained unchanged for 50 years or more, coral growth and the movement of coral debris can change depths over reefs and in channels significantly. At depths near the surface, coral growth and erosion are nearly balanced. At greater depths the growth increases, with the most rapid growth occurring in depths of more than 5 m.

2   The greatest rate of growth of live coral is attained by branching coral and is a little over 0·1 m a year, but this type of coral would probably not damage a well-built vessel. The rate of growth of massive coral reefs which could damage even the largest vessel is about 0·05 m a year.

3   The continual erosion of coral reefs causes the formation of coral sands and shingles which may be deposited and cause fluctuations in the depths on reefs or in the channels between them. Windward channels tend to become blocked by this debris and by the inward growth of the reefs, but leeward channels tend to be kept clear by the out-going tide, which is usually stronger than the in-going in these channels and deposits the debris in deep water outside the reefs.

4   The greatest recorded decrease in depths over coral reefs due to the combined growth of coral and deposit of debris is 0·3 m a year. Decrease in depths due only to the deposition of coral debris can be more rapid and is more difficult to assess.

Visibility
5.47

1   The distance at which reefs will be seen is dependent on the height of eye of the observer, the state of the sea and the relative position of the sun. If the sea is glassy calm it is extremely difficult to distinguish the colour difference between shallow and deep water. The best conditions are from a relatively high position with the sun high, at least above an elevation of 20°, and behind the observer and with the sea ruffled by a slight breeze. Under these conditions with a height of eye of 10–15 m it is usually possible to sight patches with a depth of less than 6–8 m over them at a distance of a few cables.

2   The use of polaroid spectacles is strongly recommended as they make the variations in colour of the water stand out more clearly.

If the water is clear, patches with depths of less than 1 m over them will appear to be a light brown colour, those with 2 m or more appear to be light green, deepening to a darker green for depths of about 6 m, and finally to a deep blue for depths over 25 m. Cloud shadows on the sea and shoals of fish may be quite indistinguishable from reefs, but it may be possible to identify these by their movement.

3   The edges of coral reefs are usually more uniform on their windward or exposed sides, and therefore easily seen, while the lee sides frequently have detached coral heads which are difficult to see.

Soundings
5.48
1   Coral reefs are frequently steep-to, and depths of over 200 m may exist within 1 cable of the edge of the reef. Soundings are therefore of little value in detecting their proximity. In addition, soundings shoal so rapidly on approaching a reef that it is sometimes difficult to follow the echo sounder trace, and the echo itself is often weak due to the steep sea floor profile. This steep-to nature of coral makes it particularly difficult for the surveyor to find detached coral patches, and unless it is known that the area has been fully surveyed using modern sonar systems, the possibility that undetected coral pinnacles may exist should be borne in mind. There is also the possible decrease in depth to be considered due to growth of coral and deposition of coral debris since the survey on which the chart is based.

Navigation
5.49
1   Unless navigational aids have been established, navigation among coral reefs is almost entirely dependent upon the eye. If the water is not clear, it will be almost impossible to discern the presence of reefs by eye and then the only safe method will be to sound ahead of the ship with one or more boats.

2   Furthermore, it is essential that a reliable and rapid means of communication is established between the observer aloft, or the boats ahead, and the conning position, so that avoiding action can be taken in time if dangers are detected.

3   A ground speed of 5 kn is recommended, provided that steerage way can be maintained, so that the vessel can be stopped, and anchored if necessary if no clear channel is apparent.

Coral Reef Instrumented Monitoring Platforms (CRIMP)
5.50
1   In certain areas, most notably at Kaneohe Bay in Oahu, Hawaii, research programmes are under way to monitor coral reefs. These programmes involve the use of CRIMP (Coral Reef Instrumented Monitoring Platforms), which lie on the seabed and are marked by yellow buoys.

Kelp

Growth
5.51
1   Kelp is a very large marine algae. Kelp forests occur throughout the world in shallow open coastal waters extending to both the Arctic and Antarctic Circles. The larger forests grow in water temperatures of less than 20°C, and can achieve remarkable growth rates, up to 30 cm per day in some cases. Dependant on light for growth, they rarely grow in water deeper than 15—40 m.

Navigation in kelp
5.52
1   Kelp grows on most dangers having a rocky or stony sea floor, especially in channels or inlets, and will be visible on the surface during summer and autumn. In winter and spring it cannot always be seen, especially in heavy seas. The presence of kelp should always be accepted as a sign of underwater danger and it should be avoided. Many dangers, however, are not marked by kelp; a heavy sea sometimes tears the weed from the rock, or a moderate tidal stream or current may draw the kelp below water and out of sight.

2   Growing kelp should always be considered a sign of danger, and no vessel should pass through it if it can be avoided. Kelp forms long streamers, at or just below the surface, and it should be given a wide berth if passing on the upstream side. A clear patch of water in the middle of a thick growth of kelp often indicates the position of least depth over a danger. Dead kelp which has broken away from the sea floor floats in curled masses on the surface; it may sometimes drift in long lines.

Sandwaves

Formation
5.53
1   Sandwaves are found where water is moved rapidly by strong tidal streams or heavy seas over a seabed covered by a sufficient depth of unconsolidated sediment. No sandwaves of any significance are found where the sea floor is predominantly mud, but they are found where it is sand or gravel.

  Extensive sandwave fields are known to exist in the S North Sea, including the Dover Strait and parts of the Thames Estuary, in the Persian Gulf, in the Malacca and Singapore Straits, in Japanese waters, and in the Torres Strait.

2   Sandwaves are analogous to sand dunes formed by wind action on land. The action of the water movement forms the seabed into a series of ridges and troughs, most of which are thought to be virtually stationary, but others are known to move and alter significantly in height. Recent investigations have shown that sandwaves build to their maximum vertical extent, and therefore to their most critical navigational condition, following periods of relatively calm weather. The mariner should be prepared for changes from charted depths in any area where sandwaves are known to exist, or found by the sounder recording a trace, like that in Diagram 5.54. Even in recently surveyed areas, it is possible that the surveys were not carried out when the sandwaves reached their greatest height.

3   Sandwaves form fields which may be several miles in extent, with the waves in primary and secondary patterns. The waves vary in size from ripples seen on a sandy beach at low water to waves up to 20 m in amplitude and several hundred metres in wavelength. The waves forming the primary pattern may be several miles long. They usually lie nearly at right angles to the main direction of water movement, but small waves are sometimes found lying parallel to it. Secondary patterns are usually superimposed on the primary pattern, often at an angle; it is where the crests of the patterns coincide that the shoalest depths can be expected.

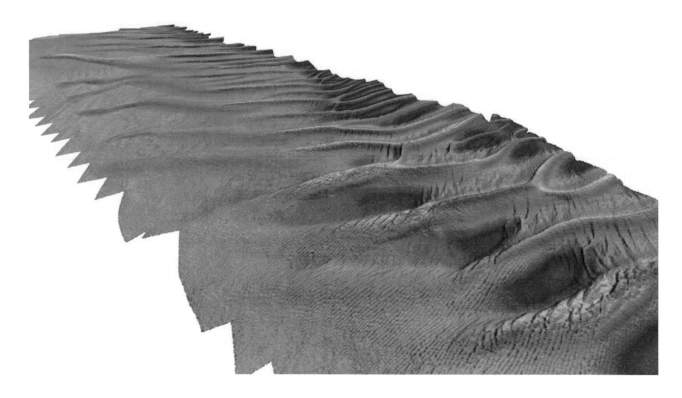

Sandwaves – Swathe image (5.53)

Detection
5.54

1   A line of soundings run at right angles to a navigational channel to fix its sides will usually run parallel to any primary pattern of sandwaves, and thus may well fail to obtain the least depth over the waves, or even to locate them at all. Further lines of soundings at right angles to the others will increase the chances of obtaining the least depth, but even these may be inadequate if the secondary pattern is complicated.

2   An echo sounder trace obtained by a surveying launch crossing a field of sandwaves in the S North Sea, at right angles to the primary pattern is shown in Diagram 5.53. The sandwaves are 5 m in amplitude with wavelengths of 150 m, rising from general depths of 40 m.

A sidescan sonar trace illustrating sandwaves, also in the S North Sea, with primary and secondary patterns is shown in Diagram 5.54.

Navigation
5.55

1   Areas where the sea floor is liable to change because of the movement of sandwaves are indicated on Admiralty charts by the appropriate symbol, or a suitable legend. Known details of such areas are given in *Admiralty Sailing Directions*.

Since the position of sandwaves and the depth of water over them are liable to change, ships with little under-keel clearance should treat the areas in which they are known to exist with due caution.

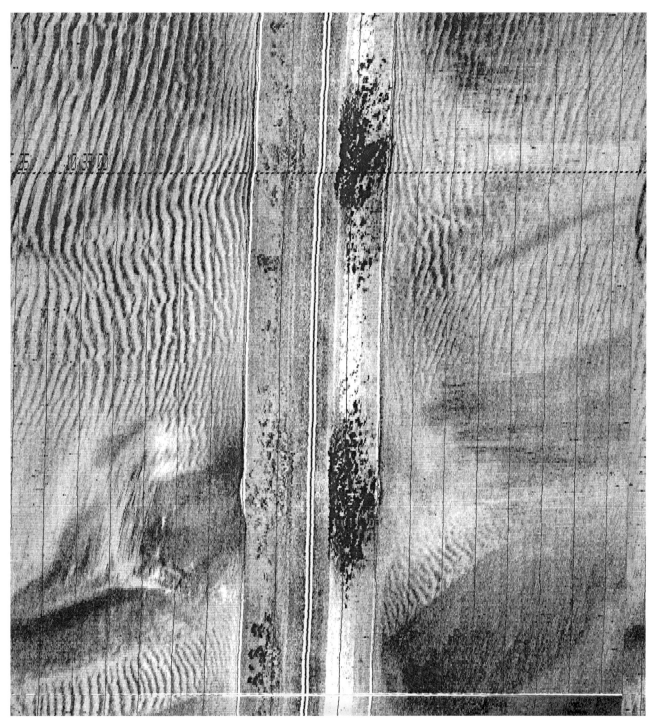

Sandwaves – Sidescan Sonar trace (5.54)

NOTES

Chapter 6

ICE

Sea ice

Formation, deformation and movement

Nomenclature
6.1

1   A comprehensive glossary, containing definitive descriptive terms for the various kinds of ice likely to be encountered by the mariner, can be found on page 373, separate from the main glossary. It is based on *WMO Sea-Ice Nomenclature* published by the World Meteorological Organization in 1970 (with subsequent amendments). A summary of terms used to describe types and forms of ice is after 6.22.

Floating ice
6.2

1   Several forms of ice may be encountered at sea. By far the most common type is that which results from the freezing of the sea surface, namely sea ice. The other forms are icebergs (6.14) and river ice. River ice is sometimes encountered in harbours and off estuaries during the spring break-up, but it is then in a state of decay so generally presents only a temporary hindrance to shipping.

Freezing of saline water
6.3

1   The freezing of fresh and salt water does not occur in the same manner. This is due to the presence of dissolved salts in sea water. The salinity of water is usually expressed in International Standard Units: sea water typically has a salinity of 35, though in some areas, especially where there is a considerable discharge of river water, the salinity is much less. In the Baltic, for example, the salinity is less than 10 throughout the year.

2   When considering the freezing process, the importance of salinity lies not only in its direct effect in lowering the freezing temperature, but also in its effect on the density of the water. The loss of heat from a body of water takes place principally from its surface to the air. As the surface water cools it becomes more dense and sinks, to be replaced by warmer, less dense water from below in a continuous convection cycle.

3   Fresh water reaches its maximum density at a temperature of 4°C; thus when a body of fresh water is cooled to this temperature throughout its depth convection ceases, since further cooling results in a slight decrease in density. Once this stable condition has been reached, cooling of the surface water leads to a rapid drop in temperature and ice begins to form when the temperature falls to 0°C.

4   With salt water the delay due to convection in the lowering of the temperature of the water to its freezing point is much more prolonged. In some areas where there is an abundant supply of relatively warm water at depth, such as SW of Spitsbergen, convection may normally prevent the formation of ice throughout the entire winter despite the very low air temperatures.

5   This delay is, in part, due to the great depths of water found in the oceans, but is mainly due to the fact that the density of salt water continues to increase with cooling until the surface water freezes. In fact the theoretical maximum density of sea water of average salinity (which can be achieved by super-cooling in controlled laboratory conditions) is well below its freezing temperature.

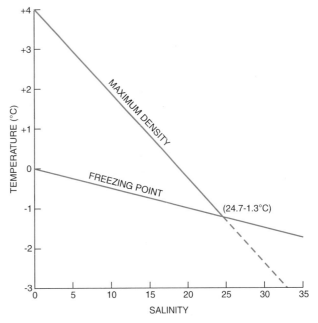

Maximum Density and Freezing Point related to Temperature and Salinity (6.3)

6   Diagram 6.3 shows the relationship between temperature, salinity and maximum density. It can be seen that in water with salinity of less than 24·7, the maximum density is reached before the freezing temperature and where the salinity is greater than 24·7 the freezing point is reached before the density attains its theoretical maximum value.

7   The greatest delay in reaching the freezing temperature occurs when the sea water, throughout its depth, is initially at an almost uniform density. In some areas, however, the density profile is not uniform. In these cases, discontinuities occur where a layer of lower salinity overlies a layer of higher salinity (at temperatures between about 3°C and freezing,

variations in density are more dependent on variations of salinity than on changes in temperature).

8   The increased density at the surface of the upper layer, achieved by cooling, may still be less than the density of the lower layer. The salinity discontinuity between the two layers then forms a lower limit to convection; the delay in reaching the freezing temperature is then dependent upon the depth of the upper layer. This is particularly so in the Arctic Ocean where there is a salinity discontinuity between the surface layer, the Arctic water, and the underlying more saline Atlantic water. Cooling of the surface water around the periphery of the basin, and within, where there is open water, leads to convection in a shallow layer which may extend to only 50 m in depth.

Initial formation
6.4

1   The first indication of ice is the appearance of ice spicules or plates, with maximum dimensions up to 2·5 cm, in the top few cm of water. These spicules, known as frazil ice, form in large quantities and give the sea an oily appearance. As cooling continues the frazil ice coalesces to form grease ice (photograph 6.4.1), which has a matt appearance. Under near-freezing, but as yet ice-free conditions, snow falling on the surface and forming slush may induce the sea surface to form a layer of ice. These forms may break up, under the action of wind and waves to form shuga (photograph 6.4.2). Frazil ice, slush, shuga and grease ice are classified as new ice.

2   With further cooling, sheets of ice rind (photograph 6.4.3) or nilas (photograph 6.4.4) are formed depending on the rate of cooling and on the salinity of the water. Ice rind is formed when water of low salinity freezes slowly, resulting in a thin layer of ice which is almost free of salt, whereas when water of high salinity freezes, especially if the process is rapid, the ice contains pockets of salt water giving it an elastic property which is characteristic of nilas. This latter form of ice is subdivided, according to age, into dark and light nilas; the second, more advanced form reaches a maximum thickness of 10 cm.

3   Again, the action of the wind and waves may break up ice rind and nilas into pancake ice (photograph 6.4.5) which later freezes together and thickens into grey ice and grey-white ice, the latter attaining thicknesses up to 30 cm. These forms of ice are referred to as young ice. Rough weather may break this ice up into cakes or floes (photograph 6.4.6).

First-year ice
6.5

1   The next stage of development, known as first-year ice, is sub-divided into thin, medium and thick; medium first-year ice has a range of thickness from 70 to 120 cm. At the end of the winter thick first-year ice may obtain a maximum thickness of approximately 2 m.

Should this ice survive the summer melting season, as it may well do within the Arctic Ocean, it is designated second-year ice at the onset of the next winter.

2   Subsequent persistence through summer melts warrants the description multi-year ice which, after several years, attains a maximum thickness, where level, of approximately 3·5 m; this maximum thickness is attained when the accretion of ice in winter balances the loss due to melting in summer.

Subsequent formation
6.6

1   The buoyancy of level of sea ice is such that approximately 1/7 of the total thickness floats above the water.

Ice increases in thickness from below, as the sea water freezes on the under-surface of the ice. The rate of increase is determined by the severity of the frost and by its duration.

2   As the ice becomes thicker, the rate of increase in thickness diminishes due to the insulating effect of the ice and its overlying snow cover in reducing the upward transport of heat from the sea to the very cold air above. Under extreme conditions, when the air temperature may suddenly fall to between −30°C and −40°C, it is possible that a layer of ice can form and grow to a thickness of about 10 cm in a day, 20 cm in 2 days and 30 cm in 4 days. However, the rate of growth decreases with the passage of time and it would take almost a month at such temperatures to reach a thickness of 60 cm.

3   Two other factors contribute to the growth of sea ice, particularly in the Antarctic due to the climatic and oceanographic conditions of that area:

Snow cover. Once its depth reaches approximately 50 cm or more, its weight may depress the original ice layer below the surface of the sea so that the snow becomes waterlogged. In winter the wet snow gradually freezes, thus increasing the depth of the ice layer.

4   Super-cooling. Water super–cools as it flows under the deep ice shelves which are typical of the Antarctic coastline. It is prevented from freezing by the pressure at this depth. Observations have shown that the flow of water under the ice shelves is often turbulent resulting in some of the super-cooled water rising towards the surface as it leaves the vicinity of the ice shelf. The consequent reduction in pressure may lead to the rapid formation of frazil ice in the near-surface layer.

5   The same process can also result in the accumulation of a relatively deep layer of porous ice beneath an original ice layer. In this way, recently broken fast ice over 4 m thick, encountered in the approaches to Enderby Land in autumn (March) was observed to consist only of 30 cm of solid ice and 4 m of porous ice, the whole offering little resistance to a ship's progress. This effect is almost entirely confined to the fast ice zone.

Salinity
6.7

1   At the first stage of its development sea ice is formed of pure water and contains no salt. The downward growth of ice crystals from the under-surface of the ice results in a network of crystals and small pockets of sea water. Eventually these pockets become cut off from the underlying water, and with further cooling they shrink in size as some of the water in these pockets freezes out. The residual solution which now has a higher salt content, is called brine.

Grease ice (6.4.1)

(Photograph - British Antarctic Survey)

Shuga, with growlers. Bergy bits and icebergs in the background (6.4.2)

(Photograph - British Antarctic Survey)

Rind ice with ice flowers (hoar frost) on top (6.4.3)

(Photograph - British Antarctic Survey)

Finger rafting in light nilas (6.4.4)

(Photograph - British Antarctic Survey)

Pancake ice (6.4.5)

(Photograph - British Antarctic Survey)

Ice cake and small floes with some bergy bits from the ice shelf in the background (6.4.6)

(Photograph - British Antarctic Survey)

2   The salinity of the brine is highly dependent on temperature. Since there exists, at least in winter, a substantial positive temperature gradient downwards through the ice, it follows that the temperature at the top of a pocket of brine is lower than at its base. This leads to freezing at the top of the brine pocket and melting at the base resulting in a slow downward migration of the brine through the ice. This brine is drained from the ice at a very slow rate.

3   As cooling continues the salt content is gradually deposited out of solution. There are certain preferred temperatures where this process becomes more apparent, notably at −8°C and −23°C. As the salt is deposited out, leaving pure ice containing pockets of pure salt, the ice gains in strength, so that, at temperatures below −23°C sea ice is a very tough material.

4   This process is reversed in summer, when, as a result of rising temperatures, the deposited salts go back into solution as brine. The pockets containing the brine gradually enlarge as the surrounding ice begins to melt so that the ice becomes honeycombed once more with pockets of brine. Eventually a great number of these pockets interlink and some break through the lower surface of the ice resulting in an accelerated rate of brine drainage.

5   It is at this stage that most of the salt trapped in the process of freezing is drained from the ice. Should this ice survive the summer melt and become second-year ice its salt content will be small. Survival through another summer season when more salt is drained away results in multi-year ice which is almost salt-free. Because of its very low salt content, multi-year ice, in winter, is extremely tough, so much so that little impression is made on it even by powerful icebreakers.

6   The age of floes may often be judged by the presence of coloured bands at their edges. During the summer, diatoms adhere to the underside of floating ice which may be slowly growing through the freezing of fresh water derived from the melting of the upper side. In the winter, the ice grows more rapidly, and diatoms are absent owing to the lack of sunlight. Thus yellow strata of frozen diatoms mark the interval between two winters freezings.

7   Ordinarily, first-year ice found floating in the sea at the end of 6 months is too brackish for making good tea, but is drinkable in the sense that the fresh water in it will relieve more thirst than the salt creates. When about 10 months old and floating in the sea, the salt water ice has lost most of its milky colour and is nearly fresh. A chunk of last year's ice that has been frozen into this year's ice will give water fresh enough for tea or coffee. Usually the water from sea ice does not become as "fresh as rain water" until the age is 2 or more years.

8   When salt ice thaws in such a way that there are puddles on top of it, these are fresh enough for cooking, provided there are no cracks or holes connecting them with the salt water under the floes, and the water can be pumped into a ship from the ice through a hose, which was ordinary sealer and whaler practice. However, water should not be pumped from a puddle that is so near to the edge of a floe that spray has been mixed with it. Whalers usually liked to go about 10 m or more from the edge of a floe to find a puddle from which to pump.

Different types of sea ice
6.8

1   Sea ice is divided into two main types according to its mobility. One type is drift ice (photographs 6.8.1 to 6.8.5), which is reasonably free to move under the action of wind and current; the other is fast ice (photograph 6.8.6), which does not move.

2   Ice first forms near the coasts and spreads seaward. A certain width of fairly level ice, depending on the depth of water, becomes fast to the coastline and is immobile. The outer edge of the fast ice is often located in the vicinity of the 25 m depth contour. A reason for this is that well-hummocked and ridged ice may ground in these depths and so form offshore anchor-points for the new season's ice to become fast.

3   Beyond this ice lies the drift ice, formed, to a small but fundamental extent, from pieces of ice which have broken off from the fast ice. As these spread seaward they, together with any remaining old ice floes, facilitate the formation of new, and later young, ice in the open sea. This ice, as it thickens, is continually broken up by wind and waves so that it consists of ice of all sizes and ages from giant floes of several years growth to the several forms of new ice whose life may be measured in hours.

4   In open ice, floes turn to trim themselves to the wind. In close ice, this tendency may be produced by pressure from another floe, but since floes continually hinder each other, and the wind may not be constant in direction, even greater forces, some rotational, result. This screwing or shearing effect results in excessive pressure at the corners of floes, and forms a hummock of loose ice blocks. Ice undergoing such movement is said to be "screwing", and is extremely dangerous to vessels.

Deformation
6.9

1   Under the action of wind, current and internal stress drift ice is continually in motion. Where the ice is subjected to pressure its surface becomes deformed. In new and young ice this may result in rafting as an ice sheet over-rides its neighbour; in thicker ice it leads to the formation of ridges and hummocks according to the pattern of the convergent forces causing the pressure.

2   During the process of ridging and hummocking, when large pieces of ice are piled up above the general ice level, vast quantities of ice are forced downward to support the weight of ice in the ridge or hummock. The downward extension of ice below a ridge is known as an ice keel, and that below a hummock is called a bummock. The total vertical dimensions of these features may reach 55 m, approximately 10 m showing above sea level. In shallow water the piling up of ice floes against the coastline may reach 15 m above mean sea level.

3   Cracks, leads (photograph 6.9) and polynyas may form as pressure within the ice is released. When these openings occur in winter they rapidly become covered by new and young ice, which, given sufficient time, will thicken into first-year ice and cement the old floes together. Normally, however, the younger ice is subjected to pressure as the older floes move together resulting in the deformation features already described.

4   Offshore winds drive the drift ice away from the coastline and open up shore leads. In some ice

Open ice (6.8.1)

(Photograph – British Antarctic Survey)

Close ice (6.8.2)

(Photograph – British Antarctic Survey)

Very close ice (6.8.3)

(Photograph - British Antarctic Survey)

Consolidated ice (6.8.4)

(Photograph - British Antarctic Survey)

Very open ice (6.8.5)

(Photograph - British Antarctic Survey)

Fast ice, with ice shelf cliffs in the background (6.8.6)

(Photograph - British Antarctic Survey)

Lead (6.9)

(Photograph - British Antarctic Survey)

regions where offshore winds are persistent through the ice season, localised movement of shipping many be possible for much of the winter. Where there is fast ice against the shore, offshore winds develop a lead at the boundary, or flaw as it is known, between the fast ice and the drift ice: this opening is called a flaw lead. In both types of lead, shore and flaw, new ice formation will be considerably impeded or even prevented if the offshore winds are strong. On most occasions, however, new or later stages of ice forms in the leads and when winds become onshore the refrozen lead closes up and the younger ice is completely deformed. For this reason, the flaw and shore leads are usually marked by tortuous ice conditions, especially when onshore winds prevail.

Clearance
6.10

1   From a given area in summer, the clearance of ice may occur in two different ways. The first, applicable to drift ice only, is the direct removal of the ice by wind or current. The second method is by melting *in situ* which in its turn is achieved in several ways.

2   Where the ice is well broken (open ice or lesser concentrations) wind again plays a part in that wave action will cause a considerable amount of melting even if the sea temperature is only a little above the freezing point.

Where drift ice is not well broken or where there is fast ice, the melting process is dependent on incoming radiation.

3   During the winter ice becomes covered with snow to a depth of approximately 30–60 cm. When this snow cover persists, almost 90% of the incoming radiation is reflected back to space. Eventually, however, the snow begins to melt as air temperatures rise above 0°C in early summer and the resulting fresh water forms puddles on the surface. These puddles now absorb about 60% of the incoming radiation and rapidly warm up, steadily enlarging as they melt the surrounding snow and, later, ice.

4   Eventually the fresh water runs off or through the ice floe and, where the concentration of ice is high, it will settle between the floes and the underlying sea water. At this stage the temperature of the sea water will still be below 0°C so that the fresh water freezes on to the under-surface of the ice, thus temporarily reducing the melting rate.

5   Meanwhile as the temperature within the ice rises, the ice becomes riddled with brine pockets, as described earlier. It is considerably weakened and offers little resistance to the decaying action of wind and waves. At this stage the fast ice breaks into drift ice and eventually the ice floes, when they reach an advanced state of decay, break into small pieces called brash ice (photograph 6.10), the last stage before melting is complete.

6   Wind, waves and rising temperatures combine to clear the ice from areas which are affected by first-year ice. In other areas, mainly within the Arctic Ocean, the summer melting probably accounts for a reduction in ice floe thickness of about 1 m.

7   The break-up of fast ice by puddling seems to be limited to the Arctic. It has not been observed in the Antarctic where the fast ice is usually broken up by the swell of the surrounding storm-ridden ocean,

Brash ice, partly covered with snow (6.10)

(Photograph - British Antarctic Survey)

particularly after the drift ice has been removed by the offshore winds which prevail on Antarctic coasts. In addition, diatoms in the lower layers of the fast ice may, because of their dark colour, absorb solar radiation passing through any snow-free ice, leading to weakening and melting from the lower surface.

Movement

6.11

1   **General information.** Drift ice moves under the influence of wind and current; fast ice stays immobile.

The wind stress on drift ice causes the floes to move in an approximately downwind direction. Coriolis force (5.7) causes the floes to deviate to the right of the surface wind direction in the N hemisphere and to the left in the S hemisphere, so that their direction of movement, due to wind drift, can be considered parallel to the isobars.

2   The rate of movement, due to wind, varies not only with the wind speed, but also with the concentration of drift ice and the extent of ridging. In very open ice (1/10 to 3/10 cover) there is much more freedom to respond to the wind than in close ice (7/10 to 8/10) where free space is very limited. The extent of ridging is often expressed in tenths of the total area. The ratio of ice movement to the geostrophic wind speed producing it is known as the "wind drift factor". The table below gives approximate values of wind drift factor for certain concentrations and extents of ridging.

Extent of Ridging (in tenths)	Concentration of ice		
	2/10	5/10	8/10
	Very Open Ice	Open Ice	Close Ice
0	1/240	1/350	1/480
3	1/55	1/80	1/140
6	1/30	1/41	1/70
More than 6	1/27	1/39	1/63

Table of Wind Drift Factors

3   The total movement of drift ice is the resultant of wind drift component and current component. As regards the latter, since the ice is immersed in the sea it will move at the full current rate except in narrow channels where it may form an ice jam. When the wind blows in the same direction as the current, the latter will run at an increased rate and therefore movement, under these conditions, due to wind and current, may be considerable. This is particularly so in the Greenland Sea and to a lesser extent in the Barents Sea and off Labrador.

4   Another effect of the wind is that when it blows from the open sea onto the drift ice, it compacts the floes into higher concentrations along the ice edge which now becomes well-defined. Conversely, an "off-ice" wind moves the floes out into the open sea at varying

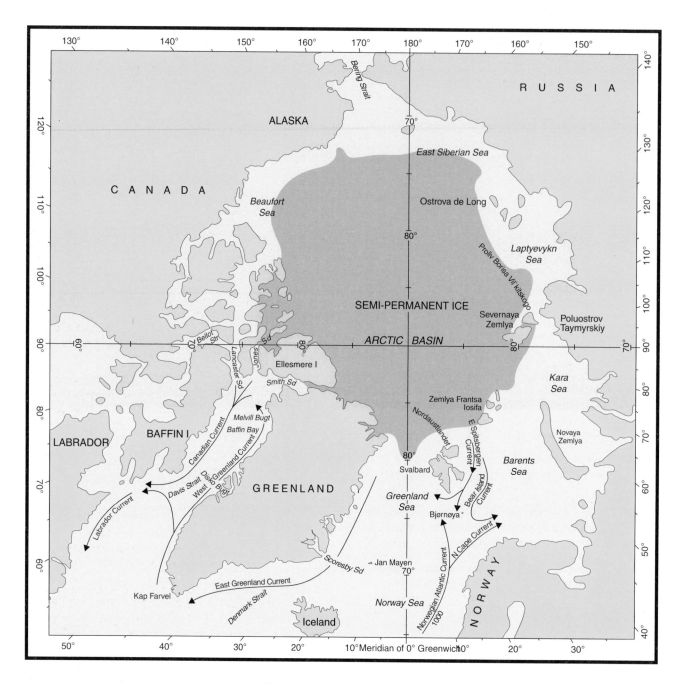

Movement of Arctic Ice (6.11)

rates, dependent on their size, roughness and age, resulting in a diffuse ice edge.

5 **In the Arctic Ocean** the main flow of ice occurs across the pole from the region of the East Siberian Sea towards the Greenland Sea (diagram 6.11). On the Eurasian side of this transpolar stream ice moves under the influence of the counter-clockwise current circulations within the seas of that area, and on the North American side it drifts in a clockwise direction under the influence of the currents of the Beaufort Sea.

6 The bulk of the ice is carried out of the polar basin by the East Greenland Current. Some passes into Baffin Bay through Smith Sound and also through Lancaster and Jones Sounds. Ice formed off the Siberian coast takes from 3 to 5 years to drift across the polar basin and down to the coast of Greenland. Ice of this age, therefore, becomes pressed and hummocked to a degree unknown in ice formed in lower latitudes. The warmth of the Arctic summers also has its effect and the result is worn down, more or less level, floes of great thickness, known as 'polar cap ice'.

1   **In Antarctic waters** there is a N tendency in the drift of ice: it therefore travels W and NW in the zone of E winds near the continent, and into and around Weddell Sea, with a clockwise motion, before gathering in a belt at the meeting of the SE and NW winds in the vicinity of the 60th parallel.

2   In lower latitudes the ice comes under the influence of the W winds and Southern Ocean current. In the Antarctic it is unusual for sea ice to be more than one or two years old, though in some places, particularly in the drift from the Weddell Sea, multi-year ice may be encountered.

The outstanding difference between Arctic and Antarctic sea ice, apparent to the mariner, is the softer texture of the latter due to the greater coverage of new and first year ice.

Limits of drift ice
6.12

1   In the Arctic the months of greatest extent are usually March or April, and of least extent, August or September; in the Antarctic they are September or October, and February or March respectively.

Considerable year-to-year variations in the limits of the ice occur due to temporary changes in the direction and speed of currents and prevailing winds, and to the occurrence of abnormally warm or cold seasons in high latitudes. Detailed information on ice conditions in the several parts of the world affected is given in the appropriate volume of Sailing Directions.

2   The procedure for obtaining ice information, including up-to-date reports, forecasts and developments, is given in *Admiralty List of Radio Signals Volume 3.*

Ice of land origin

General information

Polar comparisons
6.13

1   Due to the physical dissimilarities of the Arctic and Antarctic regions their climates and ice regimes differ greatly. The Arctic region contains a basin about 3000 m deep which is covered by a thin shell of ice about 4 m thick. The Antarctic, similar in extent, is a continent covered by an ice cap which is up to 3000 m thick.

2   The annual mean temperature at the South Pole is −49°C (the lowest temperature yet recorded in Antarctica is −88·3°C), whereas at the North Pole the annual mean temperature is estimated to be −20°C (the lowest temperature yet recorded in the Arctic is only a little below −50°C).

3   The ice cap covering the Antarctic continent accounts for more than 90% of the Earth's permanent ice. The ice constituting the ice cap is constantly moving outward towards the coasts where many thousands of icebergs are calved each year from glaciers and ice shelves which reach out over the sea. As a consequence large numbers of icebergs are to be found in a wide belt which completely surrounds the continent.

4   In contrast, the icebergs of the Arctic region are almost entirely confined to the sea areas off the E and W coasts of Greenland and off the E seaboard of Canada. The Arctic Ocean remains almost completely covered by drift ice throughout the year, whereas the greater part of the drift ice surrounding Antarctica melts each summer.

Description of icebergs
6.14

1   Icebergs (photographs 6.19 and 6.21) are large masses of floating ice derived from floating glacier tongues or from ice shelves. The density of iceberg ice varies with the amount of imprisoned air and the mean value has not been exactly determined, but it is assumed to be about $0·900 g/cm^3$ as compared with $0·916 g/cm^3$ for pure fresh water ice, that is approximately 9/10 of the volume of an iceberg is submerged. The depth of an iceberg under water, compared with its height above the water varies with different types of icebergs.

2   Icebergs diminish in size in three different ways; by calving, when a piece breaks off, by melting or by erosion.

An iceberg is so balanced that calving, or merely melting of the under-surface, will disturb its equilibrium, so that it may float at a different angle or it may capsize. When large sections are calved, they may fall into the water and bob up to the surface again with great force, often a considerable distance away. Vessels and boats should therefore keep well clear of icebergs that show signs of disintegrating.

3   In warm water an iceberg melts mainly from below and calves frequently.

Erosion is caused by wind and rain.

Cautions.

(1) Icebergs may possess underwater spurs and ledges at a considerable distance from the visible portions, and should be given a wide berth at all times.

(2) Where the sea floor is uneven or jagged, icebergs may be driven by wind or current against pinnacle rocks. It should not therefore be assumed from their appearance that when aground they are necessarily surrounded by deep water.

Arctic icebergs

Origins and movements
6.15

1   In the Arctic, icebergs originate mainly in the glaciers of the Greenland ice cap which contains approximately 90% of the land ice of the N hemisphere. Large numbers produced from the E coast glaciers, particularly in the region of Scoresby Sund, are carried S in the East Greenland current (diagram 6.11).

2   Most of those surviving this journey drift round Kap Farvel and melt in the Davis Strait, but some follow S or SE tracks from Kap Farvel, particularly in the winter half of the year, so that the maximum limit of icebergs (occurring in April in this region) lies over 400 miles SE of Kap Farvel.

3 However, a much larger crop of icebergs is derived from the glaciers which terminate in Baffin Bay. It has been estimated that more than 40 000 icebergs may be present in Baffin Bay at any one time: by far the greatest number being located close in to the Greenland coast between Disko Bugt and Melville Bugt where most of the major parent glaciers are situated.

4 Some of this vast number of icebergs become grounded in the vicinity of their birthplace where they slowly decay; others drift out into the open waters (in summer) of Baffin Bay and steadily decay there, but a significant proportion each year is carried by the predominant current pattern in an anti-clockwise direction around the head of Baffin Bay. Of these some ground in Melville Bugt and along the E coast of Baffin Island and there slowly decay. The remainder slowly drift S with the Canadian and Labrador currents, their numbers continually decreasing by grounding, or, in summer, melting in the open sea.

5 The number of icebergs passing S of the 48th parallel in the vicinity of the Grand Banks of Newfoundland varies considerably from year to year. Between 1946 and 1970 the number of icebergs sighted S of 48°N in that area varied from 1 in 1958 to 931 in 1957, and averaged 213 per year: the greatest number were usually sighted in April, May and June; none were sighted between September and January.

6 Little is known about the production of icebergs in European and Asiatic longitudes. With the exception of small glaciers in Ostrova De Long, it is probable not a single iceberg is produced along the North Siberian coast E of Proliv Borisa Vil'kitskogo. Severnaya Zemlya probably produces more icebergs than Svalbard or Zemlya Frantsa Iosifa (Franz Josef Land): icebergs from its E coast are carried by the current S to Proliv Borisa Vil'kitskogo and down the E side of Poluostrov Taymyrskiy.

7 The small icebergs typical of Zemlya Frantsa Iosifa and Svalbard which do not reach a height of more than about 15 m are probably not carried far by the weak currents of this region, though some may enter the East Greenland current. Svalbard icebergs, probably those from the E coast of Nordaustlandet, also drift SW in the East Spitsbergen and Bjørnøya (Bear Island) currents and are usually found in small numbers in the vicinity of Bjørnøya from May to October. The N half of Novaya Zemlya produces some icebergs, mainly small.

Characteristics
6.16

1 In the Arctic, the irregular glacier iceberg of varying shape constitutes the largest class. The height of this iceberg varies greatly and frequently reaches 70 m, occasionally this is exceeded and one of 167 m has been measured. These figures refer to the height soon after calving, but the height quickly decreases.

2 The largest iceberg so far measured S of Newfoundland was 80 m high, and the longest 517 m. Glacier icebergs exceeding 1 km have been seen farther N.

The following table has been derived from actual measurements of glacier icebergs S of Newfoundland by the International Ice Patrol:

Type of Iceberg	Proportion Exposed:Submerged
Blocky	1:5
Rounded	1:4
"Picturesque" Greenland	1:3
Pinnacled and ridged	1:2
Last stages, horned and winged	1:1

3 An entirely different form of iceberg is the blocky iceberg, flat-topped and precipitous-sided, which is the nearest counterpart in the Arctic to the great tabular icebergs of the Antarctic (6.19). These icebergs may originate either from a large glacier tongue or from an ice shelf. If of the latter origin, they are true tabular icebergs, but in either case they are tabular in form. Blocky icebergs encountered S of Newfoundland usually have submerged five times the amount exposed.

4 The colour of Arctic icebergs is an opaque flat white, with soft hues of green or blue. Many show veins of soil or debris; others have yellowish or brown stains in places, due probably to diatoms. Much air is imprisoned in ice in the form of bubbles permeating its whole structure. The white appearance is caused by surface weathering to a depth of 5 to 50 cm or more and also to the effect of the sun's rays, which release innumerable air bubbles.

Ice islands
6.17

1 Ice island (photograph 6.17) is a name popularly used to describe a rare form of tabular iceberg found in the Arctic. Ice islands originate by breaking off from ice shelves, which are found principally in North Ellesmere Island and North Greenland.

2 They are usually characterised by a regularly undulating surface which gives a ribbed appearance from the air, and stand about 5 m out of the water. They have a total thickness of about 30 to 50 m, and may exceed 150 square miles in area: in contrast, the tabular icebergs of the Antarctic commonly stand about 30 m out of the water, having a total thickness of about 200 m.

3 The larger ice islands have hitherto been found only in the Arctic Ocean where they drift with the sea ice at an average rate of from 1 to 3 miles per day. The best known, named T3 or Fletcher's Ice Island, was sighted in 1947 and has been occupied by United States scientific parties on several occasions for periods of up to 2 years. Since it was first discovered, and probably for many years previously, T3 has been drifting in a clockwise direction in the Beaufort Sea current system.

4 Small ice islands have been sighted in the waters of the islands of the Canadian Arctic and off Greenland, where they have been carried out of the Arctic Ocean by wind and current. In addition, tabular

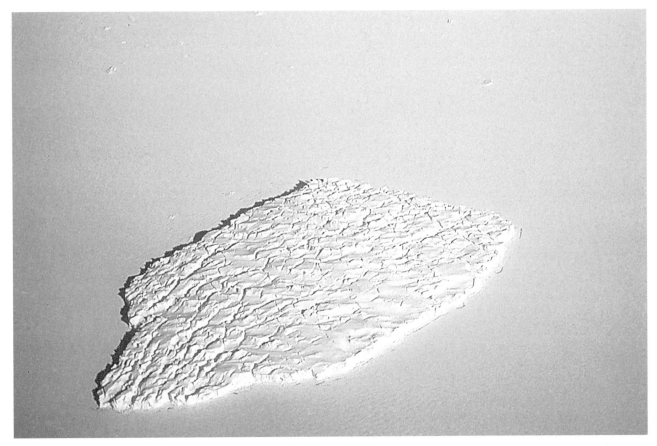

Ice island (6.17)

(Photograph - British Antarctic Survey)

icebergs, some of which may well be small ice islands, have been reported in the vicinity of Svalbard and in waters N of Russia.

Antarctic icebergs

Origin and form
6.18

1   The breaking away of ice from the Antarctic continent takes place on a scale quite unknown in the Arctic, so that vast numbers of icebergs are found in the adjacent waters. Icebergs are formed by the calving of masses of ice from ice shelves or tongues, from a glacier face, or from accumulations of ice on land near the coast, fed by the flow from two or more glaciers.

2   Antarctic icebergs are of several distinctive forms. The following descriptions should be regarded as covering only those terms which are likely to be of use to the mariner.

Tabular icebergs
6.19

1   This is the most common form (photograph 6.19) and is the typical iceberg of the Antarctic, to which there is no exact parallel in the Arctic. These icebergs are largely, but not all, derived from ice shelves and show a characteristic horizontal banding.

2   Tabular icebergs are flat-topped and rectangular in shape, with a peculiar white colour and lustre, as if made from plaster of Paris, due to their relatively large air content. They may be of great size, larger than any other type of iceberg found in either of the polar regions. Such icebergs, exceeding 500 m in length, occur in hundreds.

3   Some have been measured up to 20 or 30 miles in length, while icebergs of more than twice this length have been reported. The largest iceberg authentically reported is one about 90 miles long, observed by the whaler *Odd I* on 7th January 1927, about 50 miles NE of Clarence Island, South Shetland Islands. This great tabular iceberg was about 35 m high. The majority seen on Scott's last expedition varied in height from 10 to 35 m, the highest measured being 42 m.

4   The number of icebergs set free varies in different years or periods of years. There appears to have been an unusual break-up of ice shelf in the Weddell Sea region during the years 1927–1933, when the number and size of the tabular icebergs in that region was exceptional. The giant iceberg above described was one of these. Heights up to 50 or 60 m were measured during this period. There were also significant break-ups in the S Weddell region in the 1980s and in the Larson ice shelf in the 1990s.

Glacier icebergs
6.20

1   These are usually of an opaque flat white colour, with soft hues of green or blue, but appear dazzling white under certain conditions of light. The whiteness is caused by surface weathering to a depth of a few cm or more, and also by the effect of the sun's rays which release innumerable air bubbles.

2   They usually have a more irregular surface than the tabular icebergs and are often broken up by crevasses into sharp knife-edged ridges, known as seracs. They

Tabular iceberg (6.19)

(Photograph – British Antarctic Survey)

Weathered iceberg (6.21)

(Photograph – British Antarctic Survey)

frequently show silt bands of sand and debris. Glacier icebergs are of higher density than the tabular ones and so are more resistant to weathering.

Weathered icebergs
6.21

1   This name is given to any iceberg in an advanced state of disintegration (photograph 6.21). Large variations occur. The length of life of an iceberg is determined partly by the time spent on the ice before it emerges into the open sea.

Thereafter its period of survival is determined largely by the rapidity of its transport to lower latitudes. If stranded, an iceberg may occasionally survive as long as 3 years or more, but normally an iceberg stranded through one winter has disintegrated sufficiently to clear the shoal as soon as the sea ice has broken out in the following spring.

2   Melting of the underwater surface is a continuous process and this, aided by the mechanical action of the sea, produces caves or spurs near the waterline. This finally leads to the calving of a portion of the iceberg or to a change in its equilibrium, whereby tilting or even complete capsizing may occur, thus presenting new surfaces to the sea and the weather.

3   The presence of crevasses, earth particles or rock debris greatly enhances the process of melting or evaporation and produces planes of weakness, along which further calving occurs. In grounding, a much crevassed iceberg may be wrecked.

Other icebergs, in passing over a shoal, may develop strain cracks, which later accelerate their weathering.

Capsized icebergs
6.22

1   The underwater section of most icebergs is smooth and rounded, often with well defined blue stripes layered into the natural opaque colouration. A unique form of capsized iceberg of a dark colour, called black and white iceberg, has been observed N and E of the Weddell Sea. They are of two kinds, which it is difficult to distinguish at a distance: morainic, in which the dark portion is black and opaque, containing mud and stones; and bottle-green, in which the dark part is of a deep green colour and translucent, mud and stones appearing to be absent.

2   In both kinds the demarcation of the white and dark parts is a clear-cut plane, and the dark portion is invariably smoothly rounded by water action. Such icebergs have frequently been mistaken for rocks; before reporting a suspected above-water rock a close examination should be made, preferably with soundings round it, to ensure that it is not an iceberg.

Summary of ice forms				
Type of Ice	Form of Ice	Thickness (cm)	Ice Photograph Number	Remarks (for further information see Ice Glossary)
New ice	Frazil ice			Ice spicules
	Grease ice	≤2·5	6.4.1	Soupy layer on sea surface giving matt appearance
	Slush			Saturated snow on ice surfaces, or viscous floating mass in water after a snowfall
	Shuga		6.4.2	Spongy white ice lumps
Nilas	Dark & light nilas	≤10	6.4.4	Thin elastic crust of ice with matt surface
	Ice rind	≤5	6.43	Brittle shiny crust of ice
These types of ice are relatively soft and pliable and will not normally damage the hull of modern steel vessels except small craft. However they may block cooling water intakes.				
Young ice	Grey ice	10–15		Less elastic than nilas and breaks on swell. Usually rafts under pressure. Dark grey or light grey, becoming whiter with age
	Grey-white ice	15–30		More likely to ridge than to raft. Still containing some salt and relatively soft, but growing thicker and gradually becoming harder
First-year ice	Thin	30–70		Generally white or milky-white in colour
	Medium	70–120		Gradually changes colour as it becomes older and acquires a greenish tint after about 1 year depending on temperatures
	Thick	≥120		
Old ice	Second-year ice	≥250		Thicker than first-year ice so stands higher out of the water. Most features smoother than first-year ice. Regular pattern of small puddles produced by summer melting
	Multi-year ice	≥300		Hummocks even smoother than second–year ice. Almost salt-free. Large inter-connecting regular puddles produced by summer melting
All old ice has a green or greenish tint changing to blue-green, or intense blue with age as in the case of bare multi-year ice. The ice navigator should beware of ice of this colour. It is extremely hard and very dangerous to shipping, including ice breakers.				

Summary of ice forms *(continued)*				
Type of Ice	Form of Ice	Thickness (cm)	Ice Photograph Number	Remarks (for further information see Ice Glossary)
Floating ice	Pancake ice		6.4.5	Circular pieces of floating ice 30 cm to 3 m in diameter with raised rims. Formed from grease ice, slush, shuga, nilas or ice rind
	Ice cake		6.4.6	Flat piece of floating ice less than 20 m across
	Floe		6.4.6	Flat piece of floating ice 20 m or more across
	Floeberg	≤10		Massive piece of sea ice composed of a hummock or group of hummocks frozen together, separated from ice surroundings and protruding up to 5 m above sea level
	Floebit			Similar to floeberg but smaller, normally not more than 10 m across
	Ice Breccia			Ice at different stages of development frozen together
	Brash ice		6.10	Accumulations of floating ice made up of fragments not more than 2 m across
Ice of land origin	Iceberg	>500	6.19, 6.21, 6.4.2	Opaque white or flat white on the surface, green-blue or intense blue where bare. Virtually as hard as multi-year ice
	Bergy bit	100–500	6.4.2, 6.41.1	
	Growler	≤100	6.4.2, 6.41.2	

Navigation in ice

Passage planning

Ice and the navigator
6.23

1   Sea ice has posed a problem to the navigator since antiquity. During a voyage from the Mediterranean to England and Norway, sometime between 350 BC and 300 BC, Pytheas of Massalia sighted a strange substance which he described as, neither land nor air nor water, floating upon and covering the northern sea over which the summer Sun barely set. Pytheas named this lonely region Thule, hence Ultima Thule, farthest north or land's end.

2   Ice is of direct concern to the navigator because it restricts and sometimes controls his movements; it affects his dead reckoning by forcing frequent changes in course and speed; it affects piloting by altering the appearance or obliterating the features of landmarks; it hinders the establishment and maintenance of aids to navigation; it affects the use of electronic equipment by affecting the propagations of radio waves; it produces changes in surface features and in radar returns from these features; it affects celestial navigation by altering the refraction and obscuring the horizon and celestial bodies either directly or by the weather it influences, and it affects the charts by introducing several plotting problems.

3   Because of his direct concern with ice, the prospective polar navigator must acquaint him/herself with its nature and extent in the area it is expected to navigate. In addition to the following paragraphs, books, articles, and reports of previous polar operations and expeditions will help acquaint the polar navigator with the unique conditions at the ends of the earth.

4   As marine navigation pushes back the frontiers, transit in ice regimes will continue to be a challenge that must be met with skill, knowledge and innovation. The skills necessary to ensure a safe and efficient ice transit take years to develop over numerous encounters with challenging ice conditions. Specialists who possess those skills and knowledge will continue to be required to meet the needs of commercial shipping that by necessity or choice must transit ice-covered waters.

Essential reading
6.24

1   Operators and Management Companies of all vessels intending to operate in polar ice-covered waters should be familiar with the following publications:

IMO Guide-lines For Ships Operating In Arctic and Antarctic Ice-Covered Waters;
Admiralty Manual of Seamanship, Volume III;
Manual of Ice Seamanship, published by the U.S. Defense Mapping Agency;
Ice Seamanship and Handling Ships in Ice, published by the Nautical Institute;
Navigating in Ice, Section 1 STCW Training DVD from Videotel International.

IMO guidelines for ships operating in Arctic ice-covered waters
6.25

1   It has been recognised since the earliest incursion by mariners into ice covered waters that specialized skills are required to transit these regions safely and effectively. As stated by Captain William Scoresby in 1820:

"...the navigation of the polar seas, which is peculiar, requires in a particular manner, an

extensive knowledge of the nature, properties and usual motions of the ice, and it can only be performed to the best advantage by those who have long experience with working a ship in icy conditions."

2   The IMO have recognised that, despite tremendous advances in technology, it remains necessary for mariners to have the specific skills and knowledge necessary for safe transit of ice regimes, and has accordingly issued guidelines for ships (IMO MSC/Circ.1056/MEPC/Circ.399 dated 23 December 2002).

3   These guidelines recommend that at least one qualified Ice Navigator is carried in ships operating in Arctic ice-covered waters, and that all of the ship's officers and crew are made familiar with cold weather survival.

4   **Ice Navigators.** An Ice Navigator should have documentary evidence of having satisfactorily completed an approved training programme in ice navigation. The training programme should provide knowledge, understanding and proficiency required for operating a ship in Arctic ice-covered waters, including:

Recognition of ice formation and characteristics.
Ice indications.
Ice manoeuvring.
Use of ice forecasts, atlases and codes.
Hull stress caused by ice.
Ice escort operations.
Ice-breaking operations.
The effect of ice accretion on vessel stability.

5   Such training programmes are currently known to be offered in Russia, Canada, Finland, Denmark, Holland and Argentina.

6   As an example, the Canadian course covers the following subject matter in its syllabus:

Ice physics, including ice types and forms with particular attention to the more dangerous glacial and multi-year ice that may be encountered.
Visual interpretation of the conditions all around the vessel and the signs in the vicinity, as well as the interpretation of the various ice imagery, charts and reports that are available.

7   The interaction of weather conditions, currents and ice, along with the prevailing conditions that should be expected at particular periods of the transit;
How to combine all the above knowledge with the more traditional aspects of passage planning in order to develop the most effective and safe routeing under, at times, very dynamic conditions.

8   Full knowledge of the limitations of vessels based on ice class, due to hull strengthening, power, manoeuvrability, that are necessary to approach and enter polar ice regimes safely and successfully and direct a vessel through even the most hostile ice regimes.

9   The skills necessary to avoid besetment, the methods of freeing a beset vessel and handling a vessel damaged by besetment.
Handling operations with icebreaker assistance, including communications requirements.

10   **Ice advisors.** It has become practice for an Ice Navigator to be placed on board a vessel in a supernumerary capacity as an ice advisor, able to provide the latest ice information prior to transits of ice-covered waters, to recommended both strategic and tactical routeing and to advise the vessel's management team on cold weather precautions.

COMNAP guidelines for ships operating in Antarctic waters
6.26

1   COMNAP (The Council of Managers for National Antarctic Programmes), has, under ATCM XXVII (2004), adopted Decision 4 which provides guidelines for ships operating in Antarctic ice-covered waters, and passed it to IMO for consideration. Decision 4 is, in essence, a modified version of the IMO guidelines for ships in Arctic waters, to expand the provisions to cover Antarctic waters, noting that the environment differs:

"Whilst Arctic and Antarctic waters have a number of similarities, there are also significant differences. The Arctic is an ocean surrounded by continents, while the Antarctic is a continent surrounded by water. The Antarctic sea ice retreats significantly during the summer season or is dispersed by permanent gyres in the two major seas of the Antarctic: the Weddell and the Ross. Thus there is relatively little multi-year ice in the Antarctic. Conversely, Arctic sea ice survives many summer seasons and there is a significant amount of multi-year ice."

Guidelines
6.27

1   Do not enter ice if a longer but ice-free route is available. Using all ice information and weather forecasts obtained, choose a track where the least ice-pressure is to be expected, taking into account the following:

2   The position of the drift ice edge.
The prevailing wind direction and strength.
Areas where the least ice pressure can be expected, especially at the beginning and end of the season.
The ice concentration.
Where areas of new ice exist.
Where area of rotten ice are more likely to be encountered.

3   Avoid areas of pressure ice with ridging and hummocking.
Always highlight areas of shoal water, taking account of the vessels ice navigation draught.
Plot all waypoints given by shore authorities and icebreaker navigators.
The validity of local traffic separation schemes and zones.
The experience of the Master, Ice Pilot and ice navigation team.

Conduct of Navigation

The polar environment
6.28

1   In high latitudes, directions change fast with movement of the observer. Near the poles, meridians converge, and excessive longitudinal curvature renders the meridians and parallels impracticable for use as navigational references. All time zones meet at the poles, and local time has little significance. Sunrise and sunset, night and day, as they are known in the temperate regions, are quite different in polar regions.

2   At the poles the sun rises and sets once a year, slowly spiralling for three months to a maximum altitude of 23°27′ and then decreasing in altitude until it sets again three months later. The Moon rises once each month and provides illumination when full, though sometimes the aurora gives even more light; and the planets rise and set once each sidereal period, 12 years for Jupiter, 30 years for Saturn.

3   Fog is most frequent when the water is partly clear of ice. Low cloud ceilings are prevalent. White-outs occur from time to time, when daylight is diffused by multiple reflection between a snow surface and an overcast sky, so that contrasts vanish and neither the horizon nor surface features can be distinguished. All these conditions, combined with the ice itself, add to the difficulties of navigation.

Polar Charts
6.29

1   Polar charts used to be based largely on aerial photography. They are now based largely on satellite imagery which may be without proper ground control, except in a relatively few places where modern surveys are available, e.g. in the approaches to bases and similar frequented localities. Even then, the conditions under which these surveys have been carried out are such that their accuracy is unlikely to be of the same standard as that of surveys conducted at lower latitudes.

2   The geographical positions of features may therefore be unreliable and, even when they are correctly placed relative to adjacent features, considerable errors may accumulate when they are separated by appreciable distances. In general, soundings, topography and all other navigational information are sparse in most polar regions.

3   Visual and radar bearings of objects which are at a considerable distance may, at high latitudes, require to be treated as great circles. If used on a Mercator chart, bearings should be corrected for half-convergency in the same way as radio bearings. See *Admiralty List of Radio Signals Volume 2*.

4   Natural landmarks are plentiful in some areas, but their usefulness is restricted by difficulty in identifying them, or locating them on the chart. Along coasts, many points and inlets bear a marked resemblance to each other. The appearance of a coast is often very different when its features are masked by a heavy covering of snow or ice.

Compasses
6.30

1   **Gyro compasses** lose all horizontal directive force as the poles are approached and unusable N or S of 85° of latitude. They are generally reliable up to 75° but thereafter should be checked by the azimuths of celestial bodies at frequent intervals (approximately every 4 hours and more frequently in higher latitudes).

2   **Magnetic compasses** are of little value for navigation near the magnetic poles. Large diurnal changes in variation, sometimes as much as 10°, attributed to the continual motion of the poles, have been reported.

   In other parts of the polar regions, however, the magnetic compass can be used, provided that the vessel has recently been swung, the compass adjusted in low latitudes, and the process repeated when approaching higher latitudes.

3   **Compass errors.** Frequent comparisons of magnetic and gyro compasses should be made and logged when azimuth checks are obtained.

Echo sounders
6.31

1   The echo sounder should be run continuously to detect signs of approaching shoal water, though in many parts of the polar regions depths change too abruptly to enable the mariner to rely solely on the sounder for warning.

   In some better surveyed areas, the depths may give an indication of the vessel's position, or of the drift of the ice, and in these areas vessels should make use of all enforced stops to obtain a sounding.

2   When working in drift ice, the echo sounder trace may be lost due to ice under the ship or hull noises. If necessary, the vessel should be slowed to obtain a sounding.

Forward-looking sonar
6.32

1   Forward-looking sonar detects obstacles ahead of the ship and provides the range, bearing and depth information in sufficient time for them to be avoided and navigate safely in shallow water. Following recent cruise ship groundings and a sinking in the Antarctic, this equipment is becoming more widely fitted in commercial vessels.

   A typical system will provide a three dimensional, high resolution 90° image, updating the display every 1–2 seconds with each transmission.

Celestial navigation
6.33

1   The mariner cannot rely on obtaining accurate celestial observations. For much of the navigational season clouds hide the sun, and long days and short nights in summer preclude the use of stars for observations. In summer when, apart from the moon at times, only the sun can be used for observations, transferred position lines must be used, and as accurate dead reckoning in ice is impossible, the accuracy of the resulting positions must always be questioned.

2   The best positions are usually obtained from star observations during twilight. As the latitude increases twilights lengthen, but with this increase come longer periods when the sun is just below the horizon and the stars have not yet appeared.

   In polar regions the only celestial body available for observations may not exceed the altitude of 10° for several weeks on end, so that, contrary to the usual practice, observations at low altitudes must be accepted.

3   **Taking sights when navigating in ice.** Sights must be taken with great care as, when navigating in ice, the true horizon may be hard to define. It is normal in polar regions for the atmosphere to differ considerably from the standard, particularly near the sea surface. This affects both refraction and dip. Refraction variations of 2° or more are not uncommon and an extreme value of 5° has been reported.

4   The sun has been observed to rise as much as ten days earlier than it should. A wise precaution is to apply corrections for air temperature and atmospheric

pressure, particularly for altitudes of less than 5°. Because of the low temperature, the refraction correction for sextant altitudes may require to be taken from the appropriate table in *The Nautical Almanac*.

5   When attempting to obtain vertical sextant angles of celestial bodies with ice on the horizon, the angle so obtained should be corrected by subtracting the estimated height of the ice on the horizon from the height of eye of the observer: the maximum error this may cause is 4′. A bubble sextant, or a sextant used with an artificial horizon set up on the ice, will, however, be found to give better results.

6   Mariners are reminded that refraction elevates both the celestial body and the visible horizon, so that the error due to abnormal refraction is minimised if the visible horizon is used for observations. The position of a large tabular iceberg or an ice shelf on the relevant section of the horizon may require the navigator to possess an ability to obtain a position line by back angle sights.

7   Most celestial observations in polar regions produce satisfactory results, but in high latitudes the navigator should be on the alert for abnormal conditions.

Radio aids, electronic position-fixing systems and GNSS
6.34

1   Radar will be found to be a most valuable instrument for safe navigation if used judiciously. However it should not be relied upon so completely that the rules of good seamanship are relaxed.

Global Navigation Satellite Systems (GNSS) (11.23) such as GPS, GLONASS and GALILEO when available, are as satisfactory in polar regions as in other parts of the world.

Dead reckoning
6.35

1   Whilst GPS, DGPS and GLONASS systems have much reduced the need, a careful reckoning should be kept of all alterations of course and speed together with the times at which they were made, so that a large scale plot of the vessel's track can be maintained. The lack of information on tides and other factors usually prevents the most accurate dead reckoning from giving the exact position of the vessel, but a carefully kept reckoning will considerably help to avoid errors.

2   Icebergs, which may be regarded as effectively stationary for the period of the navigational plot, can be of great value as temporary marks. For example, at the time of obtaining a celestial position, if the position of a conspicuous iceberg ahead on the intended line of advance is plotted, it can then be used as a navigational mark until subsequent icebergs can be plotted and used in a similar fashion.

Icebergs may also mark shoals.

3   In keeping the reckoning, the fundamental components of course and speed change continually and make accurate calculation difficult. Even if a gyro compass and course recorder are fitted, speed relative to the ice is required, and this can rarely be measured continuously with accuracy.

4   To check the resultant of the vessel's course and speed through the ice, and the drift of the ice, every opportunity should be taken to obtain fixes or observed positions. The speed at any moment can be measured by timing the passage of an ice floe down a known length of the ship's side, in a similar manner to a Dutchman's log. The speed through the ice should be obtained as frequently as practicable, and at least twice an hour.

Material preparations for operations in ice

General information
6.36

1   Operations in ice-prone regions necessarily require considerable advanced planning and many more precautionary measures than those taken prior to a typical open ocean voyage.

Training
6.37

1   The ship's staff of a polar bound vessel should be thoroughly indoctrinated in the fundamentals of polar operations, utilising the best information sources available. The subjects should include, but not be limited to:

Training in ship handling in ice.
Polar navigation.
The effects of low temperatures on materials and equipment.
Damage control procedures.
Communications problems inherent in polar regions.
Ice observation and reporting procedures.
Polar survival.

Personal cold weather and survival equipment
6.38

1   Equipment necessary to meet the basic needs of the crew and to ensure the successful and safe completion of the polar voyage should not be overlooked. A minimum list of essential items should include polar clothing and footwear, protective sun-glasses, food, vitamins, medical supplies, fuel, storage batteries, anti-freeze, and survival kits containing sleeping bags, rations, firearms, ammunition, fishing gear, emergency medical supplies and a repair kit.

Vessel winterisation
6.39

1   The ship's staff should take early precautions to avoid damage to hull and machinery, and to minimise risk of commercial loss whilst in port by carrying out items on the following check-list, not necessarily fully comprehensive, with respect to operations in ice:

2   Ice-operations draught, trim and stability permitting, empty or slack off all wing and double bottom

water ballast and fresh tanks, and slack all fresh water tanks.

3   However, ensure that draughts, trim and stability are in accordance with ice classification, allowing for icing.

Ensure all the heating and air bubble tank systems are in working order.

Check bunker status, especially with respect to quantities of Diesel/Marine Gas Oil, taking into account the increased manoeuvring, and add cold temperature additives as required.

4   Ensure that the rudder and rudder angle indicators are in alignment.

All radars are fully operational and scanner heating arrangements functioning.

All searchlights are operational and availability of spare lamps.

Ensure functionability of main and spare Not–Under Command lights.

Bridge window heating and wiper/clear view screen/window wash heating systems fully functional.

5   Protect mooring equipment and ropes from icing; Test satisfactory operation of any superstructure heating arrangements.

Ensure all heating systems to deck machinery spaces are fully functional.

Drain external fire–main and deck line systems; Ensure all deck machinery is protected by low temperature grease and anti–freeze.

Ensure all life saving equipment will be available in freezing conditions, lifeboats fitted with working heaters, engines with anti–freeze, water tanks slack.

6   Ensure all ship's staff supplied with cold weather and survival equipment.

Consider additional requirements for abandoning ship in what may be consolidated pack ice.

Order salt, or proprietary products, for melting ice and sand for anti–slip.

Ensure sufficiency and availability of wooden mallets/mawls, snow shovels etc for ice removal; Consider employment of additional deck hands to permit relief systems in freezing conditions.

7   Ensure all rigging is set up correctly to withstand the shock of ice collisions.

Ensure availability of lower sea suctions, check heating/compressed air clearance systems and sea-water recirculation systems.

Ensure bunker tank heating systems fully functional.

Ensure all main/auxiliary/steering/thruster/cpp machinery space heating systems fully functional; Ensure status of cathodic protection, impressed current, is set for ice operations.

In port, never stop the hydraulic pumps for controllable pitch propellers.

Approaching ice

Readiness for ice
6.40

1   Experience has shown that vessels that are not ice-strengthened and with a speed in open water of about 12 kn often become firmly beset in light ice conditions, whereas adequately powered ice-strengthened vessels should be able to make progress through 6/10 to 7/10 first-year ice.

2   The engines and steering gear of any vessel intending to operate in ice must be reliable and capable of quick response to manoeuvring orders. The navigational and communications equipment must be equally reliable and particular attention should be paid to maintaining radar at peak performance.

3   Vessels operating in ice should be ballasted and trimmed so that the propeller is completely submerged and as deep as possible, but without excessive stern trim which reduces manoeuvrability. If the tips of the propeller are exposed above the surface or just under the surface, the risk of damage due to the propeller striking ice is greatly increased.

Indications of the proximity of icebergs
6.41

1   There are no infallible indications of the proximity of an iceberg. Complete reliance on radar can be dangerous. The only sure way is to see it.

2   **Visibility of icebergs.** Despite their size, icebergs can be very difficult to distinguish under certain circumstances, and the mariner should invariably navigate with caution in waters in which they may be expected.

In fog, with the sun shining, an iceberg appears as a luminous white mass, but with no sun it appears close aboard as a dark mass. The first sign may well be the sea breaking on its base.

3   On a clear night with no moon, icebergs may be sighted at a distance of 1 to 2 miles, appearing as black or white objects, but the vessel may, by then, be among the bergy bits (photograph 6.41.1) and growlers (photograph 6.41.2) are often found in the vicinity of an iceberg. On a clear night, therefore, lookouts and radar operators should be particularly alert, and there should be no hesitation in reducing speed if an iceberg is sighted without warning.

4   On moonlit nights icebergs are more easily seen provided the moon is behind the observer, particularly if it is high and full.

At night with a cloudy sky and intermittent moonlight, icebergs are more difficult to see and to keep in sight. Cumulus or cumulonimbus clouds at night can produce a false impression of icebergs.

5   **Likely signs.** The following signs are useful when they occur, but reliability cannot be placed on their occurrence. In the case of large Antarctic icebergs, the absence of sea in a fresh breeze indicates the presence of ice to windward if far from the land.

When icebergs calve, or ice otherwise cracks and falls into the sea, it produces a thunderous roar, and sounds like the distant discharge of guns.

6   The observation of growlers or smaller pieces of brash ice is an indication that an iceberg is in the vicinity, and probably to windward; an iceberg may be detected in reduced visibility in this way.

When proceeding at slow speed on a quiet night, the sound of breakers may be heard if an iceberg is near and should be constantly listened for.

7   **Unreliable signs.** Changes of air or sea temperature cannot be relied upon to indicate the vicinity of an iceberg. However, the sea temperature, if carefully monitored, will indicate when cold ice-bearing waters are entered.

Bergy bit, with very open ice (6.41.1)

(Photograph - British Antarctic Survey)

Growler, surrounded by grease ice and shuga (6.41.2)

(Photograph - British Antarctic Survey)

Echoes from a whistle or siren are unreliable because the shape of the iceberg may be such as to prevent any echo, and also because echoes are often obtained from fog banks.

8 Sonar has been used to locate icebergs, but the method is unreliable since the distribution of water temperature and salinity, particularly near the boundary of a current, may produce such excessive refraction as to prevent a sonar signal from reaching the vessel or iceberg.

Indications of drift ice
6.42

1 There are two reliable indications of the presence of drift ice; ice blink, and an abrupt smoothing of the sea.

Ice blink (photograph 6.42) has a characteristic light effect in the sky, which once seen, can never be mistaken. On clear days, with the sky mostly blue, ice blink appears as a luminous yellow haze on the horizon in the direction of the ice. It is brighter below, and shades off upward, its height depending on the proximity of the ice field. On days with overcast sky, or low clouds, the yellow colour is almost absent, and the ice blink appears as a whitish glare on the clouds.

2 Under certain conditions of sun and sky, both the yellowish and whitish glares may be seen simultaneously. It may sometimes be seen at night.

Ice blink is observed some time before the ice itself appears over the horizon. It is rarely, if ever, produced by icebergs, but is always distinct over consolidated and extensive pack ice.

In fog, white patches indicate the presence of ice at a short distance.

3 **Abrupt smoothing of the sea** and the gradual lessening of the ordinary ocean swell is a sure indication of drift ice to windward.

Isolated fragments of ice often point to the proximity of larger quantities.

There is frequently a thick band of fog over the edge of drift ice. In fog, white patches indicate the presence of ice at a short distance.

4 **Less reliable indications.**

Wildlife. In the Arctic, if far from land, the appearance of walruses, seals and birds may indicate the proximity of ice.

In the Antarctic, the Antarctic Petrel and Snow Petrel are said to indicate the proximity of ice, the former being found only within 400 miles of the ice edge, and the latter considerably closer to it.

5 Sea surface temperatures give little or no indication of the near vicinity of ice. When, however, the surface temperature falls to +1°C, and the vessel is not within one of the main cold currents, the ice edge should, for safety, be considered as not more than 150 miles distant, or 100 miles if there is a persistent wind blowing off the ice, since this will cause the ice temporarily to extend and become more open. A surface temperature of −0·5°C should generally be assumed to indicate that the nearest ice is not more than 50 miles away.

Lookout
6.43

1 When nearing the ice edge, an experienced lookout should be posted, with specific instructions to report all sightings, but especially those ahead of the vessel. At

Ice blink (6.42)

(Photograph - British Antarctic Survey)

night searchlights, preferably mounted forward of all upper works to prevent reflections, should be turned on and trimmed.

Radar
6.44

1 A radar data processing system which converts raw analogue radar signals into a digital format and which can display the resulting picture in real time on the screen of a PC is a very useful aid. The main advantage is that, due to higher resolution, the images are sharper with improved target discrimination. However, operators must be trained to obtain the maximum advantage from the clutter settings.

2 **When operating without icebreaker support.** Both the 10 cm (S-band) and 3 cm (X-band) radars should be in operation. It is recommended that the 10 cm radar is used for longer range detection, set on the 12 or 24 mile range scale, and the 3 cm radar is used for shorter range detection, set on the 3 or 6 mile range scale.

3 In very close, fast, or level ice, the 3 cm radar is the better set to use for finding and following leads in ice, due to its better target discrimination. The most forward scanner should preferably be utilised with this transceiver.

4 For detecting ice in open waters, the 10 cm radar has a greater capability than the 3 cm radar, which picks up too much sea clutter, particularly in the detection of ice of land origin, the ice edge and ice fields. Once in ice this radar is better for identification of other vessels and icebergs. The highest scanner should preferably be utilised with this transceiver.

5 **When operating with icebreaker support.** The ability to combine both 10 cm and 3 cm radar pictures on one screen with the 3 cm displaying the view ahead and the 10 cm displaying the view astern, is very beneficial. However, it is essential, when using electronic radar displays, to ensure that they are correctly stabilised on a fixed landmark, as buoys can drift or be confused with raised ice returns.

6 The following radar settings have been found to work well:

Vessel speed of advance	Radar	Pulse Length	Range scale	Centre/ Off-centre
8-13 kn	3 cm (X-band)	short	1·5 miles	Off-centre
	10 cm (S-band)	short	6 miles	Off-centre
>14 kn	3 cm (X-band)	short	3 miles	Off-centre
	10 cm (S-band)	short	12 miles	As required

Detection of ice by radar
6.45

1 Though an invaluable aid, the limitations of radar in detecting ice should always be borne in mind. Absence of an indication of ice on the radar screen does not necessarily mean that there is no dangerous ice in the vicinity. The strength of the echo received from an iceberg depends as much on the inclination of its reflecting surfaces as on its size and range.

2 Mariners navigating in the vicinity of forecast drift ice should maintain a continuous visual lookout in addition to a radar watch.

Mariners should also be aware of the limitations given below and that less than full operating efficiency of any radar will greatly reduce the chance of detecting ice.

The following operational parameters have been drawn from experience, however, abnormal weather conditions may substantially reduce detection ranges.

3 In a calm sea, all ice formations should be detected, from large icebergs, (photographs 6.19 and 6.21), at ranges of from 15 to 20 miles down to small bergy bits (photograph 6.41.1) at a range of possibly 2 miles. However, bergy bits and growlers, smoothed by weathering, weighing several tonnes, and protruding up to 3 m out of the water, are unlikely to be detected at a range greater than 2 miles. As warnings of the presence of ice are short, radars should be operated continuously in reduced visibility.

4 In any conditions other than flat calm, it is unsafe to rely solely on radar, especially when sea clutter extends beyond 1 mile, as no warning will be given of the presence of bergy bits and growlers that may be of a size capable of doing damage to a vessel, and drift ice, equally dangerous, becomes confused with sea clutter. On the other hand, in conditions where sea clutter is well marked, the cessation of such echoes may indicate the presence of pack ice.

5 Fields of concentrated hummocked ice should be detected in most sea conditions at a range of at least 3 miles.

Ridges show clearly, but shadow areas behind ridges are liable to be mistaken for leads or the closed tracks of vessels, and the large area of weak echoes given by a flat floe may be mistaken for a polynya. It is difficult to distinguish between 10/10 hummocked or rafted ice and 3/10 small floes and ice cakes.

6 Large floes in the midst of brash ice (photograph 6.10), will usually be distinguishable on radar.

Leads through static ice will normally be detected on radar, especially if the lead is at least 2½ cables wide and free from brash ice.

Areas of open water and smooth floes appear very similar, but in an ice field the edge of a smooth floe is prominent, while the edge of open water is not.

7 Snow, sleet and rain squalls can sometimes be detected. Lookouts can then be increased, and speed or track altered to avoid the squalls.

Indications of open water
6.46

1 **Water sky**, distinguished by dark streaks on the underside of low clouds such as stratus and stratocumulus indicates the direction of leads or patches of open water. A dark band reflected on the underside of high stratocumulus and altostratus clouds indicates the existence along this line of small patches of open water which may connect with a larger distant area of open water. If low on the horizon, water sky may possibly indicate the presence of open water up to about 40 miles beyond the visible horizon.

2 **Fog**. Dark spots in fog give a similar indication, but are only visible at considerably shorter distances than reflections on clouds. However, when navigating in close pack ice, ice of land origin and ridged/hummocked ice may appear as darker spots.

 Swell. Any surge in the surrounding drift ice indicates the presence of expanses of more open conditions in the vicinity. A noticeable increase in the prevailing swell conditions normally means that more open ice conditions lie within 30 miles in the direction from which the swell is building.

Effect of abnormal refraction
6.47

1 In normal meteorological conditions, radar echoes from most bergs may be detected at a useful range, however, in certain meteorological conditions, a very pronounced temperature lapse-rate and/or an increase of humidity with height, sub-refraction may occur and normal detection ranges be appreciably reduced.

2 Ice or open water in the distance may often be detected by super-refraction (7.43) raising the horizon. The image of the ice or areas of open water, or a mixture of the two, may be seen as an erect or inverted image. Alternatively, both images may be seen at once, one above the other and usually in contact, in which case the erect image is the higher of the two. Allowance must be made for the fact that the refraction causing the mirage will increase the apparent dimensions of small ice, sometimes so greatly as to make small pieces appear like icebergs. The areas of open water are dark relative to the ice.

Master's duties

Conduct in the vicinity of ice
6.48

1 *The International Convention for the Safety of Life at Sea (SOLAS), 1974*, requires the Master of every vessel, when ice is reported on or near his track, to proceed at a moderate speed at night or to alter course to pass well clear of the danger zone.

Reports
6.49

1 The following reports are required to be made.
 On meeting dangerous ice:
 Type of ice.
 Position of the ice.
 UT (GMT) and date of observation.

2 On encountering air temperatures below freezing associated with gale force winds causing severe ice accumulation on vessels:
 Air and sea temperatures.
 Force and direction of the wind.
 Position of the ship.
 UT (GMT) and date of observations.

Ice reports

Details
6.50

1 Information on ice is promulgated by national authorities in whose waters ice is prevalent. Details of these warning services are contained in *Admiralty List of Radio Signals Volume 3*, and further information can be found in the appropriate volumes of *Admiralty Sailing Directions*.

 Updated information in various languages can also be obtained from the following websites:
 European waters:

2 www.bsh.de/en/Marine%20data/Observations/Ice/index.jsp
 www.fimr.fi/en.htm
 www.smhi.se/
 www.vtt.fi
 Canadian waters:
 www.ice-glaces.ec.gc.ca
 Antarctic and Arctic waters:
 www.polarview.org/services/simf.htm
 www.natice.noaa.gov

Ice accumulation

General information
6.51

1 In certain conditions ice, formed of fresh water or sea water, accumulating on the hulls and superstructures of vessels can be a serious danger. Ice accumulation may occur from three causes:
 Fog, including fog formed by evaporation from a relatively warm sea surface, combined with freezing conditions.
 Freezing drizzle, rain or wet snow.
 Spray or sea water breaking over a vessel when the air temperature is below the freezing point of sea water, about $-2°C$.

Icing from fresh water
6.52

1 From fog, drizzle, rain or snow, the weight of ice which can accumulate on the rigging may increase to such an extent that it is liable to fall and endanger those on deck.

 Radio and radar failures, due to ice on aerials, insulators and scanners, may be experienced soon after ice starts to accumulate.

 The amount of ice, however, is small compared with the amount which accumulates in rough weather with low temperatures, when heavy seas break over a vessel.

Icing from sea water
6.53

1 When the air temperature is below the freezing point of sea water and the vessel is in heavy seas, considerable amounts of water will freeze on to the superstructure and those parts of the hull which are sufficiently above the waterline to escape being frequently washed by the sea. The amounts so frozen to surfaces exposed to the air will rapidly increase with falling air and sea temperatures, and have in extreme cases lead to the capsizing of vessels.

2 The dangerous conditions are those in which strong winds are experienced in combination with air temperatures of about $-2°C$ or below; freezing rain or snowfall increases the hazard. The rapidity with which ice accumulates increases progressively as the wind increases above force 6 and as the air temperature falls further below about $-2°C$. It also increases with decreasing sea temperatures. The rate of accumulation also depends on other factors, such as the vessel's speed and course relative to the wind and waves, and the particular design of each vessel.

Forecasting of icing conditions
6.54

1 Extensive observations have been made of ice accumulation due to sea water, mainly on fishing vessels around Iceland, Greenland, Labrador, and in the Barents Sea and North Pacific Ocean. The nomograms in diagram 6.54 are derived from the work of J R Overland, C H Pease, R W Preisendorfer and A L Comiskey. They indicate the rate of ice accumulation to be expected on a slow moving vessel with the wind ahead or on the beam. They are for different values of wind speed and air temperature at a selection of sea temperatures. They are reproduced by permission of NOAA/Pacific Environmental Laboratory.

Avoiding ice accumulation
6.55

1 It will be appreciated that it is very difficult to forecast accurately the three variables involved. Furthermore, the region of icing often moves at such a rate that mariners may not be able to take evasion action unless warning of impending icing conditions is received sufficiently in advance.

2 The mariner is therefore advised to exercise all possible caution whenever gales are expected in combination with air temperatures of −2°C or below. These conditions are most likely to occur with winds from polar regions, but the direction may be any that will transport sufficient cold air. If these conditions are expected, the prudent course is to steer towards warmer conditions, or to seek shelter, as soon as possible.

3 If unable to reach shelter or warmer conditions, it has been found best to reduce spray to a minimum by heading into the wind and sea at the slowest speed possible to maintain steerage way, or if weather conditions do not permit that manoeuvre, to run before the wind, equally at the least speed that will maintain steerage way.

For obligatory reports on encountering severe icing, see 6.49.

Operations in ice

General rules
6.56

1 Ice is an obstacle to any vessel, even an icebreaker. The inexperienced ice navigator is advised to develop a healthy respect for the latent power and strength of ice in all its forms. However, well-found vessels in capable hands can operate successfully in ice-covered waters.

2 The first principle of successful passage through ice is to maintain freedom of manoeuvre. Once a vessel becomes trapped, she goes wherever the ice goes. Operating in ice requires great patience and can be a tiring business with or without icebreaker escort. The ice-free long way round a difficult area whose limits are known is often the quickest and safest way.

3 When navigating in ice the following golden rules apply:
Keep moving, even if very slowly.
Try to work with the ice movement and not against it.
Excessive speed leads to ice damage.
Always attempt to achieve a right angle approach to any floe.
Ensure rudder is amidships before making any sternboard.
Avoid anchoring in moving close pack ice.

Ice identification
6.57

1 Mariners should note that, before attempting any passage through ice, it is essential to determine its type, thickness, hardness, floe size and concentration. This can only be achieved visually.

It is very easy and extremely dangerous to underestimate the hardness of ice.

2 After a snow fall, ice thickness can be very difficult to identify. Hence, mariners should exercise due diligence, based on experience, when making a passage through ice.

Ice is seldom uniform. There can be every type/age of ice amongst drift ice.

Changes in ice conditions
6.58

1 Ice moves continually under the influence of wind and current; floating ice is much influenced by the wind. With a change of wind, ice conditions can change completely, often within hours, depending on the concentrations.

Ice fuses when the temperature falls below freezing. An area of separate ice floes and loose fragments can quickly turn into a solid mass of ice and pose serious problems, even for icebreakers.

2 When practicable, a look-out from aloft will frequently detect the best strategic route to utilise, and open water not distinguishable from the bridge. However, the tactical control of both track and engine movements/power, especially if not available aloft, remain on the bridge.

Considerations before entering ice
6.59

1 Ice should not be entered if an alternative, although longer, route is available. Before deciding to enter the ice the following factors need to be considered:
Latest ice report detailing the type and concentration of the ice in the area.
Time of year, weather and temperature.

2 Area of operation.
Availability of ice manoeuvring modes from all equipment and machinery spaces.
Availability of icebreakers.
Availability of any airborne support.
Availability of potential mutual support/advice from other vessels in the area.
Vessel's ice class in relation to the type of ice expected.
State of hull, machinery and equipment, and quantity of bunkers and stores available.
Draught, with respect to any ice strengthened belt, and depth of water over the propeller tips and the rudder.
Ice experience of the person in charge on the bridge.

ICING CONDITIONS
For vessels with the wind ahead of or on the beam

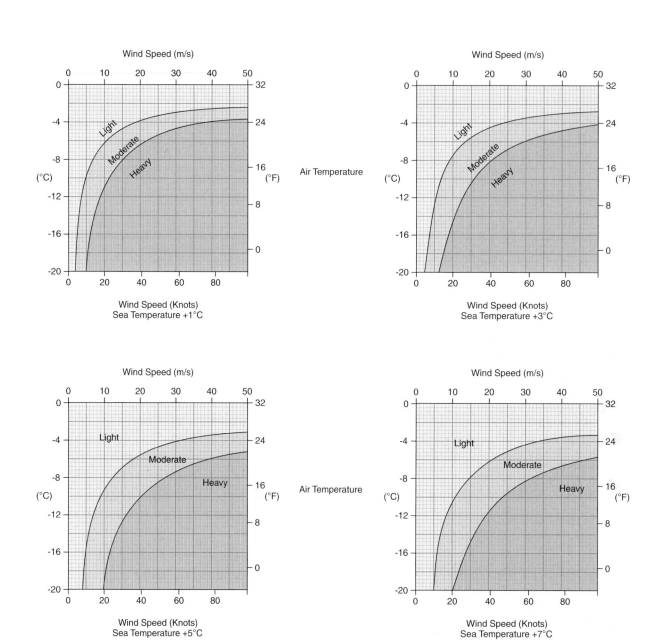

Light Icing	Less than 0.7cm/hour
Moderate Icing	0.7-2.0cm/hour
Heavy Icing	Greater than 2cm/hour

Icing nomograms (6.54)

3　Thin new ice allows passage to be made through it by modern steel vessels on the original intended route. Thick first year ice or old ice which cannot safely be negotiated, given the vessels ice classification, requires the prudent mariner to stop and wait until either conditions improve with a change of wind or tide, or an icebreaker becomes available.

Shiphandling in ice

Drift ice
6.60
1　Ice fields consisting of thick broken floes, especially those that bear signs of erosion by the sea on their upper surface, should be avoided. The floes may have underwater spurs, extraordinarily strong and hardly affected by melting.

2　If a large floe blocks the vessel's intended course, no attempt should be made to break it unless it is very rotten. It is best to go round it, if possible, or to put the stem against it, and then increase power until the floe is forced ahead and begins to swing to one side, whence the power should be reduced to allow it to pass clear.

3　If collision with a floe cannot be avoided, it should be hit squarely with the stem. A glancing blow may damage bow plating, and by throwing the vessel off course, cause another bow glancing blow from a nearby floe, or the stern to swing into ice, with potential damage to rudder and propellers.

Mariners navigating in extensive fields of thin or light ice, particularly in polar waters, must remain alert to the fact that multi year floes and ice of land origin are to be found frequently in such fields and are difficult to distinguish.

4　At night or in reduced visibility when passing through fields of drift ice, speed must be reduced or the vessel stopped until the mariner can distinguish and identify the ice ahead. Navigation in drift ice in darkness should only be attempted with the aid of well positioned searchlights to assist in the interpretation of the radar picture. See 6.43.

Ice of land origin
6.61
1　All forms of glacial ice and dirty ice broken away from coastal regions should be given a wide berth.

Icebergs are usually current-driven while the icefield will have a wind drift component (6.11).

With a strong current icebergs may travel upwind. Under these circumstances, open water will be found to leeward and pressured pack ice will be found to windward of the iceberg.

2　Similar conditions have been observed with a weak current and a strong wind, when the floes overtaking an iceberg were heaped up to windward, while a lane of open water lay to leeward of the iceberg.

Any vessel, observing such situations, and experiencing difficulty in advancing through the prevailing drift ice concentrations, should monitor the relative situation very closely, and make every available effort to manoeuvre to the leeward side of the berg.

3　When navigating in pack ice, advantage may be taken of leads created by the relative movement of icebergs through the pack ice.

Leads
6.62
1　When navigating in pack ice every opportunity should be taken to use all leads and any open water available, however, without icebreaker support, it is unwise to follow a shore lead with an onshore wind blowing or expected. A flaw lead is not as hazardous in offshore winds but is not recommended.

A vessel stopped in ice close inshore should always be pointed to seaward unless it is intended to anchor.

Making an entry
6.63
1　The following principles govern entry into the ice:
Where the existence of pressure is evident from hummocking and rafting, entry should not be attempted.
The ice should be entered from leeward, if possible, as the windward edge of an icefield is more compact than the leeward edge, and wave action is less on the leeward edge.

2　The ice edge often has bights separated by projecting tongues. By entering at one of the bights, the surge will be found to be least.
Ice should be entered at very low speed and at right angles to the ice edge to receive the initial impact, and once into the ice speed should be increased to maintain headway and control of the vessel.

Speed in ice
6.64
1　The force of the impact on striking ice depends on the tonnage and speed of the vessel. It varies as the square of the speed. Speed in ice therefore requires careful consideration. If a vessel goes too slowly she risks being beset, and if too fast she risks damage from collision with floes.

2　Where concentrations of ice vary, and a vessel passes from close pack ice through patches of open drift ice or open water and back to close pack ice, engine revolutions should be reduced on entering the more open patches. If revolutions are maintained, the vessel will gather way as she passes through the clearer water, and her speed may become too great to re-entering the close pack ice safely.

Use of engines and rudder
6.65
1　The propeller(s) and rudder(s) are the most vulnerable part of any vessel, and particularly so in ice. Engines must be prepared to go full astern at any time, and should a vessel be required to go astern in ice, it should be done with extreme care, and always with the rudder amidships.

2　If a vessel is stopped by a very close concentration of pack ice, the rudder should be put amidships and the engines kept turning slowly ahead. This will wash the ice clear astern. Once checks of the propeller have been made, the vessel can come astern.

When a vessel is working in very close pack ice, floes submerged by the bow often pass under the vessel. If this occurs, speed should immediately be reduced to dead slow, thereby reducing the flow of water/ice into the propellers.

3　Violent rudder movements should only be used in emergency, such as when beset, as they may cause the stern to swing heavily into ice, particularly when navigating in drift ice which is comprised of multi year floes.

Frequent use of the rudder, especially in the hard-over position, can be employed both as a means of slowing the vessel's advance in drift ice, whilst maintaining the flow past the rudder, which would be lost with a reduction of propeller revolutions, and as a means of making the vessel roll in very close pack ice, reducing the static friction of ice against the ship's side, and helping to maintain advance.

4 Too much use of the rudder, however, when pushing through pack ice, or following an icebreaker, may bring the vessel to a complete stop.

Anchoring
6.66

1 In close or more compact concentrations of pack ice, anchoring should be avoided.

If ice is moving, its tremendous force may break the cable. When conditions permit anchoring, such as in light brash ice, rotten ice, or among widely scattered floes, the windlass and main engines should be kept at immediate notice, and the anchor weighed as soon as wind threatens to close the drift ice around to the vessel.

Ramming and backing
6.67

1 Forcing a passage through very close or more compact pack ice to reach open water, or an area where the ice is less concentrated, may sometimes be essential. The method employed involves ramming the ice to break floes by sheer impact and weight, and then to back out into the water and broken ice astern before becoming stuck. To avoid the risk of becoming stuck in the ice, the propeller should be turning astern before the vessel stops. To avoid propeller and rudder damage, the propeller should be turning ahead before any stern contact with ice takes place.

2 By repeatedly carrying out this procedure, a slow advance can be made, dependent on the ice pressure from wind or current. It is not advisable, therefore, to continue forcing such a passage unless the channel so made exceeds the beam of the vessel and remains sufficiently wide to allow her to move freely out astern.

3 This procedure is dangerous and should be used with the utmost discretion as heavy damage to a vessel can result. Only in extreme emergency should it be used by vessels with a low or no polar ice class. Mariners on ice–strengthened vessels with a bulbous bow which employ forward buoyancy instead of displacement to break up the floes must equally be aware of their vessel's limitations and the thickness of the floes about to be rammed.

Beset
6.68

1 The most serious danger is from ice under pressure which can nip the vessel and may crush the hull. Dramatic indications of when a vessel is nipped are changes of the angles of heel and trim. The risk is far greater when navigating in ice concentrations of 7/10 or more in any current or in strengthening winds.

2 A vessel beset in consolidated pack ice is, in addition to the risk of becoming nipped, also at risk from drifting with the moving ice against icebergs, ice fronts, shoals and the shore. Hence every precaution should be taken to avoid this situation.

3 Should it be possible to manoeuvre the vessel under the lee of an iceberg whilst being swept along, this may provide a safe haven until conditions improve. However, the possibilities of the iceberg either collapsing or capsizing, or being held on a shoal, must be considered.

4 Mariners on board any vessel beset in pack ice, in the presence of bergs/bergy bits, should also note that all relative motion is likely to be due to the fact that it is the pack ice and the vessel which are in motion, and the bergs/bergy bits which are static.

For caution on dangers near icebergs, see 6.14.

5 When a vessel proceeding independently becomes beset, it usually requires icebreaker assistance to free her (see 6.77). However, a vessel can sometimes be freed by going full ahead and full astern alternately with full helm one way and then the other in order to swing her. This may loosen the vessel sufficiently to enable her to move ahead through the ice. If the vessel starts moving astern, the rudder must be amidships. In any event, when a vessel, escorted or not, becomes beset, she should normally keep her engines moving slowly ahead to keep ice away from the propellers.

6 Vessels can sometimes free themselves from the static friction of the ice against the ship's sides by pumping and transferring ballast and it may need very little change in trim or list to break free. Transferring a heavy weight from side to side on the end of a derrick or crane may have the same beneficial effect.

Deadman (6.68)

(Photograph - Captain S J Lawrence MBE)

7 The utilization of deadmen (photograph 6.68) buried in the ice and/or ice anchors may be helpful. With deadmen or ice anchors attached to the ice astern, it may be possible to warp the vessel off the ice by winching whilst the propeller is turning at maximum revolutions astern, or to lay out anchors on each beam and heave first on one and then on the other with the propeller is turning at maximum revolutions astern.

8 As a last resort, explosives placed in holes cut nearly to the bottom of the ice, approximately 10 to 12 m off the vessels beam and detonated whilst the propeller is turning at maximum revolutions astern

might succeed in freeing the vessel. A vessel may also possibly be sawed out of the ice if the air temperature is above the freezing point of sea-water.

9   Finally, in order to conserve fuel, the best advice may be patience, as a change of wind force/direction, tidal flow or current may improve conditions naturally.

Icebreaker assistance

Control
6.69

1   Masters of icebreakers are highly skilled and experienced in the specialist fields of ice navigation, icebreaking and ice escorting. It is therefore the Master of the icebreaker who directs any ice escorting operation.

Icebreakers use air reconnaissance, when available, to locate leads and open water. Some carry helicopters which are able to guide vessels by direct communication, along the best routes through the ice.

2   Escorted vessels must:

Follow the path cleared by the icebreaker and not venture into the ice on their own.

Have towing gear rigged at all times.

Have officers on the bridge thoroughly acquainted with the Icebreaker Signals given in *The International Code of Signals.*

Acknowledge and execute promptly signals made by the icebreaker, whether by RT, light or sound.

3   After requesting icebreaker assistance, a vessel must maintain continuous radio watch, and keep the icebreaker informed of any change in her ETA at the position where escorting is to commence.

Procedural information on how to obtain icebreaker assistance through selected port or harbour radios is given in *Admiralty List of Radio Signals Volume 6.*

Mariners likely to be involved in ice navigation with icebreaker assistance are advised to study the comprehensive guide *Handling Ships In Ice,* published by the Nautical Institute.

Creating a channel in ice
6.70

1   When an icebreaker is breaking a channel through large heavy floes at slow speed, the resulting channel will be about 30 – 40% wider than the beam of the icebreaker. If, however, the ice is of a type which can be broken by the stern wave of the icebreaker proceeding at high speed, the width of the channel may be as much as three times her beam.

2   In the channel there may be pieces of ice and small floes which the icebreaker has broken off the floes at the sides of the channel. These may greatly reduce the speed of a vessel following the icebreaker, or may even block the channel.

3   Rams (photograph 6.70) sometimes project into the channel from old ice. A vessel unable to keep off the ice should request the icebreaker to widen the channel. In the narrow channel left by an icebreaker in heavy ice, rams are less likely to be encountered.

Ram with very open ice (6.70)

(Photograph - British Antarctic Survey)

Convoys
6.71

1 If several vessels are to be assisted at the same time, a convoy will be formed. The sequence of vessels in the convoy and their distance apart will be ordered before entering the ice by the Master of the icebreaker.

Particular attention must be paid to maintaining the distance ordered: it will vary with the ice conditions.

If a vessel's speed is reduced, the vessel astern must be informed immediately.

2 Vessels ahead and astern, as well as the ice, must be carefully watched.

Light and sound signals made by the icebreaker must be promptly and correctly repeated by vessels in the column in succession.

Distance between vessels
6.72

1 The master of the icebreaker will order the minimum and maximum distances that escorted vessels should keep from the icebreaker, and from each other when in convoy.

The minimum distance is determined by the distance that a vessel requires to come to a complete stop after reversing her engines from full ahead to full astern. The maximum distance depends on the ice conditions and the distance for which the channel will remain open in the wake of the icebreaker.

If escorted vessels cannot maintain the distance ordered, the icebreaker should be informed at once.

2 In drift ice concentrations of 7/10 and less, vessels can usually keep station on the icebreaker with little difficulty. With a pack ice concentration of 10/10, however, the track will tend to close quickly behind the icebreaker necessitating a very close escort distance. If such ice is under pressure, the distance must be reduced to a few metres since the channel will be quickly covered with ice, leaving only a small lead astern of the icebreaker narrower than her beam. If there is considerable pressure, progress may be impossible.

3 To force a passage through large floes and icefields, the icebreaker may require to increase speed to strike the ice and crush and break it ahead of her. A vessel following her must then watch the distance carefully and try to enter the channel made by the icebreaker before it closes.

Alterations of course
6.73

1 Before entering the ice the Master of the icebreaker will decide on the route to be taken and tracks to be followed.

When any change of track is required by the icebreaker, an escorted vessel must attempt to follow as closely as is practicable.

2 All alterations by the icebreaker will be made as gradually as practicable as any attempt to turn too tightly could result in an escorted vessel swinging into floes at the side of the channel, or leaving the channel at the risk of becoming beset.

Convoy speed
6.74

1 The speed of an escorted vessel is ordered by the icebreaker. In open ice speeds from 6 to 7 kn can be expected to be maintained, but only if it is certain that vessels will not collide with ice floes. In close pack ice, when the escorting distance is reduced, a speed not greater than 5 kn should be maintained.

2 A useful rule of thumb is that 8 kn can be maintained in a drift ice concentration of 4/10 and that the speed will be reduced by 1 kn for each additional 1/10 of concentration. However, thickness and hardness of the ice, snow cover, puddling and ice under pressure may need to be taken into consideration in addition to the ice concentration.

Stopping
6.75

1 When an icebreaker comes to a standstill and is unable to make farther progress without coming astern, she shows and sounds the appropriate signals. These signals should be treated with extreme urgency. Engines should immediately be put astern and the rudder used to reduce headway.

2 In a single-screw escorted vessel navigating a narrow cleared channel when suddenly required to remove all headway by going astern, mariners should be aware of the damage potential to both rudder and propellers, as the vessel will rapidly slew out of the channel.

3 Hence, rather than risk an astern movement to avoid collision with a vessel ahead, mariners may be prefer to ram the ice to one side of the channel, especially if the ice is sufficiently thin to embed the bow without damage. However, this manoeuvre will not work in heavy ice, as the bow will tend to bounce of the side of the channel back into the stern of the vessel ahead.

4 **Caution.** Mariners must be aware that due to unexpected conditions or in an emergency, an icebreaker may stop or manoeuvre ahead of an escorted vessel without any warning signal.

Towing
6.76

1 All icebreakers are fitted with towing winches with a towing wire reeled on each winch drum. Each towing wire, which has at its end an eye and a hauling-in pendant, is led over an indentation in the stern. The winches are sited as far forward as possible to minimise the vertical angle of tow, and to allow the stem of the vessel being towed to be hove close into the indentation in the stern of the icebreaker.

2 Icebreakers tow at either long or short stay. When towing at short stay, the towed vessel is hauled close-up into the indentation, or yoke, at the stern. This is the most usual method, particularly when the ice is uneven and the speed of the icebreaker varies. Certain vessels, however, because of their size or the construction of their stem, can only be towed at long stay.

3 Once an icebreaker decides to tow, the assisted vessel must quickly prepare to take on board and secure the towing wires, particularly if there is ice screwing or ice pressure. Heaving lines passed to the after deck of the icebreaker are used to bring inboard the hauling-in pendants of the towing wires. These are brought to the escorted vessel's capstan, so that the eyes of the towing wires can be hauled aboard and secured. When the towing wires are fast, the icebreaker is informed and the forecastle cleared of all personnel.

4   When towing, the icebreaker will order the engines of the towed vessel to be run at an appropriate speed. The towed vessel should expect her rudder to be used to assist the icebreaker in holding her course and in other manoeuvres.

Casting off the tow must be done promptly, particularly if towing from the ice into a heavy sea.

Assistance to beset vessels from icebreakers
6.77

1   Depending on the ice thickness and pressure, wind direction, the type of icebreaker (propulsion configuration, power and beam), particulars of the vessel beset and traffic density, the icebreaker's master or duty officer will decide on the most appropriate method for breaking-out the beset vessel. The three most common are the sternboard and forward methods, and the quarter pass.

2   **The sternboard method.** In thin ice, the icebreaker usually comes astern along the channel and cuts out ice on either bow of the vessel. The icebreaker then goes astern close along the whole length of the lee side of the beset vessel, and then goes ahead, simultaneously ordering the vessel to follow her.

3   **The forward method.** In heavier ice, vessels can usually be broken out by the icebreaker turning through 180°, going back to the beset vessel and passing close aboard her leeward side. The icebreaker then turns through 180° astern of her, and returns along either, her leeward side to thin out the ice or her windward side to relieve pressure on that side, at the same time ordering the vessel to follow her.

4   **The quarter pass.** The icebreaker approaches the beset vessel on either quarter, passes along her side, and crosses ahead of her at an angle of between 20° and 30° to the beset vessel's course. In moderate winds, the manoeuvre may be made on either side: in strong winds, the side will be determined by which vessel is most influenced by the wind.

5   Having crossed ahead of the vessel, the icebreaker goes astern to crack any floe fragments left near the beset vessel's stem, and then goes ahead ordering the beset vessel to follow, keeping in her propeller wash.

Mariners should recognize that regardless of the method used, breaking-out will often be time consuming, and will require them to be prepared at all times to respond immediately to instructions given by the icebreaker.

Effects on the body of exposure to cold

Wind chill
6.78

1   The limitations imposed by winds at low temperatures are shown in diagram 6.78. They apply to those with special clothing for use in low temperatures, which protects all skin areas from direct wind with sufficient thickness to prevent undue coldness; without proper clothing, the limitations are significantly greater.

2   The point of intersection of the appropriate wind speed and temperature values gives the Wind Chill Factor, eg Temperature −10°C and Wind Speed 20 kn give a Wind Chill Factor of III.

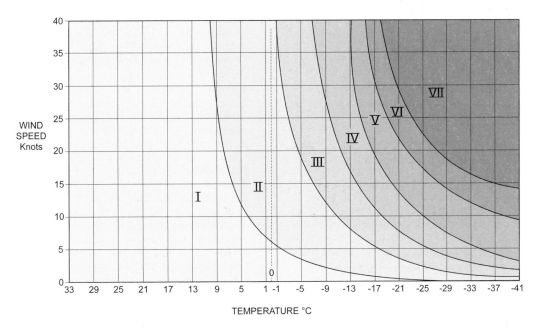

Wind chill diagram (6.78)

Wind Chill Factor	Indicates
I	Comfortable with normal precautions.
II	Work becomes uncomfortable on overcast days unless properly clothed.
III	Work becomes more hazardous even on clear days unless properly clothed. Heavy outer clothing is necessary.
IV	Unprotected skin will freeze with direct, exposure over a prolonged period, depending on degree of activity, amount of solar radiation and state of skin and circulation. Heavy outer clothing becomes mandatory.
V	Unprotected skin can freeze in 1 minute with direct exposure. Multiple layers of clothing are mandatory. Adequate face protection becomes important. Work alone is not advisable.
VI	Adequate face protection becomes mandatory. Work alone must be prohibited and supervisors must control exposure time by careful scheduling.
VII	Survival efforts are required. Personnel become easily fatigued, and mutual observations of companions is mandatory.

Immersion
6.79

1 In polar waters the dangers of immersion experienced elsewhere are accentuated by the colder water. Without special clothing such as immersion suits, even short periods of immersion in extremely cold water can be fatal. Arrangements for abandoning ship should make provision therefore for entry into lifeboats or liferafts by scrambling nets or other means without entering the water.

2 The clothing worn, morale, physical fitness, injury or loss of body heat at the time of immersion may cause wide variations in the times of survival from unconsciousness or from death.

For further details see, A Pocket Guide to Cold Water Survival, published by IMO.

3 Approximate likely times of survival for those immersed in light clothing are as follows:

Water Temp (°C)	Survival Time
0°	20 minutes to 1½ hours.
5°	30 minutes to 2½ hours.
10°	1 hour to 4 hours.
15°	Unconsciousness may occur about 2 hours after immersion but death may not result even after several hours.
20°	Unconsciousness and death are unlikely to result from cold exposure.

4 Rescuers of victims of immersion in cold water must persist with resuscitation attempts for even longer than after warm water immersion. One to two hours is recommended. Signs of life are harder to detect because cold slows all the body's functions, and a cold victim has more chance of surviving a long period before the heart is restarted.

It is not uncommon for survivors, apparently unharmed when rescued from the sea at low or even moderate temperatures, to die subsequently from heart failure attributed to hypothermia.

Protective clothing
6.80

1 Modern protective clothing, designed specifically for use in cold weather, is particularly effective if worn correctly, and provided its limitations are understood. However, its properties can quickly become degraded if it becomes wet or damaged. Hoar-frost, which is almost invisible, should be removed as soon as it is detected.

2 Perspiration should be avoided since it soaks into the clothing and ruins insulation qualities, as will any form of moisture. Before starting arduous work, clothing should be removed or opened up so that work is commenced "cold". As the work progresses, clothing should be replaced or closed up until a comfortable body temperature is reached.

3 Gloves should always be worn, even for delicate tasks, noting that contact with steel at temperatures of -7°C and below will cause instant blistering

Suitable footwear that does not fit too tightly is essential.

Hypothermia
6.81

1 Hypothermia is the medical term used to describe an abnormally low body temperature. Under normal circumstances, when wearing adequate protective clothing, hypothermia is unlikely to occur in a healthy individual.

2 But in extreme conditions, hypothermia is quite likely to occur if an individual is exhausted, if the insulating properties of clothing are impaired by tearing or wetting from sweat or water, or if the body is immobilised because of injury. It may be recognised by an intense feeling of cold, abnormal behaviour patterns, uncoordinated muscle movements which may result in stumbling and the like, and if untreated can lead to unconsciousness and death.

3 Treatment consists of moving the victim into shelter, out of the cold environment, replacing wet clothing with dry, wrapping in blankets for insulation, and provision of extra heat for the body. If the victim is conscious, plenty of hot sweet drinks and food if available should be provided. Relapses are very likely to occur unless special precautions are taken.

Frostbite
6.82

1 Frostbite is the direct result of low temperature and is due to the freezing of the fluid in tissue. Its initial stages are painless and may only be detected by a companion noticing the typical white patch on the skin or by the person affected feeling a hard spot on the face. The usual parts of the face to be affected are the nose, cheek bones, chin or ears. Minor cuts and skin abrasions provide a ready entry for frostbite.

2 Such patches can easily be cured by warming them with the hand until the frozen fluid is melted, but it should be realized that it will only be a matter of time before the trouble will recur unless precautions such as using a hood or wind shield for the face are taken.

Care should be taken not to allow the hands to get wet with petrol or oil.

3   The feet are also liable to frostbite and this is more serious as they cannot be seen and the person affected will only be warned after a while by the lack of feeling; immediate action should then be taken to restore the circulation. A frostbitten part should never be massaged.

4   Panting, and the intake of large masses of cold air, can lead to internal frostbite, and should therefore be avoided. Frequent rest between spells of work and breathing only through the nose will help in this respect.

Snow-blindness
6.83

1   Snow-blindness is caused by the burning of the cornea of the eye by ultraviolet light. The ultraviolet reflected from snow and ice must be excluded from the eyes whenever the sun is above the horizon by wearing protective goggles or glasses.

In an emergency, effective substitute goggles can be made with cardboard or any other material cut into two ovals, with narrow horizontal eye-slits and held in position with string or cloth. Some protection may also be gained by blackening the face about the eyes, nose and cheeks with dirt, charcoal or soot.

2   One can become snow-blind in overcast or cloudy conditions as easily as in direct sun since the ultraviolet light is always present; one attack predisposes to another. Symptoms appear some time after exposure when the eyes smart and water, and soon feel as though they are full of sand, and even blinking is painful. Severe pain will last at least 24 hours, and during this time it is best to remain in darkness, or keep the eyes bandaged.

Immersion foot
6.84

1   Feet should be properly protected to prevent immersion foot, a condition of painful swelling with inflammation and open lesions caused by prolonged exposure to low temperatures and moisture. Immersion foot may be avoided by keeping the feet warm and dry, which is also the only treatment possible should the complaint be contracted. When treating the feet they should not be rapidly re-warmed, and care should be taken to avoid damaging the skin or breaking blisters; they should not be massaged.

NOTES

Chapter 7

METEOROLOGY

General maritime meteorology

Sources and further reading
7.1

1   Most of the information in this section is based on *Meteorology for Mariners*, published by the Met Office, which should be consulted for further information. Other useful publications, also published by the Met Office, which contain valuable information for the mariner include *Cloud Types for Observers* and *The Marine Observer's Handbook*.

Pressure and wind

Atmospheric pressure
7.2

1   Atmospheric pressure is the pressure which the weight of the atmosphere exerts on the surface of the earth. This pressure varies from place to place depending on the density of the air of which it is comprised.

2   Pressure is measured by means of the barometer, and is usually expressed in hectopascals (hPa). The millibar (mb) is an alternative unit of measurement numerically equal to the hectopascal. Mean value at sea level is about 1013 hPa with extremes of around 950 and 1050 hPa. Pressure decreases with height; in the near surface layers of the atmosphere, across a rate of about 1 hPa every 30 ft. In order to compare the pressures at a network of observing stations which may be at different heights, it is necessary to use a "standard" level. A correction is applied to the observed barometer reading to calculate the corresponding pressure at MSL.

Wind
7.3

1   Wind is the movement of air caused by differences in atmospheric pressure between two localities. The atmosphere is always trying to achieve a uniform pressure distribution by transfer of air from a region of higher pressure to a region of lower pressure. However, the observed surface wind does not blow directly from high to low pressure, it moves roughly parallel to the isobars. This effect is caused by the Coriolis Force. Friction at the surface of the earth also affects the surface wind. The result of friction is a weakening of the wind strength and a slight backing of the wind direction from the isobars. In the N hemisphere, air flows out of an anticyclone in a clockwise circulation with the winds blowing slightly outwards across the isobars at an angle of about 15°-20°. Air moves anticlockwise around an area of low pressure with the wind blowing slightly inwards across the isobars at an angle of around 10°-20°.

2   In the S hemisphere the circulations are reversed with air diverging in an anticlockwise flow around an anticyclone and converging in a clockwise circulation around a depression.

3   **Buys Ballot's Law** simplifies the matter as follows: face the wind; the centre of low pressure will be from 90° to 135° on your right hand in the N hemisphere and on your left hand in the S hemisphere.

The wind speed is governed by the pressure gradient (or rate of change of pressure with distance) in locality: this is shown by the spacing between the isobars; the closer the spacing the greater the pressure gradient and the stronger the wind.

The Beaufort Wind Scale (Table 7.3) gives criteria for describing the force of the wind.

BEAUFORT WIND SCALE

Table (7.3)

(For an effective anemometer height of 10 m above sea level)

Beaufort Number	Descriptive term	Mean Wind Speed Equivalent		Deep Sea Criterion	Likely mean wave height (m) *
		Knots	m/s		
0	Calm	<1	0–0·2	Sea like a mirror	0
1	Light Air	1–3	0·3–1·5	Ripples with the appearance of scales are formed, but without foam crests	0·1 (0·1)
2	Light breeze	4–6	1·6–3·3	Small wavelets, still short but more pronounced; crests have a glassy appearance and do not break	0·2 (0·4)
3	Gentle breeze	7–10	3·4–5·4	Large wavelets; crests begin to break; foam of glassy appearance; perhaps scattered white horses	0.6 (1·0)
4	Moderate breeze	11–16	5·5–7·9	Small waves, becoming longer; fairly frequent white horses	1·0 (1·5)
5	Fresh breeze	17–21	8·0–10·7	Moderate waves, taking a more pronounced long form; many white horses are formed (chance of some spray)	2·0 (2·5)
6	Strong Breeze	22–27	10·8–13·8	Large waves begin to form; the white foam crests are extensive everywhere (probably some spray)	3·0 (4·0)
7	Near Gale	28–33	13·9–17·1	Sea heaps up and white foam from breaking waves begins to be blown in streaks along the direction of the wind	4·0 (5·5)
8	Gale	34–40	17·2–20·7	Moderately high waves of greater length; edges of crests begin to break into spindrift; foam is blown in well-marked streaks along the direction of the wind	5·5 (7·5)
9	Strong Gale	41–47	20·8–24·4	High waves; dense streaks of foam along the direction of the wind; crests of waves begin to topple, tumble and roll over; spray may affect visibility	7·0 (10·0)
10	Storm	48–55	24·5–28·4	Very high waves with long overhanging crests; the resultant foam, in great patches, is blown in dense white streaks along the direction of the wind; on the whole, the surface of the sea takes a white appearance; the tumbling of the sea becomes heavy and shock-like; visibility affected	9·0 (12·5)
11	Violent Storm	56–63	28·5–32·6	Exceptionally high waves (small and medium sized ships might be for a time lost to view behind the waves); the sea is completely covered with long white patches of foam lying along the direction of the wind; everywhere the edges of the wave crests are blown into froth; visibility affected	11·5 (16·0)
12	Hurricane	64 and over	32.7 and over	The air is filled with foam and spray; sea completely white with driving spray; visibility severely affected	14 and over

* The figures in this column are only intended as a rough guide to indicate what might be expected in the open sea, remote from land. Those in brackets indicate the likely maximum heights. Photographs 5.26.1–5.26.14 are illustrative of the sea states that can be expected for a given wind speed offshore. They should not be used for logging or reporting the state of the sea; figures for this purpose can be found at 5.26. In enclosed waters, or when close to land, with an offshore wind, wave heights will be smaller and the waves steeper.

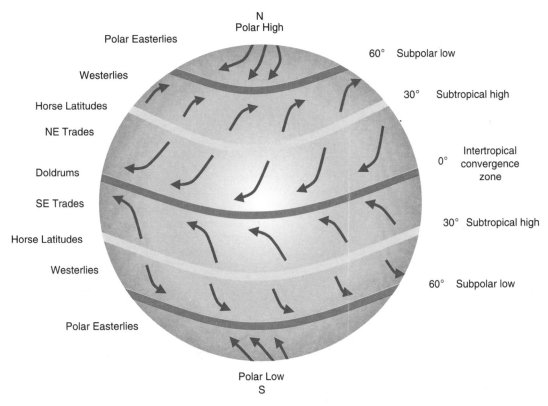

N
Polar High

Polar Easterlies

60°   Subpolar low

Westerlies

30°   Subtropical high

Horse Latitudes

NE Trades

Intertropical
0°   convergence
zone

Doldrums

SE Trades

30° Subtropical high

Horse Latitudes

Westerlies

60°   Subpolar low

Polar Easterlies

Polar Low
S

Pressure and wind belts (7.4)

General global circulation
7.4
1   Diagram 7.4 shows the pressure belts and associated surface wind systems which would exist over a uniform Earth. These idealised global systems are particularly evident over the large expanses of ocean; substantial modifications are introduced by large land masses.

Effect of change of declination of the sun
7.5
1   The annual cycle of change in the sun's declination is followed by corresponding movement of the pressure belts and associated winds. Movement varies in different localities but the pressure systems generally migrate about 5°–8° in latitude, lagging some 6 to 8 weeks behind the sun.

Effects of land and sea distribution
7.6
1   Over large land masses the temperature becomes very high in summer and low in winter; over the oceans the variation is comparatively much less. This leads to relatively high pressure over land in winter and low pressure in summer; the resulting large seasonal pressure variations are a dominating feature over continental areas and produce large scale modifications to winds over neighbouring oceans. A notable example is the monsoon wind cycle over the Indian Ocean and W Pacific Ocean which is caused by the large seasonal pressure oscillation over Asia.

General climate

Intertropical Convergence Zone
7.7
1   A broad belt of shallow low pressure and weak pressure gradients towards which the trade wind air streams of the N and S hemispheres flow is termed the Intertropical Convergence Zone (ITCZ) or doldrums. The ITCZ moves N and S seasonally and in some regions, particularly in the vicinity of large land masses, its seasonal migration takes it well outside equatorial latitudes.

2   Within the ITCZ, the areas where the winds from the two hemispheres converge are marked by lines or zones of massive cumulonimbus cloud and associated torrential rain, thunderstorms and squalls. Although a convergence zone may have some characteristics of a middle latitude cold front, there is normally little or no air mass contrast across the boundary nor is there any consistent frontal movement. A convergence zone is liable to disperse in one area and be replaced by a new development some distance away.

3   Thus the weather to be expected in the doldrums is variable light or calm winds alternating with squalls and thundery showers, but on occasion a vessel may experience only fine weather. Conditions are generally worst when the trade winds (7.8) are strongest.

It is noteworthy that the ITCZ is often the birthplace of disturbances which, as they move to higher latitudes, can develop and intensify to become tropical storms.

Trade winds

7.8

1   Air streams originate in the sub-tropical oceanic anticyclones of the N and S hemispheres and blow on the E and equatorial flanks of the anticyclones towards the ITCZ. General direction is NE in the N hemisphere; SE in the S hemisphere. They are encountered and blow with remarkable persistence over all major oceans of the world, except the N Indian Ocean and the China Seas where the monsoon winds (7.12) predominate. The trade wind zones migrate seasonally, and in each hemisphere extend to about 30°N or 30°S in the respective summers, 25°N or 25°S in winter.

2   Average wind strength is force 3–4, and in each hemisphere maximum strength is reached in spring; of the two trade wind air streams the SE trade winds are considerably the stronger and the highest average wind speeds, force 5 are found in the S Indian Ocean. In each hemisphere the winds tend to weaken on approaching the ITCZ; on the W flanks of the anticyclones the winds turn polewards becoming SE in the N hemisphere and NE in the S hemisphere.

3   Weather in the trade wind zones is generally fair and invigorating with the sky often cloudless or with well-broken small cumulus clouds. On the E sides of the oceans visibility is sometimes impaired due to fog and mist over cold ocean currents or by dust carried offshore by the wind. Cloud amounts and incidence of rain increase towards the ITCZ and also on the W sides of the oceans especially in summer.

Variables

7.9

1   Over the areas covered by the oceanic anticyclones, between the trade winds and the Westerlies farther towards the poles, there exist zones of light and variable winds which are known as the Variables; the N area is sometimes known as the Horse Latitudes (30°N–40°N). The weather in the zones is generally fair with small amounts of cloud and rain.

Westerlies

7.10

1   On the polar sides of the oceanic anticyclones lie zones where the wind direction becomes predominantly W. These zones, although mobile, generally lie N of 40°N and S of 40°S. Unlike the trade winds, the winds in these zones are known as the Westerlies, and are far from permanent. The continual passage of depressions from W to E across these zones causes the wind to vary greatly in both direction and strength. In the S hemisphere, gales are so frequent that the zone has been named the Roaring Forties. In the N hemisphere fog is common in the W parts of the oceans in this zone in summer.

Polar regions

7.11

1   Lying on the polar side of the Westerlies, the polar regions are often unnavigable on account of ice. The prevailing wind is generally from an E direction and gales are common in winter, though less so than in the zones of the Westerlies. The weather is usually cloudy and fog is frequent in summer.

Seasonal winds and monsoons

General information

7.12

1   There is a regular cycle of winds over certain ocean areas, as explained above, which results from seasonal pressure changes over neighbouring land masses due to heating and cooling. Most important and best known examples are the monsoon winds of the N Indian Ocean, China Seas and Eastern Archipelago.

2   In the N hemisphere winter, an intense anticyclone develops over the cold Asian continent and from around October or November until March, a persistent NE Monsoon wind blows over the N Indian Ocean and South China Sea; over the W Pacific Ocean the wind is NNE. The winds are generally moderate to fresh but can reach gale force locally as surges of cold air move S and particularly where funnelling occurs (Taiwan Strait, Palk Strait, for example). Weather is generally cool, fair and with well-broken cloud though the coasts of S China and Vietnam are frequently affected by extensive low cloud and drizzle. The NE Monsoon winds may extend across the equator changing direction to N or NW to become the N Monsoon off E Africa and the NW Monsoon of N Australian waters.

3   In the N hemisphere summer, pressure over Asia falls with the lowest pressure near the W Himalayas. The anticlockwise circulation gives persistent SW Monsoon winds from May until September or October over the N Indian Ocean and South China Sea, and SSW or S winds over the W Pacific Ocean. Winds are generally fresh to strong and raise considerable seas. Warm humid air gives significant amounts of cloud and rain on windward coasts and islands.

4   Similar regular and persistent winds, also known by the name of "monsoon" occur in other parts of the world, although the areas affected are by comparison far more limited. An example is the Gulf of Guinea where a SW Monsoon wind blows from June to September.

The seasons of the principal monsoons and their average strengths are shown in Table 7.12.

Local winds

Land and sea breezes

7.13

1   The regular daily cycle of land and sea breezes is a well-known feature of tropical and sub-tropical coasts and large islands. These breezes also occur at times in temperate latitudes in fine weather in summer though the effects are weaker. The cause of these breezes is the unequal heating and cooling of the land and sea. By day the sun rapidly raises the temperature of the land surface whereas the sea temperature remains virtually constant. Air in contact with the land expands and rises, and air from the sea flows in to take its place producing an onshore wind known as a "sea breeze". By night the land rapidly loses heat by radiation and becomes colder than the

	Area	General Wind Direction	Jan	Feb	Mar	Apr	May	Jun	Jul	Aug	Sep	Oct	Nov	Dec
Northern Hemisphere	South China Sea	NE	5-6	4-5	4								5-6	5-6
	Eastern China Sea	NE-N												
	Yellow Sea	N-NW	5	5	4							4-5	5	5
	Sea of Japan	N-NW												
	North Indian Ocean	NE	4	4	4								4	4
	South China Sea	SW					3	4	4	4-5				
	Eastern China Sea	SW-S												
	Yellow Sea	SW-SE						3-4	3-4					
	Sea of Japan	SW-S-E												
	N Indian Ocean	SW						5-6	6	6	5			
South Hemisphere	Indonesian waters	W-NW	3	3	3									3
	Arafura Sea	NW	5	5	3-4									3-4
	N and NW Australian Waters	W-NW	4-5	4-5										
	Indonesian waters	SE						4-5	4-5	4-5	4-5			
	Arafura Sea	SE						4	4	4	4	4		
	N and NW Australian Waters	SE-E				3-4	4-5	4-5	4-5	4-5	3-4			

Seasonal Winds - normal periods

Seasonal Winds - variable periods at onset and termination

Figures indicate typical wind force (Beaufort)

Table showing principal areas and months in which monsoon winds normally occur (7.12)

adjacent sea; air over the land is cooled and flows out to sea to displace the warmer air over the sea and produces the offshore wind known as a "land breeze".

2 Sea breezes usually set in during the forenoon and reach maximum strength, about force 4, occasionally 5 or 6, by mid-afternoon. They die away around sunset. Land breezes set in late in the evening and fade shortly after sunrise; they are usually weaker and less well marked than sea breezes. The following factors favour development of land and sea breezes:

3 Clear or partly cloudy skies.
Calm conditions or light variable winds.
Desert or dry barren coast as opposed to forests or swamps.
High ground near the coast.
In windy conditions the effect of a land or sea breeze may be to modify the prevailing wind by reinforcing, opposing or causing a change in direction.

Katabatic winds
7.14
1 When intense radiation, perhaps on clear nights, causes cooling over sloping ground, the colder denser air will flow downhill under the influence of gravity producing a breeze known as a "katabatic" or "downslope" wind.

2 In mountainous regions cold air may accumulate over high ground; onset of a light wind can displace the cold air and initiate cascading down a slope to lower ground or into a valley to give a strong wind which in exceptional cases can reach gale or storm force.

3 Where mountains rise close inshore such a katabatic wind can be a serious hazard to small craft or ships at anchor; onset of the strong offshore wind is often without warning and may arrive as a sudden severe squall. The wind may extend several miles offshore.

Among the areas where katabatic winds are common are Greenland, Norway, N Adriatic Sea, E Black Sea and Antarctica.

Cloud formations

Classification
7.15
1 Clouds are continually changing and appear in a variety of forms. It is possible however to define a limited number of characteristic forms, observed all over world, into which clouds can be broadly grouped.

Stratus (St) (7.15.1)

(Photograph - P. K. Pilsbury, Courtesy of the Met Office)

Stratus (St) (7.15.2)

(Photograph - Kevin Monk)

Stratocumulus (Sc) (7.15.3)

(Photograph - Kevin Monk)

Cumulus (Cu) (7.15.4)

(Photograph - Kevin Monk)

Towering Cumulus (TCu) (7.15.5)

(Photograph - Kevin Monk)

Cumulonimbus (Cb) (7.15.6)

(Photograph - Jimmy Deguara from www.australiasevereweather.com)

Cumulonimbus (Cb) (7.15.7)

(Photograph - Kevin Monk)

Altostratus (As) (7.15.8)

(Photograph - Michael Bath from www.australiasevereweather.com)

Altocumulus (Ac) (7.15.9)

(Photograph – P. K. Pilsbury, Courtesy of the Met Office)

Altocumulus (Ac) (7.15.10)

(Photograph – Kevin Monk)

Cirrus (Ci) (7.15.11)

(Photograph – P. K. Pilsbury, Courtesy of the Met Office)

Cirrus (Ci) (7.15.12)

(Photograph – Kevin Monk)

Cirrostratus (Cs) (7.15.13)

(Photograph - P. K. Pilsbury, Courtesy of the Met Office)

Cirrostratus (Cs) - Note the halo around the sun (7.15.14)

(Photograph - Michael Bath from www.australiasevereweather.com)

Cirrocumulus (Cc) (7.15.15)

(Photograph - P. K. Pilsbury, Courtesy of the Met Office)

Level	Designation	Type	Abbreviation	Photograph
Low <6500 ft	C_L	Stratus	St	7.15.1 and 7.15.2
		Stratocumulus	Sc	7.15.3
		Cumulus	Cu	7.15.4 and 7.15.5
		Cumulonimbus	Cb	7.15.6 and 7.15.7
Medium >6500 and <20 000 ft	C_M	Altostratus	As	7.15.8
		Altocumulus	Ac	7.15.9 and 7.15.10
		Nimbostratus	Ns	
High >20 000 ft	C_H	Cirrus	Ci	7.15.11 and 7.15.12
		Cirrostratus	Cs	7.15.13 and 7.15.14
		Cirrocumulus	Cc	7.15.15

Depressions

Description

7.16

1   A depression (or Low) (Diagram 7.16) appears on a meteorological chart as a series of isobars roughly circular or oval in shape around the centre where pressure is lowest. Depressions are frequent in middle latitudes and give unsettled weather conditions; they are often, though not always, accompanied by strong winds. They vary in size from very small features to very large circulations over 2000 miles in diameter; central pressure in extreme cases may be as low as 950 hPa. The extent and power of a deep and large depression can not only produce gale force winds but raise very high, persistent and dangerous seas. In the N hemisphere the wind circulation around a depression is anticlockwise and slightly inwards across the isobars towards the low pressure; in the S hemisphere the circulation is clockwise. See 7.3.

2   Depressions may move in any direction though most middle latitude systems move in a generally E direction. There is no normal speed of movement. A small developing and perhaps very active depression can travel very quickly indeed, possibly 30–60 kn; but as a depression deepens into a large system it usually moves much more slowly and especially so when decaying and filling.

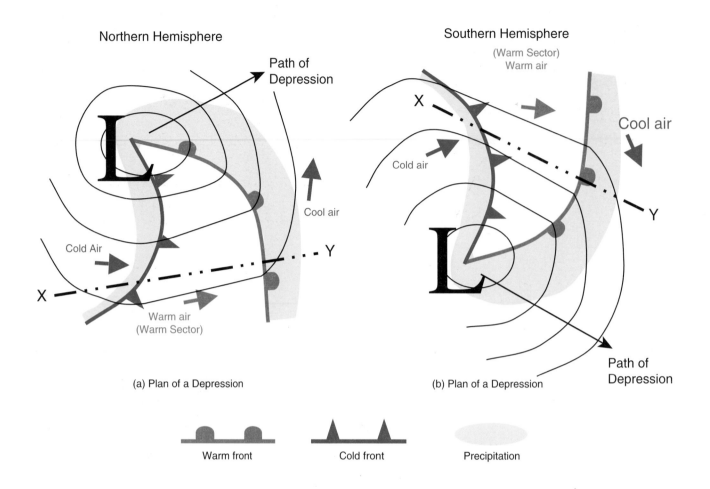

Northern Hemisphere

Path of Depression

Cool air

Cold Air

X

Y

Warm air
(Warm Sector)

(a) Plan of a Depression

Southern Hemisphere
(Warm Sector)
Warm air

Cold air

X

Y

Cool air

L

Path of Depression

(b) Plan of a Depression

Warm front

Cold front

Precipitation

DIRECTION OF MOVEMENT

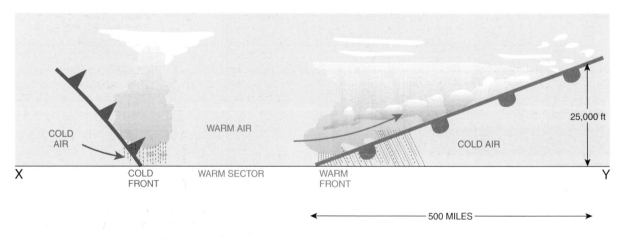

COLD AIR

WARM AIR

COLD AIR

25,000 ft

X

COLD FRONT

WARM SECTOR

WARM FRONT

Y

500 MILES

(c) Section through Depression at XY

Depressions (7.16)

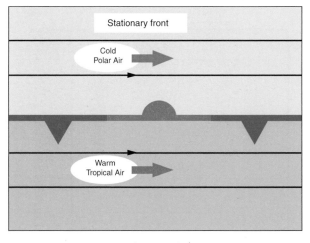

(7.17.1.1)

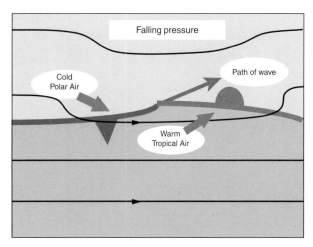

(7.17.1.2)

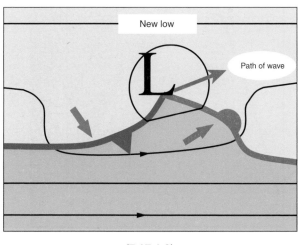

(7.17.1.3)

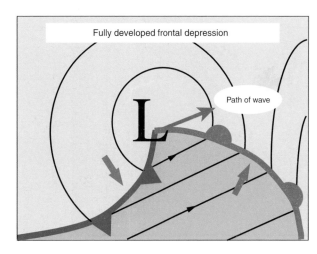

(7.17.1.4)

Formation of fronts in the N hemisphere (7.17.1)

Fronts
7.17

1   Depressions often originate on a front which is the boundary zone between two contrasting air masses. In middle latitudes, air moving from the polar regions encounters warm air from the sub-tropics moving in the opposite direction. At the frontal boundary where the two meet there is a tendency for small disturbances to develop on the front where the warm air makes incursions into the cold air mass and vice versa; the warm air rises over the cold air.

2   The process is illustrated in Diagram 7.17.1 A disturbance appears as a wave on the frontal boundary and travels E along the front as it increases in magnitude. Pressure falls in the vicinity of the crest of the wave and a depression circulation develops.

3   A front takes its name from the temperature of the air behind it when compared to the air ahead of it. Thus, a warm front is the boundary between the warmer air mass behind it and the cooler air ahead of it. Conversely, a cold front has cooler air behind it and warmer air ahead.

4   The configuration of fronts within the depression circulation as shown in Diagram 7.17.1.4 is a typical feature of middle latitude depressions.

5   **Warm front.** When the air in the warm sector (Diagram 7.16) of the depression meets the denser, cold air on the frontal boundary, the warm air overrides it; extensive cloud and precipitation covering a wide area result as the warm air ascends. The slope of the frontal discontinuity is about 1 in 100 so that the ascending warm air eventually reaches the upper atmosphere some 500 miles ahead of the surface frontal boundary. Cirrus cloud at around 25 000 to 30 000 ft is often the first sign of an approaching system.

6   **Cold front.** The cold air behind the front undercuts the warm air of the warm sector, causing the less dense warm air to rise; often quite suddenly so that a belt of large cumulus or cumulonimbus cloud may result. Associated weather are squalls and heavy thunder showers but the frontal belt of heavy precipitation is usually much narrower than on a warm front. As no frontal cloud precedes the cold front there may be little warning of its approach. The "tail" of a cold front trailing behind a depression is commonly the place of origin for further wave depressions.

7   **Occlusion.** In a frontal system the cold front generally moves faster than the warm front and eventually overtakes it, thereby closing or occluding

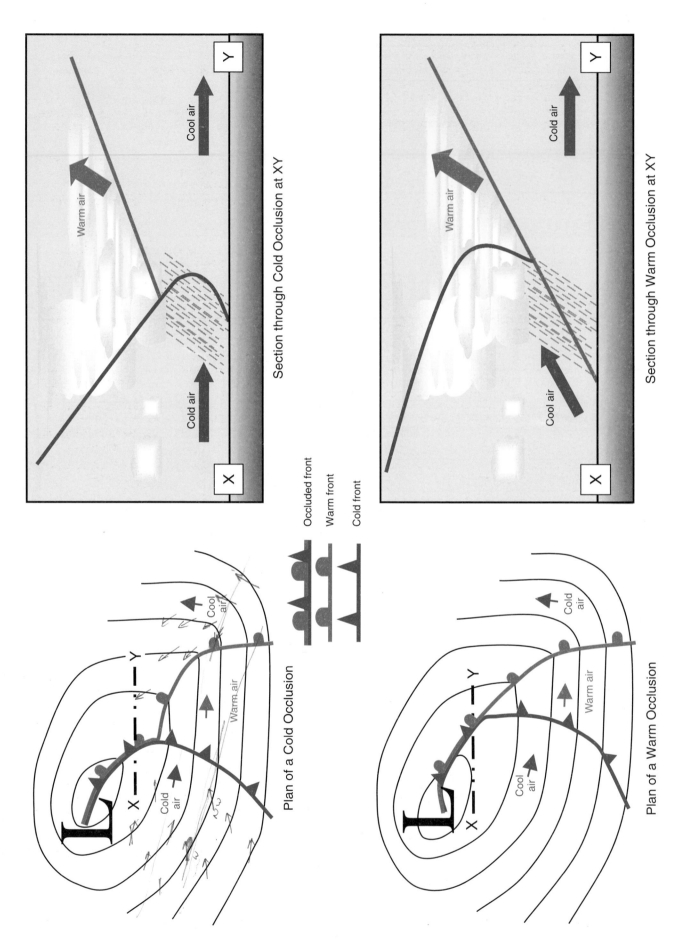

Section through Cold Occlusion at XY

Section through Warm Occlusion at XY

Occluded front

Warm front

Cold front

Plan of a Cold Occlusion

Plan of a Warm Occlusion

Warm and cold occlusions in N hemisphere (7.17.2)

the warm sector of the depression. Thereafter the cold front may displace the warm front (Diagram 7.17.2) effectively leaving a surface cold front with mixed characteristics of both warm and cold fronts: a "cold occlusion". Alternatively when the air behind the cold front is less dense than the air ahead of the warm front, the cold front will rise up the warm front, leaving a warm front at the surface but again with mixed characteristics of both warm and cold fronts: a "warm occlusion".

8   In both cases the air in the warm sector is lifted from the surface and the depression subsequently becomes less active and starts to fill.

Typical weather sequence
7.18

1   Tables 7.18.1, 7.18.2 and Diagram 7.18.3 describe typical sequences of weather likely to be experienced by mariners at sea as depressions approach in both hemispheres.

	Approaching warm front	Warm sector (behind warm front)	Approaching cold front	At cold front
Wind (N Hemisphere)	Backs to SW or S and freshens.	Veers and may freshen.	Backs slightly and freshens.	Veers markedly to W or NW. May be accompanied by sudden squalls.
Wind (S Hemisphere)	Veers N or NW and freshens.	Backs and may freshen.	Veers slightly and abates.	Backs to W or SW. May be accompanied by sudden squalls.
Cloud	Thickens and cloudbase lowers. Overcast skies obscure the sun.	Medium and high-level cloud breaks up. Typically, lower level cloud remains.	Increase in medium and high-level cloud. Often obscured by thickening of low-level cloud.	Thick bank of cloud breaks up as front clears to E.
Weather	Intermittent light precipitation increases moderate to heavy just ahead of front.	Precipitation eases and may turn to drizzle. Fog banks may develop if sea surface temperature is high compared to dewpoint.	Precipitation recommences.	Moderate or heavy precipitation followed by clearer conditions as front clears to E. Showers may develop behind the front.
Change in barometric pressure	Increased rate of fall.	Rate of fall slows and may become steady.	Fall.	Sharp rise.
Change in temperature	Very slow increase.	Sharp increase.	Steady.	Sharp decrease.
Change in dewpoint	Very slow increase. Higher rate of increase in precipitation.	Sharp increase.	Steady. May rise in precipitation.	Sharp decrease.
Visibility	Steady reduction in increasing precipitation.	Moderate or poor.	Moderate.	Sharp increase.

Typical weather experienced with depression approaching from W and passing between the observer and the nearer pole (7.18.1)

Elements	Movement of depression	Ahead of system	As system passes	Behind system	Remarks
Wind (N Hemisphere)	E or NE.	SE backing E then NE.	NE backing N	N backing NW.	Often referred to as "cyclonic" in forecasts. Changes in wind speed and direction are gradual. Winds may fall light and variable near centre of depression before rapid onset of strong or gale force winds.
Wind (S Hemisphere)	E or SE.	NE veering E then SE.	SE veering S.	S veering SW.	
Weather		Skies gradually cloud over. Showers become more frequent and increase in intensity.	Long periods of continuous precipitation with heavy squalls, low cloud and poor visibility.	Precipitation gradually breaks into showers. Visibility improves.	
Change in barometric pressure		Increased rate of fall.	Sudden drop.	Gradual increase.	

Typical weather experienced with depression approaching from W and passing between the observer and the farther pole (7.18.2)

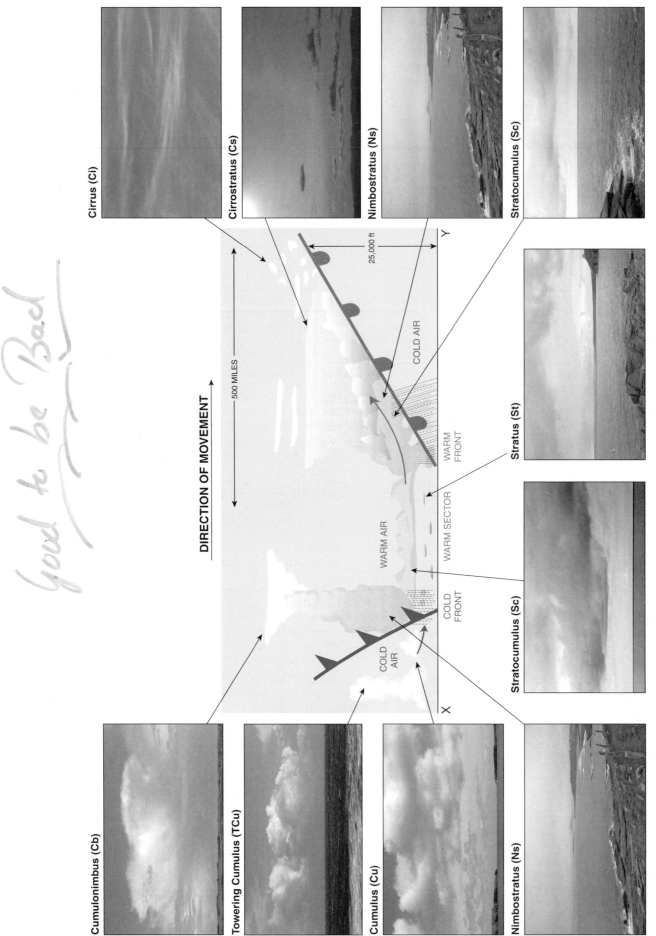

Cirrus (Ci)

Cirrostratus (Cs)

Nimbostratus (Ns)

Stratocumulus (Sc)

DIRECTION OF MOVEMENT

25,000 ft

500 MILES

COLD AIR

WARM FRONT

WARM AIR

WARM SECTOR

COLD FRONT

COLD AIR

Y

X

Stratus (St)

Stratocumulus (Sc)

Section through a mid-latitude frontal system (7.18.3)

Cumulonimbus (Cb)

Towering Cumulus (TCu)

Cumulus (Cu)

Nimbostratus (Ns)

good to be Bad

Tropical storms

General information
7.19

1   Tropical storms are intense depressions which develop in tropical latitudes; they are often the cause of very high winds and heavy seas. Although the pressure at the centre of a tropical storm is comparable to that of an intense middle latitude depression, the diameter of a tropical storm is much smaller, typically 400 to 500 miles compared with 1000 to 1200 miles, resulting in correspondingly greater pressure gradients and wind speeds. The wind blows around the centre of a tropical storm in a spiral flow inwards, anticlockwise in the N hemisphere and clockwise in the S hemisphere: hence the occasional alternative name "tropical revolving storm".

2   Within the circulation of a tropical storm the wind is often very violent and the seas are high and confused; considerable damage may be done even to large and well-found ships. The danger is especially enhanced when ships are caught in restricted waters without adequate room to manoeuvre and early action may be essential to preclude such a situation arising.

Characteristics
7.20

1   Winds of gale force, above 34 kn, are likely up to 100–200 miles from the centre of a storm at latitudes of less than 20°; as a storm moves to higher latitudes it tends to expand and by the time a system has reached 30°–35° (N or S) these distances may be doubled. Hurricane force winds, above 64 kn, are likely within 80 miles of a storm centre in the tropics and mean wind speeds of well over 100 kn have been recorded in major storms. Winds are extremely gusty and the wind speeds in gusts may be some 30–50% higher than the mean; gusts exceeding 175 kn have been reported. At the centre of a well-developed storm is a characteristic area, known as the "eye" of the storm, within which winds are light or moderate variable, the sky partly cloudy but with a heavy sometimes mountainous, and confused swell. The diameter of the eye tends to be about 10% of the overall diameter of the storm. It can vary from less than 10 miles in small intense storms to 30–40 miles in the very large storms. Surrounding the eye is the dense dark wall cloud extending to a great altitude and with very heavy rain beneath; maximum wind speeds are attained at the inner margin of the wall cloud in a belt averaging about 5–15 miles in width. In this zone visibility is almost nil due to the spray and torrential rain.

Occurrence
7.21

1   The localities, seasons, average frequencies and local names of these storms are shown in Table 7.21. They are most frequent during the late summer and early autumn of each hemisphere; they are comparatively rare from mid-November to mid-June in the N hemisphere and from mid-May to November in the S hemisphere. However it is stressed that no month is entirely safe and that storms can occur at any time.

Formation and movement
7.22

1   Tropical storms only develop over oceans, and formation is especially frequent near the seasonal location of the ITCZ (7.7). In the N hemisphere, storms form mostly in the belt 5°–15°N early and late in the storm season, and between 10°N and 25°N at the height of the season; in the North Atlantic Ocean, storm formation between 25°N and 30°N is fairly common. In the S hemisphere most storms develop between 5°S and 18°S. Those which affect the W Pacific, S Indian and North Atlantic Oceans are usually first reported in the W part of these oceans; there are exceptions such as in the North Atlantic Ocean during August and September when an occasional storm originates near Arquipélago de Cabo Verde.

2   Tracks followed are variable in all areas and individual tracks may be erratic. In the N hemisphere a storm will move off in a direction between 275° and 350° though most often within 30° of due W. When near latitude 25°N storms usually recurve away from the equator and by the time they reach 30°N movement is in a NE direction. In the S hemisphere initial movement is between WSW and SSW, usually the former, to recurve between 15°S and 20°S and thence follow a SE path. Many storms, however, do not recurve but continue in a WNW direction in the N hemisphere, or WSW in the S hemisphere. When a storm moves inland it weakens and eventually dissipates; but if it should re-emerge to follow an ocean track again it may re-intensify. Storms move at about 10 kn in their early stages increasing slightly with latitude but seldom exceeding 15 kn before recurving. A speed of 20–25 kn is usual after recurving, although speeds of over 40 kn have been recorded. When storms move erratically, sometimes making one or more complete loops, their speed of movement is usually slow; less than 10 kn.

Detection and tracking
7.23

1   Detection and tracking of tropical storms is greatly assisted by weather satellites. Most storms are detected at a very early stage of development, and thereafter each storm is carefully tracked. In some areas storms are monitored by weather reconnaissance aircraft which fly into the circulations to record observations.

Storm warnings
7.24

1   Storm warnings of the position, intensity and expected movement of each storm are broadcast at frequent and regular intervals. Details of stations which transmit warnings, the areas covered and transmission schedules are given in *Admiralty List of Radio Signals Volume 3.*

2   The following terms are in general use to describe tropical circulations at various stages of intensity:

Tropical Depression	Winds of force 7 or less
Tropical Storm	Winds of force 8 and 9
Severe Tropical Storm	Winds of force 10 and 11
Typhoon, Hurricane, Cyclone	Winds of force 12 or more

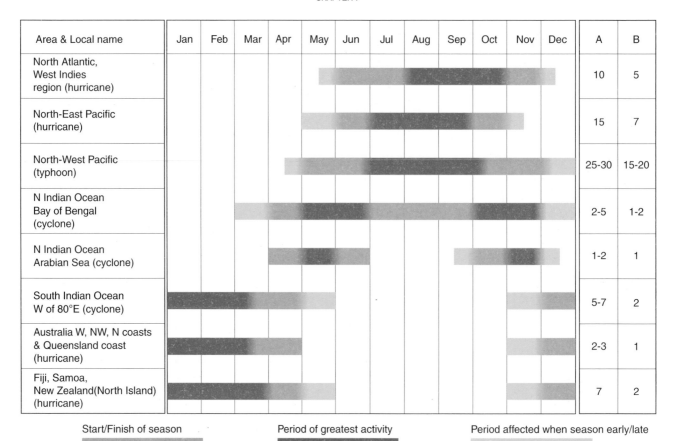

Area & Local name	Jan	Feb	Mar	Apr	May	Jun	Jul	Aug	Sep	Oct	Nov	Dec	A	B
North Atlantic, West Indies region (hurricane)													10	5
North-East Pacific (hurricane)													15	7
North-West Pacific (typhoon)													25-30	15-20
N Indian Ocean Bay of Bengal (cyclone)													2-5	1-2
N Indian Ocean Arabian Sea (cyclone)													1-2	1
South Indian Ocean W of 80°E (cyclone)													5-7	2
Australia W, NW, N coasts & Queensland coast (hurricane)													2-3	1
Fiji, Samoa, New Zealand(North Island) (hurricane)													7	2

Start/Finish of season   Period of greatest activity   Period affected when season early/late

Column A: Approximate average frequency of tropical storms each year
Column B: Approximate average frequency of tropical storms each year which develop Force 12 winds or stronger

Table showing principal areas affected by tropical storms and the months in which they normally occur (7.21)

3   The Saffir Simpson Scale was developed in the USA and is also used in many parts of the world to grade hurricane wind strength. The following table shows the categories of hurricanes according to this scale.

Saffir-Simpson Scale for Hurricane Classification

Strength	*Wind speed (Kn)*	*Pressure (hPa)*
Category 1	64 – 82	> 980
Category 2	83 – 95	965 – 979
Category 3	96 – 113	945 – 964
Category 4	114 – 135	920 – 944
Category 5	> 135	< 919

4   Weather Centres issuing Storm Warnings and advisory messages are generally manned by competent forecasters of long experience with an optimum supply of available information at their disposal. However it is sometimes difficult to identify the precise position of a storm centre, even with modern tracking facilities; and in view of the uncertain movement of storms, prediction of the future path of a storm may be liable to appreciable error particularly when forecasting for several days ahead. Appropriate allowances are therefore prudent when considering what action is necessary to avoid a storm.

Mariners should pay particular attention to their own observations when in the vicinity of a storm and act in accordance with advice given below.

Precursory signs
7.25

1   The following signs may be evidence of a storm in the locality; the first of these observations is a very reliable indication of the proximity of a storm within 20° or so of the equator. It should be borne in mind, however, that very little warning of the approach of an intense storm of small diameter may be expected.

2   If a corrected barometer reading is 3 hPa or more below the mean for the time of year, as shown in the climatic atlas or appropriate volume of *Admiralty Sailing Directions*, suspicion should be aroused and action taken to meet any development. The barometer reading must be corrected not only for height, latitude, temperature and index error (if mercurial) but also for the diurnal variation which is given in climatic atlases or appropriate volumes of *Admiralty Sailing Directions*. If the corrected reading is 5 hPa or more below normal it is time to consider avoiding action for there can be little doubt that a tropical storm is in the vicinity. Because of the importance of pressure readings it is wise to take hourly

Hurricane Katrina approaching
New Orleans - May 2005 (7.25)

(Photograph - NASA/courtesy of nasaimages.org)

barometric readings in areas affected by tropical storms.

3   An appreciable change in the direction or strength of the wind.

A long low swell is sometimes evident, proceeding from the approximate bearing of the centre of the storm. This indication may be apparent before the barometer begins to fall.

Extensive cirrus cloud followed, as the storm approaches, by altostratus and then broken cumulus or scud.

4   Radar may give warning of a storm within about 100 miles. By the time the exact position of the storm is given by radar, the ship is likely to be already experiencing high seas and strong to gale force winds. It may be in time, however, to enable the ship to avoid the eye and its vicinity where the worst conditions exist.

Path of the storm
7.26

1   To decide the best course of action if a storm is suspected in the vicinity, the following knowledge is necessary:

The bearing of the centre of the storm.
The path of the storm.

2   If an observer faces the wind, the centre of the storm will be from 100° to 125° on his right hand side in the N hemisphere when the storm is about 200 miles away, that is to say when the barometer has fallen about 5 hPa and the wind has increased to about force 6. As a rule, the nearer he is to the centre, the more nearly does the angle approach 90°. The path of the storm may be approximately determined by taking two such bearings separated by

an interval of 2–3 hours, allowance being made for the movement of the ship during the interval. It can generally be assumed that the storm is not travelling towards the equator and, if in a latitude lower than 20°, its path will be most unlikely to have an E component. On the rare occasions when a storm is following an unusual path, it is likely to be moving slowly.

3   Diagram 7.26 shows typical paths of tropical storms and illustrates the terms dangerous and navigable semicircle. The former lies on the side of the path towards the usual direction of recurvature, ie the right hand semicircle in the N and the left hand semicircle in the S hemisphere. The advance quadrant of the dangerous semicircle is known as the dangerous quadrant as this quadrant lies ahead of the centre. The navigable semicircle is that which lies on the other side of the path. A ship situated within this semicircle will tend to be blown away from the storm centre and recurvature of the storm will increase her distance from the centre.

Avoiding tropical storms
7.27

1   In whatever situation a ship may find herself, it is vital to avoid passing within 80 miles or so of the centre of the storm. If possible, it is preferable to keep outside a distance of 250 miles. If a vessel has at least 20 kn at her disposal and shapes a course that will take her most rapidly away from the storm before the wind has increased above the point at which her movement becomes restricted, it is unlikely that she will come to any harm.

Sometimes, if a tropical storm is moving slowly, a vessel ahead of it can easily outpace it or even overtake it if astern.

2   If a vessel is in an area where the presence or development of a storm is likely, frequent barometer readings should be made and corrected as at 7.25. If the barometer should fall 5 hPa below normal or if the wind should increase to force 6 when the barometer has fallen at least 3 hPa, there is little doubt that a storm is in the vicinity. If either of these criteria is met, the vessel should act as recommended in the following paragraphs until the barometer has risen above the limit just given and the wind has decreased below force 6. Should it be certain, however, that the vessel is behind the storm, or even in the navigable semicircle, it will be sufficient to alter course away from the centre keeping in mind the tendency of tropical storms to recurve towards N and NE in the N hemisphere, and towards S and SE in the S hemisphere.

3   **In the northern hemisphere**. If the wind is veering the ship must be in the dangerous semicircle. The ship should proceed with all available speed with the wind 10°–45°, depending on speed, on the starboard bow. As the wind veers the ship should alter course to starboard thereby tracing a course relative to the storm as shown in Diagram 7.26.

If the wind remains steady in direction or nearly steady so that the vessel should be in the path of the storm or very nearly in its path she should bring the wind well on to the starboard quarter and proceed with all available speed.

If the wind backs while in the navigable semicircle, the vessel should be manoeuvred to bring the wind

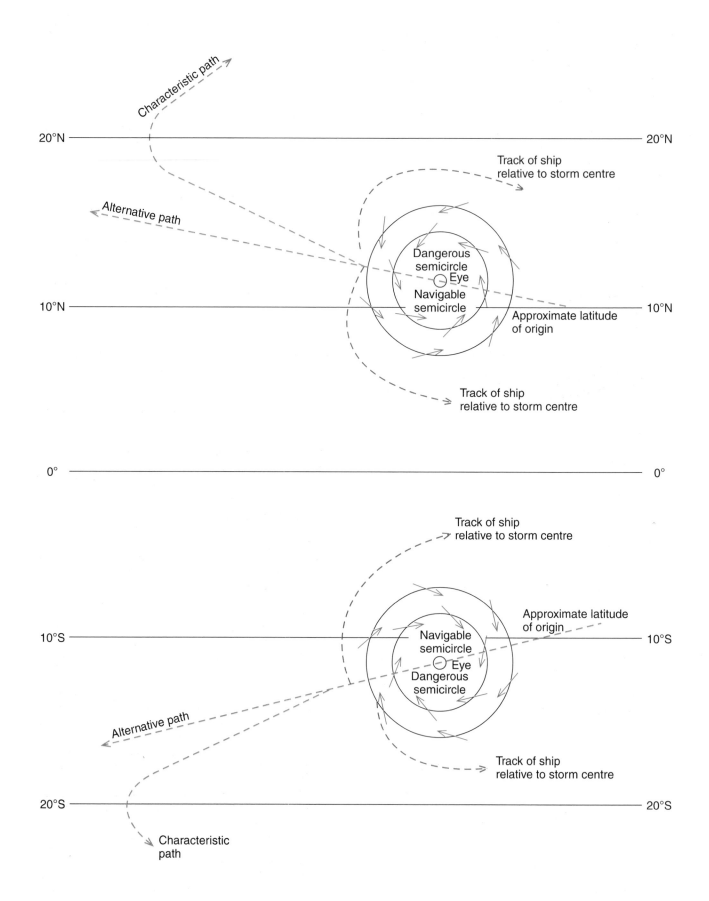

Typical paths of Tropical Storms (7.26)

onto the starboard quarter and all available speed used, turning to port as the wind backs to follow a track similar to that shown in the diagram.

4   **In the southern hemisphere**. If the wind is backing, the vessel must be in the dangerous semicircle. She should proceed with all available speed with the wind between 10°–45° on the port bow, depending on her speed. As the wind backs, the ship should alter course to port, thereby tracing a course relative to the storm as shown in Diagram 7.26.

If the wind remains steady or nearly steady in direction so that the vessel seems to be in the path of the storm, or very nearly in its path, she should bring the wind well on to the port quarter and proceed with all available speed, subsequently altering course to starboard as the wind begins to veer.

If the wind veers the ship is in the navigable semicircle. The ship should bring the wind on to the port quarter and proceed with all available speed, turning to starboard as the wind veers, following a track similar to that shown in the diagram.

5   If there is insufficient room to run when in the navigable semicircle and it is not practicable to seek shelter, the ship should heave-to with the wind on her starboard bow in the N hemisphere or on her port bow in the S hemisphere.

6   **In harbour.** When a tropical storm approaches it is preferable to put to sea if this can be done in time to avoid the worst of the storm. Riding out a tropical storm in a harbour or anchorage is an unpleasant and potentially hazardous experience when the centre passes within 80 miles or so, especially if there are other vessels close at hand. Even if berthed alongside or if special moorings are used, a vessel may be far from secure.

Obligatory reports
7.28

1   *The International Convention for the Safety of Life at Sea (SOLAS) 1974* requires that when a ship suspects the existence of or is in the vicinity of a tropical storm the Master must communicate the information by all means at his disposal to ships in the vicinity and to the nearest maritime radio station or signal station with which he can communicate; see 4.43. A report is similarly required if a ship should encounter winds of force 10 or above of which no warning has been received.

2   The report should state the following:
Position of the storm so far as it can be ascertained together with the UT (GMT) and date when it was encountered.
Position and true course and speed of the ship when the observation was made.
Barometric pressure at MSL (not corrected for diurnal variation).

3   Any change in barometric pressure during the previous 3 hours.
True direction and force of the wind.
State of the sea (5.26).
Height, length and period of the swell and the direction from which it comes (5.27–5.28).
As long as the ship is under the influence of the storm, similar messages should be transmitted at least every 3 hours if possible.

Anticyclones

General information
7.29

1   Over the E sides of the oceans the movement of anticyclones (or Highs) is generally slow and erratic and they may remain stationary for several days giving settled weather. The pressure gradient is usually slight, the winds light to moderate and the weather is often fine or partly cloudy; but in winter and in temperate latitudes skies may become overcast to give gloomy conditions. Precipitation, even as drizzle, is not uncommon near the middle of an anticyclone. Over the W parts of the oceans anticyclones are more likely to move quickly and consequently the associated weather is more changeable. Movement is generally towards the E.

Weather near the coast

Climate information
7.30

1   Each volume of *Admiralty Sailing Directions* includes climate information for a number of coastal stations in the region to which the volume refers and for which weather observations are available for a number of years.

2   However, it is important to note that the average values, frequencies and extremes given in climate tables refer specifically to the stations at which observations were made; they may not necessarily be fully representative of conditions in neighbouring localities or over the open sea and the approaches to ports in the vicinity.

Local modifications
7.31

1   Information from coastal climate stations must therefore be consulted with discretion; the following notes indicate ways in which conditions at sea may be different from those at the stations:
Wind speeds tend to be higher at sea, with a greater frequency of gales, than over the land;
Cloud amounts at a coastal station may differ considerably from those at sea.

2   Precipitation amounts recorded at a coastal station are generally applicable to nearby coastal waters but become less applicable with increasing distance from the coast. Where there is high ground near an observing station, onshore winds may induce considerably more precipitation than would be expected a few miles offshore.

3   Fog at sea is no indication that fog is present inland and vice versa: conditions favourable for fog formation in the two locations may be quite different (see 7.34–7.37). Fog statistics for coastal stations are therefore not generally applicable to neighbouring sea areas.

4   If a coastal climate station is at an appreciable altitude, the recorded temperatures and humidities can differ significantly from those at sea level. Temperatures at sea are less variable than over land. In winter temperatures over the sea are usually higher then over the land, especially at night. In summer it is usually cooler over the sea, especially during the day.

Effects of topography
7.32

1   Important modifications to the weather, especially wind conditions in coastal areas, can be caused by the local topography.

    If the coast is formed by steep cliffs, or if the ground rises rapidly inland, onshore winds are often deflected to blow nearly parallel to the coast and with increased force. Near headlands or islands with steep cliffs there may be large and sudden changes in wind speed and direction.

2   In a strait, especially if it is narrow and the sides steep, the wind will tend to blow along the strait in the direction most closely corresponding to the general wind direction in the area, even though these two directions may differ considerably. Where the strait narrows, funnelling will cause the wind strength to increase.

    Similarly in a fjord or other narrow steep-sided inlet there is a tendency for the wind to be funnelled along the inlet.

3   When a strong wind blows directly towards a very steep coast there is usually a narrow belt of contrary, gusty winds close to the coast.

    Where there is high ground near the coast, offshore winds are liable to be squally, especially when the air is appreciably colder than the sea and when the wind over the open sea is force 5 or more.

Fog

Cause
7.33

1   Fog is caused by the cooling of air to a temperature (known as the "dewpoint") at which it becomes saturated by the water vapour which is present within it. Condensation of this water vapour into minute water droplets produces fog; the type of fog depends on the means by which the air is cooled.

Sea or advection fog
7.34

1   When warm moist air flows over a relatively cold sea surface which cools it to its dewpoint, sea or advection fog is formed. This is the main type of fog experienced at sea; it may form and persist with moderate or even strong winds. It is often shallow so that mastheads of ships may protrude above it; and at times its base is a few feet above sea level with a clear layer below the fog.

2   In temperate and high latitudes sea fog is most common in spring and early summer when sea temperature is at its lowest. It is particularly frequent and prevalent where the prevailing winds transport warm moist air over areas of cold water or over the major cold ocean currents.

3   The principal parts of the world in which sea fog is prevalent are:

    Polar regions in summer.
    Grand Banks of Newfoundland (Labrador Current).
    NW Pacific Ocean (Kamchatka Current).
    The cold ocean currents off the W seaboards of continents lying within the Trade Wind belts;

notably California, Chile, Peru, SW Africa and Morocco.
British Isles, especially the SW approaches to the English Channel in spring and early summer.

Frontal fog
7.35

1   On a warm front or occlusion, fog may occur especially if the temperature of the air in advance of the front is very low. The fog is caused by the mixing of the warm and cold air on the two sides of the front; rain ahead of the front may help to raise the relative humidity to near saturation point. The fog is usually confined to a relatively narrow belt near the frontal boundary, but sea fog may develop in the warm moist air behind the front.

Arctic sea smoke
7.36

1   Also known as "frost smoke", arctic sea smoke (See photograph in Ice Glossary) occurs chiefly in high latitudes and is produced when very cold air blows over a relatively warm sea surface. Evaporation takes place from the water surface but as the air is at a much lower temperature, it is unable to hold all of the water vapour. Consequently, some water vapour immediately condenses to form a fog; the sea appears to be steaming, and the visibility may be very seriously reduced. This type of fog is encountered where a cold wind is blowing off ice or snow on to a relatively warm sea and may develop over the open water in gaps in an icefield.

Radiation fog
7.37

1   Radiation fog forms over low-lying land on clear nights, conditions for maximum radiative cooling, especially during the winter months. This fog is thickest during the latter part of the night and early part of the day. Occasionally it drifts out to sea but is found no farther than 10–15 miles offshore as the relatively high sea surface temperature causes the water droplets to evaporate.

Forecasting sea fog
7.38

1   Warnings of the likely formation of sea fog may be obtained by frequent observations of air and sea surface temperatures; if the sea surface temperature falls below the dewpoint (see Table 7.38.1), fog is almost certain to form.

2   The following procedure is recommended whenever the temperature of the air is higher than, or almost equal to that of the sea, especially at night when approaching fog cannot be seen until shortly before entering it. Sea and air (both dry and wet bulb) temperatures should be observed at least every 10 minutes and the sea surface temperature and dewpoint temperature plotted against time, as in Diagram 7.38.2.

3   If the curves converge fog may be expected when they coincide. The example shows that by 2200 there is a probability of running into fog about 2300, assuming that the sea surface temperature continues to fall at the same rate.

Dry Bulb °C	Depression of Wet Bulb	Dry Bulb °C

Dry Bulb °C	0°	0·2°	0·4°	0·6°	0·8°	1·0°	1·2°	1·4°	1·6°	1·8°	2·0°	2·5°	3·0°	3·5°	4·0°	4·5°	5·0°	5·5°	6·0°	6·5°	7·0°	7·5°	8·0°	8·5°	9·0°	Dry Bulb °C
40	40	40	40	39	39	39	39	38	38	38	38	37	36	36	35	34	34	33	32	32	31	30	29	29	28	40
39	39	39	39	38	38	38	38	37	37	37	37	36	35	35	34	33	33	32	31	31	30	29	28	28	27	39
38	38	38	38	37	37	37	37	36	36	36	35	35	34	34	33	32	32	31	30	29	29	28	27	26	26	38
37	37	37	37	36	36	36	36	35	35	35	34	34	33	32	32	31	30	30	29	28	28	27	26	25	24	37
36	36	36	35	35	35	35	34	34	34	34	33	33	32	31	31	30	29	29	28	27	26	26	25	24	23	36
35	35	35	34	34	34	34	33	33	33	33	32	32	31	30	30	29	28	28	27	26	25	24	24	23	22	35
34	34	34	33	33	33	33	32	32	32	32	31	31	30	29	29	28	27	26	26	25	24	23	22	22	21	34
33	33	33	32	32	32	32	31	31	31	31	30	30	29	28	28	27	26	25	25	24	23	22	21	20	19	33
32	32	32	31	31	31	31	30	30	30	30	29	29	28	27	26	26	25	24	23	23	22	21	20	19	18	32
31	31	31	30	30	30	30	29	29	29	29	28	28	27	26	25	25	24	23	22	21	21	20	19	18	17	31
30	30	30	29	29	29	29	28	28	28	28	27	27	26	25	24	24	23	22	21	20	19	18	19	17	16	30
29	29	29	28	28	28	28	27	27	27	27	26	25	25	24	23	22	22	21	20	19	18	17	16	15	14	29
28	28	28	27	27	27	27	26	26	26	25	25	24	24	23	22	21	20	20	19	18	17	16	15	14	13	28
27	27	27	27	26	26	26	25	25	25	24	24	23	23	22	21	20	19	18	18	17	16	15	14	13	11	27
26	26	26	25	25	25	25	24	24	24	23	23	22	22	21	20	19	18	17	16	15	14	13	12	11	10	26
25	25	25	24	24	24	24	23	23	23	22	22	21	20	20	19	18	17	16	15	14	13	12	11	10	8	25
24	24	24	23	23	23	23	22	22	22	21	21	20	19	19	18	17	16	15	14	13	12	11	9	8	7	24
23	23	23	22	22	22	21	21	21	21	20	20	19	18	17	17	16	15	14	13	12	10	9	8	7	5	23
22	22	22	21	21	21	20	20	20	20	19	19	18	17	16	15	14	13	12	11	10	9	8	6	5	3	22
21	21	21	20	20	20	19	19	19	18	18	18	17	16	15	14	13	12	11	10	9	8	6	5	3	1	21
20	20	20	19	19	19	18	18	18	17	17	17	16	15	14	13	12	11	10	9	7	6	5	3	1	0	20
19	19	19	18	18	18	17	17	17	16	16	16	15	14	13	12	11	10	9	7	6	4	3	1	0	-2	19
18	18	18	17	17	17	16	16	16	15	15	15	14	13	12	11	10	8	7	6	4	3	1	-0	-2	-5	18
17	17	17	16	16	16	15	15	15	14	14	14	13	12	11	9	8	7	6	4	3	1	-0	-3	-5	-7	17
16	16	16	15	15	15	14	14	14	13	13	12	11	10	9	8	7	6	4	3	1	0	-2	-5	-7	-10	16
15	15	15	14	14	14	13	13	12	12	12	11	10	9	8	7	6	4	3	1	0	-2	-5	-7	-10	-14	15
14	14	14	13	13	13	12	12	11	11	11	10	9	8	7	6	4	3	1	0	-2	-4	-7	-10	-13	-18	14
13	13	13	12	12	11	11	11	10	10	9	9	8	7	6	4	3	1	0	-2	-4	-7	-9	-13	-17	-23	13
12	12	12	11	11	10	10	10	9	9	8	8	7	6	4	3	1	0	-2	-4	-6	-9	-12	-16	-22	-33	12
11	11	11	10	10	9	9	9	8	8	7	7	6	4	3	1	0	-2	-4	-6	-8	-12	-15	-21	-30		11
10	10	10	9	9	8	8	8	7	7	6	6	4	3	2	0	-2	-3	-6	-8	-11	-15	-19	-27			10
9	9	9	8	8	7	7	6	6	5	5	4	3	2	0	-1	-3	-5	-8	-10	-14	-18					9
8	8	8	7	7	6	6	5	5	4	4	3	2	0	-1	-3	-5	-7	-10	-13	-17						8
7	7	7	6	6	5	5	4	4	3	3	2	1	-1	-3	-4	-7	-9	-12	-16							7
6	6	6	5	5	4	4	3	3	2	1	1	-0	-2	-4	-6	-9	-11	-15								6
5	5	5	4	4	3	2	2	1	1	0	0	-2	-4	-6	-8	-10	-14	-15								5
4	4	4	3	2	2	1	1	0	0	-1	-1	-3	-5	-7	-10	-11	-14	-18								4
3	3	3	2	1	1	0	0	-1	-2	-2	-3	-5	-7	-8	-11	-14	-17									3
2	2	2	1	0	0	-1	-1	-2	-3	-3	-4	-5	-8	-10	-13	16										2
1	1	1	0	-1	-1	-2	-2	-3	-4	-4	-5	-7	-9	-12	-15	-19										1
0	0	-1	-1	-2	-2	-3	-4	-4	-5	-6	-7	-9	-11	-14	-18											0
-1	-1	-2	-2	-3	-4	-4	-5	-6	-6	-7	-8	-10	-13	-17												-1
-2	-2	-3	-4	-4	-5	-6	-6	-7	-8	-9	-10	-12	-15	-19												-2
-3	-3	-4	-5	-5	-6	-7	-8	-9	-9	-10	-11	-14	-18													-3
-4	-5	-5	-6	-7	-7	-8	-9	-10	-11	-12	-13	-16														-4
-5	-6	-6	-7	-8	-9	-10	-10	-11	-13	-14	-15	-18														-5
-6	-7	-7	-8	-9	-10	-11	-12	-13	-14	-15	-17															-6
-7	-8	-9	-9	-10	-11	-12	-13	-15	-16	-17	-19															-7
-8	-9	-10	-11	-12	-13	-14	-15	-16	-18	-19																-8
-9	-10	-11	-12	-13	-14	-15	-17	-18	-19																	-9
-10	-11	-12	-13	-14	-15	-17	-18																			-10
-11	-12	-13	-14	-16	-17	-18																				-11
-12	-13	-14	-16	-17	-18																					-12
-13	-15	-16	-17	-18																						-13
-14	-16	-17	-18																							-14
-15	-17	-18	-19																							-15
-16	-18	-19																								-16
-17	-19																									-17

In the table, lines are ruled to draw attention to the fact that above the line evaporation is going on from a water surface, while below the line it is going on from an ice surface. Owing to this, interpolation must not be made between figures on different sides of the lines.

For dry bulb temperatures below 0°C it will be noted that, when the depression of the wet bulb is zero, i.e. when the temperature of the wet bulb is equal to that of the dry bulb, the dew-point is still below the dry bulb, and the relative humidity is less than 100 per cent. These apparent anomalies are a consequence of the method of computing dew-points and relative humidities now adopted by the Met Office, in which the standard saturation pressure for temperature below 0°C is taken as that over water, and not as that over ice.

DEWPOINT TABLE
Table (7.38.1)
(For use with marine screen)

1 In areas where a rapid fall of sea surface temperature may be encountered, which can be seen from the appropriate chartlet in *Admiralty Sailing Directions*, a reliable warning of fog will be given when the dewpoint is within 5°C of the sea surface temperature. To avoid fog a course should be set for warmer waters.

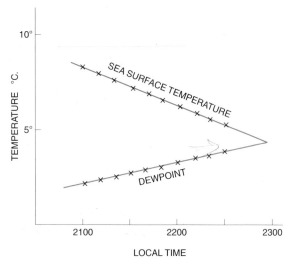

Sea Temperatures and Dewpoint readings plotted against Time (7.38.2)

Storm warning signals

Systems
7.39

1 Radio broadcasts of storm warnings are listed and described in *Admiralty List of Radio Signals Volume 3*.

Visual storm warning signals, either national or local, are shown in many countries, and these signals are described in the appropriate volumes of *Admiralty Sailing Directions*.

2 **The International System of Visual Storm Warning Signals,** prescribed by the *International Convention for the Safety of Life at Sea (SOLAS) 1974*, is in use in some countries, and members of the Convention establishing new systems are recommended to adopt it.

In the International System, day signals each consist of a shape or rectangular flag, of any colour, or two shapes or flags disposed vertically; night signals consist of lights disposed vertically; see diagram 7.39.

National or local signals may be used in conjunction with these signals, provided they do not resemble the International ones.

3 More than one day signal may be displayed simultaneously. For example, a gale expected to commence from the SW quadrant and veering is indicated by a cone, pointing down, and a single flag, the initial direction being indicated by the cone.

4 A near gale expected from the SW quadrant is indicated by a ball and a cone, point down.

The signal "Near gale expected" may be used to indicate that a strong breeze is expected if local circumstances, such as fishing activities, call for warnings of winds less strong than a near gale.

Day	Night	Meaning
●	○	Near gale expected
▲	● ●	Gale or storm expected commencing in NW quadrant
▼	○ ○	Gale or storm expected commencing in SW quadrant
▲ ▲	● ○	Gale or storm expected commencing in NE quadrant
▼ ▼	○ ●	Gale or storm expected commencing in SE quadrant
▯	Flags may be of any suitable colour	Wind expected to veer
▯ ▯		Wind expected to back
✚	● ● ●	Hurricane expected

International System of Visual Storm Warning Signals (7.39)

Weather routeing of ships

Routeing
7.40

1 The mariner planning a transoceanic passage can select either the shortest route, or the quickest route at a given speed, or the most suitable route from the point of view of weather or any other particular requirements.

2 The shortest distance from the point of departure to destination, providing no obstructions lie on the track, is the great circle between the two positions. For selected ports and positions throughout the world,

distances based on great circle routes are given in *Admiralty Distance Tables*.

3 Climate conditions, however, such as the existence of currents or the prevalence of wind, sea or swell from certain directions, may lead to the selection of a longer "climatological route" along which a higher speed can be expected to be made good. For instance, it has been estimated that the great circle route across the N Atlantic Ocean represents the fastest route only 13% of the time for E-bound ships and 2% of the time for W-bound ones. Climatological

routes are shown on routeing charts and are considered in *Ocean Passages for the World*.

Weather routeing
7.41

1   The development of weather routeing has followed advances in the collection of oceanographical and meteorological data, improved forecasting techniques and international co-operation, the introduction of orbital weather satellites, and better communications including the use of facsimile recorders to display on board the latest weather maps, ice charts and other forecasts.

2   Weather routeing makes use of the actual weather, as opposed to the expected climate conditions, and the forecast weather in the vicinity of the anticipated route. By using weather forecasts to select a route, and then modifying the route as necessary as the voyage proceeds, consideration can be given not only to the quickest route, known as the "optimum route", but also to the "strategic route" which will minimise

storm damage to the ship and her cargo, or suit any other particular requirements. Weather routeing is at present extensively used for passages across the North and South Atlantic and Pacific Oceans.

3   If a ship is on a regular run fitted with a facsimile recorder, and carries a weather forecaster with a sound knowledge of routeing methods, weather routeing can often be satisfactorily carried out on board.

4   Alternatively, if details of the ship are given, use can be made of one of the weather routeing services provided by certain governments or consultancy firms. The Met Office, Exeter, provides a routeing service for ships world-wide; a team of highly trained and experienced forecasters and Ship Masters have extensive facilities to hand for close study of a ship's individual requirements and problems. Further details and the procedure for requesting this Ship Routeing Service and similar weather routeing services are given in *Admiralty List of Radio Signals Volume 3*.

Weather related phenomena

Abnormal refraction

General information
7.42

1   The propagation of electromagnetic waves, including light and radar waves, is influenced by the lapse rate of temperature and humidity, and therefore density, with height.

2   When conditions are normal in the near-surface layers of the atmosphere there is a modest decrease of temperature with height and uniform humidity, and no significant refraction of electromagnetic waves occurs. Variations in these conditions can cause appreciable vertical refraction of light rays, and radio transmissions varying with their frequencies. Extraordinary radio propagation and optical effects can result, including abnormal radar ranges and the phenomenon known as mirage.

3   **Caution.** Whenever abnormal refraction is observed or suspected, either visually or by anomalous radar performance, the mariner should exercise caution, particularly in taking sights or in considering radar ranges.

Super-refraction

Causes
7.43

1   Super-refraction or downward bending is caused either when humidity decreases with height or when the temperature lapse rate is less than normal. When temperature increases with height, that is when an inversion is present, the downward bending of rays and signals is particularly enhanced.

2   Super-refraction increases both the optical and radar horizons, so that it is possible to see and to detect by radar objects which are actually beyond the geometrical horizon, see Diagram 7.43.

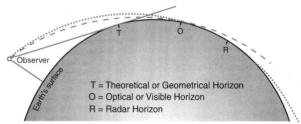

T = Theoretical or Geometrical Horizon
O = Optical or Visible Horizon
R = Radar Horizon

Super refraction (7.43)

Likely conditions
7.44

1   Super-refraction can be expected:
   In high latitudes wherever the sea surface temperature is exceptionally low.
   In light winds and calms.
   In anticyclonic conditions, particularly in the semi-permanent sub-tropical anticyclone zones over the large oceans.
   In trade wind zones.
   In coastal areas where warm air blows offshore over a cooler sea.
   Occasionally, behind a cold front.

Effect on radar
7.45

1   A modest degree of super-refraction is usually present over the sea as evaporation from the sea surface gives rise to a decrease in humidity immediately above the sea. Consequently, average radar detection ranges over the sea are often 15–20% above geometrical horizon range. When a surface temperature inversion is present extremely long ranges may be possible since the transmitted signals may be refracted downwards more sharply, to be reflected upwards from the sea surface, and then again bent downwards, and the process repeated. The signals thus effectively travel and return along a duct parallel to the Earth's surface. See Diagram 7.45.

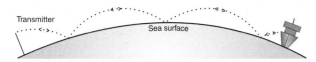

Duct propagation (7.45)

Optical effect
7.46

1 Objects beyond the geometrical horizon may become visible, so that lights may be raised at much greater distances than expected.

2 **Superior mirage,** when an inverted image is seen above the real object, is an occasional effect produced when the air is appreciably warmer than the sea. Sometimes an erect image is seen immediately above and touching the inverted one. The object and its images in this instance are well-defined, in contrast with the shimmering object and image of an inferior mirage (7.50).

3 Superior mirage is most often experienced in high latitudes and wherever the sea surface temperature is exceptionally low.

Sub-refraction

Causes
7.47

1 Sub-refraction or upward bending occurs when humidity increases and temperature decreases abnormally rapidly with height.

Likely conditions
7.48

1 Sub-refraction may occur when:
Cool air flows over a relatively warmer sea. This is most likely in coastal waters and especially polar regions in the vicinity of very cold land masses or ice fields:

2 In warm moist air over the sea when an increase in humidity with height may occur. In this case a temperature inversion will usually accompany the humidity inversion, but when the humidity factor is dominant sub-refraction will result. These conditions may sometimes be found in the warm sector of a depression in temperate latitudes.

Effect on radar
7.49

1 Sub-refraction reduces the distance of radar horizons, occasionally to an extent that a clearly visible object cannot be detected by radar. See Diagram 7.50.

Sub-refraction effects can be difficult to determine on radar, but may be suspected when poor results are obtained from a set otherwise performing well.

Optical effect
7.50

1 The ranges at which objects are visible are decreased.

Inferior mirage appears as a shimmering horizon, possibly having the appearance of water, and may be seen over hot surfaces, such as desert sand, rock or road surfaces when a hot sun is beating down with comparatively cool air above them. Objects such as an island, a coastline or a ship may appear to be floating in air above a shimmering horizon. The lower features of the object, for example the hull of a ship, may be either invisible or have an inverted image underneath. Inferior mirage is uncommon at sea and is more likely to be observed near the coast than offshore.

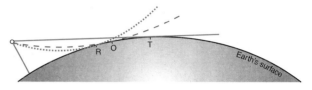

T = Theoretical or Geometrical Horizon
O = Optical or Visible Horizon
R = Radar Horizon

Sub-refraction (7.50)

Aurora

General information
7.51

1 Aurora means dawn and indeed the normal appearance of the phenomenon when seen in the latitudes of Britain is a dawn-like glow on the N horizon. The light of the aurora is emitted by the atmospheric gases when they are bombarded by a stream of electrically charged particles originating in the sun. As the stream of particles approaches the Earth it is directed towards the two magnetic poles by the Earth's magnetic field and so it normally enters the upper atmosphere in high latitudes in each hemisphere. The aurora therefore occurs most frequently in two zones girdling the Earth about 20°–25° from the N and S magnetic poles. The aurora of the N hemisphere is called aurora borealis and that of the S hemisphere aurora australis.

2 The emission of the light that is seen as aurora, takes place at heights above 60 miles, so that it may be seen at distances of about 600 miles from the place where it is overhead. The auroral glow that is seen on the N horizon in Britain is the upper portion of a display that is overhead between Føroyar and Iceland.

3 **Northern hemisphere.** The zone of maximum frequency of aurora borealis crosses Hudson Bay and the Labrador coast at about 58°N. It runs S of Kap Farvel, along the S coast of Iceland and passes just N of Nordkapp and Novaya Zemlya, over Mys Chelyuskina, and into the N part of Alaska.

4 **Southern hemisphere.** Much of the S auroral zone is within the continent of Antarctic. It extends into the adjacent oceans passing near Macquarie Island and reaching its lowest latitude, 53°S, at approximately 140°E. Aurora australis is thus seen more frequently over the SE parts of the Indian Ocean and in Australian waters than at the same latitudes in the South Atlantic Ocean.

Great aurora
7.52

1 While overhead aurora is mainly confined to the two auroral zones, where it may be seen at some time on every clear dark night, there are times when it moves towards the equator from each zone; on rare occasions it has been visible in the tropics. Departures of aurora from its usual geographical position occur at

Ray (7.53.1)

Surfaces (7.53.2)

Rayed Band (7.53.3)

Homogenous Arc (7.53.4)

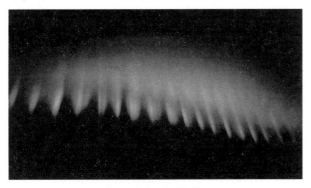

Rayed Arc (7.53.5)

Homogenous Band (7.53.6)

times of great solar activity, when large sunspots appear on the sun's disc. The great aurora that is seen widely over the Earth usually follows about a day after a great flare or eruption has occurred in the central part of the sun's disc. It is at this time that observers in lower latitudes may see aurora, not as the familiar unspectacular glow on the horizon, but in the many striking forms that it may assume when it is situated nearly overhead.

Auroral forms
7.53

1 The various auroral forms, arcs, bands and rays, are illustrated above. Auroral rays are always aligned along the direction of the lines of force of the Earth's magnetic field so that when they cover a large part of the overhead sky, they appear to radiate from a point to form a crown or corona. The point from which they radiate lies in the direction in which the S pole of a freely suspended magnetic needle, a dip needle, points in the N hemisphere, or the N pole in the S hemisphere. In the latitudes of Britain, this point, called the magnetic zenith, is 70° above the S horizon and so is 20°S of the true zenith.

2 The luminance of the normal aurora is below the threshold of colour perception of the eye, so the forms appear grey-white in colour. A brilliant display however may be strongly coloured, greens and reds being

Corona (7.53.7)

predominant and when the forms also are in rapid movement, the phenomenon is of a magnificence that defies description.

Solar activity and associated terrestrial events
7.54

1   Being closely associated with solar activity, the intensity and frequency of auroral displays are greatest at the time of maximum of the 11 year sunspot cycle and least at the time of sunspot minimum. During a year of maximum sunspot activity aurora may be seen on about 200 nights in latitudes of Shetland Isles and only about 10 nights in the English Channel; during a year of minimum activity these figures reduce to 125 and nil respectively.

2   Especially at the time of sunspot minimum, aurora shows a tendency to recur at intervals of 27 days, which is the period of rotation of the sun as observed from the Earth. This suggests that a particular local area of the sun is the source of a continuous stream of particles, which is sprayed out, rather like water from the rotating nozzle of a hose, and sweeps across the Earth at intervals of 27 days. Associated with a great aurora, therefore, there is invariably marked disturbance in the Earth's magnetic field which is called a magnetic storm when it is of exceptional severity.

Magnetic and ionospheric storms

General information
7.55

1   Disturbances on the sun may cause disturbances of the magnetic compass needle and interference with radio communications. See 11.30 for a description of the effects on Global Navigation Satellite Systems (GNSS).

2   At the time of an intense solar flare or eruption, a flash of ultraviolet light and a stream of charged particles are emitted from the sun.

3   The flash of ultraviolet light takes only 8 minutes to reach the Earth, where it produces great ionisation, electrification, at abnormally low layers of the upper atmosphere. Short radio waves which travel round the Earth by being reflected from a higher layer of the upper atmosphere cannot penetrate this barrier of ionisation and a radio "fade out" is experienced. Long radio waves however may be reflected more strongly from the base of the lower layer of ionisation. Since these short range radio fade outs and long wave enhancements are caused by the effects of ultraviolet light from the sun, they are confined to the sunlit side of the Earth and are almost simultaneous with the flare, lasting on the average for about 20 minutes.

4   The stream of charged particles, travelling much more slowly than light, arrives at the Earth, if it is suitably directed, at from 1 to about 3 days after it leaves the sun; it visibly signals its arrival by producing a bright and active aurora. It too causes great ionisation in the upper atmosphere, which is much more prolonged than that caused by the ultra-violet light. There is again deterioration in short wave radio communications, which may be a complete "blackout" in higher latitudes. At this time currents of the order of a million amperes may circulate in the upper atmosphere. The magnetic field of the fluctuating currents is appreciable at the Earth's surface and may deflect a compass needle noticeably from its normal position. The effects on these so-called magnetic and ionospheric storms, which may persist with varying intensity for several days, are usually greatest in higher latitudes. Radio blackouts and simultaneous deviations of the magnetic compass needle by several degrees are not uncommon in and near auroral zones. When a great aurora is seen in abnormally low latitudes, it is invariably accompanied by a magnetic and ionospheric storm. Unlike the fade out which occurs only on the sunlit side of Earth, the interference with radio communications which accompanies an aurora and magnetic storm may occur by day and at night.

5   All these effects occur most frequently, and in most intense forms, at the time of sunspot maximum.

Increases in solar activity could affect the reliability of GPS and other satellite systems; for further details see *Admiralty List of Radio Signals Volume 2*.

SECTION III

REGULATION OF THE MARITIME ENVIRONMENT

NOTES

Chapter 8

INTERNATIONAL ORGANISATIONS

International Maritime Organisation (IMO)

History
8.1

1   Through the latter part of the 19th century, seafaring nations started to become aware of the need to develop international regulations for the improvement of safety at sea, and some of the earliest maritime treaties date from this period. Later, the first safety of life at sea (SOLAS) convention was initiated following the loss of RMS *Titanic* in 1912.

2   However it was not until 1948, following two world wars and the establishment of the United Nations, that the Convention establishing the Inter-Governmental Consultative Organisation (IMCO) was adopted in Geneva. The Convention came into force in 1958, and met for the first time in London the following year.

3   The name was changed to the International Maritime Organisation (IMO) in 1982, and it is now (2009) a specialised agency of the United Nations with 168 Member States, and 3 Associate Members.

Purpose
8.2

1   The IMO exists to play a key role in ensuring that lives at sea are not put at risk, and that the marine environment is not polluted by shipping.

Structure
8.3

1   The Organisation consists of an Assembly, a Council and four standing Committees, along with sub-committees and working groups to support and assist the main committees.
   Assembly. The Assembly is the highest governing body of the organisation. It consists of representatives of all Member States and meets once every two years in regular session; it can, however, meet in extraordinary session if necessary. The Assembly is responsible for approving the work programme, voting the budget and determining financial arrangements. It also elects the Council.

2   **Council.** The Council consists of 40 Member State representatives, made up of 10 nations with the largest interest in providing international shipping services, 10 states with the largest interest in international seaborne trade, and 20 states not elected in the other categories which have a special interest in maritime transport or navigation, and whose election to the Council will ensure the representation of all major geographical areas of the world.

Committees
8.4

1   There are four main committees:
   The Maritime Safety Committee (MSC). The MSC is the highest technical body of the IMO, consisting of representatives of all Member States. The function of the MSC is to consider any matter within the scope of the IMO concerned with aids to navigation, construction and equipment of vessels, manning from a safety standpoint, rules for the prevention of collisions, handling of dangerous cargoes, maritime safety procedures and requirements, hydrographic information, log-books and navigational records, marine casualty investigations, salvage, rescue, and any other matters directly affecting maritime safety.

2   **The Marine Environment Protection Committee (MEPC).** The MEPC, which consists of all Member States, is empowered to consider any matter within the scope of the IMO concerned with the prevention and control of pollution from ships. In particular, it is concerned with the adoption and amendment of conventions and other regulations and measures to ensure their enforcement.

3   **Legal Committee.** The Legal Committee is empowered to deal with any legal matters within the scope of the IMO. It consists of representatives of all Member States. It was originally established in 1967 as a subsidiary body to deal with legal questions arising from the *Torrey Canyon* disaster.

4   **Technical Cooperation Committee.** The Technical Cooperation Committee is required to consider any matter within the scope of the IMO concerned with the implementation of technical cooperation projects for which the Organisation acts as the executing or cooperating agency and any other matters relating to activities in the field of technical cooperation.
   A Facilitation Committee and a number of sub-committees support the work of the main technical committees.

5   **Facilitation Committee.** The Facilitation Committee is a subsidiary body of the Council, established in 1972 dealing with the elimination of "Red Tape" and unnecessary formalities in international shipping. Participation in the work of the Committee is open to representatives of any Member State.

6   **Sub-committees.** There are nine sub-committees whose work assists the MSC and the MEPC:
   Bulk Liquids and Gases (BLG).
   Carriage of Dangerous Goods, Solid Cargoes and Containers (DSC).
   Fire Protection (FP).
   Radio Communications and Search and Rescue (COMSAR).
   Safety of Navigation (NAV).

7   Ship Design and Equipment (DE).
   Stability, Load Lines and Fishing Vessels Safety (SLF).
   Standards of Training and Watchkeeping (STW).
   Flag State Implementation (FSI).

Activities
8.5

1   IMO strives for the highest standards of safety at sea, in navigation, and in all other maritime matters. It consults, discusses and advises on any maritime question submitted by a member state, or any member of the United Nations Organization. It calls conferences when necessary, and drafts such maritime conventions and agreements as may be required.

2   International Conventions which have resulted from its work, and whose measures have been ratified and adopted by almost all the world's shipping nations, include, in addition to those mentioned above, others on the following subjects: Load Lines, Tonnage Measurement, the introduction of a new International Code of Signals, and other maritime matters.

International Hydrographic Organisation (IHO)

Objectives
8.6

1   The International Hydrographic Organization is an inter-governmental consultative and technical organization. The object of the Organization is to bring about:

   The co-ordination of the activities of national hydrographic offices.

   The greatest possible uniformity in nautical charts and documents.

   The development of the sciences in the field of hydrography and the techniques employed in descriptive oceanography.

History
8.7

1   International co-operation in the field of hydrography began with the International Congress of Navigation held in Saint Petersburg (Leningrad) in 1908 and the International Maritime Conference held in the same venue in 1912. In 1919, 24 nations met in London for a Hydrographic Conference at which it was decided that a permanent body should be created. The resulting Hydrographic Bureau began its activity in 1921 with 19 member states and with headquarters in the Principality of Monaco, to which the Bureau had been invited by HSH Prince Albert I of Monaco.

2   In 1970 an inter-governmental convention entered into force which changed the Organization's name and legal status, creating the International Hydrographic Organization (IHO), with its headquarters, the International Hydrographic Bureau (IHB), permanently established in Monaco (4 quai Antoine 1er, B.P. 445, MC 98011, MONACO CEDEX, Principality of Monaco) (Email: info@ihb.mc) (IHO web site: www.iho.shom.fr). In December 2007 the Organization had 84 member states.

Conferences
8.8

1   The official representatives of each member government within the IHO is normally the national Hydrographer, or Director of Hydrography, and these persons, together with their technical staff, meet at five yearly intervals in Monaco for an International Hydrographic Conference. The Conference reviews the progress achieved by the Organization and adopts the programmes to be pursued during the next five years. A Directing Committee of three senior Hydrographers is elected to guide the work of the Bureau during that time.

Administration
8.9

1   The Directing Committee, together with a small international staff of technical experts, co-ordinates the programmes and provides advice and assistance to member states. All member states have an equal voice in arriving at agreed solutions to problems of standardization and in programming the work of the Bureau, whilst any member state may initiate proposals for IHO consideration.

Activities
8.10

1   The IHO has worked towards standardization in the specifications, symbols, style and formats used for nautical charts and related publications since 1921. A significant milestone in standardization was reached by adoption of the *Chart Specifications of the IHO* in 1982. The permanently established Chart Standardization and Paper Chart Working Group (CSPCWG) keeps specifications under continuous review.

   The practical benefits of the IHO's work are most directly seen in such developments as International Charts (2.34) and co-ordinated Navigational Warning Services (4.6).

2   The advent of exceptionally deep-draught ships, the recognition of the need to protect the environment, the changing maritime trade patterns, the growing importance of sea bed resources, and the Law of the Sea Convention affecting areas of national jurisdiction have all served to highlight the inadequacies of existing nautical charts and publications. Charts which served well just a few years ago now require re-compilation to incorporate new data, and this data must be gathered by hydrographic survey operations. The deficiency is not limited to sparsely surveyed waters of developing nations, but also exists in the coastal waters of major industrial states.

3   Reliable charts can be produced only from reliable hydrographic surveys. The IHO's tasks include the promotion of training for surveyors, and technical assistance to less developed countries.

Regional Hydrographic Commissions
8.11

1   The IHB encourages the establishment of Regional Hydrographic Commissions or Groups, composed of representatives from member states' hydrographic services within defined geographic areas, who meet at intervals to discuss mutual hydrographic and chart production problems, plan joint survey operations, and resolve schemes for medium and large scale International chart coverage of their regions.

Publications
8.12

1   The IHO Secretariat produces a series of technical publications, available from the IHO website (www.iho.int) by subscription and also on CD-ROM from the Secretariat. Some periodical publications are available in printed form.

International Association of Marine Aids to Navigation and Lighthouse Authorities (IALA)

Introduction
8.13

1   IALA is a non-profit, non-governmental organisation (NGO) devoted to the harmonization of marine aids to navigation. IALA was formed in 1957 as a technical association to provide a framework for aids to navigation authorities, manufacturers and consultants from all parts of the world to work with a common effort to harmonize standards for aids to navigation systems worldwide, facilitate the safe and efficient movement of shipping and enhance the protection of the maritime environment.

Membership
8.14

1   IALA has 4 types of membership:

National. Available to the national authority of any country that is legally responsible for the provision, management, maintenance or operation of marine aids to navigation.

Associate. Available to any other service, organisation or scientific agency concerned with aids to navigation or related matters.

Industrial. Available to manufacturers and distributors of marine aids to navigation equipment for sale, or organisations providing aids to marine navigation services or technical advice under contract.

Honorary membership, which may be conferred by the IALA Council to any individual who is considered to have made an important contribution to the work of IALA.

Council
8.15

1   IALA is administered by a Council of up to 18 elected, and 2 non-elected members. The elected positions are determined by a ballot of all national members attending a General Assembly. Only one member from any country may be elected, and the aim is to achieve as broad a representation from around the world as possible.

Committees
8.16

1   The permanent programme of work is maintained by a number of committees:

Aids to Navigation Management (ANM). This committee deals with the management aspects of aids to navigation services, aiming to develop and review related IALA documentation on issues such as channel design, management of services relating to AIS networks, the Maritime Buoyage System, and quality management. It is also responsible for the maintenance of the *IALA*

NAVGUIDE, a comprehensive reference document, published every 4 years.

2   **Engineering, Environmental and Preservation (EEP).** This committee deals with engineering, design, maintenance and conservation issues relating to aids to navigation. It develops and reviews related IALA documentation on issues such as optics, light and colour for aids to navigation, design and maintenance of equipment, remote control and monitoring of environmental considerations. In addition, the work of the committee covers further development of the certification process and promotion of international research and development into issues such as light measurement and conspicuity. It also provides guidance on the conservation and alternative uses of traditional aids to navigation.

3   **e-NAV.** The e-NAV committee deals with the aspects of e-navigation relating to aids to navigation. It reviews and develops related IALA documentation on issues such as AIS (as applied to aids to navigation), future DGNSS systems, the impact of new radar technology on radar aids to navigation and the impact of electronic shipborne navigation aids on aid to navigation systems. It also works with other international organisations to develop the overall e-navigation concept.

4   **Legal Advisory Panel (LAP).** The panel was established by the IALA Council in June 2005 to address potential liability issues pertaining to the provision of aids to navigation and related services (e.g. advice given by a VTS, the use of aids to navigation and the provision of navigation warnings). It deals with IALA's legal responsibilities and liabilities, such as the need for disclaimers for recommendations, guidelines, e-mails and websites.

5   **Pilotage Authority Forum (PAF).** This forum provides a mechanism for IALA members with responsibility for the delivery of pilotage services to discuss issues of common interest and to work towards the international harmonization of pilotage services. The PAF develops documentation, including guidelines, on items of common concern to IALA members who are "competent pilotage authorities" as defined in IMO Assembly Resolution A.960(23), paragraph 2.1 "...the national or regional governments legally responsible for the provision of a pilotage system."

6   **Policy Advisory Panel (PAP).** This committee is made up of the Chairman and Vice-chairman of each of the main committees and provides a harmonizing mechanism to ensure the effectiveness and efficiency of the work of each committee.

7   **Vessel Traffic Services (VTS).** The VTS Committee deals with all aspects of VTS, including the expanding role of vessel monitoring for maritime safety, environmental protection and security. The committee aims to develop and review VTS related IALA documentation on issues such as the training of personnel, operational procedures, equipment requirements, the impact of AIS on VTS and the role of VTS in security and global traffic monitoring systems. The committee also reviews and updates the IALA *VTS Manual,* a

comprehensive reference document, of which a new edition is published every 4 years.

Navigation meeting groups
8.17
1   In addition to the committees, there are two standing meeting groups, the Navigation Services Advisory Committee (NSAC) and the Strategy and Operations Working Group (SOWG).

Publications
8.18
1   IALA publications take 3 forms:
Recommendations: provide the strongest possible guidance.
Guidelines: provide frameworks for specific topics.
Manuals: provide an overall view of a topic and often indicate where further information can be found.

Chapter 9

CONSTRAINTS ON NAVIGATION

United Nations Convention on the Law of the Sea (UNCLOS) and international boundaries

UNCLOS

General information
9.1

1   UNCLOS was opened for signature on 10 December 1982 and finally came into force on 16 November 1994. The convention is a very wide ranging publication and provides a thorough definition of, and guidelines for, the establishment of maritime zones by coastal states and the jurisdiction such states may exercise in their claimed maritime zones as well as establishing the rights of mariners to enjoy freedom of navigation. A list of states that have ratified UNCLOS is published in Annual Notice to Mariners No 12; this notice is re-issued on a six monthly basis in the relevant weekly summary of Notices to Mariners. UNCLOS is produced by the UN Division for Ocean Affairs and Law of the Sea Office of Legal Affairs and published by UN Publications in New York [ISBN 92–1–133522–1]. Website:

http://www.un.org/Depts/los/convention_agreements_overview_convention.htm

Archipelagic states
9.2

1   UNCLOS describes an Archipelagic State as a state constituted wholly by one or more archipelagos and this may include other islands. These states may draw straight archipelagic baselines joining the outermost islands and drying reefs of the archipelago providing the rules and conditions of UNCLOS are met. The territorial sea of such states is then drawn to seaward of the archipelagic straight baselines. States claiming archipelagic status are listed in Annual Notice to Mariners No 12.

2   See 9.6 for further details.

Baselines
9.3

1   **General information.** Annual Notice to Mariners No 12 lists the known baseline regime used by coastal states. Not all of these claims are recognised by the United Kingdom and without detailed knowledge of the national legislation establishing straight baselines, this information can only be considered as a guide. Where available, further information is available in the appropriate volume of *Admiralty Sailing Directions*. Mariners are advised that as a general rule, there is insufficient information available in navigational publications to allow accurate construction of a state's territorial sea limit. It is a requirement of UNCLOS that details of straight baselines used to control territorial seas are published by coastal states. For the United Kingdom, the UKHO "D" series of charts provides this

information; these are listed in the *Catalogue of Admiralty Charts and Publications.*

2   **Normal baseline.** The normal baseline for measuring the breadth of a territorial sea is the low water line along the coast marked on large scale charts officially recognised by the coastal State.

Straight baseline. In localities where the coastline is deeply indented and cut into, or if there is a fringe of islands or reefs in its immediate vicinity, the method of straight baselines joining appropriate points may be employed in drawing baselines from which the breadth of the territorial sea is measured.

3   **Archipelagic baseline.** An archipelagic State (9.2) may draw straight archipelagic baselines joining the outermost points of the outermost islands and drying reefs of the archipelago. Detailed provisions are contained within UNCLOS.

Bay closing line. Straight lines may be used to close the entrance to a bay provided that the line does not exceed 24 miles in length and provided that the area enclosed is greater than a semi-circle of diameter equal to the length of the bay closing line. Some special circumstances allow historic bays greater than 24 miles across to be closed with straight lines.

4   **River closing line.** If a river flows directly into the sea, the baseline shall be a straight line across the mouth of the river between points on the low-water line of its banks.

Roadstead. Special provisions are made for roadsteads within UNCLOS.

Innocent Passage
9.4

1   UNCLOS Article 19 defines in full the meaning of innocent passage. The general provision accords foreign vessels the right of innocent passage through territorial seas without making a port call or to and from a roadstead or port. Innocent passage does not include stopping or anchoring except as far as it is incidental to normal navigation or is rendered necessary by *force majeure*. The right of innocent passage also extends to internal waters enclosed by straight baselines where these waters were recognised as a route used for international navigation prior to the formation of the straight baselines. UNCLOS clarifies the meaning of innocent passage by stating that passage is innocent so long as it is not prejudicial to the peace, good order or security of the coastal state. The convention further states that passage of a foreign vessel shall be considered prejudicial to these conditions if it engages in any of the following activities:

2   Any threat or use of force against the sovereignty, territorial integrity or political independence of the

coastal state, or in any other manner, in violation of the principles of international law embodied in the charter of the United Nations.

Any exercise or practice with weapons of any kind. Any act aimed at collecting information to the prejudice of the defence or security of the coastal state.

3   Any act of propaganda aimed at affecting the defence or security of a coastal state.

Launching, landing or taking on board of any military aircraft.

Launching, landing or taking on board of any military device.

Loading or unloading of any commodity, currency or persons contrary to the customs, fiscal, immigration or sanitary laws and regulations of the coastal state.

4   Any act of wilful and serious pollution contrary to UNCLOS.

Any fishing activities.

The carrying out of research or survey activities.

Any act aimed at interfering with any systems of communication or any other facilities or installations of the coastal state.

Any other activity not having a direct bearing on passage.

5   In territorial seas, submarines and other underwater vehicles are required to navigate on the surface and show their flag.

6   States may, without discrimination among foreign vessels, temporarily suspend innocent passage in specified areas of their territorial sea, provided that it is essential for the protection of its security. This suspension must be duly published before taking effect.

Transit passage
9.5

1   It is internationally recognised that there shall be no suspension of passage through straits which are used for international navigation between one part of the high seas or EEZ and another part of the high seas or an EEZ, or between the territorial seas of a foreign state or states. UNCLOS contains detailed provisions about the transit of straits that are used for international navigation. Foreign vessels and aircraft have the right of unimpeded passage so long as it is continuous and expeditious; this includes the right of submerged passage. However, it should be noted that not all coastal states are parties to UNCLOS; those who have ratified the convention are again noted in Annual Notice to Mariners No 12. This right is, however, considered to be customary international law.

Archipelagic Sea Lanes (ASL) and passage
9.6

1   ASLs and air routes are routes through and above the territorial sea and archipelagic waters of an Archipelagic State (9.2) from one part of the high seas or EEZ to another part of the high seas or EEZ. They are defined by a series of continuous axis lines from the entry points of passage routes to the exit points.

2   The axis lines are delimited by a series of geographic co-ordinates of latitude and longitude, referred to a geodetic datum. Vessels and aircraft exercising archipelagic sea lanes passage shall not deviate more than 25 miles to either side of the axis

lines, provided that such vessels and aircraft shall not navigate closer to the coast than 10% of the distance between the axis line and the nearest points on islands bordering the sea lanes.

3   **Purpose.** An Archipelagic State may designate sea lanes and air routes thereabove, suitable for the continuous and expeditious and unobstructed transit of foreign vessels and aircraft through or over its archipelagic waters and adjacent territorial seas between one part of the high seas or an EEZ to another part of the high seas or an EEZ. All vessels and aircraft enjoy the right of Archipelagic Sea Lane passage in such sea lanes and air routes in their normal mode.

4   **ASLs adopted by the IMO.** When an Archipelagic State submits proposed ASLs to the IMO, the recognized competent international organisation, the IMO will ensure that the proposed sea lanes are in conformity with the relevant provisions in UNCLOS. The IMO will also determine whether the submission is a full or partial sea lanes proposal.

5   It should be noted that within ASLs traffic is not separated except in TSS. It should also be noted that the axis of an ASL does not indicate the deepest water, or any route or recommended track. The first partial system of archipelagic sea lanes in Indonesian archipelagic waters was adopted in 1998 and came into force in December 2002.

National maritime limits

Internal waters
9.7

1   Waters enclosed on the landward side of the baseline are internal waters over which the coastal state has complete sovereignty. An Archipelagic State may draw closing lines for the delimitation of internal waters within its archipelagic waters. See 9.2.

Archipelagic waters
9.8

1   The waters enclosed within archipelagic straight baselines are termed archipelagic waters. Foreign vessels enjoy rights of innocent passage (9.4) through archipelagic waters. Within archipelagic waters, states may enclose internal waters with straight lines using the provisions of UNCLOS for bays, rivers and ports. Archipelagic States may also declare ASLs (9.6).

Territorial sea
9.9

1   The sovereignty of a coastal state extends beyond its land territory and internal waters and, in the case of an archipelagic state, its archipelagic waters, to an adjacent belt of sea described as the territorial sea. This sovereignty extends to the air space over the territorial sea as well as to its sea floor and subsoil. Sovereignty over the territorial sea is exercised subject to UNCLOS and to other rules of international law. Every state has the right to establish the breadth of its territorial sea up to a limit not exceeding 12 miles measured from the baseline determined in accordance with UNCLOS. The outer limit of the territorial sea is the line, every point of which is at a distance from the nearest point of the baseline equal to the breadth of the territorial sea. A list of known claims for territorial sea limits is published in Annual Notice to Mariners No 12.

Contiguous Zone

9.10

1   UNCLOS makes provision for a coastal state to claim a contiguous zone adjacent to the territorial sea and extending up to 24 miles from the baseline from which the territorial sea is measured. Within the contiguous zone, states may exercise control to prevent infringements of customs, immigration, fiscal or sanitary regulations. Details of claimed contiguous zones are listed in Annual Notice to Mariners No 12.

Exclusive Economic Zone

9.11

1   UNCLOS establishes the right of a coastal state to establish an EEZ out to 200 miles from the territorial sea baseline. Within the EEZ the coastal state has sovereign rights for the purpose of exploring, exploiting, conserving and managing the natural resources, whether living or non-living, of the waters superadjacent to the sea floor, the sea floor and the subsoil thereof, and with regard to other activities for the economic exploitation of the zone, such as the production of energy from the water, currents and winds. The coastal state has jurisdiction over the establishment of artificial islands, installations and structures within the zone, and control of marine scientific research and the protection and preservation of the marine environment. Coastal states claiming an EEZ are noted in Annual Notice to Mariners No 12.

Continental shelf

9.12

1   UNCLOS defines the continental shelf as comprising the sea floor and subsoil of the submarine areas that extend beyond its territorial sea throughout the natural prolongation of its land territory to the outer edge of the continental margin, or to a distance of 200 miles from the territorial sea baseline where the outer edge of the continental margin does not extend to that distance.

2   It further describes the outer edge of the continental margin as the submerged prolongation of the land mass of the coastal state comprising the sea floor and subsoil of the shelf, the slope and the rise but excluding the deep ocean floor with its oceanic ridges and the subsoil thereof. In the area between the outer limit of the EEZ and the outer limit of the continental shelf, coastal states have sovereign rights for the purpose of exploring, exploiting, conserving and managing the natural resources comprising mineral and other non-living resources of the sea floor or subsoil together with living organisms belonging to sedentary species.

3   Sedentary species are further defined as organisms which, at their harvestable stage, are either immobile on or under the sea floor or are unable to move except in constant physical contact with the sea floor or subsoil.

4   The rights of the coastal state in the continental shelf area do not affect the legal status of the superadjacent waters or air space above those waters in which the freedom of the high seas exists. In exercising the sovereign rights that are allowed in the continental shelf area, the coastal state may not infringe or unjustifiably interfere with the freedom of the high seas.

Safety zones

9.13

1   In the territorial sea, the EEZ and the Continental Shelf, any installation erected for the exploration or exploitation of resources by the coastal state may have safety zones established, generally to a distance of 500 m. Moored installations operating in deep water may require safety zones in excess of 500 m in order to keep other vessels clear of moorings and obstructions. For further information see 13.140.

Fishery limits

9.14

1   Some States which do not claim an EEZ (9.11) exercise fisheries jurisdiction beyond the territorial sea to distances up to 200 miles from territorial sea baselines. Known claims to fisheries jurisdiction limits are listed in Annual Notice to Mariners No 12. Admiralty charts show UK fisheries limits on coastal charts of suitable scale (about 1:200 000). The UKHO also publishes details of the fisheries limits in UK waters on Charts Q6353 and Q6385.

International boundaries

International land boundaries

9.15

1   The international land boundaries shown on Admiralty charts are approximate only and may not represent changes in sovereignty, whether recognised or *de facto*, which occur after the publication of the chart.

International maritime boundaries

9.16

1   International maritime boundaries may be depicted on Admiralty charts provided they do not interfere with navigational safety. International maritime boundaries are generally only charted if they have been agreed by treaty.

Ships' Routeing

General information

Objective

9.17

1   The purpose of Ships' Routeing is to improve the safety of navigation in converging areas and in areas where the density of traffic is great or where the freedom of movement of shipping is inhibited by restricted sea room, the existence of obstructions to navigation, limited depths or unfavourable meteorological conditions. Ships' Routeing may also be used to prevent or reduce the risk of pollution or other damage to the marine environment caused by vessels colliding or grounding in or near environmentally sensitive areas.

Routeing systems
9.18

1   Following the implementation of the first routeing system in the Dover Strait in 1967, many similar systems have been established throughout the world.

2   IMO is recognised as the sole body responsible for establishing and recommending measures on an international level concerning ships' routeing. These measures, together with details of all routeing systems adopted by IMO (which include deep-water routes, TSS, precautionary areas, inshore traffic zones and areas to be avoided by certain vessels) are given in *Ships' Routeing*, published by and obtainable from IMO.

3   National governments are responsible for decisions concerning ships' routeing where schemes lie wholly within their territorial waters, but such schemes may also be submitted to IMO for approval.

Traffic Separation Schemes

General information
9.19

1   Following the implementation of the first TSS in the Dover Strait in 1967, many similar schemes have been established throughout the world. Details are shown on Admiralty charts and referred to in *Admiralty Sailing Directions*.

2   Routeing systems are intended for use by day and by night in all weathers, in ice-free waters or under light ice conditions where no extraordinary manoeuvres or assistance by icebreaker or icebreakers are required.

They are recommended for use by all vessels unless stated otherwise.

Authority
9.20

1   The IMO is the body responsible for establishing and recommending measures on an international level concerning ships' routeing. Where schemes lie wholly within territorial waters, decisions concerning routeing rest with the national government but such schemes may also be submitted for IMO approval and adoption.

Traffic separation schemes adopted by the IMO
9.21

1   The details of schemes adopted by IMO are set out in the IMO publication "Ships' Routeing", 9th Edition 2008, and in subsequent amendments and IMO circulars. Compliance with Rule 10 of the International Regulations for Preventing Collisions at Sea, 1972, is mandatory for all vessels when operating in or near schemes which have been adopted by IMO. In some schemes, special provisions are included governing their use by all vessels or by specified classes of vessels. On the charts relevant information is given, or there is a recommendation for chart users to consult Admiralty Sailing Directions for details.

Traffic separation schemes not adopted by IMO
9.22

1   Authorities establishing a routeing system that is not adopted by IMO lay down the regulations governing its use. Such regulations may not only modify Rule 10 of the *International Regulations for Preventing Collisions at Sea 1972* but also other Steering and Sailing Rules.

Applicability of International Collision Regulations in traffic separation schemes
9.23

1   While vessels using the traffic lanes in schemes adopted by IMO must, in particular, comply with Rule 10 of the *International Regulations for Preventing Collisions at Sea 1972*, they are not thereby given any right of way over crossing vessels; the other Steering and Sailing Rules still apply in all respects, particularly if risk of collision is involved.

2   Specific guidance on the application of the *International Regulations for Preventing Collisions at Sea 1972* in TSS have been published by the UK Maritime and Coastguard Agency as follows:

Subject area	Rule
Application	10(a)
Procedure within a Traffic Lane	10(b), 10(c)
Inshore Zones	10(d)
Anchoring within a Separation Zone	10(e), 10(g)
Vessels not using a Scheme	10(h)
Fishing vessels	10(b), 10(c), 10(e), 10(i)
Sailing Vessels and small craft	10(j)
Vessels engaged in safety of navigation operations (Signal YG)	10(k)

Charting
9.24

1   It is UKHO policy to insert on Admiralty charts not only the IMO–adopted routeing measures but also those established by coastal states or other competent national authorities concerned with the safety of navigation. On the charts, the IMO–adopted schemes are not normally differentiated from the other routeing schemes. The portrayal of national TSS on Admiralty charts is solely for the safety and convenience of shipping and implies no recognition of the international validity of the relevant regulations.

2   Routeing Systems are also shown diagrammatically on Mariners' Routeing Guide charts: *5500 — English Channel and Southern North Sea*, *5501 — Gulf of Suez* and *5502 — Malacca and Singapore Straits*.

3   **New TSS.** When a new TSS is to be implemented, New Editions (or occasionally New Charts) will be published showing the new scheme up to 8 weeks prior to the implementation date. A note will be shown on the face of the chart indicating the exact implementation date.

4   **Amended TSS.** When the UKHO has sufficient notice of an intended amendment to a TSS which is to be implemented on a given date, a Preliminary Notice to Mariners ((P)NM) will be issued detailing the changes and promulgating the implementation date. New Editions of the more significant scales of paper and ARCS charts showing the changes will be published 4-8 weeks prior to the implementation date; this enables the mariner to hold both a copy of the existing chart and a copy of the New Edition depicting the amended TSS. The existing versions of the charts will be renumbered as X versions, having their numbers prefixed with an X to distinguish them from the New Edition. When the TSS changes are implemented, the X version of the charts will be independently withdrawn and other charts affected by

the routeing measure amendments will be updated by textual NM or Block.

5 During the short life of the X versions, any other significant changes to charted detail on these charts will be promulgated by Temporary Notice to Mariners. The (P)NM will normally remain in force for a few weeks after the implementation date to cover any delays in distributing NEs of the relevant products.

6 The procedure for updating UK ENCs is fully described at 2.93.

Admiralty Sailing Directions
9.25

1 Admiralty Sailing Directions mention all TSS, state whether or not a scheme has been adopted by IMO, and give the appropriate regulations for their use.

Deep-draught vessels
9.26

1 Masters of deep-draught vessels should note that the existence of a scheme does not imply that the traffic lanes have been adequately surveyed; charted depths and source diagrams (if available) should be studied when planning a passage where depths are critical.

2 Bearing in mind the need for under-keel clearance, a decision to use a routeing system must take into account the charted depth, the possibility of changes in the sea floor since the time of the last survey, and the effects of meteorological and tidal conditions on water depths.

Vessel Traffic Services (VTS) and Port Operations

General information
9.27

1 A VTS is a service implemented by a competent authority, designed to improve safety and efficiency of vessel traffic and to protect the environment. The service should have the capability to interact with traffic and respond to traffic situations developing within the VTS area.

2 VTS have been established in many principal ports and their approaches, both to reduce the risk of collisions and to expedite the turn-round of vessels.

Where VTS exist, they provide a number of services from one or more Traffic Centres, including:

Information to vessels operating in the area on the arrival, berthing, anchoring and departure of other vessels.

Details of any navigational hazards.

Local weather.

Information regarding port operations.

3 Reporting points are usually designated along the approach routes for vessels to report as they pass them and so enable Traffic Centres to keep track of all shipping movements. In most places, radar and AIS surveillance are used to present a continuous picture of the traffic situation to traffic centres.

The Services also handle boarding and disembarkation arrangements for pilots, and the enforcement of local regulations.

Sources of information
9.28

1 Admiralty Sailing Directions identify where Traffic Services are established, information required when approaching the areas, and pilots arrangements, as they do for other ports.

2 Admiralty List of Radio Signals Volume 6, which are kept up-to-date by Weekly Editions of Admiralty Notices to Mariners give the latest details of VTS, Reporting Systems, Pilot Services and Port Operations. It includes the frequencies to be used for communications, details of reporting points, restrictions that may apply to certain vessels, and procedures to be carried out in the event of accidents.

3 Pilot boarding stations and certain VTS information are also shown diagrammatically on the following Mariners' Routeing Guide charts:

5500 — English Channel and Southern North Sea,
5501 — Gulf of Suez
5502 — Malacca and Singapore Straits.

International Port Traffic Signals

Introduction
9.29

1 The International Port Traffic Signals consist of signals recommended by the International Association of Lighthouse Authorities (IALA) in 1998.

It is expected that the signals will be introduced at ports as and when need for change arises, so that eventually all ports throughout the world will have uniform basic traffic signals. In addition to controlling port traffic, the signals may be used to control movements at locks and bridges. Further information is available at the IALA website at www.iala-aism.org.

At some ports the full range of signals may not be used. eg Only Signals 2 and 4, or only Signal 1 may be used.

Traffic signals in use at any particular place are given in the appropriate volume of Admiralty Sailing Directions.

Signals
9.30

1 The signals, indicated in the accompanying table, consist only of lights. They may be recognised as traffic signals because the main signals are always three lights exhibited vertically.

There are three types of signal: Main, Exemption and Auxiliary.

2 **Main signals** consist of one of five signals which are shown continuously by day and night (unless Signal 1 is the only one used by a port).

Signal 5 is used when a vessel or special group of vessels must receive specific instructions in order to proceed. No other vessels may proceed when this signal is shown. Specific instructions may be given by Auxiliary Signal or by other means such as radio, signal lamp or patrol boat.

3 **Exemption signals** consist of an additional yellow light, fixed or occulting, always exhibited to the left of the top main light. They allow smaller vessels to disregard the instructions contained in the Main Signals to which they refer.

Signals 2 and 5 may be used with Exemption Signals 2a or 5a by some port authorities.

4 **Auxiliary signals**, normally consisting of white or yellow lights, or both, are always exhibited to the right

Main Signals	Main Messages
1	Serious Emergency- All vessels to stop or divert according to instructions.
Flashing	
2	Vessels shall not proceed.
3	Vessels may proceed. One-way traffic.
4	Vessels may proceed. Two-way traffic.
5	A vessel may proceed only when it has received specific orders to do so.

Exemption Signals ‡	Exemption Messages
2a	Vessel shall not proceed, except that vessels which navigate outside the main channel need not comply with the main message.
5a	A vessel may proceed only when it has received specific orders to do so, except that vessels which navigate outside the main channel need not comply with the main message.

Auxiliary Signals †	Auxiliary Messages
Normally white and yellow lights, or both.	Local meanings

‡ Displayed to the left of top main light.

† Displayed to the right of main lights.

International Port Traffic Signals (9.30)

of the Main Signals. They may be used for special messages at ports with a complex layout, or complicated traffic situation. They convey local meanings: eg. added to Signal 5 to instruct a particular vessel to proceed; or to give information about the situation of traffic in the opposite direction; or to warn of a dredger operating in the channel. Port Regulations and *Admiralty Sailing Directions* should be consulted for full details.

Emergency signals
9.31
1   The flashing of the red lights (Diagram 9.30 Signal 1) is used to indicate an emergency. All other lights are fixed or, to differentiate them from background glare, occulting slowly (eg. every 10 seconds).

Other areas where restrictions apply

Areas To Be Avoided
9.32
1   Certain areas are designated to be avoided by certain vessels. They may be established for any of a number of reasons; for example, the area being inadequately surveyed, or local knowledge being required to navigate in it, or because unacceptable damage to the environment might result from a casualty.
2   Such ATBA, except those which have not been approved by IMO lying outside territorial waters, are shown on Admiralty charts. Details of the vessels affected by the prohibitions (on account of their class, size, cargo, or other determining factor) are usually given in *Admiralty Sailing Directions* with appropriate references on the chart.

Particularly Sensitive Sea Areas
9.33
1   **General information.** The Maritime Environment Protection Committee (MEPC) of the IMO began its study of the question of Particularly Sensitive Sea Areas in response to a resolution of the *International Conference on Tanker Safety and Pollution Protection* of 1978. Discussions of the concept between 1986 and 1991 culminated in the adoption of *Guidelines for the Designation of Special Areas and the Identification of Particularly Sensitive Sea Areas* by IMO Resolution A.720(17) in 1991. Further resolutions were adopted in subsequent years in a continuing effort to provide a clearer understanding of the concept. The most recent resolution (A.982(24) of 2006) issued revised guidelines for the identification and designation of PSSAs.
2   A PSSA is an area which needs special protection through action by IMO because of its significance for recognised ecological, socio–economic or scientific attributes where such attributes may be vulnerable to damage by international shipping activities.
    A PSSA may lie within a Special Area (10.7), and vice versa.
3   There are currently (2009) twelve designated PSSAs:
    The Great Barrier Reef (Australia) (designated a PSSA in 1990);

Sabana-Camagüey Archipelago (Cuba) (1997);
Malpelo Island (Colombia) (2002);
The sea around the Florida Keys (United States of America) (2002);
The Wadden Sea (Denmark, Germany, The Netherlands) (2002);

4   Paracas National Reserve (Peru) (2003);
Western European Waters (2004);
Extension of the existing Great Barrier Reef PSSA to include the Torres Strait (proposed by Australia and Papua New Guinea) (2005);

Canary Islands (Spain) (2005);
The Galapagos Archipelago (Ecuador) (2005);
The Baltic Sea area (Denmark, Estonia, Finland, Germany, Latvia, Lithuania, Poland and Sweden) (2005);

5   Papahänaumokuäkea Marine National Monument (Hawaii, United States of America) (2007).

Details. For additional regulations which affect specific Special Areas or PSSAs, *Admiralty Sailing Directions* or the Convention should be consulted.

Minefields

General information
9.34

1   Minefields were laid in many parts of the world during the World Wars of 1914-18 and 1939–45, during the Korean War of 1950–51, and in a number of less extensive conflicts since then including the Gulf War of 1990-91. The vast majority of these historic minefields have now been cleared. In particular, the North Sea and English Channel have been subject to extensive mine clearance efforts since 1945. The few minefields that remain uncleared are now considered safe for surface navigation. It should be noted however, that in such areas, a real danger of encountering unexploded historic ordnance still exists with regard to anchoring, demersal trawling or any form of submarine or seabed operations. In the Northern Gulf in particular, anchoring within former mine danger areas is not recommended.

2   It is important to recognise a distinction between:
Mine Danger Areas in which the responsible charting authority specifies that there is a hazard from mines to the safety of navigation of surface vessels; Mine Danger Areas will normally be charted if up-to-date details are available and can be kept corrected.
Former Mined Areas where, due to the lapse of time since the mines were laid, the responsible charting authority accepts that, whether the minefields have been swept or not, the danger to surface navigation from such mines is now no greater than the normal hazards of marine navigation, although there is still a risk involved in anchoring, fishing or any form of sea floor activity. Former Mined Areas are mentioned in appropriate volumes of Sailing Directions, with full details in an Appendix. In the rare instances where these historic minefields are still considered dangerous, they are denoted on the Admiralty chart as Mine Danger Areas, and detailed in the appropriate Sailing Directions. In addition, mariners should note that uncharted wrecks and shoals may lie in these areas as the danger from mines will have inhibited hydrographic surveying.

3   **Caution.** Many modern minefields have been cleared and others have had routes cleared through them. For surface navigation, these routes are typically marked by buoys and have been used safely by shipping for many years. However, even in cleared waters and routes there is a remote risk that mines may still remain having failed to be detected by mine-clearance effort. Mariners are therefore advised there is still a risk involved in anchoring, fishing or any form of seabed activity. This risk remains particularly high in the approaches to the Kuwaiti and Iraqi coasts, where anchoring anywhere within Mine Danger Areas or Former Mined Areas is not recommended.

4   Mine Danger Areas will normally be charted if up-to-date details are available and can be kept corrected. Former Mined Areas are mentioned in appropriate volumes of Sailing Directions, with full details in an Appendix.

Mines
9.35

1   The majority of drifting buoyant mines sighted on the surface will *probably* be lost exercise mines. Notwithstanding this, *all* drifting mines should be reported immediately to the Naval Authorities via the Coastguard Service or the normal ship/shore communication channel. An "All Ships" broadcast should also be made on VHF Channel 16 to communicate the information to ships in the vicinity. The time of sighting and position of the mine is important in the reporting information. A drifting mine must be left for naval explosive ordnance disposal experts to deal with. Under no circumstances are drifting mines to be shot at using a firearm: this may pierce the casing and sink the mine without detonating it. The mine will then migrate on the seabed or be submerged in the water column, and potentially end up in a trawl or washed up on the beach, still in a lethal state. If possible, a lightly weighted marker float or dan buoy should be laid in the vicinity of the mine to assist in re-location should the vessel finding the mine be unable to remain within visual range. No attempt to secure a line to the mine should be made.

2   Detailed guidance regarding recommended actions and precautions to be taken if mines or other explosives are picked up in fishing nets or as a result of other under-sea operations are contained in the fishery section at 13.115.

Offshore renewable energy installations (OREI)

General information

Development
9.36

1   The number of offshore renewable energy installations in the waters of coastal states is increasing. At present most are wind farms, though tidal and wave energy installations are being developed and some prototype installations have been established, which may be close to shipping routes.

2   **Wind farms.** In UK waters by mid-2008, five offshore wind farms were operational with a further 24 under construction or at various stages of planning. These are mainly located in three strategic areas - E Irish Sea, the Greater Wash and the Thames Estuary. There are also sites in other English, Welsh, Scottish and Northern Ireland areas. In the future, other strategic wind farm sea areas may be designated.

3   Early wind farms generally consisted of not more than 30 turbines and lay entirely within UK territorial waters. New developments may see up to 300 turbines in a single field, which may extend beyond territorial waters.

4   Wind farms can be very large, some approaching 100 nm². The sites may be irregular in shape and adjacent developments can be in close proximity to each other. In addition, wind turbines may be established as single units.

5   **Wave and tidal energy devices** are currently sited on an *ad hoc* basis, where wave or tidal stream conditions are optimum and where interference with other marine activities is minimal.

Charting
9.37

1   All wind farms off the UK coast are charted by the UKHO either by a group of black wind turbine chart symbols (Admiralty Chart 5011 (INT1) L5.1) or by an outer limit with an encircled black wind turbine symbol (Admiralty Chart 5011 (INT1) L5.2). The outer limit will be a black dashed line, or a magenta T-shaped dashed line if there are navigational or other restrictions in the area. Whether all submarine cables associated with wind farms will be charted depends upon the scale of the chart. As with all submarine cables, mariners should note the hazards associated with anchoring or trawling near them. Heed should also be taken of any chart notes relating to wind farms.

2   The UKHO will continue to liaise with the relevant offshore renewable energy developers and other authorities in order to promulgate safety-related information and to update charts.

Passage planning
9.38

1   The following information will enable masters and skippers to make an informed risk assessment for the intended voyage. This should be taken into account together with the guidance on voyage planning found in other publications relating to the implementation of SOLAS V Regulation 34 ("Voyage Planning"). Reference should also be made to the MCA publication "Safety of Navigation, Implementation of SOLAS Chapter V, 2002" (Second Edition with amendments - June 2007) which is accessible on the MCA website.

2   MCA and IMO Guidance on Voyage Planning is contained in Annexes 24 and 25 of that document. Further reference should also be made to MGN 371 (M+F) "Offshore Renewable Energy Installations (OREIs) - Guidance on UK Navigational Practice, Safety and Emergency Response Issues".

3   Any urgent maritime safety information relating to OREIs will be promulgated by Notices to Mariners and Navigational Warnings.

Safe navigation
9.39

1   Mariners are reminded of the requirement to navigate safely at all times. The following guidance aims to assist in carrying out that obligation. OREIs are a new development and this guidance is of a general nature, based on the information available to date. It should be noted that specific details of individual sites may vary. As additional information becomes available in the light of experience, the guidance will be reviewed and updated. Notes on Admiralty charts and in the appropriate volumes of Sailing Directions, and in other relevant publications, should be studied.

Wind turbines and farms

Appearance
9.40

1   Wind farms are readily identifiable both visually and by radar from a considerable distance in good meteorological conditions. The turbines typically comprise a foundation below sea level, a yellow transition section not less than 15 metres high measured above HAT, above which is a platform forming the base of the turbine tower, which may be typically 70 - 80 m in height. At the top of the turbine tower is the nacelle, a box shaped structure, housing the generator. The turbine blades are located opposite the nacelle. Each turbine blade can be more than 60 m in length. The structures above the yellow transition section are usually painted matt grey. The total height of a turbine and rotors is currently up to about 150 m.

2   Theoretically, an observer with a height of eye of 3 m would be able to see the tips of the blades at 28 miles. A more substantial nacelle, if 70 m high, would be visible to the same observer at 20 miles in clear visibility.

Sub-surface structures
9.41

1   The foundations may be a mono-pile sunk into the seabed, an anchored tripod, or a caisson (basket) filled with aggregate. The foundations themselves may be surrounded by rocks which protect them from the scouring action of currents. The network of cables from individual turbines may, in some cases, be connected to a separate platform containing electrical switchgear, transformers and other equipment which condition the power ready for transmission along a cable to an onshore substation.

Kentish Flats wind farm (9.40)

(Original dated prior to 2009)

(Photograph - Chris Laurens)

Aids to navigation
9.42

1   **Wind farm boundaries.** The outer perimeters of offshore wind farms will be marked and lit in accordance with IALA Recommendation 0-117 (May 2000). This requires offshore wind generators to be marked so as to be conspicuous by day and night, with consideration given to prevailing conditions of visibility and vessel traffic. In certain cases, cardinal marks may also be permanently placed adjacent to wind farms. During construction standard cardinal marks will be used around the area.

2   A corner structure, or other significant point on the boundary of the wind farm, is called a Significant Peripheral Structure (SPS). Every SPS is marked with lights visible from all directions in the horizontal plane. These lights are synchronized to display an IALA "special mark" characteristic, flashing yellow, with a range of not less than 5 miles. Aids to navigation on individual structures are placed below the arc of the rotor blades, typically at the top of the yellow section.

3   As a minimum, each SPS must show synchronised flashing characteristics. In some cases there may be synchronisation of all SPSs. In the case of a large or extended wind farm, the distance between SPSs should not normally exceed 3 miles.

4   Selected intermediate peripheral structures (IPS) on the boundary of a wind farm between SPSs, should be marked with flashing yellow lights which are visible from all directions horizontally. The characteristics of these lights should be distinctly different from those

displayed on the SPSs, with a range of not less than 2 miles. The distance between such lit structures or the nearest SPS should not exceed 2 miles. The characteristics of the lights and marks will be shown on the chart.

5   **Single structures,** not part of a group of turbines, should be marked, according to the IALA Recommendation O-114 on the marking of offshore structures, with a white light flashing Morse code "U".

6   **Other illumination and identification aids.** In addition to the navigational aid lights marking the SPSs and selected IPS of a wind farm, IALA permits:

Illuminating of peripheral structures and all structures within the wind farm (see below).

Racons, which may have the morse characteristic "U".

Radar Reflectors and Radar Target Enhancers.

AIS as an Aid to Navigation (as per IALA Recommendation A-126).

Mariners should consult the largest scale chart available for details.

7   **Sound signals.** Where required on a wind farm, the typical range of such a sound signal should not be less than 2 miles. Details will be given on the chart.

Marking of individual turbines
9.43

1   Individual turbines will be marked with a unique alphanumeric identifier which should be clearly visible at a range of not less than 150 m. At night, the identifier will be lit discretely, (e.g. with down-lighters),

enabling it to be seen at the same range. Wind turbines should therefore be readily visible in good conditions; however it should be remembered that they may not be so easily seen at night or in reduced visibility from the wind farm interior. Fixed red aviation lights on the tops of the nacelles may be visible to surface craft, and care must be taken not to confuse these with vessels' sidelights or marine navigational aids, despite the possibility of them appearing to have a flashing characteristic when seen through rotating turbine blades.

Effects of wind farms and turbines on routeing
9.44

1 **Spacing.** Turbines within a wind farm are generally spaced 500 m or more apart, depending on the size of the turbine. In order to make best use of the wind resource, turbine spacing is proportional to the rotor size and the down-wind wake effect created. In general terms, the larger the rotor the greater the spacing. Small craft may be able to navigate safely within the wind farm boundaries, while larger craft will need to keep clear.

2 **Depth of water.** The majority of wind turbines now operating or planned are located in relatively shallow water, e.g. on shoals or sand banks. The limited depth of water therefore provides a natural constraint between larger vessels and turbines. However it is expected that new generations of wind farm will be constructed in deeper water, where navigable channels in the vicinity may restrict vessels to a particular route passing close to a wind farm boundary.

3 **Seabed changes.** Wind farm structures could, over time, affect the depth of water in their vicinity. In dynamic seabed areas with strong tidal streams, changes in the scouring of the seabed may occur. This may result in depth information being unreliable. Once a wind farm has existed for a few years there will be a better appreciation of any tidal scour or changes of depth. Wind farm developers are required to make an assessment of any potential changes in sedimentation that may occur as a consequence of their plans. Development may be permitted where the assessed effect is considered tolerable. In practice the actual effect could differ, so mariners should bear this in mind and allow sufficient under-keel clearance with a suitable margin of safety. Some wind turbines have scour protection in the form of boulders and/or concrete mattresses placed around their base.

4 **Tidal streams.** Wind farm structures may obstruct tidal streams locally, creating eddies nearby. Mariners should be aware of the likelihood of such eddies which are only likely to be significant very close to the structures.

5 **Small craft.** Vessels involved in turbine maintenance and safety duties may be encountered within or around a wind farm. Fishing vessels may also be operating in the area. Mariners should be alert to the likely presence of such vessels and be aware that the structures may occasionally obscure them. This is particularly relevant at night. Large vessels may also become obscured, for example if they are on the opposite side of a wind farm. A good lookout should be therefore be maintained at all times by all available means, as required by the International Regulations for the Prevention of Collision At Sea (COLREGS).

6 **Shore marks.** In coastal areas shore marks may also become obscured by wind farm structures. Mariners should be particularly alert to this. In particular, the characteristics of lights at night may need careful verification if turbines temporary mask them. The vessel's position should be checked by other means when a wind farm obscures coastal marks.

7 **Transformer stations.** In or adjacent to larger wind farms offshore, electrical transformer-stations may be present. These are of similar appearance to small offshore production platforms. Submarine cables link turbines to this transformer-station from where the generated power is exported to the shore. Whether all submarine cables are charted depends upon the scale of the chart; in some cases only the export cable may be shown. Small craft operating within a wind farm should therefore avoid anchoring except in emergencies, as the anchor could easily become fouled.

Effects on communications and navigation systems
9.45

1 In 2004, the MCA and Qinetiq conducted trials at the North Hoyle wind farm to determine any impact of wind turbines on marine communications and navigation systems. The results, from the full report (available on the MCA website), are summarised below.

2 **Effects on radio transmissions.** The trials indicated that there is minimal impact on VHF radio, Global Positioning Systems (GPS) receivers, cellular telephones and AIS. UHF and other microwave systems suffered from the normal masking effect when turbines were in the line of the transmissions.

3 **Radar echoes.** The turbines produced strong radar echoes giving early warning of their presence. At close range however the trials showed that they may produce multiple reflected and side lobe echoes that can mask real targets. These develop at about 1½ miles, with progressive deterioration in the radar display as the range closes. Target size of the turbine echo increases close to the turbine with a consequent degradation of target definition and bearing discrimination. These effects were encountered on both 3 and 10 cm radars.

4 Similar effects were found during trials undertaken off the Kentish Flats wind farm in 2006. Radar antennae which are sited badly with respect to items of the vessel's structure can enhance these effects. Adjustment of radar controls can suppress some of these spurious radar returns but mariners are warned that there is a consequent risk of losing targets with a small radar cross section, such as buoys or small craft, particularly yachts or GRP constructed craft, therefore due care should be taken when making such adjustments.

5 If these interfering echoes develop, the requirements of the COLREGS Rule 6 (Safe Speed) are particularly applicable and must be observed with due regard to the prevailing circumstance. In restricted visibility, Rule 19 (Conduct of vessels in restricted visibility) applies and compliance with Rule 6 becomes especially

relevant. In such conditions mariners are required, under Rule 5 (Lookout) to take into account information from other sources which may include sound signals and VHF information (for example from a VTS, or AIS). Mariners should bear in mind that not all vessels are equipped with AIS.

6   Mariners should be aware that other radar targets may be obscured when close to a wind turbine field.

Where adequate safe water exists, it may be prudent in the planning of a voyage to set tracks at least 2 miles clear of turbine fields.

Rotor effects
9.46

1   Offshore wind turbines located around the UK are required to have the lowest point of the rotor sweep at least 22 metres above MHWS. This clearance should be ample for the majority of small craft. Those with a greater masthead height should take appropriate care. It would, in any case, be imprudent for larger vessels to be this close to a turbine, other than in an emergency.

2   In harvesting energy, turbines "de-power" the wind. Research indicates that a 10% reduction in wind velocity may be expected. This wind-shadow effect is predicted to exist within the vertical air column up to heights of 15 m. The impact of the wind-shadow reduces with distance in the lee of a turbine. The inter-turbine spacing affects the impact of rotor wash or wake. The width of the rotor wake is about 150 m, which is broadly similar to the rotor diameter. As the rotor wake interacts with the sea surface further shadow effects are predicted. The wind, having changed its flow through the rotors, will be expected to recover downwind of the turbine. Consequently, wind-sheer may occur as the wind back fills.

3   In simple terms, the effect of a turbine rotor harvesting the wind can be pictured as a horizontal cone, centred on the rotor hub with the approximate diameter of the rotor. The cone extends down-wind, attenuating to a point at a distance proportional to the wind velocity. This down-wind effect will also be dependent upon the azimuth of the rotor. The impact on a vessel will be proportional to its windage area and, for a sailing vessel, the mast height.

4   Mariners, and particularly yachtsmen, need to be aware of these effects. By day the normal visual clues should be noted and changes in leeway or the balance of tidal stream to wind power anticipated. Extra care should be taken at night, when visual clues are not so easily detected.

Offshore wave and tidal energy installations

General information
9.47

1   Unlike wind farms, systems using wave or tidal energy may not be clearly visible to the mariner.

Wave energy converters
9.48

1   Wave energy converters (WECs) capture kinetic energy carried by waves. They are likely to be located at or near the surface, held in position by an attachment mooring point on the seabed. WECs may be visible on the surface or semi-submerged.

2   The following definitions are used:

Attenuator. A floating device which works in parallel to the wave direction and effectively rides the waves. Movements along its length can be selectively constrained to produce energy. One example consists of large, linked floating cylinders which are connected to a hydraulic system. Potential energy is stored via hydraulic rams which operate as the hinged units move in the waves. The generated pressure is used to drive turbine generators inside the cylinders.

3   **Point absorber.** A floating structure which absorbs energy in all directions through its movements at or near the sea surface.

Oscillating Wave Surge Converter. An arm which oscillates as a pendulum mounted on a pivoted joint in response to the movement of water in the waves.

4   **Oscillating water column.** A partially submerged hollow structure. Waves cause the water column to rise and fall, allowing trapped air to flow to and from the atmosphere via a turbine. The rotation of the turbine is used to generate electricity.

Overtopping device. Captures water from waves which is then held in a reservoir above sea level before being returned to the sea through conventional turbines which generate power.

5   **Submerged pressure differential.** These devices are typically located near the shore, and are attached to the seabed. The motion of the waves caused the sea level to rise and fall above the device, the pressure differential being used to generate electricity.

Other devices may have unique and very different designs to the more well-established technologies.

Tidal energy converters
9.49

1   Tidal energy converters (TECs) capture potential energy from the movement of large bodies of water as the tides ebb and flow. TEC devices may be surface or sub-surface structures incorporating a generator fixed or moored to the seabed which captures the potential energy present in the moving body of water associated with tidal stream. Power take-off is normally via cables to an electrical terminal. TECs take a variety of forms, the most common being:

2   **Horizontal axis turbine.** This type of device extracts energy from moving water in much the same way as wind turbines extract energy from the movement of air, using a vertical plane rotor.

Horizontal axis turbine (enclosed blade tips). A funnel-like collecting device which uses the Venturi Effect to accelerate the water column, sits submerged in the current. The flow of water can drive a turbine directly or the induced pressure differential can drive an air-turbine.

3   **Vertical axis turbine.** This device extracts energy from moving water in a similar fashion to the horizontal axis turbine, but with the turbine mounted on a vertical axis.

Oscillating hydrofoil. A hydrofoil attached to an oscillating arm, whose motion is caused by the current flowing either side of the wing, creating lift,

Methods of fixing WECs and TECs to the seabed
9.50

1   From the mariner's perspective, it is important to understand that there are various methods by which devices can be fixed to the seabed, which will affect their visibility above the surface.

Seabed mounted/gravity base devices. These sit on the seabed by virtue of the weight of the combined device/foundation. In some cases there may be additional fixing to the seabed.

2   **Pile mounted.** This principle is analogous to that used to mount most wind turbines, whereby the device is attached to a pile penetrating the ocean floor.

Floating flexible mooring. The device is tethered via a cable/chain to the seabed, allowing considerable freedom of movement. This allows a device to swing as the direction of the tidal stream/current changes.

3   **Floating rigid mooring.** The device is secured in position using a fixed mooring system, allowing minimal movement.

Hydrofoil inducing downforce. The device uses a number of hydrofoils mounted on a frame to induce a positioning downforce from the tidal stream/current.

Marking
9.51

1   The visibility of WEC and TEC installations depend on the device type. Some installations are totally submerged while others may only protrude slightly above the sea surface.

WEC and TEC energy extraction devices should be marked as a single unit or as a block or field as follows:

When structures are fixed to the seabed and extend above the surface, they should be marked in accordance with the IALA recommendations for the marking of offshore wind farms (see 9.42).

2   Areas containing surface or sub-surface energy extraction devices (wave and/or tidal) should be marked by appropriate navigation buoys in accordance with the IALA Buoyage System, fitted with the corresponding topmarks and lights. In addition, active or passive radar reflectors, retro-reflecting material, racons and/or AIS transponders should be fitted as the level of traffic and degree of risk requires.

3   The boundaries of the wave and tidal energy extraction field should be marked by lit navigational buoys, so as to be visible to the mariner from all relevant directions in the horizontal plane, by day and by night. Taking the results of a risk assessment into account, lights should have a nominal range of at least 5 miles. The N, S, E and W boundaries should normally be marked with the appropriate IALA cardinal mark. However, depending on the shape and size of the field, there may be a need to deploy intermediate lateral or special marks.

4   In the case of a large or extended energy extraction field, the distance between navigation buoys that mark the boundary should not normally exceed 3 miles.

5   Taking into account environmental considerations, individual wave and tidal energy devices within a field which extend above the surface should be painted yellow above the waterline. Depending on the boundary marking, individual devices within the field need not be marked. However, if marked, they should have flashing yellow lights so as to be visible to the mariner from all relevant directions in the horizontal plane. The flash character of such lights should be sufficiently different from those displayed on the boundary lights with a range of not less than 2 miles.

6   Consideration should be given to the provision of AIS as an Aid to Navigation (IALA Recommendation A-126) on selected peripheral wave and/or tidal energy devices.

7   A single wave and/or tidal energy extraction structure, standing alone, that extends above the surface should be painted black, with red horizontal bands, and should be marked as an Isolated Danger as described in the IALA Maritime Buoyage System.

8   If a single wave and/or tidal energy device which is not visible above the surface but is considered to be a hazard to surface navigation, should be marked by an IALA special mark yellow buoy with flashing yellow light with a range of not less than 5 miles, in accordance with the IALA Buoyage System. It should also be noted that many tidal concepts have fast-moving sub-surface elements such as whirling blades.

9   The Aids to Navigation described herein should comply with IALA Recommendations and have an appropriate availability, normally not less than 99·0% (IALA Category 2).

Establishment of fields
9.52

1   The relevant Hydrographic Office should be informed of the establishment of an energy extraction device or field, to permit appropriate charting.

Notices to Mariners should be issued to publicise the establishment of a wave and/or tidal energy device or field. The Notice to Mariners should include the marking, location and extent of such devices/fields.

Contingency Plans
9.53

1   Operators of wave and/or tidal energy extraction devices or fields should develop contingency plans and emergency response plans which address the possibility of individual devices breaking loose and becoming floating hazards. Automatic location and tracking devices should be considered.

Developers and/or operators should have a reliable maintenance and casualty response regime in place to ensure the required availability targets are met. This will include having the necessary spares on hand, with provision made at the design stage, where necessary, to ensure safe access.

Safety and exclusion zones

General information
9.54

1   There are currently a few temporary exclusion zones around some UK offshore wind farms currently under construction. It is likely that safety zones will be introduced at other wind farm sites in the near future, and they will be monitored and policed.

Temporary Safety Zones
9.55

1   Temporary Safety Zones may be established during construction as and when required. Such Safety Zones will be promulgated by Notices to Mariners and Navigational Warning broadcasts. Safety zones will be monitored by support craft which may include fishing vessels employed by developers as Guard Vessels. Mariners should give such zones a wide berth. Skippers of fishing vessels operating in the area should make themselves aware of information promulgated by the local OREI Fishing Liaison Officer.

Permanent Exclusion Zones
9.56

1   Permanent Exclusion Zones are not expected to be established around wind farms, as compelling risk-assessed arguments would be required for their establishment. The nominal safety zone around an operational wind turbine is expected to have a 50 m radius (the UKHO will not be able to show a limit of this size on charts or ENCs due to scale of coverage).

2   Additionally, it may be necessary to limit access for specific activities (such as trawling) where the infrastructure requires restriction of such activity. In such cases the requirements will be promulgated separately. Fishermen should be aware of anti-scouring material, often large rocks, which may extend considerable distances from the base of wind turbines. The UKHO will publish information for specific sites on charts and in their publications when the extent of this change is known.

Exclusion Zones around wave and tidal installations.
9.57

1   With respect to other types of offshore renewable installation, the establishment of safety zones may be more proscriptive, since wave and tidal devices may not be fixed in position, may extend horizontally for considerable distances on or below the sea surface, and may have potentially dangerous moving parts. Their low profiles may make them difficult to detect visually or by radar. Operational developments will include research and trial units whose positions may vary at short notice.

Access
9.58

1   Mariners should be aware that there is no right of access to any type of OREI. They are private property and appropriate warning signs are displayed. In any event access requires skill and is limited by sea state, and should only be undertaken in controlled circumstances by trained personnel.

Emergencies in proximity to an OREI
9.59

1   In emergencies such as engine or steering failures close to or within OREI, mariners should immediately inform HM Coastguard and be prepared to use anchors if necessary, being aware of the likelihood of the presence of submarine cables and other seabed obstructions.

Refuge in OREIs
9.60

1   Mariners may, in extreme emergency, seek refuge on wind turbine towers. Access is via vertical ladders which may be encrusted with marine growth in the inter-tidal zone. Boarding turbines is risky and difficult, but the towers can provide refuge if the circumstances require. Some shelter from the elements can be obtained pending rescue, however internal access to the turbine tower will not be possible.

2   If taking refuge on a turbine tower mariners are warned that the rotors will continue to turn until others become aware of their plight. In such circumstances mariners should alert HM Coastguard by the best means available, remembering that the turbine tower may obscure line of sight communications, so they may need to adjust their position on the platform.

3   Once alerted, HM Coastguard can contact the wind farm operations control room which can remotely shut down individual turbines. Wind farms have an active safety management system requiring them to park rotor blades in a suitable configuration to permit helicopter operations, although there may be occasions when the prevailing conditions preclude helicopter rescue from turbines. In such conditions distressed mariners may have to wait for evacuation by sea, when sea conditions permit.

     Mariners in extreme emergency are unlikely to be able to use wave or tidal generators as places of refuge.

4   **Responding to emergencies.** When responding to a distress call or alert from within a wind farm or other OREI, mariners should make a careful assessment of the risks associated with entering the area, taking into consideration the guidance outlined above. Large vessels may be unsuitable for requisitioning but all mariners should initially respond as required by law and immediately relay the details to the nearest Coastguard station.

Voyage planning through waters which contain OREIs
9.61

1   Mariners planning routes through waters where OREIs have been established should be aware that there is no laid down safe distance at which to pass, and have, in simple terms, three options:

     Avoid the OREI area completely. Where there is sufficient sea room, this is the prudent option.
     Navigate around the edge of the OREI.
     In the case of a wind farm, navigate with caution through the array.

2   The choice will be influenced by a number of factors including the characteristics of the vessel (type, tonnage, draught, manoeuvrability etc), the weather and prevailing and forecast sea conditions.

Additional information
9.62

1   In some areas, additional information may be available from VTS.

Submarine pipelines and cables

Protection

Regulations
9.63

1 *The International Convention for the Protection of Submarine Cables, 1884*, as extended by the *Convention on the High Seas, 1958*, stipulates:

Vessels shall not remain or close within 1 mile of vessels engaged in laying or repairing submarine cables or pipelines, and vessels engaged in such work shall show the signals laid down in the *International Regulations for Prevention of Collisions at Sea 1972*.

2 Fishing gear and nets shall also be removed to, or kept at, a distance of 1 mile from vessels showing those signals, but fishing vessels shall be allowed 24 hours after the signal is first visible to them to get clear.

Buoys marking cables and pipelines shall not be approached within 2½ cables, and fishing gear and nets shall be kept the same distance from them.

3 It is an offence to break or damage a submarine cable or pipeline except in emergency.

Owners of vessels who can prove they have sacrificed an anchor, net or other fishing gear, to avoid damaging a submarine cable or pipeline, shall receive compensation from the owner of the cable or pipeline. See also 9.70.

Submarine pipelines

General information
9.64

1 Submarine pipelines are laid on the seabed for the conveyance of water, oil or gas and may extend many miles into the open sea, and between offshore platforms and production wells. They may be buried, trenched, or stand as much as 2 m above the sea floor, thus effectively reducing the charted depth by as much as 2 m.

Pipelines which were originally buried may have become exposed with time. Some pipelines have associated joints (known as sub-sea tees), valves and manifolds, which are often protected by guard domes of steel or concrete rising up to 10 m above the sea floor. These structures are shown on charts, if known, by a danger circle with the least depth over the structure, if known, and an appropriate legend.

2 Where pipelines are close together, only one may be charted. They may span across sea floor undulations; the size and positions of such spans are not constant and may vary due to tide and wave action.

Caution
9.65

1 Pipelines may contain flammable oil or gas under high pressure. A vessel causing damage to a pipeline could face an immediate hazard by loss of buoyancy due to gas aerated water or fire/explosion, and result in an environmental hazard. In addition to these the damage to the pipeline could lead to prosecution where it could be shown to have been done wilfully or through neglect.

Every care should therefore be taken to avoid anchoring, trawling, fishing, dredging, drilling or carrying out any activity close to submarine pipelines.

2 It is possible for fishing gear to become snagged under a pipeline so that it is irrecoverable, which could present a serious hazard to the fishing vessel. In the event that masters or skippers suspect that they have fouled a pipeline with gear or anchors, they should not place excessive weight on their gear, which could damage the pipeline and endanger their vessel and crew.

3 For the regulations to protect submarine pipelines, see 9.63.

On charts, pipelines carry an appropriate legend (Water, Gas or Oil), where known, and in the case of oil or gas pipelines a cautionary note.

Submarine cables

General information
9.66

1 Submarine cables, many carrying high voltage electric currents, are laid across rivers and harbours, offshore to islands and structures and between them, and across the oceans. Mariners should note that seabed mobility may leave cables spanning undulations of the seabed, increasing the likelihood of fishing or other gear becoming irrecoverably snagged, and potentially putting the vessel in severe danger.

2 Submarine cables of modern optical fibre design, some with digital circuit multiplication systems, may have a capacity in excess of 50 000 circuits. Modern long-distance telephone cables are fitted with submarine repeaters at frequent intervals to improve clarity; the repeaters contain components designed to function unattended for 25 years at depths of 3 miles or more. Damage to telecommunication cables can lead to extensive disruption of international communications, whilst damage to power cables will interrupt electricity supplies, and could endanger life.

3 Where cables are known to be power transmission cables, charts are noted accordingly. Submarine cables without such a note, however, must not be assumed to be of low voltage; many countries do not distinguish between cables of different voltages. Also, high voltages are fed into certain submarine cables other than power transmission cables.

Caution
9.67

1 Submarine cables may conduct high voltages and contact with (or proximity to) them poses an extreme danger.

Every care should therefore be taken to avoid anchoring, trawling, fishing, dredging, drilling, or carrying out any other activity in the vicinity of submarine cables which might damage them. Damage to a submarine cable can lead to prosecution where it can be shown to be done wilfully or through neglect.

2 If a vessel fouls a submarine cable whilst anchoring, fishing or trawling, every effort should be made to clear the anchor gear by normal methods,

taking care to avoid any risk of damaging the cable. If these efforts fail, the anchor/gear/trawl should be slipped and abandoned, and ideally, a marking buoy should be deployed, to aid possible future salvage operations.

Particular care should be exercised should a vessel's trawl/fishing gear foul a cable and raise it from the sea floor. This may lead to a capsize situation due to the excessive load. Before any attempt to slip or cut gear from the cable is made, the cable should first be lowered to the seabed.

3 In all cases care should be taken to avoid damaging the cable. It is obligatory that gear should be sacrificed rather than risk such damage.

Submarine cables should NEVER be cut. As all power cables and most telecommunications cables carry dangerous voltages, cutting them is likely to endanger life or cause serious injury.

4 Furthermore, no claim in respect of injury or damage sustained through such interference with a submarine cable is likely to be entertained.

Charting
9.68

1 Areas where anchoring, fishing and other underwater activities are prohibited on account of cables are, where known, usually charted and mentioned in *Admiralty Sailing Directions.*

The UKHO charts most power and telecommunications cables to a depth of 2000 m but these may not appear on derived charts, as other hydrographic authorities may not consider it necessary to chart every cable, or the relevant source information may not be available.

2 Disused cables are depicted on the largest scale chart of the area (to depths of 20 m), and, to promote greater safety, may also be charted in areas of offshore installations or where there is known sea floor activity, e.g. trawling.

All types of submarine cables may be depicted on charts adopted by the UKHO.

3 For UK waters, information on the cable operators may be found on the United Kingdom Cable Protection Committee (UKCPC) website at www.ukcpc.org. Precise positions and details of cables can be obtained from Kingfisher Information Service – Cable Awareness at www.kisca.org.uk

Fouling of submarine pipelines and cables

Reporting
9.69

1 Incidents involving the fouling of submarine cables or pipelines should be reported immediately to the appropriate authorities. In most cases this will be the local Coastguard, who should be advised as to the nature of the problem and the position of the vessel.

Claims for loss of gear
9.70

1 In UK waters, in order to claim the above-mentioned compensation a statement supported by the evidence of the crew must be drawn up immediately after the occurrence, and an entry made in the Deck Log. In addition, the Master must, within 24 hours of reaching a port in the United Kingdom, make a declaration on Department of Transport Form FSG 10 (Submarine cables) or FSG 10A (Submarine pipelines), giving full particulars, to one of the following authorities:

2 A MCA Marine Officer, or in ports where there is no such officer, a Chief Officer of Customs and Excise, or in ports where there is neither of these officers;

An Officer of the Coastguard; or

In England and Wales, a Sea Fisheries Inspector of the Department for Environment, Food and Rural Affairs; or

3 In Scotland, a Fisheries Officer of the Scottish Fisheries Protection Agency; or

In Northern Ireland, a Fisheries Officer of the Department of Agriculture and Rural Development, Northern Ireland.

4 The authority informed will pass the information to the Consular authorities of the country to which the owner of the cable or pipeline belongs.

Bridges and overhead power cables

Clearances
9.71

1 High voltages in overhead power cables sometimes make possible a dangerous electrical discharge or electrical arcing between a cable and a vessel passing under it.

To avoid this danger some authorities require a clearance of 2 to 5 m to be allowed when passing under a cable, depending on the conditions affecting the particular cable. This safety margin, when subtracted from the physical vertical clearance of the cable gives its Safe Vertical Clearance measured from Highest Astronomical Tide (HAT), as defined by the responsible authority. Reference should be made to the explanatory notes under the chart title to determine the applicable Height Datum.

2 However, many nations do not distinguish between cables carrying different voltages, and even when they do it may not be certain that a safety margin has been taken into account in the clearance shown on their charts.

Safe Vertical Clearance is given on charts in magenta, where known; otherwise, the physical vertical clearance is shown in black. For methods of showing clearances on older charts, see Chart 5011. The clearance is also given in Sailing Directions.

3 If the Safe Vertical Clearance is not specifically stated, nor is obtainable from local authorities, 5 m less than the vertical clearance should be allowed by vessels passing under any power cable.

4 Inevitably, the centre of a channel does not always lead under the lowest part of a cable in catenary over it. Should an appreciably greater clearance exist elsewhere in the channel, this will be stated in Sailing Directions, where known.

Effect on radar
9.72

1 For warning on the effect on radar echoes caused by overhead power cables, see 11.17.

NOTES

Chapter 10

MARITIME POLLUTION AND CONSERVATION (MARPOL)

MARPOL Regulations

General information

Background
10.1

1 In response to a growing awareness of the environment, and the potentially catastrophic effects of major pollution incidents at sea, of which the *Torrey Canyon* (1967), *Amoco Cadiz* (1978) and the *Exxon Valdez* (1989) are probably the best known recent examples, the international community has developed conventions which regulate the carriage of substances with potential for pollution, and restrict or ban the discharge overboard of materials damaging to the environment, including funnel gases and other emissions.

Conventions
10.2

1 The most important convention regulating and preventing marine pollution by ships is the IMO *International Convention for the Prevention of Pollution from Ships (1973),* as modified by the Protocol of 1978 relating thereto (MARPOL 73/78). It covers accidental and operational oil pollution as well as pollution by chemicals, goods in packaged form, sewage, garbage and air pollution.

2 IMO's Intervention Convention affirms the right of a coastal state to take measures on the high seas to prevent, mitigate or eliminate danger to its coastline from a maritime casualty. The *International Convention on Oil Pollution Preparedness, Response and Co-operation (OPRC) (1990)* provides a global framework for international co-operation in combating major incidents or threats of marine pollution. A protocol to this convention *(HNS Protocol)* covers marine pollution by hazardous and noxious substances.

3 IMO also has Secretariat responsibilities for the *Convention on the Prevention of Marine Pollution by Dumping of Wastes and Other Matter (1972),* generally known as the *London Convention,* which has been updated by the 1996 Protocol.

National and local regulations
10.3

1 In addition to these international Conventions, national governments are increasingly introducing legislation to protect the environment in their own territorial waters, and port and harbour authorities may also have their own regulations. Where legislation and regulation of this nature exists, it is contained in the appropriate volume of *Admiralty Sailing Directions.*

Reports
10.4

1 Actual or probable discharges of oil or noxious substances or sightings of pollution should be reported to the coastal authorities. See also 4.44.

Specific instructions on reporting, where known, are given in *Admiralty List of Radio Signals Volume 1.*

MARPOL 73/78

Adoption
10.5

1 The *International Convention for the Prevention of Pollution from Ships, 1973* was adopted by the International Conference on Marine Pollution convened by IMO in 1973. It was modified by the Protocol of 1978 relating thereto and adopted by the International Conference on Tanker Safety and Pollution Prevention convened by IMO in 1978. The Convention, as modified by the Protocol, is known as MARPOL 73/78.

Annexes
10.6

1 The Convention consists of six Annexes, see 10.9 to 10.21, each containing regulations for prevention or control of different types of pollution:

Annex I (Regulations for the Prevention of Pollution by Oil).

Annex II (Regulations for the Control of Pollution by Noxious Liquid Substances).

Annex III (Regulations for the Prevention of Pollution by Harmful Substances in Packaged Form).

Annex IV (Regulations for the Prevention of Pollution by Sewage from Ships).

Annex V (Regulations for the Prevention of Pollution by Garbage from Ships).

Annex VI (Regulations for the Prevention of Air Pollution from Ships).

2 Under Article 14, signatories to the Convention are bound by the provisions of Annexes I and II. However Annexes III, IV, V and VI are considered "optional", and the IMO maintains a list of countries showing which of the Annexes each has ratified, which can be viewed on the IMO website (www.imo.org).

Special areas
10.7

1 Special Areas are designated in the Annexes. They are defined under MARPOL 73/78 as areas which, for technical reasons relating to their oceanographic and ecological condition and to their sea traffic, require the adoption of special mandatory methods for the prevention of sea pollution.

Special Area	Applicable Annex(es)
The Mediterranean Sea area means the Mediterranean Sea proper including the gulfs and seas therein with the boundary between the Mediterranean and the Black Sea constituted by the 41°N parallel, and bounded to the west by the Straits of Gibraltar at the meridian of 5°36'W.	I, V
The Baltic Sea area means the Baltic Sea proper with the Gulf of Bothnia, the Gulf of Finland and the entrance to the Baltic Sea bounded by the parallel of latitude of The Skaw in the Skagerrak at 57°44'·8N.	I, V, VI
The Black Sea area means the Black Sea proper with the boundary between the Mediterranean and the Black Sea constituted by the parallel 41°N.	I, V*
The Red Sea area means the Red Sea proper including the Gulfs of Suez and Aqaba bounded at the S by the rhumb line between Ras Siyyân (Ras si Ane) (12°28'·5N 43°19'·6E) and Ḥiṣn Murād (Husn Murad) (12°40'·4N 43°30'·2E).	I*, V*
The Gulfs area means the sea area located NW of the rhumb line between Ra's al Hadd (22°30'N 59°48'E) and Damāgheh-ye Pas Bandar (Ra's Fasteh) (25°04'N 61°25'E).	I, V
The Gulf of Aden area means that part of the Gulf of Aden between the Red Sea and the Arabian Sea bounded to the west by the rhumb line between Ras Siyyân (Ras si Ane) (12°28'·5N 43°19'·6E) and Ḥiṣn Murād (Husn Murad) (12°40'·4N 43°30'·2E), and to the east by the rhumb line between Raas Caseyr (Ras Asir) (11°50'·0N 51°16'·9E) and Ras Fartak (15°35'·0N 52°13'·8E).	I*
The Antarctic area means the sea area south of latitude 60°S.	I, II, V
The North West European Waters include the North Sea and its approaches, the Irish Sea and its approaches, the Celtic Sea, the English Channel and its approaches; and part of the North East Atlantic immediately to the west of Ireland. The area is bounded by lines joining the following points: 48°27'N on the French coast, 48°27'N 6°25'W, 49°52'N 7°44'W, 50°30'N 12°00'W, 56°30'N 12°00'W, 62°00'N 3°00'W, 62°00'N on the Norwegian coast and 57°44'·8N on the Danish and Swedish coasts.	I
The Oman area of the Arabian Sea means the sea area enclosed by the following coordinates: 22°30'·00N 59°48'·00E 23°47'·27N 60°35'·73E 22°40'·62N 62°25'·29E 21°47'·40N 63°22'·22E 20°30'·37N 62°52'·41E 19°45'·90N 62°25'·97E 18°49'·92N 62°02'·94E 17°44'·36N 61°05'·53E 16°43'·71N 60°25'·62E 16°03'·90N 59°32'·24E 15°15'·20N 58°58'·52E 14°36'·93N 58°10'·23E 14°18'·93N 57°27'·03E 14°11'·53N 56°53'·75E 13°53'·80N 56°19'·24E 13°45'·86N 55°54'·53E 14°27'·38N 54°51'·42E 14°40'·10N 54°27'·35E 14°46'·21N 54°08'·56E 15°20'·74N 53°38'·33E 15°48'·69N 53°32'·07E 16°23'·02N 53°14'·82E 16°39'·06N 53°06'·52E.	I*
The North Sea area means the North Sea proper including seas therein within the boundary between (i) The North Sea southwards of latitude 62°N and eastwards of longitude 4°W; (ii) The Skagerrak, the southern limit of which is determined east of the Skaw by latitude 57°44'·8N; and (iii) The English Channel and its approaches eastwards of longitude 5°W and northwards of latitude 48°30'N.	V, VI

Special Area	Applicable Annex(es)
The Wider Caribbean Region, as defined in article 2, paragraph 1 of the *Convention for the Protection and Development of the Marine Environment of the Wider Caribbean Region* (Cartagena de Indias, 1983), means the Gulf of Mexico and Caribbean Sea proper including the bays and seas thererin and that portion of the Atlantic Ocean within the boundary constituted by the 30°N parallel from Florida eastward to the 77°30'W meridian, thence a rhumb line to the intersection of 7°20'N parallel and 50°W meridian, thence a rhumb line drawn southwesterly to the eastern boundary of French Guiana.	V*
The Southern South African waters means the sea area enclosed by the following positions: 31°14'S 17°50'E 31°30'S 17°12'E 32°00'S 17°06'E 32°32'S 16°52'E 34°06'S 17°24'E 36°58'S 20°54'E 36°00'S 22°30'E 35°14'S 22°54'E 34°30'S 26°00'E 33°48'S 27°25'E 33°27'S 27°12'E	I

Note. * The Special Area requirements for these areas have not yet taken effect because of a lack of notifications from MARPOL. Parties whose coastlines border the relevant Special Areas on the existence of adequate reception facilities (Regulations 38.6 of MARPOL Annex I and 5(4) of MARPOL Annex V).

Nearest land

10.8

1 Frequent use is made throughout MARPOL 73/78 of the expression "from the nearest land", which means from the baseline from which the territorial sea in question is established in accordance with international law (see 9.9), except that, for the purposes of this Convention (MARPOL 73/78), "from the nearest land" off the NE coast of Australia shall mean from the line drawn from a point on the coast of Australia in position 11°00'S 142°08'E through the following coordinates:

2
10°35'S 141°55'E.
10°00'S 142°00'E.
 9°10'S 143°52'E.
 9°00'S 144°30'E.
10°41'S 145°00'E.
13°00'S 145°00'E.
15°00'S 146°00'E.
17°30'S 147°00'E.
21°00'S 152°55'E.
24°30'S 154°00'E,

to a point on the coast of Australia in position 24°42'S 153°15'E.

Annex I - Regulations for the prevention of pollution by oil

General information

10.9

1 This Annex contains regulations for the prevention of pollution by oil. The United Kingdom domestic legislation to implement this Annex is the *Merchant Shipping (Prevention of Oil Pollution) Regulations 1983*.

Discharging of oil

10.10

1 The regulations govern the discharges, except for clean or segregated ballast, from all ships. They require *inter alia* all ships to be fitted with pollution prevention equipment to comply with the stringent discharge regulations.

Discharge into the sea of oil or oily mixtures, as defined in an Appendix to the Convention, is prohibited by the regulations of Annex I except when all the following conditions are satisfied.

2 **From the machinery space bilges of all ships**, except from those of tankers where the discharge is mixed with oil cargo residue:

The ship is not within a Special Area.
The ship is more than 12 miles from the nearest land.
The ship is *en route*.
The oil content of the effluent is less than 15 parts per million (ppm).

3 The ship has in operation an oil discharge monitoring and control system, oily-water separating equipment, oil filtering system or other installation required by this Annex.

These restrictions do not apply to discharges of oily mixture which without dilution have an oil content not exceeding 15 ppm.

4 **From the cargo area of an oil tanker** (discharges from cargo tanks, including cargo pump rooms; and from machinery space bilges mixed with cargo oil residue):

The tanker is not within a Special Area.
The tanker is more than 50 miles from the nearest land.
The tanker is proceeding *en route*.
The instantaneous rate of discharge of oil content does not exceed 30 litres per mile.

5 The total quantity of oil discharged into the sea does not exceed for existing tankers 1/15 000 of the total quantity of the particular cargo of which the residue formed a part, and for new tankers (as defined in the Annex) 1/30 000 of the total quantity of the particular cargo of which the residue formed a part.

6   The tanker has in operation, except where provided for in the Annex, an oil discharge monitoring and control system and a slop tank arrangement.

Special Areas and PSSAs
10.11

1   Annex I applies to all such areas.

Shipboard Oil Pollution Emergency Plans (SOPEP)
10.12

1   Regulation 26 of Annex 1 to MARPOL 73/78 requires every oil tanker of 150 gt and above and every other vessel of 400 gt and above, to carry on board a SOPEP approved by the vessel's flag administration. Regulation 26 came into force on 4 April 1995 for all existing vessels. IMO has produced guidelines, as IMO Resolution MEPC 54(32), for the development of SOPEPs. This regulation also applies to offshore installations engaged in gas and oil production, seaports and oil terminals.

Annex II - Noxious liquid substances in bulk

General information
10.13

1   This Annex contains regulations for the control of pollution by noxious liquid substances carried in bulk. This is the first attempt to control, on an international basis, the discharge of tank washings and other residues of liquid substances (other than oil) which are carried in bulk. These substances are mainly petro-chemicals, but include other chemicals, vegetable oils, coal-derived oils, and other substances categorised as noxious liquid substances in accordance with defined guidelines. This Annex also contains requirements for standards of construction of chemical tankers and other ships carrying these substances, in order to minimise accidental discharge into the sea of such substances.

2   The United Kingdom domestic legislation to implement this Annex is the *Merchant Shipping (Control of Pollution by Noxious Liquid Substances in Bulk) Regulations 1987*.

Applicability
10.14

1   The regulations apply to all ships carrying noxious liquid substances in bulk and contain, *inter alia*, provisions to reduce operational and accidental pollution from ships and require ships to be fitted with equipment to reduce the amount of residues of noxious liquid substances in the ship's cargo tanks to the minimum when unloading. The regulations impose restrictions on the quantities of residues that can be discharged into the sea, the rate of discharge and where they can be discharged. Discharges into the sea of the most noxious of these liquid substances are prohibited and ships have to make use of reception facilities ashore in order to dispose of residues. Ships are required to carry and comply with a Manual of approved procedures and arrangements, and to record all operations involving these substances in a cargo record book.

Categorisation of Noxious Liquid Substances
10.15

1   Substances are listed in the regulations and divided according to their potential environmental hazard into four categories as follows.

2   **Category A.** Noxious liquid substances which if discharged into the sea from tank cleaning or deballasting operations would present a major hazard to either marine resources or human health or cause serious harm to amenities or other legitimate uses of the sea and therefore justify the application of stringent anti-pollution measures.

3   **Category B.** Noxious liquid substances which if discharged into the sea from tank cleaning or deballasting operations would present a hazard to either marine resources or human health or cause harm to amenities or other legitimate uses of the sea and therefore justify the application of special anti-pollution measures.

4   **Category C.** Noxious liquid substances which if discharged into the sea from tank cleaning or deballasting operations would present a minor hazard to either marine resources or human health or cause minor harm to amenities or other legitimate uses of the sea and therefore require special operational conditions.

5   **Category D.** Noxious liquid substances which if discharged into the sea from tank cleaning or deballasting operations would present a recognisable hazard to either marine resources or human health or cause minimal harm to amenities or other legitimate uses of the sea and therefore require some attention in operational conditions.

6   The regulations also list substances which have been evaluated and found to fall outside these categories and to which the regulations do not apply. Other liquid substances may not be carried in bulk unless they have been evaluated.

Special Areas and PSSAs
10.16

1   Annex II applies to the Antarctic, Baltic and Black Sea Special Areas (10.7) and the Particularly Sensitive Sea Areas.

Annex III - Harmful substances carried at sea in packaged form

General information
10.17

1   This Annex contains regulations which include requirements on packaging, marking, labelling, documentation, stowage and quantity limitations. It aims to prevent or minimise pollution of the marine environment by harmful substances in packaged forms or in freight containers, portable tanks or road and rail tank wagons, or other forms of containment specified in the schedule for harmful substances in the International Maritime Dangerous Goods (IMDG) Code.

Annex IV- Sewage from ships

General information
10.18

1   This Annex applies to vessels engaged in international voyages, and sets out in detail how sewage should be treated or held aboard ship, and

the circumstances in which discharge into the sea may be allowed.

2   This Annex applies to all vessels of 400 gt and over, and to vessels of less than 400 gt which are certified to carry more than 15 persons.

Annex V- Garbage from ships

General information
10.19

1   This Annex contains regulations for the prevention of pollution by garbage which apply to all ships.

They prohibit the disposal into the sea of all plastics, including but not limited to synthetic ropes, synthetic fishing nets and plastic garbage bags.

2   They restrict the disposal into the sea of garbage, which includes all kinds of victuals, and domestic and operational waste generated during the normal operation of the ship.

The disposal into the sea of the following garbage shall be made as far as practicable from the nearest land, but in any case is prohibited if the distance from the nearest land is less than:

3   25 miles for dunnage, lining and packing materials which will float.

12 miles for food wastes and all other garbage including paper products, rags, glass, metal, bottles, crockery and similar refuse.

If passed through a cominuter or grinder, garbage in this category may be disposed into the sea not less than 3 miles from the nearest land (10.8).

Special Areas and PSSAs
10.20

1   Annex V applies to all sea areas. Additional more stringent regulations apply to Special Areas (10.8), except the Gulf of Aden Area, and to PSSAs.

Annex VI - Air pollution

General information
10.21

1   This Annex sets limits on sulphur oxides (SOx) and nitrogen oxides (NOx) emissions from ships exhausts.

It contains provisions allowing for special "SOx Emission Control Areas" to be established. In these areas, the sulphur content of the fuel oil used on board must not exceed 1·5% m/m. Alternatively, ships must fit an exhaust gas cleaning system or use any other technological method to limit SOx emissions.

The Baltic Sea and the North Sea are designated as SOx Emission Control Areas in the Protocol.

2   The Annex also prohibits the deliberate emissions of ozone depleting substances, which include halons and chlorofluorocarbons (CFCs), and prohibits the incineration on board ship of certain products such as contaminated packaging materials and polychlorinated biphenyls (PCBs).

Details
10.22

1   For further information the full text of the Annexes should be consulted.

Pollution of the sea

Ballast water management

Ballast Water Management for Ships
10.23

1   International Guidelines have been adopted by the IMO to prevent the introduction of unwanted aquatic organisms and pathogens from ships' ballast water and sediment discharges into marine eco-systems. The Guidelines include the retention of ballast water onboard, ballast exchange at sea, ballast management aimed at preventing or minimising the uptake of contaminated water or sediment and the discharge of ballast ashore. Attention is particularly drawn to the hazards associated with exchanging ballast at sea.

2   Ship Owners and Agents are strongly advised to comply with these Guidelines which were introduced under IMO Resolution A.868 (20), entitled *1997 Guidelines for the Control and Management of Ships' Ballast Water to Minimize the Transfer of Harmful Aquatic Organisms and Pathogens*.

3   In February 2004 a Diplomatic Conference adopted an *International Convention for the Control and Management of Ships' Ballast Water and Sediments*. The Ballast Water Management (BWM) Convention will come into force world-wide 12 months after it has been signed by 30 states, representing 35 % of world merchant shipping tonnage.

4   Individual States are currently in the process of introducing national legislation in accordance with the BWM Convention, introduced above. On implementation, this legislation will be applicable to ships that carry out ballast water discharge within a state's jurisdictional waters.

5   Typical legislation requires that all ships intending to discharge ballast water within a state's jurisdictional waters shall conduct any exchange at least 200 miles from the coast and in water at least 200 m in depth. If this is not possible exchange should be carried out as far as possible from the nearest land and in all cases at least 50 miles from the coast. In cases where the ship is unable to comply, ballast water must be retained on board, and only a minimum amount may be authorised for discharge, with the prior authorisation of the appropriate national Maritime Authority.

6   Ballast water management will be conducted in accordance with a *Ship's BWM Plan*. In addition, a *Ballast Water Reporting Form*, may be required by the relevant authority, as directed, prior to the ETA. The *Ship's BWM Plan* will be approved by the flag administration or relevant classification societies.

Violations of the legislation will be sanctioned according to national law, which can include warnings, fines, detention or prohibition of the ship's entry into a port or terminal.

Further information can be obtained through National Authorities, the IMO, or the UK Maritime and Coastguard Agency (UK MCGA).

Oil slicks

Movement

10.24

1   In the event of an oil spillage at sea, measures to reduce the resulting pollution call for immediate consideration of the probable movement of the consequent oil slick. Slicks are moved by tidal streams, surface currents and surface winds. The relative importance of these factors will depend on the position of the slick, but in the course of a few days the effect of the surface wind can be expected to predominate.

2   Tidal streams have a net effect over 24 hours of returning a slick to approximately the position where it started. Their effect is therefore most important when a slick is near the shore or when forecasting its movement during darkness to enable it to be found again at dawn.

    Surface currents (5.1 to 5.11) also carry a slick along with them; their strength and direction can be obtained from the appropriate volume of Sailing Directions.

3   Surface winds also impart a movement to a slick, additional to that of any wind drift current. The oil slick, being lighter than the water and lying on it in a layer 2–3 cm deep, is more easily moved by the wind. A slick therefore moves farther than the surrounding water and is affected sooner by changes of wind. When forecasting the movement of an oil slick around the British Isles, its speed due to surface wind is assessed as 3·3% of that of the wind speed, and its direction of movement is considered to be deflected by the Coriolis effect so that it follows the surface isobars of the prevailing weather system.

The London Convention 1972 and Protocol 1996

General information

10.25

1   The London Convention, or more correctly *The Convention on the Prevention of Marine Pollution by Dumping of Wastes and Other Matter* (1972), was one of the first global conventions to protect the marine environment from human activities. It has been in force since 1975.

2   **Objective.** The objective of the convention was to promote the effective control of all sources of marine pollution and to take all practicable steps to prevent pollution of the sea by dumping of wastes and other matter.

    1996 Protocol. Known as *The London Protocol,* it was agreed to further modernise the 1972 Convention, and eventually to replace it. It came into force in 2006.

Dumping

10.26

1   **Definition.** Dumping is defined, *inter alia,* as any deliberate disposal into the sea of wastes or other matter from vessels, aircraft, platforms or other man-made structures at sea. However it specifically excludes wastes or other matter incidental to, or derived from the normal operations of vessels, aircraft, platforms or other man-made structures at sea.

2   **Regulations pertaining to dumping.** Under the Protocol, dumping at sea is prohibited by Article 4.

However the following material may be considered for dumping providing that a permit (see below) has been obtained:

    Dredged material.

    Sewage sludge.

    Fish waste, or material resulting from industrial fish processing operations.

    Vessels, platforms and other man-made structures at sea; such material may only be considered for dumping provided that material capable of creating floating debris or otherwise contributing to the pollution of the maritime environment has been removed to the maximum extent, and provided that the material dumped poses no serious obstacle to fishing or navigation.

    Inert, inorganic geological material.

    Organic material of natural origin.

3   Bulky items primarily comprising iron, steel, concrete and similarly unharmful materials for which the concern is physical impact, and limited to those circumstances where such wastes are generated at locations, such as small islands with isolated communities, having no practical access to disposal options other than dumping; such material may only be considered for dumping provided that material capable of creating floating debris or otherwise contributing to the pollution of the maritime environment has been removed to the maximum extent, and provided that the material dumped poses no serious obstacle to fishing or navigation.

4   Carbon dioxide streams from carbon dioxide capture processes for sequestration. Dumping may only be considered if disposal is into a sub-seabed geological formation, if they consist overwhelmingly of carbon dioxide. They may contain incidental associated substances derived from the source material and the capture and sequestration processes used, and provided that no wastes or other matter are added for the purpose of disposing of them.

5   **Radioactive waste.** Any of the materials listed above containing levels of radioactivity greater than *de minimis* (exempt) concentrations as defined by the International Atomic Energy Agency (IAEA) and adopted by the Contracting Parties, shall not be considered eligible for dumping.

6   **Permits.** Permits may be issued by a national authority. Any permit issued will contain provisions to ensure that, as far as practicable, environmental disturbance and detriment are minimised and the benefits maximised. They will specify:

    The types and sources of materials to be dumped.

    The location(s) of the dump-site(s).

    The method of dumping.

    Any monitoring and reporting requirements.

Incineration at sea

10.27

1   Under the Protocol, incineration at sea is defined as the combustion, on board a vessel, platform or other man-made platform at sea, of wastes or other matter for the purpose of their deliberate destruction by thermal destruction. It does not include the incineration of wastes or other matter if such waste or other matter were generated during the normal operation of that vessel, platform or other man-made platform at sea.

Conservation

General information
10.28

1   Lack of conservation has led in the last hundred years to more than 100 species of birds and mammals alone being exterminated. At sea in the last century all species of whale reached the verge of extinction, the herring fishery of the North Sea was drastically diminished, and in the Baltic the herring was almost wiped out by overfishing and pollution.

2   Consequently, many nations have passed legislation to protect the flora and fauna of their coasts by establishing nature reserves where marine life, birds and mammals can live and breed undisturbed. Other nations, largely those depending on their fishing industry for their food and trade, have sought to extend their jurisdiction seaward to prevent stocks of fish approaching their shores from being unduly depleted by foreign fishing vessels.

3   Nature reserves, fish havens, shellfish beds and certain fishing limits are shown on charts where these concern the mariner. Further details and any restrictions affecting these areas and limits are given in Sailing Directions, but specialised legislation on matters such as fisheries, minerals or leisure activities, are only mentioned if it is likely to affect the general mariner.

4   The mariner should not only comply strictly with the legislation and avoid nature reserves, but avoid disturbing any wildlife unnecessarily, particularly on their breeding grounds, and by special care when visiting secluded islands where some species may be unique.

5   Most countries have quarantine regulations to prevent the import of undesirable forms of life. The mariner should strictly observe such laws as pests can be carried in unexpected ways.

    The mariner can sometimes assist the progress of conservation by reports on subjects as divergent as the sightings of whales or turtles (4.70 to 4.71), or the movements recorded by echo sounder of the deep scattering layer.

Marine Environmental High Risk Areas (MEHRAs)
10.29

1   32 locations around the UK coast have been identified as Marine Environmental High Risk Areas (MEHRAs). The locations of these areas have been identified after taking into account shipping risk, environmental sensitivity and other environmental protection measures already in place at each location and follow recommendations made by the late Lord Donaldson in his report Safer ships, Cleaner Seas.

2   MEHRAs are an essential aid to passage planning since their primary purpose is to inform ships' masters of areas where they need to exercise even more caution than usual. This is just part of the information available to mariners to enable them to navigate UK waters safely.

3   For further information, see Annual Notice to Mariners No 26.

Historic and dangerous wrecks

Regulations
10.30

1   In waters around the United Kingdom, the sites of certain wrecks are protected by the Protection of Wrecks Act, 1973, from unauthorised interference on account of the historic, archaeological or artistic importance of the wreck or anything belonging to it.

    The term "unauthorised interference" includes the carrying out, without a special licence from the Secretary of State, of any of the following actions within the site of a wreck: tampering with, damaging or removing any part of the wreck; diving or salvage operations; or depositing anything (including an anchor) on the sea floor.

2   Certain other wrecks, considered potentially dangerous, are also protected by the same Act, which declares their sites prohibited areas. Entry into these areas, above or below water, is prohibited.

    The positions and limits of the prohibited areas round these wrecks are announced by Notices to Mariners, and listed in Annual Summary of Admiralty Notices to Mariners. The areas are charted in magenta on appropriate charts and described in Sailing Directions.

3   To prevent the disturbance of the dead, similar protection applies to certain other wrecks, including aircraft, both in United Kingdom and international waters under the terms of the Protection of Military Remains Act, 1986.

NOTES

SECTION IV

OPERATIONS AT SEA

NOTES

Chapter 11

NAVIGATION AND AIDS TO NAVIGATION

Fixing the position

General information
11.1

1   The position of a ship at sea can be found by several means. Traditional methods have involved two or more position lines obtained with reference to terrestrial or celestial objects and resulting position lines may be plotted on a chart or converted to latitude and longitude. It must be emphasised that a fix by only two position lines is the most likely to be in error and should be confirmed with an additional position line or by other means.

2   Satellite navigation methods are being increasingly used for many types of navigation with the output of a position. However, the fact that the position may be referred to a datum other than that of the chart in use **must** be taken into account. See 1.33.

3   On coastal passages a ship's position will normally be fixed by visual bearings, angles or ranges to fixed objects on shore, corroborated by the Dead Reckoning or Estimated Position. The accuracy of such fixes depends on the relative positions and distances from the ship of the objects used for the observations.

4   Radar or one of the radio position-fixing systems described below may often give equally, or more accurate, fixes than visual ones, but whenever circumstances allow, fixing should be carried out simultaneously by more than one method. This will confirm the accuracy of both the observations and the systems.

Magnetic variation

General information
11.2

1   Due allowance for the gradual change in the variation is required in laying down positions by magnetic compass bearings on charts. In some cases, such as with small scales, or when the position lines are long, the displacement of position arising from neglect of this change may be important.

2   The geographical change in variation in some parts of the world is sufficiently rapid to need consideration. For instance, in approaching Halifax from Newfoundland the variation changes by 10° in less than 500 miles, and in the English Channel by about 5° in 400 miles. In such cases the appropriate Magnetic Variation chart should be consulted. These charts show the amount and rate of change of the variation and the intensity of its components throughout the world.

3   Magnetic variation values for points on the Earth's surface are calculated every 5 years. The periods between calculations are known as Magnetic Epochs, which start on 1st January 2000, 2005, etc.

The Magnetic Variation Charts, as listed in *Catalogue of Admiralty Charts and Publications*, are corrected and republished as early as possible in each magnetic epoch.

4   Magnetic variation information on nautical charts containing isogonals (lines of equal magnetic variation) is updated by New Edition for each new epoch if the variation, corrected by the annual change shown on the chart, differs by more than about 1° from the value for the new epoch. Otherwise, the magnetic variation information is normally updated by New Edition every 10 years (i.e. every second epoch).

5   Magnetic variation information on nautical charts containing compass roses with magnetic north arrows is updated whenever a New Edition is published.

Overlapping charts, published or revised in different Magnetic Epochs, may give different values for the variation in the same position. In such cases the value calculated from the most recently published chart (or New Edition), or from the appropriate Magnetic Variation chart, should be used.

6   Deflections may also be caused by wrecks lying in moderate depths; however investigations have shown that it is unlikely that such deflections will exceed 7° or will be experienced, nor should the disturbance be felt beyond a distance of 250 m. Deflections of an unpredictable amount may occur when very close to such wrecks.

7   Greater deflections may be experienced when in close quarters with a ship carrying a large cargo such as iron ore, which readily reacts to induced magnetism.

8   Power cables carrying direct current can cause deflection of the compass needle. The amount of the deflection depends on the magnitude of the electrical current and the angle the cable makes with the magnetic meridian. Small vessels with an auto-pilot dependent upon a magnetic sensor may experience some steering difficulties while crossing such a cable. See also 7.55 for the effect of magnetic and ionospheric storms on the compass needle.

Local magnetic anomalies
11.3

1   In various parts of the world, magnetic ores on or just below the sea floor may give rise to local magnetic anomalies resulting in the temporary deflection of the magnetic compass needle when a ship passes over them. The areas of disturbance are usually small unless there are many anomalies close together. The amount of the deflection will depend on the depth of water and the strength of the magnetic force generated by the magnetic ores. However, the magnetic force will seldom be strong enough to deflect the compass needle in depths greater than about 1500 m. Similarly, a ship would have to be within

8 cables of a nearby land mass containing magnetic ores for a deflection of the needle to occur.

2   **Charting and description.** Local magnetic anomalies are depicted by a special symbol on Admiralty charts and are mentioned in Sailing Directions. The amount and direction of the deflection of the compass needle is also given, if known.

Visual fixes

Simultaneous bearings
11.4

1   A fix using only two observations is liable to be affected by undetected errors in taking the bearings, or in applying compass errors, or in laying off the bearing on the chart. A third bearing of another suitably placed object should be taken whenever possible to confirm the position plotted from the original bearings.

Simultaneous bearing and distance
11.5

1   In this method the distance is normally obtained by radar, but an optical rangefinder or vertical sextant angle (see below) may be used. An approximate range may also be obtained by using the "dipping distance" of an object of known height and the Geographical Range Table given in each volume of *Admiralty List of Lights*, or in other nautical tables or almanacs.

It should be noted that the charted range of a light is not, except on certain older charts, the geographical range. See 11.84.

Running fix
11.6

1   If two position lines are obtained at different times the position of the ship may be found by transferring the first position line up to the time of taking the second, making due allowance for the vessel's ground track and ground speed. Accuracy of the fix will depend on how precisely these factors are known.

Transit
11.7

1   To enable a transit to be sufficiently sensitive for the movement of one object relative to another to be immediately apparent, it is best for the distance between the observer and the nearer object to be less than three times the distance between the objects in transit.

Horizontal sextant angles
11.8

1   Where great accuracy in position is required, such as the fixing of a rock or shoal, or adding detail to a chart, horizontal sextant angles should be used when practicable. The accuracy of this method, which requires trained and experienced observers, will depend on the availability of three or more suitably placed objects. Whenever possible about five objects should be used, so that the accuracy of both the fix and the chart can be proved.

2   A horizontal sextant angle can also be used as a danger angle when passing off-lying dangers, if suitably placed marks are available. This method should not be used where the chart is based on old or imperfect surveys as distant objects may be found to be incorrectly placed.

Vertical sextant angles
11.9

1   Vertical sextant angles can be used for determining the distances of objects of known height, in conjunction with nautical tables. A vertical angle can also be used as a danger angle.

It should be noted that the charted elevation of a light is the height of the centre of the lens, given above the level of MHWS or MHHW and should be adjusted for the height of the tide if used for vertical angles.

The height of a light structure is the height of the top of the structure above the ground.

2   Vertical angles of distant mountain peaks should be used with circumspection owing to the possibility of abnormal refraction.

Astronomical observation

General information
11.10

1   An accurate position may be obtained by observations of at least four stars suitably separated in azimuth at evening or morning twilight, or by observation of a bright star at daybreak and another shortly afterwards of the sun when above the horizon (not less than 10°). The position lines obtained from the bodies observed should differ in azimuth by 30° or more. Care should be taken in obtaining a probable position if it has been possible to observe only three stars in the same half circle of the horizon.

2   Moon sights are sometimes available when stars are obscured by light cloud, or in daytime. A good position may often be obtained in daytime by simultaneous observations of the Sun and Moon, and of the planet Venus when it is sufficiently bright.

The value of even a single position line from accurate astronomical observations should not be overlooked. A sounding obtained at the time of the observation may often indicate the approximate location on the position line.

Radar

Fixing
11.11

1   It is important to appreciate the limitations of a radar set when interpreting the information obtained from it. For detailed recommendations on fixing by radar, see *Admiralty Manual of Navigation*.

2   In general the ranges obtained from navigational radar sets are appreciably more accurate than the bearings on account of the width of the radar beam. If therefore radar information alone is available, the best fixes will be derived from use of three or more radar ranges as position arcs.

3   For possible differences between radar ranges and charted ranges when using charts based on old surveys, see 1.29.

Radar clearing ranges

11.12

1   When proceeding along a coast, it is often possible to decide on the least distance to which the coast can be approached without encountering off-lying dangers. Providing the coast can be unmistakably identified, this distance can be used as a clearing range outside of which the ship must remain to proceed in safety. A radar clearing range can be particularly useful off a straight and featureless coast.

Parallel index

11.13

1   Parallel index technique is a refinement of the radar clearing line applied to the radar display. It is a simple and effective way of monitoring a ship's progress by observing the movement of the echo of a clearly identified mark with respect to lines drawn on the radar display parallel to the ship's track. It is of particular use in the preparation of tracks when planning a passage.

Radar horizon

11.14

1   The distance of the radar horizon under average atmospheric conditions over the sea is little more than one third greater than that of the optical horizon. It will of course vary with the height of the aerial, and be affected by abnormal refraction (7.42).

No echoes will be received from a coastline beyond and below the radar horizon, but they may be received from more distant high ground: this may give a misleading impression of the range of the nearest land.

Quality and accuracy of radar returns

11.15

1   Radar shadow areas cast by mountains or high land may contain large blind zones. High mountains inland may therefore be screened by lower hills nearer the coast.

Fixes from land features should not be relied upon until the features have been positively identified, and the fixes found consistent with the estimated position, soundings, or position lines from other methods.

2   Metal and water are better reflectors of radar transmissions than are wood, stone, sand or earth. In general, however, the shape and size of an object have a greater effect on its echoing properties than its composition. The larger the object, the more extensive, but not necessarily the stronger the echo. Visually conspicuous objects are often poor radar targets. The shape of an object dictates how much energy is reflected back to the radar set. Curved surfaces, such as conical lighthouses and buoys, tend to produce a poor echo. Sloping ground produces poorer echoes than steep cliffs, and it is difficult to identify any portion of a flat or gently shelving coastline such as mud flats or sand dunes. Moreover, the appearance of an echo may vary considerably with the bearing.

Radar image enhancement

11.16

1   **Radar beacons,** either racons or ramarks, give more positive identification, since both transmit characteristic signals.

Racon. A racon is a type of radar transponder beacon which, on receipt of a radar pulse, will respond on the same frequency, leaving an image on the radar display in the form of a series of dots and dashes representing a Morse character, radiating away from the location of the beacon. Most racons respond to both 3 centimetre (X-band) and 10 centimetre (S-band) radar emissions, but some respond to 3 centimetre emissions only.

2   **Ramark.** A ramark is a radar beacon which transmits continuously without having to be triggered by an incoming radar pulse. The image on the radar display is a line of dots and/or dashes radiating from the centre to the edge, with no indication of range. Only a few ramarks remain in existence, and those only in Japanese and Chinese waters.

3   Radar beacons should be used with caution as not all are monitored to ensure proper working. Furthermore, reduced performance of a ship's radar may fail to trigger a racon at the normal range. The displayed response of radar beacons may also be affected by the use of rain clutter filters on radar sets to the point where the displayed response signal is degraded or eliminated. Particular care is required when using sets fitted with auto clutter adoptive rain and sea clutter suppression smart circuits.

4   When depending solely on a radiobeacon or radar beacon transmitting from a LANBY, light vessel or light float, it is essential, to avoid danger of collision, that the bearing of the beacon should not be kept constant.

5   Radar beacons usually operate initially on a trial basis, and charts are not updated until their permanent installation is considered justified. Details of both temporary and permanent radar beacons are included in *Admiralty List of Radio Signals Volume 2,* which should be consulted for all information on radar beacons.

6   **Radar reflectors** fitted to objects such as buoys improve the range of detection and assist identification. Most important buoys and many minor buoys are now fitted with radar reflectors, which are often incorporated within the structure of the buoy and so not visible to the mariner. In consequence certain countries no longer show such radar reflectors on their charts, so that Admiralty charts based on those charts cannot show radar reflectors either. Radar reflectors on buoys of the IALA Maritime Buoyage Systems are not charted, for similar reasons, and to give more clarity to the important topmarks.

Overhead power cables

11.17

1   Overhead power cables which span some channels give a radar echo which may mislead ships approaching them. The echo appears on the scan as a single echo always at right angles to the line of the cable and can therefore be wrongly identified as the radar echo of a ship on a steady bearing or "collision course". If avoiding action is attempted, the echo remains on a constant bearing, moving to the same side of the channel as the vessel altering course. This phenomenon is particularly apparent from the cables spanning İstanbul Boğazı (The Bosporus) (41°04′N 29°03′E).

Electronic position-fixing systems

General information
11.18

1   It is important to realise that accurate equipment is no guard against the vagaries of the propagation of radio waves. Systems operating on medium and low frequencies are liable to "night effect" in areas where the ground and sky waves are received with equal strength; these areas will occur at ranges depending upon the particular frequency used by any system.

2   Information from radio aids can be misleading and should, whenever possible, be checked by visual or other methods. A fix which is markedly different from the dead reckoning or estimated position should be treated with suspicion, particularly if it is unconfirmed by other means.

    When depending solely on a radar beacon transmitting from a LANBY, light vessel or light float, it is essential, to avoid danger of collision, that the bearing of the beacon should not be kept constant.

3   The velocity of propagation of radio waves varies when passing over differing surfaces; over sea it is up to 0·5% greater than over land, but the velocity is also affected to an unknown extent by hills and features such as cliffs. Radio position-fixing transmitters are positioned where possible close to the shore to give the maximum possible sea paths, but long land paths are sometimes inevitable. Due to the varying paths, mean velocities are used when drawing most lattices, but additional fixed errors which vary from place to place will still exist.

Radio direction-finding (RDF)
11.19

1   **QTG service.** Coast Radio Stations which will transmit signals on request for use with ship's DF apparatus are listed under this heading in *Admiralty List of Radio Signals Volume 2.* Such stations are indicated on Admiralty charts by the abbreviation R.

2   Radio waves are usually subject to refraction when crossing the coast. At best, MFDF is likely to give a bearing accuracy of 3°, but only by day and within about 100 to 150 miles of the station. The range is reduced to about 75 miles at night.

    A diagram for obtaining half-convergency to apply to observed bearings is contained in *Admiralty List of Radio Signals Volume 2.*

3   Geographical positions of radiobeacons are normally referred to the geodetic datum of the largest scale chart on which the station is shown. There are exceptions where the position relates to the latest accepted geodetic datum, which may differ from that of the chart. It is advisable to use only those stations which are charted.

4   **Radio direction-finding stations.** These are radio stations established on shore and equipped with apparatus enabling them to ascertain the direction of signals transmitted from ships or other stations. Such stations are indicated on Admiralty charts by the abbreviation RG. For details see *Admiralty List of Radio Signals Volume 2.*

5   **VHF direction-finding stations.** A number of coastguard stations in the UK and abroad operate direction-finding antennæ which can determine the direction of vessels which are within range and which are transmitting on VHF.

6   On request from a vessel in distress, the coastguard station will transmit the bearing of the vessel from the station's direction-finding antenna.

    Mariners should note that this service is available for use in emergencies only.

Loran-C
11.20

1   Loran-C is an electronic position-fixing system with chains of transmitters providing coverage in the North Atlantic Ocean, Caribbean Sea, NW Europe, Red Sea, Persian Gulf and around the Arabian peninsula and in the Northern Pacific Ocean.

2   Each system consists of a series of chains, each of which is made up of a master transmitter and two or more slaves. The pulsed transmissions can be received either by groundwave at ranges of up to 1200 miles, and at longer ranges by skywave.

3   The accuracy of a fix obtained using this system will depend on three factors:

    The distance of the observer from the transmitter;

    The bearing of the observer from the baseline joining the pair of stations which he is using;

    The angle of intersection of the hyperbolic position lines.

    Furthermore, a small inherent equipment error, or a minor error in operating the receiver, has the potential to cause a positional error, the extent of which will depend on the observer's position.

4   Since the velocity of propagation of Loran-C signals depends on the terrain over which they pass, they are subject to resulting fixed errors. As the system is not intended for precise coastal navigation these are not of great importance. However, on US Charts which still have Loran-C lattices, the fixed errors are incorporated in the hyperbolae and a note to this effect is shown.

5   Full system details and area coverage diagrams are given in *Admiralty List of Radio Signals Volume 2.*

eLoran
11.21

1   eLoran was developed in the USA as a result of disquiet over the vulnerability of GNSS. Based on Loran-C infrastructure, it uses an additional data channel to provide real-time differential corrections via reference stations which detect variations in the eLoran signal, in a similar manner to differential GNSS reference stations, allowing receivers to correct for these variations as well as providing information regarding signal integrity. It is capable of providing positional accuracy to within 10 m.

2   **System availability.** eLoran uses high powered transmitters and low-frequency signals (the opposite of GNSS) and is thus most unlikely to be affected by the same causes of disruption or interference to a GNSS signal. Receivers will be operable in all areas where an eLoran service is provided.

Eurofix
11.22

1   **General information.** Researched and developed in the Netherlands and sponsored by the Northwest European Loran-C System (NELS) grouping of Denmark, France, Germany, the Netherlands, Norway and the United Kingdom, Eurofix is an integrated radio-navigation and communications system which combines Loran-C and Differential GPS (DGPS) by

sending differential satellite corrections to users as time modulated signal information. Loran-C or Chakya (the Russian Loran-C equivalent) stations are upgraded to broadcast low-speed data over ranges of up to 1000 km.

2 **Technical description.** Data is separated into 8 channels which are assigned to DGPS, GLONASS, DLoran-C/DChakya, navigation integrity messages and a short message service. Three channels are reserved for future applications.

The normal operational mode of Loran-C is preserved which gives the Eurofix user, next to accurate DGPS positions, improved navigational reliability. If either GPS or Loran-C fail, the other system continues to provide positional information, but at a reduced accuracy of between 100-300 m. As Loran-C and GPS are highly dissimilar in operational control and signal propagation characteristics, the chance of both systems failing simultaneously are very small.

3 **System status.** Test transmissions from the Loran-C station at Sylt in Germany have been successful, and coverage throughout the NELS area will soon (2009) be made available with Eurofix transmissions from three further stations at Lessay in France and Vælandet and Bø in Norway, and approval has been given to expand system availability with transmissions from all Loran-C stations. Subject to full implementation, there is the potential for further expansion in Europe by making use of the existing Loran-C coverage in the Mediterranean Sea and the Russian Chakya infrastructure.

4 **System capability.** Eurofix can act as a DGPS receiver when using a Loran-C standard GPS correction output message fed into a suitable GPS receiver. It also allows position calculation using both DGPS and Loran-C, and comparison of the two systems. If either system fails, the other can take over, thus improving availability and continuity. The system will also allow full DGPS/Loran-C integration which, in a given situation, will make Loran-C act as a satellite source. A user would, in these circumstances, be able to calculate a 3-dimensional position with only three satellites available.

5 **Coverage and accuracy.** The coverage of Eurofix is estimated to be at least 1000 km from each Eurofix-equipped Loran-C transmitter. When fully implemented, an absolute accuracy of better than ±5 m and availability of 99·9996% per month is achievable.

Satellite navigation systems

General information

Global Navigation Satellite Systems (GNSS)
11.23

1 Global Navigation Satellite Systems (GNSS) is the standard generic term for Satellite Navigation Systems that provide autonomous geo-spatial positioning with global coverage. A GNSS allows small electronic receivers to determine their location (longitude, latitude and altitude) to within a few metres using microwave ranging signals transmitted from satellites.

Current Global Navigation Satellite Systems
11.24

1 The United States NAVSTAR Global Positioning System (GPS) (11.36) and the Russian GLOBal'naya NAvigatsionnaya Sputnikovaya Sistema (GLONASS) (11.44) are the only operational GNSS.

Proposed Global Navigation Satellite Systems
11.25

1 China intend to expand their regional navigation system, called BeiDou or Big Dipper, into the global COMPASS Navigation System (11.47) by 2020. The European Union's GALILEO Positioning System (11.45) is scheduled to be operational in 2013.

Other regional navigation systems
11.26

1 The Indian Regional Navigation Satellite System (IRNSS) (11.48) is an autonomous regional satellite navigation system being developed by Indian Space Research Organisation under the total control of the Indian government. The system is expected to be completed and operational by 2012.

GNSS classification
11.27

1 GNSS that provide enhanced accuracy and integrity monitoring usable for civil navigation are classified as follows:

GNSS-1 is the name given to a first generation system and includes existing satellite navigation systems (GPS and GLONASS) which, when used with Satellite (SBAS) or Ground Based Augmentation Systems (GBAS) have improved accuracy and are known as Differential GPS (11.41).

2 In the United States, the satellite based component is the Wide Area Augmentation System (WAAS). in Europe it is the European Geostationary Navigation Overlay Service (EGNOS) and in Japan it is the Multi-Functional Satellite Augmentation System (MSAS). All of these systems were originally developed for the aviation industry and have been adapted for use in the maritime environment. Development is ongoing and some systems are better suited to maritime use than others. Ground based augmentation is provided by systems like the Nationwide Differential GPS (NDGPS) (11.59). **GNSS-2** are the second generation of systems such as GALILEO, which will provide accurate satellite navigation with system integrity monitoring for civilian use.

Datum shifts in satellite navigation systems
11.28

1 Most GPS receivers now have the facility to permit the transformation of positions from WGS84 Datum to a variety of local horizontal datums. The generalised parameters used in the software may differ from those used by the UKHO, resulting in the possibility that positions may not agree with the chart, even if the horizontal datum is stated to be the same.

2 It is therefore recommended that the GPS receiver is kept referenced to WGS84 Datum and the GLONASS receiver to PZ90 Datum and the position shift values provided are applied before plotting on the chart.

3 Receivers capable of using signals from both GPS and GLONASS are available and these combined

sources of positional information should lead to greater confidence of accuracy and are capable of displaying the position in one of several selected horizontal datums.

See also 1.33 for further detail on positions from satellite navigation systems.

Error sources

General information
11.29

1   Positions obtained using satellite navigation systems can be affected by several potential sources of error. These errors can vary in magnitude and are not fixed as they depend on the prevailing conditions.

Example error budgets for GPS and DGPS are shown in the following table (figures are approximate):

	Typical error (m)	
	GPS	*DGPS*
Ionosphere	±5·0	±0·4
Troposphere	±0·5	±0·2
Orbit Errors	±2·5	0
Satellite clock	±1·5	0
Multipath	±0·6	±0·6
Receiver	±0·3	±0·3
TOTAL ERROR	**±10·0-15·0**	**±0·5-3·0**

Ionospheric errors
11.30

1   The most significant errors experienced by GNSS are due to the effect of solar activity on the ionosphere. As the microwave signals transmitted by satellites pass through the charged particles (electrons) of the ionosphere, the propagation speed and direction of the signal are changed in proportion to the varying electron density along the line of sight between the satellite and the receiver.

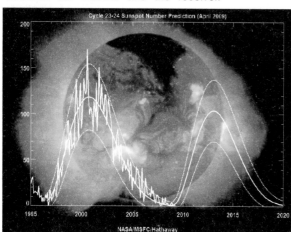

Sunspot number prediction (11.30.1)

2   The magnitude of the effect of the ionosphere varies in both time and spatial extent. The effect is much greater during the day than during the night. The magnitude also has a cyclical period of approximately 11 years (see diagram 11.30.1). For the current cycle, sunspot activity and its effects on the

ionosphere reached a minimum in 2008, will rise to a peak in 2013, and fall to the next minimum in 2018.

3   The effects of these disturbances will be most prominent in the equatorial (essentially following the geomagnetic equator) (see diagram 11.30.2) and polar regions. However during moderate or severe conditions, GNSS users in mid-latitudes can also be affected. The effects of the ionosphere, if not mitigated, can introduce measurement errors of greater than 10 m (even for DGPS users) and in severe conditions, the receiver can lose lock on the signal. Users of dual and multiple frequency GNSS receivers will be less affected.

4   Adverse conditions can persist for several hours, presenting a significant issue for navigation. The Space Weather Prediction Center (SWPC) in the United States of America provides alerts and warnings on their website at www.swpc.noaa.gov/index.html to show GNSS users where problems may occur and the potential effects on their operations.

5   In some receivers, the effect of the ionosphere is reduced by the use of a mathematical model. With the approximate knowledge of the density of the charged particles in the ionosphere (which is broadcast by the satellites), the effect of the ionosphere can be reduced by about 50%. However the residual error may still be significant. The effect of the ionosphere can be virtually eliminated by using a dual frequency receiver.

Tropospheric errors
11.31

1   The lower level of the earth's atmosphere, which contains water vapour, is called the troposphere. It has the effect of slowing the microwave signals emitted by satellites. However, weather systems in the troposphere create complex and volatile changes in pressure, temperature, density and humidity and it is impossible to accurately predict the precise effect on the signals. The effects of the troposphere cannot be overcome by the use of dual frequency receivers.

Satellite orbit error
11.32

1   The orbits of satellites are monitored continuously from ground stations around the earth, and their predicted orbital information is transmitted to the satellites. They in turn transmit the information to receivers. The accuracy of the orbital prediction is in the order of a few metres. These errors may result in inaccuracies within the calculated position. These errors can be removed by using differential positioning techniques.

Satellite clock error
11.33

1   Satellites are equipped with atomic clocks. Although these clocks are highly accurate, they are not perfect. The errors and drift of satellite clocks are calculated by ground stations and are included in the messages transmitted by the satellites. Satellite clock errors cannot, however, be precisely determined or predicted.

Multipath error
11.34

1   Multipath errors are caused by signals reflected from surfaces near the receiver antenna. The signal, instead of following a direct path to the antenna, bounces off adjacent obstructions, increasing the time taken for the signal to reach the receiver, and

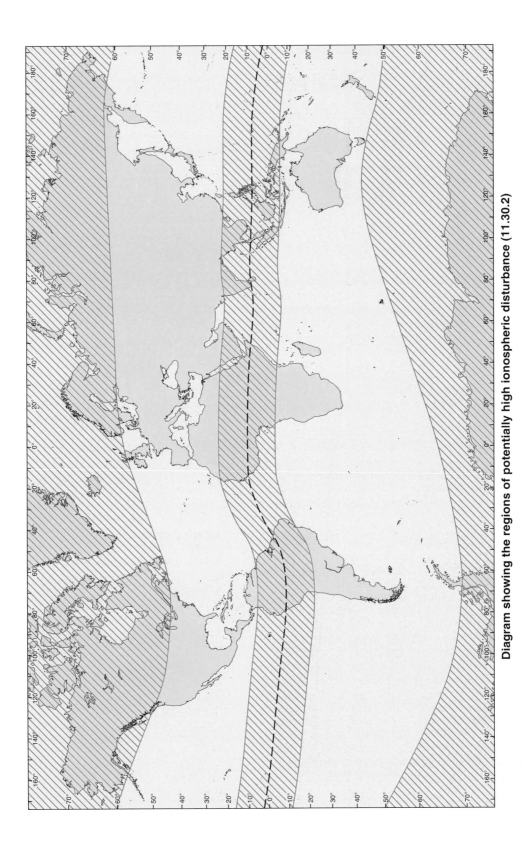

Diagram showing the regions of potentially high ionospheric disturbance (11.30.2)

interfering with the direct path signal. Typical examples of such obstructions are adjacent buildings, ships structure, cranes and derricks etc, sited above or close to the antenna. Multipath errors can be significantly reduced by careful siting of the receiver antenna, and to some extent by signal processing techniques.

Receiver errors
11.35

1   Receivers themselves may introduce some errors in measuring signals from satellites. However, in high quality receivers, these errors are minimal.

NAVSTAR Global Positioning System (GPS)

General information
11.36

1   The United States NAVSTAR Global Positioning System (GPS) is a GNSS developed originally for military purposes by the United States. It is now extensively used in the non-military environment, and particularly by mariners for navigational purposes. It comprises a constellation of between 24 and 32 satellites that transmit precise signals which allow GPS receivers to determine their current location, the time and their velocity. Its official name is NAVSTAR GPS.

Obtaining a position
11.37

1   A GPS position fix is obtained by measuring the ranges from a series of selected satellites to a receiver. Ranges are determined by measuring the propagation time of the satellite data transmissions. However, it is not possible to precisely synchronise the satellite and receiver clocks, the ranges measured are not true ranges, but are termed "pseudoranges" since they contain a receiver clock offset error. In order to achieve a two-dimensional (2D) fix on the Earth's surface at least three "pseudoranges" must be obtained; the receiver microprocessor can then resolve the three range equations to remove the effects of receiver clock offset error. Similarly four "pseudoranges" would be required to obtain a 3D fix.

2   Each satellite transmits data on two frequencies in the L-band; L1 = 1575·42 MHz and L2 = 1227·60 MHz. Both frequencies are integer multiples of the basic 10·23 MHz clock frequency. Dual-channel receivers are able to use both frequencies to correct for the effects of ionospheric refraction. Data transmitted on the L1 and L2 frequencies is encoded by a Pseudo Random Noise (PRN) modulation. A new L5 frequency (1176·45 MHz) will benefit civilian users, providing better quality range measurements and improving the tracking performance of the receiver.

Accuracy
11.38

1   GPS provides two levels of positioning capability; the Precise Positioning Service (PPS) and the Standard Positioning Service (SPS). The PPS is derived from the Precise (P) code whilst the SPS is derived from the Coarse Acquisition (C/A) code. The P code which is primarily for military use is transmitted on the L1 and L2 frequencies. The C/A code is transmitted on the L1 frequency only at present but in the future will also be transmitted on the L2 frequency to provide the second civil signal. In order to protect the military use of the L1 and L2 signals, the Y code has been developed to be spectrally separate from the C/A code. The Y code is an improvement on the P code, broadcasting on a regional basis.

2   The accuracy quoted in SPS mode is conservatively estimated at 95% (20 m) for a user equipped with a typical single-frequency receiver. Differential GPS (11.41) has been developed to improve the accuracy of a determined position.

Gaps in coverage
11.39

1   All radio navigation systems including GNSS are susceptible to interference and environmental effects which can adversely affect availability or render the system unusable.

2   Such effects have created gaps in coverage which have been reported as being particularly noticeable in the following areas:

Croatia - Entrance to Rijeka.
France (Atlantic Coast) - Approaches to Saint Malo.
France (Mediterranean Coast) - Golfe du Lion (Gulf of Lions).
Italy - Golfo di Genova (Gulf of Genoa) and Golfo di Napoli (Bay of Naples).
United Kingdom - NW Entrance to the Menai Strait.
United States (Atlantic Coast) - Chesapeake Bay.

Supporting information
11.40

1   The US Department of Commerce transmits recorded time information through Fort Collins (WWV) and Kekaha (Kauai) (WWVH) on 2·5, 5, 10, 15 and 20 MHz frequencies. During the 40 second interval between time ticks, atmospheric and navigation information is announced by voice. GPS status and outage information is transmitted at minutes 14 and 15 on WWV and minutes 43 and 44 on WWVH. For further information see www.navcen.uscg.gov.

Differential GPS (DGPS)

Introduction
11.41

1   Differential GPS (DGPS) services have been developed in response to the inherent and previously imposed limitations of GPS. Standard GPS does not provide the level of accuracy required for some operations such as navigation in harbours and their approaches.

Principle
11.42

1   The fundamental principle of DGPS is that corrections are applied to GPS-derived positions in order to remove the majority of errors and improve accuracy and integrity. The corrections are calculated by placing a receiver on a known fixed point called a Reference Station. Instead of using the GPS signals to calculate its position, it uses the known position of the Reference Station to calculate the errors. These errors are then broadcast to users to correct their measurements and improve the accuracy of their position.

Broadcast of corrections
11.43

1   A correction message known as RTCM SC104 has become the industry standard for encoding DGPS corrections. There are two methods of transmitting the corrections to the user:

Satellite based Augmentation Systems (SBAS) (11.50). Geostationary satellites are used to provide corrections on a global basis.

Ground based Augmentation Systems (GBAS) (11.58). Medium frequency radio beacons operating in the 283·5 - 325 kHz band are used to transmit correction data. These broadcasts are limited in range and subject to attenuation as a result of weather.

2   Several commercial companies provide a DGPS service, but encrypt the RTCM format signals so that either a special receiver or decoding device is necessary before the position can be obtained.

Full details of radio-beacons transmitting DGPS corrections are given in *Admiralty List of Radio Signals Volume 2*.

Global Navigation Satellite System (GLONASS)

General information
11.44

1   The Russian GLObal'naya NAvigatsionnaya Sputnikovaya Sistema (GLONASS) is similar to GPS in that it is a space-based navigation system designed to provide global, 24 hour, all weather access to precise position, velocity and time information to a properly equipped user. The fully operational system consists of 24 satellites in 3 orbital planes.

2   When operating at full effectiveness, the system's SPS provides a horizontal positional accuracy of 57-70 m with a 99·7% probability.

For further information on GLONASS see www.glonass-ianc.rsa.ru, which gives details of the current status of the system.

GALILEO

General information
11.45

1   The European global navigation system GALILEO is being built (2009) by the European Union (EU) and the European Space Agency (ESA). The system was named after the Italian astronomer Galileo Galilei and is officially referred to as just GALILEO. It is sometimes described as GALILEO Positioning System, however, since this abbreviates to GPS, the shorter astronomer's name is preferred to avoid confusion with the United States GPS. The project is an alternative, and complementary to, GPS and GLONASS. GALILEO is intended to provide more precise measurements than those available through GPS or GLONASS.

2   The constellation will consist of up to 30 satellites in Medium Earth Orbit (MEO), enabling coverage to be provided worldwide. In addition to its navigation payload, each satellite will carry a search and rescue transponder.

System description
11.46

1   The system will provide the following services:
Open Service (**OS**) will be free for anyone to access. Signals will be broadcast in two bands, 1164-1214 MHz and 1563-1591 MHz providing an accuracy of <4 m horizontally and <8 m vertically if both bands are used. Receivers using only a single band will still achieve <15 m horizontally and <35 m vertically, comparable to GPS.

2   **Commercial Service** (**CS**) will be encrypted and available for a fee. It will provide an accuracy of <1 m. The CS can also be complemented by ground stations, improving the accuracy to <0·1 m. This signal will be broadcast using the two OS signals as well as a third at 1260-1300 MHz.

3   **Public Regulated Service** (**PRS**) and **Safety of Life Service** (**SoL**) will be encrypted and provide an accuracy comparable to the OS. It will be robust against jamming. These services are designed to be used by police, military and air traffic control.

For further information see:
http://www.esa.int/esaNA/galileo.html
http://ec.europa.eu/dgs/energy_transport/galileo/index_en.htm

COMPASS

General information
11.47

1   The Chinese BeiDou2 Navigation System is named after the Big Dipper constellation. BeiDou means Northern Dou which are the 7 brightest stars of the constellation Ursa Major (Great Bear).

2   The current BeiDou1 system (made up of 4 satellites) is experimental and has limited coverage and application. However, China plans to develop a global GNSS similar to GPS and GLONASS. Known as COMPASS (BeiDou2) Navigation Satellite System (CNSS), the system will be capable of providing continuous, real-time passive 3D geo-spatial positioning and speed measurement. The complete system is expected to comprise 27 Medium Earth Orbit (MEO) satellites and 4 geostationary satellites. COMPASS will cover all of China by 2011, and could expand to a global network by 2020.

3   The system will provide the following services:
The free service, available to civilian users, will provide positioning accuracy to within 10 m, speed accuracy to within 0·2 m/s and timing accuracy to within 50 nanoseconds.

A licensed service with higher accuracy for authorized and military users.

Text messages in remote maritime areas largely beyond the reach of other satellites.

Authorised services for military users.

4   For further information see www.cast.cn/

Indian Regional Navigational Satellite System (IRNSS)

General information
11.48

1   The Indian Regional Navigational Satellite System (IRNSS) is an autonomous regional satellite navigation

system being developed by the Indian Space Research Organisation (ISRO).

The proposed system will consist of a constellation of 7 satellites and a support ground segment. It will provide coverage throughout the sub-continental land area. The extent of maritime coverage has yet to be fully determined.

2 Three of the satellites in the constellation will be placed in geostationary orbit; the remaining four will be in quasi-zenith orbits.

The system will provide position accuracies of <20 m. For further information see website: http:/www.isro.org/

Augmentation systems

General information

Introduction
11.49

1 Augmentation systems have been developed to provide corrections to GNSS which provide improved navigational accuracy to the mariner as well as high quality data regarding the reliability and accuracy of the position obtained. When augmentation Systems are used, the GPS system is known as Differential GPS (DGPS). There are two main types of augmentation:

Satellite based Augmentation Systems (SBAS) (11.50);

Ground based Augmentation Systems (GBAS) (11.58).

2 The advantages of SBAS are that they provide more extensive coverage, have no range limitations and are less susceptible to the vagaries of weather and signal interference.

Satellite based (SBAS)

Introduction
11.50

1 Geostationary satellites are used to broadcast integrity messages and differential corrections. SBAS provide corrections over specific areas. Although not originally designed as an aid to maritime navigation, mariners on a suitably equipped vessel will be able to determine her position to a better accuracy than by using GNSS alone. Use of an SBAS improves the positional accuracy to such an extent as to make it suitable for safety critical applications such as navigating through a narrow channel.

2 The lack of global coverage of most SBAS makes it essential to ensure that the system being used is appropriate for the position of the observer.

SBAS include the following:

The United States Wide Area Augmentation System (WAAS) (11.51).

The European Geostationary Navigation Overlay Service (EGNOS) (11.52);

The Indian GPS Aided Geo-Augmented Navigation (GAGAN) (11.53);

3 The Japanese Multi-functional Satellite Augmentation System (MSAS) (11.54);

The Japanese Quasi-Zenith Satellite System (QZSS) (11.55);

Canada-wide DGPS (CDGPS) (11.56).

4 Some SBAS have global coverage and are optimised for maritime use. Most of these are commercially operated. See 11.57.

Wide Area Augmentation System
11.51

1 The United States Wide Area Augmentation System (WAAS) is operated by the Federal Aviation Administration (FAA). Although designed primarily for aviation users, WAAS is widely available for other Positioning, Navigation and Timing (PNT) users.

WAAS consists of 25 ground reference stations positioned across the USA which monitor GPS satellite data. Two master stations, one on each coast, collect data from the reference stations and create a GPS correction, consisting of satellite orbit errors, clock drift and signal delays caused by the troposphere and the ionosphere.

2 The corrected differential message is then broadcast through one of two geostationary satellites with a fixed position over the equator. This information is compatible with the basic GPS signal structure, which means that any WAAS enhanced receiver can read it.

WAAS provides positional accuracy to <8 m at 95% probability.

For further information see website: http://www.faa.gov.

European Geostationary Navigation Overlay Service
11.52

1 European Geostationary Navigation Overlay System (EGNOS) is Europe's first venture into satellite navigation. It is a joint project of the European Space Agency (ESA), the European Union (EU) and Eurocontrol (the European Organization for the Safety of Air Navigation).

It provides a regional augmentation service for the United States GPS and the Russian GLONASS systems. EGNOS is a precursor to GALILEO (11.45).

2 Consisting of three geostationary satellites and a network of 40 positioning stations and 4 control centres, EGNOS transmits a signal containing information on the reliability and accuracy of the positioning signals sent out by GPS and GLONASS. It allows users in Europe and beyond to determine their position to <5 m compared with about 20 m for GPS and 57 m for GLONASS. The elements that make up the EGNOS system include Ranging and Integrity Monitoring Stations (RIMS) which pick up GPS signals, Master Control Centres (MCCs) to process the data delivered by the RIMS and uplink stations which send the signal to the three geostationary satellites which then relay it back to users on the ground.

3 There are two operational EGNOS services with a third due to become operational in 2010:

Open Service. This service is free.

Safety-of-Life Service. Once EGNOS becomes certified as compliant with international satellite navigation standards, scheduled for 2010, the safety of life service will become operational.

4 EGNOS Data Access Service (EDAS). Launched in 2009 on a trial basis, EDAS provides access to raw EGNOS location data via a link to a dedicated computer server.

For further information see: http://www.esa.int/esaNA/egnos.html.

GPS Aided Geo Augmented Navigation
11.53

1   GPS Aided Geo Augmented Navigation (GAGAN) covers Indian airspace and is operated by the Airport Authority of India with the help of the Indian Space Research Organization (ISRO) (11.48).

    The final operational phase of GAGAN is likely to be completed by 2011 and will be compatible with other SBAS systems such as EGNOS, MSAS and WAAS.

2   GAGAN will offer high positional accuracies of <8 m which could be further enhanced with GBAS (11.58).

    For further information see website: http://www.isro.org/.

Multi-functional Satellite Augmentation System
11.54

1   Multi-functional Satellite Augmentation System (MSAS) provides GPS augmentation information through Multi-functional Transport Satellite (MTSAT).

    Designed for the use by the aviation industry, it is not yet recommended for marine navigation. Presently (2009), MSAS signals achieve their intended purpose and performance only if processed by an airborne receiver. The degree of accuracy improvement has not yet been determined. Mariners should note that use of MSAS may not improve positional accuracy.

2   An SBAS enabled receiver that is compatible with WAAS may or may not process the augmentation information transmitted by MSAS.

    For further information see: http://www.kasc.go.jp/_english/msas_01.htm.

Quasi-Zenith Satellite System
11.55

1   The Japanese Quasi-Zenith Satellite System (QZSS) is a proposed 3-satellite regional time transfer system and enhancement for GPS in Japanese waters, scheduled to be operational by 2013. QZSS can only provide limited accuracy on its own and is not currently required to work in a stand alone mode. The system will be capable of transmitting both position and correction signals and other information regarding GNSS availability.

2   QZSS will be capable of enhancing standalone GPS for any mariner who tracks one or more of the system satellites. This enhancement will be particularly beneficial to those mariners in Japanese waters, but users in many other Asia-Pacific regions may also benefit as a result of the enhanced geometric arrangement made possible by QZSS, which increases both the area and the times at which positioning is possible.

3   The system will also be capable of improving positional accuracy by transmitting signals that are equivalent to modernised GPS signals.

    QZSS is designed to improve reliability by means of failure monitoring and system health data notification, as well as providing other support data.

    For further information see website: http://www.jaxa.jp

Canada-wide DGPS Correction Service
11.56

1   The Canada-wide DGPS Correction Service (CDGPS) is a free wide-area DGPS service which broadcasts corrections throughout Canada via the MSAT-1 and MSAT-2 satellites. It provides metre-level accuracy with single-frequency receivers and sub-metre level accuracy with dual-frequency receivers.

    The system covers North America from 75°N to Mexico. Corrections can be accessed using CDGPS-enabled receivers or legacy MSAT CDGPS radios.

2   For further information, see www.cdgps.com/index.htm.

Commercial systems
11.57

1   Some high performance global SBAS are available commercially on subscription. Some of these systems utilise NASA Global Differential GPS data products. Such systems can provide global positional accuracy to within 10 cm and sub-nanosecond time transfer accuracy, independent of local infrastructure.

Ground-based (GBAS)

Introduction
11.58

1   The IALA maritime beacon system has been the standard ground-based augmentation system for maritime application for over a decade. It uses transmissions in the 300 kHz radio-navigation band in accordance with ITU-R recommendations. For further information, see *Admiralty List of Radio Signals Volume 2* and www.iala-aism.org.

2   GBAS include:
    Nationwide Differential GPS System (NDGPS) (11.59).
    eLoran (11.60).

Nationwide Differential Global Positioning System
11.59

1   The Nationwide Differential Global Positioning System (NDGPS) is a GBAS operated by the United States Coast Guard, the Federal Railroad Administration and the Federal Highway Administration that provides a positional accuracy of 1-3 m and integrity of GPS information to users on land and sea. Modernization efforts include the High Accuracy NDGPS (HA-NDGPS) system, currently under development, to enhance the performance and provide 10-15 cm accuracy throughout the coverage area.
For further information see website: http://www.uscg.mil/

eLoran
11.60

1   eLoran utilises the latest technology to provide substantial improvements to the accuracy of Loran-C, and accuracies of 8-20 m are now achievable. See 11.21 for more details. eLoran has a function enabling it to transmit auxiliary data, including GPS corrections which give the system GBAS functionality.

Automatic Identification System (AIS)

General information

System description
11.61

1   AIS is a shipboard broadcast system which acts like a transponder, operating in the maritime VHF band, which transmits own ship data (see 11.67) to other vessels, VTS and other control centres, and receives the same categories of information from other vessels. The system is capable of handling over 4500 reports per minute, and is capable of updating information as often as every 2 seconds.

2   A typical installation for a Class A vessel (one meeting the mandatory SOLAS carriage requirements (SOLAS Chapter V Rule 19) for vessels over 300 gt) will consist of a VHF transmitter, 3 VHF receivers, a GNSS receiver, an interface unit to shipborne sensors and displays, and a manual input device. The mandatory minimum carriage requirement for a display in a Class A vessel is the Minimum Keyboard Display (MKD).

3   It is important to bear in mind that not all vessels are equipped with AIS. Of those vessels which are equipped, displays can range from none at all on some Class B vessels (those not covered by the mandatory carriage requirements), through the mandatory minimum MKD, to a full ECDIS and radar overlay.

4   Additionally, mariners should be aware that manufacturers build ECDIS and radar equipment to differing specifications which may cause variance in the information which can be displayed.

Function
11.62

1   AIS has four principal functions:
    Collision avoidance (11.72).
    VTS (11.73).
    Aid to navigation (11.75).
    Search and rescue (11.76).

Mandation
11.63

1   AIS is now mandatory on all international voyages by tankers, vessels of 150 gt and more while carrying more than 12 passengers, and other vessels of 300 gt or more (SOLAS V/19.2.4).

Objectives of AIS
11.64

1   AIS is intended to enhance:
    Safety of life at sea.
    Safety and efficiency of navigation.
    Security of vessels and port facilities.
    Protection of the marine environment.

2   SOLAS regulation V/19 requires that AIS exchange data ship-to-ship and with shore based facilities in order to help identify vessels, assist in target tracking, simplify information exchange (e.g. reduce verbal mandatory ship reporting), and provide additional information to assist situation awareness.

3   In general, data received from AIS improves the quality of information available to the OOW, whether at a shore surveillance station or on board ship. AIS is a useful source of supplementary information to that derived from navigational systems (including radar) and therefore an important "tool" in enhancing situation awareness.

Operation
11.65

1   AIS should always be in operation when vessels are underway or at anchor. If the master believes that the continual operation of AIS might compromise the safety or security of the vessel, or where security incidents are imminent, the AIS may be switched off.

2   Unless it would further compromise safety or security, if the vessel is operating in a mandatory reporting system, the master should report this action and the reason for doing so to the competent authority. Action of this nature should always be recorded in the vessel's official logbook together with the reason for doing so. For example, this might be the case in sea areas where pirates or armed robbers are known to operate.

3   The master should, however, restart the AIS as soon as the source of danger has disappeared. If the AIS is shut down, static data and voyage related information remains stored. The system is restarted by switching on the power to the AIS unit. Ship's own data will be transmitted after a two minute initialization period. When alongside in harbour, AIS operation should be in accordance with port requirements.

Operational guidance
11.66

1   AIS contributes to the safety of navigation and improves the monitoring of passing traffic by coastal states. Mariners should take careful note of the following guidelines:
    Shipborne AIS must be capable of the following:
    Transmission of ship's own data continuously to other vessels and VTS stations.
    Reception of data from other vessels and VTS stations continuously.
    Display of this data.

2   When used with an appropriate graphical display, shipborne AIS enables provision of fast, automatic information by calculating Closest Point of Approach and Time to Closest Point of Approach from the positional information transmitted by target vessels. AIS detects ships within VHF/FM range around bends and behind islands, provided that land masses are not too high. A typical range at sea is 20 to 30 miles depending on antenna height can be expected; with the help of repeater stations, the coverage for both ship and VTS stations can be improved.

Information from a shipborne AIS is transmitted continuously and automatically without the intervention of a watchkeeping officer.

AIS data input
11.67

1   The AIS data transmitted by a ship is of three different types:
    Static information, which is entered into AIS on installation, and need only be changed if the ship changes its name or undergoes a major conversion from one ship type to another. The

OOW should check this data whenever there is a valid reason, and once per voyage or once per month, whichever is the more frequent. This data may be only be changed on the authority of the master.

2 **Dynamic** information, which, apart from "Navigational Status" information, is automatically updated from the ship sensors.

Voyage related information, which needs to be manually entered and updated during the voyage. This information includes ship's draught, any hazardous cargo, destination and ETA, route plan with appropriate way points, the correct navigational status and any safety related short messages.

Inherent limitations of AIS
11.68

1 The information given by AIS may not be a complete picture of the situation around the ship for a number of reasons.

Other vessels, and in particular leisure craft, fishing boats and warships, and some coastal stations including VTS might not be fitted with AIS. The mariner should also be aware that other vessels, fitted with AIS as a mandatory carriage requirement, may have the equipment switched off under certain circumstances according to the professional judgement of the master (11.65).

2 The accuracy of AIS information received depends upon the accuracy of the information input in the target vessel. Poorly configured or calibrated ship sensors (position, speed, or heading sensors) might lead to incorrect information being transmitted. Incorrect information about one ship displayed on the bridge of another could be dangerously confusing.

3 If a particular ship's data input sensor (e.g. the gyro compass) fails to provide data, the AIS automatically transmits the "not available" data value. However, the built in integrity check cannot validate the contents of the data processed by AIS. It should not be assumed that information received is of a comparable quality and accuracy as that which might be available in one's own vessel.

4 Mariners remain responsible for all information entered into the system and for the information input by the sensors, and must be aware that transmission of erroneous information can create risk to other vessels as well as their own.

Target information
11.69

1 AIS is designed to provide target information to existing radar or ECDIS displays, comprising identification together with static and dynamic information. Mariners should, however, use this information with caution, noting the following important points:

2 Not all ships are fitted with AIS, particularly small craft and fishing boats. AIS positions are derived from the target's navigation system and will not necessarily coincide precisely with the radar target. Faulty data input to AIS will lead to incorrect or misleading information being displayed in other vessels.

3 Collision avoidance must always be carried out in strict compliance with the Collision Regulations. There is no provision in the Collision Regulations

for the use of AIS information; decisions should always be taken based primarily on visual and/or radar information. See 11.72.

4 Mariners should remember that information derived from radar plots relies solely upon the data measured by the own-ship's radar and provides an accurate measurement of the target's relative course and speed, which is the most important factor in deciding upon action to avoid collision. The use of VHF to discuss action to take between approaching ships is fraught with danger. Identification of a target by AIS does not remove that danger.

5 Existing ships of less than 500 gt which are not required to fit a gyro compass are unlikely to transmit heading information.

11.70

1 **Caution.** The OOW should always be aware that AIS fitted on other ships as a mandatory carriage requirement might, under certain circumstances, be switched off on the master's professional judgement (11.65).

AIS in UK waters
11.71

1 The UK AIS network comprises around 50 base stations around the coast. The system operates within IMO guidelines and is capable of receiving all message types, in particular, message types 1, 2, 3 and 5. Automated procedures enable identification and tracking of suitably equipped vessels without further intervention of either the vessel's crew or of the Coastguard.

2 **Advice to AIS users at sea.** Mariners are advised to:

Initiate early action to correct improper installation. Ensure that the correct information on identity, position and movements (including voyage-specific) is transmitted.

Ensure that AIS is in operation, at least within 100 miles of the UK coast.

Ensure that routine updating of of data into AIS is part of the navigating officer's checklist.

3 **Data input.** The following data should be manually input at the start of the voyage:

Ship's draught.

Hazardous cargo.

Destination and ETA.

Route plan (waypoints).

The correct navigation status.

Short safety-related messages.

4 It is recommended that the UN/LOCODE is used for destination names to avoid ay confusion that may be caused by mis-spelling.

Further information. See MGN 324(M+F) – *Operational Guidance on the Use of VHF Radio and Automatic Identification Systems (AIS) at Sea,* published by the UK Maritime and Coastguard Agency (MCA).

Collision avoidance

Use of AIS in collision avoidance
11.72

1 AIS information is a useful tool when used to assist in collision avoidance decision making. However, mariners should note the following cautionary points:

AIS is an additional source for navigational information. It does not replace, but only supports, navigational systems such as radar target tracking and VTS.

2   The use of AIS does not negate the responsibility of the mariner to comply, at all times, with the Collision Regulations. The mariner should not rely on AIS as the sole information system, but make use of all available relevant safety information.

The use of AIS is not intended to have any special impact on the composition of the navigational watch, which should continue to be determined in accordance with the Standards of Training, Certification, and Watchkeeping Convention.

3   Once a vessel has been detected, AIS can assist in tracking it as a target. By monitoring the information broadcast by that target, its actions can also be monitored. Changes in heading and course are, for example, immediately apparent, and many of the problems common to tracking targets by radar, namely clutter, target swap as ships pass close by, and target loss following a fast manoeuvre, do not affect AIS. AIS can also assist in the identification of targets, by name or call sign and by ship type and navigational status.

VTS

Use of AIS in Ship Reporting
11.73

1   AIS reduces the work of the watchkeeper by automatically providing coastal stations with the information required under mandatory or voluntary reporting schemes as well as for VTS purposes. Therefore it is essential that the Static and Voyage information is at all times correctly programmed and that the Dynamic inputs are functioning correctly.

2   Additionally, the mariner must consider the following:
The coastal station may not be equipped to monitor AIS.
The ship may be within a reporting system but out of VHF range of the coastal station.
Reporting requirements may require more information than AIS transmits.

Mandatory ship reporting systems
11.74

1   AIS can play a major role in ship reporting systems. The information required by coastal authorities in such systems is typically included in the static voyage related and dynamic data automatically provided by the AIS system.

Aid to navigation

AIS as an aid to navigation
11.75

1   AIS, when fitted to select fixed and floating aids to navigation can provide information to the mariner such as:
Position.
Status.
Tidal and current data.
Weather and visibility conditions.

2   A future development of AIS is the ability to provide safety related messages and also "pseudo" navigation marks. Pseudo navigation marks will enable coastal authorities to provide an AIS symbol on the display in any position. Mariners should bear in mind that this ability could lead to the appearance of "spurious" AIS targets and therefore take particular care when an AIS target is not accompanied by a radar target. It should be noted though that AIS will sometimes be able to detect targets which are in a radar shadow area.

Search and rescue

AIS in SAR operations
11.76

1   AIS may be used in search and rescue operations, especially in combined helicopter and surface searches. AIS enables the direct presentation of the position of the vessel in distress on other displays such as radar or ECS/ECDIS, which facilitates the task of SAR craft. For ships in distress not equipped with AIS, the On Scene Commander could create a pseudo AIS target.

Long-range Identification and tracking (LRIT)

General information
11.77

1   LRIT ws established by IMO Resolution MSC.202(81) in May 2006, which amends SOLAS Chapter V Regulation 19-1, and binds all governments contracted to IMO.

The SOLAS regulation establishes a multi-lateral agreement to share LRIT information amongst contracting governments for security and SAR purposes, in order to meet the maritime security needs and other concerns of such governments.

2   It maintains the right of flag States to protect information about vessels entitled to fly their flag where appropriate, while allowing coastal states access to information regarding vessels navigating off their coasts.

Applicability
11.78

1   The regulations came into force on 1st January 2009, and apply to all vessels on international voyages as follows:
All passenger vessels including high-speed craft.
All cargo vessels over 300gt, including high-speed craft.
Mobile offshore drilling units.

LRIT data
11.79

1   In order to comply with the regulations, vessels must be fitted with equipment capable of automatically transmitting their identity, location and date and time of the position. Vessels are required to report their positions at least every 6 hours.

LRIT Data Centres
11.80

1   Contracting governments are required to implement a LRIT Data Centre or join a Regional/Cooperative LRIT Data Centre such as that established by the European Union.

These Data Centres receive and process positional information from vessels at sea, and thus maintain an up-to-date database of all their flagged vessels.

Sharing of information
11.81

1   Data Centres are capable of communicating amongst themselves, and exchanging position reports upon request. In particular, a vessel having notified a port of impending arrival can be tracked by that particular port using this system.

2   The regulations establish a contracting government's entitlement to track any vessel within 1000 miles of its coastline, regardless of which flag it is flying.

Exemption
11.82

1   The regulations exempt vessels operating exclusively in GMDSS Area A1 (13.102) from the requirement to transmit LRIT information, since such vessels are already fitted with AIS.

Lights

Sectors
11.83

1   Arcs drawn on charts round a light are not intended to give information as to the distance at which the light can be seen, but to indicate the arcs of visibility, or, in the case of lights which do not show the same characteristics or colour in all directions, the bearings between which the differences occur.

2   The stated limits of sectors may not always be the same as those appearing to the eye, so that they should invariably be checked by compass bearing.

When a light is cut off by sloping land the bearing on which the light will disappear will vary with distance and the observer's height of eye.

3   The limits of an arc of visibility are rarely clear cut, especially at a short distance, and instead of disappearing suddenly the light usually fades after the limit of the sector has been crossed.

At the boundary of sectors of different colour there is usually a small arc in which the light may be either obscured, indeterminate in colour, or white.

4   In cold weather, and more particularly with rapid changes of weather, the lantern glass and screens are often covered with moisture, frost or snow, the sector of uncertainty is then considerably increased in width and coloured sectors may appear more or less white. The effect is greatest in green sectors and weak lights. Under these conditions white sectors tend to extend into coloured and obscured sectors, and fixed or occulting lights into flashing ones.

5   White lights have a reddish hue under some atmospheric conditions.

Ranges
11.84

1   There are two criteria for determining the maximum range at which a light can be seen. Firstly, the light must be above the horizon; secondly, the light must be powerful enough to be seen at this range.

Geographical range is the maximum distance at which a light can reach an observer as determined by the height of eye of the observer, the height of the structure and the curvature of the earth.

2   **Luminous range** is the maximum distance at which a light can be seen, determined only by the intensity of the light and the visibility at the time. It takes no account of elevation, observer's height of eye, or curvature of the earth.

Nominal range is normally the luminous range for a meteorological visibility of 10 miles.

Details of these ranges, and diagrams for use with them, are given in each volume of *Admiralty List of Lights*.

3   On charts, the range now shown for a light is the luminous range, or the nominal range in countries where this range has been adopted. Authorities using nominal ranges are listed in the front of the appropriate volume of *Admiralty List of Lights*. New charts and New Editions of charts published on or after 31st March 1972 show one or other of these ranges.

4   Until 1972, the geographical range of a light (for an observer's height of eye of 5 m or 15 ft) was inserted on charts unless the luminous range was less than the geographical range, when the luminous range was inserted.

Until the new policy can be applied to all charts, which will take many years, the mariner must consult *Admiralty List of Lights* to determine which range is shown against a light on the chart.

The distance of an observer from a light cannot be estimated from its apparent brightness.

5   The distance at which lights are sighted varies greatly with atmospheric conditions and this distance may be increased by abnormal refraction (7.42). The loom of a powerful light is often seen far beyond the appropriate geographical range. The sighting distance will be reduced by fog, haze, dust, smoke or precipitation: a light of low intensity is easily obscured by any of these conditions and the sighting range of even a light of very high intensity is considerably reduced in such conditions. For this reason the intensity or nominal range of a light should always be considered when estimating the range at which it may be sighted, bearing in mind that varying atmospheric conditions may exist between the observer and the light.

6   It should be remembered that lights placed at a great elevation are more often obscured by cloud, etc, than those nearer sea level.

On first raising a light from the bridge, by at once lowering the eye and noting whether the light is made to dip, it may be determined whether the vessel is near the appropriate geographical range or unexpectedly nearer the light.

Aero lights
11.85

1   The intensity of aero lights is often greater than that of most marine navigational lights, and they are often

placed at high elevations. They may be the first lights, or looms of lights, sighted when approaching land. Those likely to be visible from seaward are charted and included in *Admiralty List of Lights*.

2 Aero lights are not maintained in the same manner as marine navigational lights and may be extinguished or altered without warning to the mariner.

Obstruction lights
11.86

1 Radio towers, chimneys, tall buildings, mobile drilling rigs, offshore platforms and other objects which may be dangerous to aircraft are marked by obstruction lights.

2 Obstruction lights are usually red. Those of low intensity are indicated on charts as "(Red Lt)", without a light-star, and may be mentioned in the Remarks column of *Admiralty List of Lights*. Those of known high intensity are charted as aero lights with a light-star; full details usually appear in *Admiralty List of Lights*.

Obstruction lights are not maintained in the same manner as marine navigational lights and may be extinguished or altered without warning to the mariner.

Fog signals

General information
11.87

1 Sound is conveyed in a very capricious way through the atmosphere and the following points should be borne in mind:

Fog signals are heard at greatly varying distances. Under certain atmospheric conditions, if a fog signal is a combination of high and low tones, one of the notes may be inaudible.

2 There are occasional areas around a station in which the fog signal is wholly inaudible.

Fog may exist at a short distance from a station and not be observable from it, so that the signal may not be sounded.

Some fog signal emitters cannot be started at a moment's notice after signs of fog have been observed.

3 Mariners are warned therefore that fog signals cannot be relied upon implicitly. Particular attention should be given to placing lookouts in positions in which ship-generated noise is least likely to interfere with the hearing of a fog signal. Experience shows that, though a fog signal may not be heard from the deck or bridge when the engines are operating, it may be heard when the engines are stopped, or from a quiet position.

Homing on a fog signal
11.88

1 It is dangerous where there is a radar beacon at a navigational mark, in addition to a fog signal, to approach on a bearing of it relying on hearing the fog signal in sufficient time to alter course to avoid danger.

2 It is IALA policy that sound fog signals are nowadays used in a hazard warning role or for the protection of aids to navigation and are not position fixing aids. It is therefore considered that there is no longer a general requirement for high power fog signals. Mariners are therefore advised that any fog signal detected should be treated as a short range hazard warning and that a close quarters situation exists.

Buoyage

General information

Use of moored marks
11.89

1 A vessel's position should be maintained with reference to fixed marks on the shore whenever practicable. Buoys should not be used for fixing but may be used for guidance when shore marks are difficult to distinguish visually; in these circumstances their positions should first be checked by some other means.

2 Buoy symbols on charts may be displaced in an appropriate direction allowing the true position of the danger to be shown.

Pillar buoys
11.90

1 On Admiralty charts, if the shape of a buoy is not known the symbol for a pillar buoy is usually used, as the shape of this buoy has no significance.

Avoidance
11.91

1 Care should be taken to pass light vessels, LANBYs and other navigational buoys at a prudent distance, particularly in a tideway. In fog the mariner should not rely solely on sound signals to warn him of his approach to aids to navigation (see 11.88).

2 The mariner is particularly cautioned to give LANBYs a wide berth. Not only are they extremely expensive to repair, but because of their immense size, which may not be immediately realised from their charted symbol, they may cause damage to any ship colliding with them.

3 Should an aid to navigation be struck accidentally, it is imperative for the safety of other mariners that the fact be reported to the nearest coast radio station. Though collision with a buoy may not cause damage to it apparent at the time, it may lead to subsequent failure of its sensitive and costly equipment.

4 It should also be noted that it is an offence under Section 666 of the *Merchant Shipping Act, 1894*, to make fast to a light vessel or navigational buoy.

Sound signals
11.92

1   The bell, gong, horn or whistle fitted to some buoys may be operated by machinery to sound a regular character, or by wave action when it will sound erratically. The number of strokes of the bell or gong, or the number of blasts of the horn or whistle, is shown on charts to distinguish a signal that is sounded regularly from one dependent on wave actions.

The IALA Maritime Buoyage System

Description
11.93

1   The IALA Maritime Buoyage System which is now widely used throughout the world is described in Annex C. Details of the actual buoyage system used in any particular area are given in *Admiralty Sailing Directions*.

2   Chart symbols and abbreviations used with the IALA Maritime Buoyage System are given on Chart 5011 and in *IALA Maritime Buoyage System*.

Other buoyage

Ocean Data Acquisition Systems (ODAS)
11.94

1   **General information.** The term Ocean Data Acquisition System (ODAS) describes a wide range of devices for collecting weather and oceanographical data. The systems vary from ocean-going vessels, such as Ocean Weather Ships, to plastic envelopes and drift bottles for measuring currents.

2   **Purpose.** Meteorological models routinely utilise observations from various sources around the world to make their forecasts. Buoy data are crucial to this process, because the buoys are deployed in ocean areas where no other source of data is available. For the same reason, buoy data is essential for producing improved marine forecasts.

3   Sea surface temperature is an important tool for finding many different species of fish. The buoys provide this information to weather centres which produce charts of sea surface temperature and distribute them to fishermen.

    Several nations have successfully used surface wind and ocean current information from the buoys to help locate missing or overdue vessels.

4   Researchers use the data from the buoys to assist in establishing patterns of climate change and thence to enable prediction of future changes. For example, buoys are deployed to learn how to predict the El Niño and La Niña phenomena, which cause seasonal climate variations in many areas of the world's oceans.

    Buoy systems carrying instruments are however the devices of most concern to the mariner, and these may be expected to become more numerous each year.

5   **Types.** ODAS buoys are either moored or drifting, and may have instruments either in the float or slung beneath them to any depth.

    They are coloured yellow, marked "ODAS" with an identification number, and carry a small plate showing whom to inform if the buoy is recovered.

6   **Moored buoys** may be as much as 12 m in diameter, 2–3 m in height and 18 tonnes in weight, and may be anchored in any part of the oceans, irrespective of depth.

    The larger moored buoys for use in deep water are can-shaped, the smaller ones for use closer inshore (usually 2–3 miles offshore) are toroidal. They all carry visible aerials.

7   A flashing yellow light, showing 5 flashes every 20 seconds is exhibited from moored buoys.

    As far as possible, positions of moored instrument systems are always widely promulgated, and if considered to be of a permanent enough nature, are charted.

8   The large buoys and floats should be given a berth of 1 mile, or 2½ miles by vessels towing underwater gear. In the event of collision, they may not only suffer costly damage, but may cause structural damage or foul the propellers or rudders of ships hitting them, or damage any fishing gear that fouls them.

9   **Drifting buoys** are about 0·75 m in diameter and about 2 m from top to bottom. They do not exhibit lights or carry visible aerials.

10 **ATLAS** (Autonomous Temperature Line Acquisition System) buoys have been deployed across the central and eastern Pacific Ocean both North and South of the equator, and also in the tropical Atlantic Ocean to collect and transmit information relating to ocean currents, temperatures, and related meteorological data. They are toroidal in shape, orange and white striped with a mast containing a radar reflector and quick flashing light, and a mooring cable beneath them carrying instrumentation and an anchor. These buoys should be given a clear berth of at least 6 miles. For current positions occupied by these buoys, see *Admiralty Notices to Mariners*.

11 **TRITON** (Triangle Trans-Ocean Buoy Network) buoys have been deployed in the western tropical Pacific Ocean and also in the eastern Indian Ocean to collect and transmit information relating to ocean currents, temperatures, and related meteorological data. They are large steel buoys, coloured yellow above and blue below, with a steel mast containing a radar reflector and flashing light, and a mooring cable carrying instrumentation and an anchor below. These buoys should be given a clear berth of at least 6 miles.

Reporting and recovery of ODAS buoys
11.95

1   Mariners encountering any uncharted yellow buoy should make an Obligatory Report (4.43) giving the position, together if possible with the buoy's identity code number.

2   ODAS stations may be met with in unexpected areas, often in deep water where navigational buoys would not be found. The mariner's initial reaction may be that the buoy is adrift and lost, but this is not necessarily so, and no attempt should be made at recovery unless the buoy is in imminent danger of being washed ashore. It should be noted that valuable instruments are often suspended beneath these systems or attached to the mooring lines; cases have occurred of the moorings being cut close beneath the

buoy by unauthorised salvors, with consequent loss of the most valuable part of the system.

3   The International Hydrographic Bureau issued an advisory note to fishermen and mariners in 2004, pointing out that drifting and moored data buoys provide valuable information to many communities, including fishermen and mariners. The advisory included the following guidance:

Keep a good lookout for moored data buoys; these should be readily detectable by radar and can be avoided.

4   Do not pick up drifting buoys. Buoy operators do not refurbish drifting buoys once deployed, and a buoy recovered to the deck of a vessel would continue to transmit false and misleading positional, meteorological and oceanographic data.

Do not moor to, damage or destroy any part of a data buoy.

5   Do not deploy fishing gear close to a data buoy, despite possible concentrations of fish in the vicinity. In the event that fishing gear becomes entangled with a data buoy, do not cut or damage any part of the buoy in order to retrieve the gear.

Deep-ocean Assessment and Reporting of Tsunami (DART) buoys
11.96

1   A network of 39 DART buoys are stationed around the Pacific Rim, in the NE Indian Ocean and in the Caribbean Sea. With their associated Bottom Pressure Recorders they provide information which analysts are able to use to provide more accurate tsunami forecasts. For a full description of the DART system, see 5.30.

DART buoys are coloured in red and white quarters, bearing the legend "NOAA TSUNAMI". They are generally 2·4 m in diameter, displace 4000 kg and have a latticed superstructure to carry lights, antennae and weather sensors.

Coral Reef Instrumented Monitoring Platforms (CRIMP) buoys
11.97

1   See 5.50.

Echo soundings

Sounders

General information
11.98

1   To obtain reliable depths from his echo sounder, the mariner must ensure that it is correctly adjusted. He should also be aware that echoes, other than those correctly showing the sea floor, may appear on the trace from time to time.

Transmission line
11.99

1   When the sounder is operating, its transmissions are picked up almost instantaneously by its receiving transducer, forming a line on the trace known as the transmission line. This effectively represents the depth of the transducer below the surface of the water. The position of this transmission line should be adjusted to match the depth of the transducer, the method being described in the maker's handbook. Echo sounders that have a purely digital output will have a transducer draught setting, which should be set to the known depth of the transducer.

Velocity of sound
11.100

1   The velocity of sound in sea water varies, depending primarily upon temperature, pressure (depth) and salinity. Even at the same location, temperature and salinity may vary significantly with both depth and time due to factors such as tidal and ocean currents. Velocity of sound in water can vary from about 1445 to 1535 m/s.

2   With the exception of survey standard equipment, echo sounders are usually designed to record depths using a velocity of sound in water of 1500 m/s, which is generally regarded as the standard velocity. Set for this velocity, depths recorded should be within 5% of true depths even if extreme values for the velocity of sound are encountered, and should be sufficiently accurate for safe navigation since the magnitude of any error will obviously decrease with depth. If necessary, depths can be corrected using *Echo-Sounding Correction Tables*.

Adjustments to sounder
11.101

1   **Draught setting.** The first adjustment to be made is for draught, applied using either the transmission line or the digital draught value. If the leading edge of the transmission line or the digital draught value is set to the depth of the transducer, the displayed depths will be referenced to the surface of the sea; if it is set to zero, depths will be referenced to the depth below the transducer. If the transducer is higher than the keel, say by 1 m, then setting the transmission line/digital draught value to –1 m will provide depths below the keel.

2   To avoid continual adjustments due to changes in draught, the transmission line/digital draught value is often set so that the scale reads depths below the keel.

In ships whose draughts do not vary greatly, however, it may be preferable to set the transmission line/digital draught value to the depth of the transducer for ready comparison between the measured depth and the charted depth corrected for tide.

When using these settings, consideration should be given to changes in the draught of the vessel caused by factors such as changes in salinity, squat, consumption of fuel, adjustment of ballast, change of trim, etc.

3   **Speed of sound.** After adjusting for draught, the speed of the sounder should be adjusted to correspond with a velocity of sound in water of 1500 m/s, or such speed as the makers recommend. On stylus driven sounders, this will be achieved by adjusting the motor speed on the stylus belt according

to the manufacturer's instructions. On digital echo sounders, a simple value may be entered in the sounder's settings.

Stylus sounders will often require a short warm-up period before calibrations are undertaken.

4   Provided that these two adjustments are correctly made, the depths displayed should be accurate for navigational purposes.

Some echo sounders are manufactured so that neither of the above adjustments are possible, and the depth displayed will always be the depth below the transducer.

Checking recorded depths

Precision checking
11.102

1   For depths to about 40 m, the precise calibration of echo sounders in surveying ships is carried out by the "Bar Check" method described in *Admiralty Manual of Hydrographic Surveying Volume II, 1969*.

Briefly, the method is as follows.

2   A metal bar is lowered on marked lines below the transducer and the actual depth, from the marked lines, compared with the depth from the sounder (applying separation correctly if necessary). The results are plotted graphically, depth by measured lines against difference between marked lines and sounder depth (diagram 11.102).

3   The gradient of the line can be adjusted by varying the speed used for sound in water which should be altered (reduced in diagram 11.102) to bring the line parallel with the depth axis. (It will pivot about the depth of the transducer.) Any residual error can then be removed by adjusting the transmission line setting.

4   If adjustments cannot be made the graph can still be used for correcting soundings.

Where the water is too deep to rely on Bar Check settings for sound velocity correction, temperature/salinity probes or sound velocity probes may be lowered and the velocity profile recorded. Alternatively, an Expendable BathyThermograph (XBT) may be used.

5   Many modern survey vessels are fitted with multibeam (or swathe) echo sounders, which measure many simultaneous depths in an across-track fan-shaped swath beneath the transducer. These systems are capable of collecting millions of depths per hour and collecting 100% bathymetry during a survey, as opposed to the succession of individual profiles achieved by earlier equipment.

6   These systems require very accurate sound velocity profiles, as the sound energy is not only transmitted directly downwards through the water column, but also at angles of up to 85° from the vertical.

Different layers of water will have different velocities, and refraction occurs at the interfaces between these layers. An accurate sound velocity profile is therefore required in order to calculate the precise location where the "sounding" struck the sea floor.

7   These systems have a complex calibration procedure, and must also be fully compensated for the orientation and movement of the vessel.

Checking for navigational accuracy
11.103

1   Few ships, other than surveying ships, have the facilities or opportunities to use the Bar Check method for calibration. To guard against gross errors, however, it is advisable to ensure that a sounder is set correctly, as in 11.100 and 11.101.

2   Once the sounder has been correctly adjusted, it is good practice to check the readings against soundings made with the leadline. This should be done at a location where the sea floor is known to be flat, or in a berth free from rough terrain or sloping sea floor. A flat dock sill or similar location is ideal for a leadline check.

False echoes

"Round-the-clock" echoes
11.104

1   False readings may be obtained from a correctly adjusted sounder when the returning echo is not received until after the stylus has completed one or more of its cycles, and so repassed the transmission line and the next pulse has been transmitted.

2   If a sounder has its scale divided so that one complete cycle of the stylus corresponds to a depth of 300 m, an indicated depth of 10 m, could be a sounding of 10, 310 or even 610 m. Such false readings can sometimes be recognized if the trace

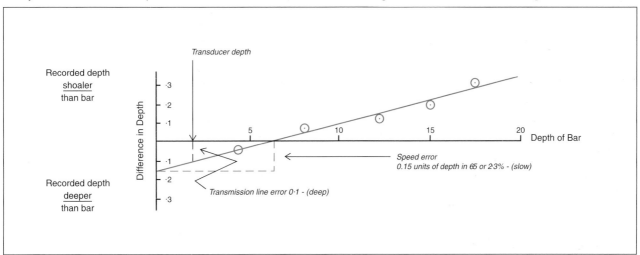

Bar Check Calibration Diagram (11.102)

appears weaker than normal for the depth recorded, or passes through the transmission line, or has a feathery appearance.

3 This type of error is unlikely to occur with digital echo sounders.

Double echoes
11.105

1 With many types of sounder, an echo may be received at about twice the actual depth. This mark on the trace is caused by the transmission pulse, after reflection from the sea floor, being reflected from the surface and again from the sea floor, before reaching the receiving transducer. It is always weaker than the true echo, and will be the first to fade out if the sensitivity of the receiver is reduced. Its possible existence must always be borne in mind when a sounder is started in other than its first phase setting.

2 The diagram at 4.55 illustrates such echoes.

Multiple echoes
11.106

1 The transmission pulse in depths as great as several hundred metres may be reflected, not once but several times, between the sea floor and the surface of the sea or the ship's bottom before its energy is dissipated, causing a number of echoes to be recorded on the trace. These multiple echoes can be faded out by reducing the sensitivity of the set. In the first phase setting, multiple echoes are too obvious to cause confusion, but should be guarded against in the second or subsequent phase setting. The sounder should always be switched on in the first phase and then phased deeper to find the first echo.

2 Echoes other than sea floor echoes seldom have the reflective qualities to produce strong multiple echoes, and may sometimes be distinguished from the sea floor echo by increasing the sensitivity of the set and comparing the multiple echoes.

Other false echoes
11.107

1 Echoes, other than those showing the true sounding, may appear on the trace of an echo sounder for a variety of reasons. They do not usually obscure the echo from the sea floor, but their correct attribution often requires considerable experience.

The following are some of the known causes of false echoes:

2 Shoals of fish.
Layers of water with differing speeds of sound;
The deep scattering layer, which is a layer, or set of layers in the ocean, believed to consist of plankton and fish, which attenuate, scatter and reflect sound pulses. It lies between about 300 and 450 m below the surface by day, ascending to near the surface at sunset and remaining there till sunrise. By day it is more pronounced when the sky is clear than when overcast. It seldom obscures the trace of the sea floor beneath it;

3 Submarine springs (5.42).
Seaweed.
Side echoes from an object not immediately below the vessel, but whose slant depth is less than the depth of water.
Turbulence from the interaction of tidal streams, or eddies with solid particles in suspension.
Electrical faults or man-made noises.

4 For fuller details of false echoes, see *Admiralty Manual of Hydrographic Surveying Volume II, 1969.*

Interaction

General information

Introduction
11.108

1 Interaction is the name given to the effects of change of water pressure on the hull of a vessel. Interaction forces can be enormous; they can change rapidly and can greatly exceed the capability of rudders and engines to counteract them. They take a number of forms:
Shallow water effect (11.111).
Squat (11.113). Squat is the decrease in under-keel clearance which occurs when a vessel is making way, or is stationary in moving water (eg berthed or anchored in a current or tidal stream).

2 Canal effect (11.119).
Ship proximity interaction (11.125).
Mariners who require greater detail should consult the *Admiralty Manual of Navigation (2008) Volume 1 - The Principles of Navigation, Chapter 12.*

Pressure and Suction
11.109

1 The Bernouilli Theorem shows that zones of high and low pressure are created around any body moving in a fluid or gas. In the case of a vessel moving through water, three such zones occur:
Around and ahead of the bow, a pressure zone.
Amidships, a suction zone.
Around and abaft the stern, a pressure zone.
These zones of pressure and suction extend laterally and vertically from a vessel. The after pressure zone is usually less powerful than that at the bow.

Magnitude of interactive forces
11.110

1 In a flow of water, the decrease in pressure of the flow varies with the square of its velocity. Interaction is dependent on pressure, so it also varies with the square of the speed of the vessel, or the rate of the current or stream of a stationary vessel. Thus, even a small reduction in speed will cause a significant reduction in its effect.

Shallow water effect

Onset depth
11.111

1 The Onset Depth for shallow water effect (SWE) depends on the speed of a vessel and her displacement. The following formula can be used to

determine the depth of water in which SWE is likely to start to occur for a single vessel in open water (known as 100% Onset Depth):

100% Onset Depth (m) =
Speed (kn) x 0·17 $\sqrt[3]{\text{Displacement (tonnes)}}$

2   Depths of less than 100% Onset Depth calculated by this formula may be referred to by their percentage (ie 50% Onset Depth).

Consequences
11.112
1   Once Onset Depth is reached, SWE causes a loss of speed for a given power setting, which starts to become apparent at around 50% Onset Depth. The effect increases as the depth reduces and becomes significant at around 25-30%. SWE also impairs steering. Additionally, it takes longer in both time and distance to accelerate/decelerate to the desired speed, even when astern power is applied. This effect is known to have caused a number of berthing incidents.

Squat

Definition
11.113
1   Squat is the decrease in Under-Keel Clearance (11.128) which occurs when a vessel is making way, or is stationary (berthed or anchored) in moving water, assuming a level seabed. It is one specific element of SWE, caused by increased velocity of water flow under a hull and the consequent reduction of pressure.

Squat by the bow or by the stern
11.114
1   In vessels with zero trim when stationary, and a Block Coefficient (11.115) of less than 0·7, squat is usually greater at the stern than at the bow. When greater than 0·7, it is usually greater at the bow. For a vessel not in zero trim when static, squat when under way will generally be greater towards whichever end was deeper when static.

Block coefficient
11.115
1   The shape of a vessel's hull governs its resistance to motion and a numerical indicator of this is known as its Block Coefficient (Cb). It assumes that a rectangular block would have a Cb of 1·0 and that an infinitely thin streamlined shape would have a Cb of 0·0. It can be calculated for any hull using the following formulae:

Block Coefficient (Cb) =
$$\frac{\text{Volume of Displacement}}{\text{Length x Beam x Draught (m)}}$$

Volume of Displacement =
$$\frac{\text{Displacement Weight (tonnes)}}{\text{Water Density}}$$

Effect of speed on Squat
11.116
1   As with Interaction more generally, squat varies with the square of the speed of the vessel. Thus a vessel passing over a shallow patch at high speed may be in

danger of grounding. Equally, a small reduction in speed has a significant effect in reducing squat, which in turn may rapidly reduce the risk of grounding.

Squat in very shallow open water
11.117
1   The following formula for calculating squat in very shallow open water (depths of 1·1-1·4 times draught) is not fully proven, and will only provide an estimate. It should be used with particular care.

Very shallow open water squat (m) =

Cb x $\dfrac{(\text{Speed (kn)})^2}{100}$

Squat in shallow open water
11.118
1   Reliable formulae are not available for the calculation of squat in water depths greater than 1·4 times draught, although evidence indicates that it may reduce sharply. Experience suggests that in water depths of 2 x draught, squat reduces to around 50-75% of that calculated by the formula at 11.117, and at depths of 3 x draught to between 25-50%. It is emphasised, however, that these calculations must be used with great circumspection.

Canal effect

Description
11.119
1   When in a narrow channel, canal or river, horizontal interaction (known as canal effect) causes lateral forces which can throw a vessel off course if they become significantly out of balance. This is particularly likely if a vessel gets too close to one side, or the bank profile changes on one side. A sheer off course can also occur if the vessel passes near a submerged shoal with deeper water on the other side. If the water is shallow, as is normally the case in a channel, canal or river, these effects are magnified.

Effects
11.120
1   The hydrodynamic forces on a vessel are intensified in a canal or similarly constrained waterway because the water is both shallow and confined, with the hull continuously close to solid banks and the bottom. In addition to the SWE experienced in confined water (11.112), the loss of speed is more substantial, a powerful wave pattern is generated both ahead and astern, and the lateral forces arising from the movement of the vessel in relation to the banks (known as bank effect - see below) can have a profound effect on steering.

Bank effect
11.121
1   If a vessel moves away from the centre-line of a canal towards one of the banks, the flow of water between her side and the nearer bank becomes confined, and therefore lower pressure (greater suction) will occur on that side. This suction will tend to pull the vessel towards the nearer bank.

However these suction forces are not evenly distributed along the length of the hull and their resultant tends to act somewhere aft of amidships.

2   This is equivalent to a force acting aft of the centre of gravity which creates a turning moment, deflecting

the ship's head away from from the nearer bank. In practice, this turning moment overrides the bodily suction towards the nearer bank and the vessel will start moving away from it, sometimes so violently that a sheer towards the opposite bank is generated.

3   The effect of a vessel being thus deflected away from a solid bank or wall is sometimes said to be being "pushed off by the bow pressure zone". This is a convenient analogy, but not an exact description of the cause of the phenomenon.

Smelling the ground
11.122

1   A similar phenomenon to Bank Effect, known as "smelling the ground", can occur when in proximity to a shoal and in rivers and canals with channels which shelve steeply on one side only. Passing close to a shallow patch or shoal, the change in water flow caused by the presence of the shoal generates unequal pressures on the hull which can cause the vessel to sheer away from it.

Wave generation in canals
11.123

1   Some of the propulsion energy of a vessel under way generates a wave pattern both ahead and astern of a vessel. In shallow, confined water (ie a canal or river), a high energy 'Wave of Translation' is generated, which can travel some distance ahead of the ship. A substantially enhanced stern wave can also be generated. Both of these waves have the potential to cause damage to the waterway itself and disruption to other users. In addition, when a vessel slows down, her stern wave can overtake her and cause shiphandling difficulties at a time when delicate manoeuvring may be necessary.

Canal speed
11.124

1   The shallow water in a canal or river reduces the efficiency of the propulsion, sometimes by as much as 20%. This can lead to more power being applied in a mistaken attempt to correct it. For a given canal, a vessel has a critical speed, known as canal speed, which cannot be safely exceeded because handling and steering become erratic. Speed limits in canals and rivers take canal speed into account and should be strictly obeyed.

Ship proximity interaction

Description
11.125

1   Close proximity to other vessels can produce a similar situation to canal effect, particularly when passing or overtaking in a narrow channel, canal or river, or for warships, when conducting under way replenishment. Large forces are generated which affect steering, speed and squat. Again, if the water is shallow, these effects are magnified (eg squat can double) and other enhanced effects of SWE will also be experienced. If there is significant disparity in the sizes of vessels in close proximity, the effect on the smaller vessel will be greater.

Overtaking or passing in shallow open water
11.126

1   In shallow open water great care must be taken when overtaking or passing, as interaction can have an effect over substantial distances, and has the potential to pull vessels together.

Overtaking or passing in shallow confined water
11.127

1   In shallow confined water such as a canal, the interaction effects will be further enhanced, and the utmost care must be taken. Safe passing or overtaking in these circumstances may not be possible.

Under-keel clearance

Need for precise consideration
11.128

1   All mariners at some time have to navigate in shallow water. Vessels with draughts approaching 30 m in particular have to face the problem of navigating for considerable distances with a minimum depth below the keel (under-keel clearance) in offshore areas.

2   Though considerable effort has been expended recently in surveying to a high standard a number of routes for deep-draught vessels, it should be realised that in certain critical areas depths may change quickly, and that present hydrographic resources are insufficient to allow these long routes to be surveyed frequently.

3   When planning a passage through a critical area, full advantage should be taken of such co-tidal and co-range charts as are available for predicting the heights of the tide. However, as mentioned at 1.21, charted depths in offshore areas should not be regarded with the same confidence as those in inshore waters, or those in the approaches to certain ports where special provision is made to enable under-keel clearance to be reduced to a minimum.

4   The possibility of increasing the vessel's under-keel clearance by transhipment of cargo (lightening) to reduce draught should also be considered for a passage through such an area.

Under-keel Allowance
11.129

1   Prudent mariners navigate with adequate under-keel clearance at all times, making due allowances for all the factors that are likely to reduce the depth beneath their keels. However, it is becoming increasingly apparent that economic pressures are causing mariners to navigate through certain areas using an inadequate Under-keel Allowance. To ensure a safe under-keel clearance throughout a passage, an Under-keel Allowance may be laid down by a competent authority or determined on board when planning the passage. Such an allowance is expressed as a depth below the keel of the ship when stationary.

2   The amount of this allowance should include provision for the following:

Reliability of the chart. In particular, the possibility that depths may have changed since the last survey, especially where the seabed is unstable and/or prone to sandwaves (5.53) eg S North Sea, Thames Estuary, Persian Gulf, Malacca Strait, Torres Strait, Japanese waters etc;

3   The amount of this allowance should include provision for the following:

Obstructions. Depths over pipelines may stand as much as 2 m above the seabed;

The vessel's course relative to prevailing weather for each of the various legs of the passage;

The vessel's movement in heavy weather, and in waves and swell derived from a distant storm. For example, a large ship with a beam of 50 m can be expected to increase her draught by about 0·5 m for every 1° of roll;

4   Negative tidal surges (5.20);

Long period swell waves (5.32);

Squat at a given speed (11.116);

Possible inaccuracies in offshore tidal predictions (1.21).

Mandated Under-keel Allowance
11.130

1   In certain areas, like Dover Strait, national authorities have conducted extensive investigations and recommend Under-keel Allowances based on scientific enquiry for each leg of the route. Some port authorities require Under-keel Allowances, similarly based or determined empirically, while others stipulate the under-keel clearance to be maintained. In neither case should they be used as a criterion for offshore passages elsewhere where conditions are likely to be very different.

2   When an Under-keel Allowance is laid down by a competent authority, the maximum speed taken into consideration should be given.

Calculation
11.131

1   The Under-keel Allowance can also be used to find the least charted depth a vessel should be able to pass over in safety at a particular time from the formula:

Under-keel Allowance + Squat + Draught = Least charted depth + Predicted Tide + any meteorological effects on the height of tide.

NOTES

Chapter 12

MILITARY OPERATIONS

General information

Warship navigation lights

Positioning
12.1

1 Vessels which by nature of their construction cannot comply fully with the requirements of the *International Regulations for Preventing Collisions at Sea 1972*, as to the number and positioning of lights, comply as closely as possible in accordance with Rule 1(e).

2 There are certain warships, apart from aircraft carriers (12.2) and submarines (12.12), of 50 m in length or over, which cannot be fitted with a second masthead light, and others which though fitted with a second masthead light do not comply strictly with the horizontal and vertical distances specified in Annex I of the Regulations.

Aircraft carriers
12.2

1 Aircraft carriers have their masthead lights placed permanently off the centreline of the ship, and at considerably reduced horizontal separation. Their sidelights may be placed either at each side of the hull, or on each side of the island structure, in which case the port sidelight may be as much as 50 m, or possibly even more, from the port side of the ship.

2 Anchor lights exhibited by certain aircraft carriers consist of four white lights situated as follows:

In the forward part of the vessel at a distance of not more than 1·5 m below the flight deck, two lights in the same horizontal plane, one on the port side and one on the starboard side.

3 In the after part of the vessel at a height of not less than 5 m lower than the forward lights, two lights in the same horizontal plane, one on the port side and one on the starboard side.

4 Each light is visible over an arc of at least 180°. The forward lights are visible over a minimum arc of from 11¼° on the opposite bow to 11¼° from right astern on their own side, and after lights from 11¼° on the opposite quarter to 11¼° from right ahead on their own side.

Exercise areas

Firing and exercise areas

Precautions
12.3

1 Firing and bombing practices and other military exercises take place in many parts of the world.

Annual Summary of Admiralty Notices to Mariners describes the principal types of practices carried out near British waters, the warning signals used, and precautions a vessel should take if she finds an exercise inadvertently being carried out while she is in the practice area.

Charts and publications
12.4

1 It is the responsibility of range authorities to avoid accidents, and ranges are only used intermittently. Since the beginning of 2000, the limits of Firing Practice areas (FPAs) have been included on all new editions of charts covering United Kingdom home waters as they are issued. FPAs in other parts of the world will be added to new editions of the relevant charts as information becomes available from the National Hydrographic Offices concerned. Limits of exercise areas in British waters, and the type of exercise for which they are used, will continue to be shown on *Practice and Exercise Area (PEXA) Charts*. These are listed in *Catalogue of Admiralty Charts and Publications*.

2 In British coastal waters appropriate magenta legends are being placed on the navigational charts to indicate the presence of FPAs. Each legend refers to a note on the chart giving further information, and drawing attention to *Admiralty List of Radio Signals Volume 3, Annual Admiralty Notices to Mariners*, and the PEXA charts. These changes are being made by new edition, and therefore some charts which include ranges do not yet carry this information. Mariners should continue to consult PEXA charts.

3 Range beacons, lights and marking buoys which may be of assistance to the mariner, or targets which may be of danger to navigation, are shown on the navigational charts, and, where appropriate, mentioned in *Admiralty Sailing Directions*. Methods used to advise shipping, and signals displayed in connection with Firing Practice Areas, when known, are described in *Admiralty Sailing Directions*, and lights are mentioned in *Admiralty List of Lights*.

4 *Admiralty List of Radio Signals Volume 3* contains details of warning broadcasts for Firing and Practice Exercise Areas which take place around the coasts of the United Kingdom. Also included within this volume are broadcast details for GUNFACTS. GUNFACTS is a warning broadcast service providing information to the mariner of practice firing intentions, including planned or known controlled underwater explosions, gunnery and missile firing by naval authorities.

Submarine exercise areas

General information
12.5

1   The locations and extent of Submarine Exercise Areas in UK waters are given in *Admiralty List of Radio Signals Volume 3.* The legend "Submarine Exercise Area" on certain charts should not be interpreted as meaning that submarines do not exercise outside such areas.

For information concerning submarines and signals used by them, see 12.10.

SUBFACTS
12.6

1   SUBFACTS is a warning service providing information to the mariner of planned or known submarine activity within the waters of the United Kingdom. Details of this warning service are given within *Admiralty List of Radio Signals Volume 3.* It should be noted that submarines might operate for the entire period or part thereof, in each area notified within the broadcasts. Submarines on the surface will act strictly in accordance with the International Regulations for Preventing Collisions at Sea.

Operation of echo sounders
12.7

1   In order to provide early detection of surface contacts by dived submarines it is recommended that vessels operating within Submarine Exercise Areas, as marked on certain charts, operate their echo sounders.

Minelaying and mine clearance exercise areas

Details of areas
12.8

1   Certain areas in the North Sea, English Channel and waters around the British Isles are used for minelaying and mine clearance practices.

Details of the areas and procedures used are given in *Annual Summary of Admiralty Notices to Mariners.* The areas are not as a rule shown on navigational charts nor described in *Admiralty Sailing Directions.* They are however shown for UK waters on PEXA charts (12.4).

Caution
12.9

1   Ships engaged in mineclearance operations show the lights or shapes prescribed by the *International Regulations for Preventing Collisions at Sea 1972.* They may be operating divers and should not be approached within 1000 m. See also 12.30.

Submarines

General information

Characteristics
12.10

1   Submarines are instruments of war which are designed and operated to optimise their capabilities in that environment. In particular, that optimisation is focussed on their ability to operate in a totally covert manner.

In order to be effective in wartime, they must operate and train at sea in a peacetime environment, but many of their design features and capabilities are inconsistent with the requirements of normal practice for surface vessels at sea.

2   Additionally, their operating environment is more hazardous than for surface vessels and requires additional precautions and procedures to ensure their safety.

In particular, their vulnerability to collision when proceeding on the surface and the fact that many are nuclear powered dictates particular caution when approaching them.

Appearance
12.11

1   Submarines on the surface have a low freeboard, a streamlined shape and low surface buoyancy, with the largest part of the hull under water. Aspect and range can therefore be difficult to assess visually and the low radar reflectivity of the streamlined shape can cause its range to be difficult to assess by radar, giving the false impression that the submarine is at a much greater distance than in reality.

Navigation lights
12.12

1   The positioning of navigation lights on submarines are constrained by the shape of the hull and fin, are therefore unusual and may well give the impression, even to the experienced eye, of being exhibited by a markedly smaller and shorter vessel. Their positioning can cause lights to be obscured for prolonged periods in rough conditions.

2   Masthead lights and sidelights of submarines are placed well forward and very low over the water in proportion to their length and tonnage. The forward masthead light may be lower than the sidelights and the after masthead light may be well forward of the mid-point of the submarine's length.

Sternlights are placed very low indeed and may at times be partially obscured by spray and wash. They are are generally at about the same height as the sidelights.

3   At anchor or at buoy by night, submarines exhibit an all-round white light amidships in addition to the normal anchor lights. The after anchor light of nuclear submarines is mounted on the upper rudder which is some distance astern of the hull's surface waterline.

Care must be taken to avoid confusion with two separate vessels of less than 50 m in length.

Special lights
12.13
1   All submarines are fitted with a flashing light to indicate to an approaching vessel the need for caution. The characteristics of this additional light varies from country to country but are typically yellow, orange or amber, flashing at 70-180 flashes per minute or flashing (3) at a short interval. Some NATO countries have specified more precisely how the flashing light should be displayed as shown in the table below. Care should be taken not to confuse this light with that shown by a hovercraft (120 flashes per minute).

Country	Light
2 Canada	All round rotating amber, group flashing 3, 10 times per minute
France	All round rotating yellow, flashing 100-120 times per minute
Germany	All round orange, showing about 100 flashes per minute, visible for 3 miles
Greece	All round orange, showing about 80 flashes per minute
Italy	All round rotating amber, showing about 90 flashes per minute
3 Netherlands	All round rotating amber, showing about 90 flashes per minute
Norway	All round amber, showing 90 flashes per minute
Poland	All round orange, showing about 100 flashes per minute, visible for 3 miles
Portugal	All round rotating beacon showing 94 flashes per minute
Spain	All round rotating amber, showing 120-180 flashes per minute
4 Turkey	All round rotating amber, showing 90 flashes per minute
United Kingdom	All round flashing amber, showing 90 flashes per minute, on some submarines
United States	Intermittent flashing amber or yellow, with a sequence of one flash per second for 3 seconds followed by a 3 second period

5   The showing of these yellow/amber/orange lights is intended to indicate to an approaching vessel the need for added caution rather than to give immediate identification of the type of vessel exhibiting the light.

Warning signals

General information
12.14
1   Mariners are warned that considerable hazard to life may result from the disregard of signals which denote the presence of submarines.

Visual signals
12.15
1   British warships and auxiliaries fly the International Code Group "NE2" to denote that submarines, which may be submerged, are in the vicinity. Vessels are cautioned to give a wide berth to any vessel flying this signal. If for any reason it is necessary to approach her a good lookout must be kept for submarines whose presence may be indicated only by their periscopes or other masts showing above the water.

2   It must not be inferred from the above that submarines exercise only when in company with escorting vessels.

Pyrotechnics and Smoke Candles
12.16
1   The following signals are used by submerged submarines:

Signal	Meaning
White smoke candle (with or without flame) (may be accompanied by yellowish green fluorescent dye)	Indicates position in response to request from vessel or aircraft as required
Yellow smoke candle	As above
Green flare (grenade) launched about 60-90 m into the air. Burns for about 5 secs	In exercises, used to simulate the firing of a torpedo
Red flare (grenade) (characteristics as for green flare above)	Submarine carrying out emergency surfacing procedure. Keep clear Do not stop propellers Clear area immediately Stand by to render assistance
Two white or yellow candles released singly about 3 minutes apart	Keep clear. I am preparing to surface Do not stop propellers Clear the area immediately

2   **Note.** If the red flare (grenade) signal is sighted and the submarine does not surface within 5 minutes, it should be assumed that the submarine is in distress and has sunk. An immediate attempt should be made to fix the position in which the signal was sighted, after which action in accordance with paras 12.25 and 12.26 should be taken.

Characteristics of pyrotechnic stores and sonobuoys
12.17
1   The pyrotechnic stores and sonobuoys described at 12.16 and shown in diagrams 12.17.1 to 12.17.4 have the following characteristics:

2 **White Smoke Candles** (see 12.17.1) burn for up to 10 minutes emitting white smoke and flame and can be seen by day or night; they can easily be confused with aircraft marine markers and floats, smoke and flame. The candle can also give off a yellowish green dye indicating that a message carrier is attached at its top end. The candle canister is green.

3 **Yellow Smoke Candles** (see diagram 12.17.1) burn for about 5 minutes emitting yellow smoke. They can be seen more easily than the white smoke candles in rough weather but cannot be seen at night. The candle canister is green with a red band.

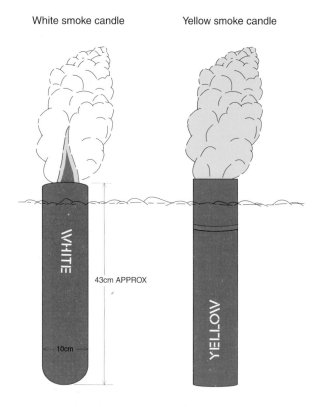

Smoke candles fired from British submarines (12.17.1)

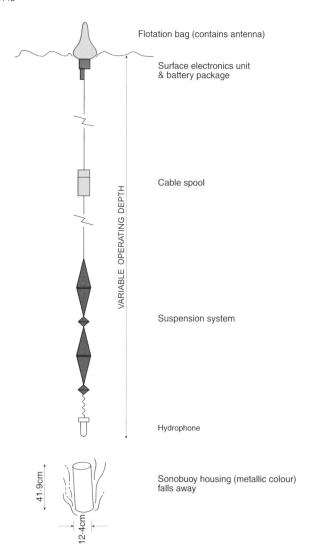

Typical deployed sonobuoy (12.17.2)

4 **Sonobuoys** (see diagram 12.17.2) are dropped from aircraft to detect submarines and may be encountered anywhere at sea. The sonobuoy has a yellow flotation bag.

5 **Smoke and Flame Flares and Marine Markers** (see diagrams 12.17.3 and 12.17.4) are dropped from aircraft to aid in search operations. They burn for varying durations as shown in the diagrams. The flares and markers have pale blue and luminous orange tops. Other versions are in service and may be encountered.

6 All of the above may be encountered in areas where warships and aircraft exercise, whether or not submarines are present. They should not be confused with submarine indicator buoys. In case of doubt the object should be approached to confirm visually whether or not it is a submarine indicator buoy before reporting it.

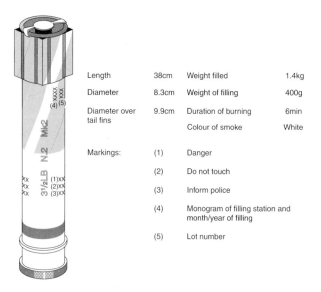

Length	38cm	Weight filled	1.4kg
Diameter	8.3cm	Weight of filling	400g
Diameter over tail fins	9.9cm	Duration of burning	6min
		Colour of smoke	White
Markings:	(1)	Danger	
	(2)	Do not touch	
	(3)	Inform police	
	(4)	Monogram of filling station and month/year of filling	
	(5)	Lot number	

Smoke and Flame flare (12.17.3)

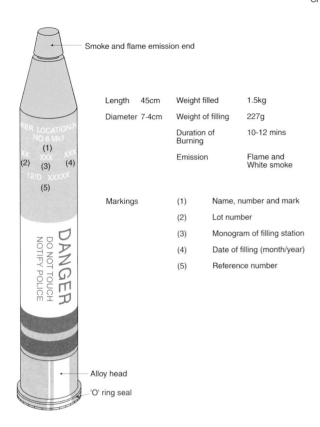

Length	45cm	Weight filled	1.5kg
Diameter	7·4cm	Weight of filling	227g
		Duration of Burning	10-12 mins
		Emission	Flame and White smoke
Markings		(1)	Name, number and mark
		(2)	Lot number
		(3)	Monogram of filling station
		(4)	Date of filling (month/year)
		(5)	Reference number

Marker, Location, Marine (12.17.4)

Submarines operating on the surface

General information
12.18

1 Submarines may be met on the surface at any time. In UK waters, an encounter is particularly likely in the following areas and their approaches:

Clyde.
North Channel.
Minches.
Plymouth.
Irish Sea.

Towed arrays
12.19

1 Submarines occasionally tow sonar equipment and other vessels are recommended to remain at least 1500 m clear when crossing astern of a surfaced submarine.

Dived submarines

General information
12.20

1 When dived, submarines operate at a depth calculated either to be deep enough to enable them to pass safely underneath any vessel likely to be encountered ("Deep"), or near the surface with masts and periscopes raised to allow observation of the surface ("Periscope Depth" (PD)).

2 At PD, a submarine will show no lights by night and will always assume that it has not been detected by any vessel that it may encounter. Therefore it will not follow the *International Regulations for the Prevention*

of Collisions at Sea and will independently adjust its course, speed or depth to avoid collision.

3 Submarine periscopes and masts are designed to be difficult to detect by radar or visual means, hence a careful lookout is necessary when it is believed that a dived submarine is in the vicinity.

Interaction of submarines and fishing vessels

Code of practice
12.21

1 A number of incidents in recent years have demonstrated the potential for danger when submarines operate in the vicinity of vessels engaged in fishing. In order to mitigate such danger, UK submarines, and those of other nations operating in UK waters, have been issued with a Code of Practice which mandates procedures to be followed. The key features are:

The prime responsibility for the safe conduct of operations lies with the submarine.

Routine passages through coastal waters will be conducted on the surface.

Essential dived transits through coastal waters will be conducted at PD, or when below PD at slow transit speeds and only for short periods.

Submarine exercises will, wherever possible and appropriate, be conducted offshore and remote from areas where vessels engaged in fishing may be operating.

2 If it is known or suspected that there may be fishing vessels operating in the vicinity of a submarine, it must be assumed that the fishing vessel(s) are or will be working along the intended track of the submarine unless the captain of the submarine can satisfy himself to the contrary.

Operating procedures
12.22

1 The following operating procedures have been established to ensure that submarines do not come into close proximity with vessels engaged in fishing:

Submarines on the surface will comply fully with the *International Regulations for the Prevention of Collisions at Sea,* showing all appropriate navigation lights and shapes, and comply with the steering rules.

Submarines transiting from the surface to PD will maintain a continuous "all round look" and maintain a mandatory minimum separation of not less than 1500 yds from vessels engaged in fishing.

Submarines operating at PD and not maintaining an "all round look" will maintain a minimum separation of not less than 4000 yds (2 miles) from all vessels classified as possible fishing vessels, whether or not they are believed to be engaged in fishing.

2 **Submarines operating at PD operating an "intermittent all round look" with an established on board radar safety cell** will maintain a minimum separation of not less than 1500 yds from vessels engaged in fishing.

Submarines when "deep" will maintain a minimum separation of not less than 4000 yds (2 miles) from all vessels classified as possible fishing vessels, whether or not they are believed to be engaged in fishing.

Shipping and navigation constraints
12.23

1   When shipping and navigation constraints arise, and it becomes impractical, for whatever reason, for a submarine below PD to maintain 4000 yds separation, it must return to PD in as short a time as possible, commensurate with the safety of adjacent shipping and the submarine, maintaining a minimum of 1500 yds separation. If the submarine cannot maintain 1500 yds separation, it must establish communications with the fishing vessel(s) before proceeding, or, failing that, come to the surface. If a warship or aircraft, which is exercising with the submarine, observes a fishing vessel in the vicinity of the submarine, it will warn the submarine and the fishing vessel by the most expeditious means possible.

2   When submarines intend to operate dived in waters where the geography or navigation constraints do not permit compliance with the separation rules, or if submarines are knowingly going to operate in waters where shipping constraints may prevent full compliance, a surface craft with a Fishing Vessel Safety Officer (FVSO) embarked will be present. The surface craft will assist in facilitating the safe navigation of all vessels and will, where appropriate, act as a communications link between the submarine and fishing vessels. It will also provide an information link between other surface and air assets and the submarine with regard to fishing vessel dispositions and movements.

Communications
12.24

1   Before diving or "going deep", submarines will take every opportunity to communicate with fishing vessels operating in the same area, either directly or through an FVSO. Additionally, the submarine will attempt to establish an agreed point of contact for fishing vessels observed to be operating as a fleet, so that operating intentions can be passed and agreed. If an objection is received, or if communications cannot be established, or if there is any doubt about respective intentions, the submarine must operate in full compliance with the procedures at 12.22, indicating her intention to do so, or surface (or remain on the surface) whilst further instructions are received from her operating authority.

2   Fishing vessels over 12 m in length are required to maintain a listening watch on VHF Channel 16, and those over 24 m are additionally required to maintain a continuous watch on VHF Channel 70. Smaller fishing vessels are only required to carry a handheld VHF radio (a DSC type is recommended).

It should be noted that not all submarines are fitted with GMDSS equipment and therefore cannot send or receive DSC messages.

Submarine emergencies

Contact with the surface
12.25

1   A bottomed submarine which is unable to surface will try to indicate her position by one or more of the following methods:

Releasing an indicator buoy (12.27) as soon as the accident occurs.

On the approach of surface vessels, and at regular intervals, by firing candles which give off a white flame and white smoke or just yellow smoke.

Pumping out oil fuel or lubricating oil.

Blowing out air.

2   **Notes:**

1. A partially flooded submarine may have only a certain number of her smoke candles available and searching vessels should not therefore expect many to appear. It some circumstances, it may be impossible for a submarine to fire any smoke candles.

2. Some submarine pyrotechnics can be fitted with message carriers. If a message has been attached, the pyrotechnic will be fitted with a dye marker, discharging a yellowish green dye into the water on reaching the surface. Such a pyrotechnic should be recovered as soon as it has finished burning.

3   3. Since oil slicks or debris may be the only indication of the presence or whereabouts of the sunken submarine, it is vitally important that surface vessels refrain from discharging anything that might appear to have come from a submarine while they are in the submarine probability area. Searching vessels and aircraft can waste many valuable hours investigating these false contacts.

Rescue
12.26

1   The saving of personnel in a sunken submarine involves the use of specialised submersibles, support craft and personnel. It is likely to take some time before they can all be assembled at the scene; the first assisting personnel on the scene are likely to be parachuted in with their own inflatable boats.

2   At any time between the accident and the arrival of assisting or rescue forces, conditions in the bottomed submarine may deteriorate to the point where the crew have to escape. The precise time at which an escape may be conducted will not be known in the early stages of any operation, and thus it is important that any vessel finding an indicator buoy should stand by ready to receive survivors until relieved by naval forces.

3   In order that those trapped in the submarine know that help is at hand, naval vessels drop patterns of very small explosive charges, the meanings of which are known to the submarine. Rather than do this, other vessels can indicate their presence by the intermittent running of an echo sounder on high power, or by banging on the outer skin of an underwater portion of the vessel's hull with a hammer. Such sounds are likely to be heard by the submarine and should be carried out at frequent intervals. The submarine may if possible acknowledge this by releasing a flare that gives off a flame or smoke once reaching the surface. Once naval forces arrive, such noisemaking should be stopped so as not to interfere with other underwater communications.

4   Once a rescue operation gets underway it is vital that vessels not involved keep well clear. Most

submarines are now fitted to receive rescue vehicles, but for those that are not, escape is the only option.

5 If the escape option is chosen, escapees will start to ascend nearly vertically from the bottomed submarine, either individually or in small groups. On arrival on the surface, it is likely that they will be exhausted or ill, and the presence of an already lowered boat to assist in their recovery is very desirable. Some individuals may require recompression treatment, and naval authorities will endeavour to provide recompression chambers at the scene as soon as possible, or arrange evacuation, probably by helicopter, to the nearest available facility.

6 UK Naval authorities are always on alert to respond to a submarine accident, but because response times will vary, any vessel finding evidence of a submarine in distress will be in a unique position to assist with lifesaving by taking the action described above.

Submarine indicator buoys

General information
12.27

1 British and some Allied submarines are fitted with two indicator buoys, one each end of the vessel, which can be released from inside in case of emergency or if for any reason the submarine is unable to surface.

2 In any submarine accident, time is the most vital factor affecting the chances of rescue of survivors, and as the sighting of an indicator buoy may be the first intimation that an accident has in fact occurred, it is vital that no time should be lost in taking action.

3 The sighting of any buoy answering the attached description should at once be reported by the quickest available means to the Navy, coastguard, or police. However, if vessels are unable to establish communications without leaving the vicinity of the indicator buoy, it should be borne in mind that the primary consideration should be for vessels to remain standing by to recover survivors and not leave the scene of the accident. Every effort should be made to include in the report the serial number of the buoy; this number is affixed below the word "Forward" or "Aft", as shown in diagram 12.28.

4 Indicator buoys are attached to the submarine by a 1000 m length of braid line. Buoys found in areas where the depth of water is less than 1000 m may be secured to a sunken submarine. In areas where strong tidal streams or currents are prevalent the depth from which the buoy may be expected to watch is considerably reduced and in these areas it is possible that a buoy may only watch at slack tide.

5 It is possible that indicator buoys may break adrift accidentally even though the parent submarine may not have sunk; similarly, a buoy found to be adrift is not necessarily an indication that all is well since it may have broken adrift after being deliberately released following an accident. In any case it is therefore important to establish whether or not the buoy is adrift and it is considered that the only practical means of determining movement is by observing its behaviour in a tidal stream or seaway, or periodically fixing its position. In any event it is absolutely vital that the mooring wire is not parted nor any tension applied to it. Boats should not secure to it.

Appearance
12.28

1 **Size and shape.** The British Type 0070 buoy (diagram 12.28) is made of expanded plastic foam, and covered with a 3 mm GRP skin for physical protection. It is hemispherical in shape, 76 cm in diameter and 90 cm deep. There is an anchorage for a 5 mm braided nylon rope mooring at the bottom of the buoy which is slightly offset from the centre. The buoy floats upright with a freeboard of about 15 cm in slack water.

2 **Markings.** It is covered with longitudinal strips of reflective tape, alternately red and white, although a programme is under way (2009) to change the colour scheme of these indicator buoys to a uniform international orange. It is therefore possible that either type may be encountered. For identification purposes each buoy is allocated a three digit serial number (eg 043) which is displayed on each side under the words "Forward" or "Aft". Also inscribed around the top of the buoy are the words: FINDER INFORM NAVY, COASTGUARD OR POLICE. DO NOT SECURE TO OR TOUCH.

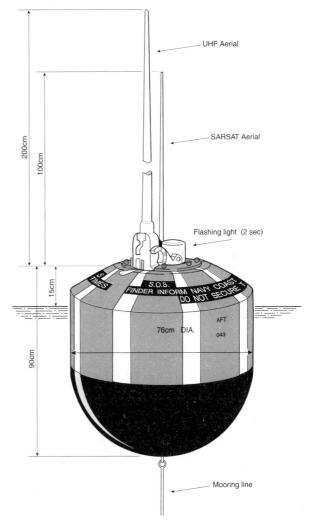

Type 0070 Submarine indicator buoy (12.28)

3 **Lights.** A light which flashes approximately every 2 seconds is mounted in the centre of the top surface. In darkness and during good weather, the unassisted visibility of the light is 5 miles. The buoy has a power

supply which will enable the light to operate for up to 72 hours,

4 **Radio Transmitter Unit.** The buoy is fitted with two automatic radios which transmit on 243·0 and 406·0 MHz via two UHF whip aerials (200 cm and 100 cm long respectively). The transmitter is automatically activated when the indicator buoy is released and the transmission sequences is as follows:

The 243·0 MHz SARBE emission will consist of 3 audio sweeps from 1600 Hz down to not lower than 300 Hz, for a period of 1·2 sec followed by a 0·8 sec period of silence.

5 The 406·0 MHz emission will consist of a SARSAT transmission. There is sufficient power to enable these transmissions to continue for at least 72 hours.

Mine countermeasures

Minefields

General information
12.29

1 Minefields remaining from past coflicts can still pose a threat to mariners, despite concerted international effort over many years to clear them. A full background and description of the threat can be found at 9.34.

Mine Clearance

Mine clearance
12.30

1 Vessels engaged in mine clearance display the signals prescribed in Rule 27(f) of the *International Regulations for Preventing Collisions at Sea 1972*. Other vessels should not approach within 1000 m.

Minehunters
12.31

1 Small boats or inflatable dinghies, from which divers may be operating or controlling a wire guided submersible, may be used in conjunction with minehunters. These may be up to 1000 m from the minehunter.

When operating divers, small boats or dinghies show flag A of the International Code by day, or exhibit the lights prescribed in Rule 23(c) or Rule 25(d) (ii) of the *International Regulations for Preventing Collisions at Sea 1972*, at night.

2 Mariners should navigate with caution in the proximity of a mineclearance vessel, or any small boat or inflatable dinghy operating in the vicinity, and avoid passing within 1000 m whenever practicable.

Buoys
12.32

1 Mineclearance operations may require the ship engaged to lay small buoys which normally carry a radar reflector and a flag. By night these buoys exhibit a white, red or green flashing light, visible all round the horizon for a distance of 1 mile.

Other military activity at sea

Formations and convoys

Caution
12.33

1 The mariner should bear in mind the danger to all concerned which is caused by single vessels approaching a formation of warships, or merchant vessels in convoy, so closely as to involve risk of collision, or attempting to pass ahead of, or through such a formation or convoy. Single ships should adopt early measures to keep out of the way of a formation or convoy.

2 Although a single ship is advised to keep out of the way of a formation or convoy, this does not entitle vessels sailing in company to proceed without regard to the movements of the single vessel. Vessels sailing in formation or convoy should accordingly keep a careful watch on the movements of any single vessel approaching them and should be ready, in case she does not keep out of the way, to take such action as will best avert collision.

Under way replenishment

Manoeuvrability
12.34

1 Warships in conjunction with auxiliaries frequently conduct under way replenishment of stores, fuel and water. Whilst doing so, two or more participating vessels will be connected by jackstays and hoses, preparing to pass them or in the process of disengaging. In any event, they will be severely restricted in both manoeuvrability and speed.

They display the signals prescribed by Rule 27(b) of the *International Regulations for Preventing Collisions at Sea 1972*. Other vessels should keep well clear in accordance with Rules 16 and 18.

Vessels operating aircraft

Movements
12.35

1 The uncertainty of the movements of ships when aircraft or helicopters are operating to or from their

decks should be borne in mind. Under these circumstances, vessels are usually constrained to steering courses determined by the speed and direction of the wind (13.153).

Lights
12.36

1   While operating aircraft or helicopters from their decks ships show the lights and shapes prescribed by Rule 27(b) of the *International Regulations for Preventing Collisions at Sea 1972*. Other vessels should keep well clear in accordance with Rules 16 and 18.

During night flying operations ships may use red or white floodlighting; aircraft carriers may use similar coloured deck lighting.

NOTES

Chapter 13

COMMERCIAL OPERATIONS

Security

International Ship and Port Facility Security Code (ISPS)

Introduction
13.1

1 The ISPS Code is an internationally agreed protective security regime for the maritime sector and was adopted in a resolution on 12 December 2002 by a Diplomatic Conference of Contracting Governments to the International Convention for the Safety of Life at Sea (SOLAS) 1974. Another resolution was adopted which made necessary amendments to SOLAS Chapter V and the new Chapter XI-2 (the original chapter XI was amended and split into XI-1 and XI-2) of SOLAS by which compliance with the ISPS Code became mandatory on 1 July 2004.

Applicability
13.2

1 The ISPS Code covers all internationally trading passenger ships carrying 12 or more passengers, cargo ships of 500 gt and above (as measured by the International Convention on Tonnage Measurement of ships, 1969); mobile offshore drilling units and all port facilities (ship/port interfaces) serving these vessels.

Objectives
13.3

1 The International Ship and Port Facility Security Code (ISPS) establishes an international framework between Governments, Government agencies, local administrations, port and shipping industries to detect/assess security threats and take preventative measures. It establishes the respective roles and responsibilities of all the parties concerned, at the national and international level, for ensuring maritime security; to ensure the early and efficient collation and exchange of security related information; to provide a methodology for security assessments so as to have in place plans and procedures to react to changing security levels (13.7), and to ensure confidence that adequate and proportionate maritime security measures are in place.

2 The objectives are achieved by the designation of appropriate officers/personnel on each ship, in each port facility and in each shipping company to prepare and put into effect the security plans that are approved for each ship and port facility.

Organisation
13.4

1 **Company Security Officer.** The company security officer (CSO) is responsible for ensuring that a ship security assessment is carried out for each vessel which is required to comply with the code and is also responsible for ensuring that a ship security plan is in place for each vessel having identified the particular features of the vessel and the potential threats and vulnerabilities.

Ship Security Officer. The ship's security officer (SSO) is responsible for implementing the ship's plan at each of the three escalating threat levels.

Port Security Officer. Each port facility will have a designated Port Security Officer (PSO) who may cover more than one facility.

Details
13.5

1 Details of the requirements and responsibilities of port facilities and ships are laid down in the *ISPS Code 2003 Edition*

Compliance by UK flagged vessels
13.6

1 With specific regard to UK vessels, ISPS requires the preparation and subsequent agreement with TRANSEC or MCA of a Ship Security Plan, following the completion of a ship security assessment. The Ship Security Plan must cover both the protective security measures required on the ship and the appropriate response to a security incident. Once the Ship Security Plan has been approved and a verification inspection has been conducted, vessels meeting UK requirements are issued with an International Ship Security Certificate. The Code also requires the appointment and training of a Ship Security Officer for each ship and a Company Security Officer for the shipping company who together are responsible for delivering against the security requirements of the plan.

Security levels
13.7

1 The ISPS Code establishes 3 security levels, to be set in port facilities and on board ships as the situation dictates. These are:

Security Level 1. This is the normal level of security, the level at which a ship or port would normally operate. Minimum appropriate protective security measures should be maintained at all times.

2 **Security Level 2.** This is a heightened level of security, the level applying for as long as there is a heightened risk of a security incident. Appropriate additional security measures should be put in place and maintained for as long as there is a heightened risk of a security incident.

Security Level 3. This is an exceptional level of security, applying only for the period of time when there is a probable or imminent risk of a security incident. It is the level at which further specific protective security measures should be maintained for a limited period of time, even though it may not be possible to identify the specific threat.

3 The setting of Security Level 3 should be an exceptional measure, being applied only when there is credible information that a security incident is probable or imminent. It should only be set for the duration of the identified security threat or actual incident.

Whilst it would be normal for the security level to escalate through all three levels to Level 3 as the threat increases, it is also possible to move directly from Level 1 to Level 3.

Setting of Security Levels for UK flagged vessels
13.8

1 TRANSEC sets the security level for all UK flagged ships, determines the appropriate security level that UK flagged ships must adopt when operating in a specific country or sea area taking into account other considerations such as the threat from piracy and armed robbery. However not all Flag States will set security levels for their ships in the same way.

Piracy

Introduction

Sources of information
13.9

1 The bulk of the information and guidance in this section is based on that given by the UK Maritime and Coastguard Agency (MCA) in Marine Guidance Note 298(M).

Due to the continuing high level of pirate activity in certain parts of the world, it is considered prudent to include a general overview of activity which has taken place in 2008/09. The content has been obtained from a variety of sources involved with counter piracy operations. The ICC International Maritime Bureau, Commercial Crimes Services web page www.icc-ccs.org and associated quarterly reports have been particularly informative.

Contact table
13.10

1 A Contact Table containing details of the authorities that should be contacted when an attack takes place can be found in *Admiralty List of Radio Signals Volume 1(1) and (2)*. The specific areas of geographical responsibility have also been included.

Piracy prone areas and warnings

General information
13.11

1 Mariners are warned to be extra cautious and to take necessary precautionary measures when transiting the areas described below.

South East Asia and Indian Sub Continent
13.12

1 **Bangladesh.** Although the number of attacks has fallen, the area is still listed as very high risk. Pirates are targeting ships preparing to anchor. Most attacks reported at Chittagong anchorages and approaches.

Indonesia. Anambas/Natuna island area, Belawan, Jakarta/Tg Priok. Pirates normally armed with guns/knives/machetes. Generally be vigilant in other areas. Many attacks may have gone unreported.

2 **Malacca Strait.** Although the number of attacks has reduced due to the increase and aggressive nature of patrols by the littoral states authorities since July 2005, ships are advised to continue the maintenance of a strict anti-piracy watch when transiting the straits.

Currently, there are no indications for how long the patrols will continue.

Malaysia. Off Tioman Island/South China Sea.

Philippines. Manila – Pirates target ships at anchor and in surrounding waters.

3 **Singapore Strait.** Vessels are advised to continue to be vigilant and maintain anti-piracy watch. Pirates are attacking ships whilst underway or anchored at OPL.

Vietnam. Vung Tau.

Africa
13.13

1 **Tema (Ghana):** most attacks occur while ships are at anchor.

Lagos & Bonny River (Nigeria): Pirates are violent and have attacked and robbed vessels/kidnapped crews along the coast and rivers, in anchorages and ports and surrounding waters. Vessels are advised to be vigilant in other parts of Nigeria.

Dar es Salaam (Tanzania): Pirates continue to target ships in port, anchorages and surrounding waters.

Gulf of Aden (GOA)/Red Sea
13.14

1 Somali pirates continue to attack vessels along the northern Somali coast in the GOA using small boats despite the presence of warships and the establishment of specific military counter-piracy operations. These pirates use automatic weapons and rocket propelled grenades (RPG) in an attempt to board and hijack vessels. If an attack is successful and the vessel hijacked, it is normally sailed towards the Somali coast and a ransom is demanded for the release of the vessel and crew.

2 All vessels transiting the area are advised to take additional precautionary measures and maintain strict 24 hours visual and radar anti-piracy watch using all available means.

South and Central America and the Caribbean
13.15

1 **Brazil.** Although the number of reported attacks in Santos has reduced, ships are advised to remain vigilant.

Rest of the World
13.16

1 **Arabian Sea.** Sightings and calls from suspicious small boats. In some cases, boats chased the ships with unknown intent.

Trends in piracy activity

Background
13.17

1 A total of 293 incidents of piracy and armed robbery against ships were reported to the ICC International Maritime Bureau's Piracy Reporting Centre (IMB PRC) in 2008. This was an 11% increase on 2007, almost entirely due to the unprecedented rise in the number of attacks in the Gulf of Aden which have continued to rise in 2009.

2 2008 saw an unprecedented number of attacks in the Gulf of Aden. In addition, it saw the first hijacking of a very large tanker. Successful attacks have also been carried out at ever greater distances from shore, along the E coast of Africa. Every attack off Somalia is aimed at hijacking the vessel; hence every attempted attack is a failed hijacking. All types of vessels with varying freeboards and speeds have been targeted and attacked.

3 Worldwide in 2008, a total of 49 vessels were hijacked, with 889 crew taken hostage. A further 46 vessels reported being fired upon. 11 crew were killed, 21 were missing (presumed dead) and 32 were injured. In the first quarter of 2009, the trend continued with 34 vessels being boarded, 29 vessels fired upon and 9 vessels hijacked. A total of 178 crew were taken hostage, 9 injured, 5 kidnapped and 2 killed.

4 In the majority of incidents, the attackers were heavily armed with guns or knives, and violence against crew members continues to increase. In 2008 the number of incidents in which guns were used was double that of 2007.

Somalia and the Gulf of Aden
13.18

1 The most recent IMB report (2009) states that the number of incidents reported for the east coast of Somalia and the Gulf of Aden in 2008 represented an increase of nearly 200% compared to 2007, with several vessels being held to ransom, and their crews held hostage.

This increase in numbers is largely due to the increased ability of Somali pirates to range further out to sea than before and the inability of the Somali government to respond.

2 Recently introduced multi-national military countermeasures, described in greater detail at 13.73, are playing a key role in countering piracy in this region, with the number of attacks resulting in instances of hijacking falling significantly in late 2008 and early 2009.

Currently, the reward-to-risk ratio for the Somali pirate is so large that only robust measures by international governments and navies will enable the safety and security of this major trade route to be restored.

Nigeria
13.19

1 Nigeria has the second highest number of serious attacks and continues to be viewed as a high risk area. The main differences between E and W African pirate activity is that almost all of the incidents in Nigeria are conducted within its territorial waters whereas most of the incidents along the east coast of Africa and the Gulf of Aden occur on the high seas.

2 The motives for the attacks are also different with Somalia being completely financial whilst in Nigeria it is partly political. Forty confirmed incidents in Nigeria have been reported to the PRC, with a further 100 incidents which have not been confirmed. Under-reporting from vessels involved in incidents in the Nigerian waters remains a concern.

3 Of the 40 reported attacks in 2008, 27 vessels were boarded and 5 hijacked. A further 7 have been reported in the first quarter of 2009. Nigeria has recorded the highest number of crew being kidnapped (39), but due to under-reporting, the actual numbers are likely to be higher. The attacks and kidnapping in the Niger delta are targeted mainly against vessels supporting or connected to the oil industry, purportedly for political change. Seventeen of the incidents were against tankers, 7 on support and supply ships and the remaining on bulk carriers, general cargo and container ships. These incidents are often violent and crew members are frequently injured and kidnapped. Even ships provided with escort protection and armed security guards can fall prey to dedicated pirates.

Indonesia
13.20

1 The efforts of Indonesian authorities in curbing piracy and armed robbery in territorial waters have reduced the number of attacks significantly. Compared to 2003 when 121 attacks were reported, there were only 28 incidents in 2008, and only one in the first quarter of 2009. The majority of these attacks were judged to be opportunistic.

Malaysia, Malacca and Singapore Straits
13.21

1 The Malacca Strait has seen a marked reduction in the number of incidents, with only 2 reported in 2008 down from 7 in 2007, and only one incident in the first quarter of 2009. Incidents in the Singapore Straits were, however, up from 3 in 2007 to 6 in 2008. Malaysia has also seen a slight increase in the number of incidents.

This positive reduction has been the cumulative result of increased vigilance and patrolling by the littoral states and continued precautionary measures taken by vessels.

Bangladesh
13.22

1 Vessels approaching anchorages or at anchor off Chittagong are at particular risk. Masters are advised to maintain strict anti-piracy watches especially while approaching these anchorages and whilst at anchor. Pirates mainly steal ship's stores. There has been a slight increase in the number of attacks in the last year (2008-2009).

Considerable effort by the Bangladeshi authorities to counter the problem has resulted in a fall in the first quarter of 2009. Only one incident was reported compared to 3 during the same period in 2008.

Tanzania
13.23

1 Methods of attack in Tanzania (Dar es Salaam) are similar to those in Bangladesh (see above). Vessels at anchor and those approaching an anchorage are targeted. In Dar es Salaam, ship's cargo is generally the target. Of the 14 vessels attacked there in 2008-2009, 12 were container ships.

Attacks in the first quarter of 2009 have almost doubled compared to the corresponding period in 2008.

Peru
13.24

1 Peru has seen an increased level of incidents in its waters in which vessels were successfully attacked.

Methods of attack

Theft or robbery from vessels
13.25

1 The most common form of piracy and armed attack consists of boarding a vessel, stealing cargo or equipment and withdrawing. Half of these robberies occur when the vessel is in port or at anchor and half occur while the ship is under way (both within territorial and international waters). The majority of incidents in harbour are opportunistic; a ship in port is particularly vulnerable since it is in a fixed position, may have a skeleton crew and the attacker has more and easier escape routes than when the vessel is at sea.

2 Most thefts of stores and equipment are carried out on an opportunistic basis, particularly if crews appear to be less than alert. Professional criminal gangs will target high value goods such as cash and valuables in the ship's safe, crew possessions and any portable ship's equipment. Less valuable items can also been taken, sometimes including paint and mooring lines.

3 Where there is evidence of tampering with containers, raiders may initially have gained access while the vessel was in harbour and then escaped over the side with what they could carry, sometimes once the vessel was underway, being picked up by accomplices. In some cases, compartments may not have been fully searched or secured before the ship left harbour.

Attacks at anchor (within port limits)
13.26

1 A ship at anchor is usually boarded from a small boat under the cover of darkness. Most attacks occur between the hours of 2200 and 0600. The attackers usually board either from the stern using grappling hooks attached to the ship's rail or from the bow by climbing the anchor cable. Often the raiders will try not to alert the crew, although they will sometimes take a hostage to gain information or to intimidate and gain control over the master or other crew members, or to gain access to the crew quarters.

2 Communications equipment may be destroyed to prevent or delay the alarm being raised. Crew quarters may be raided for portable personal possessions, and cash stolen from the ship's safe. There may be some opening of containers or holds. Selective opening of containers or holds with high value cargoes may occur, implying prior knowledge of the cargo manifest. The attackers may also steal any movable ship's stores. Having removed what they can carry, the raiders depart. Attackers may previously have had access to the ship as employees of shore based cleaning or other contractors.

Attacks when berthed alongside
13.27

1 A vessel berthed alongside a quay or outboard of another vessel is usually boarded via an unmanned gangway, by climbing mooring ropes or anchor chains, or by using grappling hooks to reach the deck. Most attacks which occur when a ship is alongside are opportunistic, and statistically an attacker is less likely to resort to violence. Attackers may flee empty-handed if challenged by crew.

2 However, in the Caribbean, the favoured method of attack has been for the attackers to rush on board brandishing knives and forcing the crew to hand over valuables.

Attacks when under way
13.28

1 Attacks on vessels under way can often be more threatening and dangerous for a ship's crew than an attack in harbour, as the attack is likely to have been planned and the attackers will almost certainly be armed with personal firearms as well as more powerful devices such as RPGs. The vast majority of this type of attack take place in the Gulf of Aden and off the Horn of Africa.

2 The tactics employed by attackers in these circumstances usually follow a distinctive pattern. Under cover of darkness, one or more high speed, low profile craft close the target vessel, utilising blind spots such as approaching from the stern. The sides of the vessel may be used for boarding if she has a low freeboard. Vessels travelling at slow speeds, especially if this is combined with a low freeboard, are particularly vulnerable to attack. Access to the vessel will often be gained by climbing poles or by grappling irons.

3 Attackers often demonstrate considerable skill and daring; they have shown themselves able to board vessels with high freeboards at speeds in excess of 17 kn. They show knowledge of onboard procedures, often seeking to board when bridge and engine room personnel are fully engaged in navigating through congested or restricted waters. They seem to be aware of the general layout of the vessels attacked.

4 The small craft used by the attackers may come from adjacent coastlines (hiding behind headlands and islands until the ship is close enough to engage) or launched from "mother" ships if farther offshore. There have been incidences where larger ships steaming without lights have been reported in the vicinity of ships which have been attacked.

5 Attackers have also been known to try to merge with local fishing boats or to disguise themselves as Coastguard, Naval personnel or Pilots in order to board the ship. In the N Persian Gulf and particularly along the Iranian coast and waterways of Iraq, criminal gangs are operating from small high-speed craft and tend to conceal themselves among fishing fleets. When a target ship nears, the attackers' boats will break cover and approach the vessel, allowing the attackers to board, usually stealing valuables and particularly cash. Alternatively they may demand protection money.

Another method is to cast fishing nets across a waterway, forcing a vessel to slow and damage the nets. The vessel is then boarded by the "fishermen" who demand compensation for the nets.

6   Have boarded, attackers will normally make their way to the master's cabin, and by threats or assault, force him to open the safe. They will then depart, taking what they can with them without alerting any other members of the crew. There have been instances of crew members being seized and threatened in order to achieve compliance. In hijack incidents, the attackers will attempt to seize the entire crew, who may then be locked up.

7   Attacks on vessels under way pose a serious threat to the safety of shipping because although the duration of a typical attack is between 15 minutes and one hour, vessels have been known to be under the control of attackers for much longer with few, if any, qualified mariners manning the bridge.

8   This situation has the potential to create a significant risk of collision or grounding. If the target ship is an oil tanker or chemical carrier, this could result in a significant pollution incident.

Although the vast majority of attacks are to steal cash, crew possessions or portable equipment, there are still cases of vessels and their cargoes being seized and the entire cargo and sometimes the vessel herself, being disposed of by the attackers.

Hijacking
13.29

1   Hijacking is a complex operation requiring considerable expertise and resources, which usually puts this crime beyond the means of small opportunist groups. For example, in the late 1990s most hijacking incidents took place in the South China Sea and these were run by large organised crime syndicates until the Chinese government launched a successful crack-down.

2   Despite its complexity there has been an increase in the number of hijackings of ships to steal the cargo (usually transferring it to another ship) over the last decade. A number of violent and well organised hijackings have taken place recently in the Malacca Straits. There have been a number of well documented cases such as the *Alondra Rainbow* or the recent case of the *Natris/Paulijing,* where the ships have been physically altered and re-registered, in essence becoming "phantom" ships. Similarly there is now a trend towards targeting smaller vessels such as tugs, barges and yachts which require far less planning and fewer resources.

3   The ship's crew, and particularly the most senior members, are likely to be taken captive and held to ransom, rather than have cargo or valuables stolen. This is particularly the case at the N end of the Malacca Strait, in the Niger Delta and off the coast of Somalia. Following negotiation, ransom demands are usually met. This may contribute to an increase in attacks of this type.

4   Therefore, it is important that masters and crew are aware of the increased possibility of this type of attack when sailing in areas where ransom demands have previously been paid. If a ship is hijacked, crew members should adopt an acquiescent attitude, comply with hijacker's demands and seek to avoid any actions which may antagonise the attackers. Failure to do so may endanger the lives of crew members.

Risk factors

Cash in the ship's safe
13.30

1   Attackers are attracted by the belief that large sums of cash are carried in the ship's safe. On several occasions this belief has been justified and substantial sums have been stolen. While carrying cash may sometimes be necessary, it entices attackers, who are likely to force the master to open the safe. Even if cash is dispersed within the vessel, attackers may intimidate crew members until all the locations have been revealed.

2   Ways of eliminating the need to carry large sums of cash on board ship should be considered. If large sums of money must be carried it is advisable to locate safes in less obvious locations, or to have a number of safes each containing a smaller sum. In any event it would be prudent to keep the number of people with knowledge of the safe location(s) to a minimum.

3   Although the incidence of cruise ships being targeted is extremely low, these ships are particularly attractive on account of the cash and valuables likely to be carried by their passengers. Size (deck height) and large crews make these ships less susceptible to attack whilst underway than most other vessels. However, with more advanced tactics and increasingly sophisticated equipment being used by attackers, it is likely that the threat of attack on a cruise ship will increase. Extra vigilance should be maintained when these ships are in port, and in particularly when alongside.

Smaller crews
13.31

1   The smaller crew numbers found on board most vessels also favour the attacker. A small crew engaged in ensuring the safe navigation of their vessel through congested or confined waters may also have the additional task of maintaining high levels of security surveillance and preparedness for prolonged periods. Companies should ensure that security watches are enhanced if their ship is in waters or ports, where attacks are known to occur.

2   Companies should also consider providing surveillance systems and intruder detection equipment to assist crews and protect their vessels. The provision of piracy alarm systems on bridge wings and other vulnerable/lookout positions should be seriously considered. Companies should also consider the need to carry additional security personnel (above the normal crewing level) in areas of high risk, ensuring that if such personnel are engaged locally, that their bonafides are thoroughly checked.

Ship Security Plan

General information
13.32

1   It is now a requirement that all vessels that fall within the scope of the ISPS Code must undergo a Ship Security Assessment, which requires the development of a Ship Security Plan. This plan must be agreed with the Flag State competent authority in order to receive an International Ship Security Certificate and thereby comply with the Code. The

content of the plan will vary depending on the vessel that it covers but must include details such as the organisational structure of security for the ship, the ship's communication systems and the security measures that will be in place at each of three Security Levels (13.7). The plan is designed to be a living document which will require review and updating as circumstances change.

Restricted areas
13.33

1   The Ship Security Assessment also requires the identification and establishment of Restricted Areas (RAs) onboard which must then feature in the Ship Security Plan. The plan should specify the extent of the RA, the times of application, the security measures to be taken to control access to them and to control activity within them. The purpose of an RA is to demarcate certain areas of a ship to prevent unauthorised access, protect passengers and crew, protect sensitive security areas on the ship as appropriate and to protect the ship's cargo and stores from interference.

2   On UK flagged ships all RAs must be clearly marked to show that access is restricted and that unauthorised presence within the area constitutes a breach of security.

Ship Security Alert System (SSAS)

General information
13.34

1   The amendments to SOLAS under Chapter X1-2, Regulation 6 requires the installation of SSAS on board vessels to which SOLAS applies.

The purpose of the SSAS is to alert Flag State competent authorities and Company Security Officers that the security of a vessel is threatened or has been compromised by terrorists.

2   There are a minimum of two activation points for SSAS from which to initiate the transmission of an alert and it is for the master to decide which crew members need to be aware of the location of the activation points.

Once activated, a covert alert will be made to the relevant competent authority. Each Flag State must have procedures in place to ensure quick and effective receipt and handling of the alert (the UK's own response procedure has been separately communicated to UK flagged shipping companies). The alert will continue until it is deactivated or reset.

3   Whilst SSAS is primarily intended for counter-terrorism purposes, in the event of a pirate attack where the ship has been boarded or is very likely to be, and when all other radio procedures have either failed or there is no opportunity to use them, SSAS may be used as a last resort to alert the Flag State.

Periodic testing (once a year as a minimum) of the SSAS to test the communication process is advisable although it is important to contact those who will be involved in the test in advance to ensure that no unnecessary response activity is implemented.

4   The UK competent authority is the Maritime and Coastguard Agency and Ship Security Alerts are received at the MCA's Maritime Rescue and Co-ordination Centre in Falmouth.

Countermeasures

General information
13.35

1   The recommended countermeasures outlined below are based on reports of incidents, advice published by commercial interests and organisations and measures developed to enhance ship security. The extent to which these recommendations are followed or applied are matters solely for Company/Ship Security Officers or masters of vessels operating in areas where attacks may occur. They are not designed to replace or supersede any security measures recorded in the Ship Security Plan, but may be used in addition to the security measures required by the plan at each Security Level.

2   If possible, appropriate risk assessments should be conducted by the Company/ Ship Security Officers or the master prior to a vessel entering an area with a high incidence of piracy. The aim of any such assessment should be to determine whether additional security personnel and/or measures are required over and above those mandatory security measures specified in the Ship Security Plan for the given Security Level.

The counter-piracy plan
13.36

1   All vessels operating in waters where piracy incidents occur should hold or develop a counter-piracy plan. The plan should be prepared having regard to the risks that may be faced, the crew numbers available, their capability and training, the ability to establish secure areas on board the vessel (for crew to lock themselves into, in the event that attackers are successful in boarding the vessel) and should also cover the surveillance and detection equipment that has been provided. The plan should, among other things, cover:

2   The need for enhanced watch-keeping, and the use of lighting and surveillance, detection or perimeter protection equipment.
Crew responses if a potential attack is detected or an attack is underway.
The radio and alarm procedures to be followed.
The reports that should be made after an attack, or an attempted attack.
Training to ensure crew react consistently to an incident.

3   Counter-piracy plans should ensure that masters and crews are made fully aware of the risks involved during attacks by pirates or armed robbers. In particular it should address the dangers that may arise if a crew adopts an aggressive response to an attack.

Early detection of a possible attack is the most effective deterrent. Aggressive responses once an attack is underway, and in particular once the attackers have boarded the ship, could significantly increase the risk to the ship and those on board. The counter-piracy plan can exist as a stand-alone document or be incorporated into the Ship Security Plan (13.32) for ease of reference for relevant members of the crew. The important point is that the counter-piracy plan should supplement the Ship Security Plan but that the latter document must take precedence as a Government approved official document.

Routeing and anchoring considerations

13.37

1   If at all possible, masters should, at their discretion, route their vessels away from areas where attacks are known to take place and in particular seek to avoid bottlenecks. If vessels are approaching ports where attacks have taken place on ships at anchor and it is known that the ship will have to anchor for some time, consideration should be given to delaying anchoring by slow steaming, or by longer routeing to remain well offshore, thereby reducing the period during which the ship is at risk.

2   Charter party agreements should contain up-to-date War Clauses which include piracy provisions, and should recognise that ships may need to delay arrival at ports where attacks occur, either because no berth is available, or because offshore loading or unloading may be delayed for a protracted period.

Preparations on approaching an area where attacks are known to occur

13.38

1   Prior to a vessel entering an area where attacks have occurred, the crew should have practised and perfected the procedures set down in the Ship's Security Plan and/or Counter-piracy Plan. Communication systems, alarm signals and procedures should have been thoroughly practised. If instructions are to be given over the vessel's address systems or personal radios they must be clearly understood by those who may not have fully mastered the language in which the instructions will be given. To this end, code words could be employed to simplify the issuing of instructions and the initiation of pre-rehearsed responses.

2   Access points and any secure restricted or controlled areas must be controlled through monitoring and patrolling in port and at anchor, and as far as practicable when underway. Crews should be trained in the use of any additional surveillance or detection equipment installed on the ship. Planning and training must be on the basis that an attack will take place and not in the belief that with some luck it will not happen. Indications to attackers that the vessel has an alert and trained crew implementing an effective Counter-piracy Plan could help deter them from attacking the vessel.

Actions in harbour or at anchor

13.39

1   The ISPS Code and the UK government requires as a minimum that access to all UK flagged vessels is controlled in order to prevent unauthorised access (measures to be put in place at each access point must be listed in the Ship Security Plan (13.32) and that an identification system (for example an ID Pass system incorporating a photograph of the pass holder) must be in place for visitors. The specific measures put in place will vary according to the Flag State and the vessel herself. However extra precautions should be taken regarding certain groups of people who require access to the ship, such as stevedores.

2   It would be beneficial to site CCTV equipment (13.44) and other electronic monitoring devices in such a way as to ensure coverage of areas vulnerable to infiltration e.g. the stern, areas of low freeboard, the hawse pipe(s) and the chain locker. It would also be wise to consider greasing or installing razor wire woven through and around the anchor chain (extending up to 2 m down the hawse pipe) while the ship is at anchor to prevent climbing. Hawse pipe covers should be securely locked in place (attackers have been known to reach through covers and undo the traditional wing nut arrangement). A further measure while the vessel is at anchor could be to activate the anchor cable wash-down system (if fitted), or to aim a fire hose through the hawse pipe, turned on at full pressure.

3   In high-risk areas, a system of regular deck patrols is recommended, conducted by a sufficient number of crew to ensure personal safety. The crew members conducting the patrol should be equipped with two-way radios to ensure instant communication with the bridge, concentrating on vulnerable areas. The patrols and search patterns should be unpredictable and conducted at irregular intervals to prevent a potential attacker from establishing a routine which could be exploited.

4   Given that attackers may use knowledge of cargo manifests to select their targets, every effort should be made to limit circulation of documents which give information on cargoes and their location onboard.

5   Despite the time pressures associated with the necessity for fast turnrounds in port, the security of the vessel and her crew should not be compromised by poor procedure. Prior to leaving a port or anchorage, the vessel should be thoroughly searched and all external doors and access points secured and controlled, with priority given to the bridge. Internally, priority should be given to the engine room, steering space and other vulnerable areas. Doors and access points should be regularly checked thereafter. The means of controlling doors or access points which would need to be used in the event of an on board emergency requires careful consideration.

Watchkeeping and vigilance

13.40

1   Maintaining vigilance is essential. All too often the first indication of an attack occurs when attackers appear on the bridge or in the master's cabin. Advance warning of a possible attack will give the opportunity to sound alarms, alert other vessels and the coastal authorities, illuminate any suspect craft, undertake evasive manoeuvring or initiate other response procedures. Signs that the vessel is aware that it is being approached can deter attackers.

2   When vessels are in, or approaching, areas where attacks are known to have taken place, bridge watches and lookouts should be significantly strengthened, manpower resources allowing. Additional watches on the stern or covering radar "blind spots" should also be considered if manpower allows. Bridge staff and lookouts should use low light binoculars if available. Radar stations should be frequently manned, even though it may be difficult to detect low profile fast moving craft on a ship's radars. A yacht or I-band radar mounted on the stern may provide an additional monitoring capability to detect small craft approaching from astern. Use of an appropriately positioned radar system when the vessel is at anchor may also provide warning of the close approach of small craft.

3   It is particularly important to maintain a radar and visual watch for craft which may be trailing the vessel when underway, and which could close quickly when mounting an attack. Small craft which appear to be matching the speed of the vessel on a parallel or following course should always be treated with suspicion. If a suspect craft has been detected, it is important that an effective all round watch is maintained in case the "obvious" craft is a decoy. Decoys are used to divert the attention of the crew away from a second craft which could be used to board the ship unobtrusively.

4   Companies with vessels which frequently visit areas where attacks have occurred should consider the provision of more sophisticated visual and electronic devices in order to augment both radar and visual watch capability at night, improving early warning of a possible attack. Additional advice on more sophisticated equipment appropriate for use on UK flagged vessels will be provided on request from the UK Department for Transport (TRANSEC).

Communications
13.41

1   For detailed guidance on radio procedures, radio watch keeping advice and standard message formats, see 13.62.

Lighting when under way
13.42

1   Vessels should use the maximum lighting available consistent with safe navigation, having regard in particular to the provisions of Rule 20(b) of the 1972 Collision Regulations. Bow and overside lights should be left on if possible. Vessels must not operate deck lighting when underway as it may lead other vessels to assume the ship is at anchor. Wide beam floodlights could be used to illuminate the area astern. Signal projector lights can be used systematically to probe for suspect craft, illuminating radar contacts if possible.

2   It has been suggested that vessels underway should be blacked out except for mandatory navigation lights. This may prevent attackers establishing points of reference when making their approach. In addition, turning lights on as attackers approach will alert them to their discovery, dazzle them, and may encourage them to desist. The fitting of passive infrared (PIR) activated floodlights to the vessel could be considered to ensure that the lights do come on, even if attackers are not observed in advance.

3   In practice however, it is difficult to maintain a full blackout of a merchant ship. The effectiveness of this approach will ultimately depend on the level of moonlight, but primarily on the vigilance and the control of emitted light by of the crew. While suddenly turning on the lights may alarm or dazzle attackers it could also place the crew at a disadvantage at a crucial point, through temporary loss of their night vision.

4   To this end it is recommended that crews be instructed on how to preserve and enhance their night vision. Crew members can maximise their visual acuity by the simple expedient of not looking directly at the intended point. By focussing a few degrees in any direction away from the target, peripheral vision is utilised, and this improves both motion detection and night sight. Ensuring that crews are adequately briefed and trained is essential and thought should be given on how to warn crew members that light is about to be employed, without forewarning the attackers.

Lighting at anchor
13.43

1   Whilst at anchor or in harbour, vessels are not so constrained by the Collision Regulations, and are at liberty to light their ships as they see fit (as long as they do not dazzle other mariners). The upper decks of many vessels are often poorly lit, however, even when all of their deck lights are switched on. It is recommended that the number and placement of deck lights be reviewed in order to reduce the number of areas vulnerable to night infiltration. Lighting of vulnerable areas could be linked to an alarm system or detection/surveillance equipment.

2   Crew members on duty outside secure areas when in port, or at anchor, should remain in shadow whenever possible to avoid being silhouetted by deck lights as this may make them targets for seizure by approaching attackers.

Closed Circuit Television (CCTV)
13.44

1   As an additional deterrent, deck lighting could be augmented by effective CCTV coverage.

Companies should seek to provide CCTV coverage, with recording facilities, of the main access points to the vessel's secure areas (13.45), the passageways approaching the entrances to key areas and the bridge. If possible, the recording equipment should be housed in a secure environment or at least in an unobtrusive place, so that there is an increased chance of it surviving any attack on the ship. The ISPS Code requires that proper procedures are in place for the maintenance of CCTV systems including the documentation, reporting and repair of defects.

Secure areas
13.45

1   In accordance with the counter-piracy plan, the master and crew should ensure that they have a secure area(s) on board to which they can safely retreat if attackers successfully board and hijack the vessel. The term "secure area" should not be confused with the term Restricted Area defined by the ISPS Code, which requires access control measures to sensitive parts of a ship (13.33). However it would be logical to select secure area(s) within the vessel's Restricted Area because robust access control measures will already be in place.

2   All doors to a designated secure area(s) should be secured and/or controlled at all times and should be regularly inspected and monitored, for example by using CCTV. Consideration should be given to the installation of special access control systems to these areas. Ports, scuttles and windows, which could provide access should also be securely closed and have laminated glass installed if possible. Deadlights should be shut and clipped tightly. Internal doors within secure areas which give immediate access to key areas such as the bridge, radio office, engine room and master's cabin should be strengthened and have special access control systems and automatic alarms. Certainly basic measures such as a spy-hole or an electronic door viewer should be considered for fitting to both the master's cabin door and the internal bridge door in order to establish who is on the other side before opening. Access control measures, surveillance and patrolling should all be stepped up in accordance with the Security Level that the vessel is operating at.

3   Securing doors providing access to, and egress from, secure areas may give rise to concern over safety in the event of an accident. In any situation where there is a conflict between safety and security, safety considerations should be paramount. Nevertheless, attempts should be made to incorporate appropriate safety provisions to ensure ease of egress and to permit access by rescue or emergency parties while allowing entry and exit to be securely controlled.

4   To prevent the seizure of individual crew members by attackers (seizure and threatening a crew member is one of the more common means of attackers gaining control over a ship), all crew members not engaged on essential outside duties should remain within a secure area during the hours of darkness. Those whose duties necessarily involve working outside such areas at night should remain in constant communication with the bridge and should have practised using alternative routes to return to a secure area in the event of an attack. Crew members who fear they may not be able to return to a secure area during an attack should select places in advance in which they can take temporary refuge. There should also be designated muster areas within the vessel's secure areas where the crew can muster during an attack and communicate their location and numbers to the bridge.

Alarms
13.46

1   Alarm signals, including the ship's whistle, should be sounded on the approach of attackers. Alarms and other signs of response can discourage attackers. Alarm signals or announcements which indicate where the attackers may be about to board, or have boarded, may help crew members in exposed locations to select the most appropriate route by which to return to a secure area.

Evasive manoeuvring and use of hoses
13.47

1   Masters should consider "riding off" boats being used by attackers by use of heavy wheel movements as they approach, provided that navigational safety permits. The effect of the bow wave and wash may be enough to deter potential attackers and make it more difficult for them to use poles or grappling irons. Manoeuvres of this kind should not be used in confined or congested waters, close inshore or by ships constrained by their draught.

2   The use of water hoses should also be considered, although the use of such equipment may be counter-productive in circumstances when attackers are carrying firearms, since the use of a water hose may antagonise the attackers, causing them to start

shooting. It is entirely at the master's discretion whether such a defensive measure should be employed, and careful consideration be given to its use.

3   Hoses may be difficult to train on approaching craft if evasive manoeuvring is taking place. However, water pressures of more than 550 kilopascals(Kpa)/ 80 psi and above have successfully deterred and repulsed attackers in the past. Not only does the attacker have to fight against the jet of water, but the flow may swamp their boat, damaging engines and electrical systems. Special fittings for training hoses might be considered which would provide a measure of protection for the hose operator. Spare fire hoses could be rigged and lashed down in vulnerable areas of the vessel whilst underway, and at anchor points and gangways whilst at anchor, which could be pressurised at short notice if a potential attack is detected.

4   Successful use of evasive manoeuvring and hoses will depend on a determination to deter attackers and delay their boarding for long enough to permit all crew members to gain sanctuary in secure areas. Continued heavy wheel movements once the attackers are on board may lessen their confidence that they will be able to return safely to their craft and may persuade them to disembark quickly. However, responses of this kind could lead to reprisals by the attackers if they seize crew members, and should not be undertaken unless the master is confident that they can be used to advantage without risk to those on board. They should not be used if the attackers have already seized crew members.

Use of distress flares
13.48

1   The only flares authorised for carriage on board are those intended for use if the ship is in distress and in need of immediate assistance. As with the unwarranted use of the distress signal on the radio (13.64) use of distress flares simply to alert shipping rather than to indicate that the ship is in grave and imminent danger may reduce their effect in the situations in which they are intended to be used. Radio transmissions should be used to alert shipping of the risk of attacks rather than distress flares. Distress flares should only be used when the master considers that his vessel is being placed in grave and/or imminent danger by the attacker's actions.

Firearms
13.49

1   The carriage and use of firearms for personal protection or protection of a ship is strongly discouraged and is not authorised by the British Government for UK flagged vessels. Carriage of firearms has the potential to escalate an already dangerous situation, and any firearms on board may themselves become an attractive target for an attacker. The use of firearms requires aptitude and specialist training; the risk of accidents with firearms carried on board ship is high. In some jurisdictions, killing a national may have unforeseen consequences, even for a person who believes that they have acted in self-defence.

Action once boarded

General information
13.50

1   There will be occasions when attackers succeed in boarding, despite early detection and countermeasures. The majority of pirates and armed robbers are opportunists seeking an easy target and time may not be on their side, particularly if the crew are aware that they are aboard and are raising the alarm. However, the attackers may seek to compensate for the pressure of time they face by escalating their threats or the degree of violence that they employ.

Priorities once boarding has taken place
13.51

1   Once attackers have boarded, the actions of the master and crew should be aimed at:

Securing the greatest level of safety for those on board the ship.

Seeking to ensure that the crew remain in control of the navigation of the ship.

Securing the earliest possible departure of the attackers from the ship.

Other considerations
13.52

1   **Confined waters.** If it is possible to maintain control of the vessel, it is advisable, when navigating in confined waters, to reduce speed and/or head for open waters, reducing the risk of grounding or collision if the attackers were to gain control.

2   **Risk to the vessel and crew.** The options available to the master and crew will depend on the extent to which the attackers have secured control. If attackers gain access to the bridge or engine room, or seize crew members who they can threaten, the master or crew may be coerced into complying with their wishes. However, even if the crew are all safely within secure areas, the master will always have to consider the overall risk to the vessel, and the damage the attackers could cause outside secure areas, e.g. by using firebombs to start fires on a tanker or chemical carrier.

3   **Evasive manoeuvring.** If the master is certain that all crew members are within secure areas and that the attackers cannot gain access, and that by their actions outside secure areas they cannot place the entire vessel at imminent risk, then consideration may be given to undertaking evasive manoeuvres of the type referred to in 13.47, to encourage the attackers to return to their craft.

4   **Resisting the attackers.** The possibility of a sortie by a well-organised crew has, in the past, successfully persuaded attackers to leave a vessel, but the use of this tactic is only appropriate if it can be undertaken without risk.

For an action such as this to be attempted, the master must have clear knowledge of the whereabouts of the attackers, that they are not carrying firearms or other potentially lethal weapons and that the number of crew involved significantly outnumbers the attackers they will face. If a sortie party can use water hoses they stand an increased chance of success.

5   The intention should be to encourage the attackers back to their craft. Crew members should not seek to come between the attackers and their craft nor should they seek to capture attackers, as to do so may increase resistance, and increase the risk faced by members of a sortie party. Once outside the secure area, a sortie party should always stay together. Pursuit of an individual attacker by a lone crew member should not be undertaken, as the crew member may become isolated and be seized by the attackers.

6   Crew members should operate together, remain in constant communication with the bridge and should be recalled if their line of withdrawal to a secure area becomes threatened.

Apprehended pirates
13.53

1   Any apprehended attacker should be placed in secure confinement and well cared for. Arrangements should be made for transfer to the custody of law enforcement officers or naval authorities of a port or coastal state (depending on whether the attack occurred in territorial or international waters) at the earliest possible opportunity. Any evidence relating to the attacker's activities should also be handed over to authorities taking custody.

Action if pirates achieve control

Negotiation
13.54

1   If the attackers gain control of the engine room or bridge, seize crew members or pose an imminent threat to the safety of the vessel, the master or officer in charge should remain calm and attempt to negotiate. The aim must be to maintain control of navigation, the safe return of any hostages and the early departure of the attackers. In most circumstances, compliance with the attackers' demands will be the only safe option, particularly if it is assessed that resistance or obstruction of any kind would be futile or dangerous.

CCTV
13.55

1   In the event of attackers gaining control, crew members should leave CCTV recorders running if at all possible.

Equipment
13.56

1   There have been occasions when entire crews have been locked up. Consideration should therefore be given to placing equipment in areas where the crew could be detained, which might assist subsequently in escaping. See 13.69 for advice regarding communications equipment.

Communications
13.57

1   If ordered not to make any form of transmission informing shore authorities of the attack, any such order should be complied with. The attackers may carry equipment capable of detecting radio signals, including satellite communications. All vessels which fall within the scope of the ISPS Code should be fitted with a Ship Security Alert System (13.34), which can be activated without attracting the attention of the attackers.

Post-attack action and incident reporting

Post attack reports

13.58

1   An immediate post attack report should be made to the relevant Rescue and Co-ordination Centre (RCC) and through them to the law enforcement agencies or naval authorities of the port or Coastal State. As well as information on the identity and location of the vessel, any damage or any injuries to crew members should be reported as should the direction in which the attackers departed together with brief details of their numbers and, if possible, a description of their craft. If the crew have apprehended an attacker, that should also be reported (13.71).

2   If an attack has resulted in the death or serious injury to any person or serious damage to the vessel herself, an immediate signal in line with statutory requirements should also be sent to the ship's maritime administration. A report of an attack is vital if follow up action is to be taken by the ship's maritime administration.

3   Any CCTV or other recordings of the incident should be secured. If practicable, areas that have been damaged or rifled should be secured and remain untouched by crew members pending possible forensic examination by the law enforcement agencies of a port or Coastal State. Crew members who came into contact with the attackers should be asked to prepare individual reports on their experience noting in particular any distinguishing features, which could help subsequent identification of the attackers. A full inventory, including a description of any personal possessions or equipment taken, with serial numbers when known, should also be prepared.

4   As soon as possible after the incident a fuller report should be transmitted to the authorities of the State in whose waters the attack occurred, or if on the high seas to the authorities of the nearest Coastal State. Due and serious consideration should be given to complying with any request made by the competent authorities of the Coastal State to allow law enforcement officers to board, take statements from crew members and undertake forensic and other investigations. Copies of any CCTV recordings or photographs should be provided if available.

5   Any report transmitted to a Coastal State should also be transmitted to the vessel's maritime administration at the earliest opportunity. A complete report of the incident, including details of any follow up action that was taken, or difficulties that may have been experienced, should eventually be submitted to the vessel's maritime administration.

6   The reports received by maritime administrations may be used in any diplomatic approaches made by national authorities to the government of the port or Coastal State regarding the incident and will also provide the basis for any report to the IMO, required under the relevant IMO Assembly Resolutions on piracy and armed robbery at sea. The format required for reports to the IMO is at 13.70.

Historically, the lack of adequate and accurate reporting of attacks has directly affected the ability to secure governmental and international action. Reports may also contribute to future refining and updating of advice given to other mariners.

7   Reports to the RCC, port or Coastal State and the ship's maritime administration should also be made, even if an attack was unsuccessful.

It is hoped that using RCCs will eliminate communication difficulties. However, if a UK flagged vessel experiences difficulties in establishing, or has been unable to establish, contact with the authorities of the relevant port or Coastal State, then the UK Department for Transport should be contacted outlining the difficulties experienced.

8   Contact details are as follows:

Address:
Maritime Security Branch
Transport Security and Contingencies Directorate (TRANSEC)
Department for Transport
Zone 5/5
Southside
105 Victoria Street
London SW1E 6DT
Maritime Helpdesk (Office hours):
+44 (0) 20 7944 2844
Duty Officer (Out of hours):
+44 (0) 20 7944 5999
Fax:
+44 (0) 20 7944 2174
Email:
maritimesecurity@dft.gsi.gov.uk
General enquiries (24 hours):
+44 (0) 870 600 6505
infoline@mcga.gov.uk

Jurisdiction and intervention

General information

13.59

1   Piracy is an offence committed on the high seas, or in a place outside the jurisdiction (territorial sea) of any State. A pirate who has been apprehended on the high seas for committing an act of piracy against merchant shipping should therefore be dealt with under the laws of the Flag State of his/her captors by mutual agreement with any other substantially interested States. (See MSC Circular 622/Rev 1 for definitions and additional information/guidance).

Within territorial waters, jurisdiction over armed robbers rests solely with the Coastal State.

Military intervention

13.60

1   International law requires any warship or other government vessel to repress piracy on the high seas. Such vessels would be expected to take action if they encountered pirates, or come to the aid of any vessel under attack by pirates, on the high seas. A naval vessel of any State can pursue pirates on the high seas, but not into the territorial waters of another State without that State's prior consent.

2   Warships on innocent passage within the territorial waters of another State cannot exercise any enforcement powers or pursue attackers without prior authorisation from the Coastal State. However, they may render humanitarian assistance to a vessel in danger or distress.

3   Royal Navy vessels will take all appropriate measures to respond to incidents of piracy on the high seas, and to provide humanitarian assistance to vessels attacked in territorial waters, whenever they are on hand to do so. However, the likelihood of a Royal Navy vessel being nearby when an incident occurs, particularly in distant waters, will not be great. UK flagged vessels will therefore, need to rely on their own vigilance and resources to prevent attacks and on the capability of Coastal States to suppress piracy or armed robbery.

Role of Coastal States and Port Authorities
13.61

1   The Government of the United Kingdom calls upon Coastal and Port States to ensure the safety and freedom from attack of vessels exercising their rights of innocent passage in the territorial sea of a Coastal State and in their ports. The Government also requests and requires Coastal States to pursue, prosecute and punish pirates or armed robbers who may operate, reside or have their base of operations in their territory. The activities of pirates and armed robbers now pose a real threat not only to those on board, but also to the territory and interests of Coastal States through the threat of a major pollution incident following an attack. The Government urges companies, masters and crews to co-operate to the greatest possible extent with the authorities of Coastal States in their efforts to pursue and prosecute attackers.

Communications

General information
13.62

1   The following information is included as a general guide. Full details of all communications procedures in the event of a piracy incident are given in *Admiralty List of Rado Signals Vol 1*.

2   Guidance in the use of radio communications by ships under attack or threat of attack from pirates or armed robbers is available in Maritime Safety Committee (MSC) Circular 805 published in June 1997. This circular recommends that a Piracy/Armed Robbery Attack Message (13.67 and 13.68) should be sent through Inmarsat-C or on an available DSC or other distress and safety frequency. Given that some pirates or armed robbers may carry equipment capable of detecting all radio signals, including satellite communications, this circular also recommends that communication should not be attempted if a ship has been boarded and its crew specifically ordered to maintain radio silence.

Communications procedures
13.63

1   The Navigational Officer on Watch (OOW) should be on duty at all times and should be extra vigilant when vessels are in, or approaching, maritime transit chokepoints, potential ambush sites and areas in which piracy is prevalent. The master should not normally perform this duty, although on occasions this may be unavoidable. Since the mandatory introduction of GMDSS, the OOW now normally performs the radio watch. To ensure that a vessel's bridge is adequately manned when transiting potentially hazardous waters, it is advisable that an appropriately qualified, dedicated crew member keeps radio watch. This allows the master and OOW to concentrate on navigational duties whilst maintaining the extra vigilance that is required when operating in high-risk areas.

2   Prior to entering areas where attacks have occurred, OOWs should practice and perfect radio operational procedures and ensure that all transmitters, including satellite systems are fully operational and available for immediate use on distress and safety frequencies. Where a GMDSS installation is provided and "ship's position" data is not automatically updated from an associated electronic navigation aid, OOWs are strongly recommended to enter the ship's position manually at regular intervals into the appropriate communications equipment. Where an INMARSAT system is available, it may prove useful to draft and store "standard messages" (13.66), ready for use in an emergency, either in the equipment's memory or on a computer disk. A special code for piracy/armed robbery attack is now available for use on Digital Selective Calling (DSC) equipment. Where practicable and appropriate, DSC equipment should be modified to incorporate this facility.

Masters should ensure that all procedures to generate a distress alert on any communications equipment are clearly marked on, or near, the equipment (with the exception of the Ship Security Alert System as this is a covert system and the obvious positioning of such procedures is likely to reduce the benefits of carrying the equipment). Masters should also ensure that all appropriate crew members are briefed on the operation of such equipment.

3   Masters should bear in mind the possibility that attackers may monitor both ship to ship and ship to shore communications, using intercepted information to select their targets. Caution should therefore be exercised when transmitting information regarding intended transit tracks or details of cargo and valuables on board in areas where attacks occur. The implementation of the AIS broadcast system and the availability of AIS information online means that the location of vessels sailing within 35 miles of the shore is now more accessible to the public. Masters need to be aware of this when transiting high-risk areas.

Radio watchkeeping and responses
13.64

1   A constant radio watch should be maintained with the appropriate shore or naval authorities when in areas where attacks have occurred. Continuous watch should also be maintained on all distress and safety frequencies, particularly VHF Channel 16 and 2182 kHz. Masters should also ensure that all maritime safety information broadcasts for the area are monitored. As it is anticipated that Inmarsat's enhanced group calling system (EGC) will normally be used for such broadcasts using the SafetyNET(SM) service, companies should ensure that a suitably configured EGC receiver is continuously available when in, or approaching, areas where there is a risk of attack. Companies should also consider fitting a dedicated receiver for this purpose, i.e. one that is not incorporated into a ship earth station being used for commercial purposes, to ensure that no urgent broadcasts are missed.

2 **Note.** The IMB Piracy Reporting Centre broadcasts daily status reports to ships in Indian, Atlantic and Pacific Ocean Regions on the SafetyNET service of Inmarsat C at 0001 UTC daily.

3 The IMO recommends in MSC Circular 597 (1992) and Addendum (1993) that reports concerning attacks by pirates or armed robbers should be made to the relevant Rescue Co-ordination Centre (RCC) for the area. Information on RCCs may be found in the Search and Rescue Section of of *Admiralty List of Radio Signals Volume 5*. MSC Circular 597 also recommends that governments should arrange for the RCCs to be able to pass reports of attacks to the appropriate law enforcement agencies or naval authorities. The IMO subsequently published MSC Circular 622/Rev 1 in 1999 which gives detailed recommendations to governments to assist in the prevention and suppression of piracy and armed robbery against ships. In May 2002 the IMO published MSC Circular 623/Rev 3 as an equivalent guide to companies. Reports of attacks against UK flagged vessels should also be made to the CSO and TRANSEC via MRCC Falmouth. Other Flag States will have their own reporting requirements.

4 If masters are unable to contact the relevant RCC, it is recommended that they report the incident to the IMB Piracy Reporting Centre which will pass the message to appropriate authorities (13.79).

5 If suspicious movements are identified which raise fears that an attack may be imminent, the master is advised to contact the relevant RCC. Where the master believes such movements could constitute a direct danger to navigation, consideration should be given to broadcasting an "All Stations" "Danger Message" as a warning to other ships in the vicinity as well as advising the appropriate RCC. A danger message should be transmitted in plain language on a VHF working frequency following "safety" priority. All such messages shall be preceded by the safety signal (Securite).

6 When, in his opinion, there is conclusive evidence that the safety of his ship is threatened, the master should immediately contact the relevant RCC and, if considered appropriate, authorise broadcast of an "All Stations" "Urgency Message" on VHF Channel 16, or any other radio communications service considered to be appropriate; e.g. Inmarsat, etc. All such messages shall be preceded by the appropriate Urgency Signal (PAN PAN) and/or a DSC call on VHF Channel 70 and/or 2187.5 kHz using the "All Ships Urgency" category. If the Urgency signal has been used and an attack does not, in fact develop, the message should be cancelled as soon as it knows that action is no longer necessary. This message of cancellation should similarly be addressed to "All Stations".

7 Should an attack occur and, in the opinion of the master, the vessel or crew are in grave and imminent danger requiring immediate assistance, the master should immediately authorise the broadcast of a distress message, preceded by the appropriate distress alerts, using the radio communication systems most appropriate for the area taking into account its GMDSS designation; i.e. A1, A2, A3 or A4. The appropriate RCC should acknowledge receipt and attempt to establish communications. To minimise delay, if using a ship earth station, vessels should ensure the coast earth station associated with the RCC is used.

8 Masters should bear in mind that the distress signal is provided for use only in cases where the vessel and/or her crew are in grave or immediate danger and that its use for less urgent purposes might result in insufficient attention being paid to calls from other vessels in genuine need of immediate assistance. Care and discretion must therefore be employed in its use to prevent future devaluation. Where the transmission of the distress signal is not fully justified, use should be made of the Urgency signal. The Urgency signal has priority over all communications other than Distress signals.

Operation of AIS
13.65

1 The risk of operating AIS whilst a vessel is transiting through an area known to have a high level of piracy attacks is that the ship can easily be targeted and located. This is especially the case if potential attackers in the vicinity have been able to obtain their own receiver. Additionally, the advent of open source on-line AIS information has also increased the visibility of vessels using AIS. Whilst ISPS Regulations discourage the turning off of AIS as this may affect the safety of the ship, if a situation arises where a master feels threatened by keeping AIS turned on, UK flagged vessels should turn AIS off while the threat remains present, provided that a proper risk assessment has been conducted. Masters of vessels of other flag states should comply with national guidance.

Standard message formats

General information
13.66

1 The following standard formats were agreed by the IMO Sub-Committee on Radio Communications in 1993 and updated by MSC Circular 622/Rev 1 published in 1999, and are laid out in the following paragraphs.

Initial message – piracy attack alert
13.67

Ship's name and call sign.
Inmarsat ID (plus ocean region code), IMO number and MMSI.
MAYDAY/DISTRESS ALERT (see Note below) URGENCY SIGNAL PIRACY/ARMED ROBBERY ATTACK
Ship's position (and time of position in UTC), course and speed
Nature of Event.

Note. The position given should be as accurate as possible including latitude and longitude co-ordinates or as bearing and distance from a conspicuous landmark.

Piracy attack/sighting/suspicious act report
13.68

PIRACY ATTACK/SIGHTING/SUSPICIOUS ACT REPORT
Ship's name, callsign and IMO number
Reference: Initial **PIRACY/ARMED ROBBERY ALERT**
Position of incident
Date/time of incident (UTC)
Details of incident, including:
Method of attack
Description of suspect craft.
Number and brief description of attackers, including weapons carried and language spoken
Injuries to crew
Damage to vessel
Brief details of stolen property/cargo
Last observed movements of suspect ship(s) e.g.
Date/time/course/position/speed
Whether assistance required
Preferred communications with reporting ship e.g.
Appropriate Coast Radio Station. HF/MF/VHF, Inmarsat ID (plus ocean region code), MMSI
Date/time of report (UTC)

1 **Notes.**

(1) It is expected that this message will be a 'Distress Message' because the crew and/or vessel will be in grave or imminent danger when under attack. Where this is not the case, the word MAYDAY/DISTRESS ALERT is to be omitted.

(2) Use of distress priority (3) in the Inmarsat system will not require MAYDAY/DISTRESS ALERT to be included.

(3) If the master and crew do not have time to follow the above procedure in the event of an attack, then the covert Ship Security Alert should be activated to inform the Company Security Officer and the relevant Flag State's competent authority.

(4) The position given should be as accurate as possible including latitude and longitude co-ordinates or as bearing and distance from a conspicuous landmark.

Secreted VHF Transceiver
13.69

1 As a result of communications equipment being damaged in the past by attackers to prevent an early alarm being raised, particularly when attacks have taken place off a port, companies and masters are recommended to secrete a VHF transceiver to allow contact to be established with the shore authorities if the main communications equipment is put out of action. Consideration could also be given to the installation of handheld iridium telephones. These sets have a longer range than the traditional VHF transceiver, and would allow the master to inform, and converse with, more distant authorities as well as the authorities in the region of the attack.

Reports to the IMO
13.70

1 Following an incident/attack, a report should be rendered to the IMO in the following format:

IMO Number	
Name/Type of ship/Flag/Gross Tonnage	
Date/Time/Position of Attack	
Details of Incident	
Consequences for crew/ship/cargo	
Action taken by master and crew	
Was the incident reported to the Coastal Authority? If so, to whom?	
Reporting State or international organisation	
Action taken by Coastal State	

Note. The position given should be as accurate as possible including latitude and longitude co-ordinates or as bearing and distance from a conspicuous landmark.

Reports to the ICC-IMB
13.71

1 A post-incident report should be rendered to the ICC-IMB in the following format:

Vessel particulars/details	
1. Name of Vessel	
2. IMO Number	
3. Flag	
4. Type of Vessel	
5. Tonnages: GRT/NRT/DWT	
6. Owners (Address and contact details)	
7. Managers (Address and contact details)	
8. Last port/next port	
9. Cargo details (type/quantity)	
Details of Incident	
10. Date and time of incident (Local and UTC)	
11. Position	
12. Nearest Land mark/location	
13. Port/town/anchorage location	
14. Country/nearest country	
15. Status (berthed/anchored/steaming	
16. Own ship's speed	
17. Own ship's freeboard during attack	
18. Weather during attack (rain/fog/mist/clear etc). Wind speed/direction. Sea/swell height.	

Details of Incident (continued)	
19. Type of attack (boarded/attempted)	
20. Consequences for ship/crew/cargo (Any crew killed/injured). (Cash/items stolen)	
21. Area of ship attacked	
Details of raiding party	
22. Number of pirates/robbers	
23. Dress/physical appearance	
24. Language spoken	
25. Weapons used	
26. Distinctive details	
27. Craft used	
28. Method of approach	
29. Duration of attack	
30. Aggressive/violent	
Further details	
31. Action taken by master and crew	
32. Was incident reported to the Coastal Authority? If so, to whom?	
33. Action taken by the authorities	
34. Number of crew and nationality	
35. Please **attach** with this report a brief description/full report/master/crew statement of the attack and photographs taken (if any)	

Contact details are at 13.78.

Communications by vessels under attack in the Gulf of Aden or Red Sea
13.72
1   If Attacked by Pirates in GOA/Red Sea:
Activate the Emergency Communication Plan.
Make 'Mayday' call on VHF Ch 16 (and back-up Ch 08, which is monitored by naval units).
Send a distress message via the DSC (Digital Selective Calling) system and Inmarsat-C as applicable.

2   Establish telephone communication with UK Maritime Trade Operations **(UKMTO) Dubai**. If time permits, call in order of priority:
The UK Maritime Trade Operations (UKMTO) Dubai.
The Maritime Security Centre – Horn of Africa MSC(HOA).
The International Maritime Bureau (IMB).
Note. All contact details are contained in the Anti-Piracy Contact Table which can be found in *Admiralty List of Radio Signals Volume 1(1) and (2).*

Maritime Security Centre – Horn of Africa (MSC-HOA)

General information
13.73
1   The EU, in cooperation with Lloyd's Register – Fairplay, has established a web-based resource for ships to receive the latest alerts and register their vessels prior to transiting high risk areas in the region. Owners and operators are encouraged to register with the Maritime Security Centre – Horn of Africa MSC(HOA) at www.mschoa.org.

2   MSC(HOA) is the planning and coordination authority for European Union Forces in the Gulf of Aden and the area off the coast of Somalia. UKMTO Dubai is the first point of contact for ships in the region. The day-to-day interface between masters and the military is provided by UKMTO Dubai, who talk to the ships and liaise directly with MSC(HOA) and the naval commanders at sea. UKMTO requires regular updates on the position and intended movements (PIM) of vessels in order for naval units to maintain an accurate picture of shipping. Masters are requested to provide details of their transit, as well as the type, nature and number/quantity of passengers and cargo prior to entering high risk areas.

EU Operation ATALANTA Mission
13.74
1   The European Union Naval Force (EUNAVFOR) Anti-Piracy Operation off the coast of Somalia is named Op ATALANTA and has been established in support of the United Nations Security Council (UNSC). Resolutions 1814, 1816, 1836 and 1846 (2008). The Operation was established in December 2008 with its Headquarters in Northwood, UK. MSC(HOA) has been established and is run by the EU Naval Force (EU NAVFOR). It is the Coordination Centre with a mission to safeguard merchant shipping operating in the Gulf of Aden (GOA), off the Horn of Africa and in the Somali Basin. The website www.mschoa.org provides a huge amount of up to date advice, guidance and reporting procedures for the use of the maritime community. It also has the authority to liaise with other organisations and States involved in combating acts of piracy and armed robbery off the Somali coast.

2   EUNAVFOR ATALANTA uses military forces at its disposal, cooperating with other states operating in the region, to provide protection to all merchant vessels in the Gulf of Aden (GOA). This is achieved through close coordination of surface units, maritime patrol aircraft and helicopters, in the Internationally Recommended Transit Corridor (IRTC) (13.76), which transits through the Maritime Security Patrol Area (MSPA) (13.75), other areas of the Gulf of Aden and the Somali Basin which suffer from a high risk of piracy.

Maritime Security Patrol Area (MSPA)
13.75
1   The Commander of the U.S. Naval Central Command, coordinating CTF 150, established an MSPA in August 2008 in support of an IMO call for international assistance to discourage attacks on commercial vessels transiting the Gulf of Aden.

The MSPA is a geographic area in the Gulf of Aden, not marked or defined by navigational marks. A 'transit corridor' has been established through the MSPA to permit easier protection of merchant vessels

2   Coalition forces patrol the MSPA on a routine basis. The MSPA is not marked or defined by visual navigational means, and is a naval military term used by warships when communicating with each other. The MSPA should not be confused with the IRTC for the Gulf of Aden. The IRTC is the recommended path through the Gulf of Aden. MSPA patrols are intended to monitor activity both inside and outside the corridor. Naval vessels patrolling the MSPA provide a measure of deterrence through their presence, but due to the vast area of the Gulf of Aden and the open waters east of Somalia, and given the high volume of shipping in the region, the safety of all ships cannot be guaranteed. Masters are therefore recommended to continue to employ all available defensive measures to make their vessels less vulnerable to attack when operating in the Gulf of Aden

Internationally Recommended Transit Corridor (IRTC)
13.76

1   The IRTC is not marked or defined by visual navigational means, nor is it intended to be a dedicated traffic separation scheme but in order for warship patrols to be effective, vessels transiting the Gulf of Aden are strongly encouraged to conduct their passage through the IRTC in groups, based on their transit speed.

The corridor passes through the following coordinates:

12°15′N 45°00′E
12°35′N 45°00′E
13°35′N 49°00′E
13°40′N 49°00′E
14°10′N 50°00′E
14°15′N 50°00′E
14°35′N 53°00′E
14°45′N 53°00′E.

Action in the event of military intervention
13.77

1   In the event of military action being taken upon a vessel during a piracy incident, the crew should keep low to the deck, cover their heads with their hands (always ensure hands are visible and not holding anything) and make no sudden movements unless so directed by friendly forces, and be prepared to answer questions regarding identity and status onboard.

International Chamber of Commerce - International Maritime Bureau

General information
13.78

1   The ICC International Maritime Bureau (IMB) is a specialised division of the International Chamber of Commerce (ICC). The IMB is a non-profit making organisation, established in 1981 to act as a focal point in the fight against all types of maritime crime and malpractice. The IMO in its resolution A 504 (XII) (5) and (9) adopted on 20 November 1981, has inter alia, urged governments and all interested parties/organisations to cooperate and exchange information with each other and the IMB. The IMB also has an observer status with the International Criminal Police Organization (ICPO – INTERPOL).

Piracy Reporting Centre
13.79

1   ICC-IMB established the Piracy Reporting Centre (PRC) in October 1992 in Kuala Lumpur, Malaysia. The PRC is continuously manned and calls can be made from anywhere in the world with the assurance that each call and query will be answered by a fully trained Duty Officer.

The PRC broadcasts daily reports of pirate activity to all world piracy hotspots, using the Inmarsat SafetyNET system (see *Admiralty List of Radio Signals Volume 5* for details of the SafetyNET System). The daily warnings include details of the latest attacks, giving their locations and detailed descriptions of the number of pirates and their vessel(s). The warnings also list areas with a risk of pirate activity. The centre provides its services free of charge to all vessels irrespective of ownership or flag. Masters are requested to report all attacks and attempted attacks, in port, at anchor or underway to the PRC.

PRC Services
13.80

1   The following services are offered by the PRC:
To receive reports of suspicious or unexplained craft movements and armed robbery from vessels and to alert other vessels and law enforcement agencies in the area.
To issue status reports of piracy and armed robbery via daily broadcasts on Inmarsat C through its SafetyNET service. Vessels can also obtain these status reports by contacting the PRC.
To collate and analyse information received and issue consolidated reports to relevant bodies including the IMO.
To assist owners and crews of vessels that have been attacked.
To locate vessels that have been seized by pirates and recover stolen cargoes.

Reporting
13.81

1   The IMB strongly encourages masters and owners to report all incidents of actual and attempted piracy and armed robbery to the IMB PRC. This is the first step in the response chain, and vital in ensuring that adequate resources are allocated by governments to deal with the problem. A set of transparent statistics from an independent, non-political, international organisation such as the IMB PRC acts as an effective catalyst to achieve this goal.

Piracy Reporting Service
13.82

1   The PRC maintains a 24 hour watch every day of the year, and acts on reports of suspicious shipping movements, piracy and armed robbery at sea, worldwide. It broadcasts daily status bulletins via satellite, recording attacks on shipping worldwide.

The regular reports contain details of the location and nature of attacks on shipping and allow companies to put their masters on special alert when they are passing through waters in which recent pirate attacks have been reported.

Weekly piracy reports on the Internet

13.83

1   Weekly reports of attacks and warnings compiled from daily status bulletins are available on the internet at:

www.iccwbo.org/ccs/imb_piracy/
weekly_piracy_report.asp

Contact details

13.84

1   The IMB PRC can be contacted as follows:

Address	ICC International Maritime Bureau Piracy Reporting Centre PO Box 12559 50782 Kuala Lumpur Malaysia
Emergency reporting	Tel: +603 2078 5763
Fax	+603 2078 5769
Telex	+84 34 199 (IMBPCI MA34199)

Email	imbkl@icc-ccs.org piracy@icc-ccs.org
Helplines	Tel: +603 2031 0014 (24 hours) Email: imbsecurity@icc-ccs.org.uk
Website	www.icc-ccs.org

IMB Head Office

13.85

1   The IMB has its Head Office in London, and can be used as a valuable source of advice. They can be contacted as follows:

ICC International Maritime Bureau
Cinnabar Wharf
26 Wapping High Street
London E1W 1NG
United Kingdom

Telephone:	+44 (0)207 423 6960
Fax:	+44 (0)207 423 6961
Email:	imb@icc-ccs.org
Website:	www.icc-ccs.org

Safety

International Safety Management Code (ISM)

Adoption

13.86

1   The International Safety Management Code (ISM) was adopted by the IMO Assembly in 1995. It has been in force since 1998 for passenger ships, oil and chemical tankers, bulk carriers, and cargo and passenger high-speed craft, and for other cargo ships and mobile offshore drilling units since 2002.

Objectives

13.87

1   The objectives of the code are to ensure safety at sea, prevention of human injury or loss of life, and avoidance of damage to the environment, in particular to the marine environment and to property.

Functional Requirements

13.88

1   Every company should develop, implement and maintain a safety management system which includes the following functional requirements:

A safety and environmental protection policy.

Instructions and procedures to ensure safe operation of ships and protection of the environment in compliance with relevant International and flag State legislation.

2   Defined levels of authority and lines of communication between, and amongst, shore and shipboard personnel.

Procedures for reporting accidents and non-conformities with the provisions of this code.

Procedures to prepare for and respond to emergency situations.

Procedures for internal audits and management reviews.

Details

13.89

1   For further information the full text of the ISM Code should be consulted.

Tonnages and Load Lines

Traditional tonnage measurements

13.90

1   **Displacement tonnage** is the weight of water displaced by a vessel and is equal to her weight and all that is in her.

Hence, displacement in tons equals the volume of water displaced (in cubic feet) divided by 35 or 36, according to whether the water is salt or fresh respectively. Displacement may also be quoted in tonnes.

2   **Deadweight tonnage** is the weight, in tons of 2240 lb or tonnes of 1000 kilograms, of cargo, stores, fuel, passengers and crew carried by a vessel when loaded to her maximum summer load line.

Gross tonnage is measured according to the law of the national authority with which a vessel is registered.

This measurement is, broadly, the capacity in cubic feet of the spaces within the hull and of the enclosed spaces above the deck available for cargo, stores, passengers and crew, with certain exceptions, divided by 100.

Thus, 100 cubic feet of capacity is equivalent to 1 gross ton.

3   **Net tonnage** is derived from gross tonnage by deducting spaces used for the accommodation of crew, navigation, machinery and fuel.

Suez and Panama Canal tonnages. Both Canal authorities have their own rules for the measurement of gross and net tonnage and ships using the canals are charged on these tonnages.

IMO tonnage measurements
13.91

1   Current tonnage regulations give effect to the *International Convention on the Tonnage Measurement of Ships, 1969*, convened by IMO.

     Gross tonnage under these regulations is derived from the moulded volume of the enclosed spaces of the entire vessel: it is used for comparing the size of one vessel with another. Most safety regulations are based on it.

2   **Net tonnage** is derived from a formula based on the volume of the cargo spaces, the number of passengers carried, the moulded depth of the vessel, and her summer draught: it is used as an indication of earning capacity, and for assessing dues and charges.

     Units are not employed: values obtained from the formulae are expressed directly as the "gross tonnage" or "net tonnage".

Load lines
13.92

1   All vessels require to be assigned and marked with load lines. The load lines indicate the draught to which a vessel may be loaded in the various designated zones which cover the oceans, and in fresh water.

     For details of load line zones, see *Ocean Passages for the World* or *Chart D 6083 — Load line regulations — zones, areas and seasonal periods*.

Pilot ladders and mechanical pilot hoists

Safety rules
13.93

1   The *International Convention for the Safety of Life at Sea, 1974*, Chapter V, Regulation 17 contains, among other regulations, the following:

     General.

     All arrangements used for pilot transfer shall efficiently fulfil their purpose of enabling pilots to embark and disembark safely. The appliances shall be kept clean, properly maintained and stowed and shall be regularly inspected to ensure that they are safe to use. They shall be used solely for the embarkation and disembarkation of personnel.

2   The rigging of the pilot transfer arrangements and the embarkation and disembarkation of a pilot shall be supervised by a responsible officer having means of communication with the navigating bridge who shall also arrange for the escort of the pilot by a safe route to and from the navigating bridge. Personnel engaged in rigging and operating any mechanical equipment shall be instructed in the safe procedures to be adopted and the equipment shall be tested prior to use.

3   **Transfer arrangements.**

     Arrangements shall be provided to enable the pilot to embark and disembark on either side of the ship.

     In all ships where the distance from sea level to the point of access to, or egress from, the ship exceeds 9 m, and when it is intended to embark and disembark pilots by means of the accommodation ladder, or by means of mechanical pilot hoists or other equally safe and convenient means in conjunction with a pilot ladder, the ship shall carry such equipment on each side, unless the equipment is capable of being transferred for use on either side.

4   Safe and convenient access to, and egress from, the ship shall be provided by either:

(1) A pilot ladder requiring a climb of not less than 1·5 m and not more than 9 m above the surface of the water so positioned and secured that:

     (aa) it is clear of any possible discharges from the ship;

     (bb) it is within the parallel body length of the ship and, as far as practicable, within the mid-ship half of the length of the ship;

     (cc) each step rests firmly against the ship's side; where constructional features, such as rubbing bands, would prevent the implementation of this provision, special arrangements shall, to the satisfaction of the Administration, be made to ensure that persons are able to embark and disembark safely;

     (dd) the single length of the pilot ladder is capable of reaching the water from the point of access to, or egress from, the ship and due allowance is made for all conditions of loading and trim of the ship, and for an adverse list of 15°; the securing strong points, shackles and securing ropes shall be at least as strong as the side ropes.

5   (2) An accommodation ladder in conjunction with the pilot ladder, or other equally safe and convenient means, whenever the distance from the surface of the water to the point of access to the ship is more than 9 m. The accommodation ladder shall be sited leading aft. When in use, the lower end of the accommodation ladder shall rest firmly against the ship's side within the parallel body length of the ship and, as far as is practicable, within the mid-ship half length and clear of all discharges; or

6   (3) A mechanical pilot hoist so located that it is within the parallel body length of the ship and, as far as is practicable, within the mid-ship half length of the ship and clear of all discharges.

Access to the ship
13.94

1   Means shall be provided to ensure safe, convenient and unobstructed passage for any person embarking on, or disembarking from, the ship between the head of the pilot ladder, or any accommodation ladder or other appliance, and the ship's deck. Where such passage is by means of:

     (1) a gateway in the rails or bulwark, adequate handholds shall be provided;

2   (2) a bulwark ladder, two handhold stanchions rigidly secured to the ship's structure at or near their bases and at higher points shall be fitted. The bulwark ladder shall be securely attached to the ship to prevent overturning.

     Shipside doors used for pilot transfer shall not open outwards.

Mechanical pilot hoists
13.95

1   (1) The mechanical pilot hoist and its ancillary equipment shall be of a type approved by the Administration. The pilot hoist shall be designed to

operate as a moving ladder to lift and lower one or more persons on the side of the ship. It shall be of such design and construction as to ensure that the pilot can be embarked and disembarked in a safe manner, including a safe access from the hoist to the deck and vice versa. Such access shall be gained directly by a platform securely guarded by handrails.

(2) Efficient hand gear shall be provided to lower or recover the person or persons carried, and kept ready for use in the event of power failure.

(3) The hoist shall be securely attached to the structure of the ship. Attachment shall not be solely by means of the ship's side rails. Proper and strong attachment points shall be provided for hoists of the portable type on each side of the ship.

2 (4) If belting is fitted in the way of the hoist position, such belting shall be cut back sufficiently to allow the hoist to operate against the ship's side.

(5) A pilot ladder shall be rigged adjacent to the hoist and available for immediate use so that access to it is available from the hoist at any point of its travel. The pilot ladder shall be capable of reaching the sea level from its own point of access to the ship.

3 (6) The position on the ships side where the hoist will be lowered shall be indicated.

(7) An adequate protected stowage position shall be provided for the portable hoist. In very cold weather, to avoid the danger of ice formation, the portable hoist shall not be rigged until its use is imminent.

Associated equipment
13.96
1 (1) The following associated equipment shall be kept at hand ready for immediate use when persons are being transferred:

(a) two man-ropes of not less than 28 mm in diameter properly secured to the ship if required by the pilot.
(b) a lifebuoy equipped with a self-igniting light;
(c) a heaving line.

(2) When required by paragraph 13.94, stanchions and bulwark ladders shall be provided.

Lighting
13.97
1 Adequate lighting shall be provided to illuminate the transfer arrangements overside, the position on deck where a person embarks or disembarks and the controls of the mechanical pilot hoist.

Construction, fitting and testing
13.98
1 The Regulation also gives details of the construction and fitting of pilot ladders and mechanical pilot hoists, and the testing of the latter.

Distress and Rescue

General information

Introduction
13.99
1 The success of rescue operations, whether by ship, life-boat, helicopter or any rescue equipment, may often depend on the co-operation of those in distress with their rescuers. A sound knowledge of search and rescue arrangements will not only help those in distress, but will ensure that the rescuers themselves are not endangered, and are able to reach the scene with minimum delay.

2 The radio watch on the international frequencies which certain classes of ship are required to keep at sea is one of the most important factors in rescue arrangements. Since these arrangements must often fail unless ships can alert each other or be alerted from shore for distress action, every ship fitted with suitable radio equipment should guard one or other of these distress frequencies for as long as is required, and longer if practicable.

Global Maritime Distress and Safety System (GMDSS)

Administration
13.100
1 GMDSS is an international system that uses terrestrial and satellite technology and ship-board radio systems to ensure, in the event of a marine distress, the rapid, automated alerting of shore-based communication and rescue authorities in addition to other ships in the immediate vicinity.

2 GMDSS was adopted by means of amendments to the International Convention for the Safety of Life at Sea (SOLAS), 1974. The amendments, contained in Chapter IV of SOLAS on Radiocommunications, were adopted in 1988 and became fully effective on 1 February 1999. From that date, all applicable vessels had to comply with the GMDSS requirements in SOLAS.

3 Implementation of the GMDSS requirements is the responsibility of Contracting Governments to SOLAS, and of the Administrations of individual countries which have ratified the GMDSS requirements into their national law. In practice, it also means that individual ship-owners are responsible for ensuring that their vessels meet GMDSS requirements, since they are required to obtain certificates from their respective Flag States certifying conformity with all relevant international regulations.

Objectives
13.101
1 Vessels fitted with GMDSS equipment are safer at sea and more likely to receive assistance in the event of a distress, because the GMDSS provides for automatic distress alerting and locating in the event that the vessel's staff do not have time to transmit a manual distress call. The GMDSS also requires vessels to carry Emergency Position Indicating Radio Beacons (EPIRBs) which float free from a sinking vessel and alert SAR authorities with the vessel's identity and location.

2   Under the GMDSS, all cargo vessels of 300 gt and above, and all passenger vessels engaged on international voyages, must be equipped with radio equipment that conforms to international standards set out in the system. The basic concept is that search and rescue (SAR) authorities ashore, as well as shipping in the immediate vicinity of the vessel in distress, will be rapidly alerted through terrestrial and satellite communication techniques so that they can assist in a co-ordinated SAR operation with the minimum of delay.

GMDSS Sea Areas
13.102

1   For GMDSS purposes, the world's oceans are divided into four different categories of Sea Area, and equipment requirements for specific vessels are determined by the category of Sea Area (or areas) within which they operate.

Area A1. Within the radiotelephone coverage of at least one VHF coast station in which DSC alerting is available. Such a coverage could typically extend 20 to 50 miles from the coast station.

2   **Area A2.** An area, excluding Sea Area A1, within the radiotelephone coverage of at least one MF coast station in which continuous DSC alerting is available. For planning purposes this area typically extends up to 150 miles offshore, but would exclude any A1 designated areas. In practice, satisfactory coverage may often be achieved up to 250 miles offshore.

Area A3. An area, excluding Sea Areas A1 and A2, within the coverage of an Inmarsat geostationary satellite in which continuous alerting is available. This area lies approximately between the parallels of 70°N and 70°S, but excludes A1 and/or A2 designated areas.

Area A4. Any area outside Sea Areas A1, A2 or A3. This is essentially the polar regions, N and S of 70° latitude.

GMDSS equipment
13.103

1   Coastal vessels are only required to carry minimal equipment if they do not operate beyond the range of shore-based VHF radio stations, but they may also carry satellite equipment. Some coasts, however, do not have shore-based VHF radio facilities so that,

although a vessel might be close to shore, the area concerned may be classed as a Sea Area A2 or A3.

Vessels which operate beyond Sea Area A1 are required to carry MF (or satellite) equipment as well as VHF.

2   Vessels which operate beyond MF range have to carry Inmarsat satellite equipment in addition to VHF and MF.

Vessels which operate in Sea Area A4 are required to carry HF, MF and VHF equipment.

The limits of the sea areas described above are defined by the Administrations providing the shore facilities. For further details of GMDSS see *Admiralty List of Radio Signals Volume 5.*

Ship reporting systems
13.104

1   A number of nations operate ship reporting systems. Among these systems is the AMVER (Automated Mutual-assistance VEssel Rescue) System, an international maritime mutual-assistance organisation operated by the US Coast Guard. For details of these systems, see *Admiralty List of Radio Signals Volume 6.*

UK waters
13.105

1   Full details of Search and Rescue arrangements off the coasts of the United Kingdom are given in *Annual Summary of Admiralty Notices to Mariners.* They include statutory duties of the Master in assisting ships in distress or aircraft casualties at sea, in cases of collision, or in the event of casualties involving loss of life at sea, as well as information on rescue by helicopter.

Other sources of information
13.106

1   **Merchant Ship Search and Rescue Manual (MERSAR)**, published by IMO, gives guidance for those who, during emergencies at sea, may require assistance from others or who may be able to provide assistance themselves.

Admiralty Sailing Directions give details of Search and Rescue facilities, where known, in Chapter 1 of each volume.

Admiralty Manual of Seamanship 1995, obtainable from The Stationery Office, gives details of methods of rescue and treatment of survivors.

Fishing

Types of Fishing

General information
13.107

1   The following types of fishing are common in European waters and many other parts of the world. In general the method employed can be seen from the type of vessel and the rig. Figure 13.107 shows some

of the differing types of fishing vessel to be found in N European waters.

Handlining and jigging
13.108

1   Handlining is done with a weighted line and baited hook. Jigging involves lure-like hooks attached to a line which is pulled, "jigged" by hand or mechanically. Both are done from a stationary, but not necessarily anchored vessel.

Norwegian Long Liner

Purse Seine-Netter

Spanish Long Liner

Scottish Trawler

Crabber

Twin-Rig Trawler

Spanish Gill-Netter

Multi-Rig Trawler

Scottish Seine-Netter

Pair Trawlers

(Photographs - Marine Scotland) Common fishing vessel types (13.107)

Longlining
13.109

1   A long line with baited hooks about 1 m apart is anchored at both ends on the ocean bed and marked by buoys. The lines may be as much as 10 miles in length with 50 000 baited hooks. This form of fishing is carried out in depths to 180 m for ground fish. The line is shot over the stern and recovered over the bow of the fishing vessel.

* 2-3 miles in length
* Baited hooks
* Left to fish for 24 hours+
* High quality fish
* Hake, ling, tusk

Long Line (13.109)

(Diagram - Marine Scotland)

Pots
13.110

1   Pots vary in size and shape from the "inkwell" to the "parlour" type, and are made of wood, metal or plastic covered with netting. They are used to catch shellfish, especially lobster and crab. The pots are set in lines of between 10 and 60 pots depending on the capacity of the vessel. Some vessels may use up to 100 pots on a line, which will have a length of about 2 miles. The lines are marked by floats and are usually found in rocky areas near the coast, but may be found offshore as well. Pots are shot over the stern and recovered over the bow.

* Baited trap
* Targeting shellfish - lobster, crab, nephrops
* High quality catch
* Set for 24-48 hours
* Environmentally friendly
* Closes large areas of sea to mobile gear

Examples of pot types (13.110.1)

(Diagram - Marine Scotland)

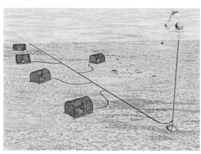

* Baited trap
* Targeting shellfish - lobster, crab, nephrops
* High quality catch
* Set for 24-48 hours
* Environmentally friendly
* Closes large areas of sea to mobile gear

Typical lay of pots (13.110.2)

(Diagram - Marine Scotland)

Gillnetting
13.111

1   Gillnetting is used to catch many different types of fish. The nets may be anchored or left to drift. Anchored nets are normally marked by a dan-buoy and supported by floats so that they stand vertically in the water. Each net is about 100 m long and a series may be joined together to give a total length measured in miles. They are shot over the stern and recovered over the bow.

2   Drift nets are supported at the surface by floats attached to a heavy rope messenger by lines the length of which is set to suit the fishing depth required. The nets are about 35 m long and 15 m deep and are attached to the messenger by short strops. Up to 100 nets may be used at a time. The drifter turns downwind to shoot the nets and pays them out one after the other. On completion sufficient messenger is paid out and the vessel turns to ride to the messenger for three or four hours before recovering the nets and shaking out the fish.

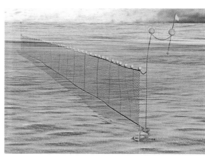

* Mesh size designed to trap target species.
* Fish cannot generate backward movement
* Up to 250m long
* Targets monkfish, hake and salmon

Moored gill-net (13.111)

(Diagram - Marine Scotland)

Seine netting
13.112

1   The seine net is used to encircle fish on or just above the sea bed. A rope warp is attached to each wing of the net varying in length depending on depth of water from 250 to 900 m in length. The gear is shot by attaching the end of one warp to a dan-buoy, paying out the warp and then the net and finally the warp attached to the other wing of the net. The vessel then circles round, recovers the dan-buoy and the end of the first warp and hauls in both warps together. The movement of the warps drives the fish into the net. This method is called Fly-dragging. The vessel may anchor to haul in the net in which case it is called Danish Anchor Seining.

* No trawl doors
* Net is not towed
* Net and ropes are laid out on seabed
* Targets haddock, cod, saithe

Seine netting (13.112)

(Diagram - Marine Scotland)

Purse seining
13.113

1 The seine net has floats on the top to support it near the surface, and a wire passed through rings at its base to enable it to be closed. As in seine netting the end of the net is marked by a dan-buoy. The net is shot over the stern by the vessel encircling a shoal of fish. The dan is recovered and the wire reeled in to close the bottom of the net which is then hauled onboard and the fish pumped into tanks. The net may be 160 m deep and extend in a circle with a diameter of 5 cables.

- Able to encompass an entire shoal
- Limited in depth (190m - 230m)
- 'Swimming fish'
- Herring, Mackerel

Purse netting (13.113)

(Diagram - Marine Scotland)

Trawling
13.114

1 There are various forms of trawling. One or two vessels may be employed up to 3 cables apart, and the trawl, which may extend up to 7 cables astern, may be towed along the sea bed, in mid-water or very close to the surface.

2 **Otter trawling** is the towing of a cone shaped net, the mouth of which is held open by water pressure on two otter boards. Speeds are normally $3\frac{1}{2}$ to $4\frac{1}{2}$ kn for mid-water and $2\frac{1}{2}$ to $3\frac{1}{2}$ kn for sea bed operations.

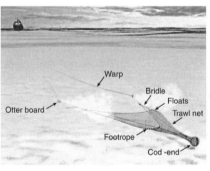

- Net kept open by trawl doors/otter boards
- Vertical opening governed by floats attached to the headline
- Targets haddock, cod, saithe, monkfish nephrops

Otter trawling (13.114.1)

(Diagram - Marine Scotland)

3 **Beam trawling**. Two nets are towed from derricks on either side of the vessel, at $2\frac{1}{2}$ to $6\frac{1}{2}$ kn. The net is held open by a beam from 4 to 14 m in length, which is towed on the sea bed on a line about three times the depth of the water. When towing the derricks are horizontal being raised to 45° when the nets are alongside and the cod ends brought inboard.

4 **Scallop trawling** is a form of beam trawling in which small individual chain bags are dragged behind the beam. Large trawlers drag up to 14 bags on each beam.

Scallop trawl (13.114.2)

(Photograph - Marine Scotland)

5 **Stern trawling** is the commonest form. The net is towed from the stern, and recovered into the vessel over a large ramp or through an opening in the stern. They can operate in almost all weather conditions and may reach 90 m in length. The trawl can be along the sea bed or in mid-water and is normally kept open by otter boards. Since the water pressure keeps the net open stern trawlers find it difficult to manœuvre.

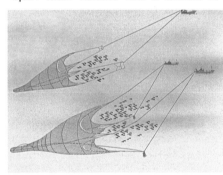

- Pelagic shoals are targeted
- Sophisticated fish finding equipment
- Very fast towing speed
- Short fishing operations
- Herring, Mackerel, Horse Mackerel, Blue Whiting

Stern trawling (13.114.3)

(Diagram - Marine Scotland)

Conventional and chemical munitions encountered or picked up at sea

General information
13.115

1 "Conventional Munitions" means all types of manufactured (not improvised) explosive weapons. "Chemical Munitions" include chemical warfare agents in any type of receptacle or weapon. Collectively these may include buoyant mines, seabed (ground) mines, torpedoes, depth charges, bombs, missiles, artillery shells, phosphorous devices and gas cylinders.

2 These weapons are sometimes picked up in trawls, or as a result of other seabed operations, particularly dredging, often in waters comparatively distant from where they were laid, fired, dropped, or dumped. These munitions are dangerous and sensitive, particularly to shock, heat or vibration, even if they have been in the water for many years. Chemical weapons may be in a particularly unstable state.

Action on encountering munitions at sea
13.116

1 The majority of drifting buoyant mines sighted on the surface will probably be lost exercise mines. Notwithstanding this, all drifting mines should be reported immediately to the Naval Authorities via the

Coastguard Service or the normal ship/shore communication channel. An "All Ships" broadcast should also be made on VHF Channel 16 to communicate the information to ships in the vicinity. The time of sighting and position of the mine is important in the reporting information. A drifting mine must be left for naval explosive ordnance disposal experts to deal with. Under no circumstances are drifting mines to be shot at using a firearm: this may pierce the casing and sink the mine without detonating it. The mine will then migrate on the seabed or be submerged in the water column, and potentially end up in a trawl or washed up on the beach, still in a lethal state. If possible, a lightly weighted marker float or dan buoy should be laid in the vicinity of the mine to assist in re-location should the vessel finding the mine be unable to remain within visual range. No attempt to secure a line to the mine should be made.

2   If a vessel, stopped in the water or at anchor, sights a drifting mine close to the side of the vessel, the best way of moving the weapon away from the vessel's side may be to use a fire hose, playing the jet on the surface of the water close to the weapon, thereby creating a current to push the weapon away. Under no circumstances is the jet to be played on the body of the weapon itself.

3   In the event of an unidentified suspect munition being picked up in trawls or as a result of other undersea operations, the following guidance should be followed:

A munition should not be landed on deck if it has been observed whilst still outboard. In the case of fishing vessels, the trawl should be lowered to the seabed, cut away and the position marked with a surface float, if possible in no more than 20m of water at least 1000m offshore and clear of any cables, pipelines or navigational aids. The local Coastguard should be contacted for assistance in determining a suitable position. Information can be passed using the reporting format as explained at 13.117.

4   In the event of the munition not being detected until the contents of the trawl have been discharged on deck, the skipper of the fishing vessel must decide whether to rid his ship of the weapon by passing it over the side, or to make for the nearest port informing the Coastguard, Harbour Authority or Naval Authority by radio without delay. The best course of action will depend on the circumstances, but should be guided by the following points:

(i) The munition should be kept on board for as short a time as possible.

5   (ii) A ship with a munition on board, or in her gear, should warn other ships in the vicinity giving her position and, if applicable, intended position of jettisoning.

(iii) Great care should be taken to avoid bumping the munition or subjecting it to shock or vibration. The primary consideration in this respect may be the motion of the vessel in relation to vessel size and sea state, weighed against the ease of handling the device over the side.

6   (iv) With due regard to points (i) and (iii), if within two or three hours steaming of the coastline the safest measure will often be to run towards the nearest port and lie a safe distance (i.e. at least 1000m) offshore to await the arrival of a Naval Explosive Ordnance Disposal (EOD) Unit.

Under no circumstances should a vessel bring recovered munitions into harbours or their approaches. It should be noted that rewards formerly paid to mariners for such recovery have been discontinued.

7   (v) If the decision is taken to pass the munition over the side, EOD Units will be greatly facilitated if the item is laid in no more than 20m water depth at least 1000m clear of any building on the foreshore, and its position marked by a suitable float and accurately plotted. Whenever possible the munition should be lowered gently back to the seabed and not dumped over the side. Impact with the seabed has been known to result in detonation of the munition resulting in casualties.

8   (vi) If retained onboard it should be stowed on deck, away from heat and vibration, firmly chocked and lashed to prevent movement. Under no circumstances is the munition to be secured using its fittings as lashing points.

(vii) The munition SHOULD BE KEPT DAMP with sea water. This is important because any explosive or firing mechanisms which may have become exposed to the atmosphere are liable to become very sensitive to shock if allowed to dry out.

9   (viii) Under no circumstances should any attempt be made to clean the munition for identification purposes, open it, or tamper with it in any way.

Reports of munitions encountered at sea
13.117

1   If a munition is encountered, the following information should be reported to the local Coastguard. This comprises information on the location and nature of the encounter, the type and state of the device encountered (if known), the action taken with the device, and, if released at sea, the location of the release.

2   1. Position of the encounter by latitude and longitude. If the contacting party is aware of the geodetic datum used for the position, and it is not World Geodetic System 1984 (WGS84), the geodetic datum should be reported as part of the location information. Where the exact position is unknown, approximate coordinates should be given, or a range and bearing from a charted feature.

3   2. Depth of water in metres.
3. Nature of the encounter. The description could include such things as: entanglement in nets; dredging activities; laying pipelines/cables; found on shore; diving/Remotely Operated Vehicle (ROV); or other details.
4. Position by latitude and longitude of disposal if released at sea (if different from i). This position needs to be as accurate as possible (ideally a GPS position) to aid relocation by diver if the munition is not marked at the surface or the mark is lost.

4   5. Details of any surface float laid to mark the munition's position and details of net and fittings if cut free and attached to munition.
6. Type of device, if known, or a description of key features if observed including sizes and colours.

7. Condition of device. The description could include:

Description	Criteria
Partly corroded	Condition where the contents cannot yet escape
Seriously corroded	Condition where substantial parts of the contents can escape
Heavily corroded	Condition where most of the contents can escape
Completely corroded	Condition where the contents can escape freely

5

8. General remarks or any amplifying comments. If an encounter is near or in a known (charted) dumping site for munitions, a reference to this should be given. If the device is located by remote means, e.g. ROV or imaging sonar operated by the offshore community, the method of detection and equipment characteristics.

9. Contact details of skipper including mobile phone number if carried.

10. Details of local tide and weather conditions, bottom type and nearest launch point for the EOD unit.

Chemical munitions and phosphorus devices
13.118

1   Chemical munitions and phosphorus devices require special care. If brought on board, it is probable that they will not be positively distinguished from other conventional weapons by an untrained individual unless the casing of the weapon has deteriorated to the extent that the agent inside is exposed to the atmosphere. In this event smouldering, smoke or liquid, sludge and vapour discharge will be observed.

2   Exposed personnel should **immediately** evacuate upwind of the device whilst stock is taken of the situation. In the case of a fishing vessel where the device would typically be brought on board in the gear aft of the crew areas, the vessel should be turned into wind such that any vapours are carried away from the crew.

3   The device should then be returned to the seabed as soon as possible by ditching the gear if necessary, the position noted and marked with a surface float, and the Coastguard informed immediately. Once the weapon has been jettisoned, crew should remain upwind until the exposed decks and surfaces have been washed down with copious quantities of sea water.

4   No attempt should be made to remove the device from the gear except where the gear cannot be ditched and it is necessary to do so to return the device to the seabed. No attempt should be made to physically touch or handle the device.

Types of chemical munitions
13.119

1   Chemical devices, which may include chlorine, phosgene or mustard gas, will generally come in two categories:

Gas filled ordnance e.g. artillery shells which are not expended. Deterioration with age of such items makes leaking chemical agent a likely hazard.

Gas filled storage cylinders. These could contain a considerable amount of chemical agent and deterioration with age of such items makes leaking chemical agent a likely hazard.

2   These were historically dumped in relatively deep areas which would be anticipated to be beyond the reach of demersal trawling or dredging; the risk of encountering such devices is relatively small but nevertheless real.

3   It should be appreciated that chemical agents in liquid and vapour form may cause burns and irritation to lungs, skin and eyes by contact (liquid or vapour) or inhalation (vapour). Commercial masks intended to provide inhalation protection against dust or industrial agents will provide little or no protection against agents intended for use in war, although heavy oilskins *may* afford some limited protection against splashes of liquid chemical.

Phosphorus devices
13.120

1   Phosphorus is an extremely hazardous chemical; aside from the risk of burns if handled, leaking phosphorus devices present a significant fire risk as they can ignite spontaneously in air once dry, and sudden exposure to atmosphere can cause an explosion. Additionally, there is a risk of chemical poisoning and the formation of highly toxic phosphoric and phosphine gases if stored.

2   Phosphorus devices will generally come in three categories:

Expended and partially expended military and civil marine pyrotechnics. These small (handheld) devices are the most common source and may contain exposed phosphorus dependent on how long they had burned. Although requiring careful handling these are not a serious threat due to their small physical size, but should still be treated with due care.

3   Phosphorus filled ordnance that has previously been dumped at sea. These devices could include artillery shells which may not be expended and could contain a considerable amount of phosphorus. Deterioration with age of such items makes leaking phosphorus a likely hazard.

4   Marine Markers are used to indicate a position by burning and smoke. The majority contain phosphorus and may have failed to ignite correctly or may appear to have burned completely. Any Marine Marker should be treated with caution as even those that appear to have functioned correctly may still contain phosphorus and re-ignite with heat, impact or on drying out.

Munitions and devices located on the seabed
13.121

1   In addition to the reports required by mariners encountering drifting mines or recovering munitions in nets or trawls (13.117), it is possible that survey vessels or others operating imaging sonar, or commercial or sports divers, may encounter munitions on the seabed. Under these circumstances, reports should also be submitted, in the prescribed format, to:

United Kingdom Hydrographic Office,
Admiralty Way,
Taunton,
Somerset, TA1 2DN,
United Kingdom.

2   This will enable the extent of areas around known dumping sites where conventional and chemical munitions are to be found, and the identification of previously unknown or unrecorded dumping sites, to be accurately shown on charts.

Aid to identification
13.122

1   A colour identification poster illustrating a representative selection of explosive ordnance which could be encountered has been prepared by the Ministry of Defence. Copies are available free from the following sources:

    Southern Diving Group, HM Naval Base Devonport, Devon, PL2 2BG.

    Northern Diving Group, HM Naval Base Clyde, Faslane, Helensburgh, Dumbartonshire, G84 8HL.

Mines
13.123

1   Drifting mines are occasionally sighted and, even though many are only exercise mines which are broken adrift, they are all best left for Naval experts to dispose of. Rifle fire can pierce the casing of a dangerous mine without causing it to explode. If it then sinks, it may subsequently be washed up on a beach or brought up in a trawl, still in a dangerous state.

2   Remoored mines, which have drifted from deeper water trailing a length of cable, are liable to become re-activated if the cable fouls an obstruction. Such mines may not appear on the surface at all states of the tide.

  If a drifting or remoored mine is sighted, the time and the position of the mine should be reported immediately to Naval Authorities via the Coastguard service or normal communication channels, and the report broadcast on VHF Channel 16 so that other shipping in the vicinity is warned. If possible, a lightly weighted marker float should be laid in the vicinity of the mine to assist in re-location should the vessel finding the mine be unable to remain within visual range.

3   If the relevant authorities are operating under the GMDSS a DSC Safety Alert will be made to all ships regarding the sighting of mines. The announcement broadcast will be carried out on one of the DSC frequencies and the message will normally be transmitted on the distress, urgency and safety frequency in the same band in which the DSC safety alert was given. Full details are given within *Admiralty List of Radio Signals Volume 5.*

4   No attempt should ever be made to recover a mine and bring it to port.

  Mines, torpedoes, depth charges, bombs, and other explosive weapons may still be dangerous, even though they may have been in the water for many years.

Aquaculture and fish havens

Aquaculture
13.124

1   Aquaculture is the term used to describe the cultivation of fish and marine vegetation for food. Differing methods are in common use, depending on the specific object under cultivation; those of particular significance for the mariner are outlined below.

2   **Fish traps.** In many parts of the world, arrangements of stakes and nets are erected in shallow coastal waters by fishermen. These structures can be very large and may sometimes extend up to several miles from the shore. They form an obstruction to navigation, and there is a risk of damage to, or by, small vessels.

3   Where their precise locations are known, and are likely to remain unchanged, they will be charted using the symbols below:

  Where fish traps occupy extensive areas, or where their positions are not known or are subject to change, the legend "Fishing Stakes" or "Fish Traps" will be shown on the chart in the appropriate position. There will usually be an accompanying explanatory note in the title area.

4   **Tunny fisheries.** Tunny nets may extend up to seven miles from the shore, and may be marked by day and night. Charts covering areas where tunny fishing is likely to be encountered may carry a cautionary note. Mariners should avoid areas where these nets are likely to be laid as, in addition to the risk of damage to the nets, they are often of sufficient strength to foul a propeller.

5   **Marine farms** are assemblages of cages, rafts and floats, or posts, where fish including shellfish are reared. In foreign waters they may be variously described as fisheries rafts, fish aggregating devices and (by the Japanese) as "floating fish havens". They are charted in black using the symbols below:

  The smaller symbol is used where space on the chart is limited. On large scale charts the actual limits of the fish farm may be shown by a black dashed line.

6   Marine farms are semi-permanent obstructions to navigation, are likely to be marked by buoys and possibly lights, and are not always confined to inshore locations. Mariners are advised to avoid these structures and their associated moorings, which may extend more than 1 mile from the structure, and which are often uncharted.

7   **Cultivated shellfish beds** (oysters, mussels) may be navigated over, depending upon draught. Claims for damage caused by vessels anchoring or grounding on them, however, can be very heavy. They are charted in magenta using the symbol below, and a cautionary note is also included on the chart

Fish Havens
13.125

1   Fish havens, also called fishery reefs, are formed artificially on the sea floor by dumping rocks, concrete, old cars, or similar materials to encourage the congregation and spawning of fish. They are typically established by private interests such as sport fishermen.

2   They are charted in the same way as obstructions in water depths of less than 20 metres, and as foul

areas in deeper water. When possible their limits, and the depth of water over them, are shown.

3   Depending upon draught, vessels may navigate in the waters over sea floor fish havens, but they represent a hazard when anchoring or engaged in sea floor operations.

Offshore oil and gas operations

General information
13.126

1   Oil and gasfields are now exploited in many parts of the oceans between the shores and the edges of the continental shelves.

2   Though the basic methods used for exploiting oil and gas have become established, details of systems and structures used vary with the requirements of the different fields and are continually being developed. This section contains terms currently in use on Admiralty charts and in *Admiralty Sailing Directions*.

3   In *Admiralty Sailing Directions,* offshore installations are usually referred to in descriptive terms, but if the specific type is known, it is also stated.

4   Navigation in the vicinity of shipping routes is often restricted by offshore installations which are used to explore and exploit offshore oil and gasfields. These installations are usually protected by Safety Zones (13.140). Submarine pipelines and cables, and sub-sea structures also usually exist on the sea floor in the vicinity of oil and gasfields See 9.64 and 9.66.

5   Vessels should navigate with particular care near areas of offshore activity.

Exploration of oil and gas fields

Surveys
13.127

1   The first stage of exploration in areas likely to contain hydrocarbon deposits is usually a magnetic, gravimetric and seismic survey. Bottom cores are usually obtained as part of this survey. For precautions in the vicinity of vessels carrying out seismic surveys, see 13.145.

Mobile offshore drilling units
13.128

1   Mobile rigs are used for drilling wells to explore and develop a field. There are three principal types of drilling rig, (see Diagram 13.128).

  Jack-up rigs which are towed into the drilling position where their steel legs are lowered to the sea floor and the drilling platform is then jacked-up clear of the water. They are used in depths down to about 120 m.

2   **Semi-submersible rigs** consist of a platform on columns which rise from a caisson submerged deep enough to avoid much of the effects of sea and swell. Some large semi-submersible rigs are self-propelled and may proceed unassisted by tugs at speeds up to 10 kn, however most are towed. They may have displacements up to 25 000 tonnes, and are used for drilling in depths to about 1700 m in the anchored mode, or in the case of dynamically positioned rigs, in excess of 1700 m.

3   **Drillships**. A typical drillship has a displacement of 14 000 tonnes, a length of 135 m and a maximum speed of 14 kn. Drillships carry a tall drilling rig

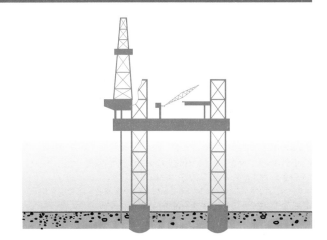

Jack-up Rig

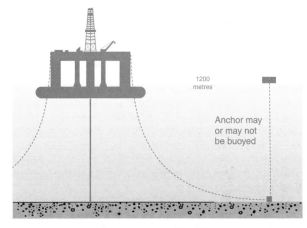

Semi-submersible Rig
(maybe dynamically positioned, no anchors)

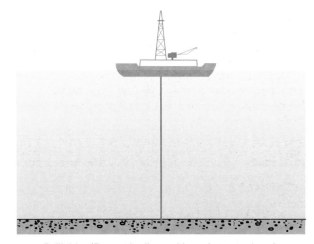

Drillship. (Dynamically positioned, no anchors)

Drilling Rigs (13.128)

amidships, and usually have a helicopter deck aft. For drilling in depths of less than about 200 m, the vessel is held by an 8-point anchor system; in greater depths a dynamic positioning system is required. Drillships can then drill in depths to about 2000 m, and to a depth of 6000 m below the sea floor.

4   Mobile rigs on station are not charted, but their positions are given in Navigational Warnings or Temporary Notices to Mariners, or both. A list of all mobile drilling rigs within NAVAREA I is promulgated weekly via SafetyNET and NAVTEX and reprinted in Section III of *Admiralty Notices to Mariners*.

5   Rigs are marked by illuminated name panels, lights, obstruction lights and fog signals, similar to those used on fixed platforms (13.132). On some rigs flares burn at times to dispose of unwanted oil or gas.

6   Buoys and other obstacles are often moored near rigs, and anchor wires, chains and obstructions frequently extend as much as 1½ miles from them. A standby vessel is normally in attendance.

Rigs should be given a wide berth.

Exploitation of oil and gas fields

Systems
13.129

1   In a typical field, oil and gas is obtained from wells drilled from fixed platforms, fitted out like a drilling rig, and usually standing on the sea floor.

2   From each wellhead, the oil or gas is carried in pipes, known as flowlines, to a production platform where primary processing, compression and pumping is carried out. The oil or gas is then transported through pipelines to a nearby storage tank, tanker loading buoy or floating terminal, or direct to a tank farm ashore. One production platform may collect the oil or gas from several drilling platforms, and may supply a number of tanker loading buoys or storage units. Such production platforms are sometimes termed field terminal platforms.

3   Converted vessels such as tankers may sometimes be permanently moored and used either as production platforms or floating terminals, or for storage.

An alternative system, to overcome some of the problems associated with deep water production operations, is the sub-sea production system (13.133) which has most of its installations on the sea floor and is maintained by divers or remotely operated vehicles (ROVs).

Development Areas
13.130

1   The development of an offshore field involves the frequent moving of large structures and buoys and the laying of many miles of pipeline, both of which are dependent on the weather. Where such operations occur it is often impossible to give adequate notice of movements, and to keep charts and publications completely up-to-date. Certain fields which are developing are designated Development Areas and their limits are shown on charts. Within these areas, construction, maintenance, standby, anchor handling and supply vessels, including submersibles, divers, obstructions possibly marked by buoys, and tankers manoeuvring may be encountered. The mariner is strongly advised to keep outside Development Areas.

Wells
13.131

1   In the course of developing a field, numerous wells are drilled.

Those which will not be required again are sealed with cement below the sea floor and abandoned. These are known as plugged and abandoned wells (P & A).

Other wells which may be required at a later date are known as Suspended Wells. They have their wellheads capped and left with a pipe and other equipment usually projecting from 2 to 6 m, but in some cases as much as 15 m, above the sea floor.

2   Wells which are in use for producing oil or gas are termed Production Wells. Their wellheads are surmounted by a complex of valves and pipes, similar to that on suspended wells.

Production wells may be protected by a 500 m exclusion zone and are usually marked by buoys or light buoys to assist recovery and to indicate a hazard to navigation or fishing. Suspended Wells are sometimes similarly marked.

3   Wells are shown on charts by a danger circle enclosing the least depth over the obstruction, if known. Production wells are marked "Production Well", suspended wells are marked "Well", or on older charts "Wellhead".

Offshore platforms
13.132

1   Several different types of platform are used for development, but they are normally piled steel or concrete structures, the latter held in position on the sea floor by gravity. Tension Leg Platforms consist of semi-submersible platforms secured to flooded caissons on the sea floor vertically below them by wires kept in tension by the buoyancy of the platform. See Diagram 13.132.

2   Platforms may serve some of a number of purposes, and may carry any of the following equipment: drilling and production equipment, oil and gas separation and treatment plants, pumpline stations and electricity generators. They may be fitted with one or more cranes, a helicopter landing deck, and accommodation for the necessary complement.

3   A number of wells may be drilled from one drilling rig by using a structure, termed a template, placed on the sea floor below the rig to guide the drill. A template may stand as much as 15 m above the sea floor.

The appearance of a platform fitted with drilling facilities is considerably altered if the drilling derrick or crane is removed.

4   Platforms may stand singly or in groups connected by pipelines to each other. Some stand close together in a complex, with bridges and underwater power cables connecting them.

The markings commonly used for platforms and rigs consist of the following:

5   A white light (or lights operated in unison) flashing Morse code (U) every 15 seconds, visible 15 miles, showing all round the horizon and exhibited at an elevation of between 12 and 30 m.

A secondary light or lights with the same characteristics, but visible only 10 miles, automatically brought into operation on failure of the above light.

6   Red lights, flashing Morse code (U) in unison with each other, every 15 seconds, visible 2 miles, and exhibited from the horizontal extremities of the structure which are not already marked by the main light or lights.

7   A fog signal sounding Morse code (U) every 30 seconds, audible at a range of at least 2 miles. Identification panels displaying the registered name or other designation of the structure in black lettering on a yellow background, so arranged that at least one panel is visible from any direction. The panels are illuminated or the background is retroreflective.

8   Unwanted gas or oil is sometimes burned from a flaring boom extending from a platform or from a nearby flare platform, and obstruction lights are exhibited where aircraft may be endangered.

Platforms are charted, where known, and may be mentioned in Sailing Directions; drilling rigs, barges and similar units which may lie as much as 1½ miles from the platform, are not charted. This ancillary equipment is sometimes marked by buoys.

9   Semi-submersible drilling rigs and tankers are sometimes converted or purpose built to act as production platforms, and are then known as Floating Production Platforms (13.134).

Platforms are normally protected by safety zones. See 13.140.

Sub-sea production systems
13.133

1   On some fields, sub-sea production systems are used. They consist of one or more wells, known as production wells, which have as much of the production equipment as possible on the sea floor instead of on a drilling platform. The output from a number of these wells may be collected in an underwater manifold centre, a large steel structure up to 20 m in height on the sea floor, for delivery to a production platform.

2   For caution on submarine pipelines, see 9.65.

Floating Production Storage and Offloading Vessels (FPSO)
13.134

1   FPSOs are used to produce oil and gas from fields which are located in a range of water depths, from very shallow (30 m) to ultra-deep (in excess of 2000 m), whereas fixed production platforms may be limited to around 400 m. These are highly specialised vessels, generally with ship-shaped hulls (converted from tankers or new construction, but are also being constructed with circular hulls. The hull provides containment and the gas and oil processing equipment is mounted on the deck. A mixture of oil, water and gas is extracted from the field, and this mixture is piped to the FPSO where it is separated, processed and stored. From the FPSO, the finished product is exported to shore by pipeline or tanker.

2   The most vital part of the FPSO is the high technology turret, which is anchored to the sea floor by chains or composite tethers, and is connected by a solid yoke to either the bow or stern of the vessel. In the most modern designs, and particularly when designed for operation in harsh environments, the turret is constructed as an internal unit within the hull of the FPSO.

Steel Production Platform

Concrete Production Platform.

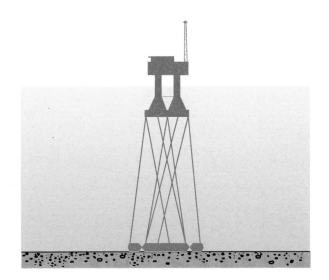

Tension Leg Platform

Offshore Platforms (13.132)

3   Process pipelines and control umbilicals pass through the turret and connect the vessel to the sub surface facilities below. The turret incorporates a swivel which permits the vessel to rotate through 360°, or "weather vane", under the influence of wind and tide.

4   In some earlier designs without turrets, the FPSO is "spread-moored", with cargo offtake being undertaken through an SBM (13.135) which may be moored up to 1000 m away from the FPSO, and connected to it with a sub-sea pipeline or "riser". Such FPSOs will typically be converted tankers, and may utilise their amidships manifolds to receive the production fluids and gases.

5   Export tankers will typically berth bow-to-bow or bow-to-stern with the FPSO, at the opposite end from any turret or SBM. These may be conventional tankers, moored at the bow and loading manifold via a floating hose through the midships, or they may have a dynamic positioning capability and through a catenary/suspended hose through a specialised bow loading connection.

As oil exploration and development activity moves into ever deeper waters, more of these vessels are being constructed and deployed all over the world.

Mooring systems

General information
13.135

1   A variety of mooring systems have been developed for use in deep water offshore oil and gasfields, and in the vicinity of certain ports, to allow the loading of large vessels and the permanent mooring of floating storage vessels or units.

These offshore systems include large mooring buoys, manned floating structures of over 60 000 tonnes designed for mooring vessels up to 500 000 tonnes, and platforms on structures fixed at their lower end to the sea floor.

2   They allow a vessel to moor forward or aft to them, and "weather vane" (13.134).

They are termed SPMs, or those which are a form of mooring buoy are termed SBMs. SBM is the generic term accepted throughout the offshore oil industry for tanker loading buoys.

3   Like production platforms, SPMs are normally marked by lights and a fog signal is sounded from them.

On charts, an offshore mooring is shown by the symbol for a tanker mooring of superbuoy size.

If the mooring is connected to the sea floor by a rigid, pivoted or articulated structure, it is shown by the symbol for an offshore platform.

The mariner should give all offshore moorings a wide berth if not intending to use them.

Types of Single Point Moorings
13.136

1   There are two main types of SPMs: Catenary Anchor Leg Moorings (CALMs) and Single Anchor Leg

Moorings (SALMs). Each type has developed a number of variations, as follows:

Type	Variations	Reference	Illustration
CALMs		13.137	13.137.1
	ELSBM		13.137.2
	Spar buoy		13.137.3
SALMs		13.138	13.138.1
	ALC		13.138.2
	SALS		13.138.3

CALMs
13.137

1   CALMs incorporate a large SBM which remains on the surface at all times and is moored by 4 or more anchors which may lie up to 400 m from the buoy.

Mooring hawsers and cargo hoses lead from a turntable on the top of the buoy, so that the buoy does not turn as the vessel swings to wind and stream.

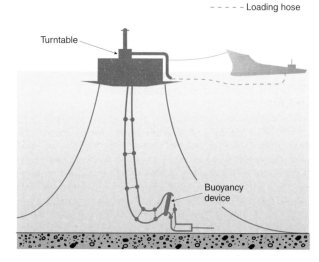

Catenary Anchor Leg Mooring (CALM) (13.137.1)

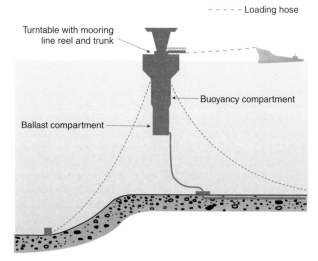

Exposed Location Single Buoy Mooring (ELSBM) (13.137.2)

2   **ELSBM** is designed for use in deep water where bad weather is common. With this type of SPM the buoy is replaced by a large cylindrical floating

structure. The structure is surmounted by a helicopter platform, has reels for lifting hawsers and hoses clear of the water, and is fitted with emergency accommodation. Its anchors may lie up to 5 cables from the structure.

3   **Spar buoy** moorings are similar to ELSBMs, but the floating structure is larger and incorporates storage facilities so that in adverse weather production can continue. They are permanently manned.

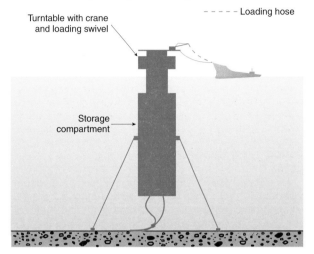

Spar buoy (13.137.3)

SALMs
13.138

1   SALMs consists of a rigid frame or tube with a buoyancy device at its upper end, secured at its lower end to a universal joint on a large steel or concrete base resting on the sea floor, and at its upper end to a mooring buoy by a chain or wire span. Oil flows into the frame through the universal joint at its lower end and out of the frame through a cargo hose connected to a fluid swivel-assembly at its upper end. When the pull of a vessel is taken by the mooring buoy, the frame inclines towards the vessel and the buoy may dip. When the vessel swings to wind or stream, the frame swings with her on the articulated joint at its foot. This type of mooring is particularly suited to loading from deep water sub-sea wellheads.

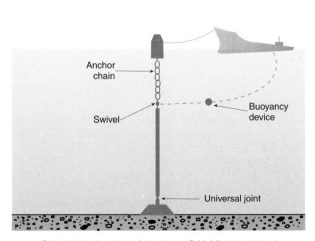

Single Anchor Leg Mooring (SALM) (13.138.1)

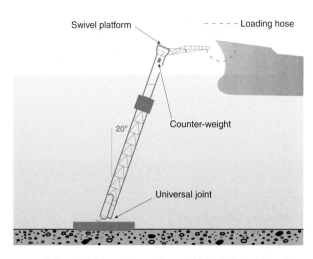

Articulated Loading Column (ALC) (13.138.2)

2   **ALCs** are a development of the SALM with the anchor span and buoyant frame or tube replaced by a metal lattice tower, buoyant at one end and attached at the other by a universal joint to a concrete-filled base on the sea floor. Some are surmounted by a platform which may carry a helicopter deck and a turntable with reels for lifting hawsers and hoses clear of the water, and have emergency accommodation. These are termed Articulated Loading Platforms (ALPs).

In bad weather, a tower may be inclined at angles up to 20° to the vertical.

3   **SALS** consist of a SALM type of mooring system that is permanently attached to the stem or stern of a storage vessel through a yoke supported by a buoyancy tank. Tankers secure to the storage vessel to load.

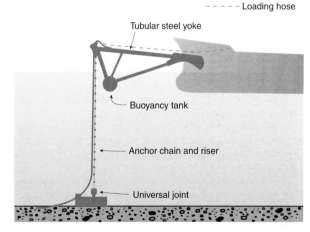

Single Anchor Leg Storage System (SALS) (13.138.3)

Other loading systems
13.139

1   **Mooring towers** are secured to the sea floor, and surmounted by a turntable to which vessels moor. At some mooring towers, a floating hose connects a fluid swivel-assembly in the turntable to the vessel, at others an underwater loading arm carries a pipe from the turntable to the vessel's midship manifold.

STL. The STL is a submerged turret, moored to the seabed, supporting production/export oil risers, which locates into the hull of a specially adapted production vessel or tanker. when configured as an export facility, dedicated tankers dock with the turret and load oil through the turret from a sub-sea system. The turret is designed to allow the vessel to rotate around it. It is particularly suitable for use in harsh environments.

Safety zones

General information
13.140
1   Safety zones prohibit unauthorised entry thereby protecting mariners and fishermen by reducing the risk of collision, but they also protect the lives and equipment of those working in the zones (divers and submersibles are particularly vulnerable).

International law
13.141
1   Under international law a coastal state may establish safety zones around installations and other devices on the continental shelf necessary for the exploration and exploitation of its natural resources. These installations include movable drilling rigs, production platforms, wellheads, single point moorings, and other associated structures.

2   Safety zones normally extend to a distance of 500 m around installations measured from their outer edges; within these zones measures can be taken to protect installations.
Vessels of all nationalities are required to respect these safety zones.

3   By a Resolution adopted in 1987, IMO recommended vessels which are passing close to offshore installations or structures to:
Navigate with care when passing near offshore installations or structures giving due consideration to safe speed and safe passing distances taking into account the prevailing weather conditions and the presence of other vessels or dangers;

4   Where appropriate, take early and substantial avoiding action when approaching such installations or structures to facilitate the installation's or structure's awareness of the vessel's closest point of approach and provide information on any possible safety concerns, particularly where the offshore installation or structure may be used as a navigational aid;
Use any designated routeing systems established in the area;

5   Maintain a continuous listening watch on the navigating bridge on VHF Channel 16 when navigating near offshore installations or structures to allow radio contact to be established between such installations or structures, standby vessels, vessel traffic services and other vessels so that any uncertainty as to a vessel maintaining an adequate passing distance from the installations or structures can be alleviated.

National laws
13.142
1   Many coastal states have made entry by unauthorised vessels into declared safety zones a criminal offence. As the type of installation subject to safety zones varies from state to state, mariners are advised always to assume the existence of a safety zone unless they have information to the contrary.

2   Some coastal states have declared prohibitions on entry into, or on fishing and anchoring within, areas extending beyond 500 m from installations. Publication of the details of such wider areas is solely for the safety and convenience of shipping, and implies no recognition of the international validity of such restrictions.

United Kingdom law
13.143
1   All oil and gas installations on the United Kingdom continental shelf and in tidal and territorial waters, which project above the sea surface at any state of the tide, including those being constructed or dismantled, are automatically protected by safety zones. An installation is defined as any floating structure or device maintained on a station by whatever means, which is involved in petroleum related activities and includes installations which are solely accommodation units. Anchor chains, wires, anchors and blocks, used to maintain a floating structure on station, may extend outside the Safety Zone associated with it.

2   Safety zones for subsea installations are established by Statutory Instruments in the form of Offshore Installations (Safety Zones) Orders. Such subsea installations may be marked by light buoys.
Safety zones around permanent installations are charted, if known, and new ones promulgated by Notices to Mariners.

3   Single Well Oil Production Systems (SWOPS) are operated for substantial periods of time by a tanker dynamically positioned over the well. When oil recovery is in progress, the tanker is protected by a Safety Zone.

4   Where an installation, such as an FPSO or tanker operating at a SWOPS is free to swing, the associated Safety Zone extends 500 m from any part of the installation. This may exceed the charted fixed Safety Zone which is based on a fixed point (e.g. the anchor point of an FPSO).

5   Entry into any United Kingdom safety zone is prohibited, except in the following cases:
To lay, work on or remove a submarine cable or pipeline near the zone.
To provide services for an installation within the zone, or to transport persons or goods to or from it, or, with proper authorisation to inspect it.
To save life or property.
On account of stress of weather.
When in distress.

6   Unauthorised entry by a vessel into a safety zone makes the owner, master, or others who may have contributed to the offence liable to a fine or imprisonment or both.

Vessels requiring special consideration

Vessels engaged in surveying

Signals
13.144

1   While carrying out hydrographic or oceanographic surveys surveying ships display the signals prescribed in Rule 27(b) of the *International Regulations for Preventing Collisions at Sea 1972*. They may also show the International Code group IR "I am engaged in submarine survey work (underwater operations). Keep clear of me and go slow."

2   While carrying out this work, which may often run across the normal shipping lanes, including traffic separation schemes where Rule 10(k) applies, surveying ships may be towing instruments up to 300 m astern. These will restrict their manoeuvrability and ability to change speed or stop quickly. Other vessels should keep well clear in accordance with Rules 16 and 18, giving a clearance of at least 2 cables if passing astern.

Vessels engaged in seismic surveys

Operations
13.145

1   Seismic surveys are undertaken in various parts of the world in connection with exploration for oil and gas. It is seldom practicable to publish details of the areas of operation except in general terms, and vessels carrying out seismic surveys may therefore be encountered without warning.

The method of carrying out such surveys is as follows:

2   The seismic vessel may tow up to three detector cables, as shown in diagram 13.145, between 3 cables and 3 miles in length and, in the case of multiple streamers, up to 300 m in width between the outer streamers. The end is marked by a tail buoy fitted with a radar reflector. "Air" or "Gas" guns are usually towed close astern of the vessel. The explosions from these guns are invisible from other craft and completely harmless to fish. A second vessel may follow the first to keep the way clear of traffic.

3   Seismic vessels usually acquire their data by steaming parallel courses over a rectangular grid. The grid size varies between 11 miles square for preliminary surveys to less than 5 cables where high definition is required. A run-in and a run-out of up to 5 miles is also required. The turning circle through 180° for a seismic vessel towing three detector cables is over a mile and vessel speeds are in the range 3 to 6 kn. Surveys vary in duration from a few days to months.

Signals
13.146

1   Seismic survey vessels are unable to move freely and generally display the signals prescribed in Rule 27(b) of the *International Regulations for Preventing Collision at Sea 1972*. Other vessels should keep well clear in accordance with Rules 16 and 18, giving them a wide berth of at least 2 miles.

Seismic survey vessels may also show the appropriate signals from the *International Code of Signals*.

2   They often keep radio silence to avoid interference with their registering equipment. Vessels called by light by a seismic survey vessel should, therefore, answer her by the same means, and not by radio.

Vessels undergoing speed trials

Avoidance
13.147

1   Vessels engaged in speed trials, usually over a measured distance, display the International Code group SM.

At the ends of a measured distance they often make 180° turns in order to steam in the opposite direction under similar conditions. Other vessels should give them plenty of room so that they can turn unimpeded and carry out each passage with a steady course and speed.

Vessels constrained by their draught

Signals
13.148

1   A vessel constrained by her draught may display the signals prescribed in Rule 28 of the *International Regulations for Preventing Collision at Sea 1972*.

The term "constrained by her draught" is defined in Rule 3(h). In certain harbours the dimensions or draught of a vessel which may display the signals are described in local bye-laws.

Dracones

Description
13.149

1   Dracones are towed flexible oil barges, consisting of a sausage-shaped envelope of strong woven nylon fabric coated with synthetic rubber. Since they float by reason of the buoyancy of their cargo, usually oil or petroleum products, they are almost entirely submerged. A typical tow would be 60 m long on a 200 m tow line.

2   Dracones and the vessels towing them display the signals prescribed in Rule 24(g) of the *International Regulations for Preventing Collisions at Sea 1972*. In addition, the vessel towing, if the circumstances require, will shine a searchlight along the length of the tow.

Incinerator vessels

General information
13.150

1   Smoke and flames, resembling those from a vessel in distress, are emitted from incinerator vessels when engaged in burning chemical waste.

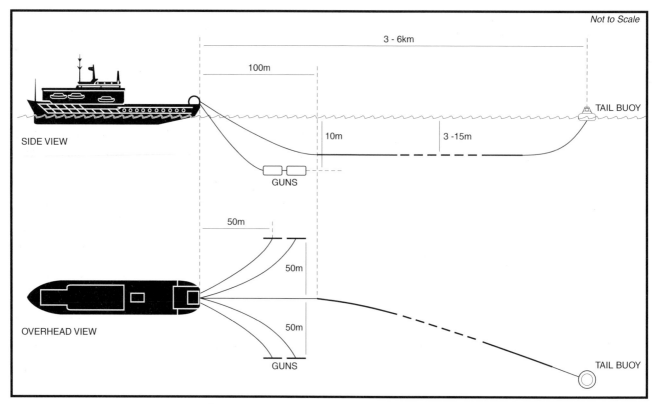

Typical Layout of Seismic Gear – Single Streamer

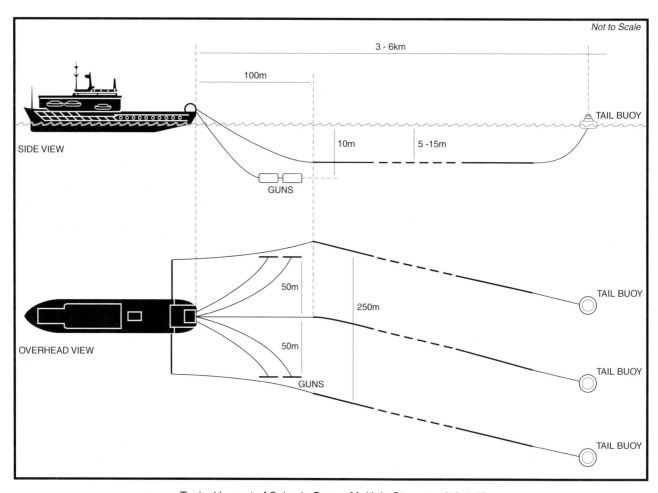

Typical Layout of Seismic Gear – Multiple Streamer (13.145)

These vessels may be at anchor or under way. They are restricted in their manoeuvrability and display the signals prescribed in Rule 27(b) of the *International Regulations for Preventing Collisions at Sea 1972*.

2 Preferably, they should be passed to windward: if passed to leeward, ships should keep clear of any smoke emitted by them.

Permanent stations used by incinerator vessels for burning operations are shown on certain charts and mentioned in Sailing Directions. Details of other selected stations may be announced by Navigational Warnings or Notices to Mariners.

Helicopter operations

General information
13.151

1 Off many of the larger ports, helicopters are frequently used for embarking and disembarking pilots. The success of such operations largely depends on good communication between ship and helicopter, agreement between the Master and helicopter pilot on a clear and simple plan for the operation, and a careful compliance with the safety regulations.

2 Guidance on these regulations is given in *Guide to Helicopter/Ship Operations*, published by The International Chamber of Shipping of 12 Carthusian St, London EC1M 6EZ, (on which the following advice is based) and various other publications.

Navigation
13.152

1 To assist the helicopter to find the vessel it may be necessary for the vessel to transmit a continuous radio homing signal for the helicopter's automatic direction finder. To assist in identification of the homing signal, it should be interspersed with the ship's call sign in Morse at slow speed.

2 In low visibility the ship may be able to use her radar to track the helicopter and inform it of its true bearing from the ship.

If it is necessary to alter course or speed during a helicopter operation, the helicopter pilot should be informed immediately.

Weather and sea conditions
13.153

1 **For routine operations** the relative wind should be from ahead or within 150° of the bow, and with a wind speed of up to 50 kn. In emergency certain types of helicopter can operate in relative wind speeds up to 70 kn.

2 Current practice in the Royal Navy is for the helicopter to approach with the relative wind between the following bearings:

Wind below 25 kn	
Area aft	45° on starboard bow to 45° on port bow
Area forward	45° on starboard bow to right astern
Wind above 25 kn	
Area aft	Right ahead to 90° on port bow
Area forward	90° on starboard beam to 135° on starboard bow

3 A course should be selected to reduce spray, roll and pitch to a minimum. This is particularly important to prevent sea and spray from entering the helicopter's engine, and for the safety of the deck party. Pitch and roll in excess of 5° may preclude helicopter landings.

4 **For winching**, the relative wind to be maintained depends on the part of the ship selected for the operation, which should be discussed with the helicopter pilot; normal optimum relative directions are:

    Area aft — 30° on port bow.
    Area midships — 30° on port bow or on the beam.
    Area forward — 120° on starboard bow.

5 If this is not possible the ship should remain stopped head to wind.

Ship operating areas
13.154

1 Details of requirements for landing and winching areas are given in *Guide to Helicopter/Ship Operations*.

Signals
13.155

1 An indication of the relative wind should be given. Flags, pendants or wind-socks, illuminated at night, are suitable for this purpose.

The ship should display the signals required by Rules 27(b) (i) and (ii) of the *International Regulations for Preventing Collision at Sea 1972*. Before all night operations in congested waters a Safety Message may be broadcast giving the ship's name, and time, expected duration and place of the intended operation.

2 **Warning signal.** A flashing red light in the operating area will indicate to the helicopter pilot that operations are to cease immediately.

Communications
13.156

1 The helicopter pilot will normally communicate by RT calling on VHF Channel 16. The officer of the watch and the officer in charge on deck should be familiar with the standard visual signals, and be in communication with each other.

Ship operating procedures
13.157

1 The officer in charge should check all operational requirements on deck shortly before the arrival of the helicopter. Different types of vessel may require specialist checks. The general requirements for all types of vessel are listed below:

2   All loose objects within and adjacent to the operating area must be secured or removed. Where necessary the deck should be washed to avoid dust being raised by the down-draught from the helicopter rotors.

All aerials and standing or running rigging above or in the vicinity of the operational area should be lowered or secured.

3   Fire pumps should be running with a minimum pressure of 80 psi on deck.

Fire hoses rigged at transfer area from separate hydrants and to be capable of making foam, ideally Aqueous Film Forming Foam (AFFF). (Hoses should be near to but clear of, and if possible upwind of, the operating area pointing away from the helicopter).

4   Foam equipment operators (at least two wearing the prescribed firemen's outfits) should be standing by, and foam nozzles pointing away from the helicopter.

A rescue party should be detailed with at least two members wearing firemen's outfits.

The man overboard rescue boat should be ready for immediate lowering.

5   The following items should be to hand:
Portable fire extinguishers.
Large axe.
Crowbar.
Wire-cutters.
Static discharge/earthing pole.
Red emergency signal/torch.
Marshalling batons (at night).
First aid equipment.

6   The correct lighting and signals (including special navigation lights) should be switched on prior to night operations.

The deck party should be ready, and all passengers clear of the operating area.

Hook handlers should be equipped with strong electricians' rubber gloves and rubber soled shoes to avoid electric shocks from static discharge.

7   All the deck crew should be wearing bright coloured life vests and protective helmets securely fastened with a chin strap, in addition the officer in charge should wear bright gloves, ideally "Dayglow" for marshalling.

Access to and exit from the operating area should be clear.

The officer of the watch on the bridge should be consulted about the ship's readiness.

8   In addition, if the helicopter is to land:
The deck party should be made aware that a landing is being made;
The operating area should be free of heavy spray or seas on deck;
Awnings, stanchions and derricks and, if necessary, side rails should be lowered or removed.
Rope messengers should be to hand in case the aircrew wish to secure the helicopter.
All personnel should be warned to keep clear of rotors and exhausts.

9   **The winch hook must NEVER be attached to any part of the ship**, and the winch wire or load must never be allowed to foul any part of the ship or rigging. If either become snagged, the helicopter crew will cut the winch wire.

Rescue and medical evacuation
13.158

1   Details of methods used for rescue of survivors and the evacuation of medical patients are given in the Notice on Distress and Rescue at Sea in *Annual Summary of Admiralty Notices to Mariners*.

Anchoring

Suitability of anchorage position
13.159

1   When anchoring, masters of vessels should always satisfy themselves that the anchor position selected is suitable, taking into consideration a range of factors. Among these are:
Is the intended position charted as an anchorage? If charted it will either be a Designated Anchorage or a reported anchorage.
Designated Anchorages are identified by national or port authorities for specific categories of vessel by size or cargo, or for quarantine or other specific purposes, and are charted in magenta. See BA Chart 5011 (INT 1).
Reported anchorages have been reported to the charting authorities as having been successfully used in the past. These are charted using a black anchor symbol. See BA Chart 5011 (INT 1).

2   Is it appropriate to the size and draught of the vessel, given proximity to shore, depth of available water at all states of the tide, and the quality of the holding ground?
In the present and forecast weather conditions, is it suitable for use throughout the planned duration of the stay?

ANNEXES

NOTES

Annex A

REQUIREMENTS FOR THE CARRIAGE OF CHARTS AND PUBLICATIONS

Regulatory instruments

SOLAS V
A.1
1 Chapter V of the International Convention for the Safety of Life at Sea 1974 (SOLAS), as amended in accordance with its Protocol of 1988 and by IMO Resolution MSC.99 (73) came into force on 1 July 2002. It is referred to below as SOLAS V.

United Kingdom Law
A.2
1 The Merchant Shipping (Safety of Navigation) Regulations 2002 give effect to the provisions of SOLAS V and came into force on 1 July 2002 (Statutory Instrument 2002 No. 1473). These Regulations require UK-registered vessels (including hovercraft and pleasure vessels of 150 GT and over) and other vessels while in UK waters, to carry nautical charts and nautical publications (defined in SOLAS V Regulation 2.2 (see A.4) in accordance with SOLAS V Regulation 19 (see A.5). SOLAS V Regulation 27 requires that those charts and publications be adequate and up-to-date (see A.6).

2 They revoke the Merchant Shipping (Carriage of Nautical Publications) Regulations 1998 (Statutory Instrument 1998 No 2647). See A.8 and A.9 for details of carriage requirements for fishing vessels.

Radio installation
A.3
1 All ships which are required to fit a radio installation must carry the International Code of Signals, published by the International Maritime Organization (IMO). In addition, all ships must carry an up-to-date copy of the International Aeronautical and Maritime Search and Rescue (IAMSAR) Manual, Volume III, jointly published by IMO and the International Civil Aviation Organization (ICAO).

Charts

Definition
A.4
1 A nautical chart or nautical publication is defined by SOLAS V Regulation 2.2 as:
"a special purpose map or book, or a specially compiled database from which such a map or book is derived, that is issued officially by or on the authority of a Government, authorized Hydrographic Office or other relevant government institution and is designed to meet the requirements of marine navigation - refer to appropriate resolutions and recommendations of the International Hydrographic Organization concerning the authority and

responsibilities of coastal States in the provision of charting in accordance with Regulation 9."

Description
A.5
1 SOLAS V Regulation 19 describes the charts and publications to be carried by the vessels specified in A.2 above, in the following sub-paragraphs:
2.1.4. "...nautical charts and nautical publications to plan and display the vessel's route for the intended voyage and to plot and monitor positions throughout the voyage; an electronic chart display and information system (ECDIS) may be accepted as meeting the chart carriage requirements of this sub-paragraph."
2.1.5. "...back-up arrangements to meet the functional requirements of sub-paragraph 4 *[that is 2.1.4 above]*, if this function is partly or fully fulfilled by electronic means - an appropriate folio of paper nautical charts may be used as a back-up arrangement for ECDIS. Other back-up arrangements for ECDIS are acceptable (see Appendix 6 to Resolution A.817(19), as amended)."

Requirements for charts
A.6
1 All charts and publications must be of the latest obtainable edition and be kept up-to-date from the latest relevant obtainable Notices to Mariners and Navigational Warnings.
The nautical charts or ECDIS referred to in Regulation 19.2.1.4 must be of such a scale and contain sufficient detail as clearly to show:
All navigational marks which may be used by a vessel when navigating the waters which are covered by the chart;
2 All known dangers affecting those waters; information concerning any vessels' routeing and vessel reporting measures applicable to those waters.

Publications

Requirement
A.7
1 The following nautical publications satisfy the requirements of SOLAS V Regulation 19.2.1.4 and should be carried by the vessels detailed in A.2:
International Code of Signals (IMO) (See notes below).
International Aeronautical and Maritime Search and Rescue (IAMSAR) Manual, Volume III (IMO & ICAO) (See notes below).
The Mariner's Handbook (NP100) (UKHO).
Merchant Shipping Notices, Marine Guidance Notes and Marine Information Notes (MCA).

2   Admiralty Notices to Mariners (UKHO).
Admiralty Notices to Mariners – Annual Summary (NP247) Parts 1 and 2 (UKHO).
Admiralty Lists of Radio Signals (UKHO).
Admiralty List of Lights (UKHO).
Admiralty Sailing Directions (UKHO).
Nautical Almanac (UKHO).
Admiralty Tide Tables (UKHO).
Admiralty Tidal Stream Atlases (UKHO).
Operating and maintenance instructions for all navigational aids carried by the ship.

3   **Notes:** In the above list, the abbreviations in brackets indicate the publisher as follows:
IMO – International Maritime Organization.
MCA – United Kingdom Maritime and Coastguard Agency.
ICAO – International Civil Aviation Authority.
UKHO – United Kingdom Hydrographic Office.
Where the UKHO is given as the publisher, any other chart or publication which meets the definition in SOLAS V Regulation 2.2 is acceptable.

4   The digital form of Admiralty Notices to Mariners is accepted by the Maritime and Coastguard Agency (MCA) as meeting the carriage requirements for Notices to Mariners. Similarly, TotalTide published by the UKHO has been approved by the MCA as meeting the requirement for Tide Tables and the Admiralty Digital List of Lights has been approved by the MCA as meeting the requirement for the Lists of Lights.

5   In the case of publications listed above, only those parts of the publication which are relevant to the voyage and operation of a vessel need be carried.

6   As stated in SOLAS V Regulation 27, nautical charts and nautical publications, such as Sailing Directions, Lists of Lights, Notices to Mariners, Tide Tables and all other nautical publications necessary for the intended voyage, must be adequate and up to date.

Modifications to Carriage Requirements for Fishing Vessels

Regulations
A.8

1   For the purposes of carriage of nautical charts and nautical publications, the provisions of SOLAS V Regulation 19.2.1.4 do not apply to fishing vessels.

2   Instead, carriage requirements for fishing vessels between 15 and 24 metres are covered by the Merchant Shipping (Safety of 15-24 Metre Vessels) Regulations 2002 and the associated code of practice contained within MSN 1770(F) – see Section 9.4.3 "Nautical Publications".

Instruments and publications
A.9

1   Fishing vessels over 24 metres are covered by the Fishing Vessels (Safety Provisions) Rules 1975 (Rule 70) and Fishing Vessels (EC Directive on Harmonised Safety Regime) Regulations 1999 and the relevant section of the Protocol to the Torremolinos Convention, 1993 – see Regulation 4 of Chapter 10 "Nautical instruments and publications".

Annex B

THE INTERNATIONAL REGULATIONS FOR PREVENTING COLLISIONS AT SEA (1972)

General information

The Regulations set out below were drawn up at a Conference sponsored by IMO. They were brought into force on 15th July 1977, and have since been amended by IMO Resolutions, the most recent of which came into force on 1st December 2009.

Copies of the Regulations can be obtained from Stationery Office Bookshops.

Associated publications

Publication	Relating to	Obtainable from
Admiralty Notices to Mariners	Details of Traffic Separation Schemes	Admiralty Distributors British Mercantile Marine Offices and Customs Offices (as listed on the UKHO website www.ukho.gov.uk)
Ships' Routeing	Details of Traffic Separation Schemes	International Maritime Organisation, 4 Albert Embankment, London SE1 7SR
CIE Publication No 2·2	Chromacity Chart mentioned in Annex I	National Illumination Committee of Great Britain, CIBS Delta House, 222 Balham High Road, London SW12 9BS
Merchant Ship Search and Rescue Manual	Distress Signals mentioned in Annex IV	International Maritime Organisation, 4 Albert Embankment, London SE1 7SR
International Code of Signals	Distress Signals mentioned in Annex IV	The Stationery Office, Kingsway Bookshop, 119 Kingsway, London WC2B 6PT or from Regional Stationery Office Bookshops.
Merchant Shipping Notices	Statutory Instruments applying the Regulations to British Ships	Finance Branch, Maritime & Coastguard Agency, Spring Place, 105 Commercial Road, Southampton SO15 1EG or IForce, Unit B, Imber Court Trading Estate, Orchard Lane, East Molesey, Surrey KT8 0BN or any MCA Marine Office

INTERNATIONAL REGULATIONS FOR PREVENTING COLLISIONS AT SEA (1972)

PART A. GENERAL

RULE 1

Application

(a) These Rules shall apply to all vessels upon the high seas and in all waters connected therewith navigable by seagoing vessels.

(b) Nothing in these Rules shall interfere with the operation of special rules made by an appropriate authority for roadsteads, harbours, rivers, lakes or inland waterways connected with the high seas and navigable by seagoing vessels. Such special rules shall conform as closely as possible to these Rules.

(c) Nothing in these Rules shall interfere with the operation of any special rules made by the

Government of any State with respect to additional station or signal lights, shapes or whistle signals for ships of war and vessels proceeding under convoy, or with respect to additional station or signal lights or shapes for fishing vessels engaged in fishing as a fleet. These additional station or signal lights, shapes or whistle signals shall, so far as possible, be such that they cannot be mistaken for any light, shape or signal authorised elsewhere under these Rules.

(*d*) Traffic Separation Schemes may be adopted by the *Organisation for the purpose of these Rules.

*i.e. IMO, as stated in Article II of the convention on the International Regulations for Preventing Collisions at Sea (1972).

(*e*) Whenever the Government concerned shall have determined that a vessel of special construction or purpose cannot comply fully with the provisions of any of these Rules with respect to the number, position, range or arc of visibility of lights or shapes, as well as to the disposition and characteristics of sound-signalling appliances, such vessel shall comply with such other provisions in regard to the number, position, range or arc of visibility of lights or shapes, as well as to the disposition and characteristics of sound-signalling appliances, as her Government shall have determined to be the closest possible compliance with these Rules in respect of that vessel.

RULE 2

Responsibility

(*a*) Nothing in these Rules shall exonerate any vessel, or the owner, master or crew thereof, from the consequences of any neglect to comply with these Rules or of the neglect of any precaution which may be required by the ordinary practice of seamen, or by the special circumstances of the case.

(*b*) In construing and complying with these Rules due regard shall be had to all dangers of navigation and collision and to any special circumstances, including the limitations of the vessels involved, which may make a departure from these Rules necessary to avoid immediate danger.

RULE 3

General definitions

For the purpose of these Rules, except where the context otherwise requires:

(*a*) The word "vessel" includes every description of water craft, including non-displacement craft, WIG craft and seaplanes, used or capable of being used as a means of transportation on water.

(*b*) The term "power-driven vessel" means any vessel propelled by machinery.

(*c*) The term "sailing vessel" means any vessel under sail provided that propelling machinery, if fitted, is not being used.

(*d*) The term "vessel engaged in fishing" means any vessel fishing with nets, lines, trawls or other fishing apparatus which restrict manoeuvrability, but does not include a vessel fishing with trolling lines or other fishing

apparatus which do not restrict manoeuvrability.

(*e*) The word "seaplane" includes any aircraft designed to manoeuvre on the water.

(*f*) The term "vessel not under command" means a vessel which through some exceptional circumstance is unable to manoeuvre as required by these Rules and is therefore unable to keep out of the way of another vessel.

(*g*) The term "vessel restricted in her ability to manoeuvre" means a vessel which from the nature of her work is restricted in her ability to manoeuvre as required by these Rules and is therefore unable to keep out of the way of another vessel. The term "vessels restricted in their ability to manoeuvre" shall include but not be limited to:

(i) a vessel engaged in laying, servicing or picking up a navigation mark, submarine cable or pipeline;

(ii) a vessel engaged in dredging, surveying or underwater operations;

(iii) a vessel engaged in replenishment or transferring persons, provisions or cargo while underway;

(iv) a vessel engaged in the launching or recovery of aircraft;

(v) a vessel engaged in mineclearance operations;

(vi) a vessel engaged in a towing operation such as severely restricts the towing vessel and her tow in their ability to deviate from their course.

(*h*) The term "vessel constrained by her draught" means a power-driven vessel which because of her draught in relation to the available depth and width of navigable water is severely restricted in her ability to deviate from the course she is following.

(*i*) The word "underway" means that a vessel is not at anchor, or made fast to the shore, or aground.

(*j*) The words "length" and "breadth" of a vessel mean her length overall and greatest breadth.

(*k*) Vessels shall be deemed to be in sight of one another only when one can be observed visually from the other.

(*l*) The term "restricted visibility" means any condition in which visibility is restricted by fog, mist, falling snow, heavy rainstorms, sandstorms or any other similar causes.

(*m*)The term "Wing-In-Ground (WIG) craft" means a multimodal craft which, in its main operational mode, flies in close proximity to the surface by utilising surface-effect action.

PART B. STEERING AND SAILING RULES

Section I. Conduct of vessels in any condition of visibility

RULE 4

Application

Rules in this Section apply in any condition of visibility.

RULE 5

Look-out

Every vessel shall at all times maintain a proper look-out by sight and hearing as well as by all available means appropriate in the prevailing circumstances and conditions so as to make a full appraisal of the situation and of the risk of collision.

RULE 6

Safe speed

Every vessel shall at all times proceed at a safe speed so that she can take proper and effective action to avoid collision and be stopped within a distance appropriate to the prevailing circumstances and conditions.

In determining a safe speed the following factors shall be among those taken into account:

(a) By all vessels:
  (i) the state of visibility;
  (ii) the traffic density including concentrations of fishing vessels or any other vessels;
  (iii) the manoeuvrability of the vessel with special reference to stopping distance and turning ability in the prevailing conditions;
  (iv) at night the presence of background light such as from shore lights or from back scatter of her own lights;
  (v) the state of wind, sea and current, and the proximity of navigational hazards;
  (vi) the draught in relation to the available depth of water.

(b) Additionally, by vessels with operational radar:
  (i) the characteristics, efficiency and limitations of the radar equipment;
  (ii) any constraints imposed by the radar range scale in use;
  (iii) the effect on radar detection of the sea state, weather and other sources of interference;
  (iv) the possibility that small vessels, ice and other floating objects may not be detected by radar at an adequate range;
  (v) the number, location and movement of vessels detected by radar;
  (vi) the more exact assessment of the visibility that may be possible when radar is used to determine the range of vessels or other objects in the vicinity.

RULE 7

Risk of collision

(a) Every vessel shall use all available means appropriate to the prevailing circumstances and conditions to determine if risk of collision exists. If there is any doubt such risk shall be deemed to exist.

(b) Proper use shall be made of radar equipment if fitted and operational, including long-range scanning to obtain early warning of risk of collision and radar plotting or equivalent systematic observation of detected objects.

(c) Assumptions shall not be made on the basis of scanty information, especially scanty radar information.

(d) In determining if risk of collision exists the following considerations shall be among those taken into account:
  (i) such risk shall be deemed to exist if the compass bearing of an approaching vessel does not appreciably change;
  (ii) such risk may sometimes exist even when an appreciable bearing change is evident, particularly when approaching a very large vessel or a tow or when approaching a vessel at close range.

RULE 8

Action to avoid collision

(a) Any action taken to avoid collision shall be taken in accordance with the Rules of this Part and shall, if the circumstances of the case admit, be positive, made in ample time and with due regard to the observance of good seamanship.

(b) Any alteration of course and/or speed to avoid collision shall, if the circumstances of the case admit, be large enough to be readily apparent to another vessel observing visually or by radar; a succession of small alterations of course and/or speed should be avoided.

(c) If there is sufficient sea room, alteration of course alone may be the most effective action to avoid a close-quarters situation provided that it is made in good time, is substantial and does not result in another close-quarters situation.

(d) Action taken to avoid collision with another vessel shall be such as to result in passing at a safe distance. The effectiveness of the action shall be carefully checked until the other vessel is finally past and clear.

(e) If necessary to avoid collision or allow more time to assess the situation, a vessel shall slacken her speed or take all way off by stopping or reversing her means of propulsion.

(f)(i) A vessel which by any of these Rules is required not to impede the passage or safe passage of another vessel shall, when required by the circumstances of the case, take early action to allow sufficient sea room for the safe passage of the other vessel.

  (ii) A vessel required not to impede the passage or safe passage of another vessel is not relieved of this obligation if approaching the other vessel so as to involve risk of collision and shall, when taking action, have full regard to the action which may be required by the Rules of this Part.

  (iii) A vessel the passage of which is not to be impeded remains fully obliged to comply with the Rules of this Part when the two vessels are approaching one another so as to involve risk of collision.

RULE 9

Narrow channels

(*a*) A vessel proceeding along the course of a narrow channel or fairway shall keep as near to the outer limit of the channel or fairway which lies on her starboard side as is safe and practicable.

(*b*) A vessel of less than 20 metres in length or a sailing vessel shall not impede the passage of a vessel which can safely navigate only within a narrow channel or fairway.

(*c*) A vessel engaged in fishing shall not impede the passage of any other vessel navigating within a narrow channel or fairway.

(*d*) A vessel shall not cross a narrow channel or fairway if such crossing impedes the passage of a vessel which can safely navigate only within such channel or fairway. The latter vessel may use the sound signal prescribed in Rule 34(*d*) if in doubt as to the intention of the crossing vessel.

(*e*)(i) In a narrow channel or fairway when overtaking can take place only if the vessel to be overtaken has to take action to permit safe passing, the vessel intending to overtake shall indicate her intention by sounding the appropriate signal prescribed in Rule 34(*c*)(i). The vessel to be overtaken shall, if in agreement, sound the appropriate signal prescribed in Rule 34(*c*)(ii) and take steps to permit safe passing. If in doubt she may sound the signals prescribed in Rule 34(*d*).

(ii) This Rule does not relieve the overtaking vessel of her obligation under Rule 13.

(*f*) A vessel nearing a bend or an area of a narrow channel or fairway where other vessels may be obscured by an intervening obstruction shall navigate with particular alertness and caution and shall sound the appropriate signal prescribed in Rule 34(*e*).

(*g*) Any vessel shall, if the circumstances of the case admit, avoid anchoring in a narrow channel.

RULE 10

Traffic Separation Schemes

(*a*) This Rule applies to Traffic Separation Schemes adopted by the *Organisation and does not relieve any vessel of her obligation under any other Rule.

(*b*) A vessel using a Traffic Separation Scheme shall:

(i) proceed in the appropriate traffic lane in the general direction of traffic flow for that lane;

(ii) so far as practicable keep clear of the traffic separation line or separation zone;

(iii) normally join or leave a traffic lane at the termination of the lane, but when joining or leaving from either side shall do so at as

small an angle to the general direction of traffic flow as practicable.

(*c*) A vessel shall, so far as practicable, avoid crossing traffic lanes but if obliged to do so shall cross on a heading as nearly as practicable at right angles to the general direction of traffic flow.

(*d*)(i) A vessel shall not use an inshore traffic zone when she can safely use the appropriate traffic lane within the adjacent traffic separation scheme. However, vessels of less than 20 m in length, sailing vessels and vessels engaged in fishing may use the inshore traffic zone.

(ii) Notwithstanding subparagraph (*d*)(i), a vessel may use an inshore traffic zone when en route to or from a port, offshore installation or structure, pilot station or any other place situated within the inshore traffic zone, or to avoid immediate danger.

(*e*) A vessel other than a crossing vessel or a vessel joining or leaving a lane shall not normally enter a separation zone or cross a separation line except:

(i) in cases of emergency to avoid immediate danger;

(ii) to engage in fishing within a separation zone.

(*f*) A vessel navigating in areas near the terminations of Traffic Separation Schemes shall do so with particular caution.

(*g*) A vessel shall so far as practicable avoid anchoring in a Traffic Separation Scheme or in areas near its terminations.

(*h*) A vessel not using a Traffic Separation Scheme shall avoid it by as wide a margin as is practicable.

(*i*) A vessel engaged in fishing shall not impede the passage of any vessel following a traffic lane.

(*j*) A vessel of less than 20 metres in length or a sailing vessel shall not impede the safe passage of a power-driven vessel following a traffic lane.

(*k*) A vessel restricted in her ability to manoeuvre when engaged in an operation for the maintenance of safety of navigation in a Traffic Separation Scheme is exempted from complying with this Rule to the extent necessary to carry out the operation.

(*l*) A vessel restricted in her ability to manoeuvre when engaged in an operation for the laying, servicing or picking up of a submarine cable, within a Traffic Separation Scheme, is exempted from complying with this Rule to the extent necessary to carry out the operation.

Section II. Conduct of vessels in sight of one another

RULE 11

Application

Rules in this Section apply to vessels in sight of one another.

RULE 12

Sailing vessels

(a) When two sailing vessels are approaching one another, so as to involve risk of collision, one of them shall keep out of the way of the other as follows:
(i) when each has the wind on a different side, the vessel which has the wind on the port side shall keep out of the way of the other;
(ii) when both have the wind on the same side, the vessel which is to windward shall keep out of the way of the vessel which is to leeward;
(iii) if a vessel with the wind on the port side sees a vessel to windward and cannot determine with certainty whether the other vessel has the wind on the port or on the starboard side, she shall keep out of the way of the other.
(b) For the purposes of this Rule the windward side shall be deemed to be the side opposite to that on which the mainsail is carried or, in the case of a square-rigged vessel, the side opposite to that on which the largest fore-and-aft sail is carried.

RULE 13

Overtaking

(a) Notwithstanding anything contained in the Rules of Part B, Sections I and II any vessel overtaking any other shall keep out of the way of the vessel being overtaken.
(b) A vessel shall be deemed to be overtaking when coming up with another vessel from a direction more than 22·5 degrees abaft her beam, that is, in such a position with reference to the vessel she is overtaking, that at night she would be able to see only the sternlight of that vessel but neither of her sidelights.
(c) When a vessel is in any doubt as to whether she is overtaking another, she shall assume that this is the case and act accordingly.
(d) Any subsequent alteration of the bearing between the two vessels shall not make the overtaking vessel a crossing vessel within the meaning of these Rules or relieve her of the duty of keeping clear of the overtaken vessel until she is finally past and clear.

RULE 14

Head-on situation

(a) When two power-driven vessels are meeting on reciprocal or nearly reciprocal courses so as to involve risk of collision each shall alter her course to starboard so that each shall pass on the port side of the other.
(b) Such a situation shall be deemed to exist when a vessel sees the other ahead or nearly ahead and by night she could see the masthead lights of the other in a line or nearly in a line and/or both sidelights and by day

she observes the corresponding aspect of the other vessel.
(c) When a vessel is in any doubt as to whether such a situation exists she shall assume that it does exist and act accordingly.

RULE 15

Crossing situation

When two power-driven vessels are crossing so as to involve risk of collision, the vessel which has the other on her own starboard side shall keep out of the way and shall, if the circumstances of the case admit, avoid crossing ahead of the other vessel.

RULE 16

Action by give-way vessel

Every vessel which is directed to keep out of the way of another vessel shall, so far as possible, take early and substantial action to keep well clear.

RULE 17

Action by stand-on vessel

(a)(i) Where one of two vessels is to keep out of the way the other shall keep her course and speed.
(ii) The latter vessel may however take action to avoid collision by her manoeuvre alone, as soon as it becomes apparent to her that the vessel required to keep out of the way is not taking appropriate action in compliance with these Rules.
(b) When, from any cause, the vessel required to keep her course and speed finds herself so close that collision cannot be avoided by the action of the give-way vessel alone, she shall take such action as will best aid to avoid collision.
(c) A power-driven vessel which takes action in a crossing situation in accordance with sub-paragraph (a)(ii) of this Rule to avoid collision with another power-driven vessel shall, if the circumstances of the case admit, not alter course to port for a vessel on her own port side.
(d) This Rule does not relieve the give-way vessel of her obligation to keep out of the way.

RULE 18

Responsibilities between vessels

Except where Rules 9, 10 and 13 otherwise require:
(a) A power-driven vessel underway shall keep out of the way of:
(i) a vessel not under command;
(ii) a vessel restricted in her ability to manoeuvre;
(iii) a vessel engaged in fishing;
(iv) a sailing vessel.
(b) A sailing vessel underway shall keep out of the way of:
(i) a vessel not under command;
(ii) a vessel restricted in her ability to manoeuvre;
(iii) a vessel engaged in fishing.

(c) A vessel engaged in fishing when underway shall, so far as possible, keep out of the way of:

(i) a vessel not under command.

(ii) a vessel restricted in her ability to manoeuvre.

(d)(i) Any vessel other than a vessel not under command or a vessel restricted in her ability to manoeuvre shall, if the circumstances of the case admit, avoid impeding the safe passage of a vessel constrained by her draught, exhibiting the signals in Rule 28;

(ii) A vessel constrained by her draught shall navigate with particular caution having full regard to her special condition.

(e) A seaplane on the water shall, in general keep well clear of all vessels and avoid impeding their navigation. In circumstances, however, where risk of collision exists, she shall comply with the Rules of this Part.

(f)(i) A WIG craft shall, when taking off, landing and in flight near the surface, keep well clear of all other vessels and avoid impeding their navigation;

(ii) A WIG craft operating on the water surface shall comply with the Rules of this Part as a power-driven vessel.

Section III. Conduct of vessels in restricted visibility

RULE 19

Conduct of vessels in restricted visibility

(a) This Rule applies to vessels not in sight of one another when navigating in or near an area of restricted visibility.

(b) Every vessel shall proceed at a safe speed adapted to the prevailing circumstances and conditions of restricted visibility. A power-driven vessel shall have her engines ready for immediate manoeuvre.

(c) Every vessel shall have due regard to the prevailing circumstances and conditions of restricted visibility when complying with the Rules of Section I of this Part.

(d) A vessel which detects by radar alone the presence of another vessel shall determine if a close-quarters situation is developing and/or risk of collision exists. If so, she shall take avoiding action in ample time, provided that when such action consists of an alteration of course, so far as possible the following shall be avoided:

(i) an alteration of course to port for a vessel forward of the beam, other than for a vessel being overtaken;

(ii) an alteration of course towards a vessel abeam or abaft the beam.

(e) Except where it has been determined that a risk of collision does not exist, every vessel which hears apparently forward of her beam the fog signal of another vessel, or which cannot avoid a close-quarters situation with another vessel forward of her beam, shall

reduce her speed to the minimum at which she can be kept on her course. She shall if necessary take all her way off and in any event navigate with extreme caution until danger of collision is over.

PART C. LIGHTS AND SHAPES

RULE 20

Application

(a) Rules in this Part shall be complied with in all weathers.

(b) The Rules concerning lights shall be complied with from sunset to sunrise, and during such times no other lights shall be exhibited, except such lights as cannot be mistaken for the lights specified in these Rules or do not impair their visibility or distinctive character, or interfere with the keeping of a proper look-out.

(c) The lights prescribed by these Rules shall, if carried, also be exhibited from sunrise to sunset in restricted visibility and may be exhibited in all other circumstances when it is deemed necessary.

(d) The Rules concerning shapes shall be complied with by day.

(e) The lights and shapes specified in these Rules shall comply with the provisions of Annex I to these Regulations.

RULE 21

Definitions

(a) "Masthead light" means a white light placed over the fore and aft centreline of the vessel showing an unbroken light over an arc of the horizon of 225 degrees and so fixed as to show the light from right ahead to 22.5 degrees abaft the beam on either side of the vessel.

(b) "Sidelights" means a green light on the starboard side and a red light on the port side each showing an unbroken light over an arc of the horizon of 112.5 degrees and so fixed as to show the light from right ahead to 22.5 degrees abaft the beam on its respective side. In a vessel of less than 20 metres in length the sidelights may be combined in one lantern carried on the fore and aft centreline of the vessel.

(c) "Sternlight" means a white light placed as nearly as practicable at the stern showing an unbroken light over an arc of the horizon of 135 degrees and so fixed as to show the light 67.5 degrees from right aft on each side of the vessel.

(d) "Towing light" means a yellow light having the same characteristic as the "sternlight" defined in paragraph (c) of this Rule.

(e) "All-round light" means a light showing an unbroken light over an arc of the horizon of 360 degrees.

(f) "Flashing light" means a light flashing at regular intervals at a frequency of 120 flashes or more per minute.

RULE 22

Visibility of lights

The lights prescribed in these Rules shall have an intensity as specified in Section 8 of Annex I to these Regulations so as to be visible at the following minimum ranges:

(*a*) In vessels of 50 metres or more in length:
— a masthead light, 6 miles;
— a sidelight, 3 miles;
— a sternlight, 3 miles;
— a towing light, 3 miles;
— a white, red, green or yellow all-round light, 3 miles.

(*b*) In vessels of 12 metres or more in length but less than 50 metres in length:
— a masthead light, 5 miles; except that where the length of the vessel is less than 20 metres, 3 miles;
— a sidelight, 2 miles;
— a sternlight, 2 miles;
— a towing light, 2 miles;
— a white, red, green or yellow all-round light, 2 miles.

(*c*) In vessels of less than 12 metres in length:
— a masthead light, 2 miles;
— a sidelight, 1 mile;
— a sternlight, 2 miles;
— a towing light, 2 miles;
— a white, red, green or yellow all-round light, 2 miles.

(*d*) In inconspicuous, partly submerged vessels or objects being towed:
— a white all-round light, 3 miles.

RULE 23

Power-driven vessels underway

(*a*) A power-driven vessel underway shall exhibit:
(i) a masthead light forward;
(ii) a second masthead light abaft of and higher than the forward one; except that a vessel of less than 50 metres in length shall not be obliged to exhibit such light but may do so;
(iii) sidelights;
(iv) a sternlight.

(*b*) An air-cushion vessel when operating in the non-displacement mode shall, in addition to the lights prescribed in paragraph (*a*) of this Rule exhibit an all-round flashing yellow light.

(*c*) A WIG craft only when taking off, landing and in flight near the surface shall, in addition to the lights prescribed in paragraph (*a*) of this Rule, exhibit a high–intensity all–round flashing red light.

(*d*)(i) A power-driven vessel of less than 12 metres in length may in lieu of the lights prescribed in paragraph (*a*) of this Rule exhibit an all-round white light and sidelights;
(ii) a power-driven vessel of less than 7 metres in length whose maximum speed does not exceed 7 knots may in lieu of the lights prescribed in paragraph (*a*) of this Rule exhibit an all-round white light and shall, if practicable, also exhibit sidelights;

(iii) the masthead light or all-round white light on a power-driven vessel of less than 12 metres in length may be displaced from the fore and aft centreline of the vessel if centreline fitting is not practicable, provided that the sidelights are combined in one lantern which shall be carried on the fore and aft centreline of the vessel or located as nearly as practicable in the same fore and aft line as the masthead light or the all-round white light.

RULE 24

Towing and pushing

(*a*) A power-driven vessel when towing shall exhibit:
(i) instead of the light prescribed in Rule 23(*a*)(i) or (*a*)(ii), two masthead lights in a vertical line. When the length of the tow, measuring from the stern of the towing vessel to the after end of the tow exceeds 200 metres, three such lights in a vertical line;
(ii) sidelights;
(iii) a sternlight;
(iv) a towing light in a vertical line above the sternlight;
(v) when the length of the tow exceeds 200 metres, a diamond shape where it can best be seen.

(*b*) When a pushing vessel and a vessel being pushed ahead are rigidly connected in a composite unit they shall be regarded as a power-driven vessel and exhibit the lights prescribed in Rule 23.

(*c*) A power-driven vessel when pushing ahead or towing alongside, except in the case of a composite unit, shall exhibit:
(i) instead of the light prescribed in Rule 23(*a*)(i) or (*a*)(ii), two masthead lights in a vertical line;
(ii) sidelights;
(iii) a sternlight.

(*d*) A power-driven vessel to which paragraph (*a*) or (*c*) of this Rule apply shall also comply with Rule 23(*a*)(ii).

(*e*) A vessel or object being towed, other than those mentioned in paragraph (*g*) of this Rule, shall exhibit:
(i) sidelights:
(ii) a sternlight:
(iii) when the length of the tow exceeds 200 metres, a diamond shape where it can best be seen.

(*f*) Provided that any number of vessels being towed alongside or pushed in a group shall be lighted as one vessel;
(i) a vessel being pushed ahead, not being part of a composite unit, shall exhibit at the forward end, sidelights;
(ii) a vessel being towed alongside shall exhibit a sternlight and at the forward end, sidelights.

(*g*) An inconspicuous, partly submerged vessel or object, or combination of such vessels or objects being towed, shall exhibit:

(i) if it is less than 25 metres in breadth, one all-round white light at or near the forward end and one at or near the after end except that dracones need not exhibit a light at or near the forward end;

(ii) if it is 25 metres or more in breadth, two additional all-round white lights at or near the extremities of its breadth;

(iii) if it exceeds 100 metres in length, additional all-round white lights between the lights prescribed in sub-paragraphs (i) and (ii) so that the distance between the lights shall not exceed 100 metres;

(iv) a diamond shape at or near the aftermost extremity of the last vessel or object being towed and if the length of the tow exceeds 200 metres an additional diamond shape where it can best be seen and located as far forward as is practicable.

(h) Where from any sufficient cause it is impracticable for a vessel or object being towed to exhibit the lights or shapes prescribed in paragraph (e) or (g) of this Rule, all possible measures shall be taken to light the vessel or object towed or at least to indicate the presence of such vessel or object.

(i) Where from any sufficient cause it is impracticable for a vessel not normally engaged in towing operations to display the lights prescribed in paragraph (a) or (c) of this Rule, such vessel shall not be required to exhibit those lights when engaged in towing another vessel in distress or otherwise in need of assistance. All possible measures shall be taken to indicate the nature of the relationship between the towing vessel and the vessel being towed as authorized by Rule 36, in particular by illuminating the towline.

RULE 25

Sailing vessels underway and vessels under oars

(a) A sailing vessel underway shall exhibit:
(i) sidelights;
(ii) a sternlight;

(b) In a sailing vessel of less than 20 metres in length the lights prescribed in paragraph (a) of this Rule may be combined in one lantern carried at or near the top of the mast where it can best be seen.

(c) A sailing vessel underway may, in addition to the lights prescribed in paragraph (a) of this Rule, exhibit at or near the top of the mast, where they can best be seen two all-round lights, in a vertical line, the upper being red and the lower green, but these lights shall not be exhibited in conjunction with the combined lantern permitted by paragraph (b) of this Rule.

(d)(i) A sailing vessel of less than 7 metres in length shall, if practicable, exhibit the lights prescribed in paragraphs (a) or (b) of this Rule, but if she does not, she shall have ready at hand an electric torch or lighted lantern showing a white light which shall

be exhibited in sufficient time to prevent collision.

(ii) A vessel under oars may exhibit the lights prescribed in this Rule for sailing vessels, but if she does not, she shall have ready at hand an electric torch or lighted lantern showing a white light which shall be exhibited in sufficient time to prevent collision.

(e) A vessel proceeding under sail when also being propelled by machinery shall exhibit forward where it can best be seen a conical shape, apex downwards.

RULE 26

Fishing vessels

(a) A vessel engaged in fishing, whether underway or at anchor, shall exhibit only the lights and shapes prescribed in this Rule.

(b) A vessel when engaged in trawling, by which is meant the dragging through the water of a dredge net or other apparatus used as a fishing appliance, shall exhibit:
(i) two all-round lights in a vertical line, the upper being green and the lower white, or a shape consisting of two cones with their apexes together in a vertical line one above the other;
(ii) a masthead light abaft of and higher than the all-round green light; a vessel of less than 50 metres in length shall not be obliged to exhibit such a light but may do so;
(iii) when making way through the water, in addition to the lights prescribed in this paragraph, sidelights and a sternlight.

(c) A vessel engaged in fishing, other than trawling, shall exhibit:
(i) two all-round lights in a vertical line, the upper being red and the lower white, or a shape consisting of two cones with apexes together in a vertical line one above the other;
(ii) when there is outlying gear extending more than 150 metres horizontally from the vessel, an all-round white light or a cone apex upwards in the direction of the gear;
(iii) when making way through the water, in addition to the lights prescribed in this paragraph, side-lights and a sternlight.

(d) The additional signals described in Annex II to these regulations apply to a vessel engaged in fishing in close proximity to other vessels engaged in fishing.

(e) A vessel when not engaged in fishing shall not exhibit the lights or shapes prescribed in this Rule, but only those prescribed for a vessel of her length.

RULE 27

Vessels not under command or restricted in their ability to manoeuvre

(a) A vessel not under command shall exhibit:
(i) two all-round red lights in a vertical line where they can best be seen;
(ii) two balls or similar shapes in a vertical line where they can best be seen;

(iii) when making way through the water, in addition to the lights prescribed in this paragraph, side-lights and a sternlight.

(b) A vessel restricted in her ability to manoeuvre, except a vessel engaged in mineclearance operations, shall exhibit:

(i) three all-round lights in a vertical line where they can best be seen. The highest and lowest of these lights shall be red and the middle light shall be white;

(ii) three shapes in a vertical line where they can best be seen. The highest and lowest of these shapes shall be balls and the middle one a diamond;

(iii) when making way through the water, a masthead light or lights, sidelights and a sternlight, in addition to the lights prescribed in sub-paragraph (i);

(iv) when at anchor, in addition to the lights or shapes prescribed in sub-paragraphs (i) and (ii), the light, lights or shape prescribed in Rule 30.

(c) A power-driven vessel engaged in a towing operation such as severely restricts the towing vessel and her tow in their ability to deviate from their course shall, in addition to the lights or shapes prescribed in Rule 24 (a), exhibit the lights or shapes prescribed in sub-paragraphs (b)(i) and (ii) of this Rule.

(d) A vessel engaged in dredging or underwater operations, when restricted in her ability to manoeuvre, shall exhibit the lights and shapes prescribed in sub-paragraphs (b)(i), (ii) and (iii) of this Rule and shall in addition, when an obstruction exists, exhibit:

(i) two all-round red lights or two balls in a vertical line to indicate the side on which the obstruction exists;

(ii) two all-round green lights or two diamonds in a vertical line to indicate the side on which another vessel may pass;

(iii) when at anchor, the lights or shapes prescribed in this paragraph instead of the lights or shape prescribed in Rule 30.

(e) Whenever the size of a vessel engaged in diving operations makes it impracticable to exhibit all lights and shapes prescribed in paragraph (d) of this Rule, the following shall be exhibited:

(i) three all-round lights in a vertical line where they can best be seen. The highest and lowest of these lights shall be red and the middle light shall be white;

(ii) a rigid replica of the International Code flag "A" not less than 1 metre in height. Measures shall be taken to ensure its all-round visibility.

(f) A vessel engaged in mineclearance operations shall in addition to the lights prescribed for a power-driven vessel in Rule 23 or to the lights or shape prescribed for a vessel at anchor in Rule 30 as appropriate, exhibit three all-round green lights or three balls. One of these lights or shapes shall be exhibited near the foremast head and one at each end of the fore yard. These lights or shapes indicate that it is dangerous for another vessel to approach within 1,000 metres of the mineclearance vessel.

(g) Vessels of less than 12 metres in length, except those engaged in diving operations, shall not be required to exhibit the lights and shapes prescribed in this Rule.

(h) The signals prescribed in this Rule are not signals of vessels in distress and requiring assistance. Such signals are contained in Annex IV to these Regulations.

RULE 28

Vessels constrained by their draught

A vessel constrained by her draught may, in addition to the lights prescribed for power-driven vessels in Rule 23, exhibit where they can best be seen three all-round red lights in a vertical line, or a cylinder.

RULE 29

Pilot vessels

(a) A vessel engaged on pilotage duty shall exhibit:

(i) at or near the masthead, two all-round lights in a vertical line, the upper being white and the lower red;

(ii) when underway, in addition, sidelights and a sternlight;

(iii) when at anchor, in addition to the lights prescribed in sub-paragraph (i), the light, lights or shape prescribed in Rule 30 for vessels at anchor.

(b) A pilot vessel when not engaged on pilotage duty shall exhibit the lights or shapes prescribed for a similar vessel of her length.

RULE 30

Anchored vessels and vessels aground

(a) A vessel at anchor shall exhibit where it can best be seen:

(i) in the fore part, an all-round white light or one ball;

(ii) at or near the stern and at a lower level than the light prescribed in sub-paragraph (i), an all-round white light.

(b) A vessel of less than 50 metres in length may exhibit an all-round white light where it can best be seen instead of the lights prescribed in paragraph (a) of this Rule.

(c) A vessel at anchor may, and a vessel of 100 metres and more in length shall, also use the available working or equivalent lights to illuminate her decks.

(d) A vessel aground shall exhibit the lights prescribed in paragraph (a) or (b) of this Rule and in addition, where they can best be seen:
(i) two all-round red lights in a vertical line;
(ii) three balls in a vertical line.

(e) A vessel of less than 7 metres in length, when at anchor, not in or near a narrow channel, fairway or anchorage, or where other vessels normally navigate, shall not be required to exhibit the lights or shape prescribed in paragraphs (a) and (b) of this Rule.

(f) A vessel of less than 12 metres in length, when aground, shall not be required to exhibit the lights or shapes prescribed in sub-paragraphs (d)(i) and (ii) of this Rule.

RULE 31

Seaplanes

Where it is impracticable for a seaplane or a WIG craft to exhibit lights and shapes of the characteristics or in the positions prescribed in the Rules of this Part she shall exhibit lights and shapes as closely similar in characteristics and position as is possible.

PART D. SOUND AND LIGHT SIGNALS

RULE 32

Definitions

(a) The word "whistle" means any sound signalling appliance capable of producing the prescribed blasts and which complies with the specifications in Annex III to these Regulations.

(b) The term "short blast" means a blast of about one seconds' duration.

(c) The term "prolonged blast" means a blast of from four to six second's duration.

RULE 33

Equipment for sound signals

(a) A vessel of 12 metres or more in length shall be provided with a whistle, a vessel of 20 m or more in length shall be provided with a bell in addition to a whistle, and a vessel of 100 metres or more in length shall, in addition, be provided with a gong, the tone and sound of which cannot be confused with that of the bell. The whistle, bell and gong shall comply with the specifications in Annex III to these Regulations. The bell or gong or both may be replaced by other equipment having the same respective sound characteristics, provided that manual sounding of the prescribed signals shall always be possible.

(b) A vessel of less than 12 metres in length shall not be obliged to carry the sound signalling appliances prescribed in paragraph (a) of this Rule but if she does not, she shall be provided with some other means of making an efficient sound signal.

RULE 34

Manoeuvring and warning signals

(a) When vessels are in sight of one another, a power-driven vessel underway, when manoeuvring as authorised or required by these Rules, shall indicate that manoeuvre by the following signals on her whistle:
— one short blast to mean "I am altering my course to starboard";

— two short blasts to mean "I am altering my course to port";
— three short blasts to mean "I am operating astern propulsion".

(b) Any vessel may supplement the whistle signals prescribed in paragraph (a) of this Rule by light signals, repeated as appropriate, whilst the manoeuvre is being carried out:
(i) these light signals shall have the following significance:
— one flash to mean "I am altering my course to starboard";
— two flashes to mean "I am altering my course to port";
— three flashes to mean "I am operating astern propulsion".
(ii) the duration of each flash shall be about one second, the interval between flashes shall be about one second, and the interval between successive signals shall be not less than ten seconds;
(iii) the light used for this signal shall, if fitted, be an all-round white light, visible at a minimum range of 5 miles, and shall comply with the provisions of Annex I to these Regulations.

(c) When in sight of one another in a narrow channel of fairway:
(i) a vessel intending to overtake another shall in compliance with Rule 9(e)(i) indicate her intention by the following signals on her whistle:
— two prolonged blasts followed by one short blast to mean "I intend to overtake you on your starboard side";
— two prolonged blasts followed by two short blasts to mean "I intend to overtake you on your port side";
(ii) the vessel about to be overtaken when acting in accordance with Rule 9(e)(i) shall indicate her agreement by the following signal on her whistle:
— one prolonged, one short, one prolonged and one short blast, in that order.

(d) When vessels in sight of one another are approaching each other and from any cause either vessel fails to understand the intentions or actions of the other, or is in doubt whether sufficient action is being taken by the other to avoid collision, the vessel in doubt shall immediately indicate such doubt by giving at least five short and rapid blasts on the whistle. Such signal may be supplemented by a light signal of at least five short and rapid flashes.

(e) A vessel nearing a bend or an area of a channel or fairway where other vessels may be obscured by an intervening obstruction shall sound one prolonged blast. Such signal shall be answered with a prolonged blast by any approaching vessel that may be within hearing around the bend or behind the intervening obstruction.

(f) If whistles are fitted on a vessel at a distance apart of more than 100 metres, one whistle only shall be used for giving manoeuvring and warning signals.

RULE 35

Sound signals in restricted visibility

In or near an area of restricted visibility, whether by day or night, the signals prescribed in this Rule shall be used as follows:

(*a*) A power-driven vessel making way through the water shall sound at intervals of not more than 2 minutes one prolonged blast.

(*b*) A power-driven vessel underway but stopped and making no way through the water shall sound at intervals of not more than 2 minutes two prolonged blasts in succession with an interval of about 2 seconds between them.

(*c*) A vessel not under command, a vessel restricted in her ability to manoeuvre, a vessel constrained by her draught, a sailing vessel, a vessel engaged in fishing and a vessel engaged in towing or pushing another vessel shall, instead of the signals prescribed in paragraphs (*a*) or (*b*) of this Rule, sound at intervals of not more than 2 minutes three blasts in succession, namely one prolonged followed by two short blasts.

(*d*) A vessel engaged in fishing, when at anchor, and a vessel restricted in her ability to manoeuvre when carrying out her work at anchor, shall instead of the signals prescribed in paragraph (*g*) of this Rule sound the signal prescribed in paragraph (*c*) of this Rule.

(*e*) A vessel towed or if more than one vessel is towed the last vessel of the tow, if manned, shall at intervals of not more than 2 minutes sound four blasts in succession, namely one prolonged followed by three short blasts. When practicable, this signal shall be made immediately after the signal made by the towing vessel.

(*f*) When a pushing vessel and a vessel being pushed ahead are rigidly connected in a composite unit they shall be regarded as a power-driven vessel and shall give the signals prescribed in paragraphs (*a*) or (*b*) of this Rule.

(*g*) A vessel at anchor shall at intervals of not more than one minute ring the bell rapidly for about 5 seconds. In a vessel of 100 metres or more in length the bell shall be sounded in the forepart of the vessel and immediately after the ringing of the bell the gong shall be sounded rapidly for about 5 seconds in the after part of the vessel. A vessel at anchor may in addition sound three blasts in succession, namely one short, one prolonged and one short blast, to give warning of her position and of the possibility of collision to an approaching vessel.

(*h*) A vessel aground shall give the bell signal and if required the gong signal prescribed in paragraph (*g*) of this Rule and shall, in addition, give three separate and distinct strokes on the bell immediately before and after the rapid ringing of the bell. A vessel aground may in addition sound an appropriate whistle signal.

(*i*) A vessel of 12 m or more but less than 20 m in length shall not be obliged to give the bell signals prescribed in paragraphs (*g*) and (*h*) of this Rule. However, if she does not, she shall make some other efficient sound signal at intervals of not more than 2 minutes.

(*j*) A vessel of less than 12 metres in length shall not be obliged to give the above-mentioned signals but, if she does not, shall make some other efficient sound signal at intervals of not more than 2 minutes.

(*k*) A pilot vessel when engaged on pilotage duty may in addition to the signals prescribed in paragraphs (*a*), (*b*) or (*g*) of this Rule sound an identity signal consisting of four short blasts.

RULE 36

Signals to attract attention

If necessary to attract the attention of another vessel any vessel may make light or sound signals that cannot be mistaken for any signal authorised elsewhere in these Rules, or may direct the beam of her searchlight in the direction of the danger, in such a way as not to embarrass any vessel. Any light to attract the attention of another vessel shall be such that it cannot be mistaken for any aid to navigation. For the purpose of this Rule the use of high intensity intermittent or revolving lights, such as strobe lights, shall be avoided.

RULE 37

Distress signals

When a vessel is in distress and requires assistance she shall use or exhibit the signals described in Annex IV to these Regulations.

PART E. EXEMPTIONS

RULE 38

Exemptions

Any vessel (or class of vessels) provided that she complies with the requirements of the International Regulations for Preventing Collisions at Sea, 1960*, the keel of which is laid or which is at a corresponding stage of construction before the entry into force of these Regulations may be exempted from compliance therewith as follows:

(*a*) The installation of lights with ranges prescribed in Rule 22, until four years after the date of entry into force of these Regulations.

(*b*) The installation of lights with colour specifications as prescribed in Section 7 of Annex I to these Regulations, until four years after the date of entry into force of these Regulations.

(*c*) The repositioning of lights as a result of conversion from Imperial to metric units and rounding off measurements figures, permanent exemption.

(*d*)(i) The repositioning of masthead lights on vessels of less than 150 metres in length, resulting from the prescriptions of Section 3(*a*) of Annex I to these Regulations, permanent exemption.

(ii) The repositioning of masthead lights on vessels of 150 metres or more in length, resulting from the prescriptions of Section 3(a) of Annex I to these Regulations, until nine years after the date of entry into force of these Regulations.

(e) The repositioning of masthead lights resulting from the prescriptions of Section 2(b) of Annex I to these Regulations, until nine years after the date of entry into force of these Regulations.

(f) The repositioning of sidelights resulting from the prescriptions of Section 2(g) and 3(b) of Annex I to these Regulations, until nine years after the date of entry into force of these Regulations.

(g) The requirements for sound signal appliances prescribed in Annex III to these Regulations, until nine years after the date of entry into force of these Regulations.

(h) The repositioning of all-round lights resulting from the prescriptions of Section 9(b) of Annex I to these Regulations, permanent exemption.

ANNEX I

Positioning and technical details of lights and shapes

1. *Definition*

The term "height above the hull" means height above the uppermost continuous deck. This height shall be measured from the position vertically beneath the location of the light.

2. *Vertical positioning and spacing of lights*

(a) On a power-driven vessel of 20 metres or more in length the masthead lights shall be placed as follows:

(i) the forward masthead light, or if only one masthead light is carried, then that light, at a height above the hull of not less than 6 metres, and, if the breadth of the vessel exceeds 6 metres, then at a height above the hull not less than such breadth, so however that the light need not be placed at a greater height above the hull than 12 metres;

(ii) when two masthead lights are carried the after one shall be at least 4·5 metres vertically higher than the forward one.

(b) The vertical separation of masthead lights of power-driven vessels shall be such that in all normal conditions of trim the after light will be seen over and separate from the forward light at a distance of 1,000 metres from the stem when viewed from sea level.

(c) The masthead light of a power-driven vessel of 12 metres but less than 20 metres in length shall be placed at a height above the gunwale of not less than 2·5 metres.

(d) A power-driven vessel of less than 12 metres in length may carry the uppermost light at a height of less than 2·5 metres above the gunwale. When however a masthead light is carried in addition to sidelights and a sternlight or the all-round light of Rule 23(c)(i) is carried in addition to sidelights, then such

masthead light or all-round light shall be carried at least 1 metre higher than the sidelights.

(e) One of the two or three masthead lights prescribed for a power-driven vessel when engaged in towing or pushing another vessel shall be placed in the same position as either the forward masthead light or the after masthead light; provided that, if carried on the aftermast, the lowest after masthead light shall be at least 4·5 metres vertically higher than the forward masthead light.

(f)(i) The masthead light or lights prescribed in Rule 23 (a) shall be so placed as to be above and clear of all other lights and obstructions except as described in sub-paragraph (ii).

(ii) When it is impracticable to carry the all-round lights prescribed by Rule 27(b)(i) or Rule 28 below the masthead lights, they may be carried above the after masthead light(s) or vertically in between the forward masthead lights(s) and after masthead light(s), provided that in the latter case the requirement of Section 3(c) of this Annex shall be complied with.

(g) The sidelights of a power-driven vessel shall be placed at a height above the hull not greater than three-quarters of that of the forward masthead light. They shall not be so low as to be interfered with by deck lights.

(h) The sidelights, if in a combined lantern and carried on a power-driven vessel of less than 20 metres in length, shall be placed not less than 1 metre below the masthead light.

(i) When the Rules prescribe two or three lights to be carried in a vertical line, they shall be spaced as follows:

(i) on a vessel of 20 metres in length or more such lights shall be spaced not less than 2 metres apart, and the lowest of these lights shall, except where a towing light is required, be placed at a height of not less than 4 metres above the hull:

(ii) on a vessel of less than 20 metres in length such lights shall be spaced not less than 1 metre apart and the lowest of these lights shall, except where a towing light is required, be placed at a height of not less than 2 metres above the gunwale;

(iii) when three lights are carried they shall be equally spaced.

(j) The lower of the two all-round lights prescribed for a vessel when engaged in fishing shall be at a height above the sidelights not less than twice the distance between the two vertical lights.

(k) The forward anchor light prescribed in Rule 30 (a)(i), when two are carried, shall not be less than 4·5 metres above the after one. On a vessel of 50 metres or more in length this forward anchor light shall be placed at a height of not less than 6 metres above the hull.

3. *Horizontal positioning and spacing of lights*

(a) When two masthead lights are prescribed for a power-driven vessel, the horizontal distance between them shall not be less than one-half of the length of the vessel but need not be more than 100 metres. The forward light shall be placed not more than one-quarter of the length of the vessel from the stem.

(b) On a power-driven vessel of 20 metres or more in length the sidelights shall not be placed in front of the forward masthead lights. They shall be placed at or near the side of the vessel.

(c) When the lights prescribed in Rule 27(b)(i) or Rule 28 are placed vertically between the forward masthead light(s) and the after masthead light(s) these all-round lights shall be placed at a horizontal distance of not less than 2 metres from the fore and aft centreline of the vessel in the athwartship direction.

(d) When only one masthead light is prescribed for a power driven vessel, this light shall be exhibited forward of amidships; except that a vessel less than 20 metres in length need not exhibit this light forward of amidships but shall exhibit it as far forward as is practicable.

4. *Details of location of direction-indicating lights for fishing vessels, dredgers and vessels engaged in underwater operations*

(a) The light indicating the direction of the outlying gear from a vessel engaged in fishing as prescribed in Rule 26(c)(ii) shall be placed at a horizontal distance of not less than 2 metres and not more than 6 metres away from the two all-round red and white lights. This light shall be placed not higher than the all-round white light prescribed in Rule 26(c)(i) and not lower than the sidelights.

(b) The lights and shapes on a vessel engaged in dredging or underwater operations to indicate the obstructed side and/or the side on which it is safe to pass, as prescribed in rule 27(d)(i) and (ii), shall be placed at the maximum practical horizontal distance, but in no case less than 2 metres, from the lights or shapes prescribed in Rule 27(b)(i) and (ii). In no case shall the upper of these lights or shapes be at a greater height than the lower of the three lights or shapes prescribed in Rule 27(b)(i) and (ii).

5. *Screens for sidelights*

The sidelights of vessels of 20 metres or more in length shall be fitted with inboard screens painted matt black, and meeting the requirements of Section 9 of this Annex. On vessels of less than 20 metres in length the sidelights, if necessary to meet the requirements of Section 9 of this Annex, shall be fitted with inboard matt black screens. With a combined lantern, using a single vertical filament and a very narrow division between the green and red sections, external screens need not be fitted.

6. *Shapes*

(a) Shapes shall be black and of the following sizes:
 (i) a ball shall have a diameter of not less than 0·6 metre;

 (ii) a cone shall have a base diameter of not less than 0·6 metre and a height equal to its diameter;
 (iii) a cylinder shall have a diameter of at least 0·6 metre and a height of twice its diameter;
 (iv) a diamond shape shall consist of two cones as defined in (ii) above having a common base.

(b) The vertical distance between shapes shall be at least 1·5 metres.

(c) In a vessel of less than 20 metres in length shapes of lesser dimensions but commensurate with the size of the vessel may be used and the distance apart may be correspondingly reduced.

7. *Colour specification of lights*

The chromaticity of all navigation lights shall conform to the following standards, which lie within the boundaries of the area of the diagram specified for each colour by the International Commission on Illumination (CIE).

The boundaries of the area for each colour are given by indicating the corner co-ordinates, which are as follows:

(i) *White*

| x | 0·525 | 0·525 | 0·452 | 0·310 | 0·310 | 0·443 |
| y | 0·382 | 0·440 | 0·440 | 0·348 | 0·283 | 0·382 |

(ii) *Green*

| x | 0·028 | 0·009 | 0·300 | 0·203 |
| y | 0·385 | 0·723 | 0·511 | 0·356 |

(iii) *Red*

| x | 0·680 | 0·660 | 0·735 | 0·721 |
| y | 0·320 | 0·320 | 0·265 | 0·259 |

(iv) *Yellow*

| x | 0·612 | 0·618 | 0·575 | 0·575 |
| y | 0·382 | 0·382 | 0·425 | 0·406 |

8. *Intensity of lights*

(a) The minimum luminous intensity of lights shall be calculated by using the formula:

$$I = 3\cdot43 \times 10^6 \times T \times D^2 \times K^{-D}$$

where I is luminous intensity in candelas under service conditions,

T is threshold factor 2×10^{-7} lux,

D is range of visibility (luminous range) of the light in nautical miles,

K is atmospheric transmissivity.

For prescribed lights the value of K shall be 0·8, corresponding to a meteorological visibility of approximately 13 nautical miles.

(b) A selection of figures derived from the formula is given in the following table:

Range of visibility (luminous range) of light in nautical miles	Luminous intensity of light in candelas for K=0·8
D	I
1	0·9
2	4·3
3	12
4	27
5	52
6	94

Note. The maximum luminous intensity of navigation lights should be limited to avoid undue glare. This shall not be achieved by a variable control of the luminous intensity.

9. *Horizontal sectors*

(a)(i) In the forward direction, sidelights as fitted on the vessel shall show the minimum required intensities. The intensities shall decrease to reach practical cut-off between 1 degree and 3 degrees outside the prescribed sectors.

(ii) For sternlights and masthead lights and at 22·5 degrees abaft the beam for sidelights, the minimum required intensities shall be maintained over the arc of the horizon up to 5 degrees within the limits of the sectors prescribed in Rule 21. From 5 degrees within the prescribed sectors the intensity may decrease by 50 per cent up to the prescribed limits; it shall decrease steadily to reach practical cut-off at not more than 5 degrees outside the prescribed sectors.

(b)(i) All-round lights shall be so located as not to be obscured by masts, topmasts or structures within angular sectors of more than 6 degrees, except anchor lights prescribed in Rule 30, which need not be placed at an impracticable height above the hull.

(ii) If it is impracticable to comply with paragraph (b)(i) of this Section by exhibiting only one all-round light, two all-round lights shall be used suitably positioned or screened so that they appear, as far as practicable, as one light at a distance of one mile.

10. *Vertical sectors*

(a) The vertical sectors of electric lights as fitted, with the exception of lights on sailing vessels underway shall ensure that:

(i) at least the required minimum intensity is maintained at all angles from 5 degrees above to 5 degrees below the horizontal;

(ii) at least 60 per cent of the required minimum intensity is maintained from 7·5 degrees above to 7·5 degrees below the horizontal.

(b) In the case of sailing vessels underway the vertical sectors of electric lights as fitted shall ensure that:

(i) at least the required minimum intensity is maintained at all angles from 5 degrees above to 5 degrees below the horizontal;

(ii) at least 50 per cent of the required minimum intensity is maintained from 25 degrees above to 25 degrees below the horizontal.

(c) In the case of lights other than electric these specifications shall be met as closely as possible.

11. *Intensity of non-electric lights*

Non-electric lights shall so far as practicable comply with the minimum intensities, as specified in the Table given in Section 8 of this Annex.

12. *Manoeuvring light*

Notwithstanding the provisions of paragraph 2(f) of this Annex the manoeuvring light described in Rule 34(b) shall be placed in the same fore and aft vertical plane as the masthead light or lights and, where practicable, at a minimum height of 2 metres vertically above the forward masthead light, provided that it shall be carried not less than 2 metres vertically above or below the after masthead light. On a vessel where only one masthead light is carried the manoeuvring light, if fitted, shall be carried where it can best be seen, not less than 2 metres vertically apart from the masthead light.

13. *High speed craft**

(a) The masthead light of high-speed craft may be placed at a height related to the breadth of the craft lower than that prescribed in paragraph 2(a)(i) of this Annex, provided that the base angle of the isosceles triangles formed by the sidelights and the masthead light, when seen in end elevation, is not less than 27°.

(b) On high-speed craft of 50 m or more in length the vertical separation between fore mast and main mast lights of 4·5 m required by paragraph 2(a)(ii) of this annex may be modified provided that such distance shall not be less than the value determined by the following formula:

$$y = \frac{(a+17\psi)C +2}{1000}$$

where:

y = is the height of the main mast light above the fore mast light in metres;

a = the height of the fore mast light above the water surface in service condition in metres;

ψ = the trim in service condition in degrees;

C = the horizontal separation of the masthead lights in metres.

* Refer to the International Code of Safety for High-Speed Craft, 1994 and the International Code of Safety for High-Speed Craft, 2000.

14. *Approval*

The construction of lights and shapes and the installation of lights on board the vessel shall be to the satisfaction of the appropriate authority of the State whose flag the vessel is entitled to fly.

ANNEX II

Additional signals for fishing vessels fishing in close proximity

1. *General*

The lights mentioned herein shall, if exhibited in pursuance of Rule 26(d), be placed where they can best be seen. They shall be at least 0·9 metres apart but at a lower level than lights prescribed in Rule 26(b)(i) and (c)(i). The lights shall be visible all round the horizon at a distance of at least 1 mile but at a lesser distance than the lights prescribed by these Rules for fishing vessels.

2. *Signals for trawlers*

(a) Vessels of 20 metres or more in length when engaged in trawling, whether using demersal or pelagic gear, shall exhibit:

(i) when shooting their nets:
two white lights in a vertical line;
(ii) when hauling their nets:
one white light over one red light in a vertical line;
(iii) when the net has come fast upon an obstruction:
two red lights in a vertical line.
(b) Each vessel of 20 metres or more in length engaged in pair trawling shall exhibit:
(i) by night, a searchlight directed forward and in the direction of the other vessel of the pair;
(ii) when shooting or hauling their nets or when their nets have come fast upon an obstruction, the lights prescribed in 2(a) above.
(c) A vessel of less than 20 m in length engaged in trawling, whether using demersal or pelagic gear or engaged in pair trawling, may exhibit the lights prescribed in paragraphs (a) or (b) of this Section, as appropriate.

3. *Signals for purse seiners*

Vessels engaged in fishing with purse seine gear may exhibit two yellow lights in a vertical line. These lights shall flash alternately every second and with equal light and occultation duration. These lights may be exhibited only when the vessel is hampered by its fishing gear.

ANNEX III

Technical details of sound signal appliances

1. *Whistles*

(a) Frequencies and range of audibility

The fundamental frequency of the signal shall lie within the range 70–700Hz.

The range of audibility of the signal from a whistle shall be determined by those frequencies, which may include the fundamental and/or one or more higher frequencies, which lie within the range 180–700Hz ($\pm$ 1 per cent) for a vessel of 20 m or more in length, or 180–2100Hz ($\pm$ 1%) for a vessel of less than 20 m in length and which provide the sound pressure levels specified in paragraph 1(*c*) below.

(b) Limits of fundamental frequencies

To ensure a wide variety of whistle characteristics, the fundamental frequency of a whistle shall be between the following limits:
(i) 70–200Hz, for a vessel 200 metres or more in length;
(ii) 130–350Hz, for a vessel 75 metres but less than 200 metres in length;
(iii) 250–700Hz, for a vessel less than 75 metres in length.

(c) Sound signal intensity and range of audibility

A whistle fitted in a vessel shall provide, in the direction of maximum intensity of the whistle and at a distance of 1 metre from it, a sound pressure level in at least one 1/3rd-octave band within the range of frequencies 180–700Hz ($\pm$ 1 per cent) for a vessel of 20 m or more in length, or 180–2100Hz ($\pm$ 1%) for a vessel less than 20 m in length, of not less than the appropriate figure given in the table below.

Length of vessel in metres	1/3rd-octave band level at 1 m in d B referred to 2×10^{-5} N/m^2	Audibility range in nautical miles
200 or more	143	2
75 but less than 200	138	1·5
20 but less than 75	130	1
Less than 20	120* 115† 111‡	0·5

* When the measured frequencies lie within the range 180–450Hz
† When the measured frequencies lie within the range 450–800Hz
‡ When the measured frequencies lie within the range 800–2100Hz

The range of audibility in the table above is for information and is approximately the range at which a whistle may be heard on its forward axis with 90 per cent probability in conditions of still air on board a vessel having average background noise level at the listening posts (taken to be 68 dB in the octave band centred on 250 Hz and 63 dB in the octave band centred on 500 Hz).

In practice the range at which a whistle may be heard is extremely variable and depends critically on weather conditions; the values given can be regarded as typical but under conditions of strong wind or high ambient noise level at the listening post the range may be much reduced.

(d) Directional properties

The sound pressure level of a directional whistle shall be not more than 4 dB below the prescribed sound pressure level on the axis at any direction in the horizontal plane within 45 degrees of the axis. The sound pressure level at any other direction in the horizontal plane shall be not more than 10 dB below the prescribed sound pressure level on the axis, so that the range in any direction will be at least half the range on the forward axis. The sound pressure level shall be measured in that 1/3rd-octave band which determines the audibility range.

(e) Positioning of whistles

When a directional whistle is to be used as the only whistle on a vessel, it shall be installed with its maximum intensity directed straight ahead.

A whistle shall be placed as high as practicable on a vessel, in order to reduce interception of the emitted sound by obstructions and also to minimise hearing damage risk to personnel. The sound pressure level of the vessel's own signal at listening posts shall not exceed 110 dB (A) and so far as practicable should not exceed 100 dB (A).

(f) Fitting of more than one whistle

If whistles are fitted at a distance apart of more than 100 metres, it shall be so arranged that they are not sounded simultaneously.

(g) Combined whistle systems

If due to the pressure of obstructions the sound field of a single whistle or of one of the whistles referred to in paragraph 1(*f*) above is likely to have a zone of greatly reduced signal level, it is recommended that a combined whistle system be fitted so as to overcome this reduction. For the purposes of the Rules a combined whistle system is to be regarded as a single whistle. The whistles of a combined system shall be located at a distance apart of not more than 100 metres and arranged to be sounded simultaneously. The frequency of any one whistle shall differ from those of the others by at least 10 Hz.

2. *Bell or gong*

(a) *Intensity of signal*

A bell or gong, or other device having similar sound characteristics shall produce a sound pressure level of not less than 110 dB at a distance of 1 metre from it.

(b) *Construction*

Bells and gongs shall be made of corrosion-resistant material and designed to give a clear tone. The diameter of the mouth of the bell shall be not less than 300 mm for vessels of 20 metres or more in length.

Where practicable, a power-driven bell striker is recommended to ensure constant force but manual operation shall be possible. The mass of the striker shall be not less than 3 per cent of the mass of the bell.

3. *Approval*

The construction of sound signal appliances, their performance and their installation on board the vessel shall be to the satisfaction of the appropriate authority of the State whose flag the vessel is entitled to fly.

ANNEX IV

Distress signals

1. The following signals, used or exhibited either together or separately, indicate distress and need of assistance:

   (a) a gun or other explosive signal fired at intervals of about a minute;

   (b) a continuous sounding with any fog-signalling apparatus;

   (c) rockets or shells, throwing red stars fired one at a time at short intervals;

   (d) a signal made by any signalling method consisting of the group $\cdots\ -\ -\ -\ \cdots$ (SOS) in the Morse code;

   (e) a signal sent by radiotelephony consisting of the spoken word "Mayday";

   (f) the International Code Signal of distress indicated by N.C.;

   (g) a signal consisting of a square flag having above or below it a ball or anything resembling a ball;

   (h) flames on the vessel (as from a burning tar barrel, oil barrel, etc.);

   (i) a rocket parachute flare or a hand flare showing a red light;

   (j) a smoke signal giving off orange-coloured smoke;

   (k) slowly and repeatedly raising and lowering arms outstretched to each side;

   (l) a distress alert by means of digital selective calling (DSC) transmitted on:
      (i) VHF channel 70, or
      (ii) MF/HF on the frequencies 2187·5 kHz, 8414·5 kHz, 4207·5 kHz, 6312 kHz, 12577 kHz or 16804·5 kHz;

   (m) a ship–to–shore distress alert transmitted by the ship's Inmarsat or other mobile satellite service provider ship earth station;

   (n) signals transmitted by emergency position-indicating radio beacons.

   (o) approved signals transmitted by radio-communications systems including survival craft radar transponders.

2. The use or exhibition of any of the foregoing signals except for the purpose of indicating distress and need of assistance and the use of other signals which may be confused with any of the above signals is prohibited.

3. Attention is drawn to the relevant sections of the International Code of Signals, the Merchant Ship Search and Rescue Manual and the following signals:

   (a) a piece of orange-coloured canvas with either a black square and circle or other appropriate symbol (for identification from the air);

   (b) a dye marker.

Annex C

IALA Maritime Buoyage System

Introduction and description

Background

General information
C.1

1   The severest test of a buoyage system occurs when the mariner is confronted unexpectedly by night or in low visibility by the lights marking an uncharted danger, such as a recent wreck; immediately he must instinctively, positively and correctly decide what he must do.

2   In the Dover Strait in 1971 the *Brandenburg* struck the wreckage of the *Texaco Caribbean* and sank, though the wreckage was appropriately marked. A few weeks later the wreckage, despite being marked by a wreck-marking vessel and many buoys, was struck by the *Niki*, which also sank. A total of 51 lives was lost. It was this disaster which gave rise to the development and implementation of the IALA Maritime Buoyage System.

3   The wreck of the *Tricolor* in the Dover Strait in 2002 highlighted once again the need to mark new dangers quickly and resulted in the introduction, on a trial basis, of the Emergency Wreck Marking Buoy. For full details, see C.51.

Development
C.2

1   The beginnings of a uniform system of buoyage emerged in 1889, when certain countries agreed to mark the port side of channels with black can buoys and the starboard side with red conical buoys.

Unfortunately when lights for buoys were introduced, some European countries placed red lights on the black port hand buoys to conform with the red lights marking the port side of harbour entrances, whilst throughout North America red lights were placed on the red starboard hand buoys.

2   Thereafter various conferences sought a single buoyage system, but without success, until 1936 when a system was drawn up under The League of Nations at Geneva. It established a Cardinal system, and a Lateral system with the principle that red buoys should be used to port and black buoys to starboard. But several countries were not signatories to this Convention and continued to develop their original, and opposite systems.

3   After World War II (1939–45) buoyage systems were re-established in NW Europe based on the system devised by the 1936 Geneva Convention, but wide differences in interpretation of that system resulted in nine different systems coming into use in those waters.

4   In 1973, observing the need for urgency, a further attempt to find a single world-wide system of buoyage was made by the Technical Committee of the International Association of Lighthouse Authorities (IALA). IALA is a non-governmental body which brings together representatives from the aids to navigation services in order to exchange information and recommend improvements to navigational aids based on the latest technology.

5   IALA decided that agreement could not be achieved immediately, but concluded that the use of only two alternative systems was practicable by dividing the world into two Regions. It proposed a system allowing the use of both Cardinal and Lateral systems in each Region, but whereas in Region A the colour red of the Lateral system is used to mark the port side of channels and the colour green the starboard side, in Region B the colours are reversed.

The boundaries of the two Buoyage Regions are shown in Diagram C.2.

Implementation
C.3

6   In 1980, at a conference convened with the assistance of the Inter-Governmental Maritime Consultative Organisation (IMCO), now the International Maritime Organisation (IMO), and the International Hydrographic Organisation (IHO), the lighthouse authorities from 50 countries and the representatives of nine international organisations concerned with aids to navigation, agreed to adopt the rules of the new combined system, and reached decisions on the buoyage Regions.

7   The IALA System has now been implemented throughout much of the world. In some parts, however, conversion to the new system is still incomplete.

In certain areas, such as North America and the inland waterways of Western Europe, the IALA system is used with modifications which are described in *Admiralty Sailing Directions*.

Alterations to charts
C.4

1   In the past, when replacement of an existing buoyage system by the IALA System involved extensive changes, careful preparations and announcements were made so that charts affected, corrected up to date for both the old and new systems, were available during the period of change.

2   However, though most major alterations of buoyage to the IALA System have now been completed, there are still some places where the buoyage does not conform to that System. Some ports will convert their buoyage piecemeal and only when other buoyage changes make it convenient; others have yet to announce plans to conform to the IALA System.

3   Progress towards completion of the change to the IALA System is, therefore, likely to be gradual, and notice of change, if given, is likely to be short.

When a system of buoyage is changed, however, corrections enabling charts to be kept up-to-date will be promulgated, as before, by the most appropriate means, either by Notices to Mariners or by issuing New Editions of affected charts.

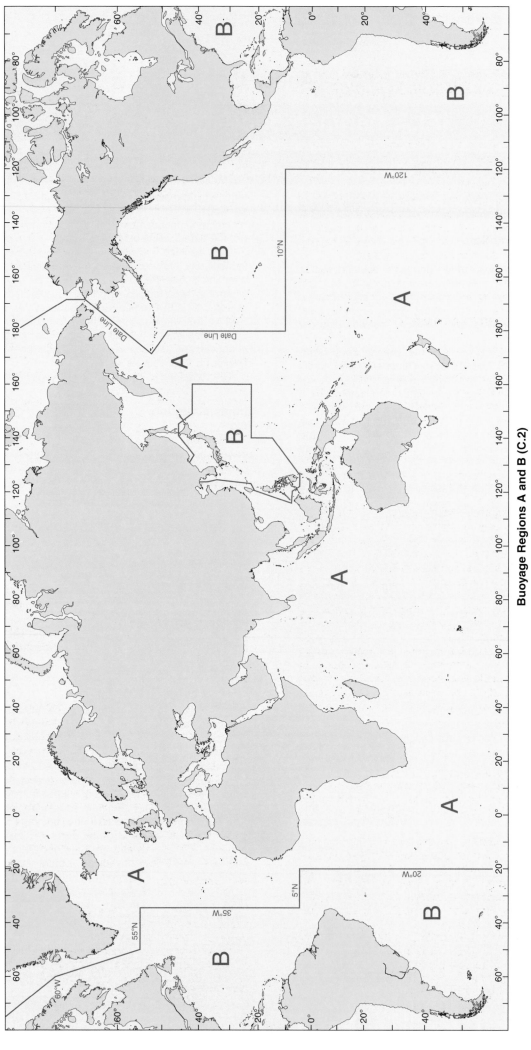

Buoyage Regions A and B (C.2)

Description of the System

Scope
C.5

1   The System applies to all fixed and floating marks, other than lighthouses, sector lights, leading lights and marks, lanbys, certain large light floats, and light vessels. It serves to indicate:

2   Sides and centrelines of navigable channels.
Navigable channels under fixed bridges (see C.25).
Natural dangers and other obstructions such as wrecks (which are described as "New Dangers" when newly discovered and uncharted).
Areas in which navigation may be subject to regulation.
Other features of importance to the mariner.

Chart symbols and abbreviations
C.6

1   To meet the needs of the IALA Buoyage System, new symbols and abbreviations, and altered ones, are being incorporated on Admiralty charts when they are corrected or reprinted for use with the System. They are given in *Chart 5011 — Symbols and Abbreviations used on Admiralty Charts* and are illustrated in Diagram C.6.

Marks
C.7

1   Six types of mark are provided by the System: Lateral, Cardinal, Isolated Danger, Safe Water, Special marks and Emergency Wreck Marking Buoys. They may be used in any combination. The way in which Cardinal and Lateral marks can be combined is illustrated in diagrams C.7.1 and C.7.2.

2   Most lighted and unlighted beacons, other than leading marks, are included in the System. In general, beacon topmarks have the same shapes and colours as those used on buoys. Because of the variety of beacon structures, the accompanying diagrams show mainly buoy shapes.

3   Until 2006, permanent and semi–permanent wrecks were marked in the same way as other dangers; no unique type of mark was reserved for them in the IALA System. In 2006, the Emergency Wreck Marking Buoy was introduced on a trial basis. For further details see C.51.

Colours
C.8

1   Red and green are reserved for Lateral marks, and yellow for Special marks. Black and yellow or black and red bands, or red and white or blue and yellow stripes are used for other types of marks as described later.

2   **On Admiralty charts,** the shading of buoy symbols to indicate the colours of buoys is no longer used. A black (ie filled-in) symbol is used for predominantly green marks and for all spar buoys and beacons; an open symbol is used for all buoys and beacon towers of other colours, but with a vertical line to indicate striped Safe Water buoys.

3   The abbreviated description of the colour, or colours, of a buoy is given under the symbol. Where a buoy is coloured in bands, the colours are indicated in sequence from the top, eg E Cardinal buoy — Black with a yellow band — BYB. If the sequence of the bands is not known, or if the buoy is striped, the colours are indicated with the darker colour first eg Safe Water buoy — Red and white stripes — RW.

4   Examples are shown in Diagram C.6.

Shapes
C.9

1   Five basic shapes were defined when the System was devised: Can, Conical, Spherical, Pillar and Spar.
To these must be added light floats, as well as buoyant beacons (which are charted as light beacons).
Variations in the basic shapes may be common for a number of years after the introduction of the IALA System to a particular locality since much existing equipment will continue in use.
Can, conical and spherical buoys indicate by their shape the correct side to pass.

2   Marks that do not rely on their shape for identification carry the appropriate topmark whenever practicable. However, in some parts of the world, including US waters, light-buoys have identical shapes on both port and starboard sides of Laterally-marked channels, and are not fitted with topmarks. Also in US waters, a buoy with a conical or truncated conical top, known as a nun buoy, is used to mark the starboard side of the channel.

3   **On Admiralty charts,** the symbol for a spar buoy is also used to indicate a spindle buoy. The symbol will, as before, be sloped to distinguish it from a beacon symbol which is upright.
If the shape of a buoy of the IALA System is not known, a pillar buoy is used. See *Chart 5011*.

Topmarks
C.10

1   Can, conical, spherical and X-shaped topmarks are the only ones used.
On pillar and spar buoys the use of topmarks is particularly important, though ice or severe weather may at times prevent it.

2   **On Admiralty charts,** topmarks are shown boldly, in solid black except when the topmark is red, when it is in outline only. See *Chart 5011*.

Lights
C.11

3   Where marks are lighted, red and green lights of the IALA System are reserved for Lateral marks and yellow lights for Special marks. Alternating blue and yellow flashing lights are used for Emergency Wreck Marking Buoys.
White lights, distinguished one from another by their rhythm, are used for other types of mark.
It is possible that some shore lights, specifically excluded from the IALA System, may, by coincidence have similar characteristics to those of the buoyage system. Care is needed on sighting such lights that they are not misinterpreted.

Retroreflectors
C.12

1   Two codes, the Standard Code and the Comprehensive Code, are used for distinguishing unlighted marks at night by securing to them, in particular patterns, retroreflective material to reflect back light. In any specified area only one of the codes is used. The code in use will, if known, be mentioned in *Admiralty Sailing Directions*.

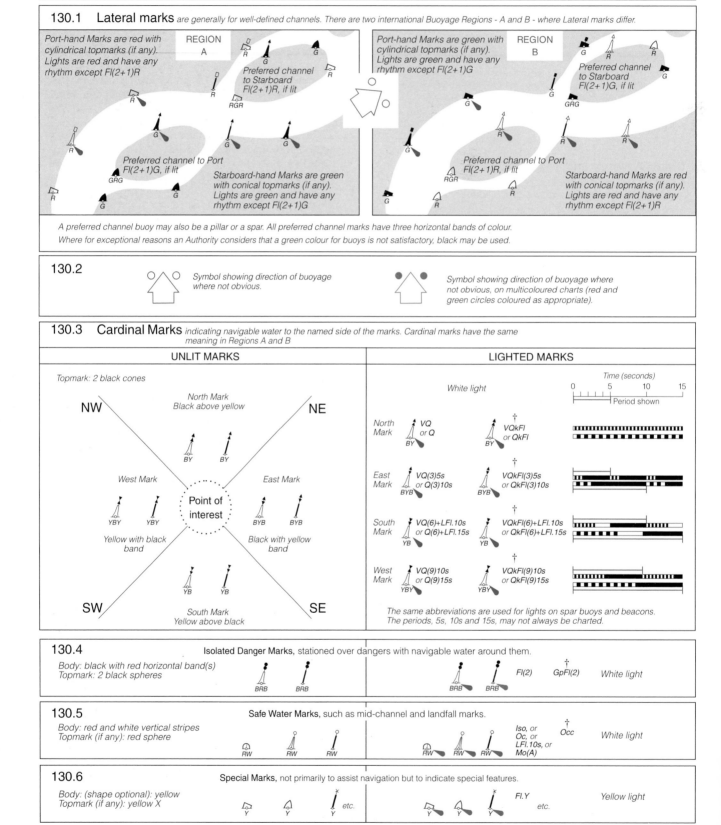

IALA Maritime Buoyage System

IALA International Association of Lighthouse Authorities

Where in force, the IALA System applies to all fixed and floating marks except landfall lights, leading lights and marks, sectored lights and major floating lights.

The standard buoy shapes are cylindrical (can) ⌐, conical △, spherical ○, pillar ⌁, and spar ⌇, but variations may occur, for example: minor light floats

In the illustrations below, only the standard buoy shapes are used. In the case of fixed beacons (lit or unlit) only the shape of the topmark is of navigational significance.

130.1 Lateral marks *are generally for well-defined channels. There are two international Buoyage Regions - A and B - where Lateral marks differ.*

REGION A

Port-hand Marks are red with cylindrical topmarks (if any). Lights are red and have any rhythm except Fl(2+1)R

Preferred channel to Starboard Fl(2+1)R, if lit

Preferred channel to Port Fl(2+1)G, if lit

Starboard-hand Marks are green with conical topmarks (if any). Lights are green and have any rhythm except Fl(2+1)G

REGION B

Port-hand Marks are green with cylindrical topmarks (if any). Lights are green and have any rhythm except Fl(2+1)G

Preferred channel to Starboard Fl(2+1)G, if lit

Preferred channel to Port Fl(2+1)R, if lit

Starboard-hand Marks are red with conical topmarks (if any). Lights are red and have any rhythm except Fl(2+1)R

A preferred channel buoy may also be a pillar or a spar. All preferred channel marks have three horizontal bands of colour.

Where for exceptional reasons an Authority considers that a green colour for buoys is not satisfactory, black may be used.

130.2

Symbol showing direction of buoyage where not obvious.

Symbol showing direction of buoyage where not obvious, on multicoloured charts (red and green circles coloured as appropriate).

130.3 Cardinal Marks *indicating navigable water to the named side of the marks. Cardinal marks have the same meaning in Regions A and B*

UNLIT MARKS	LIGHTED MARKS

Topmark: 2 black cones

NW   North Mark   NE
          Black above yellow

BY   BY

West Mark   East Mark

YBY   YBY   **Point of interest**   BYB   BYB

Yellow with black band   *Black with yellow band*

          YB   YB
SW   SE
          South Mark
          Yellow above black

White light

Time (seconds) 0 5 10 15 — Period shown

	UNLIT	LIGHTED	
North Mark	VQ or Q (BY)	VQkFl or QkFl † (BY)	
East Mark	VQ(3)5s or Q(3)10s (BYB)	VQkFl(3)5s or QkFl(3)10s † (BYB)	
South Mark	VQ(6)+LFl.10s or Q(6)+LFl.15s (YB)	VQkFl(6)+LFl.10s or QkFl(6)+LFl.15s † (YB)	
West Mark	VQ(9)10s or Q(9)15s (YBY)	VQkFl(9)10s or QkFl(9)15s † (YBY)	

The same abbreviations are used for lights on spar buoys and beacons. The periods, 5s, 10s and 15s, may not always be charted.

130.4 Isolated Danger Marks, *stationed over dangers with navigable water around them.*

Body: black with red horizontal band(s)
Topmark: 2 black spheres

BRB   BRB   BRB   BRB   Fl(2)   GpFl(2) †   *White light*

130.5 Safe Water Marks, *such as mid-channel and landfall marks.*

Body: red and white vertical stripes
Topmark (if any): red sphere

RW   RW   RW   RW   RW   RW   Iso, or Oc, or LFl.10s, or Mo(A)   Occ †   *White light*

130.6 Special Marks, *not primarily to assist navigation but to indicate special features.*

Body: (shape optional): yellow
Topmark (if any): yellow X

Y   Y   Y   etc.   Y   Y   Y   etc.   Fl.Y   *Yellow light*

Chart Symbols and Abbreviations (C.6)

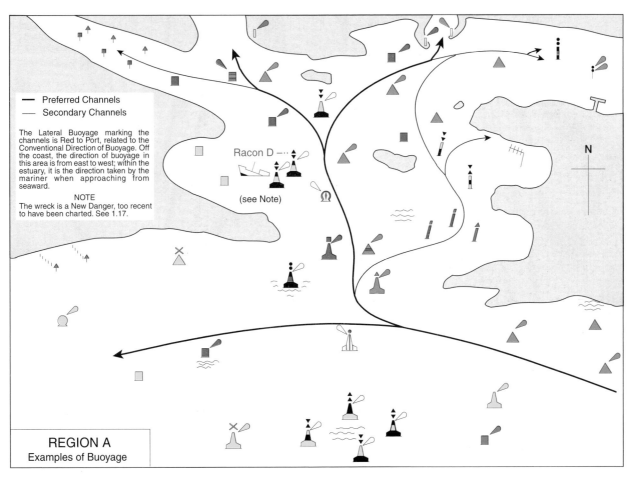

REGION A
Examples of Buoyage

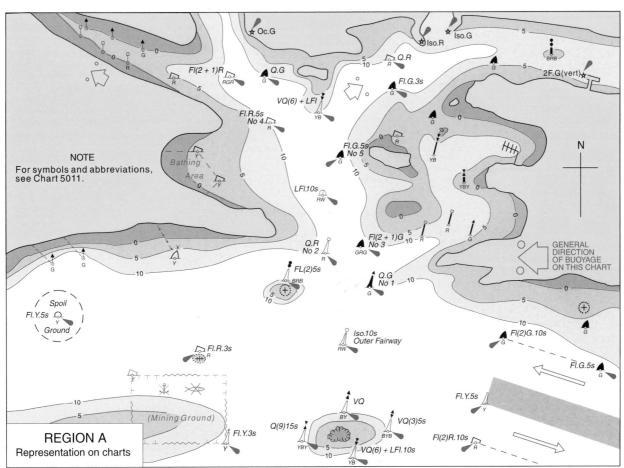

REGION A
Representation on charts

Region A (C.7.1)

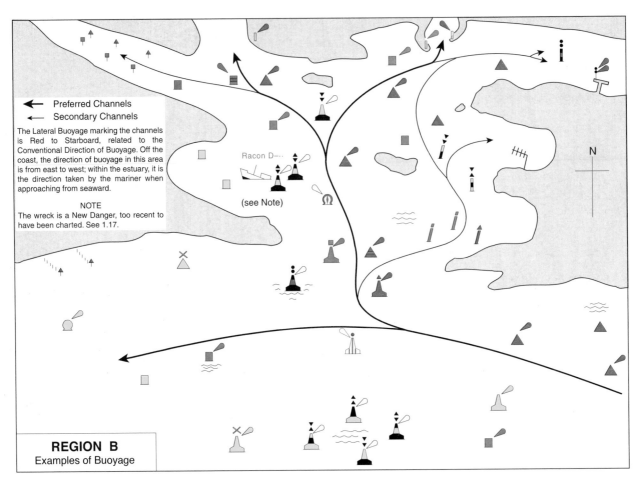

REGION B
Examples of Buoyage

Within the figure:
- Preferred Channels
- Secondary Channels

The Lateral Buoyage marking the channels is Red to Starboard, related to the Conventional Direction of Buoyage. Off the coast, the direction of buoyage in this area is from east to west; within the estuary, it is the direction taken by the mariner when approaching from seaward.

NOTE
The wreck is a New Danger, too recent to have been charted. See 1.17.

Racon D–··

(see Note)

N

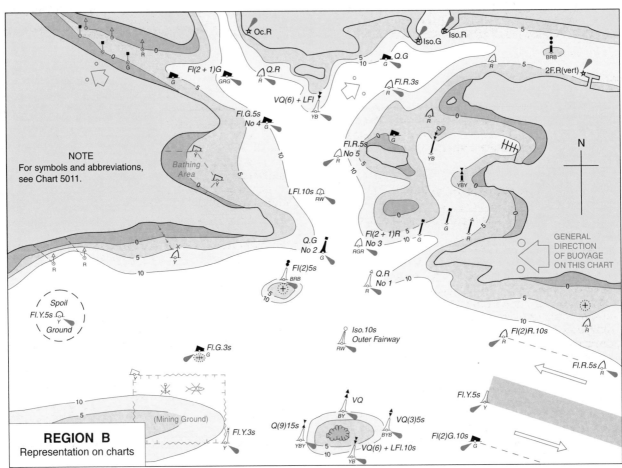

REGION B
Representation on charts

NOTE
For symbols and abbreviations, see Chart 5011.

GENERAL DIRECTION OF BUOYAGE ON THIS CHART

N

Region B (C.7.2)

2 **Standard Code** uses the following markings:

Red Lateral marks: One red band or red shape similar to the topmark.

Green Lateral marks: One green band or green shape similar to the topmark.

Preferred Channel marks: As for red or green Lateral marks, depending on the dominant colour of the mark.

Special marks: One yellow band, yellow X or yellow symbol.

Cardinal, Isolated Danger and Safe Water marks: One or more white bands, letters, numerals or symbols.

3 **Comprehensive Code** uses the same markings for Lateral and Special marks, but separate markings for distinguishing Cardinal. Isolated Danger and Safe Water marks, which are given later in the descriptions of those marks.

Radar reflectors
C.13

1 On the introduction of the System, it was decided not to chart radar reflectors. It can be assumed that most major buoys are fitted with radar reflectors.

Definition
C.14

1 A newly discovered hazard to navigation not yet shown on charts or included in Sailing Directions, or sufficiently promulgated by Notices to Mariners, is termed as a New Danger. The term covers naturally occurring obstructions such as sandbanks or rocks, and man-made dangers such as wrecks.

2 In 2006 the Emergency Wreck Marking Buoy was introduced on a trial basis (See C.51).

Marking
C.15

1 **Cardinal or Lateral marks,** one or more, are used to mark New Dangers in accordance with the IALA System.
If the danger is especially grave, at least one of the marks will be duplicated, as soon as practicable, by an identical mark until the danger has been sufficiently promulgated.

2 **A quick or very quick flashing light** will be exhibited from a New Danger mark, if it is lit. If it is a Cardinal mark, it will exhibit a white light, if a Lateral mark, a red or green light.
A racon, Morse Code (D), showing a signal length of 1 mile on a radar display, may be used to mark a New Danger.
See diagrams C.7.1 and C.7.2.

Lateral marks

Use
C.16

1 Lateral marks are generally used for well-defined channels in conjunction with a Conventional Direction of Buoyage. They indicate the port and starboard sides of the route to be followed (see Diagrams C.16.1 and C.16.2).

Conventional Direction of Buoyage
C.17

1 The Conventional Direction of Buoyage is defined in one of two ways:
Local Direction of Buoyage. The direction taken by the mariner when approaching a harbour, river, estuary, or other waterway from seaward.

2 **General Direction of Buoyage.** The direction determined by the buoyage authorities, based wherever possible on the principle of following a clockwise direction around continents. It is usually described in *Admiralty Sailing Directions* and, if necessary, indicated on charts by the appropriate symbol. Diagram C.17 illustrates how General Direction gives way to Local Direction at the outer limit of the Thames Estuary.

3 Around the British Isles the General Direction of Buoyage runs N along the W coast and through the Irish Sea, E through the English Channel and N through the North Sea.

C.18

1 On Admiralty charts, the Conventional Direction of Buoyage may be indicated by magenta arrow symbols.
In some straits (eg. Menai Strait and The Solent) and in the open sea (eg. off the Irish coast at Malin Head), where the direction changes, attention is drawn to its reversal by magenta arrow symbols confronting each other.

2 On many coasts and in some straits world-wide, buoyage authorities have not yet established or promulgated a General Directions of Buoyage, so it is not possible to chart the magenta symbol. This could be hazardous if a New Danger were to be marked by Lateral buoys.

Preferred Channels
C.19

1 When proceeding in the Conventional Direction of Buoyage, at the point where a channel divides to form two alternative channels to the same destination, the Preferred Channel is indicated by a modified Lateral mark. The System does not provide for a Preferred Channel mark where the two channels re-join.

Colours
C.20

1 Red and green are the colours reserved for Lateral marks.

Lateral Marks - Region A (C.16.1)

This diagram is schematic and in the case of pillar buoys in particular, their features will vary with the individual design of the buoys in use.

PORT HAND	STARBOARD HAND

Colour: Red.

Shape: Can, pillar or spar.

Topmark (when fitted): Single red can.

Retroreflector: Red band or square.

Colour: Green.

Shape: Conical, pillar or spar.

Topmark (when fitted): Single green cone point upward.

Retroreflector: Green band or triangle.

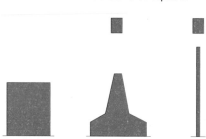

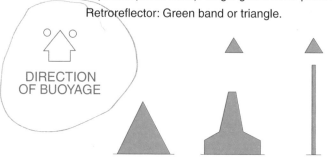

DIRECTION
OF BUOYAGE

LIGHTS, when fitted, may have any rhythm other than composite group flashing (2+1) used on modified Lateral marks indicating a preferred channel. Examples are:

Red light		Green light
Q.R	Continuous-quick light	Q.G
Fl.R	Single-flashing light	Fl.G
LFl.R	Long-flashing light	LFl.G
Fl(2)R	Group-flashing light	Fl(2)G

The lateral colours of red or green are frequently used for minor shore lights, such as those marking pierheads and the extremities of jetties.

PREFERRED CHANNELS

At the point where a channel divides, when proceeding in the conventional direction of buoyage, a preferred channel is indicated by:

Preferred channel to starboard	Preferred channel to port

Colour: Red with one broad green band.

Shape: Can, pillar or spar.

Topmark (when fitted): Single red can.

Retroreflector: Red band or square.

Colour: Green with one broad red band.

Shape: Conical, pillar or spar.

Topmark (when fitted): Single green cone point upward.

Retroreflector: Green band or triangle.

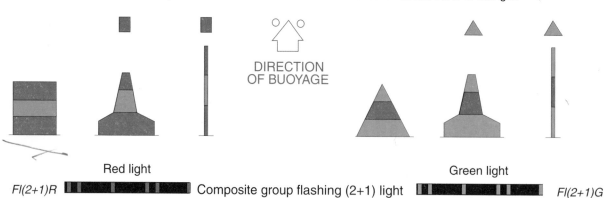

DIRECTION
OF BUOYAGE

Red light		Green light
Fl(2+1)R	Composite group flashing (2+1) light	Fl(2+1)G

NOTES

Where port or starboard marks do not rely on can or conical buoy shapes for identification, they carry the appropriate topmark where practicable.

If marks at the sides of a channel are numbered or lettered, the numbering or lettering follows the conventional direction of buoyage.

Special marks with can and conical shapes but painted yellow, may be used in conjunction with the standard Lateral marks for special types of channel marking; see 2.10

Lateral Marks - Region B (C.16.2)

This diagram is schematic and in the case of pillar buoys in particular, their features will vary with the individual design of the buoys in use.

PORT HAND	STARBOARD HAND
Colour: Green.	Colour: Red.
Shape: Can, pillar or spar.	Shape: Conical, pillar or spar.
Topmark (when fitted): Single green can.	Topmark (when fitted): Single red cone point upward.
Retroreflector: Green band or square.	Retroreflector: Red band or triangle.

DIRECTION OF BUOYAGE

LIGHTS, when fitted, may have any rhythm other than composite group flashing (2+1) used on modified Lateral marks indicating a preferred channel. Examples are:

Green light		Red light
Q.G	Continuous-quick light	Q.R
Fl.G	Single-flashing light	Fl.R
LFl.G	Long-flashing light	LFl.R
Fl(2)G	Group-flashing light	Fl(2)R

The lateral colours of red or green are frequently used for minor shore lights, such as those marking pierheads and the extremities of jetties.

PREFERRED CHANNELS

At the point where a channel divides, when proceeding in the conventional direction of buoyage, a preferred channel is indicated by:

Preferred channel to starboard	Preferred channel to port
Colour: Red with one broad green band.	Colour: Green with one broad red band.
Shape: Can, pillar or spar.	Shape: Conical, pillar or spar.
Topmark (when fitted): Single red can.	Topmark (when fitted): Single green cone point upward.
Retroreflector: Red band or square.	Retroreflector: Green band or triangle.

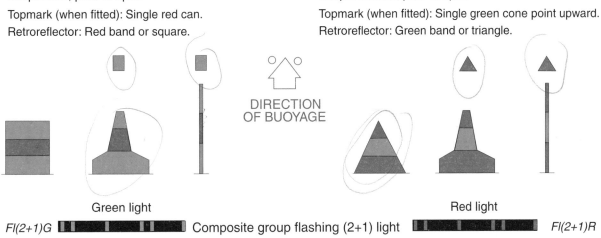

DIRECTION OF BUOYAGE

Green light		Red light
Fl(2+1)G	Composite group flashing (2+1) light	Fl(2+1)R

NOTES

Where port or starboard marks do not rely on can or conical buoy shapes for identification, they carry the appropriate topmark where practicable.

If marks at the sides of a channel are numbered or lettered, the numbering or lettering follows the conventional direction of buoyage.

Special marks with can and conical shapes but painted yellow, may be used in conjunction with the standard Lateral marks for special types of channel marking; see 2.10

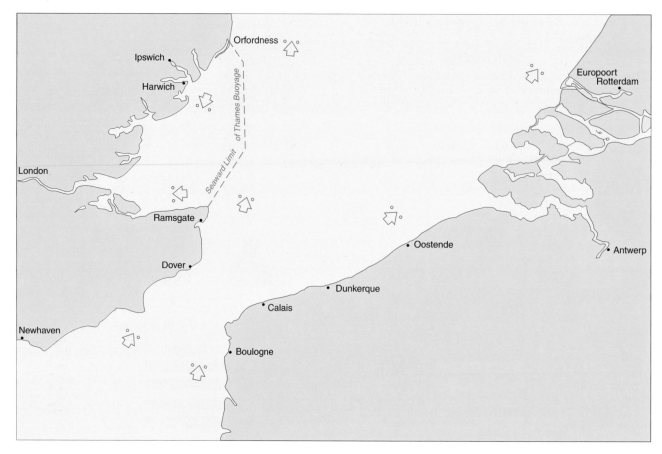

C.17 Local and General Direction of Lateral Buoyage

Topmarks
C.21

1   When fitted, port-hand marks carry can-shaped topmarks, and starboard-hand marks carry conical topmarks.

Lights
C.22

1   When exhibited, red and green lights are used for Lateral marks.

Lateral marks for certain purposes have specified rhythms:

Composite Group Flashing (2+1) for Preferred Channel marks.

Quick Flashing or Very Quick Flashing for New Danger marks.

Other Lateral marks may have lights of any rhythm.

Sequence
C.23

1   If marks at the sides of a channel are numbered or lettered, the sequence follows the conventional direction of buoyage.

Special marks
C.24

1   Yellow coloured can and cone shapes may be used as Special marks in conjunction with the Lateral marks for special types of channel marking, see C.45.

Marking of fixed bridges over navigable waters
C.25

1   **Best point of passage** is the most appropriate point to pass under a bridge, and is determined by the competent authority taking into account all relevant factors such as:

Maximum available headroom.

Water depth under the bridge, particularly where it is not uniform.

Protection of bridge piers and other obstructions.

The need to have one or two way traffic.

2   **Visual marks.** The extent of the navigable channel is marked as follows (See diagram C.25):

In Buoyage Region A: to port, a panel showing a solid red square; to starboard, a panel showing a solid green equilateral triangle, point upwards

In Buoyage Region B: to port, a panel showing a solid green square; to starboard, a panel showing a solid red equilateral triangle, point upwards.

In both Regions, the best point of passage is marked by a circular panel with red and white vertical stripes.

3   **Note.** Bridge spans other than those marked by the red and green lateral marks prescribed above (eg spans to be used by very small craft) may be indicated by Special marks (C.45).

4   **By night,** red or green rhythmic navigation lights may be used to mark the extent of the navigable channel, although in some cases the daymarks described above may be floodlit. If the navigable channel occupies the full width of a span, some authorities may floodlight the bridge piers alone.

The best point of passage is indicated by a white light or lights located under the span and exhibiting a safe water mark character (C.43).

5   **Sound signals.** One or more sound signals of any type may be used to warn the mariner of the presence of a bridge. If a number of such signals are placed at different points on the bridge, their character should be different from one another.

6   **Racons.** A short range racon may be used to mark the best point of passage under a bridge. Where two racons are used to mark either side of a bridge span they are coded:

Port: Morse Code B (—...)
Starboard: Morse Code T (—)

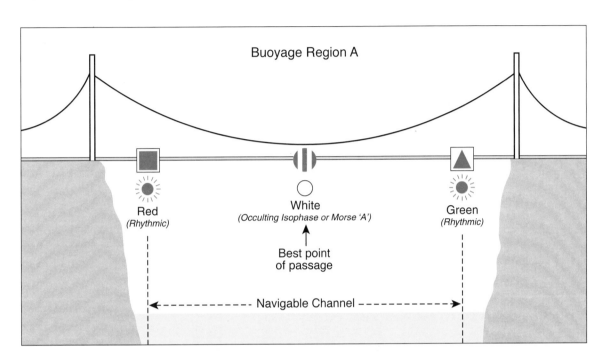

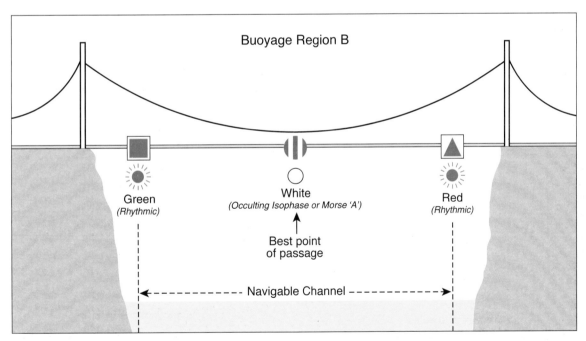

Marking of fixed bridges over navigable waters (C.25)

Cardinal marks

System description
C.26

1   Cardinal marks are used to indicate where the mariner may find the best navigable water, relative to a point of interest. They are placed in one of the four quadrants (N, E, S, W) defined as:

    N: between NW and NE.
    E: between NE and SE.
    S: between SE and SW.
    W: between SW and NW.

    Cardinal marks take their name from the quadrant in which they are placed. See Diagram C.26.

2   The mariner is safe if he passes N of a North mark, E of an East mark, S of a South mark and W of a West mark.

Uses
C.27

1   Cardinal marks may be used to:

    Indicate that the deepest water in an area is on the named side of the mark.

    Indicate the safe side on which to pass a danger.

    Draw attention to a feature in a channel such as a bend, junction, bifurcation, or end of a shoal.

Topmarks
C.28

1   **Black double-cone topmarks** are a very important feature of Cardinal marks; they are carried whenever practicable, with the cones as large as possible and clearly separated.

    The arrangement of the cones must be memorised. More difficult to remember than North (▲) and South (▼) are East (◆) and West (✕) topmarks; "W for Wineglass" may help.

Colours
C.29

1   **Black and yellow bands** are the colours used for Cardinal marks.

    The position of the black band, or bands, is related to the points of the black topmark, thus;

N	Points up	Black band above yellow band
S	Points down	Black band below yellow band
W	Points inward	Black band with yellow bands above and below
E	Points outward	Black bands above and below yellow band

Shape
C.30

1   Cardinal marks do not have a distinctive shape, but if they are buoys, will normally be either pillar or spar.

Lights
C.31

1   If Cardinal marks are lit, they will exhibit white lights, They are characterised by a group of quick or very quick flashes, which distinguish them as Cardinal marks, and indicate their quadrant as follows:

N	Uninterrupted
E	3 flashes in a group
S	6 flashes in a group followed by a long flash. The long flash (of not less than 2 seconds duration) is to ensure that 6 flashes cannot be mistaken for 3 or 9.
W	9 flashes in a group

2   To aid the memory, the number of flashes in each group can be associated with the clock face, thus:

3 o'clock	East
6 o'clock	South
9 o'clock	West

3   **Period.** The periods of the East, South and West lights are, respectively, 10, 15, and 15 seconds if a quick light, and 5, 10, and 10 seconds if a very quick light.

4   **Rate.** Quick lights flash at a rate of between 50 and 79 flashes per minute, usually either 50 or 60. Very quick lights flash at a rate of between 80 and 159 flashes per minute, usually either 100 or 120.

Retroreflectors
C.32

1   One or more white bands, letters, numerals or symbols of retroreflective material are used in the Standard Code to distinguish unlighted Cardinal marks.

2   Blue and yellow bands on the black and yellow parts of the mark are used in the Comprehensive Code, thus:

N	Blue on the black part and yellow on the yellow part
E	Two blue on the upper black part
S	Yellow on the yellow part and blue on the black part
W	Two yellow on the upper yellow part

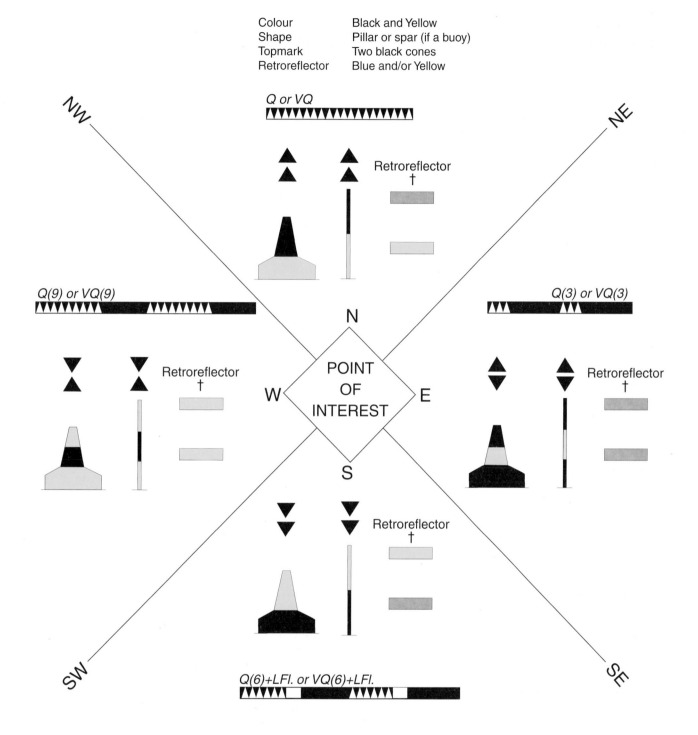

Colour   Black and Yellow
Shape   Pillar or spar (if a buoy)
Topmark   Two black cones
Retroreflector Blue and/or Yellow

Q or VQ

Retroreflector
†

NW

NE

Q(9) or VQ(9)

Retroreflector
†

Q(3) or VQ(3)

Retroreflector
†

N

POINT
OF
INTEREST

W   E

S

Retroreflector
†

SW

SE

Q(6)+LFl. or VQ(6)+LFl.

NOTES

† Retroflectors illustrated are those of the Comprehensive Code. In the Standard Code these marks are distinguished by one or more white bands, letters, numerals or symbols.

This diagram is schematic and in the case of pillar buoys in particular, their features will vary with the individual design of the buoys in use.

LIGHTS, when fitted, are white Very Quick Lights or Quick Lights; a South mark also has a Long Flash immediately following the quick flashes.

Cardinal Marks (C.26)

Isolated Danger Marks

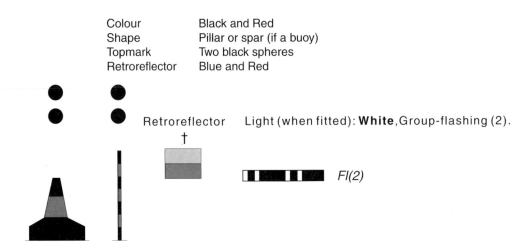

Colour	Black and Red
Shape	Pillar or spar (if a buoy)
Topmark	Two black spheres
Retroreflector	Blue and Red

Retroreflector †

Light (when fitted): **White**, Group-flashing (2).

Fl(2)

NOTES

† Retroflectors illustrated are those of the Comprehensive Code. In the Standard Code these marks are distinguished by one or more white bands, letters, numerals or symbols.

This diagram is schematic and in the case of pillar buoys in particular, their features will vary with the individual design of the buoys in use.

Isolated Danger Marks (C.33)

Use
C.33

1   Isolated Danger marks are erected on, or moored on or above, isolated dangers of limited extent which have navigable water all round them. The extent of the surrounding navigable water is immaterial: such a mark can, for example, indicate either a shoal which is well offshore, or an islet separated by a narrow channel from the coast. See Diagram C.33.

2   On Admiralty charts, the position of a danger is the centre of the symbol or sounding indicating that danger. The symbol indicating the Isolated Danger buoy will inevitably be slightly displaced.

Topmark
C.34

1   Black double-sphere topmarks, disposed vertically, are a very important feature of Isolated Danger marks and are carried whenever practicable.

Colours
C.35

1   Isolated Danger marks are black with one or more red bands.

Shape
C.36

1   No significance is attached to the shape of Isolated Danger marks, but in the case of a buoy, a pillar or spar buoy is used.

Light
C.37

1   An Isolated Danger mark exhibits a white flashing light showing a group of two flashes. The association of two flashes and two spheres of the topmark may help in remembering these characteristics.

Retroreflectors
C.38

1   One or more white bands, letters, numerals or symbols of retroreflective material are used for unlighted Isolated Danger marks in the Standard Code.

One or more pairs of blue above red bands are used in the Comprehensive Code (see Diagram C.33).

Safe Water Marks

Colour	Red and White
Shape	Pillar or spar
Topmark	Red sphere
Retroreflector	Red and White

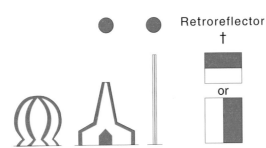

Retroreflector
†

or

Light (when fitted): **White**, Isophase, or Occulting, or Long-Flashing every 10 seconds, or Morse Code (A)

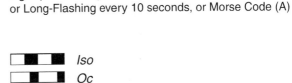

Iso
Oc
LFl.10s
Mo(A)

NOTES

† Retroflectors illustrated are those of the Comprehensive Code. In the Standard Code these marks are distinguished by one or more white bands, letters, numerals or symbols.

This diagram is schematic and in the case of pillar buoys in particular, their features will vary with the individual design of the buoys in use.

Safe Water Marks (C.39)

Use
C.39

1   Safe Water marks are used to indicate that there is navigable water all round a mark. Such a mark may be used as a centreline, mid-channel or landfall buoy, or to indicate the best point of passage under a fixed bridge.

Topmark
C.40

1   A red spherical topmark is a very important feature, particularly if the buoy is not spherical. It is fitted whenever practicable.

Colours
C.41

1   Red and white stripes are used for Safe Water marks, and distinguish them from the black-banded danger-marking marks.

Shape
C.42

1   Spherical, pillar or spar buoys are used as Safe Water marks.

Lights
C.43

1   When lit, a white light, occulting, or isophase, or showing a single long flash or Morse code (A) is used for Safe Water marks.

2   If a long flash (ie a flash of not less than 2 seconds) is used, the period of the light is 10 seconds.

Retroreflectors
C.44

1   One or more white bands, letters, numerals, or symbols of retroreflective material are used for unlit Safe Water marks in the Standard Code.

Red and white stripes or bands are used in the Comprehensive Code.

Special Marks

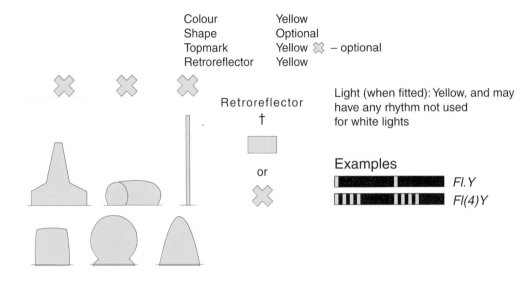

Colour   Yellow
Shape   Optional
Topmark   Yellow ✕ – optional
Retroreflector Yellow

Retroreflector
†

or

Light (when fitted): Yellow, and may
have any rhythm not used
for white lights

Examples

▬▬▬▬▬▬▬ *Fl.Y*
▮▮▮▮▬▬▮▮▮▮ *Fl(4)Y*

NOTES

† Retroflectors illustrated are those of the Comprehensive Code. In the Standard Code these marks are distinguished by one or more white bands, letters, numerals or symbols.

This diagram is schematic and in the case of pillar buoys in particular, their features will vary with the individual design of the buoys in use.

Special Marks (C.45)

Use
C.45

1 Special marks may be used to indicate to the mariner a special area or feature, the nature of which is apparent from reference to a chart, Sailing Directions or Notices to Mariners. Special marks may be lettered to indicate their purpose.

2 Uses include the marking of:
Ocean Data Acquisition System (ODAS) buoys (11.94).
Traffic Separation Schemes where use of conventional channel marking might cause confusion, though many schemes are marked by Lateral and Safe Water marks.
Spoil grounds.
Military exercise areas.
Cables or pipelines (including outfall pipes).
Recreation zones.

3 Another function of Special marks is to define a channel within a channel. For example a channel for deep-draught vessels in a wide estuary, where the limits of the channel for normal navigation are marked by red and green Lateral buoys, may have the boundaries of the deep channel indicated by yellow buoys of the appropriate Lateral shapes, or its centreline marked by yellow spherical buoys.

Topmark
C.46

1 A single yellow X is the form of topmark used for a Special mark, when one is carried.

Colour
C.47

1 Yellow is the colour for Special marks.

Shape
C.48

1 The shape of Special buoys is optional but must not conflict with that used for a Lateral or Safe Water mark. For example, an outfall buoy on the port side of a channel could be can-shaped but not conical.

Lights
C.49

1 When lit, a yellow light is exhibited from a Special mark. The rhythm may be any, other than those used for the white light of Cardinal, Isolated Danger and Safe Water marks. The following are permitted examples:
Group occulting.
Flashing.
Group flashing with a group of 4, 5 or (exceptionally) 6 flashes.
Composite group flashing.
Morse code letters, other than Morse Code (A), (D) or (U).

2 In the case of ODAS buoys, the rhythm is group flashing with a group of 5 flashes every 20 seconds.

Retroreflectors
C.50

1 One yellow band, an X, or a symbol are used as retroreflectors for unlit Special marks.

Emergency Wreck Marking Buoy

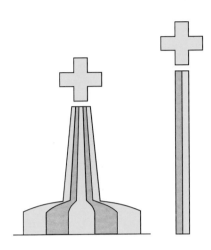

Emergency Wreck Marking Buoy (C.51)

Introduction
C.51

1   The wreck of the *Tricolor* in the Dover Strait in 2002 brought into sharp focus the effective responses required to adequately and quickly mark such new dangers and prevent collisions.

2   A new wreck can be very dangerous for shipping, not only when its exact position is unknown, but even when the position is known and the wreck properly marked.

3   Until recently, new dangers have generally been marked by Cardinal or Lateral buoys, but weather conditions, sea state and unknown facts about the danger can all hamper timely marking.

4   In addition, the volume of traffic, background lighting, and the proliferation of other aids to navigation in the area may make the deployment of Cardinal or Lateral marks difficult for Mariners to quickly identify a new danger in the early stages of an incident.

Use
C.52

1   The emergency wreck marking buoy, introduced by IMO on the recommendation of IALA, on a trial basis, in 2006, is designed to provide a highly conspicuous visual and radio aid to navigation. It will be be placed as close to the wreck as possible, or in a pattern around the wreck, and within any other marks that may be subsequently deployed.

2   The emergency wreck marking buoy will be maintained in position until:

The wreck is well known and has been promulgated in nautical publications i.e. Notices to Mariners.

The wreck has been fully surveyed and exact details such as position and least depth above the wreck are known.

A permanent form of marking of the wreck has been carried out.

Topmark
C.53

1   If fitted, the top mark is a standing or upright yellow cross.

Colour
C.54

1   The emergency wreck marking buoy is coloured in equal number and dimensions of blue and yellow vertical stripes (minimum of 4 and maximum of 8 stripes).

Shape
C.55

1   The emergency wreck-marking buoy is a pillar or spar buoy, with size dependant on location.

Lights
C.56

1   If lit, the emergency wreck marking buoy exhibits an alternating blue and yellow flashing light with a nominal range of 4 nautical miles (authorities are authorised to alter the range depending on local conditions) where the blue and yellow 1 second flashes are alternated with an interval of 0·5 seconds, e.g:

B1·0s + 0·5s + Y1·0s + 0·5s = 3·0s

If multiple buoys are deployed then the lights may be synchronised.

Other aids to navigation
C.57

1   The emergency wreck marking buoy may be fitted with a racon Morse Code "D" and/or AIS transponder.

NOTES

Annex D

Flags and Ensigns of Maritime Nations

COUNTRY	NATIONAL FLAG	MERCHANT ENSIGN	MILITARY ENSIGN
Albania			
Alderney			
Algeria			
American Samoa			
Angola			
Anguilla			
Antigua and Barbuda			
Argentina			
Aruba			
Australia			

COUNTRY	NATIONAL FLAG	MERCHANT ENSIGN	MILITARY ENSIGN
Austria			
Azores			
Bahamas			
Bahrain			
Bangladesh			
Barbados			
Belgium			
Belize			
Benin			
Bermuda			
Bolivia			

COUNTRY	NATIONAL FLAG	MERCHANT ENSIGN	MILITARY ENSIGN
Bosnia and Herzegovina			
Brazil			
British Antarctic Territory			
British Indian Ocean Territory			
British Virgin Islands			
Brunei			
Bulgaria			
Burma			
Cambodia			
Cameroon			
Canada			

COUNTRY	NATIONAL FLAG	MERCHANT ENSIGN	MILITARY ENSIGN
Cape Verde			
Cayman Islands			
Chile			
China			
Cocos (Keeling) Islands			
Colombia			
Comoros			
Congo - Brazzaville			
Congo - Kinshasa (formerly Zaire)			
Cook Islands			
Costa Rica			

COUNTRY	NATIONAL FLAG	MERCHANT ENSIGN	MILITARY ENSIGN
Croatia			
Cuba			
Cyprus			
Denmark			
Djibouti			
Dominica			
Dominican Republic			
East Timor			
Ecuador			
Egypt			
El Salvador			

COUNTRY	NATIONAL FLAG	MERCHANT ENSIGN	MILITARY ENSIGN
Equatorial Guinea			
Eritrea			
Estonia			
Ethiopia			
Faröe Islands			
Falkland Islands			
Fiji			
Finland			
France			
French Guiana			
French Polynesia			

COUNTRY	NATIONAL FLAG	MERCHANT ENSIGN	MILITARY ENSIGN
French Southern and Antarctic Lands			
Gabon			
The Gambia			
Georgia			
Germany			
Ghana			
Gibraltar			
Greece			
Greenland			
Grenada			
Guadeloupe			

COUNTRY	NATIONAL FLAG	MERCHANT ENSIGN	MILITARY ENSIGN
Guam			
Guatemala			
Guernsey			
Guinea			
Guinea Bissau			
Guyana			
Haiti			
Honduras			
Hong Kong SAR			
Hungary			
Iceland			

COUNTRY	NATIONAL FLAG	MERCHANT ENSIGN	MILITARY ENSIGN
India			
Indonesia			
Iran			
Iraq			
Ireland			
Isle of Man			
Israel			
Italy			
Ivory Coast			
Jamaica			
Japan			

COUNTRY	NATIONAL FLAG	MERCHANT ENSIGN	MILITARY ENSIGN
Jersey			
Jordan			
Kenya			
Kiribati			
Korea (North)			
Korea (South)			
Kuwait			
Laos			
Latvia			
Lebanon			
Liberia			

COUNTRY	NATIONAL FLAG	MERCHANT ENSIGN	MILITARY ENSIGN
Libya			
Lithuania			
Luxemborg			
Macao SAR			
Madagascar			
Madeira			
Malaysia			
Maldives			
Malta			
Marshall Islands			
Martinique			

COUNTRY	NATIONAL FLAG	MERCHANT ENSIGN	MILITARY ENSIGN
Mauretania			
Mauritius			
Mayotte			
Mexico			
Micronesia			
Midway Islands			
Monaco			
Montenegro			
Montserrat			
Morocco			
Mozambique			

COUNTRY	NATIONAL FLAG	MERCHANT ENSIGN	MILITARY ENSIGN
Namibia			
Nauru			
Netherlands			
Netherlands Antilles			
New Caledonia			
New Zealand			
Nicaragua			
Nigeria			
Niue			
Norfolk Island			
Northern Marianas			

COUNTRY	NATIONAL FLAG	MERCHANT ENSIGN	MILITARY ENSIGN
Norway			
Oman			
Pakistan			
Palau			
Panama			
Papua New Guinea			
Paraguay			
Peru			
Philippines			
Pitcairn Island			
Poland			

COUNTRY	NATIONAL FLAG	MERCHANT ENSIGN	MILITARY ENSIGN
Portugal			
Puerto Rico			
Qatar			
Réunion			
Romania			
Russia			
St Helena and Dependencies (Ascension - Tristan de Cunha)			
St Kitts / Nevis			
St Lucia			
St Pierre and Miquelon			
Samoa			

COUNTRY	NATIONAL FLAG	MERCHANT ENSIGN	MILITARY ENSIGN
Sao Tome and Principe			
Sark			
Saudi Arabia			
Senegal			
Serbia			
Seychelles			
Sierra Leone			
Singapore			
Slovenia			
Solomon Islands			
Somalia			

COUNTRY	NATIONAL FLAG	MERCHANT ENSIGN	MILITARY ENSIGN
South Africa			
South Georgia and South Sandwich Islands			
Spain			
Sri Lanka			
Sudan			
Suriname			
Sweden			
Switzerland			
Syria			
Taiwan			
Thailand			

COUNTRY	NATIONAL FLAG	MERCHANT ENSIGN	MILITARY ENSIGN
Togo			
Tokelau			
Tonga			
Trinidad and Tobago			
Tristan da Cunha			
Tunisia			
Turkey			
Turks and Caicos Islands			
Tuvalu			
Ukraine			
United Arab Emirates			

COUNTRY	NATIONAL FLAG	MERCHANT ENSIGN	MILITARY ENSIGN
United Kingdom			
United States of America			
Uruguay			
US Virgin Islands			
Vanuatu			
Venezuela			
Vietnam			
Wake Island			
Wallis and Futuna			
Yemen			

NOTES

Glossary

Scope

Definitions given are those in UKHO use and have no significance in International Law. Only terms which are not already defined in English Dictionaries, or which may be used with a significantly different connotation are included in this glossary.

Exceptions to the definitions of certain terms in this glossary, due to local custom and long usage, may occasionally be met.

Foreign and local terms will be found in the glossaries of the appropriate volumes of *Admiralty Sailing Directions*.

Lights, and terms used in association with lights, light structures and fog signals, are described with equivalent terms in 13 languages in *Admiralty List of Lights*.

Weather reporting terms, with their equivalents in French and Spanish are given in *Admiralty List of Radio Signals Volume 3(2)*.

Terms

A

abeam. See **beam, on the**.

abnormal magnetic variation. Designation applied to any anomalous value of the magnetic variation of which the cause is unknown. See also **local magnetic anomaly**.

aboard. In the sense used in pilotage and ship handling means "near". e.g. "To keep the E shore aboard". "Close aboard" means "Very near". See also **borrow.**

above. Uptide or upstream of a position.

above-water. A shoal, rock or other feature is termed above-water if it is visible at any state of the tide. See also **awash, dries, below-water.**

abrupt. Steep; precipitous. See also **bold**.

abyssal. Relating to the greatest depths of the ocean (literally, without bottom).

abyssal gap. A narrow break, in a ridge or rise, or separating two abyssal plains.

abyssal hill(s). An isolated, or tract of, small elevation(s) on the deep sea floor.

abyssal plain. An extensive, flat, gently sloping or nearly level at abyssal depths.

accretion or **deposition.** The depositing of material on the sea floor or the coast by water movement; the opposite to **erosion**.

active plan. A passage plan during execution or in the process of being edited.

Admiralty Pilot. Commonly used to describe a volume of Sailing Directions published by the UKHO. Also, the title given to a **pilot** employed by the Queen's Harbour Master in one of the naval dockyard ports in UK.

advance. For a specific alteration of course, advance is the distance moved from the wheel–over position, along the original course, to the point where a vessel is steady on her new course. See also **transfer.**

aeronautical radiobeacon. A radiobeacon primarily for the use of aircraft. Usually abbreviated to "aero radiobeacon".

afloat. Floating, as opposed to being aground.

age of the Moon. The interval in days and decimals of a day since the last New Moon.

agger. See **double tide.**

agonic line. A line joining points on the Earth's surface where there is no magnetic variation.

aground. Resting on the seabed.

aid to navigation. A device or system external to the vessel that is designed and operated to enhance the safe and efficient navigation of vessels and/or vessel traffic. Examples include buoys, beacons, lights, leading marks, and radio position fixing systems. See also **navigation aid.**

ALC. Articulated Loading Column. See 13.138.

alertpoint. In voyage planning, the location wherer the navigator attaches notes pertaining to the voyage being planned.

ALP. Articulated Loading Platform. See 13.138.

alongside. A ship is alongside when side by side with a wharf, wall, jetty, or another ship.

amphidrome. A point in the sea where the tide has no amplitude. Co-tidal lines radiate from an amphidromic point and co-range lines encircle it.

anchorage. Water area which is suitable and of depth neither too deep nor too shallow, nor in a situation too exposed, for vessels to ride in safety. Also, an area set apart for vessels to anchor, such as:
    examination anchorage. Used by ships while awaiting examination.
    quarantine anchorage. A special anchorage set aside, in many ports, for ships in quarantine.
    safety fairway anchorage. An anchorage adjacent to a **shipping safety fairway**.

anchor buoy. Small buoy occasionally used to mark the position of the anchor when on the sea floor; usually painted green (starboard) or red (port), and secured to the crown of the anchor by a buoy rope.

angle of cut. The lesser angle between two position lines.

aphelion. The point in the orbit of a planet which is farthest from the Sun. See also **perihelion.**

apogee. The point in the orbit of the Moon, or any satellite, which is farthest from the Earth. See also **perigee.**

approaches. The waterways that give access or passage to harbours, channels, and similar areas.

apron. The portion of a wharf or quay lying between the waterside edge and the sheds, railway lines or road. Also, oceanographically, a gently dipping surface, underlain primarily by sediment, at the base of any steeper **slope.**

arch. Geologically, a covered passage cut through a small headland by wave action.

archipelagic apron. A gentle **slope** with a generally smooth surface of the sea floor, characteristically found around groups of islands or **seamounts.**

arc of visibility. The sector, or sectors, in which a light is visible from seaward.

arm (of a jetty, or similar structure). A narrow portion projecting from the main body.

arm of the sea. A comparatively narrow branch or offshoot from a body of the sea.

arming the lead. Placing tallow in the recess in the bottom of the sounding lead to ascertain the nature of the sea floor.

artificial harbour. A harbour where the desired protection from wind and sea is obtained from moles, jetties, breakwaters, and similar structures. (The breakwater may have been constructed by sinking concrete barges, vessels, or other suitable objects to form a temporary shelter.)

artificial horizon. A horizon produced by bubble, gyro or mercury trough to allow measurement of altitude of celestial bodies.

astronomical twilight. The period between the end of **nautical twilight** and the time when the Sun's centre is 18° below the horizon in the evening, and the period between the time when the Sun's centre is 18° below the horizon in the morning and the beginning of nautical twilight in the morning.

ATBA. See **routeing system** and 9.32.

atoll. A ring-shaped coral reef which has islands or islets on it, the shallow rim enclosing a deeper natural area or lagoon; often springing from oceanic depths.

awash. A shoal, rock or other feature is termed awash when its highest part is within 0·1 m, or with fathoms charts within 1 foot, of **chart datum**. Also, **awash at high water.** May be just visible at MHWS or MHHW. See also **dries, above-water.**

B

back. The wind is said to back when it changes direction anticlockwise in the N hemisphere. See also **veer.**

backwash. Waves reflected from obstructions such as cliffs, seawalls or breakwaters, running seaward and combining with the in-coming waves to cause a steep and confused sea.

backwash marks. Small scale oblique reticulate pattern sometimes produced by the return swash of the waves on a sandy beach. See also **ripple marks, beach cusps.**

backwater. An arm of the sea, usually lying parallel with the coast behind a narrow strip of land, or an arm of a river out of the main channel, and out of the main tidal stream or current.

bank(s). Oceanographically, an isolated, or group of, elevation(s) of the sea floor over which the depth of water is relatively shallow, but sufficient for safe surface navigation. Also, the margin of a watercourse such as a river, lake, or canal. Note. The right bank of a river is the one on the right hand when facing downstream.

bar. A bank of sand, mud, gravel or shingle near the mouth of a river or at the approach to a harbour, causing an obstruction to entry.

bar buoy. A buoy indicating the position of a bar.

barrier. An obstruction, usually artificial, in a river. e.g. Thames Barrier.

barrier reef. A coral reef, lying roughly parallel with the shore, but separated from it by a channel or lagoon. The distance offshore may vary from a few metres to several miles.

basalt. Dark green or brown igneous rock, often in columnar strata.

bascule bridge. Lifting bridge. See also **bridge.**

basin. An almost land-locked area leading off an **inlet, firth** or **sound**. Also, an area of water limited in extent and nearly enclosed by structures alongside which vessels can lie. Oceanographically, a depression, in the sea floor, more or less equidimensional in plan and of variable extent. Also:

> **tidal basin.** A basin without caisson or gates in which the level of water rises and falls with the tide. Sometimes called an open basin.
> **non-tidal basin.** A basin closed by a caisson or gates to shut it off from open water, so that a constant level of water can be maintained in it. Also called a wet dock.
> **impounding basin.** A basin in which water can be held at a certain level, either to keep craft afloat or to provide water for sluicing.
> **turning basin.** An area of water or enlargement of a channel in a port, where vessels are enabled to turn, and which is kept clear of obstructions such as buoys for that purpose.

bathymetry. The science of the measurement of marine depths. Submarine relief.

bay. A comparatively gradual indentation in the coastline, the seaward opening of which is usually wider than the penetration into the land. See also **bight, gulf.**

bayou. Term used in Florida for a small bay, and in Mississippi and Louisiana for a waterway through lowlands or swamps, connecting other bodies of water, and usually tidal or with an imperceptible current.

beach. Any part of the shore where mud, sand, shingle, or pebbles accumulate in a more or less continuous sheet. The term is not used to describe areas of jagged reef, rocks or coral. Also, **to beach.** To run a vessel or boat ashore. To haul a boat up on a beach.

beach cusps. Triangular ridges, or accumulations, of sand or other detritus regularly spaced along the shore, the apex of the triangle pointing towards the water, giving a serrated form to the water-edge.

beach ridges. The seaward boundaries of successive positions of beaches on seaward-advancing shores. The intervening depressions may be extensive and contain features such as lagoons, marshes or mangrove swamps, or be narrow and consist of sand. See also **storm beach.**

beacon. A fixed artificial navigational mark, sometimes called a daybeacon in the USA and Canada. It can be recognised by means of its shape, colour, pattern or topmark. It may carry a light, radar reflector or other navigational aid.

beacon tower. A major masonry beacon the structure of which is as distinctive as the **topmark**.

beam, on the. An object is said to be on the beam, or abeam, if its bearing is approximately 90° from the ship's head.

beam sea. The condition where the sea and swell approach the ship at approximately 90° from the ship's head.

bearing:
    anchor bearing. The bearing of a shore object from the position of the anchor.
    check bearing. The bearing of an extra object taken to check the accuracy of a fix.
    clearing bearing. The bearing of an object, usually taken from a chart, to indicate whether a ship is clear of danger.
    line of bearing. A ship runs on a line of bearing if she makes good a ground track on a constant bearing of an object.

bed. The **sea floor** composition and sub-strata of the ocean, sea, lake or river. Usually qualified, e.g. seabed, river bed.

bell-buoy. A buoy fitted with a bell which may be actuated automatically or by wave motion.

below-water. A shoal, rock or other feature is termed below-water or underwater if it is not visible at any state of the tide. See also **above-water.**

bench. See **terrace.**

benchmark. A mark, such as an arrow cut in masonry, a bolthead, or a rivet fixed in concrete, whose height relative to some particular datum is exactly known. (See Admiralty Tidal Handbook No 2 (NP 122(2))

berm. An horizontal ledge on the side of an embankment or cutting to intercept falling earth or to add strength. Also, a narrow, nearly horizontal shelf or ledge above the foreshore built of material thrown up by storm waves. The seaward margin is the crest of the berm.

berth. The space assigned to or taken up by a vessel when anchored or when lying alongside a wharf, jetty, or other structure.
    to give a wide berth. To keep well away from another ship or any feature.

berthpoint. In voyage planning, the first and last points of a berth-to-berth passage. Indicates locations where significant activities take place which naturally punctuate a voyage and usually involves the stopping of engines i.e. port calls for loading/discharging cargo or bunkers.

bight. A crescent-shaped indentation in the coastline, usually of large extent and not more than a 90° sector of a circle. See also **bay, gulf.**

bilge (or keel) blocks. A row of wooden blocks on which the bilges, or keel, of a ship rest when she is in dry dock or on a slipway.

bill. A narrow promontory.

blather. Very wet mud, a feature of estuaries and rivers; of a dangerous nature such that a weight will at once sink into it.

blind rollers. When a swell wave encounters shoal water it is slowed and becomes steeper. If the depth or extent of the shoal or rock is sufficient to cause the wave to steepen markedly but not to break, the resulting wave is termed a blind roller.

bluff. A headland or short stretch of cliff with a broad perpendicular face. Also, as an adjective, having a broad perpendicular or nearly perpendicular face.

boat camber. See **camber.**

boat harbour. An area of sheltered water in a harbour set aside for the use of boats, usually with moorings, buoys, or other facilities.

boat house. A shed at the water's edge or above a slipway for housing a boat or boats.

boat pound. See **pound.**

boat slip. A slipway designed specifically for boats.

boat yard. A boat-building establishment.

bog. Wet spongy ground consisting of decaying vegetation, which retains stagnant water, too soft to bear the weight of any heavy body. An extreme case of swamp or morass.

bold. Rising steeply from deep water. Well-marked. Clear cut. See also **abrupt.**

bollard. A post (usually steel or reinforced concrete) firmly embedded in or secured on a feature such as a wharf or jetty, for mooring vessels by means of wires or ropes extending from the vessel and secured to the post. See also **dollie.**

boom. A floating barrier of timber used to protect a river or harbour mouth or to enclose a boat harbour or timber pound. Also, a barrier of hawsers and nets supported by buoys used in the defence of a port or anchorage.

booming ground. A term used mainly in Canadian waters, and similar to timber **pound** where logs are temporarily held and stored for making up into rafts. The area is usually enclosed by a boom to retain the logs.

borderland. A region adjacent to a continent, normally occupied by, or bordering a **shelf** and sometimes emerging as islands, that is irregular or blocky in plan or profile, with depths well in excess of those typical of a **shelf.**

bore. A tidal wave which propagates as a solitary wave with a steep leading edge up certain rivers. Formation is most apparent in wedge-shaped shoaling estuaries at times of spring tides. See Admiralty Manual of Tides.

borrow. In the sense used in pilotage means "keep towards, but not too near", e.g. "To borrow on the E side of the channel". See also **aboard.**

bottom, nature of the. The material of which the seabed is formed, e.g. mud, stones.

boulders. Water-rounded stones more than 256 mm in size, i.e. larger than a man's head, See also **cobbles.**

brackish. Water in which salinity values range from approximately 0·50 to 17·00.

breakers. Waves or swell which have become so steep, either on reaching shoal water or on encountering a contrary current or by the action of wind, that the crest falls over and breaks into foam.

breaking sea. The partial collapse of the crests of waves, less complete than in the case of breakers, but from the same cause; also known as White Horses.

breakwater. A solid structure, such as a wall or mole, to break the force of the waves, sometimes detached from the shore, protecting a harbour or anchorage. Vessels usually cannot lie alongside a breakwater.

bridge. Structure erected over a depression, or over an obstacle such as a body of water or a railroad, to provide a roadway for pedestrians or vehicles. Bridges are either fixed or movable. Movable bridges are usually either swing bridges, or bascule bridges.

> **swing bridges** may pivot about a point, either in mid-channel or on one bank.
> **bascule bridges** may have either single or double leaves, depending on whether they lift from one or both banks. They hinge upwards and are counterweighted for ease of operation. The name is from the French word meaning *rocker* or *seesaw.*

broach. To slew around inadvertently broadside on to the sea, when running before it.

broadside on. Beam on, e.g. to wind or sea.

broken water. A general term for a turbulent and breaking sea in contrast to comparatively smooth and unbroken water in the vicinity.

brook. A small stream.

brow. An arrangement of wooden planking to give passage between ship and shore when the ship is alongside. Also called a **gangway.**

bubble curtain. A length of perforated submarine pipeline from which compressed air is released, forming bubbles on the surface which discourage the formation of ice. Bubble curtains may be found in Norwegian waters, particularly around marine farms and small craft harbours.

building slip. A space in a shipbuilding yard where foundations for launching ways and keel blocks exist and which is occupied by a ship when being built.

buoy. A floating, and moored, artificial navigation mark. It can be recognised by means of its shape, colour, pattern, topmark or light character, or a combination of these. It may carry various additional aids to navigation. See also **LANBY, light buoy.**

buoyant beacon. A floating mark coupled to a sinker either directly or by a cable that is held in tension by the buoyancy of the mark. Its appearance above the water generally resembles a beacon rather than a buoy; it does not rise and fall with the tide; and it normally remains in a vertical or near-vertical position. Formerly known as a Pivoted Beacon.

C

cable. A nautical unit of measurement, being one tenth of a sea mile. See **mile.** Also, a term often used to refer to the chain cable by which a vessel is secured to her anchor. Also used to refer to submarine, or overhead, power or telephone cables.

cable buoy. A buoy marking the end of a submarine cable on which a cable ship is working. Also used in the sense of a **telegraph buoy.**

cabotage. The passage of a cargo on a domestic voyage and therefore not subject to international agreements.

cairn. A mound of rough stones or concrete of pyramidal or beehive shape used as a **landmark.**

caisson. A structure used to close the entrance to dry docks, locks and non-tidal basins. They are of two kinds: floating caissons which are detachable from the entrance they close, and sliding caissons which slide into a recess at the side of the dock. Some dry docks are closed by raising a flap-type door, hinged at the outer side of the dock sill. See also **cofferdam.**

calcareous. Formed of, or containing, carbonate of lime or limestone.

caldera. A collapsed, or partially–collapsed **seamount,** commonly of annular shape.

calling-in point. See **reporting point.**

CALM. Catenary Anchor Leg Mooring. See 13.137.

calving. The breaking away of rock, stones, earth, or other material from the face of a cliff. See also Ice Glossary for use of term in relation to icebergs.

camber. A small basin usually with a narrow entrance, generally situated inside a harbour. e.g. Boat camber: a small basin for the exclusive use of boats.

camel. A tank filled with water and placed against the hull of a stranded or sunken vessel. It is well secured to the vessel and then pumped out, the buoyancy thus added helping to lift the vessel.

can buoy. A nearly cylindrical buoy moored so that a flat end is uppermost.

canal. A channel dredged or cut through dry land or through drying shoals or banks and used as a waterway. See also **ship canal.**

canal port. A port so situated that the waterway is entirely artificial.

canyon. A deep gorge or ravine with steep sides, at the bottom of which a river flows. Oceanographically, an isolated relatively narrow, deep depression with steep sides, the bottom of which generally deepens continuously, developed characteristically on some continental **slopes.**

cape. A piece of land, or point, facing the open sea and projecting into it beyond the adjacent coast.

Capesize. Used to describe cargo ships which are too large to traverse either the Suez or Panama Canals.

cargo transfer area. See **transhipment area**.

cast. To turn a ship to a desired direction without gaining headway or sternway.

catamaran. A floating stage or raft used in shipyards, for working from, and sometimes used as a fender between ship and wharf. The name is taken from various native-built craft common in the East Indies and some other parts of the world. Also, a type of twin-hulled yacht.

catwalk. A narrow footway forming a bridge, e.g. connecting a mooring dolphin to a pierhead. Also known as a walkway.

causeway. A raised roadway of solid structure built across low or wet ground or across a stretch of water.

cay. A small insular feature usually with scant vegetation; usually of sand or coral. Often applied to smaller coral shoals.

centreline controlling depth. See **controlling depths.**

channel. A comparatively deep waterway, natural or dredged, through a river, harbour, strait, or a navigable route through shoals, which affords the best and safest passage for vessels or boats. The term is given to certain wide straits or arms of the sea, e.g. English Channel, Bristol Channel. Also, oceanographically, an elongated depression like a river valley in ocean basins, commonly found in **fans**.

character or **characteristic of a light**. The distinctive rhythm and colour, or colours, of a light signal that provide the identification or message, See Admiralty List of Lights.

chart datum. A level so low that the tide will not frequently fall below it. In the United Kingdom, this level is normally approximately the level of Lowest Astronomical Tide. It is the level below which soundings are given on Admiralty charts, and above which are given the drying heights of features which are periodically covered and uncovered by the tide. Chart datum is also the level to which tidal levels and predictions are referred in Admiralty Tide Tables. See 5.14.

cill. See **dock sill.**

cinders. Fragments formed when magma is blown into the air; larger in size than volcanic ash.

circular radiobeacon. A radiobeacon which transmits the same signal in all directions.

civil twilight. The periods of the day between the time when the Sun's centre is 6° below the horizon and Sunrise (morning twilight), or between sunset and the time when the Sun's centre is 6° below the horizon (evening twilight).

claw off. To beat or reach to windward away from a lee shore.

clay. A stiff tenacious sediment having a preponderance of grains with diameters of less than 0·004 mm. It is impossible to differentiate between clay and silt by eye, but a sample of wet clay, when dried in the palm of the hand, will not rub off when the hands are rubbed together.

clean. Applied to the floor of the sea, harbour or river, means free from rocks or obstructions. See also **foul.**

clearing bearing. See **bearing.**

clearing marks. Selected marks, natural or otherwise, which in transit clear a danger or which mark the boundary between safe and dangerous areas for navigation.

cliff. Land projecting nearly vertically from the water or from surrounding land, and varying from an inconspicuous slope at the margin of a low coastal plain to a high vertical feature at the seaward edge of high ground. Can be formed by a fault in geological strata (inland).

cliffy. Of cliff–like appearance. See **cliff.**

close (verb). To approach near.

close aboard. Very near.

coast. The meeting of the land and sea considered as the boundary of the land. See also **shore.** Also, the narrow strip immediately landward of the waterline of MHWS, or sometimes a much broader zone extending some distance inland.

coastal plain. A strip of flat consolidated land varying in width which may occur immediately landward of the coastline.

coastal waters. The sea in the vicinity of the coast (within which the coasting trade is carried out).

coasting. Navigating from headland to headland in sight of land, or sufficiently often in sight of land to fix the position of the ship by land features.

coastland. The strip of land with a somewhat indeterminate inner limit, immediately landward of the coastline. It may include such features as sand dunes or **saltings** which are associated with proximity to the sea, and merges into the hinterland where the features cease.

coastline. The landward limit of the beach. The extreme limit of direct wave action, such as occurs in onshore gales during Equinoctial Spring Tides. See also **backshore.** It may be some distance above the waterline of MHWS, but for practical hydrographic purposes the two are usually regarded as coincident.
Also, a general term used in describing the shore or coast as viewed from seaward, eg a low coastline.

coastwise (adjective and adverb). Near to the coast, e.g. Coastwise traffic is that which sails round the coast, and to sail coastwise means coasting as opposed to keeping out to sea.

cobbles. Water-rounded stones of from 64 mm to 256 mm in size, i.e. from the diameter of a man's clenched fist when viewed sideways to slightly larger than the size of a man's head. See also **pebbles, boulders.**

cocked hat. The triangle sometimes formed by the intersection of three lines of bearing on the chart. See also **cut.**

cofferdam. Watertight screen or enclosure used in laying foundations underwater. Sometimes called a **caisson.**

combers. Steep, long swell waves with high breaking crests.

cone. See **fan.**

confused sea. The disorderly sea in a race; also when waves from different directions meet, due normally to a sudden shift in the direction of the wind.

conformal projection. Another name for **orthomorphic projection.**

conical buoy. A cone-shaped buoy moored to float point up. See also **can buoy, nun buoy.**

conspicuous object. A natural or artificial mark which is outstanding, easily identifiable, and clearly visible to the mariner over a large area of sea in varying conditions of light. If the scale is large enough they will normally be shown on charts in bold capitals, or on older charts by the note "conspic". See also **prominent.**

constants (harmonic). The phase-lag (g) and the amplitude (H) of a constituent of the tide.

constants (non-harmonic). The average time and height difference of high and low water, referred to the times and heights at a standard port; the time can also be referred to the time of Moon's transit.

constituent (of the tide). The tidal curve can be considered as being composed of a number of cosine curves, having different speeds, phase-lags and amplitudes, the speed being determined from astronomical theory and the phase-lags and amplitudes being determined from observation and analysis. These cosine curves are known as constituents of the tide. See Admiralty Tidal Handbook No 1 (NP122(1)).

container. A rigid, non-disposable, cargo-carrying unit, with or without wheels. Standard lengths are: 6·1 m (Twenty-foot Equivalent Unit (teu)) and 12·2 m (Forty-foot Equivalent Unit (feu)): both width and height are standardised at 2·44 m.
The main types of container are:
    collapsible: Can be stowed when not in use;
    dry bulk: For cargoes such as dry chemicals or grain;
    dry cargo: For general cargo;
    flat rack: For timber, large items or machinery;
    refrigerated: Insulated and usually fitted with its own refrigeration systems.

container terminal. A specially equipped berth with storage area, where standard cargo containers are loaded or unloaded.

continental borderland. A province adjacent to a continent, normally occupied by or bordering a continental shelf, that is highly irregular, with depths well in excess of those typical of a continental shelf.

continental margin. The zone, generally consisting of the shelf, slope and rise, separating the continent from the deep sea sea floor or **abyssal plain.** Occasionally a **trench** may be present in place of a **continental rise.**

continental rise. A gentle slope rising from the oceanic depths towards the foot of the continental **slope.**

continental shelf. A zone adjacent to a continent, or around an island, and extending from the low water line to a depth at which there is usually a marked increase of slope towards oceanic depths. Conventionally, its edge is taken as 200 m, but it may be between about 100 m and 350 m. See **shelf.**

continental slope. The slope seaward from the shelf edge to the beginning of a continental rise or the point where there is a general reduction in slope.

contour. A line joining points of the same height above or depths below, the datum. See also **fathom line.**

controlling depth. The least depth within the limits of a channel: it restricts the safe use of the channel to draughts of less than that depth. Depths in a channel are designated as follows:
    centreline controlling depth. A depth which applies only to the channel centreline: lesser depths may exist in the remainder of the channel.
    mid-channel controlling depth. A depth which applies only to the middle half of the channel.

convergence. The boundary or region where two converging currents meets, with the result that the water of the current of higher density sinks below the surface and spreads out at a depth which depends on its density.

conveyor. Belt of buckets or similar contrivance for transporting cargo, especially ores or coal, from ship to shore or vice versa.

coping. The top course of masonry in a wall: the waterside top edge of a wall.

coral. Hard calcareous substance secreted by many species of marine polyps for support, habitation. It may be found either dead or alive. See 5.46.

coral island. An island principally or entirely formed of coral. It may be one of three kinds: an elevated coral reef forming an island; a reef island formed by the accumulation of coral debris on a submerged fringing or barrier reef; or an atoll.

coral reef. Reefs, often of large extent, composed chiefly of coral and its derivatives. See **atoll, barrier reef, fringing reef.**

co-range lines. Lines on a tidal chart joining points which have the same tidal range or amplitude; also called co-amplitude lines. Usually drawn for a particular tidal constituent or tidal condition, e.g. mean spring tides.

cordillera. An entire mountain province, including all the subordinate ranges and groups and the interior plateaux and basins.

coriolis force. An apparent force acting on a body in motion, due to the rotation of the Earth, causing deflection, e.g. of winds and currents, to the right in the N hemisphere and to the left in the S hemisphere.

co-tidal chart. A chart combining **co-range lines** with **co-tidal lines**; co-tidal charts may refer to the tide as a whole or to one or more tidal constituents.

co-tidal lines. Lines joining points at which high water (or low water) occurs simultaneously. The times may be expressed as differences from times at a standard port or as intervals after the time of Moon's transit.

course. The intended direction of the ship's head.

course made good. The resultant horizontal direction of actual travel. The direction of a point of arrival from a point of departure.

cove. A small indentation in a coast, usually a cliffy one, frequently with a restricted entrance and often circular or semi-circular in shape.

cradle. A carriage of wood or metal in which a vessel sits on a slipway.

craft. A term applied to small vessels and boats.

harbour craft. Boats, barges, lighters, etc., used on harbour work.

crane. A mechanical contrivance for lifting weights. The main types are:

cargo crane. For transferring cargo between a ship's hold and the shore or lighter;

container crane. Specifically intended for handling containers;

fixed crane. Built on the shore for use in one place only;

floating crane. Mounted on a lighter or pontoon. See also **crane lighter**;

gantry crane. Mounted on a frame or structure spanning an intervening space. See also **transporter**;

luffing crane. Can move a load nearer or farther from the base of the crane by raising or lowering the jib;

mobile or **crawler crane.** Self-propelled on wheels or caterpillar tracks;

portal crane. A type of gantry crane with vertical legs giving sufficient height and width for vehicles or railway trucks to pass between them;

wharf crane. Located on a wharf or pier specifically for serving vessels alongside it.

Cranes are normally described by their lifting capacity, e.g. a 15-tonne crane.

crane lighter. A lighter especially fitted with a crane. May be self-propelled or towed.

crater. A bowl-shaped cavity; in particular, at the summit or on the side of a volcano.

creek. A comparatively narrow inlet, of fresh or salt water, which is tidal throughout its course.

crest. Of a hill, the head, summit or top: of a mountain range, the line joining the highest points. Similarly, of an elevation of the sea floor, or of a swell or wave.

crib. A permanent marine structure usually designed to support or elevate pipelines; especially a structure enclosing a screening device at the offshore end of a potable water intake pipe. The structure is commonly a heavy timber enclosure that has been sunken with rocks or other debris.

cross-sea. A wave formation imposed across the prevailing waves. See also **confused sea.**

cross-swell. Similar to **cross-sea** but the waves are longer swell waves.

culvert. A tunnelled drain or means of conveying water beneath a canal, railway embankment or road, sometimes the size of a small bridge, i.e. up to about 3 m across. Also, a channel for electric cables.

current. The non-tidal horizontal movement of the sea which may be in the upper, lower or in all layers. In some areas this movement may be nearly constant in rate and direction while in others it may vary seasonally or fluctuate with changes in meteorological conditions. The term is often used improperly to denote tidal streams. See 5.1.

current diagrams use arrows to indicate predominant direction, average rate and constancy, which are defined as follows:

predominant direction. The mean direction within a continuous 90° sector containing the highest proportion of observations from all sectors.

average rate. The rate to the nearest ¼ kn of the highest 50% in predominant sectors as indicated by the figures on the diagrams. It is emphasised that rates above or below those shown may be experienced.

constancy. The colour and thickness of the arrows is a measure of its persistence; e.g. low constancy implies marked variability in rate and particularly direction.

cut. The intersection on the chart of two or more position lines.
Also, an opening in an elevation or channel. Similar to a canal but shorter. May constitute a straightening of a bend in a winding channel.

cut tide. A tide which fails to reach its predicted height at high water.

D

dam. A bank of earth or masonry, built to obstruct the flow of water, or to contain it.

dan buoy. An anchored float, ballasted to float upright, carrying a stave through its centre with a flag, a light or other distinguishing mark.

danger. The term is used to imply a danger to surface navigation.

danger angle: horizontal or vertical. The angle subtended at the observer's eye, by the horizontal distance between two objects or by the height or elevation of an object, which indicates the limit of safe approach to an off-lying danger.

danger line. A dotted line on the chart enclosing, or bordering, an obstruction, wreck, or other danger.

dangerous wreck. A **wreck** submerged at such a depth as to be considered dangerous to surface navigation. See **derelict**.

Date Line. The International Date Line, accepted by international usage, is a modification of the 180° meridian to include islands of any group, on the same side of the line. Its position is shown on *Chart 5006 The World — Time Zone Chart* and described in *Admiralty List of Radio Signals Volume 2*. See also **time zones.** When the Date Line is crossed on an E course the date is put back one day, on a W course the date is advanced one day.

datum. See **horizontal datum, vertical datum.**

daybeacon. A term used in the USA and Canada for a beacon: in the USA it is restricted to unlighted beacons.

daymark. The identifying characteristics of an aid to navigation which serve to facilitate its recognition in daylight. On those structures that do not by themselves present an adequate viewing area to be seen at the required distance, the aid is made more visible by affixing a daymark to the structure. A daymark so affixed has a distinctive colour and shape depending on the purpose of the aid. An unlighted navigational mark.

deep. An isolated, or group of, localised deep area(s) within the confines of a larger feature, such as a **trough, basin** or **trench.** See also **hole.**

deep-water route. See **routeing system.**

defile. A narrow mountain pass or gorge.

degaussing range. An area about 2 cables in extent set aside for measuring ship's magnetic fields. Sensing instruments are installed on the sea floor in the range with cables leading to a control position ashore. The range is usually marked by buoys.

degenerate amphidrome. A terrestrial point on a tidal chart from which co-tidal lines appear to radiate.

delta. A tract of alluvial land, generally triangular, enclosed and traversed by the diverging mouths of a river.

departure; point of. The last position fixed relative to the land at the beginning of an ocean voyage of passage.

deposition. See **accretion.**

depth. The vertical distance from the sea surface to the sea floor, at any state of the tide. Hydrographically, the depth of water below chart datum. See also **sounding.**

derelict. Any property abandoned at sea, often of sufficient size as to constitute a menace to navigation; especially an abandoned vessel. See **wreck.**

derrick. A contrivance for hoisting heavy weights. Usually consisting of a wooden or metal spar with one end raised by a topping lift from a post or mast and the other end pivoted near the base.

diatom. Microscopic **phytoplankton**, especially common in the polar seas; develops delicate cases of silica.

diatom ooze. A siliceous deep-sea ooze formed of the shells of **diatoms.**

diffuser. An arrangement of multiple outlets for distributing liquid at the seaward end of a pipeline or outfall.

digital chart. Generic term for any electronic chart which does not conform to the definition of an **ENC.** See 2.88.

dike. See **dyke.**

dilution of precision. A dimensionless number that takes into account the contribution of relative satellite geometry to errors in position determination.

discoloured water. See 5.37.

distributary. One of several outlet streams draining a river, especially on a delta.

diurnal inequality. The inequality, either in the heights of successive high waters or in the intervals between successive high or low waters.

diurnal stream. A tidal stream which reverses its direction once during the day.

diurnal tide. A tide which has only one high water and one low water each day; that part of a tide which has one complete oscillation in a day.

dock. The area of water artificially enclosed in which the depth of water can be regulated. See also **basin.**

    to dock. To be admitted to a dock.

    to dock a ship. To receive a ship into dock, or dry dock.

docks. The area comprising the basins, quays, wharves and offices of a port; the dock area.

dock sill. The horizontal masonry or timber work at the bottom of the entrance to a dock or lock against which the caisson or gates close. The depth of water controlling the use of the dock is measured at the sill.

dockyard. That part of a port which contains the facilities for building or repairing ships.

dollie. A very small bollard for the use of barges and harbour craft. See also **bollard.**

dolphin. A built-up post, usually of wood, erected on shore or in the water.

berthing dolphins. Dolphins against which a ship may lie. Also known as breasting dolphins.

mooring dolphins. Dolphins which support bollards for a ships's mooring lines. The ship does not come in contact with them as they are set clear of the berth.

deviation dolphin. Dolphin which a ship may swing around for compass adjustment.

double tide. A tide which, due to a combination of shallow water effects, contains either two high waters or two low waters in each tidal cycle.
At Hook of Holland, this phenomenon occurs with the low waters and is known as the **Agger.**

downstream. In particular, the direction in which the stream is flowing; in general, in rivers and river ports, whether tidal or not, the direction to seaward.

drag. A ship is said to drag (her anchor) if the anchor will not hold her in position.
Also commonly used by mariners to describe the retardation of a ship caused by shallow water.

drag sweep. To tow a wire or bar set horizontally beneath the surface of the water to determine the least depth over an obstruction or to ascertain that a required minimum depth exists in a channel. Used as a noun, to denote the apparatus for this.

draught. The depth of the keel below the waterline at any point along the hull.

dredge. To deepen or attempt to deepen by removing material from the sea floor.
Also an apparatus for bringing up sea floor samples, gathering deep water organisms.

dredged area. Area where the depths have been increased by the removal of material from the sea floor.

dredger or **dredge.** A special vessel fitted with machinery for dredging, employed in deepening channels, harbours and removing obstructions to navigation such as shoals and banks. The various types include: Bucket dredgers, Grab dredgers and Suction dredgers.

dredging anchor. A vessel is said to be dredging anchor when moving, under control, with her anchor moving along the sea floor.

dries. A feature which is covered and uncovered by the tide is said to dry. The drying height is the height above chart datum, which is indicated on charts by a bar under the figure, or the legend "Dries" which may be abbreviated to "Dr". See also **awash.**

drift. The distance covered by a vessel in a given time due solely to the movement of current, tidal stream, or wind, A combination of any of these. Also, a detached and floating mass of soil and growth torn from the shore or river bank by floods, often mistaken for an islet. Common in the East Indies. Also, as a verb, to move by action of the current, tidal stream or wind without control.

drift angle. The angle between the ground track and water track.

drift current. A horizontal movement in the upper layers of the sea, caused by wind. See 5.7.

drilling rig. A movable float platform used to examine and develop a possible oil or gasfield. See 13.128.

drillship. A ship specially designed for offshore drilling of the seabed. See 13.128.

dry dock. An excavation in the ground, faced with masonry or concrete, into which a ship is admitted for underwater cleaning and repairs. The entrance can be closed by a **caisson** or gate. The water is pumped out after a vessel has entered, leaving her dry, resting on blocks and generally also supported by shores. See also **graving dock** and **floating dock.**

dry harbour. A small harbour which dries out, or nearly so, at LW. Vessels using it must be prepared to take the ground on the falling tide.

drying heights. Heights above chart datum of features which are periodically covered and exposed by the rise and fall of the tide. See also **awash.**

dumb lighter. A lighter incapable of self-propulsion.

dumping ground. An area similar to a **spoil ground**.

dune. A ridge or hill of dry wind-blown sand which may, or may not, be in a state of migration. Vegetation, frequently planted on purpose, often stabilises previously migrating dunes. Coastal dunes may occur in the vicinity of sandy shores, but cannot survive wave action. Consequently they are features of the coastland rather than of the foreshore.

duration (of rise or fall of the tide). The time interval between successive high and low waters.

dyke or **dike.** A causeway or loose rubble embankment built in shallow water in a similar way to a **training wall**, but not necessarily for the same purpose. Sometimes built across shallow banks at the side of an estuary to stabilise the sandbanks by protection against wave action, and to prevent silting in the channel. In the Netherlands: an embankment to prevent flooding and encroachment by the sea. In Orkney and Shetland Islands: a wall. Also used to mean an artificial ditch.

E

ebb channel. See **flood channel.**

ebb tide. A loose term applied both to the falling tide and to the out-going tidal stream.

ECDIS. Electronic Chart Display and Information System. See 2.81.

ECS. Electronic Chart System. Any digital chart navigation system which does not conform to the definition of an **ECDIS**. See 2.78.

ED50. European Datum 1950. A horizontal datum used on some charts of European waters. See 2.9.

eddy. A circular movement of water, usually formed where currents pass obstructions, between adjacent currents, or along the edge of a permanent current. See **whirlpool.**

elbow. A change of direction in the contour of a submerged bank or shoal; a sharp change in the direction of a channel, breakwater, pier.

elevation. The vertical distance of a point or a level on or affixed to the surface of the earth, measured from MSL. On Admiralty charts, the elevation is its height above the level of MHWS or MHHW, whichever is quoted in Admiralty Tide Tables.

ELSBM. Exposed Location Single Buoy Mooring. See 13.137.

embankment. A sloping structure of stone, rubble or earth, raising the height of a river bank, or used as the foundation for, or strengthening of, a **causeway** or **dyke**.

embayed. To be in such a position, or under such adverse conditions, in a bay that extrication is difficult if not impossible.

ENC. Electronic Navigational Chart. See 2.87.

entrance lock. A lock situated between the tideway and an enclosed basin when their levels vary. It has two sets of gates by means of which vessels can pass either way at all states of the tide. Sometimes known as a tidal lock.

equilibrium tide. The hypothetical tide which would be produced by the lunar and solar tidal forces in the absence of ocean constraints and dynamics.

equinoctial spring tide. A spring tide, greater than average, occurring near the equinox, in March and September.

equinox. Either of the two points at which the Sun crosses the equator: or the dates on which these occurrences take place.

erosion. The wearing away of the coast, or banks of a river, by water action; the opposite of **accretion**.

escarpment. An elongated, characteristically linear, steep slope separating horizontal or gently sloping sectors of the sea floor in non-**shelf** areas. Also abbreviated to **scarp**.

established direction of traffic flow. See **routeing system**.

estuary. An arm of the sea at the mouth of a tidal river, usually encumbered with shoals, where the tidal effect is influenced by the river current.

estuary port. A port built at the tidal mouth or estuary of a river.

ETRS89. European Terrestrial Reference System 1989. A horizontal datum used for charting which is fully compatible with **WGS84**. See 2.10.

even keel. The state of a ship when her draught forward and aft are the same. Loosely applied when a ship is floating at her designed draught marks.

eyot. A small island in a river.

F

fairway. The main navigable channel, often buoyed, in a river, or running through or into a harbour.

falling tide. The period between high water and the succeeding low water.

fan. A relatively smooth, fan-like, depositional feature normally sloping away from the lower termination of a canyon or canyon system. Also termed a **cone.**

fastener. See **snag.**

fathom. A unit of measurement used for soundings. Equal to 6 feet or 1·8288 m.

fathom lines. Submarine contour lines drawn on charts, indicating equal depths in fathoms.

ferry. A boat, pontoon, or any craft, used to convey passengers or vehicles to and fro across a harbour or river. See also **train ferry.**

To ferry. To convey in a boat, to and fro over a river or across a harbour.

fetch. The area of the sea surface over which seas are generated by a wind having a constant direction and speed.
Also, the length of the generating area, measured in the direction of the wind, in which sea is generated.

firth. An arm of the sea; a river estuary. Used principally in Scotland.

fish aggregating device. A term used to describe a moored or floating object ranging in construction from a collection of buoys or rough bamboo rafts through to large rafts on which lights and radar reflectors are fitted. All these devices have plastic streamers or palm fronds hanging below them, the purpose of the device being to attract algae and marine growths on which small fish feed and in turn attract shoals of larger fish.

fish farm. See **marine farm.**

fish haven. An area where concrete blocks, hulks, disused car bodies and similar items of scrap material are placed on the sea bed in order to provide suitable conditions for fish to breed in. In Japanese waters, the term "floating fish haven" may be used instead of **marine farm.** Draught permitting, vessels may navigate over sea floor fish havens, but they are a danger to anchoring or sea floor operations.

fish pound. A barrier across the mouth of a creek placed to retain fish in a creek.

fish stakes. A row of stakes set out from the shore, frequently to a considerable distance; often terminating in a partly decked enclosure from which a net can be lowered.

fish trap. An enclosure of stakes set in shallow water or a stream as a trap for fish.

fish weir. An enclosure of stakes set in a stream or on the shoreline as a trap for fish.

fishing ground. Area wherein craft congregate to fish; most particularly those areas occupied periodically by the large fishing fleets.

fishing harbour or port. One especially equipped for the convenience of the fishing industry, the handling of fish and the maintenance of its vessels.

fitting-out basin. A basin in a shipyard sited and equipped, to accommodate ships to complete the installation of machinery, after launching.

fix. The position of the ship determined by observations and/or navigational aids.

flat. An extensive area, level or nearly so, consisting usually of mud, but sometimes of sand or rock, which is covered at high water and is attached to the shore. Sometimes called Tidal flats. See also **ledge.**

floating beacon. A moored or anchored floating mark ballasted to float upright, usually displaying a flag on a tall pole, and sometimes carrying a light or radar reflector; used particularly in hydrographic surveying.

floating bridge. A power-worked pontoon used as a ferry which propels itself across a harbour, river or canal, by means of guide chains.

floating crane. See **crane.**

floating dock. A watertight structure capable of being submerged sufficiently, by admission of water into the pontoon tanks, to admit a vessel. The tanks are then pumped out, the dock and vessel rising until the latter is clear of the water, thus serving the same purpose as a dry dock.

flood channel. A channel in tidal waters through which the flood (in-going) tidal stream flows more strongly, or for a longer duration of time, than the ebb. It is characterised by a sill or bar of sand or other consolidated matter at the inner end, ie the least depth in the channel occurs close to the inner end. Ebb channels occur in close association with, and usually alongside, flood channels: they have a sill at their outer end.

flood-mark. A mark, consisting usually of a horizontal line and a date, sometimes found on riverside buildings or dock walls, to mark the highest level reached by flood waters at the date indicated.

flood tide. A loose term applied both to the rising tide and to the in-going tidal stream. See also **ebb tide.**

flow. The combination of tidal stream and current; the whole water movement.
Also a loose term for flood (e.g. ebb and flow).

following sea. One running in the same direction as the ship is steering.

foraminifera. Single-celled animals consisting of a mass of jelly-like flesh with no definite organs or parts of the body; covered with a casing of carbonate of lime: common in the surface waters of the sea.

forced tide. A tide which exceeds its predicted height at high water.

foreland. A promontory or headland.

foreshore. A part of the shore lying between high and low water lines of Mean Spring tides.

form lines. Lines drawn on a chart to indicate the slope and general shape of the hill features; generalised contour lines which do not represent any specific or standardised heights. See also **hachure.**

foul area, foul sea floor or foul patch. An area where the sea floor is strewn with wreckage or other obstructions, no longer dangerous to surface navigation, but making it unsuitable for anchoring.

forty-foot equivalent unit. See **container**.

foul ground. An area where the holding qualities for an anchor are poor, or where danger of striking or fouling the ground or other obstructions exist.

foul bottom. The bottom of a ship when encrusted with marine growth.

fracture zone. An extensive linear zone of irregular topography, mountainous or faulted, characterized by steep–sided or assymetrical **ridges,** clefts, **troughs** or **escarpments.**

free port. A port where certain import and export duties are waived, unless the goods pass into the country, to facilitate re-shipment to other countries. See also **transit port.**

freshet. An abnormal amount of fresh water running into a river, estuary or the sea, caused by heavy or prolonged rain or melted snow.

fringing reef. A reef, generally coral, closely attached to the shore with no lagoon or passage between it and the land.

furrow. Oceanographically, a fissure which penetrates, roughly perpendicularly to the run of the contours, into the continental or island shelf or slope. See also **canyon.**

G

GALILEO. A satellite navigation system owned and operated by the European Union. See 11.45.

gangway. Similar to a **brow**. Sometimes called a gangplank. Also, the opening in the ship's side by which a ship is entered or left. Also, a passage-way inside a ship.

gap. See **passage.**

gat. A **swashway**, **gut** or natural channel through shoals.

gazetteer. A directory of information about places and place names, including positional information. Can be represented visually on a cartographic backdrop.

geodesic. The shortest distance between two points on the spheroid. It is equivalent to a great circle on the sphere.

geodetic datum. See **horizontal datum.**

geographical mile. See **mile.**

geoid. An imaginary surface which is everywhere perpendicular to the plumb line, and which on average coincides with MSL in the open ocean. Its shape approximates to that of a spheroid, but it is irregular due to the uneven distribution of the Earth's mass.

gird. To gird a ship is to prevent her from swinging to wind and tide. Of a tug, to be towed broadside on through the water by her tow-rope.

globigerina ooze. Ooze which has the limy skeletons of **foraminifera** as its principal constituent, the dominant element being the calcareous tests of the globigerina, a spherical shelled organism.

GLONASS. GLObal NAvigation Satellite System. The satellite navigation system owned and operated by the Russian Federation. See 11.44.

GMDSS. Global Maritime Distress and Safety System. See 13.100.

GNSS. Global Navigation Satellite System. The generic term for a satellite navigation system with global coverage. Includes such systems as **GPS**, **GLONASS** and **GALILEO**.

godown. A term used in eastern ports for a warehouse or store. Originates from the Indian Telugu word "gidagi" meaning "a place where goods lie".

gong-buoy. A buoy fitted with a gong which may be actuated automatically or by wave motion.

GPS. Global Positioning System. The satellite navigation system, the full name of which is NAVSTAR GPS, owned and operated by the United States Department of Defense. See 11.36.

gradient currents. Currents caused by pressure gradients in the water. See 5.9.

gravel. Coarse sand and small water-worn or rounded stones; varying in size from about the diameter of the top of a man's thumb to the size of a pinhead. See also **sand, pebbles.**

graving dock. Another name for a **dry dock**. To grave is an old term meaning to burn off the accretions on a ship's bottom before tarring.

Greenwich Meridian. See **prime meridian.**

grid. A systematic rectangular network of lines superimposed on a chart or map and lettered and numbered in such a way that the position of any feature can be defined with any required degree of precision.

grid reference. The position of a feature given in grid letters and numbers.

gridiron. A flat framework, usually baulks of timber placed parallel with each other, erected on the foreshore below the high water line, and in such a position that a vessel can be moved over it at high water and left dry and resting on it at low water.

ground. A portion of the Earth's crust which may be submerged or above water, e.g. spoil ground, middle ground, swampy ground, landing ground.

to ground. To run ashore or touch the sea floor.

ground speed. The speed of a vessel over the ground.

ground swell. A long ocean swell; also this swell as it reaches depths of less than half its length and becomes shorter and steeper; i.e. influenced by the ground.

ground track. See **track.**

groyne. A low wall-like structure, generally of wood or stone, usually extending at right angles from the shore, to prevent erosion. Frequently erected in estuaries and rivers to direct the flow of the water and prevent silting or encourage accretion.

gulf. A portion of the sea partly enclosed by land; usually of larger extent and greater relative penetration than a **bay**.

gut. A natural narrow inlet of deep water in a bank or shoal, sometimes forming a channel through it. It may also refer to the main part of a channel.

guyot(s). An isolated (or group of) **seamounts** having a comparitively smooth, flat top. Also called **tablemounts.**

H

hachures. Shading lines sometimes used on charts and maps to indicate the general slope and shape of hill forms. See also **form lines.**

half tide. See **tide**.

half-tide basin. A basin the gates of which are open for entry and departure some hours before and after high water.

half tide level. See **tide**.

half-tide rock. Formerly used to describe rocks which are awash at about mean tide level.

harbour. A stretch of water where vessels can anchor, or secure to buoys or alongside wharves, and obtain protection from sea and swell. The protection may be afforded by natural features or by artificial works. See also **artificial harbour, island harbour.**

harbour board. See **Port Authority.**

harbour reach. Reach of a winding river or of an estuary which leads directly to the harbour. See **reach**.

hard. A strip of gravel, stone or concrete, built on a beach across the foreshore to facilitate landing or the hauling up of boats.

harmonic analysis. An analysis of tidal observations, carried out to determine the harmonic constituents of the tide, as a basis for tidal predictions.

harmonic constants. See **constants (harmonic).**

harmonic constituent. See **constituent (of the tide).**

harmonic prediction. Prediction of the tide by combining harmonic constituents.

HAT. Highest Astronomical Tide. See **tide.**

haven. A harbour for vessels from the violence of wind and sea. In the strict sense it should be accessible at all states of the tide and conditions of weather.

head. A comparatively high promontory with a steep face. An unnamed head is usually described as a headland. Also, the inner part of a bay or creek, e.g. the head of the bay. Also, the seaward end of a jetty or pier.

head sea. A sea coming from the direction in which a ship is heading; the opposite to a **following sea**.

heading. Synonymous with ship's head.

headland. See **head.**

headway. Motion through the water in a forward direction.

heavy sea. A rough, high sea.

height. The vertical distance between the top of an object and its base.
Also, the height of a vessel is the height of the highest point of a vessel's structure (e.g. radar aerial, funnel, cranes, masthead) above her waterline.

height of the tide. See **tide.**

heights. A comparatively level plateau at the summit of a precipitous mountain.

high focal plane buoy. A light buoy on which the signal light is fitted particularly high above the waterline. Used as fairway or landfall buoys. See also **LANBY.**

higher high water. See **tide.**

high water datum or **datum for heights.** The high water plane to which elevations of land features are referred. On Admiralty charts this datum is normally the level of MHWS when the tide is predominantly semi-diurnal, MHHW when the tide is predominantly diurnal, and MSL where there is no appreciable tidal range.

high water springs. See **tide.**

high water stand. See **tide.**

hill(s). An isolated (or group of) elevation(s), smaller than a **seamount.** See also **abyssal hill(s) and knoll(s).**

holding ground. The sea floor of an anchorage is described as good or bad holding ground according to its capacity for gripping the anchor and chain cable. In general, clay, mud and sand are good; shingle, shell and rock are bad.

hole. A small local depression, often steep-sided, in the sea floor.

hollow sea. A very deep and steep sea.

hopper. A barge used in harbours, for conveying sullage or spoil to a spoil ground (where it is discharged through the bottom of the barge).

horizontal clearance. The horizontal distance between two perpendiculars e.g. bridge pillars, canal banks.

horizontal datum. A reference for specifying positions on the Earth's surface. Each datum is associated with a particular reference spheroid. Positions referred to different datums can differ by several hundred metres. See 2.5.

hurricane haven. A port where vessels may seek shelter from a tropical cyclone.

HW. High Water. See **tide.**

hydrography. The science and art of measuring the oceans, seas, rivers and other waters, with their marginal land areas, inclusive of all fundamental elements which have to be known for the safe navigation of such areas, and the publication of such information in a form suitable for the use of mariners.

I

impounding basin. A basin in which water can be held by means of a sluice, weir or gate. Used for keeping craft afloat when the tide drops below a certain level, or to provide water for sluicing a channel which is very shallow and tends to collect silt.

index chart. An outline chart on which the limits and numbers of navigational charts, volumes of Admiralty Sailing Directions, are shown.

Indian Spring Low Water. See **tides.**

indraught. A draught of air or flow of water setting inward.

infopoint. In **voyage** planning, a position on or associated with a **passage leg** where some non-navigational activity is required, or to denote a contingency safe area.

inland waterways. The navigable systems of waters comprising canals, rivers, lakes, within the land territory.

inlet. A small indentation in the coastline usually tapering towards its head. See also **creek.**

inner harbour. A harbour within a harbour, provided with quays, at which vessels can berth.

inshore. Close to the shore. Used sometimes to indicate shoreward of a position in contrast to seaward of it.

inshore traffic zone. A routeing measure comprising a designated area between the landward boundary of a **traffic separation scheme** and the adjacent coast, to be used in accordance with the provisions of Rule 10(d), as amended, of the International Regulations for Preventing Collisions at Sea, 1972 (Collision Regulations).

inshore traffic zone. See **routeing system**.

ironbound coast. A rock-bound coast without anchorage or harbour.

island harbour. A harbour formed, or mainly protected, by islands.

island shelf. The zone around an island and extending from the low water line to a depth at which there is usually a marked increase in slope towards oceanic depths.

island slope (shoulder or talus). The declivity from the outer edge of the island shelf into deeper water.

island terminal or structure. Deep-water structure not connected to the shore by a causeway or jetty. Submarine pipelines or overhead cableways are used to transport cargoes between the island and the shore.

isobathic. Of equal depth.

isogonic. Of equal magnetic variation (declination).

J

jetty. A structure generally of wood, masonry, concrete or iron, which projects usually at right-angles from the coast or some other structure. Vessels normally lie alongside parallel with the main axis of the structure.
Also, term used in the USA and Canada for a **training wall**. See also **pier**.

K

key. See **cay**.

knoll. An elevation somewhat smaller than a **seamount** and of rounded profile, characteristically isolated or as a cluster on the sea floor. See also **hill(s).**

knot. The nautical unit of speed, i.e. 1 nautical mile (of 1852 m) per hour.

L

lagoon. An enclosed area of salt or brackish water separated from the open sea by more or less, but not completely, effective obstacles, such as low sandbanks. The name is most commonly used for the area of water enclosed by a barrier reef or atoll.

LANBY. Large Automatic Navigational BuoY. A very large light buoy, used as an alternative to a light vessel, to mark offshore positions important to the mariner. Lanbys vary in size up to a displacement of 140 tonnes and a diameter or height of 12 m. Racons or radar reflectors may be fitted to them. Full details of lanbys are given in *Admiralty List of Lights.*

land levelling system. A network of benchmarks, connected by levelling to a common datum.

land survey datum. The point of origin of a land levelling system giving the plane to which elevations of features shown on maps are referred. The most usual plane for land survey datums is an approximation to **MSL**.

landfall. The first sight, or radar indication, of land at the end of a passage.

landfall buoy. A buoy with a tall superstructure, marking the seaward end of the approach to a harbour or estuary. It may be situated out of sight of land.

landing. A place where boats may ground in safety; a contraction of "landing place used by boats". May be artificial, consisting of a platform or steps, or the equivalent in natural rock.

landing stage. A platform or pontoon connected with the shore, for landing or embarking passengers or goods. Ships can berth alongside the larger landing stages.

landlocked. Sheltered by land from all or very nearly all directions.

landmark. A prominent artificial or natural feature on land such as a tower or church, used as an aid to navigation.

landslip. Sliding down of a mass of land on a cliff, mountain or cutting.

lanes, shipping. Much frequented shipping tracks crossing an ocean or sea.

LASH. Lighter Aboard SHip. A cargo-carrying system using specially built ships and lighters. Cargoes are loaded into LASH lighters which are towed to a LASH ship where the loaded lighters are embarked. At their destination the LASH lighters are disembarked and towed away to their unloading berths. Special berths or anchorages are sometimes designated for LASH ships.

LAT. Lowest Astronomical Tide. See **tide**.

launching. The sliding of a newly-built ship by the action of its own weight into the water down on a specially prepared slipway - stern first or beam on (side launch).

launching cradle. The frame in which a ship is supported for launching.

lava. An igneous rock. It is formed by the cooling of magma, i.e. matter flowing from a volcano or fissure in the ground, on the Earth's surface.

layering. A method of emphasising on a chart differences of height or depth by the use of varying tints.

lead. A narrow channel; especially through pack ice, or in rock or coral-studded waters (pronounced "leed").
Also, the weight used in sounding with a leadline (Pronounced "led").

leading lights. Lights at different elevations so situated as to define a leading line when brought into transit.

leading line. A suitable line for a vessel to follow through a given area of water as defined by leading marks located on a farther part of the line.

leading mark. One of a set of two or more navigation marks that define a leading line.

ledge. A flat-topped ridge or narrow flat of rocks, extending from an island or coast. See also **continental shelf** and **island shelf.**

lee shore. The shore towards which the wind is blowing.

lee side. The side of the ship or object which is away from the wind and therefore sheltered.

lee tide. A tidal stream running in the same direction as the wind is blowing.

leg. The basic component of a **passage.** Each leg is terminated by two points which may be **waypoints, berthpoints or pilotpoints.**

levee. Large river embankment built to prevent flooding. Oceanographically, A depositional natural embankment bordering a **canyon, valley** or **seachannel** on the ocean floor.

light beacon. A beacon from which a light is exhibited. See also **buoyant beacon.**

light buoy. A buoy carrying a structure from which is exhibited a light, which may have any of the characteristics of a light exhibited from a lighthouse other than sectors. See also **lanby, light float.**

light float. An unmanned fully-automated vessel, comparable in size to a light vessel, or a boat-shaped unmanned float carrying a light and sometimes sounding a fog signal. The former is a major navigational light; the latter may sometimes be used instead of a light buoy where there are strong tidal streams or currents.

lightening area. See **transhipment area.**

lighter. A general name for a broad flat-bottomed craft used for transporting cargo and other goods between vessels and the shore. Lighters may be self-propelled but are usually towed. There are also lighters rigged for special purposes, See also **dumb lighter, mooring lighter, crane lighter.**

lighthouse. A distinctive structure from which a light or lights are exhibited as an aid to navigation.

lighthouse buoy. A name formerly used for a lanby.

lights. A comprehensive term including all illuminated aids to navigation, other than those exhibited from floating structures.

lights in line. Two or more lights so situated that when in transit they define the limit of an area, the alignment of a cable, or an alignment for use of anchoring. Unlike leading lights they do not mark a direction to be followed.

light vessel. A manned vessel, secured in a designated locality carrying a light of high luminous intensity and usually sounding a fog signal to assist navigation. Also known as **lightship.**

linkspan. A pontoon carrying a ramp placed between a **RoRo** vessel and a wharf to enable vehicles to embark or disembark from the wharf.

LNG. Liquid Natural Gas. Gas, predominantly methane, from oilfield sources. Held in liquid state at atmospheric pressure at a temperature of about $-162°C$ for transport and storage.

local knowledge. The use of a pilot, local seafarer competent to act as a pilot or past experience.

local magnetic anomaly. A **magnetic anomaly** covering a small area. See 11.3.

lock. An enclosure at the entrance to a tidal basin, or canal, with caissons or gates at each end by means of which ships are passed from one water level to another without materially altering the higher level.
  to lock a vessel. To pass a vessel through a lock.

loom. The vague appearance of land or vessels, when first sighted in darkness, or through fog, smoke or haze. Also, the diffused glow of a light seen when the light itself is below the horizon or obscured by an obstacle.

low water neaps. See **tides.**

lower low water. See **tides.**

loxodrome. See **rhumb line.**

LPG. Liquid petroleum gas. Light hydrocarbon material, gaseous at normal temperatures and pressures. By-product of petroleum refining and oil production. Held at liquid state under pressure for transport and storage. Liquid petroleum gases include propane and butane.

LRIT. Long Range Identification and Tracking. A development of the AIS system which allows the monitoring of vessels at distances of up to 1000 miles offshore. See 11.77.

lunitidal interval. The time interval between the transit of the Moon and the next following high or low water; hence high water lunitidal interval, low water lunitidal interval, mean high water interval and mean low water interval.

LW. Low Water. See **tide.**

M

madrepore. A common form of perforate coral; probably the most wide-spread of reef-building corals.

magnetic anomaly. An effect, permanently superimposed on the Earth's normal magnetic field and characterised by abnormal values of the elements of compass variation, dip, and geomagnetic force. See **abnormal magnetic variation,** and 11.3.

magnetic variation. The angle which the magnetic meridian makes with the true meridian. Called "magnetic declination" by physicists.

main ship channel. The channel having the greatest depth and easiest navigation.

mainland. A term applied to a major portion of land in relation to off-lying islands.

make the land. Make a **landfall** . To sight and approach the land after being out of sight of land at sea.

mandatory routeing system. See **routeing system.**

manganese. A black mineral used in glass-making, found as a sea floor sediment.

mangrove swamp. A flat low-lying area of mud and silt, lying between the high and low water lines of spring tides, covered by the stilt-like roots of the mangrove and associated vegetation. A feature of tropical waters.

marina. An area provided with berthing and shore facilities for yachts.

marine farm. A structure, on the surface or submerged, in which fish are reared or seaweed cultivated. They may obstruct navigation and are sometimes marked by buoys (special) which may be lighted. They are not necessarily confined to inshore locations and may be moved. See also **fish haven, fish aggregating device.**

marine protected areas. Areas of inter-tidal or sub-tidal terrain together with their overlying waters and associated flora, fauna, historical and cultural features, which have been reserved to protect part or all of the enclosed environment. There is a wide variety of marine protected areas indicated in the terms used such as 'marine sanctuary', 'marine reserve', 'marine park', 'protected seascape' or 'wildlife sanctuary'.

marine railway. A term sometimes applied to a **patent slip**, more particularly in Canada and the USA.

maritime radio station. See radio station.

mark. A fixed feature on land or moored at sea, which can be identified on the chart and used to fix a ship's position.

marl. A crumbling earthy deposit, particularly one of clay mixed with sand or decomposed shells. A layer of marl is sometimes quite compact.

mean tide level. See **tide.**

measured distance. The shortest distance between two or more sets of parallel transits set up on shore to determine the speed of a vessel. The length and direction of the distance are charted.

median valley. The axial depression of the mid-oceanic ridge system. Also called a Rift or Rift Valley.

MEHRA. Marine Environmental High Risk Area. An area in UK waters established to inform ships' masters that they need to exercise even more caution than usual. See 10.29.

meridian. A semi–Great Circle on the surface of the earth whose ends lie at oposite poles. See also **prime meridian** and **Greenwich Meridian.**

MHHW. Mean Higher High Water See **tide.**

MHLW. Mean Higher Low Water See **tide.**

MHW. Mean High Water. See **tide.**

MHWN. Mean High Water Neaps. See **tide.**

MHWS. Mean High Water Springs. See **tide.**

mid-channel controlling depth. See **controlling depth.**

mid–oceanic ridge. See **ridge** and **rise.**

mile.
　The **international nautical mile** is 1852 m. The unit used by the United Kingdom until 1970 was the British Standard nautical mile of 6080 feet or 1853·18 m.
　The **sea mile** is the length of 1 minute of arc, measured along the meridian, in the latitude of the position; its length varies both with the latitude and with the dimensions of the spheroid in use.
　The **statute mile** is the unit of distance of 1760 yards or 5280 feet (1609·3 m).

MLHW. Mean Lower High Water. See **tide.**

MLLW. Mean Lower Low Water. See **tide.**

MLW. Mean Low Water. See **tide.**

MLWN. Mean Low Water Neaps. See **tide.**

MLWS. Mean Low Water Springs. See **tide.**

moat. An annular depression that may not be continuous, located at the base of many **seamounts**, oceanic islands and other isolated elevations.

mole. A breakwater alongside the sheltered side of which vessels can lie.
Also, a concrete or stone structure, within an artificial harbour, at right-angles to the coast or the structure from which it extends, alongside which vessels can lie.

monobuoy. Term sometimes used for a **Single Buoy Mooring**.

moor. To secure a vessel, craft, or boat, or other floating objects by ropes, chains, to the shore or to anchors.
Also, to ride with both anchors down laid at some distance apart, and the ship lying midway between them.

mooring buoy. A buoy of special construction which carries the ring of the moorings to which a vessel secures.

mooring lighter. A lighter especially fitted for handling, laying and weighing moorings.

mooring tower. A metal tower standing on the sea floor to which ships can moor. See 13.139.

moorings. Gear usually consisting of anchors or clumps, cables, and a buoy to which a ship can secure.

morse code light. A light in which flashes of different duration are grouped in such a manner as to reproduce a Morse code character.

MSL. Mean Sea Level. See **tide.**

mud. A sediment having predominance of grains with diameters less than 0·06 mm. The term is a general term referring to mixtures of sediments in water and applies to both clays and silts. The geological name is "lutite".

N

NAD83. North American Datum 1983. A horizontal datum used for charting which is fully compatible with **WGS84**. See 2.10.

narrows. A contracted part of a channel or river.

natural scale. The ratio between a measurement on a chart or map and the actual distance on the surface of the Earth which that measurement represents. It is expressed as a ratio with a numerator of one, e.g. 1/25 000 or 1:25 000.

nautical mile. See **mile**.

nautical twilight. The period between the end of **civil twilight** and the time when the Sun's centre is 12° below the horizon in the evening, and the period between the time when the Sun's centre is 12° below the horizon and the beginning of civil twilight in the morning. See also **astronomical twilight**.

navigable. Affording passage for ships or boats.
Also, capable of being navigated.

navigation. The art of determining a ship's position and of taking her in safety from one place to another.

navigation aid. An instrument, device, chart, method, internal to the vessel and intended to assist in the navigation of the vessel. Examples include compass, sextant, chronometer, chart. See also **aid to navigation.**

neap tide. See **tide**.

neck (of land). A narrow isthmus or promontory.

no anchoring area. See **routeing system**.

no sea floor sounding. A depth obtained at which the lead or sounder has not reached the sea floor.

nodal point. The point of minimum tidal range in an amphidromic system. An amphidromic point.

noise range. An area set aside for measuring the underwater noise generated by a ship. Acoustic sensing instruments are installed on the sea floor with cables leading to a control position ashore. The area is often marked by buoys.

nun buoy. A buoy in the shape of two cones, base to base, and moored from one point so that the other is more or less upright. Used in the USA for a buoy with a conical or truncated conical-shaped top.

O

observation spot. A position at which precise astronomical observations for latitude and longitude have been obtained.

obstruction. A danger to navigation, the exact nature of which is not specified or has not been determined.

ocean. The great body of water surrounding the land masses of the globe, or more specifically one of the main areas into which the body of water has been divided by geographers. Any of the major expanses of salt water on the surface of the globe.

ocean swell. A swell encountered in the open ocean in great depths.

oceanography. The study of the oceans especially of the physical features of the sea water and sea floor and of marine flora and fauna.

offing. The part of the sea distant but visible from the shore or from an anchorage.

offshore. To seaward of, but not close to, the shore, as in "offshore fishing". Also, from the shore, as in "offshore wind". Oceanographically, the region extending seaward from the low water line of Mean Spring tides to the continental or island slope.

offshore installation. Any structure such as a drilling rig, production platform, wellhead or **SPM**, set up offshore.

ogival buoy. A buoy with an arch-shaped vertical cross-section above the waterline.

ooze. Very soft mud, slime; especially on the bed of a river or estuary. Oceanographically, fine-grained soft deposits of the deep-sea, formed from the shells and skeletons of planktonic animals and plants. See **diatom, globigerina ooze, pteropod ooze, radiolarian ooze.**

open (adjective). Two marks are said to be open when they are not exactly in transit.

open (verb). To bring into view, e.g. "to open the land eastward of a cape".

open basin. See **basin**.

open coast. An unsheltered, harbourless coast open to the weather.

open harbour. An unsheltered harbour, exposed to the sea.

open roadstead. An anchorage unprotected from the weather.

open water. Waters where in all circumstances a ship has complete freedom of manoeuvre. See also **restricted waters.**

opening. A general term to indicate a gap or passage. eg an opening in a reef.

Ordnance Datum. The datum, or series of datums, established on the mainland and adjacent islands of the British Isles as the point of origin for the **land levelling system**.

Ordnance Datum (Newlyn). This **point of origin** corresponds to the average value of **MSL** at Newlyn during the years 1915 to 1921.

Ordnance Survey. The Government survey of the land area of Great Britain; the responsible authority for Ordnance Survey maps.

orthodrome. A great circle track.

orthomorphic or **conformal projection.** Charts and maps on this type of projection have the property that small areas on the Earth's surface retain their shape on the chart or map, the meridians and parallels being at right-angles to one another and the scale at any one point being the same in all directions. Mercator's and stereographic projections are examples used in hydrography.

outer harbour. A sheltered area, even in bad weather, outside the harbour proper, the inner harbour and the docks.

outfall. A narrow outlet of a river into the sea or a lake, as opposed to the opening out at a mouth. Also, the mouth of a sewer or other pipe discharging into the sea.

outfall buoy. Buoy marking the position where a sewer or other pipe discharges into the sea.

overfalls. Also known as tide-rips. Turbulence associated with the flow of strong tidal streams over abrupt changes in depth, or with the meeting of tidal streams flowing from different directions.

overhead clearance. The clearance between the highest point of a vessel and an obstruction. See **vertical clearance.**

overtide. Harmonic constituents of short period, associated with shallow water effect.

P

Panamax. Used to describe the largest ships capable of fitting through the Panama canal, typically a maximum beam equal to 32·2 m (106 ft).

parallel. Small circle on the Earth's surface parallel with the equator.

pass. A comparatively narrow channel often with high ground or cliff on either side, leading to a harbour or river. Also, a passage through or over a mountain range.

passage. A navigable channel, especially one through reefs or islands. Also, a sea journey between defined points; one or more passages may constitute a voyage. Oceanographically, a narrow break in a **ridge** or **rise**. Also called a **gap.**

patch. A portion of water or land which has distinctive characteristics, e.g. drying patch (of land, ground, sand), shoal patch (of water), and discoloured patch (of water or rock). In British hydrographic usage, may be used as an alternative to **shoal**, both being limited to a detached area which constitutes a danger.

patent slip. A cradle supported on carriages running on rails on the shore from about the level of High Water Springs to the level of Low Water Springs. The cradle can be run into the water to receive a small or medium-sized vessel and then hauled up until the vessel is clear of the water for bottom cleaning and repair.

pay off. A ship is said to pay off when her head falls away from the wind.

peak(s). An isolated (or group of) prominent elevation(s), either pointed or of a very limited extent across the summit.

pebbles. Water-rounded material of from 4 to 64 mm in size, ie from the diameter of the top of a man's thumb to the diameter of his clenched fist when viewed sideways.

pens. A series of parallel jetties for berthing small craft.

perch. A small beacon, often an untrimmed sapling, used to mark channels through mud flats or sandbanks; may or may not carry a topmark; often of a temporary nature.

perigee. The point in the orbit of the moon (or any satellite) which is nearest to the Earth. When the Moon is in perigee the tidal range is increased. See also **apogee.**

perigee tide. See **tides.**

perihelion. The point in the orbit of a planet which is nearest to the Sun. See also **aphelion.**

phase (of the Moon). The appearance at a given time of the illuminated surface of the Moon.

phosphorescence. The name formerly applied to bioluminescence. See 5.38.

phytoplankton. The microscopic floating plant life of the oceans; the basic food source for most marine life.

pier. A structure, usually of wood, masonry, concrete or iron, extending approximately at right-angles from the coast into the sea. The **pierhead**, alongside which vessels can lie with their fore-and-aft line at right-angles to the main structure, is frequently wider than the body of the pier. Some piers, however, were built solely as promenades. See also **jetty.** Also, the structure joining a wharf to the land. Also, supports for the spans of a bridge.

pierhead. The seaward end of a pier, frequently set at right-angles to the pier in the form of a T or L.

pile. A heavy baulk of timber or a column of reinforced concrete, steel or other material, driven vertically into the bed of the sea or of a river. It may be used to mark a channel or to serve as part support for construction work such as a pier, wharf or jetty.

pile beacon. A beacon formed of one or more piles.

pile fender. A pile driven loosely into the seabed in front of a wharf to absorb the shock of a vessel going alongside.

pile lighthouse. A lighthouse erected on a pile foundation.

pile moorings. Permanent moorings to which a vessel is secured fore and aft between piles.

pillar buoy. A buoy of which the part of the body above the waterline is a pillar, or of which the greater part of the superstructure is a pillar or a lattice tower.

pilot. The individual qualified to take charge of ships entering, leaving, and moving within certain navigable waters. See also **Admiralty Pilot.**

pilotage. The conducting of a vessel within restricted waters. Also, the fee for the services of a pilot.

pilotage waters. Those areas covered by a regular pilotage service.

pilotpoint. In **voyage** planning, a point on the vessel's **route** where a pilot is intended to be embarked/disembarked.

pinnacle (rock). A rock, which may or may not be dangerous to navigation, rising sheer from the sea floor, and of which no warning is given by sounding. Oceanographically, a discrete (or group of) high tower or spire–shaped pillar(s) of rock, or coral, isolated or cresting a summit.

pitch. Angular motion of a ship in the fore-and-aft plane. See also **roll, scend.**

pitching. The facing of the sloping sides of a breakwater, which may be paved, or consist of stones, tetrapods or rubble.

pivoted beacon or tower. See **buoyant beacon.**

plain. Oceanographically, a flat gently sloping or nearly level region of the sea floor.

plankton. Collective name for the microscopic floating and drifting plant and animal life found throughout the world's oceans. A distinction can be made between neretic (coastal) and oceanic (deep-water) plankton. See **phytoplankton, zooplankton.**

plateau. Extensive elevated region with level (or nearly level) surface. See also **tableland.**
Oceanographically, a flat or nearly flat area of considerable areal extent which is relatively shallow, dropping off abruptly on one or more sides.

PLEM. Pipe Line End Manifold. A steel frame secured to the sea floor with piles for the purpose of anchoring the end of a submarine pipeline. PLEMs are usually associated with pipelines which terminate at offshore tanker berths; they will often be fitted with valves, operated either by divers or remotely from the surface. Semi–flexible hoses rise upwards from the PLEM and connect directly to the tanker, or to the underside of a tanker mooring system, e.g. an **SBM.**

point. A sharp and usually comparatively low piece of land jutting out from the coast or forming a turning-point in the coastline.

point of origin. A fixed point in a co-ordinate system or grid to which all measurements are referred.

polyzoa. Minute creatures of the sea, which always live in colonies, some of which are small and branching and others large and with strong lime skeletons which give them the appearance of corals.

pontoon. A broad, flat-bottomed floating structure (often of heavy timber baulks) rectangular in shape, used for many purposes in a port, as a ferry landing place, a pierhead, or alongside a vessel to assist in loading or discharging.

port. A commercial harbour or the commercial part of a harbour in which are situated the quays, wharves, facilities for working cargo, warehouses, docks, repair shops, etc. The word also embraces, geographically, the city or borough which serves shipping interests. See also ports named after location, e.g. **canal port, estuary port, seaport, river port.**

Port Authority. Persons or corporation, owners of, or entrusted with or invested with the power of managing a port. May be called a Harbour Board, Port Trust, Port Commission, Harbour Commission, Marine Department, etc.

port radio station. See **radio station.**

port of refuge. A legal term meaning: When a vessel suffers from stress of weather or other unforeseen hazards of the sea it may be necessary for her to put into an intermediate port, or even put back into her loading or discharge port. In these circumstances deviation to such a port for the purpose of effecting necessary repairs in order to continue the voyage is justifiable so far as a Charter Party or Insurance is concerned.

position line. A line on a chart, representing a line on the Earth's surface, on which a ship's position can be said to lie, such as might be obtained from a single bearing, the observations of one heavenly body, or an arc of a range circle.

pound (or pond). Small body of still water in the form of a camber or small basin in a dockyard, used for the storage of boats or other gear afloat. e.g. **boat pound, timber pound.**

pratique. Permission granted to a vessel on arrival in a port to have dealings ashore, once the requisite health authorities are satisfied that the state of health on board is good and that there are no cases of notifiable diseases on board. Vessels remain in **quarantine** until pratique is granted. Some vessels, usually warships, may be granted **free pratique**, exempting them from the normal rules.

precautionary area. See **routeing system.**

prime meridian. The **meridian** which passes through the Greenwich Observatory in London, UK. It is the starting point (0°) for the measurement of longitude E and W. Also known as the **Greenwich Meridian.**

production platform. A offshore structure sited on an oil or gasfield. See 13.132.

project depth. The designed dredging depth of a channel.

projection. A geometrical representation of a plane on a part of the Earth's surface.

prominent object. An object which is easily identifiable, but does not justify being classified as conspicuous.

promontory. A major **spur**-like protrusion of the continental **slope** extending to the deep seafloor. Characteristically, the **crest** deepens seaward.

province. Oceanographically, a region identifiable by a number of similar physiographic characteristics that are markedly in contrast with those in the surrounding areas.

pteropod ooze. Limy deposits formed from the dead bodies of small swimming snails or sea butterflies, commonest near the equator. Found in shallower water than globigerina ooze, and especially near coral islands and on submerged elevations far from land.

pumice. A light, porous or cellular type of lava, occasionally to be found floating on the sea surface.

Q

quadrature. A term applied principally to the Sun and Moon when their longitudes differ by 90° (i.e. halfway between full and new Moon).

quarantine. Isolation imposed on an infected vessel. All vessels are considered to be in quarantine until **pratique** is granted.

quarantine anchorage. See **anchorage.**

quartz. Crystalline silica. Usually colourless and transparent, but varies considerably in opaqueness and colour, the most common solid mineral.

quay. A solid structure usually of stone, masonry or concrete (as distinguished from a pile structure) alongside which vessel may lie to work cargoes. It usually runs along or nearly along the line of the shore of the inner part of a port system.

quayage. Comprehensive term embracing all the structures in a port alongside which vessels can lie. Also, the charge made for berthing on a quay. See also **wharfage.**

quoin. A wedge; sometimes used to describe the shape of an island or hill.

R

race. Fast-running water, frequently tidal, caused by passage through a constricted channel, over shallows, or in the vicinity of headlands, etc. Eddies are often associated with races.

radar conspicuous object. Any object that is readily distinguishable and outstanding on a radar screen on most bearings from seaward.

radar assistance. The communicating to a vessel of navigational information determined by a shore radar, when requested.

radio. Wireless Telegraphy (WT) and Radio Telephony (RT). The internationally agreed prefix to all appliances operated by wireless or radio.

radio bearing. The bearing of a radio transmission.

radio calling-in point. See **reporting point.**

radio fog signal. Special transmissions provided by a radiobeacon as an aid to navigation during periods of fog and low visibility.

radio lighthouse. See **rotating pattern radiobeacon.**

radio station.

maritime radio stations are normally open for public correspondence through which ships can pass messages for onward transmission. These stations are usually connected to the national telephone system. See *Admiralty List of Radio Signals Volume 1.*

port radio stations normally operate in the VHF band through which messages can be passed to Port Authorities. These messages are restricted to the movement, berthing and safety of ships, and in emergency to the safety of persons. Port radio stations may be associated with radar surveillance and traffic control centres in large ports. See *Admiralty List of Radio Signals Volume 6.*

radiolaria. Forms of **foraminifera** having skeletons of silica.

radiolarian ooze. A siliceous deep-sea ooze formed of the skeletons of radiolaria.

radome. A dome, usually of glass reinforced plastic, housing a radar aerial. On shore installations these domes are often conspicuous or prominent. Term is also used for domes or pods housing similar equipment in ships and on aircraft.

raise the land. To sight the land by approaching to the point where it appears above the horizon. Similarly, to raise a light or another ship.

raised beach. An old beach, raised appreciably beyond the inshore limit of wave action, by earth movements which have caused the sea to recede.

ramp. A sloping road or pathway from the sea or river bed to above high water, in place of steps; eg the roadway from a beach to the top of a seawall. Also, an inclined platform between the shore and a vessel, with one end adjustable for height, to enable vehicles to drive on and off the vessel.

range. Term used in the USA and Canada for **transit.**

range of the tide. The differences in level between successive high and low waters or vice versa.

rate (of tidal streams and currents). The velocity, usually expressed in knots.

ratio of ranges. A factor, found on or deduced from a co-tidal chart, whereby the range of the tide offshore can be calculated.

reach. A comparatively straight part of a river or channel, between two bends. See also **harbour reach.**

recommended. A term used on Admiralty charts, and in associated publications, in conjunction with various chart symbols, mostly to do with tracks and routeing. Such recommendations derive from a variety of sources, but should not be taken as recommendations by the UKHO. The word 'recommended' is retained because it is part of the IMO definition of the feature depicted by a particular symbol. For details of IMO definitions of **recommended direction of traffic flow, recommended route** and **recommended track,** see **routeing system.**

recommended anchorage. An expression formerly used to describe an anchorage which had been recommended by users as having good holding or other advantages. They are not designated by a regulatory authority, nor are they recommended by the UKHO. They are shown on the chart by a black anchor symbol (Chart 5011 Symbol N10) and are now referred to as **reported anchorages**.

rectilinear stream. A tidal stream which runs alternately in approximately opposite directions, with a period of slack water in between. See also **rotary streams.**

reduction of soundings. The adjustment of soundings to the selected chart datum by correction for the **height of the tide**, which gives charted depths.

reef. An area of rocks or coral, detached or not, the depth over which constitutes a danger to surface navigation. Also, sometimes used for a low rocky or coral area, some of which is above water. Oceanographically, a mass (or group) of rock(s) or other indurated material lying at or near the sea surface that may constitute a hazard to surface navigation.

reef island. See **coral island.**

reflector. A device fitted to buoys and beacons to reflect radar transmissions.

refuge harbour. An artificial harbour built on an exposed coast for vessels forced to take shelter from the weather.

refuge hut. A hut containing emergency rations and clothing, maintained on some barren and isolated coasts for the use of shipwrecked persons.

reported anchorage. An anchorage which had been recommended by users as having good holding or other advantages. Not designated by a regulatory authority.

reporting point. A position in the approaches to certain ports where traffic is controlled by a vessel traffic service at which ships entering or leaving report their progress as directed in the relevant Admiralty List of Radio Signals. Also known by certain authorities as a Calling-in Point or **waypoint**.

restricted waters. Areas which, for navigational reasons such as the presence of sandbanks or other dangers, confine the movements of shipping to narrow limits, See also **open waters.**

retroreflector. A surface or device from which most of the reflection of light can occur as retroreflection.

rhumb line or **loxodrome.** Any line on the Earth's surface which cuts all meridians at the same angle, ie a line of constant bearing.

ride to the anchor. To lie at anchor with freedom to yaw and swing.

ridge. Oceanographically, it has three meanings:
An isolated (or group of) elongated narrow elevation(s) of varying complexity having steep sides.
An isolated (or group of) elongated narrow elevation(s), often separating ocean **basins.**
The linked major mid-oceanic mountain systems of global extent. Also called **mid-oceanic ridge.**

rift valley. See **median valley.**

ripple marks. Small ridges caused by wave action on sandy or silty shores, and on the sea floor. See also **backwash marks, beach cusps.**

rips: tide. See **overfalls.**

rise. Oceanographically, a broad elevation that rises gently and generally smoothly from the sea floor. The linked major mid-oceanic mountain systems of global extent. Also called **mid-oceanic ridge.** A synonym for the last-listed definition of **ridge.**

rising tide. The period between low water and the succeeding high water.

river basin. A region which contributes to the supply of water to a river or rivers. The catchment area of a river.

river port. A port that lies on the banks of a river. See also **canal port, seaport, estuary port.**

road, roads. An open anchorage which may, or may not, be protected by shoals or reefs affording less protection than a harbour. Sometimes found outside harbours.

roadstead. Alternative name for **road.**

rock. An extensive geological term, but limited in hydrography to hard, solid masses of the Earth's surface rising from the, sea floor either completely submerged or projecting permanently, or at times, above water.

roll. The angular motion of a ship in the athwartship plane. See also **pitch.**

root. The landward end of the structure of a jetty, pier, etc.

RoRo Term, abbreviated from ROll-on ROll-off, applied to ships, wharves, berths and terminals, where vehicles can embark or disembark by driving on or off a vessel.

rotary streams. Tidal streams, the direction of which gradually turn either clockwise or anti-clockwise through 360° in one tidal cycle.

route. Specific sequence of geographical positions defining the **legs** which constitute a **passage.**

routeing system. Any system of one or more routes or routeing measures aimed at reducing the risk of casualties; it includes **traffic separation schemes, two-way routes, recommended tracks, areas to be avoided, inshore traffic zones, roundabouts, precautionary areas and deep-water routes.**

> **mandatory routeing system.** A routeing system adopted by IMO in accordance with the requirements of Regulation V/10 of the International Convention for the Safety of Life at Sea 1974, for mandatory use by all vessels, certain categories of vessel or vessels carrying certain cargoes.
>
> **TSS.** Traffic Separation Scheme. A routeing measure aimed at the separation of opposing streams of traffic by appropriate means and by the establishment of **traffic lanes.**
>
> **separation zone or line.** A zone or line separating the traffic lanes in which vessels are proceeding in opposite or nearly opposite directions; or separating a traffic lane from an asdjacent sea area; or separating traffic lanes designated for particular classes of vessel proceeding in the same direction.
>
> **traffic lane.** An area within defined limits in which one-way traffic is established. Natural obstacles, including those forming separation zones, may constitute a boundary.

> **roundabout.** A routeing measure comprising a separation point or circular separation zone and a circular traffic lane within defined limits. Traffic within the roundabout is separated by moving in a counterclockwise direction around the separation point or zone.
>
> **inshore traffic zone.** A routeing measure comprising a designated area between the landward boundary of a **traffic separation scheme** and the adjacent coast, to be used in accordance with the provisions of Rule 10(d), as amended, of the International Regulations for Preventing Collisions at Sea, 1972 (Collision Regulations).
>
> **two-way route.** A route within defined limits inside which two-way traffic is established, aimed at providing safe passage of vessels through waters where navigation is difficult or dangerous.
>
> **recommended route.** A route of undefined width, for the convenience of vessels in transit, which is often marked by centreline buoys. See **recommended.**
>
> **recommended track.** A route which has been specially examined to ensure so far as possible that it is free of dangers and along which vessels are advised to navigate. See **recommended.**
>
> **deep-water route.** A route within defined limits which has been accurately surveyed for clearance of sea bottom and submerged obstacles as indicated on the chart.
>
> **precautionary area.** A routeing measure comprising an area within defined limits where vessels must navigate with particular caution and within which the direction of traffic flow may be recommended.
>
> **ATBA** Area to be Avoided. A routeing measure comprising an area within defined limits in which either navigation is particularly hazardous or it is exceptionally important to avoid casualties and which should be avoided by all vessels, or certain categories of vessel.
>
> **no anchoring area.** A routeing measure comprising an area within defined limits where anchoring is hazardous or could result in unacceptable damage to the marine environment. Anchoring in a no anchoring area should be avoided by all vessels or certain classes of vessel, except in the case of immediate danger to the vessel or persons on board.
>
> **established direction of traffic flow.** A traffic flow pattern indicating the directional moverment of traffic as established within a **traffic separation scheme**.
>
> **recommended direction of traffic flow.** A traffic flow pattern indicating a recommended directional movement of traffic where it is impractical or unnecessary to adopt an **established direction of traffic flow**.

rubble. Waste fragments of stone, brick, concrete, etc, or pieces of undressed stone, used as a foundation or for protecting the sides of breakwaters and seawalls. See **pitching.**

run. The distance a ship has travelled through the water.
> **run of the coast.** The trend of the coast.
> **run down a coast.** To sail parallel with it.
> **run before the wind.** To steer a course downwind.

runnel. A depression in a beach usually roughly parallel with the waterline for much of its course; frequently associated with rills debouching over the beach, but also occurring when there is a sudden change in the gradient, eg as caused by breakers during the stand of the tide near high or low water.

running survey. A survey in which the greater part of the work is done from the ship sounding and moving along the coast, fixed by dead reckoning, astronomical observations, or other means, and observing angles, bearings and distances to plot the general configuration of the land and offshore details. Similarly, a running survey of a river by boats.

S

saddle. A broad pass or col, resembling in shape a riding saddle, in a **ridge** or between contiguous elevations.

saddlehill. A hill with two summits separated by a depression, appearing from some directions like a saddle.

safe vertical clearance. The maximum height of a vessel, measured above the datum, which can pass under an overhead power cable without risk of electrical discharge from the cable to the vessel. See 9.71.

SALS. Single Anchor Leg Storage. See 13.138.

saltings. Lands in proximity to salt water, which are covered at times by the tide.

sand. A sediment consisting of an accumulation of particles which range in size from a pin's head to a fine grain. The most common sediment on the continental shelves are of two principal types:
> Terrigenous sand which is made up from the breaking up of rocks on land by weathering, the small fragments being carried out to sea by streams. (The most common constituent of terrigenous sand is quartz, but many other minerals are also included.)
> Calcarenite sand made up from shells or shell fragments, foraminifera, coral debris and other organisms that contain calcium carbonate.

Also, a shoal area of sand, sometimes connected with the shore or detached. Some sands partly dry and some are always submerged. See also **shifting sand.**

scale (on a chart or map). A graduated line used to measure or plot distances. On large scale Admiralty charts the following scales are usually provided: Latitude and Distance, Feet, and Metres; and on ungraduated plans, Longitude. See also **natural scale.**

scarp. See **escarpment.**

scend or **send:**
> **of a ship.** A ship is said to scend heavily when her bow or stern pitches with great force into the trough of the sea.
> **of waves.** The vertical movement of waves or swell alongside a wharf, jetty, cliff or rocks.

scoriae. Cellular lava or clinker-like fragments of it.

scour. The clearing of a channel by the action of water. Also, the local deepening close to an islet, rock or obstruction due to the clearing action of the tidal streams or currents.

scouring basin. A backwater or basin by the side of a channel or small harbour from which water can be released quickly near low water for the purpose of scouring the channel or harbour.

sea. The expanse of salt water which covers most of the Earth's surface. Also, a sub-division of the above, next in size to an ocean, partly and sometimes wholly enclosed by land, but usually with access to open water. Also, the waves raised by the wind blowing in the immediate neighbourhood of the place of observation at the time of observation. See 5.25.

sea floor. The interface between water and seabed.

sea mile. See **mile.**

sea reach. The most seaward reach of a river or estuary.

sea room. Space clear of the shore which offers no danger to navigation and affords freedom of manoeuvre.

sea valley(s). See **valley(s).**

sea-way. The open water outside the confines of a harbour. Also, a rough sea caused by wind, tide or both.

seaboard. Alternative name for coastal region.

seachannel(s). A continuously sloping elongated discrete (or group of) depression(s) found in **fans** or **abyssal plains** anc customarily bordered by **levees** on both sides.

seaknoll. An isolated submarine hill or elevation less prominent than a seamount.

seamark. A daymark erected with the express purpose of being visible from a distance to seaward.

seamount. A discrete (or group of) large isolated elevation(s), greater than 1000 m in relief above the sea floor, characteristically of conical form. Also known as a **seapeak.** See also **guyot.**

seamount chain. A linear or arcuate alignment of discrete **seamounts**, with their bases clearly separated. See also **seamount.**

seamount group. Three or more seamounts not in a line and with bases separated by a relatively flat sea floor.

seamount range. Three or more seamounts having connected bases and aligned along a ridge or rise.

seapeak. See **guyot** and **seamount.**

seaport. A port situated on the coast, with unimpeded connection with the sea. See also **canal port, estuary port, river port.**

seashore. See **shore.**

seasonal changes (in sea level). Variations in the sea level associated with seasonal changes in wind direction, barometric pressure, rainfall. See 5.18.

seawall. A solid structure, usually of masonry and earth, or tetrapods built along the coast to prevent erosion or encroachment by the sea. Ships cannot usually lie alongside a seawall.

sector of a light. The portion of a circle defined by bearings from seaward within which a light shows a specified character or colour, or is obscured.

sedimentation. The process of breakup and separation of particles from the parent rock, their transportation, deposition, and consolidation into another rock.

sediment trap. A device used to measure the rate and amount of sedimentation in a location.

seiche. See 5.24.

semi-diurnal (stream or tide). Undergoing a complete cycle in half a day.

send. See **scend**.

separation zone or **separation line**. See **routeing system**.

set (of the stream). The direction in which a tidal stream or current is flowing.

shackle (of cable). The length of a continuous portion of chain cable between two joining shackles. In British ships the standard length of a shackle of cable is 15 fathoms (27·432 m).

shallow. A shoal area in a river, or extending across a river, where the depths are less than those upstream or downstream of it.

shallow water effect. The effect on a hull of its speed in shallow water. It can cause loss of speed for a given power setting, impair steering and increase the time taken to accelerate and decelerate. See also **squat**, See 11.111.

sheer. A ship is said to take a sheer if, usually due to some external influence, her bows unexpectedly deviate from her course.

shelf. A zone adjacent to a continent (or around an island) and extending from the low water line to a depth at which there is usually a marked increase of slope towards the oceanic depths. See **ledge, continental shelf, island shelf**.

shelf edge or **shelf break**. The line along which there is a marked increase of slope at the seaward margin of a **continental** (or island) **shelf**. Also called **shelf edge**.

shell. A hard outer case, conch, crust, or skeleton, of many sea animals.

shifting sand. Sand of such fine particles and other conditions that it drifts with the action of the water or wind.

shingle. A descriptive term for **gravel**.

ship canal. A canal large enough to permit the passage of ocean-going vessels.

shiplift. An installation for dry docking vessels whereby they are raised clear of the water on a grid and cradle. Ship and cradle can then be transferred ashore on rails to a refitting area leaving the shiplift free to lift or refloat other vessels.

shipping safety fairway. Area designated as a fairway by USA within which no artificial island or fixed structure, whether temporary or permanent, is permitted.

ship's head or **heading**. The direction in which a ship is pointing at any moment.

shipyard. A yard or place containing facilities in the way of slips and workshops, etc, for the construction, launching, fitting-out, maintenance and repair of ships and vessels.

shoal (noun). An isolated (or group of) offshore hazard(s) to surface navigation with substantially less clearance than the surrounding area and composed of unconsolidated material. Oceanographically, an offshore hazard to surface navigation composed of unconsolidated material. The term shoal is not generally used for dangers which are composed entirely of rock or coral. See also **bank, shallow**.

shoal (verb). To become more shallow.

shore. The meeting of sea and land considered as a boundary of the sea. See also **coast**. and **foreshore**. Also, a prop fixed under the ship's bottom or at her side, to support her in dry dock.

shore up. To support by means of shores round a vessel.

shoreline. Another term for **coastline** , in a more general sense.

sill. Oceanographically, a **sea floor** barrier of relatively shallow depth restricting water movement between **basins**. See also **dock sill**.

sill depth. The greatest depth over a sill.

silt (noun). Sediment deposited by water in a channel or harbour or on the shore, in still areas, or where an obstruction is met. A finer sediment than sand. See also **clay**.

silt (verb). To choke or be choked by silt.

skerry. A rocky islet.

slack water. That period of negligible horizontal water movement when a rectilinear tidal stream is changing direction.

slake. An accumulation of mud or ooze on the bed of a river, channel or harbour. Also, such an accumulation left exposed by the tide.

slick. A local calm streak on the water caused by oil. Also, the calm patch left by the quarter of a ship when turning sharply.

slime. Fine oozy mud or other substance of similar consistency.

slip dock. A combination of patent slip and dock (the water is excluded by gates and side walls) used where there is considerable range of the tide.

slipway or **slips**. Applied loosely to a building slip. A craft or small vessel under repair may be hauled on the slips to be clear of the water.

slope. The deepening sea floor out from the **shelf edge** to the upper limit of of the **continental rise**, or the point where there is a general decrease in steepness.

snag. A small feature on the sea floor capable of damaging nets and other fishing gear. Also called a fastener.

solstices. The two points at which the Sun reaches its greatest declination N or S, or the dates on which this occurs.

solstitial spring tide. See **tide**.

sound (noun). A passage between two sea areas. A passage having an outlet at either end.
Also, an arm of the sea or large inlet.

sound (verb). To determine the depth of water.

sounding. Measured or charted depth of water or the measurement of such a depth. See also **reduction of soundings.**

spar-buoy. A buoy in the form of a pole which is moored to float nearly vertical.

speed. The speed of a vessel refers to her speed through the water unless otherwise specified. See also **ground speed.**

spending beach. The beach in a **wave basin** on which the waves entering the harbour entrance expend themselves, only a small residue penetrating the inner harbour.

spherical buoy. A buoy, the visible portion of which shows an approximately spherical shape.

spheroid. A mathematically regular surface resembling a slightly flattened sphere, defined by the length of its axes and used to approximate the geoid in geodetic computations. e.g. Airy (used in Great Britain, International, etc.).

spindle buoy. A buoy, similar in height to a spar buoy, but conical instead of cylindrical.

spit. A long narrow shoal (if submerged) or a tongue of land (if above water), extending from the shore and formed of any material.

SPM. Single Point Mooring. See 13.135.

spoil. Mud, sand, silt or other deposit obtained from the floor of a channel or harbour, by dredging.

spoil ground. An area set aside, clear of the channel and in deep water when possible, for dumping spoil obtained by dredging or sullage. A spoil ground buoy marks the limit of a spoil ground. Lesser depths may be found within the spoil ground.

spring tide. See **tide**.

spur. A projection from a range of mountains or hills or a cliff. Also, a small projection from a jetty or wharf, at an angle to its main axis. Oceanographically, a subordinate elevation or **ridge** protruding from a larger feature, such as a **plateau** or island foundation.

squat. The decrease in **under–keel clearance** which occurs when a vessel is making way, or stationary in moving water. An element of **shallow water effect**, it is caused by increased velocity of water flow under a hull and the consequent teduction in pressure.

stack. A precipitous detached rock of considerable height. Also, a pillar left when the roof of an arch collapses through continued weathering or wave action.

staith or **staithe.** A berth for ships alongside where the walls or rails project over the ship, enabling cargo (in most cases coal) to be tipped direct from the railway trucks into the vessel's holds.

stand of the tide. See **tide**.

stand on. To continue on the same course.

Standard Time. The legal time common to a country or area, normally related to that of the time zone in which it wholly or partly lies. See *Admiralty List of Radio Signals Volume 2.*

statute mile. See **mile.**

steep-to. Any part of the shore or the sides of a bank or shoal which descends steeply to greater depths is described as a steep-to. Boat landings are described as steep-to when the gradient is steeper than about 1 in 6.

steerage way. The minimum speed required to keep the vessel under control by means of the rudder.

stem the tide. To proceed against the tidal stream at such a speed that the vessel remains stationary over the ground. Also, to turn the bows into the tidal stream.

stippling. The graduations of shade or colour produced on a chart by means of dots.

stones. A descriptive term for any loose piece of broken rock lying on the sea floor, ranging in size from that of pebbles to boulders. Used in place-names to indicate large detached rocks or islets, e.g. Seven Stones, Mewstone.

storm beach. A beach covered with coarse sand, pebbles, shingle or stones, as a result of storm waves above the foreshore, and usually characterised by berms or beach ridges.

strait. A comparatively narrow passage connecting two seas or two large bodies of water.

strath. Oceanographically, a broad elongated depression with relatively steep walls located on a continental shelf. The longitudinal profile of the floor is gently undulating with the great depths often found in the inshore portion.

strip light. A light whose source has a linear form, generally horizontal, which can reach a length of several metres. Used on heads of piers, along quay walls, at the corners of quays and on dolphins. It may have a rhythmic character and be coloured.

submarine valley(s). See **valley(s).**

submerged. A feature is said to be submerged if it has sunk under water, or has been covered over with water.

Suezmax. Used to describe the largest ships capable of fitting through the Suez canal, typically maximum draught 16 m (53 ft).

sullage. Refuse, silt or other sea floor deposit for disposal on a spoil ground, open sea, or some place clear of the channel.

sullage barge. The lighter or barge used for the conveyance of sullage.

surf. The broken water between the outermost line of breakers and the shore. Also used when referring to breakers on a detached reef.

surface current. A current of variable extent in the upper few metres of the water column. See 5.2.

surge. The difference in height between predicted and observed tides due to abnormal weather conditions. See 5.18–5.21 and Admiralty Tide Tables.

to surge. A rope or wire is surged round the revolving drum of a winch when it is desired to maintain or ease the strain without heaving in at the speed of the winch.

surging. The horizontal movement of a ship alongside due to waves or swell.

suspended well. An oil or gas well, not in use, but whose wellhead has been capped at the sea floor for possible subsequent use. See 13.131.

S-VDR. Simplified Voyage Data Recorder. See **VDR**.

swamped mooring. A non-operational mooring when the mooring buoy has been temporarily removed and the mooring chain lowered to the sea floor.

swash. The thin sheet of water sliding up the foreshore after a wave breaks. Also, a shoal in a tideway or estuary close enough to the surface to cause overfalls.

swashway or **swatchway**. A channel across a bank or through shoals. See also **gut**.

SWE. Shallow Water Effect. The general term used to describe to the effect on the draught and handling of a vessel caused by the relationship between the speed of that vessel and the depth of water. See 11.111. See also **squat**.

Also, A general term descriptive of the distortion of the tidal curve from that of a pure cosine curve, most marked in areas where there is a large amount of shallow water.

sweep. Commonly used contraction of **drag sweep**.

swell. See 5.27.

syzygy. An astronomical term denoting that two celestial bodies have the same celestial hour angle, or celestial hour angles differing by 180°. When the sun and Moon are in syzygy, **spring tides** occur.

T

tableknoll. A knoll having a comparatively smooth, flat top with minor irregularities.

tableland. An extensive elevated region with a flat-topped level surface.

tablemount. A seamount having a comparatively smooth, flat top. See **guyot(s).**

tank farm. A large group of oil storage tanks, usually near an oil terminal or refinery.

telegraph buoy. A buoy marking the position of a submarine telegraph cable. See also **cable buoy.**

terminal. A number of berths grouped together and provided with facilities for handling a particular form of cargo, e.g. oil terminal, container terminal.

terrace(s). An isolated (or group of) relatively flat horizontal or gently inclined surfaces, sometimes long and narrow, which is(are) bounded by a steeper ascending slope on one side and by a steeper descending slope on the other. See also **bench**.

tetrapods. Concrete masses the size of boulders, cast with four stump-legs so that the masses interlock. Used for the pitching of breakwaters and seawalls.

thalweg. The deepest part of a channel.

tidal angles and factors. Astronomical data, combining the effects of several tidal constituents, used for the prediction of tides by the Admiralty Method. See Admiralty Tide Tables.

tidal harbour. A harbour in which the water level rises and falls with the tide as distinct from a harbour in which the water is enclosed at a high level by locks and gates.

tidal stream. The alternating horizontal movement of water associated with the rise and fall of the tide.

tide. The periodic rise and fall of the surface of the sea, due principally to the gravitational interactions between the sun, moon and earth. The science of tidal prediction is discussed in detail in the Admiralty Manual of Tides. Daily predictions of the times and heights of **high** and **low water** for ports around the world, and the times, height differences and harmonic constants for all ports where they are known, are contained in Admiralty Tide Tables. For further details see 3.27. The following measures of tidal activity are some of those most frequently used when involved with tides and tidal prediction:

HW. High Water. The highest level reached by the tide in one complete cycle.

MHW Mean High Water. The average of all high water heights over the period of a year.

higher high water. The higher of two successive high waters where diurnal inequality is present.

MLHW. Mean Lower High Water. The height of the mean of the lower of the two daily high waters over a long period of time.

MHHW. Mean Higher High Water. The height of the mean of the higher of the two daily high waters over a long period of time. When only one high water occurs on a day this is taken as the higher high water. Used where the tide is predominantly diurnal.

MHWN. Mean High Water Neaps. The height of mean low water neaps is the average, throughout a year when the average declination of the Moon is 23½° of the heights of two successive high waters during those periods (approximately once a fortnight) when the range of the tide is least.

MHWS. Mean High Water Springs. The height of mean high water springs is the average, throughout a year when the average maximum declination of the Moon is 23½°, of the heights of two successive high waters during those periods of 24 hours (approximately once a fortnight) when the range of the tide is greatest.

HAT. Highest Astronomical Tide. The highest tidal level which can be predicted to occur under average meteorological conditions and under any combination of astronomical conditions.

LW. Low Water. The lowest level reached by the tide in one complete cycle.

MLW. Mean Low Water. The average of all low water heights over the period of a year.

lower low water. The lower of two successive low waters where diurnal inequality is present.

MHLW. Mean Higher Low Water. The height of the mean of the higher of the two daily low waters over a long period of time.

MLLW. Mean Lower Low Water. The height of the mean of the lower of the two daily low waters over a long period of time. When only one low water occurs on a day this is taken as the lower low water. Used where the tide is predominantly diurnal.

MLWN. Mean Low Water Neaps. The height of mean low water neaps is the average height obtained from two successive low waters during the same periods.

MLWS. Mean Low Water Springs. The height of mean low water springs is the average height obtained by two successive low waters during the same periods.

LAT. Lowest Astronomical Tide. The lowest tidal level which can be predicted to occur under average meteorological conditions and under any combination of astronomical conditions. See 5.14.

MSL. Mean Sea Level. The average height of the surface of the sea at a **tide station** for all stages of the tide over a 19 year period, usually determined from hourly height readings measured from a fixed, predetermined reference level (**chart datum**).

mean tide level. The level mid-way between **MHW** and **MLW**. My differ slightly from **MSL**. Also known as **half tide level**.

The folowing expressions are commonly used to describe differing states and conditions of tide or tidal activity:

spring tide. A tide of relatively large range occurring near the times of new and full Moon.

neap tide. A tide of relatively small range occurring near the times of the Moon's first and last quarters.

half tide. The **height of the tide** halfway between high water and low water. See also. **mean tide level.**

stand of the tide. A prolonged period during which the tide does not rise or fall noticeably. In some cases this is a normal feature of the tidal conditions; in others it is caused by certain unusual meteorological conditions. See also **high water stand.**

height of the tide. The vertical distance at any instant between sea level and chart datum.

high water stand. A prolonged period of negligible vertical movement near high water, this being a regular feature of the tides in certain localities while in other places stands are caused by meteorological conditions.

solstitial spring tide. The spring tide (greater than average) occurring near the solstices.

tidepole. A graduated vertical staff used for measuring the **height of the tide**.

tide gauge. An instrument which registers the **height of the tide** against a scale.

automatic tide gauge. An instrument which measures and records the tidal data.

pressure tide gauge. An instrument which measures the pressure below the sea surface; this pressure may be converted to water depth if the air pressure, the gravitational acceleration and the water density are known.

tide-pools. Pools worn in seashore rocks, left full of water when the tide level has fallen below them.

tide race. See **race**.

tide-raising forces. The forces exerted by the Sun and Moon which cause the tides.

tide-rip. See **overfalls**.

tide-rode. An anchored or moored ship is tide-rode when heading into the tidal stream. See also **wind-rode**.

tideway. Where the full strength of the tidal stream is experienced, as opposed to inshore where only weak tidal streams may be experienced.

Also, the channel in which the tidal stream sets.

timber pound. See **pound**.

time signal. A special signal, usually by radio for the purpose of checking the errors of chronometers. See the relevant Admiralty List of Radio Signals.

Time Zones. Longitudinal zones of the Earth's surface each 15° in extent, for which a Zone Time is designated. The zones are shown on Chart 5006 (The World — Time Zone Chart) and described in *Admiralty List of Radio Signals Volume 2*. See also **Standard Time, Date Line.**

tongue. A long, narrow and usually low, salient point of land. See also **spit**.

topmark An identification shape, fitted on the tops of beacons and buoys. See also **daymark.**

topography. Detailed description in a book, or representation on a chart or map, of the natural and artificial features of a district.
Also the features themselves.

toroidal buoy. A buoy shaped like a ring in the horizontal plane, usually with a central support with shape, mainly used for oceanographical purposes

track. The path followed, or to be followed, between one position and another. This path may be the ground track, over the ground, or the water track, through the water. Used in the sense of ground track in the term **recommended track**.

trackpoint. In voyage planning, a point representing a vessel's geographic position along a particular historic **track**.

traffic lane. See **routeing system**.

train ferry. A ferry fitted with railway lines to transport railway carriages and wagons across the water.

training wall. A mound often of rubble, frequently submerged, built alongside the channel of an estuary or river to direct the tidal stream or current, or both, through the channel so that it may assist in keeping it clear of silt. Termed **jetty** in the USA and Canada.

transfer. For a specific alteration of course, transfer is the lateral distance that a vessel moves in a direction towards the new course at right angles to the original course. See also **advance**.

transfer of datum. The method of determining a new chart datum by reference to an established datum whereby the tide will fall to the datum at the new position when it falls to datum at the old one.

transhipment area or **lightening area**. Area designated for transfer of cargo from one vessel to another to reduce the draught of the larger vessel. Also known as cargo transfer area.

transit. Two objects in line are said to be "in transit". See also **range**.

transit port. A port where the cargo handled is merely en route to its destination and is forwarded by coasters or river craft. The port itself is not the final destination before distribution.

transit shed. A structure or building on a wharf or quay for the temporary storage of cargo and goods between ship and rail or warehouse, and vice versa. There is a legal difference between a transit shed under the shipowner's control and a warehouse which may not be.

transporter. A type of travelling **crane** consisting of a movable bridge or gantry which runs on rails, straddling a cargo (usually coal) dump and projecting over the quay side. A small crane or grab runs along the gantry transporting the cargo from dump to vessel or vice versa.

transporter bridge. A type of **bridge** which may be erected over a waterway consisting of a tower either side of the water connected by a girder system along which a carriage runs. A small platform at road level is suspended from the carriage and on this the road traffic is transported across the waterway.

trench. Oceanographically, a long characteristically very deep and asymmetrical depression of the sea floor, with relatively steep sides.

trend of a coast. The general direction in which it extends.

triangulation. The measurement of a system of triangles connecting control stations in an area to be surveyed, in order to ascertain the correct relative positions of those stations.
Also, the geometrical framework (also called horizontal control) thus obtained.

trilateration. The measurement of a system of triangles connecting control stations in an area to be surveyed, by measuring the sides of the triangles rather than their angles as in a triangulation.

trot. A line or system of mooring buoys between which a number of small ships or craft can be secured, head and stern.

trough. The hollow between two waves.
Oceanographically, a long depression of the sea floor characteristically steep-sided and normally shallower, than a **trench**.

TSS. Traffic Separation Scheme. See **routeing system**.

tufa. A porous concretionary or compact form of calcium carbonate, which is deposited from solution around springs.

turning basin. See **basin**.

turn-round (turn–around). The turn-round of a vessel in a port is the complete operation comprising arrival, discharge and loading of cargo, and departure.

twenty-foot equivalent unit. See **container**.

twilight. See **astronomical, nautical** and **civil twilight**.

two-way route. See **routeing system**.

typhoon haven. A port where vessels may seek shelter from a tropical cyclone.

U

uncovered. Exposed; not covered by water.

undercurrent. A current below the surface, particularly one flowing in a direction or at a speed differing from the **surface current**.

under way. The term used in the International Regulations for Preventing Collisions at Sea 1972 to mean that a vessel is not at anchor, or made fast to the shore, or aground.

undercliff. A terrace or lower cliff formed by a landslip.

under–keel clearance. The difference between the **draught** of a vessel and the available depth of water. See also **squat**. See 11.128.

undertow. A sub-surface current setting into the deeper water when waves are breaking.

underwater. See **below-water**.

unexamined. A potential danger to navigation is marked unexamined when the least depth of water over it has not been rigorously determined.

unwatched light. A light without any personnel permanently stationed to superintend it.

upstream. The opposite direction to **downstream**.

V

VDR. (Voyage Data Recorder). An approved device which records voyage data for later analysis in the event of an accident. Mandated by IMO for all passenger and **RoRo** vessels since 2004 and all cargo vessels of greater than 3 000 gt built since 1 July 2002. Older vessels must have a minimum of **S–VDR** fitted at the first scheduled dry–docking after 1 July 2007 and not later than 1 July 2010.

valley. Oceanographically, an isolated (or group of) relatively shallow, wide depression(s), the bottom of which usually has a continuous gradient. This term is generally not used for features that have canyon–like characteristics for a significant portion of their extent. Also called **submarine valley(s)** or **sea valley(s)**.

variation. See **magnetic variation**.

veer. The wind is said to veer when it changes direction clockwise in the northern hemisphere.

vertical clearance. The minimum height of the underside of the span of a bridge, or an overhead cable. It is measured from Highest Astronomical Tide (HAT) where there is an appreciable tidal range, and above Mean Sea Level (MSL) where the range is negligible. Notes on charts should always be checked to ascertain the vertical datum in use.

vertical datum. A horizontal plane to which heights, depths or levels are referred. See **chart datum, high water datum, Indian Spring Low Water datum, Land Survey datum** and **Ordnance datum**.

Vessel Traffic Service (VTS). A service implemented by a competent authority to improve the safety and efficiency of vessel traffic and protect the environment. The service shall have the capability to interact with the traffic and respond to traffic situations developing in the VTS area.

vigia. A reported danger, usually in deep water, whose position is uncertain or whose existence is doubtful. A warning on the chart to denote that undiscovered dangers may exist in the neighbourhood.

volcanic ash. Uncemented pyroclastic material consisting of fragments mostly under 4 mm in diameter. Coarse ash is 0·25 to 4 mm in grain size; fine ash is less then 0·25 mm.

voyage. An entire journey by sea, comprising one or more discrete **passages**.

W

waiting area. An area with designated limits within which ships must wait for a pilot or representative of the shore authorities.

walkway. See **catwalk.**

warp (noun). A hawser by which a ship can be moved when in harbour, port, etc. The warp is secured to a buoy or some fixed object and brought inboard and hauled upon to move the ship.

warp (verb). To move a ship from one place to another by means of a warp.

warping buoy. Mooring buoys specially laid to assist ships hauling off a quay or jetty.

wash. The accumulation of silt and alluvium in the estuary. Soil carried away by water.
Also, the visible and audible motion of agitated water, especially that caused by the passage of a vessel.

watch buoy. A buoy placed to mark a special position; in particular, near a light vessel, to check its position.

water boat. A boat (usually self-propelled) fitted with large water tanks and its own pump and hose connections, used in harbours for supplying fresh water to sea-going ships.

water track. See **track.**

waterborne. Floating; particularly of a ship afloat after being aground, or on being launched.

watercourse. A natural channel for water, which may sometimes dry.

waterline. The actual junction of the land and water at any instant.
Also, the line along which the surface of the water touches a vessels' hull.

waterway. A water feature (river or channel) which can be utilised for communication or transport.

wave basin. A device to reduce the size of waves which enter a harbour, consisting of a basin close to the inner entrance to the harbour in which the waves from the outer entrance are absorbed.

wave trap. A device used to reduce the size of waves which enter a harbour before they penetrate as far as the quayage. Sometimes it takes the form of diverging breakwaters, and sometimes of small projecting breakwaters situated close within the entrance.

wave-cut shore. A shore or bare rock formed by wave erosion, or on a limestone or other soluble rock by solution. Correctly, a shore which is not a beach is wave-cut.

way. The motion of a vessel through the water.

ways. The timber sills upon which a ship is built.

waypoint. A geographic position which, together with **berthpoints** and **pilotpoints**, define the **legs** that comptrise a **passage.**

way point. See **reporting point.**

weather side. The side of a vessel towards which, or on the side of a channel from which, the wind is blowing. See also **lee side.**

weather shore. That from which the wind is blowing.

weather tide. The opposite of **lee tide.**

wellhead. The head of the pipe drawing oil from an oilfield or gas from a field of gas.

wet dock. A non-tidal basin.

WGS84. World Geodetic System 1984. The most prevalent horizontal datum used in charting, which is used for positions provided by GPS NAVSTAR. See 2.11.

wharf. A structure similar to a **quay** alongside which vessels can lie to discharge cargo. Usually constructed of wood, iron or concrete, or a combination of them, and supported on **pile**s. It may be either in continuous contact with the land or offset slightly from it, and may be connected with it by one or more approach piers.

wharfage. In a general way, a charge made against cargo passed on to or over a wharf, quay, or jetty. See also **quayage.**

whirlpool Water in rapidly rotary motion. See **eddy.**

whistle-buoy A buoy which emits a whistle, actuated by compressed air or by the compression of air in a tube by the action of the waves.

white horses. See **breakers.**

WIG (Wing-In-Ground) craft. Craft supported in their operational mode solely by aerodynamic forces which enable them to operate at low altitude above the sea surface, but out of direct contact with that surface.

wind drift current. A horizontal movement in the upper layers of the sea, caused by wind. See 5.7.

wind-rode. An anchored or moored vessel is wind-rode when heading, or riding, into the wind. See also **tide-rode.**

wire drag. See **drag sweep.**

wreck. The ruined remains of a stranded or sunken vessel which has been rendered useless,. See also **dangerous wreck** and **derelict.**

Y

yard. A waterside area constructed and fitted-out for a specific purpose usually indicated by a prefix, e.g. boat yard, dockyard, shipyard.

yard craft. See **craft.**

yaw. Unavoidable oscillation of the ship's head either side of the course being steered or when at anchor, due to wind and waves.

Z

Zone Time. The system of time-keeping used by a vessel at sea in which the time kept is that of the appropriate **Time Zone.**

zooplankton. The microscopic drifting animal life of the oceans including the larvae of the larger swimming animals and fish.

NOTES

Ice Glossary

Terms commonly used in an ice environment

Scope

This glossary defines descriptive terms in general use for the various kinds of ice likely to be encountered by the Mariner. It includes terms given in *WMO Sea-Ice Nomenclature* published by the World Meteorological Organization in 1970 (with its subsequent amendments).

Terms

A

ablation. All processes by which snow, ice or water in any form are lost from a glacier, floating ice or snow cover. These include melting, evaporation, calving, wind erosion and avalanches. Also used to express the quantities lost by these processes.

accumulation. All processes by which snow, ice or water in any form are added to a glacier, floating ice or snow cover. These include direct precipitation in the form of snow, ice or rain, condensation of ice from vapour, and transport of snow and ice to a glacier. Also used to express the quantities added by these processes.

aged ridge. A ridge which has undergone considerable weathering. These ridges are best described as undulations.

anchor ice. Submerged ice attached or anchored to the sea floor, irrespective of the nature of its formation.

area of weakness. A satellite-observed area in which either ice concentration or ice thickness is significantly less than that in the surrounding areas. Because the condition is satellite observed, a precise quantitative analysis is not always possible, but navigation conditions are significantly easier than in surrounding areas.

B

bare ice. Ice without snow cover.

belt. A large feature of drift ice arrangement; longer than it is wide; from 1 km to more than 100 km in width.

bergy bit. A large piece of floating glacier ice, generally showing less than 5 m above sea level but more than 1 m and normally about 100–300 sq m in areas. See Photographs 6.4.2, 6.4.6, and 6.41.1.

bergy water. An area of freely navigable water in which ice of land origin is present in concentrations less than 1/10. There may be sea ice present, although the total concentration of all ice shall not exceed 1/10.

beset. Situation of a vessel surrounded by ice and unable to move.

big floe. A floe 500–2000 m across.

bight. An extensive crescent-shaped indentation in the ice edge, formed by either wind or current.

brash ice. Accumulations of floating ice made up of fragments not more than 2 m across; the wreckage of other forms of ice. See Photograph 6.10.

bummock. From the point of view of the submariner, a downward projection from the underside of the ice canopy; the counterpart of a hummock.

C

calving. The breaking away of a mass of ice from an ice wall, ice front or iceberg.

close ice. Floating ice in which the concentration is 7/10 to 8/10, composed of floes mostly in contact. (Photograph 6.8.2)

compacted ice edge. Close, clear-cut ice edge compacted by wind or current usually on the windward side of an area of drift ice.

compacting. Pieces of floating ice are said to be compacting when they are subjected to a converging motion, which increases ice concentration and or produces stresses which may result in ice deformation.

compact ice. Floating ice in which the concentration is 10/10 and no water is visible.

concentration. The ratio in tenths describing the amount of the sea surface covered by ice as a fraction of the whole area being considered. Total concentration includes all stages of development that are present, partial concentration may refer to the amount of a particular stage or of a particular form of ice and represents only a part of the total.

concentration boundary. A line approximating to the transition between two areas of drift ice with distinctly different concentrations.

consolidated ice. Floating ice in which the concentration is 10/10 and the floes are frozen together. (Photograph 6.8.4)

consolidated ridge. A ridge in which the base has frozen together.

crack. Any fracture of fast ice, consolidated ice or a single floe which may have been followed by separation ranging from a few centimetres to 1 m.

D

dark nilas. Nilas which is under 5 centimetres in thickness and is very dark in colour.

deformed ice. A general term for ice which has been squeezed together and in places forced upwards (and downwards). Sub-divisions are rafted ice, ridged ice and hummocked ice.

difficult area. A general qualitative expression to indicate, in a relative manner, that the severity of ice conditions prevailing in an area is such that navigation in it is difficult.

diffused ice edge. Poorly defined ice edge limiting an area of dispersed ice; usually on the leeward side of an area of drift ice.

diverging. Ice fields or floes in an area are subjected to diverging or dispersive motion, thus reducing ice concentration and/or relieving stresses in the ice.

dried ice. Sea ice from the surface of which melt-water has disappeared after the formation of cracks and thaw holes. During the period of drying, the surface whitens.

drift ice. Term used in a wide sense to include any area of sea ice, other than fast ice, no matter what form it takes or how it is disposed. When concentrations are high, ie. 7/10 or more drift ice may be replaced by the term pack ice.

E

easy area. A general qualitative expression to indicate, in a relative manner, that ice conditions prevailing in an area are such that navigation in it is not difficult.

F

fast ice. Sea ice which forms and remains fast along the coast, where it is attached to the shore, to an ice wall, to an ice front, between shoals or grounded icebergs. Vertical fluctuations may be observed during changes of sea level. Fast ice may be formed *in situ* from sea water or by freezing of floating ice of any age to the shore, and it may extend a few metres or several hundred kilometres from the coast. Fast ice may be more than one year old and may then be prefixed with the appropriate age category (old, second-year, or multi-year). If it is thicker than about 2 m above sea level it is called an ice shelf. (Photograph 6.8.6)

fast-ice boundary. The ice boundary at any given time between fast ice and drift ice.

fast-ice edge. The demarcation at any given time between fast ice and open water.

finger rafted ice. Type of rafted ice in which floes thrust "fingers" alternately over and under the other (Photograph 6.4.4).

finger rafting. Type of rafting whereby interlocking thrusts are formed, each floe thrusting "fingers" alternately over and under the other. Common in nilas and grey ice.

firn. Old snow which has crystalised into a dense material. Unlike ordinary snow, the particles are to some extent joined together; but, unlike ice, the air spaces in it still connect with each other.

first-year ice. Sea ice of not more than one winter's growth, developing from young ice; thickness 30 centimetres to 2 m. May be sub-divided into thin first-year ice/white ice medium first-year ice and thick first-year ice.

flaw. A narrow separation zone between drift ice and fast ice, where the pieces of ice are in a chaotic state; it forms when drift ice shears under the effect of a strong wind or current along the fast-ice boundary. See **shearing.**

flaw lead. A passage-way between drift ice and fast ice which is navigable by surface vessels.

flaw polynya. A polynya between drift ice and fast ice.

floating ice. Any form of ice found floating in water. The principal kinds of floating ice are lake ice, river ice, and sea ice, which form by the freezing of water at the surface, and glacier ice (ice of land origin) formed on land or in an ice shelf. The concept includes ice that is stranded or grounded.

floe. Any relatively flat piece of sea ice 20 m or more across. Floes are sub-divided according to horizontal extent as follows:

Giant	Over 10 km across
Vast	2–10 km across
Big	500–2000 m across
Medium	100–500 m across
Small	20–100 m across

See photograph 6.4.6.

floeberg. A massive piece of sea ice composed of a hummock or a group of hummocks, frozen together and separated from any ice surroundings. It may protrude up to 5 m above sea level.

floebit. A relatively small piece of sea ice, normally not more than 10 m across composed of hummock(s) or part of ridge(s) frozen together and separated from any surroundings. It typically protrudes 2 m above sea-level.

flooded ice. Sea ice which has been flooded by melt-water or river water and is heavily loaded by water and wet snow.

fracture. Any break or rupture through very close ice, compact pack ice, consolidated ice, fast ice, or a single floe resulting from deformation processes. Fractures may contain brash ice and/or be covered with nilas and/or young ice. Length may vary from a few metres to many kilometres:

Large Fracture	More than 500 m wide
Medium Fracture	200–500 m wide
Small Fracture	50–200 m wide
Very small Fracture	1–50 m wide
Crack	0–1 m wide

fracture zone. An area which has a great number of fractures.

fracturing. Pressure process whereby ice is permanently deformed, and ruptures occur. Most commonly used to describe breaking across very close pack ice, compact pack ice and consolidated pack ice.

frazil ice. Fine spicules or plates of ice, suspended in water.

friendly ice. From the point of view of the submariner, an ice canopy containing many large skylights or other features which permit a submarine to surface. There must be more than ten such features per 30 nautical miles along the submarine's track.

frost smoke. Fog-like cloud due to contact of cold air with relatively warm water, which can appear over openings in the ice, or to leeward of the ice edge, and which may persist while ice is forming. It often occurs at dawn and dissipates as the sun rises in the sky. See photograph below.

Frost smoke
(Photograph - British Antarctic Survey)

G

giant floe. A floe over 10 km across.

glacier. A mass of snow and ice continuously moving from higher to lower ground or, if afloat, continuously spreading. The principal forms of glacier are: inland ice sheets, ice shelves, ice streams, ice caps, ice piedmonts, cirque glaciers and various types of mountain (valley) glaciers.

glacier berg. An irregularly shaped iceberg.

glacier ice. Ice in, or originating from a glacier, whether on land or floating on the sea as icebergs, bergy bits or growlers.

glacier tongue. Projecting seaward extension of a glacier, usually afloat. In the Antarctic glacier tongues may extend over many tens of kilometres.

grease ice. A later stage of freezing than frazil ice when the crystals have coagulated to form a soupy layer on the surface. Grease ice reflects little light, giving the sea a matt appearance. See photographs 6.4.1 and 6.41.2.

grey ice. Young ice 10–15 centimetres thick. Less elastic than nilas and breaks on swell. Usually rafts under pressure.

grey-white ice. Young ice 15–30 centimetres thick. Under pressure more likely to ridge than to raft.

grounded hummock. Hummocked grounded ice formation. There are single grounded hummocks and lines (or chains) of grounded hummocks.

grounded ice. Floating ice which is aground in shoal water. See **stranded ice.**

growler. Rounded pieces of glacier ice smaller than a bergy bit or floeberg, often transparent but appearing green or almost black in colour, extending less than 1 m above the sea surface and normally occupying an area of about 20 square metres. See photographs 6.4.2 and 6.41.2.

H

hoar–frost. A deposit of ice having a crystalline appearance, generally assuming the form of scales, needles, feathers or fans; produced in a manner similar to dew (ie. by condensation of water vapour from the air), but at a temperature below 0°C. See photograph 6.4.3.

hostile ice. From the point of view of the submariner, an ice canopy containing no large skylights or other features which permit a submarine to surface.

hummock. A hillock of broken ice which has been forced upwards by pressure. May be fresh or weathered. The submerged volume of broken ice under the hummock, forced downwards by pressure is termed a bummock.

hummocked ice. Sea ice piled haphazardly one piece over another to form an uneven surface. When weathered, has the appearance of smooth hillocks.

hummocking. The pressure process by which sea ice is forced into hummocks. When the floes rotate in the process it is termed screwing.

I

iceberg. A massive piece of glacier ice of greatly varying shape, protruding more than 5 m above sea level, which has broken away from a glacier, and which may be afloat or aground. Icebergs may be described as tabular, dome-shaped, capsized, sloping, pinnacled, weathered or glacier bergs. See 6.15 to 6.22 and photographs 6.19 and 6.21.

iceberg tongue. A major accumulation of icebergs projecting from the coast, held in place by grounding and joined together by fast ice.

ice blink. A whitish glare on low clouds above an accumulation of distant ice. See photograph 6.42.

ice-bound. A harbour, inlet, or similar expanse of water is said to be ice-bound when navigation by ships is prevented on account of ice, except possibly with the assistance of an ice-breaker.

ice boundary. The demarcation at any given time between fast ice and drift ice or between areas of drift ice of different concentrations.

ice breccia. Ice pieces of different stages of development frozen together.

ice cake. Any relatively flat piece of sea ice less than 20 m across. See photograph 6.4.6.

ice canopy. Drift ice from the point of view of the submariner.

ice cover. The ratio of an area of ice of any concentration to the total area of sea surface within some large geographical locale; this locale may be global, hemispheric, or prescribed by a specific oceanographic entity such as Baffin Bay or the Barents Sea.

ice edge. The demarcation at any given time between the open sea and sea ice of any kind, whether fast or drifting. It may be termed compacted or diffuse. See **ice boundary.** See photograph below.

Ice edge

(Photograph - British Antarctic Survey)

ice field. Area of floating ice consisting of any size of floes, which is greater than 10 km across. See **ice patch**.

icefoot. A narrow fringe of ice attached to the coast, unmoved by tides and remaining after the fast ice has moved away.

ice-free. No ice present. If ice of any kind is present this term should not be used.

ice front. The vertical cliff forming the seaward face of an ice shelf or other floating glacier varying in height from 2–50 m or more above sea level. See **ice wall.** See photograph below.

Ice front with some bergy bits

(Photograph - British Antarctic Survey)

ice island. A large piece of floating ice protruding about 5 m above sea level, which has broken away from an Arctic ice shelf, having a thickness of 30–50 m and an area of from a few thousand square metres to 500 sq km or more, and usually characterized by a regularly undulating surface which gives it a ribbed appearance from the air. See photograph 6.17.

ice isthmus. A narrow connection between two ice areas of very close or compact ice. It may be difficult to pass, whilst sometimes being part of a recommended route.

ice jam. An accumulation of broken river ice or sea ice caught in a narrow channel.

ice keel. From the point of view of the submariner, a downward-projecting ridge on the underside of the ice canopy; the counterpart of a ridge. Ice keels may extend as much as 50 m below sea level.

ice limit. Climatological term referring to the extreme minimum or extreme maximum extent of the ice edge in any given month or period based on observations over a number of years. Terms should be preceded by minimum or maximum. See **mean ice edge.**

ice massif. A variable accumulation of close or very close ice covering hundreds of square kilometres which is found in the same region every summer.

ice of land origin. Ice formed on land or from an ice shelf, found floating in water. The concept includes ice that is stranded or grounded.

ice patch. An area of floating ice less than 10 km across.

ice piedmont. Ice covering a coastal strip of low-lying land backed by mountains. The surface of an ice piedmont slopes gently seaward and may be anything from about ¼ cable to 30 miles wide, fringing long stretches of coastline with ice cliffs known as ice walls. Ice piedmonts frequently merge into ice shelves.

ice port. An embayment in an ice front, often of a temporary nature, where ships can moor alongside and unload directly onto the ice shelf. See photograph below.

Ice port. The vessel is moored to fast ice in a creek in an ice shelf

(Photograph - British Antarctic Survey)

ice rind. A brittle shiny crust of ice formed on a quiet surface by direct freezing or from grease ice, usually in water of low salinity. Thickness to about 5 centimetres. Easily broken by wind or swell, commonly breaking in rectangular pieces. See photograph 6.4.3.

ice shelf. A floating ice sheet of considerable thickness showing 2–50 m or more above sea level, attached to the coast. Usually of great horizontal extent and with a level or gently undulating surface. Nourished by annual snow accumulation and often also by the seaward extension of land glaciers. Limited areas may be aground. The seaward edge is termed an ice front. See photograph 6.8.6.

ice stream. Part of an inland ice sheet in which the ice flows more rapidly and not necessarily in the same direction as the surrounding ice. The margins are sometimes clearly marked by a change in direction of the surface slope but may be indistinct.

ice under pressure. Ice in which deformation processes are actively occurring and hence a potential impediment or danger to shipping.

ice wall. An ice cliff forming the seaward margin of a glacier which is not afloat. An ice wall is aground, the rock basement being at or below sea level. See photograph below.

Ice wall

(Photograph - British Antarctic Survey)

J

jammed brash barrier. A strip or narrow belt of new, young or brash ice (usually 100–5000 m wide) formed at the edge of either drift or fast ice or at the shore. It is heavily compacted mostly due to wind action and may extend 2–20 m below the surface but does not normally have appreciable topography. Jammed brash barrier may disperse with changing winds but can only consolidate to form a strip of unusually thick ice in comparison with the surrounding drift ice.

L

lake ice. Ice formed on a lake, regardless of observed location.

large fracture. More than 500 m wide.

large ice field. An ice field over 20 km across.

lead. Any fracture or passage-way through sea ice which is navigable by surface vessels. See photograph 6.9.

level ice. Sea ice which has not been affected by deformation.

light nilas. Nilas which is more than 5 centimetres in thickness and rather lighter in colour than dark nilas. See photograph 6.4.4.

M

mean ice edge. Average position of the ice edge in any given month or period based on observations over a number of years. Other terms which may be used are mean maximum ice edge and mean minimum ice edge. See **ice limit.**

medium first-year ice. First-year ice 70–120 centimetres thick.

medium floe. A floe 100–500 m across.

medium fracture. A fracture 200–500 m wide.

medium ice field. An ice field 15–20 km across.

moraine. Ridges or deposits of rock debris transported by a glacier. Common forms are: ground moraine, formed under a glacier; lateral moraine, along the sides; medial moraine, down the centre; and end moraine, deposited at the foot. Moraines are left after a glacier has receded, providing evidence of its former extent.

multi-year ice. Old ice up to 3 m or more thick which has survived at least two summers' melt. Hummocks even smoother than in second-year ice, and the ice is almost salt free. Colour, where bare, is usually blue. Melt pattern consists of large interconnecting irregular puddles and a well-developed drainage system.

N

new ice. A general term for recently formed ice which includes frazil ice, grease ice, slush and shuga. These types of ice are composed of ice crystals which are only weakly frozen together (if at all) and have a definite form only while they are afloat.

new ridge. Ridge newly formed with sharp peaks and slope of sides usually 40°. Fragments are visible from the air at low altitude.

nilas. A thin elastic crust of ice, easily bending on waves and swell and under pressure, thrusting in a pattern of interlocking "fingers" (finger rafting). Has a matt surface and is up to 10 centimetres in thickness. May be sub-divided into dark nilas and light nilas. See photograph 6.4.4.

nip. Ice is said to nip when it forcibly presses against a ship. A vessel so caught, though undamaged, is said to have been nipped.

nunatak. A rocky crag or small mountain projecting from and surrounded by a glacier or ice sheet.

O

old ice. Sea ice which has survived at least one summer's melt; typical thickness up to 3 m or more. Most topographic features are smoother than on first-year ice. May be sub-divided into second-year ice and multi-year ice. See photograph below.

Old ice with puddles forming on top

(Photograph - British Antarctic Survey)

open ice. Floating ice in which the ice concentration is 4/10–6/10, with many leads and polynyas, and the floes are generally not in contact with one another. See photograph 6.8.1.

open water. A large area of freely navigable water in which sea ice is present in concentrations less than 1/10. No ice of land origin is present.

P

pack ice. The term was formerly for all ranges of concentration. See **drift ice**.

pancake ice. Predominantly circular pieces of ice from 30 centimetres to 3 m in diameter, and up to about 10 centimetres in thickness, with raised rims due to the pieces striking against one another. It may be formed on a slight swell from grease ice, shuga or slush or as a result of the breaking of ice rind, nilas or, under severe conditions of swell or waves, of grey ice. It also sometimes forms at some depth, at an interface between water bodies of different physical characteristics, from where it floats to the surface; its appearance may rapidly cover wide areas of water. See photograph 6.4.5.

pingo. A mound formed by the upheaval of subterranean ice in an area where the subsoil remains permanently frozen.

Pingos are also found in Arctic waters, rising about 30 m from an otherwise even sea floor, with bases about 40 m in diameter and surrounded by a shallow moat; they are then termed submarine pingos.
Oceanographically, a more or less conical mound of fine unconsolidated material characteristically containing an ice core.

polynya. Any non-linear shaped opening enclosed in drift ice. Polynyas may contain brash ice and/or be covered with new ice, nilas or young ice.

puddle. An accumulation on ice of melt-water, mainly due to melting snow, but in the more advanced stages also due to the melting of ice. Initial stage consists of patches of melted snow on an ice floe.

R

rafted ice. Type of deformed ice formed by one piece of ice overriding another. See **finger rafting**.

rafting. Pressure processes whereby one piece of ice overrides another. Most common in new and young ice. See **finger rafting**.

ram. An underwater ice projection from an ice wall, ice front, iceberg or floe. Its formation is usually due to a more intense melting and erosion of the unsubmerged part. See photograph 6.70.

recurring polynya. A polynya which recurs in the same position every year.

ridge. A line or wall of broken ice forced up by pressure. May be fresh or weathered. The submerged volume of broken ice under a ridge, forced downwards by pressure is termed an ice keel.

ridged ice. Ice piled haphazardly one piece over another in the form of ridges or walls. Usually found in first-year ice. See **ridging**.

ridged ice zone. An area in which much ridged ice with similar characteristics has formed.

ridging. The pressure process by which sea ice is forced into ridges.

rime. A deposit of ice composed of grains more or less separated by trapped air, some adorned with crystalline branches, produced by the rapid freezing of super-cooled and very small water droplets.

river ice. Ice formed on a river, regardless of observed location.

rotten ice. Sea ice which has become honey-combed and which is in an advanced state of disintegration.

rubble field. An area of extremely deformed sea ice of unusual thickness formed during the winter by the motion of drift ice against, or around a protruding rock, islet, or other obstruction.

S

sastrugi. Sharp, irregular ridges formed on a snowy surface by wind erosion and deposition. On drift ice the ridges are parallel to the direction of the prevailing wind at the time they were formed. See photograph below.

Sastrugi

(Photograph - British Antarctic Survey)

screwing. See **hummocking**.

sea ice. Any form of ice found at sea which has originated from the freezing of sea water, as opposed to ice of land origin.

second-year ice. Old ice which has survived only one summer's melt; typical thickness up to 2·5 m and sometimes more. Because it is thicker than first-year ice, it stands higher out of the water. In contrast to multi-year ice, summer melting produces a regular pattern of numerous small puddles. Bare patches and puddles are usually greenish-blue.

shearing. An area of drift ice is subject to shear when the ice motion varies significantly in the direction normal to the motion, subjecting the ice to rotational forces. These forces may result in phenomena similar to a **flaw**.

shear ridge. An ice ridge formation which develops when one ice feature is grinding past another. The type of ridge is more linear than those caused by pressure alone.

shear ridge field. Many shear ridges side by side.

shore lead. A lead between drift ice and the shore or between drift ice and an ice front.

shore ice ride-up. A process by which ice is pushed ashore as a slab.

shore polynya. A polynya between drift ice and the coast or between drift ice and an ice front.

shore melt. Open water between the shore and the fast ice, formed by melting and/or as a result of river discharge.

shuga. An accumulation of spongy white ice lumps, a few centimetres across; they are formed from grease ice or slush and sometimes from anchor ice rising to the surface. See photographs 6.4.2 and 6.41.2.

skylight. From the point of view of the submarine, thin places in the ice canopy, usually less than 1 m thick and appearing from below as relatively light, translucent patches in dark surroundings. The undersurface of a skylight is normally flat. Skylights are called large if big enough for a submarine to attempt to surface through them (120 m) or small if not.

slush. Snow which is saturated and mixed with water on land or ice surfaces, or as a viscous floating mass in water after a heavy snowfall.

small floe. A floe 20–100 m across.

small fracture. A fracture 50–200 m wide.

small ice cake. An ice cake less than 2 m across.

small ice field. An ice field 10–15 km across.

snow barchan. See **snowdrift**.

snowdrift. An accumulation of wind-blown snow deposited in the lee of obstructions or heaped by wind eddies. A crescent-shaped snowdrift, with ends pointing downwind, is known as a **snow barchan**.

standing floe. A separate floe standing vertically or inclined and enclosed by rather smooth ice.

stranded ice. Ice which has been floating and has been deposited on the shore by retreating high water.

strip. Long narrow area of floating ice, about 1 km or less in width, usually composed of small fragments detached from the main mass of ice, and run together under the influence of wind, swell or current.

submarine pingo. See **pingo**.

T

tabular berg. A flat-topped iceberg. Most tabular bergs form by calving from an ice shelf and show horizontal banding. See **ice island** and photograph 6.19.

thaw holes. Vertical holes in sea ice formed when surface puddles melt through to the underlying water.

thick first-year ice. First-year ice over 120 centimetres thick.

thick first-year ice/white ice. First-year ice 30–70 centimetres thick.

thin first-year ice/white ice first stage, 30–50 centimetres thick

thin first-year ice/white ice second stage, 50–70 centimetres thick

tide crack. Crack at the line of junction between an immovable ice foot or ice wall and fast ice, the latter subject to rise and fall of the tide.

tongue. A projection of the ice edge up to several kilometres in length, caused by wind or current.

V

vast floe. A floe 2–10 km across.

very close ice. Floating ice in which the concentration is 9/10 to less than 10/10. See photograph 6.8.3.

very open ice. Floating ice in which the concentration is 1/10 to 3/10 and water preponderates over ice. See photograph 6.8.5.

very small fracture. A fracture 1–50 m wide.

very weathered ridge. Ridge with tops very rounded, slope of sides usually 20°–30°.

W

water sky. Dark streaks on the underside of low clouds, indicating the presence of water features in the vicinity of sea ice.

weathered ridge. Ridge with peaks slightly rounded and slope of sides usually 30°–40°. Individual fragments are not discernible.

weathering. Processes of ablation and accumulation which gradually eliminate irregularities in an ice surface.

white ice. See **thin first-year ice.**

Y

young coastal ice. The initial stage of fast ice formation consisting of nilas or young ice, its width varying from a few metres up to 100–200 m from the shoreline.

young ice. Ice in the transition stage between nilas and first-year ice, 10–30 centimetres in thickness. May be sub-divided into grey ice and grey-white ice.

ICE TERMS ARRANGED BY SUBJECT

Floating ice:

The principal kinds are:
Sea ice;
Lake ice;
River ice;
Ice of land origin.

Development:

New ice includes:
Frazil ice;
Grease ice (Photographs 6.4.1 and 6.41.2);
Slush and Shuga (Photographs 6.4.2 and 6.41.2);
Nilas: may be sub-divided into Dark and Light Nilas
(Photograph 6.4.4) and Ice Rind (Photograph 6.4.3);
Pancake ice (Photograph 6.4.5);
Young ice; Grey or Grey-white ice.

First-year ice. May be designated:
Thin/White;
Medium;
Thick.

Old ice. May be sub-divided into:
Second-year ice;
Multi-year ice.

Forms of Fast ice:

Fast ice (Photograph 6.8.6): called Young Coastal
ice in its initial stage;
Icefoot;
Anchor ice;
Grounded ice: includes Stranded ice and Grounded
hummock.

Drift ice:

Ice cover concentration: may be designated
Compact, Consolidated (Photograph 6.8.4);
Very Close (Photograph 6.8.3);
Close (Photograph 6.8.2);
Open (Photograph 6.8.1);
Very Open ice (Photograph 6.8.5);
Open water, Bergy water or Ice-free.

Forms of Floating ice include:
Pancake ice (Photograph 6.4.5);
Floe (Photograph 6.4.6);
Ice cake (Photograph 6.4.6);
Floeberg, Floebit, Ice Breccia, Brash ice
(Photograph 6.10);
Iceberg (Photographs 6.19 and 6.21);
Glacier berg, Tabular berg (Photograph 6.19);
Ice Island (Photograph 6.17);
Bergy bit (Photograph 6.41.1);
Growler (Photograph 6.41.2);

Arrangement: see Ice Field, Ice Isthmus, Ice Massif, Belt,
Tongue, Strip, Bight, Rubble Field, Shear Ridge Field, Ice
Jam, Ice Edge (See photograph above in main part of ice
glossary), Ice Boundary, Iceberg Tongue.

Drift Ice motion processes:
Diverging;
Compacting;
Shearing

Deformation processes:
Fracturing;
Hummocking;
Ridging;
Rafting;
Shore ice ride-up;
Weathering.

Openings in the ice:
Fracture: see Crack, Tide Crack and Flaw;
Fracture zone;
Lead (Photograph 6.9);
Polynya; includes Shore polynya, Flaw polynya and
Recurring polynya.

Ice-surface features:
Level ice;
Deformed ice: sub-divisions include: Rafted ice
Ridge and Hummock;
Standing floe;
Ram (Photograph 6.70);
Bare ice;
Snow-covered ice: includes Sastrugi (See
photograph above in main part of ice glossary) and
Snowdrift.

Stages of melting:
Puddle;
Thaw holes;
Dried ice;
Rotten ice;
Flooded ice;
Shore melt.

Ice of land origin:
Firn;
Glacier ice: (see Glacier), Ice Wall (See
photograph above in main part of ice glossary), Ice
Stream and Glacier Tongue;
Ice shelf: the seaward edge is termed an Ice Front
(See photograph above in main part of ice
glossary);
Calved ice: see Iceberg, Ice Island, Bergy bit and
Growler.

Sky and air indications:
Water sky;
Ice blink (Photograph 6.42);
Frost smoke (See photograph above in main part
of ice glossary).

Terms relating to surface shipping:
Area of weakness;
Beset;
Ice bound;
Nip;
Ice under pressure;
Difficult area;
Easy area;
Iceport.

Terms relating to submarine navigation:
Ice canopy;
Friendly ice;
Hostile ice;
Bummock;
Ice keel;
Skylight.

INDEX

METEOROLOGICAL CONVERSION TABLE AND SCALES
Fahrenheit to Celsius °Fahrenheit

	0	1	2	3	4	5	6	7	8	9
°F					Degrees Celsius					
-100	-73·3	-73·9	-74·4	-75·0	-75·6	-76·1	-76·7	-77·2	-77·8	-78·3
-90	-67·8	-68·3	-68·9	-69·4	-70·0	-70·6	-71·1	-71·7	-72·2	-72·8
-80	-62·2	-62·8	-63·3	-63·9	-64·4	-65·0	-65·6	-66·1	-66·7	-67·2
-70	-56·7	-57·2	-57·8	-58·3	-58·9	-59·4	-60·0	-60·6	-61·1	-61·7
-60	-51·1	-51·7	-52·2	-52·8	-53·3	-53·9	-54·4	-55·0	-55·6	-56·1
-50	-45·6	-46·1	-46·7	-47·2	-47·8	-48·3	-48·9	-49·4	-50·0	-50·6
-40	-40·0	-40·6	-41·1	-41·7	-42·2	-42·8	-43·3	-43·9	-44·4	-45·0
-30	-34·4	-35·0	-35·6	-36·1	-36·7	-37·2	-37·8	-38·3	-38·9	-39·4
-20	-28·9	-29·4	-30·0	-30·6	-31·1	-31·7	-32·2	-32·8	-33·3	-33·9
-10	-23·3	-23·9	-24·4	-25·0	-25·6	-26·1	-26·7	-27·2	-27·8	-28·3
-0	-17·8	-18·3	-18·9	-19·4	-20·0	-20·6	-21·1	-21·7	-22·2	-22·8
+0	-17·8	-17·2	-16·7	-16·1	-15·6	-15·0	-14·4	-13·9	-13·3	-12·8
10	-12·2	-11·7	-11·1	-10·6	-10·0	-9·4	-8·9	-8·3	-7·8	-7·2
20	-6·7	-6·1	-5·6	-5·0	-4·4	-3·9	-3·3	-2·8	-2·2	-1·7
30	-1·1	-0·6	0	+0·6	+1·1	+1·7	+2·2	+2·8	+3·3	+3·9
40	+4·4	+5·0	+5·6	6·1	6·7	7·2	7·8	8·3	8·9	9·4
50	10·0	10·6	11·1	11·7	12·2	12·8	13·3	13·9	14·4	15·0
60	15·6	16·1	16·7	17·2	17·8	18·3	18·9	19·4	20·0	20·6
70	21·1	21·7	22·2	22·8	23·3	23·9	24·4	25·0	25·6	26·1
80	26·7	27·2	27·8	28·3	28·9	29·4	30·0	30·6	31·1	31·7
90	32·2	32·8	33·3	33·9	34·4	35·0	35·6	36·1	36·7	37·2
100	37·8	38·3	38·9	39·4	40·0	40·6	41·1	41·7	42·2	42·8
110	43·3	43·9	44·4	45·0	45·6	46·1	46·7	47·2	47·8	48·3
120	48·9	49·4	50·0	50·6	51·1	51·7	52·2	52·8	53·3	53·9

Celsius to Fahrenheit °Celsius

	0	1	2	3	4	5	6	7	8	9
°C					Degrees Fahrenheit					
-70	-94·0	-95·8	-97·6	-99·4	-101·2	-103·0	-104·8	-106·6	-108·4	-110·2
-60	-76·0	-77·8	-79·6	-81·4	-83·2	-85·0	-86·8	-88·6	-90·4	-92·2
-50	-58·0	-59·8	-61·6	-63·4	-65·2	-67·0	-68·8	-70·6	-72·4	-74·2
-40	-40·0	-41·8	-43·6	-45·4	-47·2	-49·0	-50·8	-52·6	-54·4	-56·2
-30	-22·0	-23·8	-25·6	-27·4	-29·2	-31·0	-32·8	-34·6	-36·4	-38·2
-20	-4·0	-5·8	-7·6	-9·4	-11·2	-13·0	-14·8	-16·6	18·4	-20·2
-10	+14·0	+12·2	+10·4	+8·6	+6·8	+5·0	+3·2	+1·4	-0·4	-2·2
-0	32·0	30·2	28·4	26·6	24·8	23·0	21·2	19·4	+17·6	+15·8
+0	32·0	33·8	35·6	37·4	39·2	41·0	42·8	44·6	46·4	48·2
10	50·0	51·8	53·6	55·4	57·2	59·0	60·8	62·6	64·4	66·2
20	68·0	69·8	71·6	73·4	75·2	77·0	78·8	80·6	82·4	84·2
30	86·0	87·8	89·6	91·4	93·2	95·0	96·8	98·6	100·4	102·2
40	104·0	105·8	107·6	109·4	111·2	113·0	114·8	116·6	118·4	120·2
50	122·0	123·8	125·6	127·4	129·2	131·0	132·8	134·6	136·4	138·2

HECTOPASCALS TO INCHES

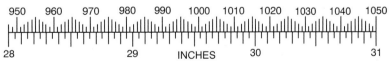

MILLIMETRES TO INCHES

(1) (for small values)

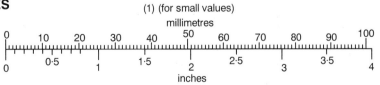

(2) (for large values)

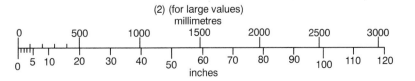

TABLE FOR CONVERTING METRES TO FEET AND FATHOMS

Metres	Feet	Fms.	Metres	Feet	Fms.	Metres	Feet	Fms.
1	3·281	0·547	51	167·323	27·887	200	656·17	109·36
2	6·562	1·094	52	170·604	28·434	300	984·25	164·04
3	9·843	1·640	53	173·885	28·981	400	1312·34	218·72
4	13·123	2·187	54	177·165	29·528	500	1640·42	273·40
5	16·404	2·734	55	180·446	30·074			
						600	1968·50	328·08
6	19·685	3·281	56	183·727	30·621	700	2296·59	382·76
7	22·966	3·828	57	186·008	31·168	800	2624·67	437·45
8	26·247	4·374	58	190·289	31·715	900	2952·76	492·13
9	29·528	4·921	59	193·570	32·262			
10	32·808	5·468	60	196·850	32·808	1000	3280·84	546·81
						2000	6561·68	1093·61
11	36·089	6·015	61	200·131	33·355	3000	9842·52	1640·42
12	39·370	6·562	62	203·412	33·902	4000	13123·36	2187·23
13	42·651	7·108	63	206·693	34·449	5000	16404·20	2734·03
14	45·932	7·655	64	209·974	34·996			
15	49·213	8·202	65	213·255	35·542	6000	19685·04	3280·84
						7000	22965·88	3827·65
16	52·493	8·749	66	216·535	36·089	8000	26246·72	4374·45
17	55·774	9·296	67	219·816	36·636	9000	29527·56	4921·26
18	59·055	9·843	68	223·097	37·183			
19	62·336	10·389	69	226·378	37·730	10000	32808·40	5468·07
20	65·617	10·936	70	229·659	38·276			

Metres	Inches
0·10	3·937
0·20	7·874
0·30	11·811
0·40	15·748
0·50	19·685
0·60	23·622
0·70	27·559
0·80	31·496
0·90	35·433
1·00	39·370

Metres	Feet	Fms.	Metres	Feet	Fms.
21	68·898	11·483	71	232·940	38·823
22	72·178	12·030	72	236·220	39·370
23	75·459	12·577	73	239·501	39·917
24	78·740	13·123	74	242·782	40·464
25	82·021	13·670	75	246·063	41·010
26	85·302	14·217	76	249·344	41·557
27	88·583	14·764	77	252·625	42·104
28	91·864	15·311	78	255·906	42·651
29	95·144	15·857	79	259·186	43·198
30	98·425	16·404	80	262·467	43·745
31	101·706	16·951	81	265·748	44·291
32	104·987	17·498	82	269·029	44·838
33	108·268	18·045	83	272·310	45·385
34	111·549	18·591	84	275·591	45·932
35	114·829	19·138	85	278·871	46·479
36	118·110	19·685	86	282·152	47·025
37	121·391	20·232	87	285·433	47·572
38	124·672	20·779	88	288·714	48·119
39	127·953	21·325	89	291·995	48·666
40	131·234	21·872	90	295·276	49·213
41	134·514	22·419	91	298·556	49·759
42	137·795	22·966	92	301·837	50·306
43	141·076	23·513	93	305·118	50·853
44	144·357	24·059	94	308·399	51·400
45	146·638	24·606	95	311·680	51·947
46	150·919	25·153	96	314·961	52·493
47	154·199	25·700	97	318·241	53·040
48	157·480	26·247	98	321·522	53·587
49	160·761	26·794	99	324·803	54·134
50	164·042	27·340	100	328·084	54·681

Factors: 1 metre = 3·280839895 feet *or* 39·370078740 inches
= 0·546806649 fathoms
1000 metres = 0·5399568 International Nautical Miles

TABLE FOR CONVERTING FEET AND FATHOMS TO METRES

Feet	Fms.	Metres	Feet	Fms.	Metres	Feet	Fms.	Metres	Feet	Fms.	Metres
1		0·305	51	8½	15·545	102	17	31·090	426	71	129·845
1·5	¼	0·457	52		15·850	108	18	32·918	432	72	131·674
2		0·610	53		16·154	114	19	34·747	438	73	133·502
3	½	0·914	54	9	16·459	120	20	36·576	444	74	135·331
4		1·219	55		16·764	126	21	38·405	450	75	137·160
4·5	¾	1·372	56		17·069	132	22	40·234	456	76	138·989
5		1·524	57	9½	17·374	138	23	42·062	462	77	140·818
6	1	1·829	58		17·678	144	24	43·891	468	78	142·646
7		2·134	59		17·983	150	25	45·720	474	79	144·475
8		2·438	60	10	18·288	156	26	47·549	480	80	146·304
9	1½	2·743	61		18·593	162	27	49·378	486	81	148·133
10		3·048	62		18·898	168	28	51·206	492	82	149·962
11		3·353	63	10½	19·202	174	29	53·035	498	83	151·790
12	2	3·658	64		19·507	180	30	54·864	504	84	153·619
13		3·962	65		19·812	186	31	56·693	510	85	155·448
14		4·267	66	11	20·117	192	32	58·522	516	86	157·277
15	2½	4·572	67		20·422	198	33	60·350	522	87	159·106
16		4·877	68		20·726	204	34	62·179	528	88	160·934
17		5·182	69	11½	21·031	210	35	64·008	534	89	162·763
18	3	5·486	70		21·336	216	36	65·837	540	90	164·592
19		5·791	71		21·641	222	37	67·666	546	91	166·421
20		6·096	72	12	21·946	228	38	69·494	552	92	168·250
21	3½	6·401	73		22·250	234	39	71·323	558	93	170·078
22		6·706	74		22·555	240	40	73·152	564	94	171·907
23		7·010	75	12½	22·860	246	41	74·981	570	95	173·736
24	4	7·315	76		23·165	252	42	76·810	576	96	175·565
25		7·620	77		23·470	258	43	78·638	582	97	177·394
26		7·925	78	13	23·774	264	44	80·467	588	98	179·222
27	4½	8·230	79		24·079	270	45	82·296	594	99	181·051
28		8·534	80		24·384	276	46	84·125	600	100	182·880
29		8·839	81	13½	24·689	282	47	85·954			
30	5	9·144	82		24·994	288	48	87·782			
31		9·449	83		25·298	294	49	89·611			
32		9·754	84	14	25·603	300	50	91·440			
33	5½	10·058	85		25·908	306	51	93·269			
34		10·363	86		26·213	312	52	95·098			
35		10·668	87	14½	26·518	318	53	96·926			
36	6	10·973	88		26·822	324	54	98·755			
37		11·278	89		27·127	330	55	100·584			
38		11·582	90	15	27·432	336	56	102·413			
39	6½	11·887	91		27·737	342	57	104·242			
40		12·192	92		28·042	348	58	106·070			
41		12·497	93	15½	28·346	354	59	107·899			
42	7	12·802	94		28·651	360	60	109·728			
43		13·106	95		28·956	366	61	111·557			
44		13·411	96	16	29·261	372	62	113·386			
45	7½	13·716	97		29·566	378	63	115·214			
46		14·021	98		29·870	384	64	117·043			
47		14·326	99	16½	30·175	390	65	118·872			
48	8	14·630	100		30·480	396	66	120·701			
49		14·935				402	67	122·530			
50		15·240				408	68	124·358			
						414	69	126·187			
						420	70	128·016			

Feet	Metres
700	213·360
800	243·840
900	274·320
1000	304·800

Fms.	Metres
200	365·760
300	548·640
400	731·520
500	914·400
600	1097·280
700	1280·160
800	1463·040
900	1645·920
1000	1828·800

Inches	Ft.	Metres	Inches	Ft.	Metres
1	0·083	0·025	7	0·583	0·178
2	0·167	0·051	8	0·667	0·203
3	0·250	0·076	9	0·750	0·229
4	0·333	0·102	10	0·883	0·254
5	0·417	0·127	11	0·917	0·279
6	0·500	0·152	12	1·000	0·305

Factors

1 Inch = 0·0254 metres
1 Foot = 0·3048 metres
1 Fathom = 1·8288 metres
or 6 feet

1 International Nautical Mile = 1852 metres

PREVIOUS EDITIONS

First published 1962
Second Edition 1966
Third Edition 1971
Fourth Edition 1973
Fifth Edition 1979
Sixth Edition 1989
Seventh Edition 1999
Eighth Edition 2004

Produced in the United Kingdom
by UKHO